MGR

R. KANNAN

MGR

A Life

PENGUIN BOOKS

An imprint of Penguin Random House

PENGUIN BOOKS

USA | Canada | UK | Ireland | Australia
New Zealand | India | South Africa | China | Singapore

Penguin Books is part of the Penguin Random House group of companies
whose addresses can be found at global.penguinrandomhouse.com

Published by Penguin Random House India Pvt. Ltd
4th Floor, Capital Tower 1, MG Road,
Gurugram 122 002, Haryana, India

Penguin
Random House
India

First published in Penguin Books by Penguin Random House India 2017

ISBN 9780143429340

Typeset in Dante MT Std by Manipal Digital Systems, Manipal
Printed at Repro India Limited

To my late father, S.K. Rajarathinam, my mother, R. Abaranji, and my sister, Nirmala Rajarajan

Contents

Preface

I owe this book to Kamini Mahadevan, who planted the seed of the idea following the publication of *Anna: The Life and Times of C.N. Annadurai*. I must confess that I was not enthusiastic initially. Although, like many of my time, I too had run to catch a glimpse of MGR—the matinee idol—followed his every move and savoured the moment, I still could not easily bring myself to write about a politician whose identity was so deeply rooted in film. Eventually, I gave in, even as author, politician and former diplomat Pavan Varma encouraged me to take up the challenge. MGR had the power to draw crowds on par with Mahatma Gandhi, Jawaharlal Nehru, Annadurai and Indira Gandhi. He was a colossus. His life is inextricably intertwined with the Dravidian movement, and I believed his biography could, in a way, tell the story of the movement up until 1987—his death.

At the end of this exercise, MGR, human and fallible, emerges as a great humanist and an incredibly fascinating man with a keen native intelligence and, unlike the popular portrayal of him, as an astute politician. His life of poverty, struggle, success and fame, and his god like status, is unique and could serve as an inspiration and an example. To me, he is much like Caliph Harun al-Rashid of the *Thousand and One Nights* fame. William Montgomery Watt writes that Caliph Harun (the honorific title 'al-Rashid' means 'the one following the right path') 'was neither a great ruler nor a man of prepossessing character, though he was a lavish patron of the arts. He owes his fame to the wealth and luxury of his court, surpassing anything previously known, and to his place in Arabic legend.'[1] Much like the caliph, MGR's renown came from his huge heart, his charisma, his parent Dravida Munnetra Kazhagam (DMK) and his carefully cultivated screen image as a do-gooder and a man who fought the mighty for the suppressed and oppressed, the weak and the poor. Yet, ironically, research studies have shown that while MGR's welfare schemes benefited the poor they failed to lift them out of the morass of poverty.

My introduction to the Dravidian movement goes back to my childhood in Washermanpet, Madras—the birthplace and the citadel of the DMK—and my family's association with its stalwarts. I have seen Perasiriyar (professor) K. Anbazhagan (general secretary of the DMK) visit my maternal grandfather, M. Ramasamy. On my paternal side, Periyar E.V. Ramasamy (EVR) apparently had been a guest in my grandfather S. Karuppiah's home at Aruppukkottai. My introduction to MGR, his films, and the DMK and post-DMK politics began with my cousin G. Lakshmanaswamy, an ardent MGR fan, and the tenants in my grandfather's house. I was so hooked on MGR's films that once, in 1976 or so, my father punished me for refusing to go out with the family, preferring instead to stay back and watch *Gulebakavali* (1955)[2] being shown on the newly launched state television, Doordarshan. The following year, I saw MGR in person, campaigning from his open-top van. He looked like a celestial being in that 4 p.m. sun.

In 1980, T. Ramalingam, an advocate and a young leader of the Janata Party, introduced me to Tamil literature, to Kannadasan's poetry, and his writings on his time with the DMK and the Janata Party's brand of nationalist politics. I owe him much. At the same time, my friend Ramalinga Jothi of the Congress (I) gave me an insight into the workings of his party. With my friend V. Jayaprakash from a Sarvodaya family, I discussed both the nationalist and the Dravidian movements. DMK poet Kaviarasar Ponnivalavan, my classmate/friend K. Shahjahan's father, Karikalan, a DMK district representative, and former DMK MP Viduthalai Virumbi shed light on the DMK's workings in the field for me. Meanwhile, Tamil savant, civil servant and public speaker Dr Avvai Natarajan took me under his wing and mentored me in public speaking with fatherly affection.

Between 1980 and 1986, as a student leader and debater, I came into contact with a number of leaders of the Dravidian movement. In 1988, on my return from the US after completing my LLM degree, Dr L. Venugopal, the son of Dr Lakshmanaswami Mudaliar, one of the celebrated Arcot doctor twins, arranged for me to call on Kalaignar (Karunanidhi was given this title, which means 'artist'). (I had the good fortune to be delivered by Dr Mudaliar in 1962.) Much like Ekalavya from the Mahabharatha, I had admired, observed and learnt from Kalaignar—but only from a distance. Finally, face-to-face with the legend, I could feel his presence and, in retrospect, understand why MGR was so preoccupied with him till the end. Professor T.K.S. Villalan, Rasipuram Vellalapatti K. Arulmani, a fellow student in the US, Dr R. Balasundaram, his late father, K. Ramasamy, and the late R.N. Nallathambi and his wife helped strengthen this relationship with the DMK leadership in the years that followed. I owe my gratitude to each and every one of them for their contribution to my formative years.

I have, however, not allowed this association to come in the way of this book. And, in retrospect, I am happy that I agreed to Kamini's proposition. Many would be happy that I agreed to write the book. Some of them are not with me today: my father, my father-in-law, Kaviarasar Ponnivalavan, Congress man Aru. Shankar, economist and civil servant S. Guhan, activist Savithri Raghavendra and a third cousin R. Prem Kumar are among them.

This book talks about MGR's life and chronicles his rise as a film star, his public career, his careful image-making, his contribution to the Dravidian movement, his break from his parent DMK and the founding of the All-India Anna Dravida Munnetra Kazhagam (AIADMK), culminating in his becoming chief minister of Tamil Nadu, his adopted state,[3] not once but thrice. MGR never lost a general election to the Legislative Assembly and, more significantly, never felt the need to buy votes. He did not depend on caste, religion or language to get him votes either. His political appeal transcended such electoral considerations. The country's highest civilian honour, the Bharat Ratna, was posthumously bestowed on him on 26 January 1988. The Union government declared a national holiday on the day of his death and in millions of Tamil homes around the world there was a sense of personal loss. For someone who had quit school after Class Three because of poverty, the extraordinary adulation he enjoyed was no mean achievement.

MGR's film and public career spanned four decades. Three decades after his death, he still seems politically and socially relevant, at least among the women of my generation and in the rural heartland. M.K. Stalin, son of Kalaignar, once friend, initiator, collaborator and party leader turned bête noire of MGR, told me that he 'likes MGR very much'. A zealous fan, he would see the first showing of MGR's films and the actor would seek Stalin's views on them. He insisted that

Stalin call him *periyappa* or 'elder father', and jocularly complained to Kalaignar when Stalin once called him 'sir' instead. In the tradition of Anna and the Dravidian movement, MGR built such personal bonds with thousands, if not tens of thousands. The screen carried this personal bonding to his fans and their families, into their homes and beyond, and he became vathiyar (teacher, a term of endearment among the poor and the working class) to some and makkal thilagam (people's darling) in general. In 1972, K.A. Krishnaswamy (KAK) elevated MGR from puratchi nadigar (revolutionary actor), the title bestowed by Kalaignar, to puratchi thalaivar (revolutionary leader). Everyone, other than his political antagonists, who came in contact with him was smitten by MGR's charisma, charm, concern, interest in them and his huge heart. As he successfully charted his own political course, his critics explained the 'MGR phenomenon' as 'cine glamour'. Yet, the truth remains that there has been no one like MGR, before or after him.

This book responds to some of those imponderables, although it is not an academic exercise. It seeks to fill the void of a dependable, standard biography on MGR in English. M.S.S. Pandian's *The Image Trap: MG Ramachandran in Film and Politics* (1992) is a good work but highly critical of the actor-politician. *MGR: The Man and the Myth* (1992) by K. Mohandas, his Intelligence point man, is helpful to some extent in understanding Chief Minister MGR. DMK patriarch, Kalaignar M. Karunanidhi's six-volume work *Nenjuku Needhi* (Justice to the Heart) is a hugely useful work to understand his relationship with MGR and what went wrong between them, from his point of view. J. Jayalalithaa's *Manam Thirandhu Solgiraen* (Baring My Heart) series that appeared in *Kumudam* in late 1978 for twenty-four weeks, her two-part 1984 interview with *Ananda Vikatan*, her 1998 interview with the *Illustrated Weekly of India*, and her 1999 interview with Simi Garewal and Rediff.com give us an insight into the mentor–mentee relationship between MGR and her.

In writing this book I have relied principally on MGR himself: His autobiography, *Naan Yaen Pirandhen?* (Why Was I Born?), that was serialized in *Ananda Vikatan* weekly from 1970 to 1972, besides his response to readers, his essays, interviews and speeches at various times in various journals and forums. It is a pity that a government that invokes his name when required has done little to perpetuate his memory and has not found it fitting to collect his speeches in the Legislative Assembly and elsewhere, and occasional writings. On the contrary, his mentee's government has done everything possible to distance itself from his memory. While MGR named institutions and programmes after his mentor Anna, his mentee delighted in naming everything after herself. Of course, the best tribute to a man whose heart was with the poor is to eliminate poverty in the state and not merely seek to enrich oneself and a select cabal. As the 14 February 2017 judgement in the Disproportionate Assets case[4] has shown, the mentee imbibed none of the selflessness of her mentor.

In narrating MGR's political career I have relied on *Murasoli* (sadly, the issues for the few years following MGR's split from the DMK are not available on the Internet and the online access to the magazine remains unstable), *India Today, Dinamani, The Hindu, Frontline, Ananda Vikatan* and other publications. The archives of *India Today* were critical in writing the chapters on MGR's three terms.

MGR was god on earth to the rural poor, and millions just wished to see him, to touch him; they were electrified by his presence and took the moment as a gift life had bestowed on them. Despite being an actor, MGR was no orator. His speeches were rambling and long-winded, and his voice was anything but appealing after the 1967 shooting incident. Following the stroke he suffered in October 1984, his speech was impaired and he cut a truly sorry figure when he attempted to speak. He wrote well, but was not a writer by any means. He was not known for his acting talent either. Yet, the man was simply adored and loved. His fans and the simple Tamil folk believed that he lived for them, and in his success, they saw theirs. They lived vicariously through him. As superstar Kamal Haasan pithily put it during the January 2017 *jallikattu* student protests, Chief Minister MGR would have gone to the Marina to meet the students and, even if he was advised against it, would have 'sat near the [police] commissioner's office and declared that he too was fasting with them'.[5] Such was his inborn ability to relate to the masses.

He was also the ultimate host.

If he was a Karna in giving, he was also like the mythical hero born with a Teflon exterior. Despite the scandals and the corruption charges that dogged his years in office, MGR's image as a clean man could not be dented.

My gratitude to a long list of people who have assisted me with this project: Professor Sachi Sri Kantha from Japan, authors Tamil Magan, V. Ramnarayan, Charukesi, R. Muthukumar, *Kumudam*'s P. Varadarajan, *India Today*'s Sandeep Unnithan, G.S. Simhanjana, B. Sushmita, *The Hindu*'s B. Kolappan, *Times of India*'s Shalini Umachandran, D. Mahalakshmi, N. Manickam, Professor T.K.S. Villalan, V. Jayaprakash, Dr S. Mohan Raj, Anand Krishna, Iniyan Sampath, Arul Natarajan, V. Kumaresan, Subha Venkat, Bala Srinivasan, M. Muthuraja, J. Gobi, Raja Gundu, Asif Niazi, D.V.N. Bose, 'Wide Angle' Ravi Shankar, V.N. Swami, V. Balakrishnan, T. Chitrarasu, Kavitha Muralidharan, Anna Arivalayam's librarian, Sa. Sundaram, Ravi Ram, 'Stills' Gnanam and last but not least, Penguin Random House India's Jyotsna Raman. I seek forgiveness from those whom I have forgotten to mention here.

My sincere gratitude goes to MGR's cabinet colleagues, the late K.A. Krishnaswamy, S. Ramachandran, R.M. Veerappan, Dr H.V. Hande, C. Aranganayagam, Su. Thirunavukkarasar (earlier S. Thirunavukkarasu), and former Speaker of the Assembly P.H. Pandian, former deputy chairman of the Legislative Council Pulavar Pulamaipithan, Dravidar Kazhagam president K. Veeramani, scriptwriter Arurdhas, artist Mohan V. Raman and industrialist Pollachi M. Manickam for their valuable time and insights. I wish to record my gratitude to the leader of the Opposition and DMK working president, M.K. Stalin, for sharing his memories of MGR.

This preface would be incomplete if I do not mention the principal driving force behind this mission, my wife, Usha. As I procrastinated about my writing, she came after me, cajoling and at times rebuking me for my dereliction of duty. Although opposed to the idea of me writing about Dravidian leaders and not following 'higher pursuits' like the UN, my sister-in-law Dr M. Vijayarani always made herself available over the phone to listen to my fears, misgivings and happiness about the trajectory of the book, my line of reasoning and the progress of the work.

My editors, Kamini Mahadevan and Ranjana Sengupta, midwifed this book. I am indebted to them. I am grateful to Ravi Singh, then publisher of Penguin Books India, and to Meru Gokhale, the current publisher of Penguin Random House India, for giving me this opportunity and privilege. I wish to record my sincere thanks to Dr Shashi Tharoor who introduced me to Penguin Books and *The Hindu*'s N. Ram for launching my writing career.

The First 'Stage'

I am overcome with shock and melancholy on hearing that my dear friend Dr MGR has passed away. Our friendship blossomed in 1945 with Jupiter Pictures' *Rajakumari*, directed by A.S.A. Samy, in which he starred as the hero and I was the scriptwriter. The memories of us staying in Coimbatore in the same house, exchanging views on politics and society, working together in the film world—our friendship maturing to the point of us serving in the same movement—cannot be forgotten and will forever remain green. Our comradeship in the film world would grow strong through our association in several films such as *Abhimanyu, Marudhanaatu Ilavarasi Mandhirikumari, Naam, Malaikallan, Kanchi Thalaivan, Engal Thangam, Pudhumaipithan* and *Arasilangkumari*. With that same sense of friendship, we were inseparable and as one in politics, up to 1972. We remained extremely friendly even in the aftermath of the changed political circumstances and through our differences.

[MGR] reigned as the unparalleled hero of Tamilagam's (Tamil Nadu) film world. He created a new era in the film arena. Few had made the film world theirs as he did and conquered it the way he did. He has the honour of making his party, the ADMK he founded in 1972, rise to power in a short span of time. There is none who would not praise his resolute will to serve tirelessly—even through his two–three years of illness—during the ten years he served as chief minister. By his ceaseless hard work and not giving up, he shone, winning people's affection.[1]

This is how Muthuvel Karunanidhi, popularly called Kalaignar, once MGR's leader, and later bête noire and political antagonist, reacted to the death of Tamil Nadu's chief minister Marudur Gopalan Ramachandran, or MGR.

J. Jayalalithaa, MGR's protégé and political heir, said she wished to commit 'sati' now that MGR who 'was everything to [her]' was no more.[2]

The matinee idol's fans had always considered their puratchi thalaivar, and the founder of the All-India Anna Dravida Munnetra Kazhagam, as immortal both on screen and in real life. They could not even stand their hero being killed in movies, to the point where an otherwise promising film like *Pasam* (Affection, 1962) died at the box office.

However, on the morning of 24 December 1987, his devoted fans woke up to a harsh reality when their leader succumbed to a cardiac arrest—like any other mortal. Overcome by grief, thirty-one people committed suicide.[3] For three years, MGR had been living on a transplanted kidney and with a speech impairment. Yet, his fans' belief in his immortality is explicable. Twice, their god had cheated death: On 12 January 1969, screen villain Madras Rajagopal Radhakrishnan, aka M.R. Radha, shot MGR and then himself, and the second occasion, when MGR's vitals failed on 5 October 1984. Even a few minutes delay would have been fatal, and yet he survived.

Fans were rapturous when in September 1967, in the aftermath of his brush with death, their hero was fittingly welcomed by heroine Jayalalithaa in *Kavalkaran* (Guard, 1967) when she sang, *'Ninaithaen vandhaai, Nooru vayadhu* (I thought of you and you showed up; you will live a hundred years)'—indicating the popular belief in MGR's longevity. In 1970, MGR himself triumphantly sang, *'Naan sethu pozhachavanda, Emaney paathu sirichavanda* (I died and came back alive; I have mocked the god of death).' The movie, *Engal Thangam* (Our Gold, 1970), featuring this song, was produced by Kalaignar's nephew Murasoli Maran and featured Jayalalithaa opposite MGR.

In 1972, he broke away from his parent party, the Dravida Munnetra Kazhagam (DMK), accusing its leader and then chief minister, Kalaignar, of corruption. Named after his late mentor and the DMK's founder, Conjeevaram Natarajan Annadurai (Anna), MGR's AIADMK created history when it captured power in Tamil Nadu in 1977, only five years after its founding. To his followers, his rise meant that the meek had inherited the earth. Their leader's success was theirs.

No actor or individual had ever possessed such a sway over Tamils in recent memory. In October 1984, as MGR, by then chief minister for a second time, fought for his life, twenty-two of his fans immolated themselves, unable to bear their hero's suffering. Twenty more had unsuccessfully attempted suicide, only to escape with burn injuries.[4] On 5 November 1984, an air ambulance flew MGR to Downstate Medical Centre, Brooklyn, New York.

MGR returned to Madras to a hero's welcome on 4 February 1985. During all this time, not a day passed without radio and television stations airing the memorable song from *Oli Vilakku* (The Lit Lamp, 1968), his hundredth film. The song by one of the most important of MGR's image-makers, lyricist Vaali, said it all about the larger-than-life figure:

> There are many lamps in your palace, oh god,
> But the jewelled one at your feet
> Is the light of my belief.
>
> Oh Lord,
> I washed your feet with tears.
> To make his life last,
> Today I beg you
> Murugaiyaa.
>
> Of your twelve eyes,
> If one or two show grace,
> There would be happiness in my eyes,
> The person who reigns in our hearts,
> The good one who gives bountifully,
> If the heavens beckon him,
> What would happen to this earth?
>
> The clouds would shed tears,
> And lightning writhe in pain,

Won't the sky melt, if the patron's face is not seen?
I am going with you to trade my life for his,
You should now command,
That our king's life be spared.*

The song had been prescient. In the movie, MGR suffers major burns. Actress 'Sowcar' Janaki, a widow, pleads for his life before the Tamil deity Murugan. The song sequence is aptly interspersed with multi-confessional prayers. Both in the state and outside, the outpouring of affection for the matinee idol was spontaneous and unprecedented. Offerings to temples went up by 40 per cent from the

---

* *Iraivaa un maaligaiyil . . .*
  Yethanaiyo mani vilakku . . .
  Thalaivaa un kaaladiyil . . .
  Yen nambikkaiyin oli vilakku . . .

  Aandavanae un paadhanggalai naan
  Kanneeril neeraattinaen
  Intha oaruyirai nee vaazha vaikka
  Indru unnidam kaiyaenthinaen
  Murugaiyaa . . .

  Pannirandu kangalilae ondrirandu malarndhaalum
  Yennirandu kangalilum inba oli undaagum
  Ullamadhil ullavarai alli tharum nallavarai
  Vinnulagam vaavendraal mannulagam yennaagum
  Maegangal kan kalangum
  Minnal vandhu thudi thudikkum

  Vaanagamae urugaadho
  Vallal mugam paaraamal

  Unnudanae varugindraen yen uyirai tharugindraen
  Mannan uyir pogaamal iraivaa nee aanaiyidu

Vaali records that MGR's wife, Janaki Ramachandran, told him at the Apollo Hospital that MGR was saved by this song. Vaali, *Naanum Indha Nootraandum*, Chennai: Kalaignan Pathippagam, 1995, p. 254.

time he fell ill until June 1985.[5] Makkal thilagam MGR was dear to all Tamils, the most prominent of whom was his friend of forty-two years, Kalaignar.

In an open letter titled 'I Too Am Offering Prayers', the DMK patriarch recalled their more than four-decade-long friendship, their sharing a small flat in Coimbatore, their horse cart ride around the town for two annas, and how they ate and hung out together. He reminisced how he had stuck to his recommendation that MGR play the lead role in *Mandhirikumari* (The Minister's Daughter, 1950) for which he had penned the dialogues. MGR would reciprocate this gesture by insisting on Kalaignar as the scriptwriter for his *Marudhanaatu Ilavarasi* (The Princess of Marudha, 1950).

Kalaignar movingly noted how MGR had carried him through the surging crowd at Egmore railway station in Madras, where he arrived after serving a six-month sentence for leading the party's historic 1953 Kallakudi agitation, and how MGR had lost his expensive watch in the process. The potent and sentimental missive said the last fifteen years of discord could not erase their earlier friendship of twenty-seven years.[6]

However, despite his jubilant return from the US, it was clear to the discerning that the once invincible hero was living on borrowed time. Yet, when his end came on Christmas Eve in 1987, the anarchy that followed and the millions that descended on the city showed that not since Anna had any leader enjoyed such affection in the state. As the several-kilometres-long cortège moved to the final resting place, the Marina in Madras, the crowd's refrain, 'MGR vazhga' (long live MGR), rent the air and women wailed and beat their breasts to express grief as if a family member had fallen. With his signature dark glasses and white fur cap, the Class Three dropout and three-time chief minister was, however, making a one-way journey this time. The second film star, after Ronald Reagan, to be elected to public office, MGR was both a phenomenon and an enigma. This is his story.

THE 'GOD OF DEATH'

Melakkath Gopala Menon was the eldest son of Angaratha Sangunni Mandradiyar, and he married Marudur Sathyabama of the Marudur *tharavad* or joint household. 'Marudur' prevailed over 'Melakkath' as the family name under the matrilineal system practised by, among others, their Nair community; the name Gopalan is patronymic. Sathyabama was Gopala Menon's third wife. He had divorced his first wife; the second wife had died. Gopala Menon and Sathyabama had two children: Thangam, a girl, and Chakrapani, a boy. Ramachandran arrived on 17 January 1917 as the last but not the least of the three children.[*7] For long, MGR's birthday was a closely guarded secret. It was Murugan Talkies Paramasiva Mudaliar, a friend, who, some sixty years later, on 17 January 1978, brought out advertisements to make public MGR's birthday.[8] MGR has said that his ancestors were originally from Pollachi, and were Mandradiyars of the Kongu Vellalars, a large middling farming community in the western part of Tamil Nadu.[9] MGR greatly resented being considered a Malayali, which would become Kalaignar's refrain after their split.[10]

On the paternal side, MGR's grandfather and father were 'multimillionaires'.[11] MGR's autobiography, *Naan Yaen Pirandhen?*, prominently features his mother, but is conspicuous for the little it says about his father. Sathyabama was from an equally affluent background. Hundreds of carts brought home the paddy from the family's holdings. Additionally, properties and a flourishing timber business spoke volumes about the family's prosperity. But that she had to be given away in marriage as the third wife indicates that the family had fallen on bad times.

Gopala Menon served as an honorary 'magistrate' in Aroor, Trichur, Karur and Ernakulam, among other places.[12] He was reputedly an upright and fearless man. Once, a party to a land dispute approached Gopala Menon to favour them. As he chose to expose them instead, they got him removed from his post. Gopala Menon responded by handing in his papers.[13] According to an apocryphal account, a Namboodri walking naked after his bath 'stopped and chatted up' a Nair girl, as was the practice. Instead of walking away from the ugly spectacle, Gopala Menon beat the Namboodri's bottom with the cane he was carrying.[14]

---

* However, MGR himself has said that he believes he was born in 1917 or 1918, but does not know the exact date. Sudangan, *Suttachu Suttachu*, Chennai: Kizhakku Pathippagam, 2005, p. 105.

Gopala Menon soon chose to move his family to the beautiful hill town of Kandy, in what was then Ceylon. The circumstances that prompted the move remain unclear. But Chakrapani has said that their father was fond of travel.[15] He found some law-related work before becoming principal of a 'college'—in all likelihood a primary-level estate school for Indian plantation workers.[16] Two-and-a-half years after MGR's birth, Gopala Menon died on their return to Kerala.[17] Thangam, the only sister passed away a year or two later. Superstitious Sathyabama slapped the moniker *mudikaalan* or the 'god of death' on her youngest child.[18]

Sathyabama inherited the children but little else. *Marumakkathayam* or the matrilineal system of inheritance had rendered her and her children 'destitute'.[19] It is likely that spurned by her husband's relatives in Kerala, Sathyabama moved to Kumbakonam in Tamil Nadu. In Kumbakonam, policeman Velu Nair, a distant relative, provided support.[20] Chakrapani and Ramachandran were admitted to the Yanaiadi elementary school in 1922.[21]

The family was poverty-stricken, and life proved extremely harsh.[22] Sathyabama often fasted so that she could feed her children. A bowl of rice gruel from a neighbour had once saved the brothers from starvation.[23] One day, observing Ramachandran's lean frame, Sathyabama expressed her anguish: 'If [you had been] a smart child, won't [you] have died as soon as [you were] born?' Later, as a star, MGR often recalled this and would remark, 'Today I am doing very well. But it is a pity that my mother is not there to rejoice over this.'[24]

Poverty gave rise to shameful situations. On one occasion, MGR saw Velu Nair brandishing a penknife at his mother. Before he could grasp the situation, Sathyabama grabbed his slippers and began beating up Velu Nair. A shocked MGR stopped his mother. Sathyabama declared to Velu Nair: 'For the last fourteen years, I had been waiting for this moment . . . When he [MGR] was barely four or five, you took him outside, despite his tender age, shut the door and beat me with his slipper. That son is now here. Yes! If you can, throw him out now and beat me. Can you?'

Fourteen years before, early one morning, Velu Nair was already high. Shouting 'What did you tell my sister?', he raised his arm to beat Sathyabama. As little Ramachandran began crying, Velu Nair took him outside. He also pushed Chakrapani out and shut the door on them. Chakrapani could simply shout, 'Amma! Run away! Come out!' Initially, Sathyabama tried to respond to Velu Nair, but as he began raining blows on her with MGR's slippers, she shrank in fear. It was the most humiliating moment for her and the children, who watched the painful spectacle helplessly through the open window. When Velu Nair was finished, he flung open the door and walked out.

The crying children rushed to hug their mother. 'Why should this happen, Mother? Let us go somewhere and take our lives,' Chakrapani sobbed.

'Before this happened, I would have been ready to die. But, from now on! No! No! I won't die. I have to live. You should grow and become adults. Then I can die . . . Okay, okay! Come! You have to have a bath and go to school.' So saying, Sathyabama wiped her tears and rose as though nothing had happened. MGR felt feverish after this incident. He had to skip school that day. All this flashed before MGR's eyes as he watched Sathyabama beating up Velu Nair.

Sathyabama had avenged the disgrace she had faced: 'I vowed to take revenge. I have done it.' The entire incident bewildered MGR. Why would his mother react to an incident so far back in time? Sathyabama said that akin to love and affection, the desire for revenge, too, never died. She explained the genesis of the quarrel. She had mentioned to Velu Nair's sister their crushing poverty and her intention to work as domestic help in some houses in order to get by. Velu Nair's sister scornfully suggested that Sathyabama take her children and go begging from one house to another. '[Begging] is part of *your* family tradition!' Sathyabama had retorted. Listening to his sister's version of events, the impetuous Velu Nair had become violent. Poverty could not erase Sathyabama's sense of self-respect or revenge.[25] It, however, led to the end of the children's schooling.

MADURAI ORIGINAL BOYS COMPANY

Ramachandran's first tryst with theatre was at the school play depicting the Hindu god-king Ram's children *Luv–Kush*. He was six and could hardly have guessed that he would make a career of the stage. In a hopeless situation, financially, Sathyabama stopped the children's schooling; Ramachandran's formal education ended with Class Three and Yettan (elder brother in Malayalam) Chakrapani's with Class Seven.[26]

When MGR was barely seven years old, his maternal uncle Narayanan Nair took the boys to the Madurai Original Boys Company (Boys Company) where he was a playback singer.[27] The boys had joined one of the best-known troupes, which would produce, among others, legends such as Pudukkottai Ulaganathan Chinnasamy or P.U. Chinnappa (PUC), K.R. Ramasamy (KRR), M.R. Radha (who was briefly associated with the company), Kali N. Ratnam and K.P. Kesavan. They would play a major role in shaping the young MGR and his brother, Chakrapani. Tamil theatre was witnessing a renaissance, thanks to Sankaradas Swamigal, who was considered its father, and scores of travelling drama troupes provided entertainment in the pre-cinema era.[28] Yet, public ambivalence to the performing arts was pronounced and performers were looked down upon.

As MGR noted, the brothers joined theatre because of one reason—'penury'.[29] 'We did not do it in order to become actors. We did it for the food and the money, and to relieve my mother from the burden of providing food for us.'[30] The little boy was the family's hope. The company, too, chose to invest in the younger of the two brothers with arresting features. As a true elder brother, Chakrapani was only too content to promote his sibling's career.[31]

True to their name, the boys companies were mostly made up of boys. A throwback to medieval and English Renaissance playing companies, these troupes only employed boys as it was considered unacceptable for women to perform. Besides, boys were easy to work with. The troupes were like a *gurukul* where all aspects of theatre—from acting to bookkeeping were taught. The brothers learnt music, dance and martial arts like silambam (stick fighting) and fencing. Their tongues lilted to metre and music, even as their feet grew nimble to dance and fight steps. The regimen was punishing. So was Sriramulu, the dance teacher, who believed that sparing the rod spoilt the child. He dealt his cane from the knees downwards, asking the student to keep his legs together so he could hit both ankles simultaneously. It was pure agony. The first time this happened, the seven-year-old MGR cried to go back to his mother. Comforting him, Chakrapani reminded

him of the reality: 'Go and do what . . .? Be a burden for Mother . . .?'
Packirisamy Pillai, a comedian, took pity and his intercession helped
free the boys from the 'torture'.[32]

KALI N. RATNAM

The boys were often part of a group cast. On other occasions, they took
on girls' roles. Initially, they had no lines to mouth. Senior artist Kali N.
Ratnam tutored the company's boys and was MGR's first teacher.[33] One
day, he asked little Ramachandran to perform as Prince Uttara of the
Virata kingdom. Little Ramachandran, as per custom, fell at Ratnam's
feet to be blessed. But, during the performance, when Uttara tripped
on Arjun unexpectedly, it elicited a cheer from the audience. Jealous,
the Uttara regular had played dirty by lending Ramachandran shoes
that were both meant for the left foot.[34] MGR would later recollect: 'If
they considered that it was your hair that landed you key roles, those
adversaries would give you a crew cut while you were asleep. That was
how competition reigned there.'[35]

Ironically, the weakling Uttara would later make a name for himself
and be compared to Hollywood's Errol Flynn and John Wayne. Early
his career at the company house in Nagapattinam, little Ramachandran
had seen a painting of two wrestlers locked in combat. Drawn to the
painting again and again, the little boy aspired to become a fighter like
them.[36]

If circumstance favoured him while playing Uttara, young
Ramachandran also proved equal to his task. The company frequently
staged *Ramayana*, a play known for its difficult and archaic Tamil
dialogues. The boy playing sage Agasthya had not returned from
leave. Little Ramachandran and two others were taught the part.
Ramachandran's performance landed him the role.

But Ramachandran was after all a boy, if not a child, and this
showed at times. In the eponymous play, he was the last of the seven
children of Nallathangaal. In folklore, let down by her in-laws and
fate, she drowns her children in a well before taking her own life.
Seeing the doom of his siblings, Ramachandran pleads sorrowfully,
'Mother, please spare me, at least to do the last rites for you.' At
this, the audience would sob. For a child of seven, it was surely a

weighty role. Nallathangaal ignores his pleas and the frightened child flees her deadly embrace. Ramachandran, however, stood still until beckoned by his prompters to withdraw backstage. It was a mistake. Stage manager Nannaiah Bhagavathar's cane fell on the child as he retreated. Additionally, playback Narayanan Nair's wooden clap landed on the child's head. For his part, dance teacher Sriramulu administered knocks exactly at the spot the wooden clap had landed earlier. Ramachandran rushed back on to the stage only to face Nallathangaal again. Terrified, he fled backstage again. This time Ratnam pinched him so hard that little Ramachandran wailed. 'That is how you should wail,' said Ratnam pushing the boy back on to the stage. Completely confused, the little boy's wails were heard long after he jumped into the well as per the storyline. The audience was terribly moved. The prompters had done their job. Later, hugging the boy, Ratnam assured him, 'You can become big in the future only if you go through such hardship.'[37] Ratnam could not have been more prophetic. Much uncertainty, hardship and humiliation would await MGR on his way to stardom.

K.P. KESAVAN, P.U. CHINNAPPA AND K.R. RAMASAMY

An incident involving a senior artist would make Ramachandran decide to learn all the parts in any script he read. P.U. Chinnappa was second only to the 'first superstar' of early Tamil cinema, Mayavaram Krishnamurthy Thyagaraja Bhagavathar, also called MKT or M.K.T. Bhagavathar.[38] PUC acted as the second hero, Taj-ul-Mulk or Dasan Mulk, in the company play *Gul-e-Bakavali* from the Arabian Nights. P.G. Venkatesan played the heroine. The gifted PUC, however, possessed an independent streak. One day, he deviated from the script and sang songs of his own. Venkatesan, who could not match PUC, became downcast and withdrew quietly. Sensing an opportunity, Ramachandran decided to memorize all the songs and parts of the others. When *Mahabharatha* was staged in Nagapattinam, Ramachandran acted as Abhimanyu, after which his monthly salary rose to a princely five rupees. Meanwhile, Ratnam had taught Ramachandran the stage nuances of delivery, hand and leg movements, including how to kick the floor and to exit the stage.[39]

Ramachandran's place in the company now seemed secure. PUC played Bharata and doyen K.P. Kesavan played Ram in the company's *Ramayana*. Kesavan would leave a major impression on Ramachandran, both as an actor and as an example of the transient nature of stardom. When *Ramayana* was staged in Trichy, PUC did not show up until the day before. And talks of PUC being wooed by another company began doing the rounds. In anticipation, Ratnam began to prepare K.R. Ramasamy, later on the first hero-politician of the DMK, for the part.[40]

KRR's benefit performances helped the DMK purchase its first headquarters 'Anbagam' (The Abode of Love). The party showed its gratitude by electing KRR to the Legislative Council in 1960, and when he became terminally ill, stood by him. Despite his promising beginning, KRR was overcome by his personal problems and would never become the DMK's alter ego, like MGR did. In the sixties, MGR would help him out and KRR's last film would be MGR's *Nam Nadu* (Our Country, 1970).[41] Within the company, however, the two contemporaries would fall out unexpectedly, with KRR mistakenly thinking that MGR had usurped his place.[42]

As he grew up, MGR began standing in for others. Besides, he could teach others their parts without the aid of the script. Naturally, proprietor Sachidanandam Pillai was quite taken with MGR. He began to play the hero in *Satyavan–Savithri*, the woman anti-hero in *Rajambal* and the 'enemy's' role in *Rajendran*. He said, in 1968, that his first performance as hero was as Manoharan in the *Manohara* play.[43] When the adolescent PUC's voice broke, MGR came to regularly perform the role of Bharata. Ratnam, however, rightly worried that all this would go to MGR's head. MGR now 'appeared as an enemy to the teacher who made him'.[44]

Perhaps the relationship was destined to be jinxed. At Salem, Ratnam thought that MGR had shirked the rehearsals with him. When MGR revealed he had rehearsed with others, Ratnam felt slighted and told MGR that he had escaped this time but he would wait to teach him a lesson. After this, Ratnam began to sideline MGR. One day, on his own, Pillai intervened to get the part of Prince Sundoor for MGR. The next day Ratnam angrily handed over the script saying: 'So you approach the proprietor to get roles?'

Yettan M.G. Chakrapani did not fare better with Ratnam either. Frugal by nature, the accountant switched off the kerosene lamps at the company house by 8 p.m. The dark house proved intolerable. Following complaints, the proprietor instructed that the lights be kept on beyond that hour. The tight-fisted accountant, however, observed the instruction in the breach. Soon the casing of the lamps began to go missing; when replaced, they went missing again. A week later, a poem lampooning the accountant showed up behind his seat. As though this was not enough, the boys read the poem aloud. When removed, a new poem took its place. Ratnam suspected that Chinnappa was behind the prank. PUC had left as his father was very ill.

Ratnam and company actor T.R.B. Rao sent the poems to the proprietor, who held an inquiry while at Vellore. Strangely, Rao's writing matched that of the poems. Unable to face Pillai's ire, Rao bolted to his home town. The truth was that PUC and M.G. Chakrapani had once practised copying Rao's elegant handwriting. The books that were inspected were, however, in PUC's original hand. Chakrapani could not tell them the truth. PUC had escaped by the skin of his teeth.

Not prepared for this turn of events, Ratnam now charged that Chakrapani had facilitated PUC's departure. Pillai, who bought the conspiracy theory, asked for a cane. PUC, who had left on account of his father's illness, had also left with the jewellery that he wore for his stage roles. 'None had left so far with the company's jewellery. You have allowed Chinnappa to abscond with the jewels? Who will compensate for this?' So saying, Pillai advanced menacingly towards Chakrapani, but was stopped in his tracks by MGR, who instinctively ran to his brother. Dropping the idea of corporal punishment, Pillai asked Chakrapani to leave, and the boy began collecting his belongings. Pillai was flummoxed as MGR, too, ran to collect his things and, hence, Chakrapani's expulsion was revoked. A hugely disappointed Ratnam began to harbour a grudge against the brothers.[45]

It did not help that having played some key roles, MGR was losing his head. But this good fortune proved to be fleeting with his voice breaking at adolescence. A 'fallen angel' now, he thought it would be better to end his life. Narayanan Nair assured him that vocal training would help restore his voice. However, Sathyabama could fully relate to her son's fears. A new pasture had to be found soon.[46]

LEAVING THE BOYS COMPANY: THE FIRST TIME

Sathyabama herself could not take the separation any more. The boys
had been away from her for seven years. Her sudden visit to Panruti
town where the company was camping led to talk that she had come
to take away the children. Ratnam and T.R.B. Rao advised the brothers
that such a move would be calamitous. They cited the example of
the talented K.B. Kamakshi's misfortunes after leaving the company.
Sathyabama mentioned another company, where there was an offer of
100 rupees a month for the brothers and they could live as a family.
When they approached Sachidanandam Pillai, moved by their mother's
pleas, he retorted:

> Boys! You have offers now from here and there after you have
> reached a stage! Where were those companies before? You are
> relatively settled now! Your mother is a woman. Don't be fooled
> by promises of more money. Listen to me; otherwise you will be
> starving again! Seeing your mother starve will hurt you! If you
> continue here, you will rise, become a well-known actor. Wear a
> bracelet, necklace and jewellery! It is up to you then!

Pillai was cruelly reminding them of their past. They were torn between
staying and leaving. MGR asked Chakrapani, 'Should we go with
Mother! Shall we stay?' Chakrapani advised, 'Good or bad we will stay
here. We will look into ways of bringing Mother to be with us. We will
cite this and ask Periyavar (the elder—here Sachidanandam Pillai) if he
can give us a pay rise.' A sceptical MGR asked, 'What if he says no . . .?'
Pat came the answer: 'We have to be patient till you become a big star!'
Chakrapani was only articulating what was well-understood all along:
MGR was the family's hope. Sathyabama, however, blamed Narayanan
Nair's magic spell for the boys' decision. She left telling her children that
they should consider that she was no more.[47]

Although the brothers stayed put for the time being, the zeal to
grow and prosper would eventually see them leave their first abode.[48]
Artists were almost bonded to the company and Pillai went to any extent
to punish the deserters, once reporting a deserter as a thief to the police
and compelling him to return. Those who managed to avoid returning

saw their prospects doomed by Pillai's machinations. A negotiated exit was the only solution. This time an irate Pillai told Sathyabama that if the boys quit, they would find themselves on the streets soon. Sathyabama's riposte was sharp. 'It won't be any different from what we went through before their joining your company!' Pillai now demanded that MGR return his gold chain and earrings. A disgusted Sathyabama threw the chain to the floor, saying, 'Let it come in handy for your medical expenses when needed.' An incensed Sachidanandam Pillai dared her to repeat her curse, and she retorted: 'Day and night you have sucked the blood of these little boys, working them and earning money; yet, you claim their just salary as yours! That is why I said it should come in handy . . .'

Sachidanandam Pillai's moustache puckered now. No one had spoken back to him; no one could even stand his gaze. He could single-handedly fight fifty thugs armed with sticks. Getting up, he roared: 'Woman! You don't possess even an inch of place! How dare you speak back to me?'

Sathyabama was not to be cowed. 'You may be a big proprietor. But, don't think that you can enslave everyone!' Pillai snarled, 'How dare you?' To which Sathyabama replied, 'This daring is part of the family tradition.' He now showed her out. She said, '[That is what] we have been saying, that we wish to go.'

Pillai threatened to have her jailed if she took the children without his permission. The frightened boys went and hugged their mother. Sathyabama fired the last salvo:

> If I wish, I can send you to prison now! If I tear my clothes and appear before the police with some bloody wounds, you will have to go to jail with your family; do you know that? Jail is not only for those like me, it is also for you! Whom do you threaten? I might be illiterate. I have not forgotten the law taught by my husband . . .

Sachidanandam Pillai was petrified.

At their workplace, the boys experienced a new kind of respect, akin to that accorded to the victorious returning from a major battle. Even Ratnam kept away from them. MGR had, however, confided their plans in a close friend and Sachidanandam Pillai came to know of them. Despite this, one day, Sathyabama was seen whisking the boys away through the main entrance of the Wall Tax Road hall in the middle of a performance.[49]

KANDASAMY MUDALIAR

The company began searching for the brothers even as they repaired to Thalakudi town where their patron Madras Kandasamy Mudaliar was training a troupe. The anxious brothers were comforted by the presence of Kandasamy Mudaliar's son M.K. Radha, PUC, P.G. Venkatesan and others. In any case, Kandasamy Mudaliar's affection and attention gave them much reassurance. In 1968, MGR listed him after Kali Ratnam as the one who taught him acting.[50] The brothers called him 'teacher'. Kandasamy Mudaliar had groomed his only son, M.K. Radha, for theatre.[51]

The troupe was to sail to Singapore, but, in the event, sailed to Burma, which had a small but significant Tamil population. There was a small problem though: The Boys Company was staging plays in Madras, and their search for the MG brothers was very much on. However, their fears proved unfounded. At sea, MGR would contemplate their unclear future. Later, in his memoirs, he would recollect Kalaignar's remarkable dialogue from their joint venture *Naam* (Us, 1953): 'What is experience? Isn't it what remains after everything has been lost!'[52]

The seafaring proved rough and P.G. Venkatesan began to cry due to the ubiquitous presence of water around. The next day, the boys grew seasick. But Kandasamy Mudaliar caringly administered medicine and made coffee for them with tinned powdered milk. The boys were touched and were happy when they reached land. Burma was in the throes of the nationalist movement and MGR refers to Saya San, a pioneer rebel hanged by the British, and the civil strife and violence which threatened to suck in the troupe. Thankfully, nothing like that happened and, after their performances in Burma, the company returned home.[53]

THE BOYS COMPANY ONCE AGAIN

Pleasantly for the brothers, their former owner Sachidanandam Pillai sent word for them on their return to Madras. He had discovered that none other than MGR could do the part in *Rathnavali* and indirectly laid the blame at Ratnam's door for his departure. MGR's salary went up by ten rupees. The change in MGR's fortune and his somewhat disrespectful behaviour antagonized Ratnam further.

Nonetheless, the family was finally reunited after a span of several years. And it was a happy family. To the brothers, their mother was god, although MGR and Sathyabama had the occasional argument. Sathyabama was proud of her son, and she justified his stubbornness saying that he had her 'dignity, speed and thoughts'. Chakrapani intervened in these quarrels only when required and, having ensured that the two had made up, he would leave quietly. In a lighter vein, he would quip that the mother and son would make up, leaving the intermediaries standing by.

MGR was almost sixteen years old by now, but he loved the attention. While acting in *Pathibakthi* (Devotion to Husband) as the villain's sidekick, Veeramuthu, an accident led to the swelling of MGR's right hand. The excruciating pain turned out to be a mixed blessing. Sathyabama had to brush his teeth, but could not reach his mouth. 'Hey, Mudikaalaa! Why you are killing me?' she complained good-naturedly. MGR would then bend down to make it easy for her. He had to recover quickly to avoid the risk of being replaced. For a week, Sathyabama fed him. 'That rare happening' soothed his pain immensely. This motherly love and wishes were the strengths that guided MGR.[54]

M.R. RADHA

Sathyabama was not the only one from whom he got an unusual gift. He would owe M.R. Radha for helping him find a new niche and guaranteeing his future on stage when adolescence had robbed him of his voice.

Sometimes a company's fortunes depended on a single artist and one such actor was to soon join the company, MGR wrote in *Naan Yaen Pirandhen?* 'He is a natural in fighting scenes, can handle any role, is not afraid of anyone, will not comply with any restrictions, moves easily with all . . .' Such were the things said about him and the boys were impatient for his arrival. 'Finally, one day he arrived; a head full of hair, muffler around the neck, coat, *veshti* and slipper . . . intrepid, fast [walker], and an uninhibited loud talker and laugher . . . Within [a] few days, he had changed the mood of the company house. Yes, he was Mr Radha, anna (the elder brother).'[55]

School did not interest the redoubtable M.R. Radha. One day, as he skipped school, his mother took him to task and refused to serve him an extra cut of fish to show her displeasure.[56] The ten-year-old walked out of his home in protest. While he stood at the Egmore railway station in Madras, not knowing what to do, a man asked him to carry his luggage. The passenger was Alandur Rangasamy Naidu, and he would take the boy into his Alandur Manamohana Rangasamy Naidu troupe. Life was very difficult and little Radha, like other children in the company, was beaten at times and he felt like a slave. However, when a relative found him and took him back, Radha, smitten by the theatre bug, wanted to return to the stage.

Radha was a born rebel. Non-Brahmins were prohibited from visiting the company's kitchen. Radha took pleasure in violating this dictum. To register his defiance, he would stop by at the kitchen to inquire about the progress of that day's cooking. Radha moved from Naidu's troupe to three other companies, before settling at Yadartham Ponnusamy Pillai Company, where K.R. Ramasamy, T.S. Balaiah and T.R. Mahalingam were present. One day, the company performed *Krishna Leela* (Krishna's Pranks) at Arani. T.R. Mahalingam played Krishna. Radha, who performed as his playmate, usually stole the audience's heart. Congress leader S. Satyamurti, who presided over that day's show, however, singled out T.R. Mahalingam for praise. Radha felt that one Brahmin was praising another. His dislike for the Congress party, to which Satyamurti belonged, and Brahmins became permanent and he began to toe Periyar E.V. Ramasamy's line.[57]

One of the most vocal devotees of Periyar, Radha displayed the backdrop *Dravida Marumalarchi Nataka Sabha* (Dravida Renaissance Drama Association) on stage and proclaimed 'Workers of the world unite!', becoming the first person to employ Dravida in the name of drama troupes. Radha made his mark as a revolutionary and a reformer on stage.[58]

His daring messages and his improvised dialogues saw his plays being frequently subjected to bans. Radha defied the bans by simply changing their titles. As he played cat and mouse with the police, they would show up to check if he was staging the approved script. Radha insisted that they buy tickets like any other; and they did.

Radha, an illiterate, was a genius and a maverick. His unorthodox zeal and fame saw Anna bring EVR and EVR's nephew E.V.K. Sampath to watch Radha's *Izhandha Kadhal* (Lost Love) at Kumarapalayam. The higher-class tickets were sold out and Radha refused to make any concessions for them. The stalwarts of the Dravidian movement sat on the floor and enjoyed the play. At the interval, Anna, on his own, took the stage to pay the highest compliment to Radha: 'We have come uninvited. Radha's one play is equivalent to a hundred Dravidar Kazhagam conferences.'[55] Radha would later become the flag bearer of the Dravidar Kazhagam.

His versatility made him one of the most popular villains and comedians on stage and in films till the 1960s. *Ratha Kanneer* (Tears of Blood, 1954) remains his most memorable movie performance ever. Only the second Radha in MGR's life, M.R. Radha's performance during his brief sojourn with the Boys Company would be a great eye-opener for MGR to reinvent himself. Little did MGR or Radha know then that they would be the most paired hero and villain on screen till the 1960s and that, three decades later, on 12 January 1967, Radha would shoot at MGR before trying to shoot himself.

K.P. Kesavan played the lead in *Pathibakthi* at the Boys Company. All major roles had been taken. A nonchalant Radha would choose on the day of the play to don the role of Veeramuthu, a sidekick to the villain. Veeramuthu would come to life like never before and outshine his boss, Gangatharan, the villain. The audience greedily lapped up Veeramuthu's every move, his manner of speech and the way he moved his cigarette from one corner of his mouth to the other.

Radha's innate insouciance had elevated the colourless role of Veeramuthu to a consequential one. The play went limp in his absence. Radha's presence of mind, quick wit and his ability to transform himself into the character made his magnetism felt. But, an independent spirit, he was unable to stand the company's restrictions. He left in a few months.

On Radha's exit, MGR came to play Veeramuthu.[60] MGR recorded that from the beginning he had veered towards fight sequences in plays:

I had always been interested in things like wrestling, boxing, silambam and sword fight. I was considered by others in the drama troupe as someone who acted tough and deftly during fights, as talented, knew tactics, and was strong and brave. Whether I possessed these traits or not, as others kept repeating this to me I grew confident that I was [indeed] daring, strong and talented.[61]

This natural predilection helped MGR perform physically dangerous roles such as Veeramuthu. Playing detective, mentor Ratnam would throw him down and box him, and the thunderous sound caused by MGR's fall would invite lusty cheers from the audience. The *thud* however, had to reach the last row of the hall. Therefore, the floor was not stacked with hay or coir to cushion the fall. It did not matter whether your head was broken or your limbs suffered a fracture. What mattered was the sound. MGR did so well as Veeramuthu that even when he suffered from diarrhoea and cholera, he was asked to perform the climax.[62]

Ratnam however, continued to entertain the impression that MGR was somewhat disrespectful towards him. MGR's actions did not help matters either. At the *Kabirdas* (Kabir's Slave) play, Ratnam wished for MGR to play Bharata. (Bharata simply held the royal umbrella for Ram.) MGR told Ratnam, 'Give me a role where I will speak some dialogue . . . Don't ask me to hold the umbrella.' Only the redoubtable P.U. Chinnappa had ever said 'no' to Ratnam in the troupe's history. Ratnam responded ingratiatingly: 'Sorry, I had made a mistake . . .' MGR felt that he had cowed Ratnam, but he was clearly mistaken. Ratnam would hit back.

In *Kadar Bhakthi* (Devotion to Homespun), chanting 'Vande Mataram' or 'long live our motherland' and 'long live Gandhi', protesters would stage civil disobedience before a store selling foreign cloth. The police would beat them up and drag them away. The scene aroused the audience so much that a repeat became mandatory, and every actor wished to be part of this highly charged scene. When MGR volunteered, Ratnam mockingly said, 'Oh! You can't be doing minor roles. Kindly be seated!' Sachidanandam Pillai, who was present, was shocked by the honorific used by Ratnam for MGR. At his request, Ratnam explained the earlier incident, but also took a jibe at him saying that his support had made MGR disobedient. As the proprietor's moustache crumpled angrily, MGR expected that he would be asked to leave. Pillai's reaction was unthinkable.

> Yaenda ('you' in singular)! Do you know why I took you? It is because you are fair-skinned and good-looking, and I thought that it would be nice if you donned the roles. Did we take you because your singing skills are out of this world? . . . Careful! If you are willing to accept the roles given by Ratnam, you can stay! Otherwise, just scoot!

Pillai had committed near murder by chiding MGR in the presence of all his fellow actors. MGR quietly left the place to sob in private. A while later, a boy showed up to thrust some pieces of paper containing dialogues, asking MGR to be prepared for the 'enemy' role. Tormented, MGR wanted to quit. But then, which other troupe would have him or give him meals at the hour and salary by the month? On the proprietor's advice, Ratnam had offered him the role and the arrangement was that the messenger and he should alternate playing the part. Pillai had reasoned with Ratnam that MGR's request for a solid role was not unreasonable; besides, he had told Ratnam to punish MGR if he deserved it, but not to deprive him of roles. MGR was touched by Pillai's graciousness. However, Ratnam had not taken kindly to what happened. He nursed his grudge and would become the brain behind the police complaint against them later.[63]

MGR'S GENEROSITY

One attribute that required no tutorship and came naturally to MGR was his innate sense of giving and hospitality. Reputedly, the fire in MGR's hearth was never allowed to die out; some fifty–sixty people would be fed at his home, at each meal, every day. 'Have you eaten?' was one of his signature greetings, one which he used unfailingly, not just with visitors but even with his driver and staff. 'He was a generous man, and never forgot his modest roots and days of poverty. He had a genuine concern for the poor,' his driver noted.[64]

He was the ultimate host and he insisted on, and enjoyed, serving his guests himself and frequently encouraged them to stuff themselves with food. He would ask everyone around him if they had eaten and would make sure they did. As chief minister, when he came to know that his drivers and aides had not eaten, when he was hosting an official dinner at a five-star hotel, he grew angry. The next day, he summoned the officials to tell them that, rules not permitting, they had two options: Either to charge the expenses to his personal account or to change the rules. The rules were changed.[65]

He seemed to have been born with this gift of generosity, like Karna. Those who came in contact with him were awestruck by the man's large heart. The *Murasoli* of yesteryears is replete with MGR's munificence and generous acts, some deliberate and calculated, but many done quietly and behind the scenes. Lyricist Vaali records a touching moment during the making of *Engal Thangam*. While writing the song '*Naan alavodu rasipavan* (I appreciate things in moderation)', Vaali struggled for a matching second line. Producer Murasoli Maran's uncle, Kalaignar, instinctively suggested, '*Edhayum alavindri koduppavan* (I give limitlessly)', clearly displaying what he thought of MGR. Kalaignar's words said it all about the man's generosity.

In 1962, MGR made history when, following Prime Minister Jawaharlal Nehru's radio appeal in the wake of the Chinese incursion, he announced a contribution of 75,000 rupees, the single largest to the war fund. (Actors Dilip Kumar, Raj Kapoor and Meena Kumari had given 50,000 rupees each.[66]) MGR rushed with a cheque for 25,000 rupees as the first tranche to Chief Minister Kamaraj's residence. Kamaraj had, however, left to catch a train. Hastening to the Egmore railway station, MGR went straight into Kamaraj's coupé. A surprised Kamaraj received the contribution saying, 'Very happy' and arranged for it to be flashed as news so that it would encourage others to contribute too.

On his return to Madras, a pressman asked Kamaraj if MGR's act was aimed at self-promotion. An upset Kamaraj retorted: 'Keep quiet. How much did you give? You might give or you might not. Why should you make light of those who give? Did he plan this? [Did he know that] Nehru was going to address the nation? I was to travel by train. How is this possible? I was stunned when I received MGR's cheque. I instructed that the media get this news.' MGR had also written to Nehru. Nehru sent him back a thank you letter.[67]

No. 556-PMO/62

New Delhi,
27th October, 1962.

Dear Shri Ramachandran,

I have received your letter of the 22nd October. I am grateful to you for your generous donation of rupees seventy five thousand for the benefit of our soldiers on the front. I note that you have given rupees twenty five thousand of this to Shri Kamaraj, Chief Minister of Madras, and the balance will be paid in due course.

Yours sincerely,

Jawaharlal Nehru

Shri M.G. Ramachandran, MLC,
160, Lloyds Road,
Madras 14.

In 1970, to the question 'Your critics accuse you of helping others for your personal gain', MGR responded as follows:

> We all agree that helping people is man's duty. But the moment an individual becomes conscious that he is helping his fellows, it ceases to be help. So why do you want to make me useless to myself and others by planting an undesirable thought in me?
>
> I am not prepared to acknowledge the existence of a selfless man. Even Mahatma Gandhi was not entirely unselfish. There could have been no more selfish a man than him in the whole world in trying to attain his goals. That is why they called him the Father of the Nation.

My selfishness may not be so grand, I do not have that kind of
stature, but I cannot deny the smidgeon of selfishness in my tiny
heart, like a sparrow that realizes its life's joy within its little nest.
I leave it to you to judge the nature of my selfishness.[68]

Modern Theatres' director, K. Somu, notes an interesting episode about
MGR's conscious acts of generosity. Once, when Somu met him at
Golden Studios, MGR, as was his wont, compelled his visitor to eat
with him. Somu saw MGR concentrating on the day's dailies. 'I was
looking for a news item. I could not find it,' he explained. Somu said, 'I
had seen it in the morning itself.' MGR asked, 'Which daily?' Somu said
MGR was holding the daily and showed him the news item. A happy
MGR pinched Somu's cheek fondly. He was looking for news of his gift
of 5000 rupees.[69]

But, for every conscious and calculated act of charity, there appear
to be many that were spontaneous, private and hidden. In 1983, actor
Sivakumar estimated that MGR's unpublicized acts of charity would
amount to more than 1 crore rupees.[70] We know now that it possibly
ran into several crores. In late April 1987, months before his death, MGR
had channelled 4 crore rupees to the Liberation Tigers of Tamil Eelam
(LTTE) from government funds.[71] When President J.R. Jayewardene
made it an issue, Prime Minister Rajiv Gandhi pulled up MGR. He took
the cheque back, only to give the money from his 'personal funds', and
this fact would not have come to light if the LTTE's Anton Balasingham
had not decided to make it public in 2003.[72] And prior to this he had
given them 2 crore rupees.[73]

Stories abound about how, even when MGR himself had little, he
would go to the aid of others. MGR and Paramasiva Mudaliar had gone
for a walk on a cold Margazhi (December–January) day. Paramasiva
Mudaliar was dressed in a full-sleeved shirt and had wrapped a shawl
over it. MGR wore a cotton vest undergarment and had a shawl
wrapped around his head. They came across an old woman, fighting
the cold by covering herself with a torn sari. At the sight of this, MGR
instinctively removed his shawl and laid it on the old woman, and
turned to his friend, completely oblivious of his gesture, to continue the
walk. Paramasiva Mudaliar mused: 'MGR gave away even his modest
belongings to the poor old woman. Why did I not think of this? So I,

from a wealthy background, am not endowed with the attribute of generosity. But MGR, who is poor, is gifted with it. In the future, he would become big and famous.'[74] Paramasiva Mudaliar was clairvoyant.

MGR's sense of generosity was already in place from the very beginning of his film career. While acting in Salem, in Modern Theatres' films, MGR would have spent half his salary by the time the film was finished. Seeking the studio staff list, he would prepare individual envelopes for each employee, with his name, and put varying amounts for each of them.[75] Later in his career, MGR cared for the studio staff and others, who were part of his movies, by ensuring the comfort and food arrangements for them were in place in outdoor shoots. He would check the menu himself and, if he felt that it was unsatisfactory, summon the cook, give him a wad of currency and tell him: 'Money is not a concern . . . These people have left their wife, children, parents and have come this far to make a living . . . I am not here as the movie's hero alone.'[76]

Every Pongal day, MGR distributed gifts to his staff and others. If he had to borrow money to celebrate Pongal this way, he did. Similarly, when there were floods or huts were gutted, MGR was the first to provide relief. Sometime in the late fifties, seeing rickshaw men pedalling, drenched in the rain, MGR spontaneously and famously gifted 6000 raincoats to them. Each plastic coat had cost ten rupees.[77]

In the 1962 general elections, a DMK propagandist song sung MGR's praise adequately thus:

Bharata Karnan's palm
Became pink thanks to his generosity.
But Dravida Karnan's entire body
Turned pink, thanks to his generosity every day.[78]

Similarly, as MGR convalesced in the US in 1984, election campaign posters aptly declared: 'Koduthu koduthu sivantha karam, kumbittu ketkirathu (The palm that has turned pink by giving, supplicates for your vote)'.

MGR himself said that he was living by what Anna had said: 'The money from the people should go back to them.'[79] In Padagoti (Boatman, 1964), Vaali aptly wrote:

He gave all that he gave
To whom did he give?
Did he give for just one?
No, he gave for everyone*

As chief minister, MGR continued to extend help to as many people who sought it—be it a girl's education or a wedding or surgery or bailing out an actor and preventing the auction of his house or, for that matter, as already mentioned, quietly giving away money to the LTTE from his 'personal funds' in 1984.[80] As chief minister, when his staff nabbed a woman who was faking as a beggar, he asked them to let her go and narrated an incident involving reformist comedian 'Kalaivanar (Lover of Arts)' N.S. Krishnan (NSK), an unparalleled giver. Once, NSK summoned back a pregnant woman and gave her another 100 rupees saying: 'The first hundred rupees was out of my sympathy for you. The second is in appreciation of your acting talent. Please take out the bundle of clothes that you have around your stomach.'[81]

His charity transcended political boundaries. When MGR's fiercest critic CPI leader A. Baladhandayutham reluctantly approached him for financial assistance for erecting a statue of P. Jeevanandam, MGR ran towards him, and warmly embraced him, moving his visitor terribly. When he knew his mission MGR said: 'You are not going to erect Jeeva's statue. I am,' and sponsored the statue all by himself.[82]

In 1977, poet Kannadasan, MGR's harshest vilifier-turned-admirer, charged that 'MGR's charity is only to buy others'.[83] Even after this, when MGR made him Poet Laureate, a visibly moved Kannadasan said: 'When I die, I will be given state honours. I wish to thank MGR in advance for honouring me thus.' On the poet's death, in 1981, Chief Minister MGR got on to the bier, lifted the poet's head and placed it on a small stool. 'Now people can see the poet's face better,' he said.[84]

---

* *Koduthathellam koduthaan,*
  Avan yaarukaaga koduthaan,
  Orutharukka koduthaan
  Illai oorukaaga koduthaan

In his will, MGR formed a charitable trust and left a major share of his Ramavaram Gardens property to house a home for the deaf and dumb.

In *Panam Padaithavan* (The Moneyed One, 1965), MGR would sing the following lines in the song '*Kan pona pokile* (Whichever direction the eye is cast)' by Vaali:

Alive or gone, fame should last
The world should say: Who like him?*

MGR lived true to those words. Traits such as generosity are inborn. Some things come easily, but others with much difficulty and uncertainty. MGR's entry into Tinseltown was one such instance of the latter.

7

---

* *Irundhaalum maraindhaalum paer solla vendum*
 Ivar pola yarendru oor solla vendum

Stepping into Cinema and Marriage

Sachidanandam Pillai of the Boys Company and his partner were making the play *Pathibakthi* as a movie. Kandasamy Mudaliar had penned the dialogues for the movie for Manorama Films. Both movies advocated abstinence from alcohol. Under alcohol and the villain's influence, M.K. Radha, the hero, ill-treats his wife, Gnanambal. One day, under the mistaken belief that he had shot his friend dead, he escapes to Ceylon. On his return, the hero is charged with murder. The climax sees an inspector turn up with evidence that proves the hero's innocence. MGR was to play that inspector.

The Boys Company had folded up. The brothers were not offered roles in the film and MGR said they were not the kind who would solicit them. One day, they ran into their teacher Kandasamy Mudaliar unexpectedly: 'We were embarrassed to say that we had no roles and afraid to say we did!' wrote MGR. (In the event, the company did not offer them any roles.) It was then that Kandasamy Mudaliar spoke about the possibility of a detective's role for MGR in *Sathi Leelavathi*.[1] MGR said:

> My role in the play [*Pathibakthi*] was as a sidekick to the villain. Believing that I would be given the same role in the film, where there was no room to shine, I met with Mr Kandasamy Mudaliar who was penning the dialogues for *Sathi Leelavathi* to seek [better] role[s] for us.[2]

Whether MGR was offered a role in *Pathibakthi* or not was not that important. What was important was that landing a 'good role' would remain his sole objective. It was the key to 'eradicate poverty' and to 'prosper'.[3]

On 28 March 1936, when the movie was released, MGR was only nineteen years old and, at the time of its making, he sported no facial hair. Despite this, he realized that if he played the role of the detective, the hero's wise friend, he would leave an impression.[4] His quest would, however, prove elusive and he would end up playing the inspector, a role he was averse to. Chakrapani would never feature in the movie.

The brothers met *Sathi Leelavathi's* producer, Marudachalam Chettiar, a tall, well-built man with a thick moustache, and Kandasamy Mudaliar at a hotel on Wall Tax Road. When Marudachalam Chettiar held out a 100-rupee note as advance, the brothers were overwhelmed. It was their first 100 rupees. *Sathi Leelavathi's* total fee would be 300 rupees.

As they walked home, MGR asked his brother if the note was authentic, to which Chakrapani said that he had never seen one before. Back home, Sathyabama held the note against the light, and declared it contained a watermark. After this, she placed it before her husband's picture, lit camphor and then applied sacred ash on her sons' foreheads.[5] MGR could not sleep that night. It felt that the house was filled with silver coins and that there was no place to put their feet.[6]

The brothers were in for a shock to learn later that M.V. Mani, a veteran with the Boys Company, had been offered the detective's role. But they worried more that M.V. Mani might innocently spill the beans about their cinema plans. On Sathyabama's advice, they brought their personal effects and filed a pre-emptive police complaint with a copy to the British commissioner of police. When the company lodged its complaint, the local Indian inspector planned to take them into custody. Sathyabama now asked her sons to send a new letter with copies of the old, this time by registered post, to the commissioner. Subsequently, the Indian inspector was directed to provide protection and obtain in writing from the brothers that they felt safe. The unlettered Sathyabama had proven that she was a worldly-wise woman.[7]

ENCOUNTERING N.S. KRISHNAN

The company's threat had been staved off, but MGR's part in *Sathi Leelavathi* remained a question mark. Marudachalam Chettiar had acted without Kandasamy Mudaliar's knowledge when he offered the detective's role to Mani. Kandasamy Mudaliar could only fret, but could not offer anything concrete just yet to the brothers. Thus, when MGR turned up on the sets of Sathi Leelavathi, he was not sure of his part. Despite this not-so-encouraging beginning, the ambience on the sets was about to greatly improve. One day, Mani and the others told MGR: 'An actor will join us tomorrow! That's it. This whole place will become fun; furthermore, no one can be lazy.'

N.S. Krishnan, for that was whom they were referring to, made his entry dramatically. Sathi Leelavathi was the first film for both MGR and NSK (although Menaka [1935] became the first for NSK as it was released earlier). Krishnan, the Charlie Chaplin of the south, and his second wife, T.A. Madhuram, peddled reform with humour. NSK's philanthropy of mythical proportions, his hero-like popularity and his gravitas made him the patriarch of Tamil cinema. When he died in 1957, the crowds at his funeral are said to have been comparable to those at Gandhi's.[8] NSK traversed both the tinsel and the public world with ease. He was close to the communists and the Dravidian movement, and was a regular at the DMK conferences.

On the sets of Sathi Leelavathi, turning to MGR, NSK said, 'My dear! I understand that your siren burst while you were still young!' referring to his throat as a siren and the breaking of his adolescent voice. MGR was irritated.[9] But there was more embarrassment in store for him.

'DID YOU SEE THE STARS?'

MGR's walk and mannerisms quickly became the butt of NSK's jokes. Unable to match his wit, MGR thought instead to wrestle with him. Strangely, NSK, the reel buffoon, agreed to the wrestling idea. On the day of the fight, he typically warned MGR that he, 'a simple comedian', could afford to lose but the 'brave' MGR could not.

MGR quickly threw NSK to the ground. But the next thing he knew was that NSK was sitting on him. Even as the painful truth that he had been tricked sank in, NSK teased him, 'What, Ramachandra! Did you see the stars?' MGR felt that he was looking at the sky more for his honour than at the stars. NSK kept rubbing it in, repeating his question and jeering, 'Big wrestler! He wished to lock me. Lock! I just locked him; that's it! Only one lock! He was biting the dust!'

MGR was now incensed and challenged NSK to a second fight, which he agreed to. As MGR sprang ragingly at him, NSK sat down suddenly. 'Get up! If you have any dignity or honour, fight me!' NSK smilingly conceded that he had no honour and also agreed that he had lost the second fight. He, however, taunted MGR, 'But, how many stars did you count? First tell me that!' Chakrapani and everyone else on the sets were in splits at this. 'He was Kalaivanar's close friend! What did he care about my defeat?' wrote MGR later.

MGR would not give up yet and he challenged NSK to a serious fight. NSK, who agreed, would stand up as though readying for a fight but would simply sit down when MGR sprang at him. When this happened some ten to fifteen times MGR resignedly told him, 'Admit it, anna, you have no guts!' An unflappable NSK said, 'Come, come! Let us bathe and go to eat! We have sand all over us', and led him to the well.

When MGR was wiping his hair dry, NSK told him, 'You should not take the enemy for granted. Never consider him as being weaker than yourself.' MGR was very upset. He felt that after insulting him, why should NSK begin to offer advice?

Over time, NSK's genuine affection and concern drew MGR close to him, and he gratefully recorded NSK's advice as laying the foundation for his development in the tinsel world. The lesson that he learnt from NSK was this: However lofty an idea, if the recipient has no trust in the advocate, it will not find acceptance. NSK himself had now earned MGR's respect. He exhorted his young charge thus:

> You should read some good magazine. You should not accept the ideas in it without due consideration. You should read the magazines that rebut those ideas. You should not read too many magazines and confuse yourself. Choose two magazines opposed to each other and read them. Compare the explanations of the magazine with the people you meet, [and] the incidents that you encounter in your life. Hold on firmly to what you consider as fair![10]

Kalaivanar had recommended 'Ayya' or EVR's weekly magazine *Kudiarasu* (the Republic). MGR recorded what happened afterwards:

I did. For the first one–two weeks I did not understand anything. Still I persisted. It had been recommended by Mr N.S.K., whom I held in high regard. How can I discontinue reading it? I read. After a few weeks, I began to understand one or two things. After reading more, I was able to talk to others about it. After a few days, I was able to also discuss the ideas therein. It was a time when even if the Almighty had come down to preach about widow marriage and inter-caste marriage, [they would have] firmly reject[ed] them, as so extreme were people's views on these ideas. As for my mother, when it came to belief in God, she was firmer than the others.

Sathyabama spoke firmly:

Don't believe that all you read will be compatible with life. We say that what was said in [the] yesteryears does not hold good now. How can we be sure that what we advocate today would be right in the future? Therefore, let those who advocate do the advocacy. You listen to them carefully. But don't reach a hasty conclusion.

She said that NSK might be a good man, but there was no harm in MGR being cautious. Sathyabama was patient with her son and his eagerness for new ideas, but wanted to contain his zeal. For the first time, however, MGR felt that his mother was unlettered.[11]

BRAHMIN–NON-BRAHMIN

Having been exposed to theatre as a boy, MGR was thus susceptible to two competing influences: The changes in the sociopolitical environment that theatre mirrored and his ultra-conservative mother.

The non-Brahmin Dravidian movement was gathering momentum during these years. Non-Brahmin elites founded the precursor to the Dravidian parties, the Justice Party, in 1916—the year of the non-Brahmin manifesto, which sought affirmative action for non-Brahmins in elections and government jobs. The extraordinary historical and literary activity in the nineteenth and early twentieth centuries had culminated in such stirrings. Professor Christopher Baker of Cambridge University suggests that while the rest of India pursued literature and arts during that period, Tamil Nadu's 'dominant intellectual interests' were centred on history and language. These interests were stoked by British administrators whose passion for the history of their colonized land saw them chronicling temple inscriptions, studying palm-leaf manuscripts and recording oral traditions of history.

The prodigious compilation by Colonel Colin Mackenzie, the first Surveyor General of India, of the south Indian manuscripts led, in turn, to the remarkable district gazetteers of local history. A collection of epigraphic material followed. The advent of the printing press and the search for Tamil literature—given up as lost or about to be lost— by giants of savants would reveal a new world. Thus, the search and republishing of early literary works by Arumuga Navalar and S.V. Damodaram Pillai of Jaffna, and U.V. Swaminatha Iyer and Pillai's finding of the two great Sangam anthologies of the *Agam* (interior) and *Puram* (exterior) would forever change the course of political discourse in the Tamil country. The Sangam period appeared a glorious one. As an example, one *Agam* song suggested that women hurled precious stone earrings to chase chickens pecking on food left to dry in the sun.

According to Baker, how such a 'utopia' was lost had to be explained and a villain, or villains, had to be found, even as the British, the Aryans and the Muslims appeared to be likely candidates.[12] Perhaps a more dispassionate appraisal would have revealed that great civilizations do lose cadence with time and that internecine fighting had been the bane of Tamils.

English education and the printing press revolutionized the dissemination of these literary and historical discoveries among the non-Brahmin elite.[13] The result was a nascent sense of non-Brahmin consciousness. If the Tamils were experiencing an identity crisis then, the European missionaries inadvertently helped alleviate it. They turned the spotlight on Tamil and its richness. With civil servant and linguist Francis Whyte Ellis's studies on comparative Dravidian linguistics, and later, missionary and linguist Robert Caldwell's *A Comparative Grammar of the Dravidian or South Indian Family of Languages*, a Tamil identity came to be forged, with its language, history and culture, ripe for the political arena.

Of the possible causes, the Brahmin, with his prayers and texts in Sanskrit, his somewhat lighter complexion and his Vadama (from the north) mark appeared more like the remnant of an affliction and the enemy within, if not easy prey. Even as the non-Brahmin Justice Party made tepid gains, a fiery revolutionary raised his head amidst the Tamils—EVR. An ardent Congress man, EVR was disillusioned with the party as it was not amenable to his radical reforms. He then quit to found his Self-respect movement in 1925, which advocated equality at birth, radical social reforms eschewing the Brahmin and his rituals in one's social life, a separate Tamil Nadu, and, alternatingly, a Dravida Nadu made up of the Dravidian south. His work had a huge impact on consolidating the non-Brahmin consciousness and creating a militant, albeit fringe, non-Brahmin identity.

The non-Brahmin, or the Dravidian, movement was yet to make a huge impact on cinema. It would have to wait until the 1940s, when the likes of poet Bharatidasan and scriptwriter Elangovan would sanitize Tamil cinema of Brahminical Sanskritized Tamil. In the 1940s, Anna and Kalaignar would herald what would be later termed as Dravidian cinema. Nonetheless, it seemed that the movement's sympathizers were already making inroads into Tamil cinema. One of its most important persons was N.S. Krishnan, who had taken it upon himself to be an early political teacher of MGR.

Sathi Leelavathi's cast were all housed in one place and a Brahmin cooked vegetarian meals for them. The Brahmin cast dined adjacent to the kitchen, while others ate in the veranda outside. NSK did not like this distinction and first took up the issue with M.V. Mani, a Brahmin. When Mani said that the practice was an established one, NSK replied that it could be changed as easily. Mani retorted: 'How is that possible? Did we establish this? These practices were established by our ancestors and should it not be they who should decide?' NSK argued: 'True. They ought to decide on an issue that they had introduced. But we are the sufferers! So, the responsibility to change should also fall on us!'

Mani said, 'This is fate. What can be done?' NSK replied: 'If we consider this fate then we should also take what is to happen as fate.' Mani was sarcastic: 'Oh! So you wish to carry on "self-respect" propaganda here too? . . . You are to change fate itself. Why don't you stop your speeches and do something good for the country.' An undeterred NSK said: 'Sure! We will first reform this house and then move to the nation.' As he stopped payments to the cook, and appointed another to prepare non-vegetarian meals, a compromise was reached. Under its terms, the Brahmin cook would cook vegetarian meals and for two days, the new cook would prepare non-vegetarian food for the others.

MGR asked NSK: 'Why annan (elder brother)! You could have withheld payments to the cook at the outset.' NSK replied, 'If they had changed, I would have not gone to this extent. I slowly tried to change them. It did not work. So, I thought it was time for the final assault and, therefore, used Ram's weapon [Ram's arrow which is used as a metaphor to indicate that it is the final recourse] and finished the job.'[14]

If Mani was conservative he was equally a connoisseur of good writing and would introduce MGR to the contemporaries of good Tamil writing.[15]

CALF LOVE

MGR, the adolescent, was also exposed to love around this time. His autobiography speaks at length about his calf love for a girl, a fellow tenant's daughter. His efforts to woo the girl bordered on the comical and the tragic as the girl hardly took notice of him. One day, he decided to up his efforts. The girl usually came out to throw away the leaves on which dinner had been eaten (plantain leaves are often used as plates in the south). Faking a headache, he lay down on his cot at 7 p.m. waiting for her. As he got up, seeing her go out, Sathyabama stopped him, asking him to apply some balm and lie down quietly so that his headache would disappear. He saw the girl smile at this.

The next evening, he mustered up the courage to hold her hand. Smiling, she took back her hand and left him. This was enough to go and brag of his progress to his friends. When they found out that the girl was yet to attain puberty, they had a hearty laugh. Some months later, when he said the matter should not be broached as 'she has attained puberty', the friends broke out into more laughter. They calmed an angry MGR down saying that he had wooed her when he should not have and now when he should, he was shying away.

Then, on their advice, he wrote a small note seeking a meeting. She refused to accept the note. The second time he tried, her hands shook as she took it. After that she avoided him. One day, when he spotted her, he held her hand and sought a response. She asked him to let go of her hand and went away.

One day, her family was going out and they left her with MGR's mother. At 2 a.m., she came slowly towards his room. As he tried to hold her hand, she forbade him and, standing firm, she spoke clearly: 'Are you going to marry me?' MGR had not expected the question. As his mind raced, she continued, 'Your caste is different. Mine is different. You are a Malayali and I am a Tamil. How can there be marriage? What would happen to my life if it were known that you write to me? Who would marry me? Henceforth, at least don't do such things based on someone's advice.' She concluded by saying that she would be happy if she were fortunate enough to marry him, but that would not happen, and she then bent down as if to touch his feet and left. In 1968, in response to being asked to name 'a major challenge in his personal life', MGR would simply say, 'It was the love a girl had for me. Please don't ask me more on this.'[16]

THE DREADED INSPECTOR'S ROLE

Initially, NSK had the role of a Brahmin with a few scenes in *Sathi Leelavathi*. He told Chakrapani that the role would not bring him recognition, and later managed to beef it up, mirroring the then famous Harold Lloyd. MGR's role, meanwhile, remained unclear. On Chakrapani's suggestion, the three of them went to seek Kandasamy Mudaliar's intercession. Kandasamy Mudaliar assured them of another weighty role, the hero's friend. However, MGR would again be in limbo then as Nammalvar, the heroine in the play, clamoured for a role and landed the hero's friend's role. In those days, the heroines were played by men. In the event, the dreaded inspector's role was on offer. MGR did not wish to become 'Inspector Ramachandran' to be stereotyped like fellow artist T.R.B. Rao who came alive when he donned the uniform and, therefore, ended up playing the inspector in plays.

Sathyabama was happy that her son was given a 'respectable' role and advised MGR to do it with a sense of responsibility. MGR yielded reluctantly.[17] As a fatherless son, MGR's world was completely dominated by his protective mother and her views. But she had also limited him in some ways. American director Ellis R. Dungan was in disbelief when he learnt that MGR could not ride a bicycle. Sathyabama had forbidden MGR to learn to ride one or to play marbles as a child. But, in the role of inspector Rengiah Naidu, MGR needed to ride a bike along with a policeman. In the end, he sat on a bike with two people balancing it, and, as the camera rolled, was given a push.[18]

N.S. Krishnan, T.S. Balaiah, MGR and director Dungan made their film debuts with Sathi Leelavathi. Dungan remembered MGR (after his death) thus:

> He started his career as a film actor in my first film, Sathi Leelavathi, as a raw recruit in the minor role of a police inspector and also acted in Meera and Mandhirikumari. I could see the improvement in his acting from picture to picture. MGR was a tall, handsome, and [an] athletic-type man, admired by all, and became extremely popular with the movie-goers.
>
> . . . Sathi Leelavathi proved to be quite a success at the box office.[19]

Pathibakthi, its twin, was also a success, and MGR had to rescue K.P. Kesavan, its hero, from his fans when they had gone to see the movie in Elphinstone Cinema, on the then Mount Road. By the time Marmayogi (The Secretive Sage, 1951) was released, the tables had turned and Kesavan would return the favour—saving MGR from the screening at the Globe Theatre in Madras on the same road.[20]

Yet, in the movie's aftermath, the future remained dark. The brothers frequented Kandasamy Mudaliar's place, and he recommended MGR for his next film Samugathondu (Public Service, 1936). When an anxious MGR inquired about his role and learnt that he would play inspector, his eyes grew moist, he felt feverish and was speechless. Fearing he would become 'Inspector Ramachandran', MGR demurred, despite Kandasamy Mudaliar and his son, M.K. Radha's, insistence.[21]

MGR was now at a dead end. The coming years would also be particularly hard on him. On at least three occasions, he almost landed good roles—but not quite. Promised a villain's role in Dungan's second film, he ended up playing a head constable—a role he detested. Another time, while he landed a contract after a well-wisher's intervention, he had to face the humiliation of hearing the producer say, 'His face is not suitable for cinema. He has a double chin. It won't work. Yet, it is because of your intervention that I am recommending him.' It was the darkest day in MGR's life. His pride from the frequent praise he got for his looks had been dealt a major blow. But Sathyabama offered her thanks to Kali for MGR getting work.

The role fell through. Frustrated, MGR, while passing by the Kali temple on their street that day, looked at the idol with anger and bitterness. He opined that Sathyabama was wasting her time fussing over a 'stone', and it should end and the idol be smashed. Sathyabama slapped her son angrily a few times, lamenting that she had borne a son who wished to 'destroy god'. MGR's profanity now overshadowed the issue of joblessness. Chakrapani intervened, asking her to stop her volley of curses, adding that MGR was the family's hope.[22]

Reminiscing about this incident, decades later, MGR compared Kali and his mentor Anna. He praised Anna for his humaneness and wondered why the omnipotent Kali could not be as compassionate.[23]

At some point, M.K. Radha came to MGR's rescue. He graciously recommended him to director Raja Chandrasekhar for his *Dakshayagnam* (Daksha's Fire Sacrifice, 1938). When Chandrasekhar asked if MGR could act, M.K. Radha said: 'I have luck on my side. Therefore, I am a hero. Ramachandran does not have luck on his side. Therefore, he is looking for work. This is the difference between the two of us . . . Whether in acting or other professional skills, there is no difference whatsoever.' MGR said he cried as he wrote about this in his autobiography: 'No one has ever said such things before; and till now . . . I am yet to have the good fortune to see another actor who would speak about my non-existent talents like anna.'[24]

   Dakshayagnam was shot in Calcutta and MGR played Indrajit in
it. M.K. Radha was to act as Daksha. He could not; M.G. Nataraja
Pillai, a district Congress president and an excellent artist, played
the role instead. However, Nataraja Pillai fell ill and was advised
to take some brandy with his meals if he wished to live. Nataraja
Pillai, a Gandhian, expectedly abhorred the idea. MGR took it upon
himself to persuade him. After much discussion, Nataraja Pillai,
surprisingly, asked for two days' time and finally gave in. MGR,
who had persuaded him to drink, would in his later years say that
drinking permits should not be issued. 'If some were to die because
of this, let them die.'[25]

   Nataraja Pillai did not live long and, with his death, MGR secured
the villain Suryakedhu's role in *Maya Macheendra* (The Illusory
Macheendra, 1939).[26] MGR's dream of doing sword-fighting sequences
came true with that role. Master Vithal, a Marathi superstar of the silent-
era movies, had captured the ten-year-old MGR's heart and mind, and
he used to try and imitate his footwork and swordplay.[27] *Dakshayagnam*
and *Veera Jagadish* (Valiant Jagadish, 1938) were released the same year.
The following year, *Maya Macheendra* and *Prahalada* were released. But
they did little for MGR's film career.

   Again, 1940 brought nothing for him. *Seethajananam* (Seetha's
Birth) and *Ashok Kumar* were released in 1941. MGR should have played
Indrajit in *Seethajananam* too. But he rejected director Chandrasekhar's
insistence that he also play Vishnu for no additional remuneration.
MGR said that only years later he realized that his film guru had taken
liberties with him, his protégé, but by his demurral then, he had burnt
another bridge. 'Henceforth I [do] not have any future in cinema; there
is no godfather either!' he lamented.[28] In two years' time, the rift would
have healed and the director brothers Chandrasekhar and Raghunath
would come in a major way to MGR's aid.

   MGR was to play the brother of M.K.T. Bhagavathar in *Ashok
Kumar*. For reasons that are unclear, both MKT and his wife were
apparently against MGR. In an effort to overcome this resistance, MGR
would wait at MKT's house day after day. He would not forget this
slight. As chief minister, he made MKT's widow, reduced to destitution
and poverty, wait for two days before he saw her and gifted her 1 lakh
rupees from his personal funds. He explained to scriptwriter Ravindar:

'I wanted that lady to realize how times change. She stood only for two days. Even then, she felt so hurt. Do you know how many days I had waited in their house compound? . . . Because of the kind-heartedness of those two (the director and his younger brother), I got to play that role! Just because you are on top now, one shouldn't undermine others' opportunities.'

Despite this, MGR also helped save MKT's house from being auctioned and gave it to the family. He also named a government hall in Trichy after MKT.[29]

ABHORRENCE TO LIQUOR

Although MGR had never explained his abhorrence to alcohol, it is likely that the cause of this was Velu Nair. Once, noticing a half-empty brandy bottle in the cabinet at the joint family home, MGR created a huge fuss, at one point insisting that there was no place for those who drank. Sathyabama retorted it was his brother's place and it was MGR who had no room there. Terribly offended, MGR declared he would not only leave the house but the world. He promptly broke the bottle before he walked out on them.

MGR must have raced, for he reached Rattan Bazaar in a tenth of the time that the brothers usually took. It was evening, and people hurried past him. MGR was upset that none seemed to care for a man who was in a rush to end his life.

As he walked around aimlessly, he heard a voice asking him to stop. It was his brother. 'What is this? Is there no limit to your madness! . . . Yaenda! Have you grown so big so as not to tolerate even Mother's words? . . . Did you leave because she said it is my house?'

MGR retorted: 'No, not because of that! I saw the brandy bottle; I was upset . . . She says she is right!' A long argument ensued now. MGR then learnt that Velu Nair had procured the liquor to help MGR's sister-in-law with the delivery of her child (as was the practice then to ease labour pains), but had gone and consumed it himself. Chakrapani told MGR that his mentor Anna had not accepted the idea of suicide even for the worthiest ends and that no rationalist would accept it.[30] But then, he would be pushed to consider suicide one more time when he lost his first wife, Thangamani.

PUSHED INTO MARRIAGE

Ironically, he would initially protest the idea of marriage. MGR revered Gandhi.[31] His prayer room would sport his portrait alongside that of Sathyabama's.[32] MGR wished to wear homespun cloth, a symbol of defiance against the British. Sathyabama thought of her son's fascination for Gandhi's advocacy as treasonous, and even tragic and evil.[33] This problem had no simple solution. The amulets and talismans that Sathyabama procured could be thrown away without her knowledge. But how could one hide homespun clothes?

The opportunity arose unexpectedly. Sathyabama conceived a plan to get MGR married. Chakrapani went along with it. She wrote to say that she had taken ill but was feeling better and would like to see Chakrapani's little daughter, Mani. She instructed Chakrapani to send Mani with MGR.

MGR left for Palakkad that very day. At Erode station, Balakrishnan, the uncle of Chakrapani's first wife, deceased by then, boarded the train. 'Where are you off to?' queried Balakrishnan. Confused, MGR reminded him that he had already mentioned his mother's illness.

Alighting at their destination, they hired a horse cart to their village. En route, when Balakrishnan revealed Sathyabama's plans, MGR shrieked and demanded that the cart return. Balakrishnan now fell at MGR's feet and begged him not to go back. MGR said they had schemed to insult him by getting him married to a girl with no means of support. He promised revenge: He would return to Madras.

Balakrishnan again clutched MGR's feet and this time tears welled up in his eyes. He reminded MGR that he had once promised to give his daughter's hand in marriage to him. If MGR were to return, it would appear that Balakrishnan had changed MGR's mind. Giving in to his pleas, MGR decided that he would not submit, even if his mother threatened to take her life.

But when he saw Sathyabama, her dull eyes and sunken cheeks, MGR grew worried. She had not brushed her teeth or had a bath. She said his arrival was good enough and if he did not like the girl, they would both leave by the noon train. Sceptical relatives accused her of having lied about MGR's willingness to them. Reading her son's mind, Sathyabama said that he had to be true to his conscience. What if the girl happened to be to his liking? Sathyabama was crying. In a little while, MGR felt like crying too. It was like a funeral.

Only an hour remained for the auspicious time for the nuptials. MGR prayed to all the gods, but they stood him up. 'Well,' he said to himself, 'the groom has said no and that is the end of the matter.' But he was also panic-stricken at the thought of his mother taking her life. The girl's home, six or seven houses away, wore a festive look, blithely ignorant of their dilemma.

A relative explained that an unsuccessful suitor in the family had spread the rumour that MGR would not show up. The man had also promised to avenge his humiliation. MGR was in a real quandary now. Should an innocent be punished and her future 'ruined'? He resolved that, regardless of the girl's situation, he would not consent to a wedding without his brother. But then Sathyabama pulled out Chakrapani's letter to show that he was an accomplice. Dusk set in over a house already dark in spirit.

MGR used his ultimate weapon: 'If I have to give my consent to the wedding . . .' Sathyabama readily bit his bait. 'Tell me . . . What do you wish . . .? Would you like to see her. . .?' Sathyabama was sure about the girl's looks. An uncle chimed in that MGR would elope with her if he saw her. While happy about his fiancée's beauty, MGR remained undeterred:

> I will only wear homespun [cloth] for the wedding. From now on, I will wear homespun [cloth] as I desire. I will spin homespun [yarn]. If you agree to this I will get married.

Hearing this, his mother, who was squatting and chatting with him, eased herself to sit on the ground.

An elderly relative shouted joyfully that MGR had saved their honour even as tears streamed down Sathyabama's cheeks. She told her nonplussed relative, '[But] he has made me live with dishonour for the rest of my life!' The poor relative had no clue about Sathyabama's conviction that homespun cloth was worn by god's enemies. Saythabama said the only thing that had remained with her—her resolve—was also lost that moment. 'He is my last child. It is natural that he is smart. I wished for him my intelligence. But he is smarter . . . Whoever gets into a confrontation with him, it is they who will be defeated, for Kali, whom I worship, will not abandon him.'

MGR's homespun clothes arrived, even as he was nagged by doubt whether the price for them was worth it.

At the wedding altar, as the elders yelled to usher in the girl, MGR felt the urge to see the bride. 'Give her the [wedding] cloth,' the elders instructed the groom and as MGR looked straight at her, he was 'transfixed'. The bride was led away. But his eyes and mind had left with her.

That night, the young groom shot a volley of questions at his bride, who kept trembling. MGR realized that his own hands were shaking as he attempted to touch her. 'Do you like me?' Bhargavi did not respond. She looked at him from the corner of her eye and then went back to staring at the floor. 'Do you wonder if I am good-looking or not?' She kept silent. 'Whom do you like the most?' She reddened at this, triggering MGR's fancy. That night was, however, one of imagination and nothing more. The next day, the couple left for Madras. The farewell proved to be a heart-rending affair.

Bhargavi, alias Thangamani, was a vegetarian, and she chose to fast on days when there was no vegetarian fare. At times, she threw up at the sight of poultry, meat or fish. For her sake, MGR, a non-vegetarian aficionado, would simply settle for vegetarian food. Slowly, Thangamani came around to making fish gravy for MGR.[34]

CHAYA ABORTS MGR

Thangamani was an ideal wife; but life was far from ideal. An advertisement for a jamedar (a non-commissioned rank with five men under his command) in the Army caught MGR's attention. The job required horse-riding skills, a chest size of thirty-two inches, height of five and a half feet, and fluency in English. The salary was a handsome 125 rupees a month. 'Please teach me English in three months. You will be rewarded in the other world,' he told his English teacher; he began chest-widening exercises and learnt music.

But before anything would come of these efforts, Narayanan and Company sent word for MGR one day. He met proprietor, Narayana Iyengar, and directors Jaswantlal Nandlal and Chandrasekhar. MGR was to play the hero in their *Chaya*. The salary was a stately 350 rupees monthly and the daily allowance was thirty-five rupees a day.[35]

Jaswantlal was known to be short-tempered and employed the term 'jungliwala' (jungle man) to express disappointment. Therefore, on the first day, as Jaswantlal inspected him, MGR sharpened his ears. The director now wished to see MGR ride a horse. Changing into a veshti from his trousers, he rode the horse, only to realize later that Jaswantlal could have justly called him a jungliwala for riding the horse wearing a veshti! Thankfully, the dreaded word was not uttered.

But *Chaya* would completely destroy MGR's dreams and 'plunge [his] career into a gorge'.[36] The company had decided to drop him, despite Jaswantlal's opposition. One day, Jaswantlal folded his hands together as a sign of respect before MGR could. 'What Mr Ramachandran! If you are not in this movie, I, too, am not there.' MGR was overwhelmed. Immersed in the Dravidian movement, MGR recorded decades later: 'What was the necessity for him to say so? Who am I? He is a north Indian; I am from the south!'

Then, one day following the shoot, Jaswantlal told MGR: 'Be brave. You should act well. Don't fear anything! Goodbye . . .' Sathyabama interpreted Jaswantlal's words as such: 'We would have to go back to Madras soon.' Jaswantlal was conspicuously absent at the next day's shoot. Some weeks later, manager Varadachari paid MGR the dues, bringing the tenuous bond to an end. Asking him to return to Madras, Varadachari promised to send word later. Both knew that he was merely being polite.[37]

THANGAMANI'S DEATH

Chaya had left a deep scar on MGR's psyche. But a personal tragedy was set to hit him harder.[38] Marital life was pleasant, but the family was in dire straits and it appears that Thangamani herself asked her parents to take her back until the situation stabilized.[39] Scriptwriter Arurdhas writes that things were so bad that MGR sold Thangamani's jewellery, earning the displeasure of his in-laws.[40] MGR himself attributes her return to the 'evacuation' of Madras that followed the Japanese bombing of Vishakapatnam, Kakinada and Colombo on 4–5 April 1942. On their way to the railway station, one of the rickshaw's lights caught fire.

Reading it as a bad omen, Thangamani rested her head against MGR's shoulder and began sobbing. Was she mantic about her impending death? She said they would meet soon.

When MGR finally repaired his way to Palakkad to see Thangamani, en route he had stopped by at his sister-in-law's place, which sported a mournful look. The sister-in-law asked if he had come because of the telegram, adding that Thangamani was not keeping well. Taking the next train to Palakkad, MGR showed up at a relative's place, who said that she had 'cheated' them, at which MGR wailed loudly. Thangamani had died of a heart attack. MGR sped to Thangamani's house, heading straight for her room. A lamp had been lit next to the cot. MGR fell down beside it and cried his heart out. After a while, the loud cries turned to a whimper.

On his return, MGR was composed when he spoke to his brother. As MGR ate his meal, his sister-in-law thought that he had reconciled himself to the loss of Thangamani. But MGR's mind was filled with her last words—that he would meet her soon. There remained only one way: To meet her in death. He raced to the Pothanur railway tracks. He felt a rage rising within him when he realized that an apprehensive Chakrapani had followed him. They sat next to each other, quietly. MGR decided to sit out his brother. The sun was slowly setting. As dusk spread, they began to speak. Chakrapani reminded MGR about their sister's death and said: 'The answer to a death does not lie in the death of another.' MGR was now angry again. He had not sought wedlock in the first place and now, he was a widower. Sensing his thoughts, Chakrapani said that some things were beyond them and that in the future MGR could decide his own course.

They went back home. MGR just drank some milk and fell asleep. At 3 a.m., he woke up only to find Chakrapani keeping vigil. MGR was touched. The next morning his sister-in-law brought Mani over to him. He hugged little Mani. Chakrapani came to tell him that NSK was at the Coimbatore Central Studios and wished to see MGR. NSK said MGR should see things in perspective, adding that the odds stacked against him intended to steel him. 'These difficulties are going to aid you to do a lot of good in the future.' MGR could not help wondering if one had to lose so much to become something. Chakrapani and MGR left for Madras, taking his advice.[41]

SADANANDAVATI

Although he had lived with Thangamani for only three years, MGR's attachment to her was so deep that he felt that there could be no room for another woman in his life. He even attempted a seance with Thangamani's spirit, paying a sum far beyond his means.[42] However, his resolve would prove weak, and yielding to his mother, he agreed to remarry the same year (1942) that Thangamani left him.

At Kuzhal Mannam, the bride's village in Palakkad district, a large crowd had assembled to see the groom, despite the rain, and MGR felt a little happy at this sight. Many had hoped to also get a glimpse of NSK, already a well-known actor by then. As Sadanadavati stepped into the wedding hall, Chakrapani was dumbstruck for his brother's bride was plain and ordinary looking. MGR himself appeared indifferent to her looks. Instead, Sadanandavati's mother's questions on his previous marriage and Thangamani's death had upset him. No one had told the in-laws about the circumstances of his wife's death.

MGR decided to step out of the house for some fresh air. It proved to be a mistake. The crowd had melted and some older children who remained shot a volley of questions at MGR. 'Can you sing?' 'Yes. I had in plays.' 'Why had you not sung with MKT?' 'I am not that talented.' This evoked much laughter from the boys, which angered MGR. But the situation was to get more difficult. 'Do you know NSK?' 'Yes.' 'Then why did he not attend the wedding?' NSK's presence would have greatly boosted his image, but then he hadn't come. Chellappan Nair, the bride's relative, asked: 'Why do you have to claim that you know someone when you don't?' MGR shot back: 'I do know NSK!' The boys were in their element now. They said they too knew NSK from the movies.

Chellappan Nair proved to be more trouble. He now wondered if MGR knew Achutan Nair, who had been cast in several films with NSK. He winked at the boys and laughed mockingly, even as MGR insisted that someone was duping them, as there was no Achutan Nair. Chellappan Nair retorted: 'You said NSK would attend the wedding; he didn't. Achutan Nair has photos from films with NSK. But you say that he is lying. We should not believe him, but we should believe you. Right?' MGR understood that he was being very cleverly called a liar.

Exasperated, he asked, if he could see Achutan Nair. But Achutan Nair was shooting with NSK. Luckily, the call to dinner saved the day for MGR. But after what had transpired, he could barely eat and Chellappan Nair would not let up. 'You won't like these meals. You would only like non-vegetarian and other things. Right?' The 'other' was an insinuation about alcohol. MGR realized that the relatives were upset that their girl had wed an upstart artist who knew no major actor, had no wealth and, worse still, was a widower. MGR swallowed the insults, resolved to bear them, and to wait for the day he would become known. Later that evening, when they were alone as a couple, Sadanandavati reassured MGR: 'One day, you are going to earn a lot. Those who mock our family will hang their heads in shame then . . .' Sadanandavati had truly spoken as a wife.

SADANANDAVATI'S ILLNESS

Sathyabama naturally wished for a grandchild from her younger son. Considered 'weak', Sadanandavati was given an injection, which MGR writes led to a miscarriage. On the other hand, scriptwriter Arurdhas records what MGR had confided in him:

> I had seen the depths of hunger and poverty. I have touched the nadir of life's existence. This was in the past. Now, I am at the apogee of fame. I am flourishing. Every day fifty to sixty people are served at each meal at my place. But I have been deprived of two things that I can never countenance. One, is that I have no children . . . I have secretly checked my horoscope with expert astrologers. Three experts were of similar opinion. They said that my horoscope showed that several women would be involved in my life. 'You would give them all that they need. But none of them would give you progeny as you desire. They cannot. The shortcoming is not with them . . .'
>
> Whenever mothers and sisters hand over their children, asking me to choose a name, my heart would tremble. But I would hide it and would name the children and fulfil their wish . . . I am not gifted enough! . . . The other [thing I feel deprived of] is that I have no formal education . . .[43]

Sadanandavati's health began to deteriorate and she was eventually diagnosed with tuberculosis of the lungs. Treatment was primitive and cruel, and lasted for months. When Sadanandavati developed sores, a second doctor confirmed the first doctor, Dr Rao's, diagnosis—that there was no cure. A third doctor, B.R. Subramaniam (BRS), took a chance and administered 120 injections. Sadanandavati healed to live for another eighteen years. BRS, who became their personal physician after this miracle, had warned that there could be no conjugal relationship. For two years, MGR complied, but, as he put it, 'how long can one practice abstinence in a marriage?'[44] While on the sets of *Marmayogi*, MGR had to rush to see Sadanandavati, whose life was saved by removing the foetus. This was the second time they had lost a child and MGR was devastated.[45]

THE POST-*CHAYA* SCENARIO

Once back home, the prospects looked bleak. However, director Chandrasekhar's brother Raghunath pleasantly surprised MGR when he sent for him and offered him a hero's part, cautioning him that the part was minor, but 'would stay in people's minds . . .' MGR agreed to a fee of 300 rupees. He had been paid 350 rupees a month for *Chaya*. But then the movie's future and his own was uncertain.

The shooting for *Tamizharium Perumal* (Perumal who knows Tamil, 1942) began. For three days, MGR had been so ill that he had no strength to even walk, let alone run. In one particular take, he had to run in anguish towards his dead lover. Tripping and falling for effect, he picked himself up and ran again. 'Cut,' said Raghunath. But the cameraman had stopped filming as soon as MGR tripped. Raghunath was upset that MGR, so unwell, would have to redo the difficult take. Brushing aside his concern, MGR ran, fell, got up and then ran again.

> I ran like this in many places.
> I could not even walk. But the running I did that day cannot be measured.
> After returning home I was struck by fever for a whole week . . .
> [I suffered] body pain. However my heart was full! Happy.
> [For] wasn't it the run to banish fate [itself] . . .?

The movie, a hit, again did nothing for MGR's career. He worked with the legendary PUC in *Harichandra* (1943). They had debuted in 1936, but PUC had graduated as a hero with *Utthama Puthiran* (The Noble Son, 1940), never to look back. Similarly, in 1944, *Poompavai* (Flower Girl) had launched MGR's peer KRR as a hero. MGR, meanwhile, was still playing minor roles.

The fortunes of superstars MKT and PUC would, however, change with circumstances. Entangled in a murder case in 1944, MKT would sadly pale into oblivion and poverty. Premature death would claim PUC in 1952, at the age of forty. These were exceptional stars, whose voice was their asset in an era of songs.

M.K.T. Bhagavathar embodied both good looks and charisma, and was a phenomenon. MGR describes his feelings about MKT as he entered C.S. Jayaraman's (Kalaignar's brother-in-law) concert. 'Though there were many lights in the area, Bhagavathar looked to me as if he was fully made of gold, studded with diamonds,' wrote MGR in a eulogy. He added, 'Anyone who sees him come, walking with a smile, would think that a golden figurine had come to life' and when he left 'people would feel an emptiness and darkness enveloping the place'.[46] Such was MKT's aura. In 1959, when MGR wrote this obituary, he had already achieved as much as MKT, if not more.[47] But it was PUC's life that seems to have left a deep impression on MGR. In 1971, in his acceptance speech for the National Best Actor Bharat Award, MGR said that his forbears always reminded him of the transient nature of things, and he singled out PUC, who had lived like a prince, but had suffered in his last days.[48]

MGR himself was an amalgamation of MKT and PUC. He had the singing talent of neither, but that era was already being consigned to history with playback singing on the rise. He certainly had MKT's looks and shine, and PUC's fighting prowess. Yet, it would take some time before he would get noticed amidst the competition. Meanwhile, *Salivahanan* and *Meera* were both released in 1945. In 1967, actor T.S. Balaiah, who played a major role in *Meera*, wrote that director Dungan had rejected MGR for his 'wooden face' and, pitying him, Balaiah used his goodwill with the director to get him the minor role of a commander in the movie.[49] If this is true, then *Salivahanan* had more humiliation in store. Ramanarayana Venkataramana Sarma, alias Ranjan, and

MGR would star in *Salivahanan*, with Ranjan as hero and MGR as villain—perhaps the only time in his film career. Ranjan, too, had quickly made it big. Debuting in *Ashok Kumar*, in two years *Mangamma Sabatham* (Mangamma's Vow, 1943) would elevate the action star to a hero. *Chandralekha* (1948) catapulted Ranjan to Bollywood. Aching for stardom in *Salivahanan*, MGR and Ranjan were fiercely competitive during the fighting sequences, and MGR felt that Ranjan was trying to hurt him. Filled with 'malice', Ranjan further saw to it that the shots where MGR excelled were shortened.[50]

Not everyone would, however, see MGR as competition and the Dravidian movement would embrace him eagerly. He, however, would initially spurn its overtures and that of his mentor Anna, only to found a party in his name three decades later.

The Lure of the Dravidian Movement

The Dravidian movement's first actor D.V. Narayanasamy (DVN) spotted MGR's talent early on and actively courted him—only to be spurned in the last minute. Ironically, neither would have guessed then that MGR would become the mascot of the movement.

As we saw earlier, NSK had recommended the writings of EVR to MGR. EVR was an inspiration to many, and DVN would read aloud from EVR's *Kudiarasu* and *Viduthalai* (Freedom) magazines to his colleagues at the T.K. Shanmugam (TKS) troupe. When DVN upped his efforts at such propaganda, the TKS management, considering him a nuisance, asked him to leave.*

DVN turned to Anna, becoming the 'first son the art mother had bequeathed', taking refuge with him during lean times.[1] 'From morning to night and from night to evening, [DVN] spoke of self-respect precepts,' wrote poet Kannadasan on DVN's attempts to convert him. Although consumed by Anna's speeches, M.G. Chakrapani would introduce the poet to the one who would finally convince him to join the choir—Kalaignar Karunanidhi.[2]

As deputy editor of *Kudiarasu*, Anna keenly watched the growing power of the stage and its potential harnessed by the Congress-led Independence movement.[3] Theatre, as we saw, was not immune to EVR's work, but Anna helped forge a marriage between the two by actively seeking out the stage—which his mentor saw as a bane for

---

* 'Latchiya Nadigar' or idealist actor S.S. Rajendran (SSR), 'Valayapathi' Muthukrishnan and KRR would be drawn to the movement, thanks to DVN's lobbying.

the Tamils. Unlike EVR, Anna accorded artists and actors a special place in the party, to mutual benefit. Kamaraj's famous remark later, 'How can there be a government by actors?'[4] showed the success of Anna's approach as well as the public's general derision for actors then. In fact, Kamaraj termed MGR a performer, even after he founded his AIADMK.[5] And so did EVR, who considered even his devoted disciple, actor M.R. Radha, a 'mountebank' till the end.[6] Anna was, however, of a different view. His genius understood the power of theatre and, with the advent of cinema, the potential of films. The irrepressible EVR would grudgingly admit in his presidential speech on the debut of Anna's propagandist *Sivaji Kanda Hindu Rajyam* (Shivaji's Hindu Kingdom) that 'Anna has imparted ideas in this play that I would convey in ten conferences'.[7] Anna himself frequently acted in his plays. His entry into cinema as scriptwriter coincided with the birth of the DMK in 1949. Anna's *Nallathambi* (The Good Brother) hit the screens on 4 February that year, followed by *Velaikaari* (Servant Maid) three weeks later. *Nallathambi* did not do well commercially, but *Velaikaari* would win critical acclaim while being a box office success. When 'Story–Dialogue: C.N. Annadurai, M.A.' appeared in the credits, the audience went into raptures. Film historian Randor Guy says that this was a new phenomenon in Indian cinema.[8]

In 1957, MGR looked back on Anna's contribution in bringing dignity to art and artists:

> Only DMK has an inseparable attachment with artists. The founder of DMK, Arignar Anna, is not only a political leader; he is an artistic political leader. No other movement in the Indian subcontinent possesses this . . . That is why Anna and the DMK have a magnetic influence over artists. That is why I am proud and exultant to say that I am a member of the DMK.[9]

INTRODUCTION TO ANNA

MGR attributes the 'good fortune' of making Anna his 'elder brother, teacher and guide' to DVN.[10]

MGR had seen Anna and DVN perform in Anna's *Chandrodayam* (Moonrise), the play, at Victoria Public Hall, Madras. MGR was so

impressed by DVN's performance that he came to look upon him as
a 'brother'. They would meet a couple of times after this. MGR liked
DVN's altruism and concern for artists, and his belief that social change
should come speedily. DVN turned a blind eye to MGR's homespun
clothes, the black-beaded chain he wore from Tirupati, his ash-smeared
forehead and the vermilion between his eyebrows. Wishing to enlist
MGR to his mission, he discussed with him the nation's state of affairs,
an area of interest to both. NSK had already prepared MGR to pay
attention to new ideas and DVN now attempted to take this further,
readying MGR to experiment with them.

DVN had seen MGR's dash and agility in the film *Maya Macheendra*.
One day, he asked if MGR would like to act in their party's play penned
by Anna. MGR quickly nodded agreement. DVN offered him the role
of Shivaji in *Sivaji Kanda Hindu Rajyam*, which Anna had written with
DVN in mind.

When they went to see Anna in 1944, at his relative Ettiappan's
house on Karuppanna Mudali Street, Chintadripet, he was on the terrace
with S.V. Lingam, a party stalwart.[11] Bare-bodied, with a shawl wrapped
around him, and in his veshti, Anna was surrounded by books, papers
and pens. MGR noted how simple Anna was. He remained so until the
very end, even after his rise to power. He cared little for his appearance
or sartorial elegance. He wore no watch and often sported stubble. It was
a major concession if he shaved. Anna had few possessions. His younger
brothers and sisters of the DMK, whom he viewed as one family, of
which he was the elder brother, were his only possession. Anna's heart
and head were in the right place, and humanism towered over all his
other attributes. He described himself as a commoner and lived as one.
As chief minister, he said that it is the common man's 'point of view that
matters most' and he claimed 'to represent him in all his ruggedness'.[12]
By then, he had already blossomed into a tall leader and a fine statesman.
His years in office were the pride of the Tamils, the renaissance of their
political power and the coming of the common man.

■

Affectionate, caring and sharp, with an incomparable talent for speech
and writing, Anna sought to preserve the idea of India's unity in diversity,

and the country's scientific and developmental progress through English, among other things. He said no language would be subservient or inferior to the other, and argued that English would ensure the odds are evenly spread and, with it, all could win. History has vindicated him. Today, we have a 160-billion dollar Indian information technology industry that makes up 9.5 per cent of the GDP[13], and English has played no small part in it, not to mention India's scientific progress. Little known outside Tamil Nadu and unknown to the younger generation of Tamils, the barely 5.3-foot tall leader remains one of the tallest postmodern Indian leaders.

Supremely self-assured and yet humble, Anna was a rare politician. His mission was not pan-Indian but pan-Tamil, and yet, he would turn out to be one of the greatest protectors of India's territorial integrity and unity. Anna advocated a truly federal India where the Centre would handle defence, finance, foreign affairs and communications, and the states, the rest. The DMK pioneered the advent of regional parties in India's polity, providing a safe and democratic outlet for regional aspirations within a united India.

For fourteen years, Anna worked under his 'political father' EVR and his Self-respect movement. The movement was humble and its followers were very modest—only drawn to it by the bitter truth behind its message and the hope of a new era. The duo's sincerity, commitment to the cause, their prodigious people skills, talent and charisma were their only resources. Their political foes had greatly underestimated them. The trickle would slowly develop into a downpour and, by the 1940s and 1950s, the duo would have made great strides in their advocacy and mission. Ambition and philosophical differences, however, led to the 'son' founding the DMK in 1949. In 1967, the DMK was voted to power.

In the US on a visit as chief minister in 1968, Anna said that no party should be in power for more than ten years—for such power would be 'intoxicating'. How perceptive indeed. Similarly, he did not rule out the possibility of the DMK as part of a coalition at the Centre, although he considered it 'far too distant'.[14]

Today's generation, and the generations to come, would find it hard to believe that a man who was not a cricketer or a movie star was considered such a cult figure. People waited for hours on end patiently to catch a glimpse of the short man who so highly represented them and their interests. The historic record crowds that paid homage to him were a vindication of his life, which remains his message.

■

In 1944, in his first meeting with Anna, MGR could not have imagined any of this about him. Providence had chosen DVN as the one to bring Anna and his *idhayakani* or 'heart's fruit' together, but not just yet. Anna made MGR feel at ease, and greeted him with the familiarity and affection reserved for a younger brother.[15] MGR's elder brother, M.G. Chakrapani, has said that although he had been attracted to the Dravidian ideals for several years already (thanks to his close association with Kalaignar Karunanidhi, poet Kannadasan and scriptwriter A.V.P. Asaithambi, all with Salem Modern Theatres), his younger brother, MGR, 'completely lacked interest' in the movement.[16]

A few days after the meeting, DVN brought the play's script to MGR. Arurdhas wrote that MGR was overwhelmed, as he felt it would take him three to four days just to memorize the dialogues. MGR suggested changes to the play for greater effect, and asked DVN if the script could be adjusted accordingly. DVN said he would inform Anna about this. Two days later, at about 10 p.m. DVN took MGR to Anna, who was busy writing at the time. 'What changes do you wish for?' he asked. As MGR explained his thoughts, Anna looked at DVN and said, 'Will do' and then said, 'Narayanasamy! Remind me later. I will write.' Turning to MGR, he asked if he had read the noted Marathi writer V.S. Khandekar, and then gave him a copy of Khandekar's novel *The Burnt Bud*, saying, 'Do read this. You will find many good ideas.'

Anna later recalled his first impressions on seeing MGR: 'I met him some eight years ago in relation to a play, through the artist Narayanasamy. When I first saw him, I suspected that he was an Aryan. Later, I grew happy on learning that he was in fact a Dravidian. There is no doubt that his looks, handsomeness, physique and shine would have caused jealousy among Brahmins. His speech is worthy. His cooperation, I believe, would bring success to our plans for the future.'[17]

Indeed. Once, next to Kovilpatti town, seeing the fluttering DMK flag on MGR's Plymouth car, the crowd grew excited, and started shouting, 'MGR flag . . . MGR . . . flag.' Anna was in the front seat, while MGR was seated behind. When a friend took exception to the crowd's behaviour later, Anna told him, 'You don't understand . . . All this popularity for MGR only flows to the party . . . It is the party that benefits.'[18]

Back to the script: MGR was shooting for the movie *Rajakumari* (Princess, 1947) in Coimbatore. He was not sure if he needed to wait for the amended script of the play or memorize the one that he had with him. Sensing MGR's predicament, A.S.A. Samy, the film's director, got in touch with DVN and, through him, got Anna's consent to carry out the necessary changes himself. (However, Kalaignar wrote later that DVN had said in several public meetings that Anna was surprised at MGR's suggestions, which he rejected, and that MGR, citing Anna's unwillingness to carry out the changes, had refused to act in the play.)[19] When M.G. Chakrapani learnt about these developments, he was very upset. He strongly chided his brother for his indiscretion and for 'insulting' Anna, especially given his magnanimity in the first place in inviting MGR to play the lead role, even though he was not part of the movement. 'Will anyone think well of you?' Chakrapani asked his sibling. MGR realized that he had hurt many because of his thoughtlessness. Chakrapani said it would be best if he did not perform in the play for the time being. 'Let the hurt inflicted by your actions heal,' he advised him.

Meanwhile, MGR's costume had already been made and the 1 April 1945 *Dravida Nadu* issue advertised his lead role in the play. In the end, a week before the play's debut, when DVN telephoned him, MGR turned down the offer. According to DVN, M.G. Chakrapani had advised MGR that his film career would be at risk if he were to perform in the propagandist play of the radical Dravidar Kazhagam.[20] Ironically, thirteen years later, in 1957, when firmly ensconced in the DMK, MGR would actually defend his relationship with the DMK and the concomitant price to be paid as one of principle:

When an actor joins the DMK, they don't join because they expect gains. It is the lively principles of the DMK that has drawn the worker, the farmer, the clerk and the intellectual from society, that equally draws an actor. Any person who evaluates which party would promote his influence, even while not interfering with his profession, and profits and engages into the profit–loss assessment and then joins the DMK—for such calculative 'geniuses' the DMK would be a disappointing party. An actor in the DMK is more like a warrior facing the enemy from all four sides . . .

DMK is the only party with the right and the credentials for actors to engage and participate. It is the DMK, which fights for Tamilagam, Tamils, Tamil, Tamil arts and Tamil civilization.[21]

SSR writes that Anna himself felt that somebody had ill-advised MGR.[22] Ever-gracious though, he never spoke about the last-minute refusal. One day, when MGR brought it up, Anna smilingly said: 'A.S.A. Samy told me everything.' MGR said that after this he felt relieved.[23] A decade later, he would tell Arurdhas in a different context that he had customarily suggested changes in the script to '[even] Anna and Karunanidhi'.[24] Villupuram Chinnaiah Ganesa Moorthy, later 'Sivaji' V.C. Ganesan, would play Shivaji and become known by that name. Ganesan said later that for 'reasons best known to him, [MGR] refused the part.'[25]

'SIVAJI' GANESAN AND ANNA

As a boy, Ganesan was picked up from the audience during a street performance of *Kattabomman*, based on the eighteenth-century chieftain who revolted against the British. Chinnaiah Mandrayar slapped Ganesan more because he was outraged that his son had played a British soldier.* Ganesan ended up both with a high fever and a passion for theatre.

Ganesan joined Yadhartham Ponnusamy's drama troupe, Madurai Shri Bala Gana Sabha, which was playing at Trichy then, by demonstrating his singing abilities and claiming he was an orphan. Ganesan debuted as Sita in the play *Ramayana*. Little Ganesan's histrionics soon made him indispensable to the troupe, so he was not permitted to go home even when two of his brothers passed away. Gifted with the ability to change

---

* Ganesan's father was imprisoned for planting dynamite on a railway track carrying British soldiers. Ganesan was born just then, so that some held that his birth was a bad augury. How much more wrong could they have been? The family moved close to Trichy, where his mother Rajamani began to eke out a living as a milkmaid.

his voice, he came to be known early on as 'simmakuralon' (with the voice of a lion). Soon, he would land male roles and, finally, the king's role.[26] It was while performing in *Khaddarin Vetri* (Homespun's Victory), a patriotic play, at the age of eleven that Ganesan first caught a glimpse of his future leader Kamaraj.[27]

At twelve, Ganesan managed to convince the management to let him go home for Deepavali. But soon, M.R. Radha came to fetch him and Ganesan left, this time with his mother's permission, to be part of Radha's Saraswathi Gana Sabha in Madras, which enacted social plays at the Thanthai Periyar Theatre at Erode. The house where the actors lived was next to EVR's and only a door separated them. The young Ganesan would rush off after his morning bath to listen to EVR's teachings. EVR took lessons in politics and ran a gurukul. Ganesan joined Anna, EVR's nephew E.V.K. Sampath and others. He forged a relationship with Anna and developed affection for Sampath. EVR's words on reform and awakening were 'imprinted in [Ganesan's] psyche and helped [him] later to shape [his] life.'

However, as the company ran into financial difficulties, one Krishnan Pillai took over the troupe. Life was tough and there were many desperate moments. At one point, with no performances for a month, they had to dig out tapioca that was then boiled, salted and eaten. Ganesan had had enough. He left the stage but came back to his parent company, which NSK had taken over. After NSK's jail term, the company split, and KRR and Ganesan left for Kanchipuram to be Anna's guests.

The seventeen-year-old Ganesan soon became attached to his host, Anna. At *Dravida Nadu*, he helped turn the manual printing press and assisted in the composing of typefaces. He also stacked the pages that Anna churned out seamlessly.

It was around this time that DVN grew very concerned at MGR's refusal to act in the play as Sivaji. K.B. Kamakshi and S.V. Subbaiah's names were initially considered, before DVN echoed a fellow actor's suggestion of Ganesan playing the role to Anna.*

---

* In 1983, in a felicitation meeting, in Ganesan's presence, MGR said that he had suggested Ganesan's name for playing Sivaji and his diary and DVN would attest to this, and that DVN, A.S.A. Samy and Ganesan himself were well aware of this. Kirubakaran, S., (ed.), *Naan Aanaiyitaal...!* Chennai: Vikatan Pirasuram, 2014, p. 248.

When Anna asked him, 'Ganesa, are you willing to act as Sivaji?' the young man broke into a sweat and timidly responded, 'Where is Sivaji and where am I? How can I?' Anna encouraged him, 'Why don't you try? You can,' and then proceeded to hand over the ninety-page script, telling him to go through it while he went home for a bit. This was around 11 a.m. By the time Anna returned at 6 p.m. accompanied by his friends Thangavelu, Puttasamy and classmate C.V. Rajagopal, Ganesan had learnt the script by heart.

Ganesan beckoned Anna to sit and began acting out the play. It was a majestic and memorable performance. When Ganesan finished, Anna rushed to hug him; his eyes were moist. 'You have memorized it in seven hours; you are Sivaji indeed.' Ganesan actually owes the title 'Sivaji' to Anna, although it would be Anna's mentor, EVR, who voiced it publically at the play's debut. MGR would note in a public meeting in 1957 on both Sivaji Ganesan and Anna thus:

> 'Sivaji' was Anna's encomium for [Ganesan] . . . Anna is always protective of artists. They could be in any party. That is why we all consider Anna as an elder brother. Why, even as a wisdom-imparting father. And a teacher.[28]

Now, with only four days to go before the play, the costumes for MGR were altered to fit the leaner Ganesan.

The play lent its name to Ganesan, one of the most gifted Indian actors ever. EVR, who presided over the play, beckoned him to ask, 'You are Ganesan, are you? From today, you are Sivaji,' and Ganesan came to be popularly known as 'Sivaji'.

The grateful Ganesan would later term the name given him by EVR as 'generous alms' to him and declare that it was only after the play 'the ordinary Ganesan became Sivaji Ganesan'. However, it would be years before the moniker would become synonymous with him. In the credits for *Parasakthi* (Goddess Parasakthi, 1952), he still appears as Ganesan. But the Dravidian movement and Anna were generous not only in giving him that moniker but also seeing that it stuck.*

---

* Thus, after Ganesan had become Sivaji, when the Sivaji Fans Association president Chinna Annamalai surprisingly sought out MGR to act as Shivaji in his historical film in the late 1960s, MGR refused. Later, he

The play *Parasakthi* would be turned into a film by AVM Studios, which bought the rights from the playwright Pavalar Balasundaram. The movie version would take the Tamil film world by storm and Ganesan would go places. Ironically, he would go through the same harrowing experience as MGR in *Rajakumari*, his debut film as hero.[29]

RAJAKUMARI, A MOVIE THAT WAS NEARLY ABORTED

In the 1930s, Tiruppur M. Somasundaram aka 'Jupiter' Somu and S.K. Mohideen founded the legendary Jupiter Pictures. Its *Sri Murugan* (1946) was shot in Coimbatore, and MGR was signed up on a monthly retainership. As Lord Shiva, MGR performed the rudra thandav and ananda thandav in the movie. *Sri Murugan* would finally lead him to the hero's role in Jupiter's *Rajakumari*. But the movie was full of false steps and, until the end, it faced the danger of being aborted.

Eventually, Jupiter would prove a good augury for not only MGR but also Kalaignar Karunanidhi. *Rajakumari* would bring them together for the first time officially, although MGR has recorded that *Abhimanyu* (1948) was when he first met Kalaignar.[30] At Jupiter, MGR met his third wife, Janaki, when they were paired together for *Mohini* (1948). *Rajakumari* would seal their friendship and they would act in support of each other's careers.

Jupiter Pictures had entrusted a film to A.S.A. Samy. Diffident about casting P.U. Chinnappa and T.R. Rajakumari, the reigning king and queen of the silver screen, as suggested by Somu, Samy recommended instead the up-and-coming MGR and Malathi. Somu had been taken by MGR's dance number in *Sri Murugan* and, besides, he was on Jupiter's payroll. MGR's role as a hero now appeared within reach.

---

turned down director Ramanna's invitation: 'Thambi Sivaji already has this title. Therefore, my conscience does not permit me to act as Shivaji in the documentary.' Anna told Ramanna who sought his intervention: 'Already the party had conferred the title Sivaji on Thambi Ganesan. Only if that title were to endure will it be an honour to the party', adding that MGR had 'made the right decision'. http://www.vikatan.com/news/miscellaneous/57771-the-reason-to-avoid-mgr-act-as-sivaji-character.art.

Nonetheless, the start to *Rajakumari* itself would prove to be disquieting. A sentimental MGR associates the film's music director, S.M. Subbiah Naidu, with his 'first break' and other important turns.[31] When Subbiah Naidu broke the news that he was cast in the film, MGR remained sceptical, especially in light of *Chaya*.[32] Besides, stalwarts like MKT, PUC and T.R. Mahalingam were reigning supreme as music and singing were prerequisites for a hero. MGR had the gift of neither. Then how could he become a hero? He did not wish to go through another harrowing period of uncertainty and decided to approach the director discreetly.[33] But neither the director nor the proprietor, whom he approached later in the director's presence gave MGR any hope. In 1972, he said that because playback singing had been introduced by this time, he could make it as a hero.[34]

MGR did, however, eventually make it.[35] The remuneration for *Rajakumari* was 2500 rupees and was paid in monthly instalments of 200 rupees. Though a fee of 1500 rupees had been agreed upon, Jupiter Pictures paid him more than 5000 rupees for *Sri Murugan*. They were generous paymasters and they would pay MGR well for his two other films later. However, the company ran into financial difficulties; MGR had to go without pay for the last months of *Rajakumari*.[36] Choreographer 'teacher' Kumar and MGR's yet-to-be most celebrated villain M.N. Nambiar made MGR's continued stay in Coimbatore possible.

Despite such support, *Rajakumari* itself turned out to be a most disconcerting experience. MGR wrote:

> The pain I had to endure to confirm my role as hero in the movie cannot be described in writing or explained . . . My hero's status was, as they say, a 'daily danger yet blessed with a long life'. Someone new with [MKT] Bhagavathar's hairdo will show up at the studios. That's it! News would reach me . . . 'Someone has come in your place. They are going to subject him to a screen test. He looks like Bhagavathar.' Hearing this, I would feel so humiliated, as if my five-and-a-half foot frame had shrunk to three.

MGR's desperation to retain the role saw him court danger on the sets of *Rajakumari*. In the movie, the disillusioned hero decides to hang himself. The ceiling beam that should have given in did not yield, leaving MGR literally hanging. With the noose strangling his neck, blood rushing to his brain, chest hurting and eyes squeezed, MGR had not smelt death that close till then. Thankfully, the beam eventually gave way, and MGR fell on to the coir-covered floor. Everyone present rushed to him, as he lay unconscious. 'Even then, the uppermost thought on my mind was they should not dismiss me as unsuitable,' wrote MGR later.'[37]

MGR did possess heroic attributes. *Rajakumari* exhibited his innate quality to help others, even though his own position remained shaky. MGR recommended 'Sando' Chinnappa Thevar, who was on the company's payroll, as villain. Samy, the director, was not thrilled: Thevar, he said was only 'an extra', preferring instead the well-known wrestler Kamaldeen. MGR stuck to his recommendation, failing which, he said, the fighting sequence could be scrapped. Thevar landed the role.

This quality, to sponsor and stand by those whom he considered deserving, drew a set of loyalists to him. MGR stuck his neck out for others, unlike Sivaji Ganesan who took no sides and treated the film world as a purely professional arena. With MGR, you were either with him or not. If you were with him, then he saw to it that you rose with him.[38] Chinnappa Thevar paid back his debt to MGR many times over when he promised not to make films with Sivaji Ganesan and, as a successful producer, produced sixteen of MGR's movies between 1956 and 1972. All of them, save one, were hits.

Rajakumari, a box office hit, gave the Tamil film world its next MKT, or demigod. Equally, it introduced Kalaignar Karunanidhi, the signature scriptwriter of the Dravidian movement. Director Samy and proprietor Somu could have hardly imagined that the two would ride the Tamil film and political worlds as colossi for half a century. Music director Chidambaram S. Jayaraman had recommended his brother-in-law to Samy for dialogue writing. On Samy's invitation, Kalaignar

---

* But even until the very end, *Rajakumari* looked perilously close to ending the way *Chaya* did. After seeing the rushes of the two-thirds shot film, S.K. Mohideen, Somu's partner, suggested they abort the project. Thankfully, Somu agreed to Samy's suggestion that only some 4000 feet remained and a decision could be made in the end. http://www.thehindu.com/todays-paper/tp-features/tp-cinemaplus/rajakumari-1947/article3023314.ece.

approached EVR, where he was assistant editor at *Kudiarasu*, who gave his consent. Kalaignar asked that he be permitted to continue his political activities, to which Samy agreed.[39]

KALAIGNAR M. KARUNANIDHI

Muthuvel Karunanidhi was born as Dakshinamurthy, in Thirukuvalai, in Thiruvarur, on 3 June 1924, to Muthuvel and Anjugam. The pious Muthuvel was a poet and a farmer, and could narrate the epic stories better than pundits. His son would turn out to be a poet, a writer, an orator and more, but not a believer. The young Karunanidhi's belief was in social and political reform. His gods would be different: EVR and Anna. He would himself turn into a leader par excellence, and achieve dizzying fame and power.

In 1936, a student ignored the peon, and rushed to meet the Thiruvarur High School headmaster. The boy threatened to drown himself in the town's pond when refused admission. The headmaster gave in. The pupil was Karunanidhi. This presence of mind and perseverance would mark Karunanidhi apart from his peers.[40]

Eight decades later, Kalaignar, of the backward Isai Vellalar community, would identify his 'Mother, father . . . and the caste discrimination that has been chasing [me] from the beginning' behind this 'obstinacy'. When it was pointed out that he had become chief minister at the young age of forty-five, and that he has since been in a position of influence for some fifty years and has been dealing with national leaders, an emotional Kalaignar said: 'Yes. Even among many of them, I have very clearly sensed caste discrimination. I have realized that behind the malice against the DMK is their inability to stomach its leadership by someone from a simple background such as me. However, the higher one rises, caste will attack you from behind.' The interviewer noted that the nonagenarian's eyes were moist while narrating this.[41]

Even at the age of fifteen, Karunanidhi was good at negotiations. The rival youth association's president suggested holding a poll between his and Kalaignar's Tamil Manavar Manram's members to choose a common leader. Three days before the poll, the rival sought help to stage his play as an artist playing the main role had stood him up. Karunanidhi agreed to stand in, provided the opponent quit the leadership race. The rival agreed to this condition and Karunanidhi took over the leadership of the merged clubs.[42]

Again at fifteen, he started a handwritten fortnightly journal *Manava Nesan* (Student's Friend) of eight pages. *Manava Nesan* came out for some seven–eight months, only to change form and grow later as his 'first child' *Murasoli* (which means 'the sound of the drum').

In the 1938 anti-Hindi agitation, Karunanidhi went on a procession with the Tamil flag, sloganeering against Hindi, praising Tamil and distributing handbills.[43]

He preferred reading EVR's *Kudiarasu* to his lessons. Not surprisingly, the precocious student failed the final year exams, not once but thrice. Clearly, his interest was in a public career. Thankfully for him, three attempts were the maximum chances a student was given.[44]

In 1942 Anna's *Dravida Nadu* had carried the young Karunanidhi's 'Ilamai Bali' (The Sacrifice of the Youth) essay in the third or fourth issue of its publication. Buoyed by his success, the writer would try his luck again with a second piece the following week. It was never published. A week later, Anna, meeting him on a visit to Thiruvarur, asked that he stop sending in essays. 'Study well. Once you finish your studies, you can involve yourself deeply in party activities,' Anna had advised. Kalaignar would say later that he listened to everything that Anna said except this, and that is why he never earned a degree.[45]

After failing school, the young lad fell in love, but the girl's parents did not want a self-respecter as their son-in-law. The resultant depression led to the penning of the *Palaniappan* play—he starred in it and later, sold it for 100 rupees. The family insisted that he find a job. But a job felt like 'poison' to the lad.

Determined to rescue their son from depression, the family hit on the idea of marriage.

The wedding to Padmavathi on 13 September 1944 brought marital bliss, but no work.[46] Furthermore, the following year at the Dravidar Kazhagam 22 July 1945 conference in Pondicherry, the young groom was beaten up badly and left unconscious close to a gutter. Later, when reunited, the fatherly EVR would administer medicine himself and take him to Erode, and make him assistant editor at *Kudiarasu*.[47]

In 1946, a year later, on Jupiter Pictures' invitation, Kalaignar moved to Coimbatore, where, at one point, MGR and Kalaignar lived

together.[48] The rent was twelve rupees. They quickly became friends
and Kalaignar would introduce Anna's works to MGR, a Congress man
at heart, who reciprocated by introducing Kalaignar to Gandhi's works.
Kalaignar recalled:

> My contact and friendship with MGR, a Gandhi devotee, who
> wore homespun [cloth] and a necklace made of lotus seeds
> began then. I would give Anna's books to him, while he gave me
> Gandhi's. We would frequently engage in debates. The result was
> that he became part of the Kazhagam.[49]

Rajakumari carried Kalaignar's name in the credits as 'assistant
writer' to A.S.A. Samy, who was credited for the story, 'scenarios',
direction, as well as the script. But when *Abhimanyu* did not carry his
name, and producer Somu assured him that once he earned some
popularity he would use Kalaignar's name, the writer's 'heart was very
troubled'. Considering it below his dignity he returned the next day to
Thiruvarur.[50]

Scriptwriter, politician and film producer Arangannal records
Kalaignar's maiden visit to Madras on MGR's invitation soon after
this. When they went to visit MGR at his house, Sathyabama served
them some gulab jamun and savoury items from a nearby restaurant,
and this would become a ritual. In his second visit, for *Marudhanaatu
Ilavarasi*, Kalaignar and Arangannal would take a tram in the evenings
to go to Elephant Gate to see MGR, who would meet them wearing his
white homespun clothes, lotus seed necklace and a handkerchief neatly
tucked behind his collar. None of them was well known, and they could
easily walk the streets of Madras to go see movies and boxing shows.[51]

By now, in 1948, *Murasoli* had become a weekly, thanks to Padma's
jewellery being pledged. The third issue cost Padma's thali. It was also,
unfortunately, Padma's last days, for she was afflicted with tuberculosis.
Going to attend a pre-scheduled meeting of Adi Dravidas at Pudukottai,
Kalaignar left Padma in a critical condition only to find her gone on his
return. (She had left behind the child M.K. Muthu.) Kalaignar himself
wondered later if it was a sense of duty or a case of heartlessness on
his part.[52] Similarly, he chose to address a local conference even as
his father was breathing his last; thus, not being next to him when he

passed away. Ironically, this is the same Kalaignar that MGR would later charge as caring for his family more than he did for the party.

His second wedding, to Dayalu, was on 15 September 1948, Anna's birthday. The groom had gone missing from the wedding altar only to be traced at a protest and brought back! Kalaignar, now a dramatist and actor, had staged his *Thookumedai* (Gallows) in Trichy, to meet the wedding expenses. Anna had presided over the function. On an earlier occasion, it was for his performance at the play that Dravidar Kazhagam's stormy petrel Pattukottai Azhagiri had conferred the title 'Kalaignar' on him. Arangannal writes that after *Mandhirikumari*'s release in 1950, the title gained currency and Karunanidhi became Kalaignar Karunanidhi.[53]

One day, at the Salem Modern Theatres' rehearsal hall, M.G. Chakrapani and K.M. Sherif introduced a tall man, his forehead smeared with holy ash, to Kalaignar. 'He too is here; he writes songs,' they said. It was poet Kannadasan and he would soon become close to Kalaignar. Even when they first met, Kalaignar had gauged that 'Kannadasan would not be fazed by anything' and that 'he considered criticizing others and inviting criticism from others as fun'. In a few weeks, Kalaignar and the poet travelled to Pollachi by bus from Coimbatore. They debated rationalism during the journey. By the time they reached their destination, in a little over an hour, Kannadasan had been converted to the cause, and he wiped the holy ash off his forehead. Kalaignar wrote correctly that it was his friendship that drew Kannadasan to the fold and concludes perhaps it was 'because of this he was not too attached to the [movement's] ideals'.

Strangely, MGR also held a similar opinion of the poet, blaming it on his impetuous nature: '[Kannadasan] is someone who possesses the attribute of speaking anything at any time . . . He would believe anything, and also not believe anything . . .'[54] In retrospect, Kannadasan was an extraordinarily gifted poet, who reached unscalable heights in cinema. But impressionable, impulsive and emotional, he became a capricious commentator of the movement, its ideals and leaders.

Kalaignar and the poet travelled to Madras for the founding of the DMK on 17 September 1949. On Anna's invite, Kalaignar joined him and the others for discussions after the founding meeting. Kannadasan had left for their lodge earlier.[55]

■

MGR considered *Rajakumari* a 'huge hit' and as his first break.[56] But, it did not change his fortunes drastically. His second break would come after a couple of films with *Marudhanaatu Ilavarasi*.

To reciprocate, MGR suggested Kalaignar pen the dialogues. Kalaignar had earlier insisted on MGR acting in *Manahirikumari*.[57] Kalaignar was barely twenty-five then and the producers worried about his relative inexperience. But MGR disabused them of their doubts and Kalaignar was in.[58]

He would write the story during the nights and meet at MGR's place in the mornings for discussions. Kalaignar would play the devil's advocate, arguing against the sequence and rationale of his own storyline. The brothers found this brave, unique and generous on the part of Kalaignar. After they would agree on the 'story so far', Kalaignar would go back to continue writing. This is how *Marudhanaatu Ilavarasi's* story was sculpted in a record one week.

Kalaignar's pen proved felicitous. Like their mentor, Anna, Kalaignar had the ability to get it right the first time itself. But Kalaignar would help with more than the script and see the movie through. Its producer had no money and so MGR, Chakrapani, director Kasilingam and Kalaignar took it upon themselves to see the movie to its completion.[59]

At this time, MGR appears to have been a staunch believer. He had written, in his own hand, 'Murugan Thunai' or 'Murugan Protects' on the agreement. Many times during the shoots, he went to Chamundeshwari temple. The movie cost 5 lakh rupees. Eighteen prints were taken and in Madras alone the movie was released in five places. It was a runaway success.[60]

V.N. JANAKI: A NEW LOVE

MGR and Janaki, the heroine, would fall in love during the making of the movie and she would leave her promising career and her husband, Ganapathy Bhat, also in cinema, for MGR. At the shoot in Mysore, Bhat laid out three conditions for letting go of Janaki: firstly, she should continue acting post-marriage; secondly, the films should be signed with him and, thirdly, he would decide the films in which MGR and Janaki could act together for the next ten years. Furious, MGR asked if he was a 'slave trader' and left. However, a development independent of Bhat would cloud the couple's plans. Polygamy was about to be forbidden.

Meanwhile, Janaki's money had been transferred to another account and a letter from Bhat said that Janaki was bound to him for ten years. Janaki had to prove the ten-year contract was fake. She asked Bhat's boss, S.S. Vasan, to intervene. Bhat's explanation was that MGR was after Janaki's money and he just wished to safeguard it. Vasan agreed to testify against Bhat and they won the case, but Bhat had squandered away the money by then.

Vasan, an exceptional man of great energy, vision and compassion, cared deeply for Janaki. When Janaki approached him for some money in order to pay her taxes as MGR was away, Vasan gave her the money—and a piece of his mind. He reminded her that MGR's situation was much like what Bhat had described and asked her not to rush into anything. A few days later, when she came back with a cheque from MGR, Vasan was pleasantly surprised. She refused his offer to keep the money and said that MGR did not like her taking money from anyone and insisted that one should live within one's means. Vasan's eyes grew moist on hearing this. 'You have gotten a man who wishes to live with self-respect . . . Even if it takes years, marry him . . .'[61]

It would, indeed, take years, and MGR became the butt of criticism from magazines and fellow artists. Janaki would cry, while MGR smarted inside. His financial and personal situation thus continued to be jinxed.

MANDHIRIKUMARI

The Kalaignar–MGR duo would better their box office success with *Mandhirikumari*. Modern Theatres T.R. Sundaram, who had suffered a major failure with his latest release, wanted to recoup his losses and wished for Kalaignar to pen *Mandhirikumari*, which became the first movie to properly credit him for his story and script. A retainership of 500 rupees a month was fixed. Kalaignar had set up home for his family at Salem now, and he began penning *Mandhirikumari* in earnest.

Released in June 1950, the movie, Kalaignar said, created a 'huge revolution'. Kalaignar's dialogues were sharp, highly imaginative and marked by exceptional turns of phrase. For the first time, posters gave prominence to the scriptwriter and, along with the song booklet, as a first, the dialogues were sold in the form of a booklet.[62] *Mandhirikumari* would see NSK approaching Kalaignar to pen the script for his *Manamagal* (Bride, 1951). It would also eventually bring him *Parasakthi*.[63]

But *Mandhirikumari* also saw some humiliating moments for MGR. In a song sequence, MGR's facial expressions were not to director Dungan's liking. An upset Dungan showed his anger towards MGR by ordering a retake. Sensitive, MGR responded in kind. He went to Dungan and, in his 'butler's English', angrily explained his position. Dungan could understand nothing of what MGR told him. He asked for Somu's help. MGR told Somu to tell Dungan the following: 'I know you; you too know me from *Sathi Leelavathi* times.' Trying to convey this in English, MGR had told Dungan earlier, 'I know you; you know I,' which had left Dungan at a loss. As Somu explained the situation, Dungan and the entire unit broke out laughing. However, Dungan would remember the rebellious behaviour. He took his revenge soon.

At Yercaud, MGR and S.A. Natarajan had a sword-fight sequence. The trolley shot of 600 metres length in the movie was shot at the rocks at the foot of Yercaud hills when the sun was at its height. As the fight progressed, MGR was to fall on a rock and the camera would zoom on him. MGR looked tired. The heat radiating from the rock had seeped through his fine silk shirt, scorching his back. No wonder MGR was uncomfortable. An indifferent Dungan ordered the entire sequence to be shot again, instead of just the close-up shot. In the second attempt, MGR could not even pull himself away from the rock as the silk shirt was stuck to his skin. His back had blisters because of the heat. Somu was moved to tears. MGR noticed them and said, 'Aandavane! [God! MGR's endearing way of address to those he respected or liked] This is a lesson for you. If you become a director, don't do such things.'[64]

Modern Theatres had signed up MGR for three movies, as was their practice; of these the last two also proved to be hits.* For *Mandhirikumari*, he got 12,500 rupees; he was paid the same amount for the two other films. MGR would address proprietor T.R.

---

* *Sarvadhikari* (Dictator, 1951) and *Alibabavum 40 Thirudargalum* (Alibaba and the Forty Thieves, 1956) were the second and third respectively.

Sundaram as 'Mudhalali' (owner) and, as a mark of respect, would not sit down in his presence. After his shots, he would sit and either read or observe other shots. Even when Sundaram told him not to show up, MGR would come to the sets to watch others. He did not like to be idle.

Artists would get ready by 7 a.m. The shooting would go on till the evening, sometimes well into the night. Sundaram would call it a day sometimes, so as not to tire out the artists. MGR would refuse him politely, 'No, Mudhalali, we will continue. We have come to act. We are willing to work all twenty-four hours. We are not tired.'

At Modern Theatres, the food was vegetarian. Any non-vegetarian dish had to be procured at one's own expense. As an avid non-vegetarian, MGR hired a cook and his food would be shared by at least four others on the sets. During the lunch interval, he would lay a towel on the floor and lie down. He did not like to sleep in the afternoons. After a short rest, he would come back to the sets. He would religiously ask the light boys and other staff who entered the sets after him if they had eaten too.

Books were his companions; he liked serious reading. If anyone wanted to borrow a book, he would obtain another copy and gift it to them. A demure MGR would not converse with female artists, even if it were the heroine, unless needed. In fact, he would walk away from them. He also preferred to do the stunts himself and not use a double.[65]

MGR considers *Marmayogi*, his third break that established him, as 'among the first tier of heroes'.[66] However, the following year, Kalaignar and Sivaji Ganesan's *Parasakthi* would be released, to set new records.

PARASAKTHI AND SIVAJI GANESAN

Mandhirikumari had shown that the fire could not be hidden, but *Parasakthi* would unleash the volcano in Kalaignar. Sivaji Ganesan performed in the play at Dindigul under the Sakthi Nadaga Sabha banner. Following the release of *Mandhirikumari*, National Pictures P.A. Perumal (PAP) travelled to Salem and asked Kalaignar to do the script. KRR, Kalaignar says, was to play the lead role, but he was busy and Sivaji Ganesan was signed up instead.[67] Thanks to producer PAP, 'Sivaji' V. Chinnaiah

Ganesan, only twenty-four years old and a cinema novice, was retained at Rs 250 a month as the screen hero for *Parasakthi*. Director duo Krishnan and Panju flew Ganesan from Trichy to Madras on a Dakota plane for a screen test. Interested in Ganesan's welfare, the directors asked him to mouth 'success' as the first word for the voice test. One sound engineer tried to convince the directors that Ganesan was instead saying 'sadat'. Another said that Ganesan opened his mouth like a fish.

Thankfully, the directors found the test rushes satisfactory. They felt they could cosmetically improve Ganesan's teeth arrangement and could make him put on some weight. The weight would bear on Ganesan's chances almost till the end of the film. Ganesan was thin, but before his performance, this appeared a small shortcoming and PAP, Kalaignar and the directors were keen on Ganesan. But not co-producer A.V. Meiyappa Chettiar (AVM), who reluctantly agreed on the condition that they first shoot 5000 feet of film for review. But even after only 1000 feet, PAP's father-in-law was against Ganesan and wanted a well-known actor in the film, namely KRR. The directors now sought out Anna, who graciously encouraged them to stick with Ganesan.[68]

But not all were so large-hearted. Ganesan could do nothing right for the others and the criticism stung the young man badly. One day, as he cried his heart out, the senior of the director duo, Krishnan, assured him: 'Don't worry, Ganesa. This is an acid test for new entrants.' He prophesied that Ganesan would be successful and that 'cinema companies will be named after [him]'.[69] Krishnan's words would come true, but not before Ganesan faced more humiliation. Seeing the rushes again, this time after 8000 feet, AVM pronounced: 'In this movie, we can enjoy the dialogues closing our eyes. One is unable to like the movie or the new faces.' But PAP and the directors stood their ground and continued to root for Ganesan. The film took two years to complete.

The movie would introduce S.S. Rajendran, noted for his pronunciation and distinct delivery of Tamil dialogues.* His devotion

---

* SSR declined an offer to act as Bharata in *Ramayana*, when it was made into a movie, saying that he did not act in mythological dramas. Since then, he came to be known as a *latchiya* or idealistic actor. *Kuladeivam* (Family Deity, 1956), *Mudhalali* (Owner, 1957), *Thai Pirandhaal Vazhi Pirakkum* (Thai Month Will Herald Light, 1958) are among his major hits.

to Anna, bordering on piety, would see him criticize MGR at times. He would also fall out with Kalaignar in 1976 and, along with his brother-in-law DVN, join MGR later.[70]

On 1 May 1952, Ganesan married his cousin's daughter, Kamala, in a simple wedding ceremony at Swamimalai, close to his cousin's place. PAP, MGR, Kalaignar, Kannadasan, T.A. Maduram, S.V. Sahasranamam, Krishnan Panju and writer Arangannal attended the wedding. It was a happy occasion as the congregation of the yet-to-be conquerors of Tamil Nadu's political, film and cultural spaces showed up. Poverty, hardship and the ambition to succeed had forged close personal bonds between them. All three—MGR, Kalaignar and Sivaji Ganesan—worshipped their mothers and the mothers saw them all as their sons. All three have recollected how they were fed, and how love and affection was showered on them by the others' mothers.

Released five-and-a-half months later, on 17 October 1952, after the wedding, *Parasakthi* was to change the lives of three of our protagonists for good. Kalaignar and Sivaji Ganesan had arrived.[71] The winning combination had heralded the era of dialogues and dialogue delivery, making the era of songs and the ability to sing to gain stardom passé. Kalaignar and Ganesan would develop a personal bond and would work together in several other films for the next three decades.* When Ganesan breathed his last, Kalaignar, in his obituary, said that death had finally torn them apart.[72]

The MGR–Ganesan relationship would go through ups and downs, and after the singular *Goondukili* (Caged Parrot, 1954) they would never unite to do a movie. Arangannal says that a highly sensitive and circumspect MGR took umbrage at Ganesan's innocuous comment at the former's wedding meal; that he did not need to perform wearing a suit when people greatly enjoyed his swashbuckling. *Andaman Kaidhi* (Andaman Prisoner, 1952), where MGR wore a suit, had not done that well. MGR took Ganesan's words to heart. He told Arangannal: 'Did you see what Ganesa asked me . . .? Umm I will show him [who I

---

* In *Panam* (Money, 1952), *Thirumbipaar* (Look Back, 1953) and, after his exit from the DMK, in *Raja Rani* (King and Queen, 1956), *Kuravanji* (1960), *Iruvar Ullam* (The Heart of Two, 1963) and *Maadi Veetu Ezhai* (The Poor of the Rich Household, 1981).

am].' Arangannal says that MGR's differences with Ganesan and their competition began from this point on.[73]

But it might have begun earlier. Ganesan has recorded that his stepping in to do Shivaji 'may have alienated us'. He wrote that he met MGR later when he joined cinema. But he also wrote that he knew MGR from 1944 onwards, when he and 'Kaakaa' Radhakrishnan would go to MGR's place and hang around during mealtimes. Sathyabama would ask that MGR wait for Ganesan, to feed them. Such was her love for Ganesan. Equally, Ganesan's mother, Rajamani, saw MGR as a son and MGR considered her 'as his own mother'. On Ganesan's invitation, MGR would unveil Rajamani's statue later. In the nights, MGR would take them to the cinemas and buy dinner on their way back. MGR, Ganesan writes 'never hesitated to spend on us'. Their friendship grew until Ganesan left for Kanchipuram to Anna.[74]

Parasakthi was the first seriously political propagandist film of the Dravidian movement.

Panam, which came to the screens on 27 October 1952, ten days after *Parasakthi*, again with Kalaignar and Sivaji Ganesan, saw NSK rooting for the DMK skilfully using the subterfuge of acronyms, homonyms and double entendres:

Theena . . . Muna . . . Kaanaa!
Engal Theena . . . Muna . . . Kaanaa!...

Pagutharivodu naatinar vazha
Thirukural thanthaar periyar!
Valluvap periyar!...

Thambimaarukuoru
Oru Anna polae...

Engal Thi Mu Ka

In Tamil, *Theena . . . Muna . . . Kaanaa* was also the acronym of the DMK (Thee Mu Ka), which the song mentions in the end and was understood as such, although in the song it referred to the Thirukural Front Association. Periyar referred to Tamil philosopher poet Thiruvalluvar in the song, but

it was understood as EVR Periyar and Anna polae (like an elder brother)
clearly referred to Anna, although it was used as an analogy for the work
of the association. Poet Kannadasan had penned the song, replete with
double entendres. NSK had included the proceedings of the DMK's first
state conference, from 13 to 16 December 1951, as part of the movie.[75]

Propaganda also meant attacking the Congress. Thus, in *Thirumbipaar*,
again scripted by Kalaignar and with Sivaji Ganesan in the lead, there
was a song that criticized the Congress administration for adulteration.
Crafted by Kannadasan and acted out by NSK, the song's popularity led to
the latter being called 'Kalapadam (adulteration) Krishnan'[76] for a while.

Even as Sivaji Ganesan was making waves, MGR was building his
public profile. In 1952, director K. Subramanyam became the catalyst
for an association for the welfare of artists. MGR got the original Junior
Actors Association (Thunai Nadigar Sangam) registered under the
Societies Act and rechristened it the Thennindhia Nadigar Sangam (the
South Indian Artistes Federation) or simply Nadigar Sangam. MGR was
one of the four vice presidents. K. Subramanyam, MGR, Sivaji Ganesan,
S.S. Vasan, Chinnappa Thevar and A.V.M. Chettiar donated funds
towards the purchase of land in T. Nagar, Madras. In November 1955,
MGR founded *Nadigan Kural* (The Voice of the Artist), the sangam's
journal, and served as its first editor. In that he wrote: 'An association
for the unity of artists, a magazine to carry the united voice, a library
to improve the knowledge of all actors, a place to socialize, improve
health by sports, exchange views and a stage for actors—these are our
dreams for the future.' After NSK's demise, MGR took over, and, after
a gap of a few years, he took over the organization again, before S.S.
Rajendran led it from 1963 to 1966.[77]

PURATCHI NADIGAR OR REVOLUTIONARY ACTOR

Kalaignar records that in the aftermath of *Malaikallan* (Mountain Thief,
1954), borrowing a car from Pakshiraja Studios, he and MGR motored to
Trichy to preside over M.S. Mani's *Oviyan* (Painter) play. Kalaignar said
on that occasion that 'MGR was wearing homespun [cloth], but inside
was clothed in a black shirt [the colour of the Dravidian movement].' It
was here that Kalaignar conferred on him the title 'Puratchi Nadigar' or
Revolutionary Actor.[78]

MGR chose the 25–26 April 1953 conference at Trichy the following year to make this commitment more open.[79] MGR was listed after NSK and before Sivaji Ganesan as speaker.

Here is an excerpt of his speech:

> I have not seen a movement, save the DMK, endeavouring to improve the lives of the artists. To jeer us and to criticize us there are many. But Anna alone respected us (artists) as humans, and realizing that we too have an interest in public affairs; he has come forward to give us a role . . . Who has such an interest [in us] and affection? What is wrong if we consider him our leader? For almost ten years, I have known Anna. He showers the same affection now, as then. For the awareness work that the DMK under his leadership carries out, I, from the Keralite part, will do my best.

MGR said that if Anna were to announce an agitation 'the first corpse to fall would be mine'.

Ganesan, for his part, said that if Anna were to command, he would tear up film agreements and get involved in the party's agitation. 'If we attain anything, we should attain Dravida Nadu or sudukadu [cremation ground],' Ganesan thundered here. 'People like me have won honour because of Anna's affection towards us. This intellectual movement is our heart. We are willing to sacrifice our soul, assets and body for it! To obtain rights, to obtain Dravida Nadu, people like me are always ready.'[80]

Poet Karunanandam said that although he joined the movement last, by planning well, MGR firmly planted himself in the party. He made no mistakes in his personal life and public career, and moved forward carefully. He said that after the Kazhagam began to contest in elections, MGR's 'indispensability was clearly evident. [Equally] the Kazhagam has been supportive of his growth. After MGR's entry, Anna was asked if actors had to be included with the Kazhagam this inseparably.'[81]

LEAVING THE CONGRESS

MGR explained later why he chose to quit the Congress. 'Why did I quit [the] Congress? Did I not like the Mahatma's principle? I would be offended if anyone asked me so. Why then? Why the change of heart?'

MGR was fascinated by Subhas Chandra Bose and considered Netaji as his 'ideal man'. In January 1939, Netaji had defeated Pattabhi Sitaramayya to the Congress presidency. Gandhi declared that 'Pattabhi's defeat is my defeat'. The thought that even the Mahatma had favourites somehow caused a 'small crack' in his image of Gandhi. Bose's resignation later brought in 'unremitting sadness' and became one of the reasons for him to 'quit' the Congress. MGR never moved away from Gandhi really and, in retrospect, the explanation appears contrived. In 1966, he said: 'I have not seen a saint like him. Even Christ and Budhha only propagated religion. But, it was Gandhi who conducted politics with honesty.'

For some years, MGR said he remained aloof and was not a member of any party. After some introspection, he wished to learn about the ideals and principles of some parties. He borrowed some books from his communist friends. The books inspired him to action. However, as a Gandhian, wedded to non-violence, he could not bring himself to accept an ideology of destruction to create a new world. His questions were not satisfactorily answered. His communist friends referred him to the writings of socialists Jayaprakash Narayan and Ashok Mehta. MGR was by then 'tired' of politics. It was now that he had the opportunity to read and reread Anna's 1949 work *Panathottam* (Money Garden) many times and slowly he was able to relate to it. Anna was able to offer many satisfactory explanations for the questions he had as a believer in Gandhian ideals.[82] 'Only true followers of Anna's socialist policies can take humanity forward to a frontier of human welfare and world peace by smashing any number of language disputes, social malaises, inequalities and religious fanaticism' he would write in 1970.[83] For nine weeks in a row, in his weekly autobiography in *Ananda Vikatan*, MGR sang the paeans of Anna's praise in his autobiography, titling a chapter 'Anna is God'.[84]

'God on Earth': The Zealous Convert

MGR exhibited the zeal of a convert with the DMK. Although a believer in the almighty,[1] he shied away from playing roles that conflicted with his movement's ideals. *Madurai Veeran* (Madurai Warrior, 1956), a subaltern hero's tale, had been changed to suit MGR. Asked whether his interference would not affect the producer, MGR declared:

> Nothing will happen. The films made according to my advice have been quite successful. Many scenes in *Madurai Veeran* are quite unrelated to the popular lore in the oral tradition. In the old story, Vellaiammal was a very poorly depicted character. The producer of the film paid heed to my suggestions on the character, and the film did very well. In the making of *Malaikallan* too I had a say in the storyline. My advice proved useful in *Alibaba* too. Don't conclude from all this that I forced my political views into my films. I make my suggestions as an artist in the first place. All I do is allow the film-makers to use my experience.[2]

However, in *Alibabavum 40 Thirudargalum* MGR may not have had his say completely. Instead of 'Alibaba vows on Allah', MGR said, 'Alibaba vows on amma', evading any religious reference. The director, the redoubtable Modern Theatres' Sundaram pulled him up for the improvisation. MGR had to yield.[3]

But the following year, he turned down *Rani Lalithangi* (Queen Lalithangi, 1957) when his suggested changes were refused. Sivaji Ganesan, who had just then come out of the DMK, stepped in.[4] MGR gave up *Kathavarayan* (1958) on 'principle' again, which was also picked up by Sivaji Ganesan.[5] Later, when he was accused of reneging on contracts, MGR said:

> I did not withdraw from my contracts citing my refusal to utter god's name. Take the film *Kathavarayan* first. I do not believe in the kind of faith healing or miracle rituals shown in that film . . .
>
> Today, I am a big actor. I am a hero to millions of young boys and girls who see me in films. The future of the country is in their hands. I do not support planting wrong ideas in their minds. I withdrew from *Kathavarayan* in a dignified way to register my protest. The other incident involved the film *Lalithangi*. In this movie, the hero treats all women as prostitutes and hates them. In the end, he has a change of heart when he falls for the beauty of a dancer in his court. I did not like this insult to womankind. Moreover, I was not happy with the way the producer treated the climax of the film. That is why I refused to act in *Lalithangi*.[6]

In keeping with the DMK's ideology of secularism, MGR wore no religious symbols, except towards the end of his life. Until then, he also wished that his close associates not sport them. He asked lyricist Vaali to refrain from wearing any religious marks, as party elders like N.V. Natarajan (NVN) would think poorly of him. At this, when Vaali retorted that he would rather leave, MGR said the issue could be closed.[7] Earlier, he had asked actress Sakunthala of his MGR drama troupe to wear her religious symbols in private and while performing in the temple town of Thiruvannamalai stopped her from visiting the shrine saying, 'If party men see this they would mistake me.'[8]

The years 1953 to 1956 were a slow period for MGR, with two out of three films following *Marmayogi* not faring well.* He founded the MGR Nataka Manram (MGR Drama Troupe). On 1 October 1953, R.M. Veerappan (RMV) joined as his manager, thanks to senior stage

---

* Earlier, *En Thangai* (My Sister, 1952), following *Marmayogi*, did relatively well and MGR's performance as a caring brother was well spoken of. However, *Andaman Kaidhi* (Andaman Prisoner, 1952) and *Kumari* (Maiden, 1952) did not fare well.

artist Narayana Pillai, after which MGR's heart grew fonder of the DMK. A man known for his political astuteness and organizational skills, RMV would see that MGR blossomed into a 'mature politician'.[9] In September 2005, Kalaignar would describe RMV as the 'sculptor' who made MGR.[10]

The MGR Nataka Manram had thirty men and nine women, and MGR had made them part of the DMK. When he found out that Sakunthala was not a member, he expressed his unhappiness and then summoned an aide to ask that a DMK flag be tied to her car.[11]

Some forty families depended on the troupe and they grew concerned when MGR landed *Malaikallan*. In response, a caring MGR took it upon himself to stage plays in the Coimbatore area in the evenings, while he would shoot for *Malaikallan* during the day.[12] Similarly, as the drama troupe began to fare better, MGR converted the monthly salary to a share from the proceeds.[13] But as MGR got busy, the troupe wound up.[14]

The troupe's play *Inbakanavu* (Sweet Dream) was debuted for the benefit performance of the DMK's 1953 Three-front Agitation case fund, in the first week of October 1953, and it was a huge hit.[15] MGR used to wave the DMK flag both at the beginning and end of the play,[16] and would address the audience on the DMK's policies in the end.[17] This DMK involvement, however, came with a price. The Madras Sabhas (associations) refused sponsorship and the state-run All India Radio ostracized him.[18] When a staffer broadcast an abridged version of *Inbakanavu*, he was promptly transferred for the indiscretion.[19] This ostracism extended to his film career as MGR made it clear that he would act only if his political propaganda was permitted in his movies. Sakunthala said that MGR lost many an opportunity and a worried Chakrapani often quarrelled with his younger brother on this account.[20] MGR himself wrote later: 'The bond is such that whatever good or bad occurs to the Kazhagam, [it] also reflects in my life.'[21]

But MGR pushed the envelope with his DMK agenda. In fact, in 1968, he testified that it was his 'job', and said that he felt vindicated when he was accused that he was politicizing cinema and vice versa.[22] *Thozhilali* (Worker, 1964) is a case in point. To indicate that the worker would one day become the owner, MGR had to speak the line: 'That is my future star of confidence.' Scriptwriter Arurdhas, a

Catholic, explained the story of the guiding star of Bethlehem. When MGR pointed out that it was the Swatantra Party's symbol, Arurdhas suggested replacing the sun with the star. Dravidar Kazhagam's M.R. Radha, the villain in the movie, made it clear to MGR that the shot with the word sun could not end with his face as was planned. The shot now ended with MGR directing the script to the image of Murugan behind M.R. Radha on the wall.[23] This would not be the first time that MGR had tried and failed.

Genova (1953) produced both in Tamil and Malayalam, with MGR in the lead, contained some early lessons for the actor. Firstly, he was aghast to learn that a former office boy at Jupiter was to score the music, but producers E.P. Eppan and F. Nagoor (also the director) stood firm with their decision. After listening to the songs, MGR went over to the composer's house in Mylapore to embrace him and said, 'From now on you are the music director for all my films.'[24] M.S. Viswanathan (MSV), poet Pattukottai Kalyanasundaram and playback singer T.M. Soundararajan (TMS) would become MGR's image-making team, which, after Kalyanasundaram's death, came to comprise poets Kannadasan and later Vaali, before Pulavar Pulamaipithan and Kavignar Muthulingam joined.

However, Genova's next surprise was not as pleasant. One day, MGR saw an actor giving a voice-over for him in Malayalam. His 'blood boiled' at this. Production manager Mathews smilingly introduced the dubbing artist who was all grace. Seething inside, MGR took Mathews aside to protest, only to hear from him that his Malayalam sounded like Tamil and that he had done him 'a favour'. Furious, MGR walked out, threatening legal action. Mathews told him that if he wished he could also dub his Tamil. He pointed out to a shocked MGR that the agreement stipulated MGR's consent only for dubbing other than in Tamil or Malayalam. A worried MGR thought of the consequences of his film career if Mathews were to dub his Tamil in Genova and felt that his own rules had trapped him. However, his impulsiveness would continue and he found himself in a similar predicament with Thaaikupin Thaaram (Wife after Mother, 1956).[25]

After Genova, MGR tended to be more careful, but when he asked producer Lena Chettiar, who had recommended him for Malaikallan, whether that film's producer was a 'trouble producer' (troublemaker), he sharply pointed out that producers should be the ones asking such questions of artists and not the other way around.[26] But MGR may have owed *Malaikallan* to Sivaji Ganesan in the end.

After *Parasakthi*, Sivaji Ganesan's star shone bright. When Pakshiraja Studios' S.M. Sriramulu Naidu wished to enlist Sivaji Ganesan for his *Malaikallan*, Ganesan pointed out that he could not even meet his commitments in Madras, so he could not imagine spending some months shooting in Coimbatore at that time. He suggested MGR's name instead. The next day, Sriramulu Naidu met MGR and signed him up.[27]

MGR considers *Malaikallan* his fourth break.[28] In the credits, his name was spelled as M.G. Ramachandran as opposed to 'M.G. Ramchandar', as he called himself till then. Kalaignar had penned its dialogues and the movie's credits showcased this as the first slide. MGR's name was listed first among the actors. Poet Ramalingam Pillai's song *'Thamizhan endror inamundu / Thaniye adhorkoru gunamundu* (Tamils are a race / The race has a distinctiveness)' essayed the pride of being a Tamil.[29] Furthermore, Thanjai Ramaiah Das's *'Innum ethanai kaalamthaan emaatruvaar indha naatile* (How much longer will they cheat us in this country)' became a super hit. Playback singer TMS had sung both the songs. His voice fit both MGR and Sivaji Ganesan like a glove.

A HOME FOR MOTHER

Soon, the brothers moved from Adyar to 160, Lloyds Road, now Avvai Shanmugam Salai, in Royapettah, because of Sathyabama's health. She had become an invalid.

The move to the new place was hugely courageous on their part as the rent was 250 rupees. Landlord A.V. Raman was a very kind soul. Two years into their tenancy, he pointed out that they had paid a cumulative 6000 rupees as rent and that after seven to eight years, the rent they would have paid would equal the house's value and yet, the house would still be his. Instead, Raman suggested that they purchase the house right away. It felt like a cruel joke in their situation, except that Raman was serious. Seeing them fall silent, he asked them to think it over.

Another year went by, and Raman repeated his offer. This time he suggested they give 9000 rupees annually for four years and the house would be theirs. Raman had rejected a Mylapore lawyer, who had offered a higher price for the house, thrusting the house on the brothers. When they were called again, Raman said that only half the amount remained and once they paid that, he would legally transfer the house to them. 'The truth is that the house had been forcibly imposed on us,' wrote a gracious MGR later. The house that Sathyabama breathed her last in had become hers after her death, thanks to Raman and her sons. 'Thaai Veedu' (Mother's House), as the brothers named it in honour of their mother, witnessed the ups and downs in MGR's life.[30]

THREE-FRONT AGITATION 1953

The young DMK party planned agitations and programmes, and, in the summer of 1953, Anna announced the party's now famous Three-front Agitation. MGR did not take part in it. Anna had exempted actors and certain professionals such as lawyers.[31] On 15 July, the batch led by Kalaignar lay on the rails of the local Kallakudi station defying the authorities and an incoming train. The train screeched to a halt just ahead of where Kalaignar and his colleagues lay. Kalaignar would be slapped with a six-month sentence for the protest. Later that day, however, six lives would be lost in police firing.

Anna was upset with Kalaignar for exceeding the party's original mandate—of just sticking the poster saying 'Kallakudi' on the name board of the station called Dalmiapuram, demanding a return to the original name—and the series of events leading to the loss of life.[32] Kallakudi left a deep impression on MGR. On 29 November, the screen hero awaited the Kallakudi hero, at the Egmore railway station, who was returning to Madras after the completion of his prison term. Kalaignar could not even alight from the train. Such were the crowds. Like in the movies, carrying him, MGR waded through the jostling crowd, only to lose his expensive watch in the process.[33]

MGR would praise Kalaignar as one of the rare leaders who had risked his life and had the train not screeched to a halt, the loss would have been irreparable.[34] In 1970, he told Vaali to 'especially include lines on Karunanidhi having kept his head on the rails' and sang in *Engal Thangam*:

Blocking the moving train [and]
Placing his head on the rails
Disregarding life, as straw
This crowd upheld Tamil honour'[35]

Furthermore, MGR had not taken a fee for the movie and had asked
Jayalalithaa to do the same to help out Kalaignar financially.[36] Although
it appeared to be the apogee of their cooperation, Vaali wrote that
he was aware that MGR and Kalaignar were having some 'small cold
wars'.[37] Producer Murasoli Maran appeared in no hurry to complete the
movie. On Jayalalithaa pointing this out, MGR would begin probing,
only to learn that the producers were deeply engaged in discussions on
Kalaignar's eldest son, M.K. Muthu's *Pillayo Pillai* (Oh! The Son, 1972).[38]
Clearly MGR was not 'Our Gold' any more. Also, the cold war would
not be cold any longer as MGR feared that Muthu was being sponsored
by his family in competition to him.

IMAGE-MAKING

MGR was considered god on earth. His widow Janaki thought he was
an 'avatar' of god.[39] Once, a Pondicherry farmer insisted on taking MGR
to his land saying, 'Your feet should touch my earth' as it would bring
him prosperity. Such was the faith among the uneducated in him. On
another occasion, a rural fan wondered if MGR had played the chieftain
Veerapandiya Kattabomman, who rebelled against the British, he would
have not allowed Major Bannerman to hang him in the movie and,
instead, would have hanged the major. In the movie, Sivaji Ganesan
had played the role of Kattabomman.[40]

Although the Kalaignar–Sivaji Ganesan combination had raised
dialogues in film and their delivery to a new level, somehow fans never
conflated Sivaji Ganesan with the message of his dialogues. MGR's
fans, on the contrary, did. *Marmayogi* was perhaps the first of MGR's

---

* *Odum rayilai idai marithu*
  Adhan paathayil thanadhu thalai vaithu
  Uyiraiyum thaan thurumbaai madhithu
  Tamizh peyarai kaatha kootamidhu

films where the dialogues were conjoined with the hero even outside of the movie. *Rajakumari*, *Marudhanaatu Ilavarasi* and *Mandhirikumari* had established MGR as a dashing hero who valiantly fought for justice. *Marmayogi* portrayed MGR's precocious fighting skills, but A.S.A Samy's dialogues were pregnant with innuendo and multilayered meanings competing for equal attention with the hero's fighting in the movie. The line, 'Naan kuri vaithaal thavara maatten! Thavarumey aanaal kuri vaikka maatten (I will not miss if I aim! I will not aim if I were to miss)!' and the hero's declaration, 'Whenever oppression and authoritarianism hurt people, I will appear there in a flash', much like Krishna in the *Gita*, resonated with the audience. In *Mandhirikumari*, MGR had mouthed Kalaignar's rousing dialogues as commander Veeramohan: 'They are few . . . We are many! They are conspirators . . . We are the daring! Oh, lion Tamils! Rise snarling!'

MGR had figured out early on that there was no difference between the screen hero and the real one—at least in his case. He portrayed what he was—or so he claimed. In 1974, MGR told the *New York Times*, 'What I say in my films, what I do, I try to live up to in my personal life.'[41] Cinema was more than a livelihood—it was his life and a vehicle for his latent aspirations. The budding hero chose his roles and lines carefully, never essaying a negative role. Sivaji Ganesan on the contrary saw movies purely as a profession and took up any role, sometimes to the detriment of his public image. For instance, *Thirumbipaar*, his fifth movie, cast him as a womanizer.

Sivaji Ganesan said in an interview in 1997:

MGR is the chief among those who understood themselves. He had decided early on to succeed in a big way in politics. Therefore, he played roles that would bring him respect from people. I thought that there was no connection between acting and politics. But people have proven that there is a connection. That is why MGR succeeded in politics. For me, politics was only secondary. I acted as a drunk, a womanizer, murderer and rowdy many times. That is why I was able to star in 300 films . . .

[Within the Congress] they did not allow my growth . . . I have not gained anything from politics. [In fact] I have only been humiliated.

I realized only later that people did not wish to see me as a politician. They had wished to see me only as an actor. So many actors have come to politics. Have all of them become leaders?[42]

In another context, Sivaji Ganesan hinted that MGR's portrayal may not have resembled the real MGR:

I acted with my Annan, MGR, in the film, Goondukili. Generally, our people regard acting as villain or hero as two different entities. The actors themselves are responsible for this mindset. The ideal hero does not smoke, drink or even look at girls. The girls should be the ones who fall all over him. He should be a man who takes care of his parents and live[s] the life of a philanthropist. Committing adultery would be blasphemous for him. Some actors took this very seriously and acted as if they never smoked, drank alcohol or looked at women. These are the expectations of the masses. I understood these things a little later.

I was not aware then that even if an actor had all the undesirable habits, he had to pose as a good man and ensconce himself in the hearts of the people to enter politics . . .[43]

Film producer A.V.M. Saravanan, however, mentioned that the real MGR was true to his screen image.[44]

As late as 1978, MGR himself said:

For any man, it is not enough what he thinks of himself. The people should believe what he is. If I was not really what I am projecting on the screen, then the people would have abandoned me long ago . . . I live as simply as possible, despite what I can otherwise afford.[45]

Thus, in Panam Padaithavan, terrified at the thought of being shown as going to a cabaret, MGR asked director Ramanna, 'What would my fans think of me? Is this necessary?' Thankfully for MGR, the sequence did not survive the censors.[46]

Poet Vaali once suggested that MGR play the role of Devdas, who takes to drinking and a courtesan because of his unfulfilled love. Declining the suggestion, MGR reasoned:

Aandavane! I have an image for myself . . . It is not something that I had constructed . . . In movie after movie and movie after movie, it happened naturally . . . Kannadasan, Pattukottai [Kalyanasundaram], you and other poets had penned such substantive songs for me . . . After singing songs that have a message for society, how can I, even if it is necessary for the plot, act as a drunk? I naturally do not have the habit. It's one thing to act as a drunk and another to pretend to be intoxicated in a scene. I have done the latter in many movies to befool villains and to find their shortcomings . . . You would've seen this. Even when the villain would give me a glass of alcohol, I would throw its contents into a nearby flowerpot and pretend as though I have consumed it.

Aandavane! There are many ways in the world to make money. Similarly, there are several ways to reach office . . . But to get a place in people's hearts, that cannot happen for all . . . If the womenfolk are celebrating me, carrying me on their heads, [it is because] I act as *kuppan* and *suppan* [a Tamil way of referring to the commoners] from the slums, I intercede with and challenge, like a just man, those who exploit the poor, using their labour and not give them their due!

Now tell me—can I act as Devdas? If I do, within a day the image that I have in the hearts of many, that I am a good person, would be completely demolished. There are many actors in cinema but let me be a man amongst the actors![47]

GOOD VS EVIL

MGR's films personify the Hindu philosophy of the triumph of good over evil, with MGR embodying the good. The evil villain could be a tyrant, counterfeiter, gangster, a rogue scientist, a feudal landlord, an imposter, a corrupt official, a press tycoon and so on. MGR, the underdog, is intelligent and physically invincible, overcoming all the plots, however, malevolent or complicated. He would single-handedly beat up the villain and his henchmen. He would intercede on behalf of the meek for a cause, always fight honourably, save damsels in distress and worship his mother. The villain's daughter, however, rich or of a higher-caste, would invariably fall in love with him. It was only a matter of time before MGR became 'vathiyar' or teacher to the working class, and the epitome of the perfect man to womenfolk. An additional reason for his movies' success was their being replete with romance, turning his young fans into voyeurs. After seeing *Anbe Vaa* (Oh Love, Come!, 1966), Anna had remarked 'It was okay in this movie. In another movie, the two tightly embraced and rolled while singing "*Javvadhu medai katti* (To build a stage with javadhu [a local perfume])".' The movie was *Panathottam* (Money Garden, 1963).[48]

As MGR rose up the ladder, producers chose stories that matched his persona, even as scriptwriters and lyricists took it upon themselves to craft lines that established and perpetuated the MGR image, turning him into a cult. In 1974, when asked about his success as opposed to the actors of the north, MGR himself noted that 'producers and film scriptwriters did not engage in a concerted way [in this direction]' as they did for him. He could have added that even if they had, it would have not congealed like it did in his case.[49]

His fans vicariously lapped up his success and glory, and, in fact, lived through him. In 1965, speaking about this, MGR said:

> I come down by the lift in this palace-like Ashoka Hotel. Yet, these people did not entertain an iota of jealousy at me. Instead, they have affection and trust in me. They believe that my very living in such status and luxury is for them.[50]

The poet Vaali, however, did not give up. He pointed out that in *Goondukili*, MGR smoked in a scene. Flashing a smile, MGR said that he was not that deeply involved in public life then and was yet to become vathiyar. In later years, the scene was removed.[51]

The film's director, Ramanna's, version of the event shows that MGR put up stiff resistance to avoid doing the scene. Finally, MGR was seen pondering with a lit cigarette in his hand and then casually throwing away the stub. MGR never smoked even on the screen![52]

Oli Vilakku posed a more serious dilemma for MGR. It was his hundredth film and the producer was the legendary S.S. Vasan. In a particular sequence, the hero had to act as a drunk and mouth a song. MGR summoned Vaali for advice, who cited an earlier P.U. Chinnappa film. Vaali said that MGR would be drunk but his conscience would emerge as four different MGRs in order to criticize his act in the song. MGR now anxiously asked Vaali for the pallavi (the first two lines of a song). Vaali came up with:

> Tell me bravely, are you a human?
> You are a beast
> When you fall into this alcohol*

MGR was overwhelmed and planted a kiss on Vaali's head.[53]

MGR was obsessed with his image. A very sensitive person, he wished to project an aura of gravitas, respect and importance around him. His interactions with others in public were also carefully crafted. Arurdhas provided insight into how MGR's and Sivaji Ganesan's styles and perspectives differed. On their second film together, *Thaaiaiy Kaatha Thanayan* (The Son Who Saved His Mother, 1962), MGR stopped a scene midway. Arurdhas, as was his wont with Ganesan, shouted across the set to prompt MGR. The take was then continued and was successfully shot. MGR later called Arurdhas to tell him:

> When you prompt me, shouting from across the sets, I don't feel anger but embarrassment. I will never allow an inch of my respect to be lost in the eyes of others. I have been thus from my youth . . . In the future, if you wish to prompt me, come close and do so, not loudly.[54]

Comedian Chandrababu felt MGR was hugely egoistic. MGR's habit was to stay aloof, reading a book during the breaks. On one occasion, when he joined them on director Ramanna's invitation, everyone except MGR laughed at a joke told by Chandrababu. As the comedian wondered why MGR could not enjoy the joke like the others did, MGR shot back saying that it was so flat that the comedian would have to physically tickle him to get a laugh out of him. That day, MGR wished to show that he alone was the great one, even in that small team. I

---

* *Dhayiriamaaga sol nee manidhan thaanaa*
  Nee thaan oru mirugam
  Indha madhuvil vizhum neram . . .

see that this "I" arrogance of his has grown, like the rise of his career,'
wrote Chandrababu. The comedian was westernized and was quite an
independent spirit. He found MGR strange. MGR, for his part, could not
relate to Chandrababu's western ways. He did not like Chandrababu
calling him Mr MGR. Nobody called him so, save actress Bhanumathi
with whom he developed a difficult relationship in *Nadodi Mannan*
(Vagabond King, 1958)*

MGR's Intelligence point man Mohandas wrote in 1992:

> MGR was a man with a king-sized ego . . . All his moves were well-
> calculated and intended to promote his self-interest. He excelled
> in the art of manipulation, whether it was cinema, the political or
> administrative field. He trusted none and was always calculating
> how to boost his image, irrespective of the consequences.[55]

He was, unsurprisingly, very selective about his public appearances and
similarly kept his trade a secret. Rarely was his shooting public. Fight
and romance sequences were filmed privately. MGR wanted cinema to
remain magical—a mystery and a wonder.[56] It was after the launch of
his AIADMK that he had to show up more often in public. The man was
so gifted that this frequent exposure only added to his image, charisma
and connection with the people.[57]

His image was partly cultivated, but, in retrospect, MGR also had
a lot of luck. The charges of him being high-handed and capricious in
the film world, the pain he inflicted on producers, on fellow actors,
like Chandrababu or S.A. Asokan, and his female companions, his
corruption, autocracy and inconsistency while in office—Teflon-like
nothing stuck to him. Just when things would appear to be going
downhill, MGR would be saved by an accident, such as the 1967
shooting or his ill health, as in 1984–85.

---

* In *Adimaipenn* (Slave Girl, 1969) Chandrababu's genuine praise on the
  sets, 'Vathiyar is dashing. He looks like a Greek god' upset MGR and
  he left the place. Jayalalithaa and Cho. Ramaswamy told the comedian
  he could have said this in Tamil. http://tamil.thehindu.com/opinion/
  blogs/என்னர="மை-தே்"ழி-24-எனக்கும்-அரசியல்-தெரியாம்/
  article9516539.ece?ref=relatedNews.

FIGHT SEQUENCES

Part of MGR's image was that he was a good fighter and a swashbuckler. Fighting sequences became a must in MGR's films, so he would lament that 'with the passage of time, it has somehow come to be established that all my movies must have fight sequences'.[58] However, when it came to fighting with animals, MGR appears to have been very careful.

Many of MGR's films are entertainers and Ramanna's *Gulebakavali* is one such film, known for its songs, dances and fights, especially the one between MGR and a tiger. A cut-up Chandrababu, who co-starred in the film, wrote about how the famous tiger fight in the movie was filmed. Coming in two hours late for the shot, MGR was keen to know that the tiger was drugged and in the cage, and he kept his gaze completely fixed on the animal. He deftly ducked and somewhat hid himself as the tiger leapt and the director said 'cut'. MGR was drenched in sweat as he left the cage and beckoned Chandrababu for a chat, even as Ramanna kept filming the tiger. 'I should not describe how this was done. That is a professional secret. MGR was next to me [all the time]. But the tiger fight [with him] was being filmed,' wrote Chandrababu impishly.[59] In *Thaaikupin Thaaram* he refused to tame a bull and a double was used instead.

If he was careful about fighting with animals, MGR equally felt the weight of his fans' adulation and the responsibility it had created. Even titles were chosen very carefully. For *Thirudaathae* (Do Not Steal, 1961) M. Lakshmanan, a scriptwriter for the film, came up with *Thirudaathae* and *Nalladhuku Kaalamillai* (Goodness Stands No Chance), recommending the latter as the title. MGR said:

> If we were to name it *Nalladhuku Kaalamillai*, people would think that MGR himself has said that goodness stands no chance, then why should we be good? *Thirudaathae* is not like that. It exhorts them not to do wrong. It has a good message. We should always convey good message[s] to people.[60]

MGR was also politically correct. He didn't want to have a title with a splash of arrogance; similarly, he did not wish for socially ill-respected themes in his films or to play such characters. His movie titles had to be clean. Of course, MGR did not choose all his movie titles. Some, like *Panathottam*, were borrowed from a play of Anna's. Others like *Rani Samyuktha* (Queen Samyuktha, 1962) or *Adimaipenn* (Slave Girl, 1969) simply had to follow the storyline. Poet Vaali chose the name *Padagoti*. However, invariably, the titles reflected his persona, message, party and political trajectory. In the seventies, this trend was on the upswing. Every fourth movie title after 1960 appears to follow this pattern.* And many a movie had the word thaai (mother) in the title.

THE SONG AS THE MESSAGE

In 1989, Rajinikanth sang the song, '*Superstaru yarunu kaetaa* (If you were to ask who the superstar is)' in the movie *Raja Chinna Roja* and, in

---

* *Nallavan Vazhavaan* (The Good Will Flourish, 1961), *Thaai Sollai Thattathey* (Don't Disobey Mother's Words, 1961), *Thirudaathae, Thayai Katha Thanayan, Kudumba Thalaivan* (The Family Head, 1962), *Pasam, Dharmam Thalaikaakkum* (Charity Saves, 1963), *Needhikkuppin Pasam* (Affection after Justice, 1963), *Kanchi Thalaivan* (Kanchi's Leader, 1963), *Deivathaai* (Godly Mother, 1964), *Thaayin Madiyil* (In Mother's Lap, 1964), *Thozhilali, Padagoti, Aayirathil Oruvan* (One in a Thousand, 1965), *Enga Veetu Pillai* (Our House's Son, 1965), *Mugarasi* (The Lucky Face, 1966), *Naan Aanaiyittaal* (If I Were to Command, 1966), *Petraal Thaan Pillayaa* (Is Only a Biological Child a Child, 1966), *Thaaiku Thalaimagan* (The First Son for the Mother, 1967), *Vivasayee* (Farmer, 1967), *Kavalkaran, Oli Vilakku, Pudhiya Bhoomi* (New Earth, 1968), *Nam Nadu, Maattukara Velan* (Cowherd Velan, 1970), *Engal Thangam, Rickshawkaran* (Rickshawman, 1971), *Oru Thaai Makkal* (The Children of One Mother, 1971), *Nalla Neram* (Good Tidings, 1972), *Annamitta Kai* (The Hand that Fed, 1972), *Urimaikural* (The Voice of Rights, 1974), *Sirithu Vaahza Vendum* (Live with a Smile, 1974), *Netru Indru Naalai* (Yesterday, Today, Tomorrow, 1974), *Ninaithathai Mudippavan* (The One Who Accomplished His Thoughts, 1975), *Naalai Namadhae* (Tomorrow Is Ours, 1975), *Idhayakani* (Heart's Fruit, 1975), *Pallandu Vazhga* (Long Live, 1975), *Needhiku Thalai Vanangu* (Bow to Justice, 1976), *Ooruku Uzhaipavan* (The One Works for Others, 1976), *Uzhaikkum Karangal* (Working Hands, 1976) and *Meenava Nanban* (Fisherman's Friend, 1977), *Maduraiai Meeta Sundarapandian* (Sundarapandian Who Retook Madurai, 1977).

2004, Kamal Hassan was referred to as 'Alwarpettai Aandava' (Alwarpet god)' in *Vasool Raja MBBS*. But these were rare occasions when the two giants of Tamil cinema today were embodied in a song. On the concerted attempt at image-making for MGR, in 1977, Kannadasan alleged, 'In every movie he would wish that lyricists scripted songs eulogizing him.'[61] However, Vaali avers that MGR never asked lyricists to do any such thing and, in fact, he was shy and embarrassed when they eulogized him.[62] Also, he was bashful about self-praise or pomposity. When a poet wrote, 'If I beckon with my finger, victory will be mine', he asked it to be changed to 'If He (god) beckons'.[63]

MGR had a keen sense for good lines and punchlines. He knew roles, dialogues and songs were central in perpetuating the MGR myth and image. While heroines sang paeans of his praise, while other characters spoke of his virtue, the most potent lines, be it a song or a script line, emanated from him. For instance, in *Chakravarthi Thirumagal* (The Emperor's Daughter, 1957), in a song sequence, NSK asks MGR what is on fire without fire and smoke. As NSK looks puzzled, MGR answers his question: 'The poor's hungry stomach.'[64] In many a song, MGR sang Anna's and the DMK's praise. After his exit from the DMK in 1972, his songs took on the DMK leadership, praised Anna and showcased his AIADMK. The song '*Thambi naan padithen Kanchiyile netru* (Younger brother, I studied in Kanchi [Anna's birthplace, Kanchipuram] yesterday)' by poet Vaali, from *Netru Indru Naalai* is a classic in this genre of songs.

Songs had a multiplier effect, as they were heard at tea stalls and at homes in that era where there was no television and no private radio stations. MGR paid a great deal of attention to songs, from the content and the music to the way they were filmed. *Malaikallan* possibly heralded the idea that MGR's songs contained a message.

The songs from *Nadodi Mannan* (The Vagabond King, 1958) bring this out powerfully:

Welcome to you, welcome to classical Tamil!
Brilliantly espousing the Adi Dravidar's life
Welcome to classical Tamil!*

---

* *Senthamizae vanakkam*
   Adi Dravidar vazhvinai seerodu vilakkum / Senthamizae vanakkam

And:

> Don't sleep younger brother, don't sleep
> Don't get the name idler*

And:

> Tell me which brings pleasure
> To work, or to get work†

And:

> To prepare the barren land,
> To plough without laziness‡

And:

> If you struggle, you will see tangible results§

After 1958, when the rising sun became the DMK's official election symbol, MGR's songs would refer to the symbol and, with the advent of colour films, MGR would often dress in black and red.

POET KANNADASAN

After Pattukottai Kalyanasundaram's early death in 1959, poet Kannadasan became integral to MGR's image-making. MGR's credentials as a Dravidian 'cultural icon' were reinforced by Kannadasan's song in *Mannadhi Mannan* (Emperor, 1960)—also the actor's favourite song by the poet.[65]

---

* *Thoongathae thambi thoongathae*
  Nee somberi endra peyar vaangathae
† *Uzhaipadhilaa uzhaipai peruvathilaa inbam*
  Undaavathengae sol thozha
‡ *Summa kedantha nelatha kothi*
  Sombalillama aer nadathi
§ *Paadupattaa thannalae palanirukudhu kai maelae*

Fear is idiocy
Fearlessness is a Dravidian asset . . .*

Tens of millions lived, tens of millions died
Who lives in people's hearts?
Great warriors, people who guard others' dignity
They live on in history.†

Songs bearing messages would become a regular feature and lasted till the very end of MGR's film career.

Arasilangkumari's (Princess, 1961) 'Chinna payale chinna payale sethi kelada (Little boy, little boy listen to [my] message)', 'Thirudaadhe paapa thirudaadhe (Don't steal child don't steal)' in *Thirudaathae*, and 'Poyum poyum manidhanikindha buthiyai koduthaanae (Alas, he had given humans this sense)' from *Thaai Sollai Thattadhe* are some examples of the early message-bearing songs. They would turn both more political in their messages and more adulatory towards their hero later.

From the sixties, songs poured praise on the hero and his fans understood that they referred to MGR. He was a handsome man—the songs spoke of his good looks, how light his complexion was, his generosity, his valour, the path he chose to walk down and his intentions.

In *Kudumba Thalaivan*, Kannadasan extolled his handsomeness thus: 'Kattaana katazhgu kanna, unnai kaanaadha pennum oru penna (Oh handsome one, can a woman who has not seen you be a woman)?'

In *Needhikkuppin Pasam*, poet Kannadasan wrote:

Teak gave you your body,
The little elephant gave you your walk,

---

* *Acham enbadhu madamaiyadaa,*
   Anjaamai, Dravidar udamaiyadaa . . .
† *Vaazhndhavar kodi maraindhavar kodi*
   Makkalin manadhil nirpavar yaar?
   Maaberum veerar maanam kaappor
   Sariththiram thanile nirkinraar.

The flowers gave you your laughter,
Gold gave you your complexion.[66]

In *Panathottam*, the heroine sang of MGR:
Is the singer a poet?
Or is he Pari's son?
Is he related to the Cheras?
Or is he the moon of the Tamils?[†]

Pari is one of the eight Tamil kings celebrated in Tamil history for their philanthropy. Of course, the Cheras are considered the precursors of the Malayalis.

Kannadasan whetted the appetite of MGR's fans with his exquisite poetry. Here are a few of his image-making songs, tailor-made for MGR.

In *Pasam*, the poet painted MGR's kingdom.

The world was born for me,
The flowing rivers are for me,
Flowers bloom for me,
The earth mother's expanse is for me.

The moon as a golden chariot,
The crown embedded with stars,
With the koel singing in the art world,
This is my kingdom![‡]

---

[*] *Theku maram udalai thanthathu*
Chinna yaanai nadaiai thanthathu
Pookal ellaam siripai thanthathu
Ponnalavo nirathi thanthathu

[†] *Paaduvathu kaviyaa?*
Illai Pari vallal maganaa?
Seranaku uravaa?
Senthamizhar nilavaa?

[‡] *Ulagham piranthathu enakkaaga*
Odum nadhigalum enakkaaga
Malargal malarvadhu enakkaaga
Annai madiyai virithaal enakkaaga . . .

In *Panathottam*, MGR sang Kannadasan's lines:

> Let whatever happens happen,
> Let justice disappear in the dark,
> It will appear on its own, don't worry,
> There is a leader, don't doubt.*

In *Dharmam Thalai Kaakkum* (Justice Will Save Your Life, 1963) the title song spoke of the virtues of charity, but was understood by his fans as extolling MGR's giving nature:

> The charity you do will save your head,
> At the right time, it will save your life . . .
> Even when those around you plot against you
> What you gave will guard you,
> The heart of the one who gives abundantly
> Is a flower garden of happiness.
> In life, good people will never fail,
> This is the verdict of the four vedas.†

> *Thavazhum nilavaam thangaradham*
> *Thaaragai padiththa manimagudam*
> *Kuilgal paadum kalaikkoodam*
> *Kondadhu enadhu arasaangam*
> * *Yenna thaan nadakkum nadakkattumae*
> *Iruttinil needhi maraiyattumae*
> *Thannaalae veli varum thayangaadhae*
> *Thalaivan irukkiraan mayangaadhae*
> † *Dharmam thalai kaakkum*
> *Thakka samayathil uyir kaakkum*
> *Kooda irundhdhae kuzhi parithaalum*
> *Koduthadhu kaathu nikkum*
>
> *Allikkoduthu vaazhpavan nenjam*
> *Aanandhdha poondhoappu*
> *Vaazhvil nallavar endrum keduvadhillai*
> *Idhu naangumarai theerppu*

In *Vettaikkaran* (Hunter, 1964), Kannadasan wrote:

> If you know yourself, if you know yourself,
> You can fight in this world.
> Whether you touch the highs or lows,
> You can live without bowing your head.
> People who live valuing honour,
> Are considered deer, [Kavarimaan, a mythical deer will die for honour],
> Those who understand themselves and enlighten the world,
> Become leaders!
>
> Those who give generously, knowing others' needs
> Are they not god's children?
> Those who live justly on earth
> Are they not equal to gods?...
>
> If you walk into a grand gathering
> You should be adorned with garlands.
> You are a blemishless king
> People should sing!*

---

* *Unnai arinthaal, nee unnai arinthaal*
  Ulagathil poraadalaam
  Uyarnthaalum thaazhnthaalum
  Thalai vanangaamal nee vaazhalaam
  Maanam periyathendru vaazhum manithargalai
  Maan endru solvathillaiya
  Thannaith thaanum arinthukondu oorukku solbavargal
  Thalaivarkal aavathillaiyaa
  Pirar thevai arinthu kondu vaari kodupavargal
  Theivathin pillai illaiya

  Bhoomiyil naeraaga vaazhbavargal ellorum
  Saamiku nigar illaya

  Maaberum sabaiyinil nee nadanthaal
  Unakku maalaigal vizha vendum
  Oru maatru kuraiyaatha mannavan ivanendru
  Potrip pugazha vendum

Despite their differences, the poet was faithful to the task of projecting MGR's image through his songs, till the end. (In 1978, MGR bestowed on him the honour of Poet Laureate.)[67]

But the differences between them were deep and Kannadasan was a maverick who could not be relied on. Another equally gifted poet had to be found. It would happen organically and the poet would craft one of the immortal songs that would fit MGR beautifully.

> He gave all that he gave
> To whom did he give?
> Did he give for just one?
> No, he gave for everyone[*]

A happy producer, G.N. Velumani of *Padagoti* said that the song had nicely captured MGR's characteristics and his fans would be enthralled. Arurdhas and MGR mistook the poet for Kannadasan. It was Vaali. The songs of Rangarajan, aka Vaali, would pitch MGR to a new level. MGR came to hugely trust Vaali's abilities, that in a public meeting he announced, 'Henceforth, for my movies, a new poet called Vaali will pen the songs!'

Thus, in the 1960s, Vaali enjoyed a monopoly over the image-making and propaganda songs. Within a couple of years, the poet had become a star[68] and his songs all helped turn MGR into a larger-than-life character.

Vaali's songs for MGR were politically pregnant, and quickly became a nightmare for the censors. Their power was such that at an event to fete his rise to power, Chief Minister Anna beckoned Vaali over to whisper, 'Your film songs have helped much in the success of the DMK.'[69] The songs were mouthed by his protégé MGR and Anna had advised the poet to be in the actor's good books. It was not just through his songs—MGR had given himself to the party and Anna.[†]

MGR, however, tried to avoid confrontation with authority. Thus, on one occasion, as Vaali explained that the censors had raised an objection to many of the pallavis of the now signature MGR song 'Naan

---

[*] *Koduthathellam koduthaan,*
  Avan yaarukaaga koduthaan,
  Orutharukka koduthaan
  Illai Oorukaaga koduthaan

[†] In 2010, Jayalalithaa said, 'It was MGR who helped DMK founder, C.N. Annadurai, to ascend the throne [chief ministership]. http://zeenews.india. com/home/im-the-political-heir-of-mgr-jayalalitha_418718.html.

aanayitaal (If I were to command)' the actor said he would have too if he was in their place. He explained that though the song was Vaali's, the censors identified the words with him and the DMK, and would not permit it. When he said 'thalaivan', or leader, the word only referred to Anna. Fondly addressing Vaali as 'aandavane', he said, 'The ruling party is allergic to this! You are a poet who, with your songs, threatens those in power.'[70] Vaali had to change many of the pallavis to please the censors. Yet, the song's potency or message was not lost and it remains one of the best songs associated with MGR.

Similarly, the censors had objected to the line 'Medaiyil muzhangu Arignar Anna pol (Deliver like scholar Anna on stage)' in the song 'Nalla nalla pillaigalai nambi (Trusting the good kids)' from Petraal Thaan Pillayaa. Vaali substituted Thiru. Vi. Ka., a Tamil savant and orator, for the word Anna. Yet, at the theatres, the fans were rapturous because Thiru. Vi. Ka. sounded like Thi. Mu. Ka. or DMK.[71] In later years the original line on Anna would be inserted.

To evade the censors Vaali chose words craftily, picking words that could easily be misheard. Once Anbe Vaa's (Oh! Love Come, 1966) producer, AVM, asked, 'Why, Mr Vaali! If we make a film with MGR, do we have to write udhaya suriyan (rising sun)?' The original 'Udhaya suriyanin paarvaiyile (In the gaze of the rising sun)' was changed to pudhiya suriyan or new sun, on the objection of the censors. When AVM wondered about the logic behind terming the sun new or old, Vaali said that when MGR enunciated the words, they would sound like udhaya suriyan, and the theatre would come crumbling down. Vaali was proved right.[72]

In Panam Padaithavan he sang Vaali's, 'Kan pona pokkile kaal pogalaama (Can the legs follow the eyes that lead astray)', where a stanza went as follows:

> Alive or gone, you should attain fame
> The country saying—none like him!'

In the song 'Nalla nalla pillaigalai nambi (Trusting the good kids)', there was a stanza that picturized him thus:

---

* Irunthaalum marainthaalum per solla vendum
  Ivar pola yaar endru oor solla vendum

If you have kindness, you become a philanthropist,
If you have the sense of duty, you become a hero,
If you have patience, you become a human,
If you have all three you can become a leader.*

From the late sixties, the songs would presage MGR's entry into politics more directly, speaking about the DMK and the government. After the 1972 split, MGR would wage a campaign against Kalaignar and the DMK through his songs. In 1968, poet Pulamaipithan would join as an image-maker with the song 'Naan yaar, nee yaar (Who am I, who are you)' with the movie Kudi Irundha Koil (The Temple that Was as an Abode, 1968) and poet Muthulingam, after the hit 'Anbuku naan adimai Tamizh panbukku naan adimai (I would submit to love, I would submit to Tamil culture)' in Indru Pol Endrum Vazhga (Live Like Now, Forever, 1977).

STOOPING DOWN TO CONQUER: GOONDUKILI

MGR often strategically stooped down to conquer. There were no permanent friends or foes as long as they helped his public life journey. Thus, he tolerated Kannadasan when he became a harsh critic in the early sixties for the poet was integral to his films' commercial success. When Pudumaipithan's (Lover of Modernity, 1957) success was attributed to Chandrababu's comedy, MGR advised that the comedian be dropped in future projects, only to invite him again to star in his Nadodi Mannan and other films.[73] He made up with Chinnappa Thevar and, in 1954, in the aftermath of his failed venture Naam,† agreed to the unthinkable—to pair with his rival Sivaji Ganesan. Despite their friendship and shared times in the Dravidian movement, their film

---

* Karunai irundhaal vallalaagalaam.
  Kadamai irundhaal veeranaagalaam,
  Porumai irundhaal manidhanaagalaam,
  Moondrum irundhaal thalaivanaagalaam!

† Marudhanaatu Ilavarasi had led to Mekala Pictures—a partnership between Kalaignar, MGR, Janaki, director A. Kasilingam and film journalist Rajaram. Their first and only production Naam did not fare well.

paths had become separate and would continue to be so. *Goondukili* remains the only movie in which the titans starred together, much to the disapproval of their fans.[74]

They maintained a correct relationship with each other on the sets. MGR would go to his chair and begin reading a book after his shots, and keep to himself. Ramanna said that MGR read several books before the completion of the film. Ganesan, for his part, would disappear from the sets regularly, but would promptly show up for his shots. 'It is nothing; I did not wish to smoke before annan and, hence, have to go out,' Ganesan explained to the director one day.

In the film, an innocent MGR has to serve a sentence, thanks to his friend Ganesan, who plays an evil character. MGR returns home to find that his friend had had designs on his wife the entire time and that she had left. When an angry MGR seeks out Ganesan and strangles him, Ganesan's eyes are about to pop out. Watching them shoot this scene, a troubled Ramanna shouted 'cut'. Actually, MGR's hands had not even touched Ganesan's neck and both had 'acted so realistically'. The scene would remain etched in public memory.[75]

The film failed and MGR wrote that it had failed because of the 'over-expectation' of viewers.[76] However, the reason was that a fan system was already in place for the two and the fans did not like their heroes coming together. In the event shows had to be discontinued in several places.[77]

MGR FANS ASSOCIATION

MGR fans associations or 'Rasikar Manrams' would grow into an institution in themselves and become a pillar of support for the DMK. The first Rasikar Manram was founded in Madurai in 1950. In the 1960s, RMV brought these bodies together as MGR Fans Associations, which would later become the All-World MGR Fans Association.[78] They did some social work and ran night schools, but since they viewed their idol as next only to god, they took it upon themselves to treat him as one. They waited for the release of their idol's movie as a parent awaits the birth of his or her baby. They tied festoons, distributed sweets and turned the opening of his films into memorable events. They passed around a coconut bearing lit camphor, in worship, at the

first appearance of their hero on screen. The coconut was then flung
to the ground and smashed, a ritual used to ward off the evil eye or to
propitiate the deities.

Fans made block bookings and occupied the front rows. Some saw
the movie even ten times, sometimes selling their blood to find the
money for the tickets, and made sure that the movie ran for 100 days,
to the extent that MGR had to expressly discourage them from selling
their blood to watch his movies. MGR gifted money for the weddings and
medical expenses of those associated with these fan clubs. MGR himself
noted:

> Films and public service are like my two eyes. There is a constant
> stream of people with great confidence in me, seeking my help.
> I can't meet all of them, but my staff takes care of them. Some
> come to me for educational aid. Those who have lost limbs come
> for financial aid as they are unable to take up employment. Some
> others seek capital to start businesses. I try to extend the assistance
> I can. How much can an individual do? So some may go away
> disappointed. At the same time, some undeserving or crooked
> people, with fraudulent intentions, get away with aid that could
> have gone to more worthy people. That is very disappointing.

The growth of the fan clubs, at one point, would become a matter of
concern as they acted as a parallel body. MGR said the following about
them:

> Yes, fan clubs are necessary. They are indispensable to the
> propagation of ideas among the people. Nobody protested
> when these clubs were first formed, but today their growth and
> popularity have caused envy of the stars concerned amongst
> some. This can be equated with a father's sense of inadequacy
> towards his daughter's intellectual growth after he has put her
> through college for her BA.[79]

What else did they do? They threw cow dung on the posters of Sivaji
Ganesan's movies. MGR himself had admitted that it was 'possible' that
they did this.[80] Ganesan appeared on top of the game in the tinsel world

and MGR's fans took it upon themselves to express their disapproval of their icon's rival. But MGR would overtake Ganesan politically first. This is how it happened.

A CYCLONE FELLS SIVAJI GANESAN

The DMK had launched a fund drive for the victims of the 1956 cyclone. Ganesan recounted what happened afterwards:

> I had been part of this movement from the time I was very young, and, without warning, I was dismissed as someone of no consequence and my anna, MGR, [was] admitted instead. He was not in the least bit connected with this movement at that point [sic. MGR had addressed the Lalgudi DMK conference in April 1953 with Ganesan]. They did this just to sideline me.[81]

Ganesan continued: '[F]or the first time, MGR was called on stage and honoured. Such irony! It was I who had collected maximum funds, but the honour went to MGR. He became 'like a mad man'. Ganesan visited the temple town of Tirupati later, in the company of the film director A. Bhimsingh, only to see 'Tirupati Ganesan Govinda' (Govinda here is shorthand for failure) written all over the walls; his car was attacked, his film posters were defaced with cow dung and stones were pelted at him on his return.[82] Posters screaming 'Tirupati Ganesa Thirumbipaar' referred to his *Thirumbipaar* movie, scripted by Kalaignar. It suggested that Ganesan had done a U-turn. The irony is that MGR, in 1968, would reveal that he had gone to Tirupati while doing *Marmayogi* and, although he said neither 'devotion nor a vow' prompted him and he 'had the urge to go there', he had visited many other temples after that.[83] He would respond to a question several years later thus: 'There's even a scene in *Periya Idathu Penn* (Girl of a Wealthy Household, 1963), where I take a group of people to a temple. Even outside movies, I recently lit the temple lamp at the Marudhamalai temple. What do you say to that?'[84]

Kalaignar wrote in the 1970s on the incident:

> Chief Minister MGR frequently visits the Moogambikai temple in another state . . .

The moment the press reported that Sivaji Ganesan, who was in the DMK, had visited Tirupati, the same MGR became the driving force behind the cabal against him![85]

Arangannal insinuated that Sampath was behind Sivaji Ganesan's exit, adding that Sampath was not happy with MGR's growth either.[86] Sampath would, ironically, find himself in Ganesan's company in the Congress later and, in 1972, after MGR quit the DMK, would greatly warm up to him. The vicissitudes of fate are hard to fathom indeed.

It was just as well for Ganesan, MGR and the party. Ganesan himself acknowledged later:

> Can two swords share a sheath? If both had the same niche, we would have had only one set of fans, but if we worked individually, we would each have a separate set of fans. He would comment on me, likewise I would comment on him. This was only about politics without a trace of personal animosity. Many took this seriously and concluded that we were enemies, but this did not irk either of us.[87]

The MGR–Ganesan relationship, however, would go through many ups and downs, and would not be as even as Ganesan described it. MGR had clearly defeated Ganesan politically. But he would have to strive hard to overtake Ganesan in the cinema world.

Ganesan came to be regarded as one of the finest actors in Tamil cinema, if not the finest in India. He began working 'twenty-four hours a day', so much so that he 'never saw [his] parents, wife or children'.[88] 'Long live, wherever you are!' was Anna's wish for Ganesan.[89]

For the party, the investment in MGR, a savvier political player, was worthwhile. MGR and the party grew hand in hand, reinforcing each other.

MGR was already an icon. V.R. Lakshminarayanan, then an assistant commissioner of police in Madras, describes what he witnessed on a blazing May afternoon in 1956, when MGR led a procession in honour of a Tamil writer on Mount Road, today's Anna Salai:

> Traffic for two miles was completely paralysed and virtually more than 1 lakh people were jostling, fighting and yelling to get a close-

up view of their idol. Mind you, it was no political demonstration.
In any case, the DMK in 1956 was not much of a force and the
gathering was almost impromptu . . . The unadulterated tribute
of the masses to their hero . . In flesh and blood . . .[90]

That year, *Madurai Veeran* ran for 100 days in all the thirty-six cinemas,
becoming the first Tamil film to set such a record and gross 1 crore
rupees. The movie made MGR a household name. It was already
fashionable for hairdressing saloons to hang MGR's pictures, and not a
day passed by without the vernacular press reporting on his films or his
acts of charity.[91]

1957 GENERAL ELECTIONS

MGR's growth was closely linked with that of the DMK's. MGR pointed
out, however, that at the time of the 31 March 1957 general elections,
the party neither had the backing of the press nor popular elders,
money or position. He said that traders, mill owners, landlords, mutt
pontiffs, contractors and the like were unwilling to give any money to
the Kazhagam. In late 1955, Anna had said that if the party's 'artists
were to divert their services for six months, the problem [of resources]
would be solved'.[92] A munificent MGR appears to have been one of the
major benefactors of the party.

SSR has recorded that he spoke to Navalar Nedunchezhian and
MGR on the DMK taking part in the 1957 polls, after which the three
set off to Kanchipuram to meet Anna. After hearing them out, Anna
smilingly said, 'Is younger brother MGR smitten by the desire to go
to the Assembly?', to which MGR replied that many desired that the
Kazhagam should enter the electoral fray.[93]

Udhaya Suriyan (Rising Sun) by Kalaignar was a popular propagandist
play around this time and became a major vehicle of benefit performances.
In March 1958, the party would be allotted the rising sun symbol.[94]
However, as if to presage its allocation to the DMK, MGR took the screen
name 'Udhaya Suriyan' in *Chakravarthi Thirumagal*, released just weeks
before the 1957 general elections on 18 January that year. Despite the
odds of contesting in a maiden election and the absence of an official party
symbol, P.U. Shanmugam, whom MGR described as 'an honest man'

and wanted elected, was confident of his victory and advised MGR to go and campaign in the difficult constituencies.[95] MGR addressed fifteen to twenty campaign meetings. Ganesan travelled to every nook and corner of the state to seek votes for his leader Kamaraj's Congress party.

That summer, the popular Tamil weekly *Kumudam* tried to pit the two rivals against each other with a contest titled 'The Star I Like', asking readers to evaluate the acting skills of MGR and Sivaji Ganesan. In a rare gesture of unity, both actors said that the contest would create a division between the two, their fans, and serve no useful purpose to the tinsel world.[96]

Later that year, as the Congress government celebrated the centenary of the independence movement, MGR directed and staged three short plays on Tirupur Kumaran, Muthuvadivu and V.O. Chidambaram, all freedom fighters, as requested. Sivaji Ganesan, for his part, staged a part of his *Kattabomman* play. Chief Minister Kamaraj presided over the celebrations.[97]

BLACK-FLAG PROTEST AND FOUR DAYS INTERNMENT

On 30 August that year, hepatitis would snatch the patriarch of Tamil cinema, NSK, at the age of forty-eight.[98] By the end of that year, MGR said at a public function that he was under pressure 'to sign up for more than thirty films'.[99] Anna had been arrested before he could address a meeting and preventive arrests of other leaders had followed, prior to the party's 6 January 1958 black-flag demonstration against Nehru. MGR was picked up at 2 a.m. on 4 January and he was interned for four days. He insisted, and saw to it, that many DMK men were upgraded from their C- to B-class cells, before he would accept the higher B-class cell given him. Despite moving up to the B-class, SSR, his cellmate, found the conditions unbearable and revolting. MGR, who ate the nauseating red rice on an aluminium plate, told an incredulous SSR: 'I have eaten such food in my early days. This is not new.' On their release, Anna, who was waiting for them, first took MGR home and then dropped SSR at his place.[100]

Earlier, film director K. Subramanyam had pleaded the case of the artists with Chief Minister Bhaktavatsalam, and a letter of regret was expected. MGR was overjoyed when he heard that Sadanandavati had told Chakrapani, 'Do not erase his honour by writing a letter of regret!'[101]

IDHAYAKANI OR HEART'S FRUIT

That year Emgeeyar (MGR) Pictures' *Nadodi Mannan* proved to be a milestone in the party's history and MGR's career, and also his fifth break.[102] The idea for *Nadodi Mannan* had been planted early on in MGR's career, in Calcutta where he saw *If I Were King* (1938). Ronald Colman's line 'If I were king' was deeply etched in the twenty-year-old MGR's mind. MGR said that he thought of poverty and the poor even then.[103] In the film, MGR played dual roles—one, of a man who is poisoned by his enemies and, the other, who ascends the throne because he looks like the former. The temporary king embarks on a reformist course that enthrals his poor subjects, but worries the elites. The movie proved to be a blueprint for a future DMK administration.

MGR's ambitious project cost 18 lakh rupees, took too much time and created problems that were immensely worrying for his elder brother, Chakrapani. *Dinathanthi* had called the movie '*Komali Mannan*' (Jester King).[104] Some interpreted his effort as 'arrogance' and others felt 'he would be on the streets'.[105] MGR himself declared, 'I am a king if this succeeds; if not, I will be a vagabond.'[106]

Furthermore, MGR's directorial ambitions brought him into conflict with actress Bhanumathi, who was gifted, fiercely independent and spoke her mind.[107] Bhanumathi addressed MGR as 'MGR' or 'Mr Ramachandran'. MGR, in a sense, was a perfectionist, but also headstrong. So was Bhanumathi. One day, Bhanumathi lost her temper and opined that MGR should decide on the story, bring in a good director and then she would give him the dates as needed, at no additional cost. In response, MGR simply suggested that she quit. When she did, her character in the movie was killed and Saroja Devi was introduced.[108]

Nadodi Mannan was the biggest propaganda blitzkrieg for the DMK till then. MGR described Anna's social reformist ideas as the nucleus for the movie and the movie's success was 'Sweet Dravidam's victory'.[109] It contained songs in the four major Dravidian languages and one song welcomed MGR as '*Endrum inidhana Dravida poongavil malarndha vendhe varugavae* (Oh king, who blossomed in the ever-sweet Dravida garden, welcome)'. However, the song '*Kaalai maatai paal karaka paarkiraanga* (They are trying to milk the ox)' was excluded, fearing the censors, as a pair of bullocks was the Congress's election symbol.[110] Kannadasan and Raveendar's lines such as 'Those who did not trust me and lost out are more. None have lost trusting me till today' and 'You are looking at the people from the palace. I am with the people and observe the palace', brought the cinema hall down. The Emgeeyar Pictures emblem showed a youth and a maiden holding aloft the DMK flag, making the fans cheer wildly.[111] And R.M.Veerappan's lines in the advertisements, '*Veeramaa mugam theriyudhae / Adhu vetri punnagai puriyudhae* (The brave face is seen / It is sporting the victory smile)' were memorable.[112]

The movie was released on 22 August 1958. MGR remained calm and apparently indifferent to the fate of the film.[113] Within a week, the DMK's organs came out with special numbers marking the movie. Small booklets were also published on the movie. *Nadodi Mannan* would take MGR's fame to a new high, and MGR said the movie's success was 'the success of the DMK to which I belong'.

Several celebrations were held to mark the success of *Nadodi Mannan*.[114] On 26 October 1959, MGR rode the streets of Madurai seated on the rising sun tableau on a lotus base, in a carriage drawn by four horses. A caparisoned elephant led the procession. At the end of the procession was a rotating image of the globe on which rested the memento—a three-foot-long sword made of close to a kilogram of gold. Nedunchezhian presented MGR with the gold sword. MGR spoke briefly. Commenting on the sword later, he said it symbolized that desires for gold or riches should be cut or broken.[115]

On 30 November, at a felicitation held on the SIAA Grounds in Madras, Anna described MGR's heart as large and his character as gold, and said that everyone could take part in MGR's fame.[116] 'There was a fruit at the top of the tree. When I was wondering if I would get it, it fell on my lap. Before it fell on my lap, I held it in my heart. This is my heart's fruit (idhayakani)[117] . . . Praising MGR is like me praising myself,' Anna concluded. He would also instruct R.M. Veerappan, who was estranged from MGR in the aftermath of *Nadodi Mannan*, to go back to him.[118]

MGR termed the day Anna called him 'idhayakani' as the most memorable day in his life.[119] Despite these accolades, in 1971, MGR would reveal that he was 'pained' by the non-selection of *Nadodi Mannan*, initially considered by the Government of India, for the Third Afro-Asian Film Festival in Cairo in 1960.[120]

But the movie had taken him to dizzying heights, and MGR would say later that 'after the release of *Nadodi Mannan*, I often felt that there was a big danger awaiting me.'[121] Sivaji Ganesan's *Veerapandia Kattabomman* (1959) was sent instead, and it won the best film, actor and music categories in Tamil.

MGR's foreboding soon came true when, on 16 June 1957, at a performance of *Inba Karavu* at Sirkazhi, a fellow actor fell on MGR's leg, fracturing it. On the day of the performance, MGR had told his aide Thirupathisamy that he felt that there would be a major accident.[122] After the accident, MGR ordered the curtain be brought down, made a sort of tourniquet, and told the anxious crowd that he would come back to perform. He drove at five miles an hour, till Pondicherry, when dawn broke, and thereafter, at normal speed.[123] For a week, MGR stayed at the hospital.[124]

The fracture actually brought together Sadanandavati and Janaki, who stayed at MGR's bedside and took turns to look after him. As the leg healed, so did the relationship between both women.[125] Nonetheless, once MGR was healthy again, Janaki wished to go back to her place. Chakrapani congratulated his brother at the way things had worked out between the two claimants to MGR's attention and said: 'You have won.'[126]

But MGR rued that the majority had concluded that he could not act any more, especially in fight sequences. Distributors wanted their money back and producers 'cried' to MGR figuratively. Ironically, their words of comfort revealed their difficulty and insecurity.[127] And there were others who were happy about 'the DMK guy's' misfortune. The accident was a great eye-opener, as it showed MGR who his true friends were.

During this difficult situation, K. Diraviam, a senior official with the Kamaraj administration, came over to seek MGR's advice for the Nadigar Sangam felicitating recipients of the state awards in literature, music and drama—the three facets of Tamil culture. As Diraviam said that choosing someone for music could upend the felicitation idea, an agitated MGR pointed out that K.B. Sundarambal was accomplished in music, drama and films, and was a freedom fighter. He lamented that the 'Delhi Empire' had ignored her, but felt that Tamil Nadu should not. (Sundarambal was the first film personality to be nominated to the Legislative Council; and she served as a member from 1958 to 1964).[128] MGR's suggestion was accepted and Chief Minister Kamaraj, ministers M. Bhaktavatsalam, C. Subramaniam and Governor A.J. John took part in the felicitations.[129] MGR would develop a personal friendship with Diraviam and make him his chief secretary in 1980, in his second term.[130]

THE MGR EFFECT

Despite doctors advising him against travel after the Sirkazhi accident, when Anna sent Nedunchezhian, MGR relented and agreed to attend the Kanchipuram meeting around this time. Assuring him that the speaker was not any senior leader, the organizers took MGR to the stage. On a separate stage nearby, Anna was actually delivering his speech and MGR records that 'everyone felt saddened'. As a 'little confusion' ensued, Anna turned back and without 'bitterness' or 'agitation' asked MGR to speak, and then sent him back safely. MGR recorded his gratitude later thus:

> Although he was the great exclusive leader of lakhs of youngsters, he did not consider that someone ordinary had deprived the audience of listening further to his speech and had interrupted it; instead, with motherly love and affection, he welcomed me and showed affection to me without even the slightest frustration and fault-finding. I often think of that munificence of Anna's and eulogize it.

Anna embodied rationality, affection and tolerance, said MGR, and,[131] a little later, he would describe him as a god.[132] RMV, however, records that MGR was cut up with Anna earlier for not having visited him after the accident and RMV had to clear the air between the two.[133]

It also appears that while Anna was ever gracious, MGR sometimes was not. Arurdhas wrote that MGR often tested his popularity and hold on the party. MGR's people would phone him to advise him of the situation at the meeting. The thespian would then come and join it, creating a flutter in the crowd. 'This was his habit,' records Arurdhas.

One day, MGR showed up while Anna was addressing the meeting at Kannappar Grounds, Madras, and his fans rose to cheer him with chants of 'MGR long live'. 'Those who were aware that these [situations] were prearranged by MGR were saddened.' But Anna did not lose his composure and, after the rustle settled down, he continued his speech. Anna knew that MGR was akin to an elephant—deferring to the mahout; yet, always conscious of his elephantine power. According to Arurdhas, the elephant tested the mahout: 'MGR tested Anna himself.'[134] But, in 1960, when RMV expressed concern at the idea of a state-wide MGR Fans Association jamboree. MGR assuaged his fears saying that neither he nor his actions would 'go out of control'. M.G. Chakrapani, the man behind the move, assured RMV separately: 'You should also believe this . . . There is nothing that MGR would do to harm the Kazhagam.'[135]

Around this time, in response to the question from a fan 'I adore you, but whom should I place first in my heart—you or Anna?', MGR responded with, 'Shouldn't the younger brother yield first place to the elder?'[136]

However, such senseless adulation for movie stars caused much heartburn among career politicians. Public meetings were the party's mainstay and even gifted speakers had to yield to stars. The effect of MGR's presence on the audience was electrifying, as he himself noted:

> If I were to address public meetings, whoever else was there on stage, whether they were the best speakers, philosophers or leaders with a higher stature than I, the moment I reached the stage, such zeal would erupt among the people that their speeches would be disrupted. The speaker would not even be able to continue later . . .[137]

A very self-confident and cinema-savvy Anna handled that moment, and other similar moments, with ease. He did not wish to tinker with what had become a successful formula—the harnessing of cinema and its stars for the party's benefit. But the other leaders were not as self-assured or generous as Anna. MGR pointed out, 'When [Kannadasan] was in the Kazhagam, he was very disappointed because of me.'[138]

The displeasure was caused by MGR's sheer prominence. Unable to take what he considered an insult any longer, Kannadasan 'poured his heart out' to Anna, MGR recorded. Anna made light of the issue and advised the poet to act in films so that he too could command such a 'reception'.[139] Sampath, MGR said, began to 'hate' him.

> E.V.K. Sampath was speaking when I approached the venue . . .
> Mr E.V.K. Sampath could not continue, and he stopped his speech and resumed his seat. The sadness that gripped me is immense . . .
> I severely condemned the people's action. Yet, I came to know after some time that I had lost Mr Sampath's affection and had earned his hatred.[140]

MGR's gargantuan growth would wreck the party once in 1961 and, later, in 1972.

WINNING OVER SIVAJI GANESAN'S PRODUCERS

In Tinseltown, however, Sivaji Ganesan remained formidable competition. During the making of Thaai Makalukku Kattiya Thali (The Thali the Mother Tied on Her Daughter, 1959), MGR told its scriptwriter Arangannal: 'I have a five-year plan, Mudhalali [here a term of endearment]. You [wait and] watch, all those who produce films with this Sivaji Ganesan, I will make them come over to me.' Sivaji Ganesan's career was at its peak at the time and Bhimsingh, B.R. Panthulu, G.N. Velumani and A.P. Nagarajan were considered Sivaji Ganesan's men. Bhimsingh had promised Sivaji Ganesan that he would not direct MGR. (Just as Chinnappa Thevar had pledged that he would not produce any film with Ganesan.)[141]

Perhaps, as part of the plan, MGR decided to bury the five-year-old hatchet with Thevar. The rift between Thevar and MGR happened when the actor, who was to tame a bull in Thaaikupin Thaaram's climax, had said he was not willing to take the risk. A double had to be used to finish the climax. Things got worse when MGR issued a legal notice saying that the film had been dubbed in Telugu without his consent. Aluri Chakrapani, Nagi Reddy's partner, told a worried Thevar that they could issue a notice in return saying that MGR too had not kept his part of the agreement—for a double had been used. When MGR heard of this, he shut up, fearing the damage it would do to his image.[142] Thevar, however, was so upset by all this that he said he would never see MGR again. 'I will prosper without you in the film world,' he declared [143] When they made up later, Thevar ended up producing another fifteen of MGR's films—*Thaai Sollai Thattathey* was produced in a record one month and *Thaerthiruvizha* (Car Festival, 1968) in sixteen days.[144]

MGR thus built strategic alliances. From the very beginning, unlike Sivaji Ganesan, he cultivated and promoted artists, directors, poets, music directors, producers and technicians who suited his professional and political ends. He patronized them, and their careers became inextricably linked to his. He cared for the interests of those who had cast their lot with him. In 1971, a generous MGR gave poet Pulamaipithan money to buy back his ancestral house that had been mortgaged.[145] When stunt actor Ramakrishnan broke his ankle in a scene, MGR got him the best medical care; visited him in hospital every alternate day and paid the medical expenses of 37,000 rupees, besides giving the family 10,000 rupees. He also waited for Ramakrishnan's recovery to film the shot.[146] Such positive stories (and some negative stories) abound about MGR. Sivaji Ganesan, on the other hand, did not involve himself in casting or any production issues. He did not favour or disfavour anyone. In the event, MGR built up a loyal following for himself. Sivaji Ganesan failed to do so.

It was only a matter of time before Sivaji Ganesan's producers would line up to cast MGR. Arangannal wrote: '[MGR] created the situation where those producers, considered inseparable, would do penance to get his dates. This showed how intelligent and clairvoyant he was.'*[147] Be it B.R. Panthulu, G.N. Velumani, P.S. Veerappa, A.P. Nagarajan or C.V. Sridhar, all of them moved over to MGR from Ganesan, and they went on to make hits like *Aayirathil Oruvan*, *Panathottam* and *Ananda Jothi* (Flame of Happiness 1963). Arurdhas pointed out that Sivaji Ganesan couldn't make a similar claim. At this, a saddened Ganesan's

---

* Similarly, MGR had also said that he would earn 1 crore and would establish a university in his name. Arangannal said that if MGR had not founded the AIADMK, he would have achieved this ambition. Arangannal, part 1, *Ninaivugal* (Andal Pathippagam, 2000), p.198.

eyes grew moist and said, 'What can I do? My stars are such.' Arurdhas then said that Ganesan's situation was equally perilous in the political arena. Giving it some thought, Ganesan demurred and said, 'I have confidence when it comes to politics. Let us forget my becoming chief minister, but I will show you by making ten of my men legislators.'[148] This would never happen. Sivaji Ganesan's followers saw him as a great matinee idol, but were not willing to go beyond that to make him a political figure of consequence. They were delirious seeing him, shaking his hand and getting snapped with him, but not more.[149]

CAPTURING THE MADRAS CORPORATION

The DMK had won forty-five of the 100 councillor seats in the 1959 elections to the Madras Corporation. It needed a majority, nonetheless, for its candidate to become the mayor. MGR, who lived a few doors away from party lawyer V.P. Raman, was summoned in the middle of the night to Raman's house. Anna said, 'This will require much effort. You have to help [us].' Clearly, MGR was much more than a crowd-puller.

The 'heart's fruit' subsequently put K. Rajaram, once EVR's aide and a senior leader, in touch with a friend, with instructions to assist Rajaram in getting the support of the councillors for a DMK majority. MGR and the party's understanding with the communists would lead to the party's control of the capital's administration, giving it a new status. The DMK–communist understanding continued with the election of K.R. Ramasamy, the DMK's first hero thus elected to the Legislative Council.

Arangannal mentioned MGR's contribution even at the time of the campaign, especially in relation to S. Ganesan, later the mayor of Madras, who contested from Kodambakkam. Manager Padmanabhan of MGR's Sathya Studios worked doubly hard. Sampath, C.P. Chitrarasu, DVN, Kannadasan, SSR, KRR, T.K. Ponnuvelu and Kanchi Manimozhi had all worked towards victory. Kalaignar had selected the candidates and had ensured their success. Anna had singled out Kalaignar for praise in the victory celebrations. Sampath and Kannadasan were deeply upset by this.[150]

KANNADASAN AND MGR FALL OUT

MGR, too, was not happy in the aftermath of the elections, but for other reasons. Anna's social reformist *Thaai Magaluku Kattiya Thaali* had failed. No new films had come through and MGR needed a break. Against this background, MGR was to star in the remake of the Hindi movie *Pocket Maar* (Pickpocket, 1956), a social entertainer. Titled *Thirudaathe* in Tamil, it began well until the dastardly Sirkazhi accident.[151]

Kannadasan, who wrote the story, screenplay and dialogues for *Thirudaathe,* alleged in a function that MGR's non-cooperation had left several producers begging on the streets, that his films did not do well and that the movie industry had lost 1 crore rupees because of MGR. As this news made headlines, it prompted partymen to ask MGR, 'Why so?' In MGR's words, he was akin to a sick man with a terribly contagious disease that even his friends from the film world shunned him. It was in stark contrast to the praise heaped on him in the wake of *Nadodi Mannan.*

Arurdhas tried to place Kannadasan's charges in context. He said that MGR harboured a grudge against producers and was particularly bitter that when *Chaya* was aborted, producers dubbed him a 'luckless' person and blamed him for it.[152] MGR asked new producers if the film depended on him or them in other words, whether the producer would use MGR's 'goodwill' to mobilize funding or finance it himself. If it depended on him, MGR would evaluate their relationship—if there was a past, if the person was worthy enough—and then either consent to or turn down the film. Once he had agreed to sign a film, MGR would soon establish direct contact with the financiers and, frequently, the producer would be turned into a middleman. If the producer and the financier were playing with him, MGR would figure out their motives. Then, even MGR would not know when the movie would be finished, said Arurdhas. Some had perished doing this, while others, luckily, flourished, depending upon their behaviour.[153]

In June 1977, at the time of the general elections, Kannadasan once again laid out a litany of serious charges against MGR. He said that MGR harassed Chandrababu, many a film remained unfinished because of his 'conceitedness', leaving ruined producers behind. Referring to MGR's 'income tax charades',[154] he said 'a dishonest man showcases himself as honest'[155] and that 'His only thirst was for women and fame'.[156] And, in early 1978, he called MGR 'Dr Jekyll and [Mr] Hyde'.[157]

Kannadasan further alleged that because of MGR's vengeful nature, the careers of many had been finished off and some moved to the Sivaji Ganesan camp for survival. Sivaji Ganesan, Kannadasan said, had vengeance towards none. Kannadasan alleged that soon after he left the DMK, MGR wished to destroy his career. He added that MGR tried to arm-twist producers to drop him, but failed (Vaali's account and the record prove Kannadasan wrong).[158] Kannadasan's diatribe should be seen as a flourish of his poetic licence. Arurdhas said that if one listened to MGR's side of the story, one could not but feel sympathy for him.[159] Only years later, in mid-1980, the same Kannadasan said of MGR: 'He does not practise the art of calling someone a friend in public and simultaneously backstabbing him.'[160]

Thirudaathe ran for more than 150 days and became the year's top grosser, and[161] MGR considered it his sixth break.[162] Although a social entertainer, Patukkottai Kalyanasundaram's politically loaded song '*Maathuraanga, emaathuraanga, manasu vachu makkallaiye emaathuraanga* (They are changing, they are cheating, they plan and cheat the public)' was not allowed by the censors as it appeared to be directed at the Congress government that was in power then.[163]

The seventh turning point would be equally crucial. *Thaai Sollai Thattathey*, produced in record time by Thevar Films, would help further rehabilitate MGR's image as a dutiful actor.[164] MGR cooperated so fully that Thevar not only finished all of his movies in a short time, but was also able to announce their release when the shooting began.

THE 1961 DMK SPLIT

Meanwhile, the DMK was growing in strength—but so were its factions. Sampath, who had so valiantly left his uncle EVR for Anna, was also very possessive of Anna and the party. Personal and philosophical differences in the party's strategy and trajectory saw Sampath lead a campaign against Anna and his style of leadership from the mid-1950s.

While Sampath's detractors accused him of adopting a siloed track, Kannadasan wrote that Sampath was egalitarian and wished to cure the party that was directionless, and was hostage to hero worship and film stars.[165]

Following a visit to Bombay in 1961, MGR refuted the suggestion that actors were dominating the DMK:

> I have so far not been seriously involved in DMK's party work. I have not campaigned for any member of the party in the Chennai municipal elections. I only made one visit to one of the constituencies in the recent election. It is therefore incorrect to say that film actors like me are carrying the party on their shoulders.

But it was not just Sampath and Kannadasan who thought that the actors had hijacked the party. MGR himself noted that in Delhi and elsewhere the 'wrong impression has gained ground that DMK is a film actors' party,' and that he has 'decided to emphasize in these regions that DMK is a powerful movement in the south, not a party run by film people'. And then, he declared that he would suspend political activity for sometime:

> Till now, I have not involved myself with the DMK seriously. I did not campaign for any candidate in the recent elections for the Madras Corporation I went to just one part for a night . . . We [actors] campaigned in the Chennai [Tamil Nadu] Assembly elections. We won fifteen seats. We did not campaign in the corporation election. We won more than twice the number of seats. What does this indicate? DMK will function without actors. So I have decided to stay away from politics for a while. Not that I was involved earlier, though the impression was created that I was. This doesn't mean that I have left DMK. I am a DMK member—without doubt, I will remain in the party till death do us part. I'll have the slogan 'Vaazhga Dravidam' on my lips even as I breathe my last.[166]

MGR's decision to lie low for the time being showed that he was clearly cut out for politics. Sivaji Ganesan's remark is pertinent here:

When a man's talents and hard work earn him respect, many would like to see him pulled down. Those who are alert during those moments are the ones who hold on to a lasting career in politics. My brother MGR and I stood out as prime examples. MGR was alert and he remained in politics, while I was thrown out of it.[167]

Giving in to Sampath, Anna had volunteered to give up the powers and authority of his position and had instructed Kalaignar to support Sampath's resolution on reforms. Sampath consequently became the party's first presidium chairman.[168] MGR noted that despite the distribution of authority, Anna remained tall, for the workers considered no one else as deserving.[169]

Despite this, Kannadasan was 'very bitter' that Anna condoned Kalaignar's ways, while Sampath was under the impression that Kalaignar's actions had Anna's blessings. Kalaignar writes that Sampath had a group behind him, which had opposed Nedunchezhian initially, later him and then Anna himself. He and the others saw to it that the party was not affected.[170]

However, the differences within the party took an ugly turn on 21–22 June 1961, when the DMK's executive and general council convened in Vellore. Kalaignar records that, unable to bear the condemnation he faced in the forums, Sampath submitted his resignation. Kannadasan has detailed his version of events: According to him, the atmosphere was charged and Sampath's shirt was pulled by one of the members. Importantly, MGR and SSR showed up during the commotion from an adjacent room, and stood there. The accounts of what happened after that between the Kannadasan and the Anna camp vary considerably.[171] Anna's 25 June statement, disabusing the press reports of violence, also suggests that Sampath had painted himself into a corner. Kannadasan said that the actors took offence at the statement as Sampath had earlier implicated them in the violence. Anna was 'confused' and issued a placatory statement, and they were all back to square one. Referring to Anna as 'inconsistent', Sampath wondered how his promises could be trusted. The following week, Kannadasan caricatured these actors in a piece entitled 'Forgiveness' in Thenral, portraying the parlous state of affairs in the party.[172] But, in the interim, on 20 February, an attack on

Kannadasan was attempted in Trichy, while addressing a public meeting with Sampath. Anna quickly condemned it. However, Sampath began a fast in protest against this incident. A greatly pained and worried Anna implored him to end it, and succeeded in bringing him around.

On 26 February, a 'guards meeting' at Thiruvottiyur saw a rapprochement that did not last. Kannadasan said that when he complained that the party cadres almost walked over party seniors to get a glimpse of the actors, Anna said that Kalaignar had brought MGR into the party, and that Kalaignar and the poet had bestowed titles on him and that MGR's popularity was a result of their actions. He allegedly added that MGR should not be blamed henceforth as nothing would stick and there was no way that he could be sent away. If the account is authentic, then Anna was indeed prescient. Kannadasan concluded that Anna was right and that it was their fault that they had disingenuously praised MGR—not a 'deserving man'—because of the crowds behind him.[173]

Sampath left the party on 9 April to found his own outfit, before he crossed over to Kamaraj. Anna wondered how, within forty-two days of the Thiruvottiyur meet, the 'Kazhagam had decayed beyond redemption'. Following MGR's exit in 1972, and the charges he laid against him and the DMK, Kalaignar wrote: 'The country is asking the same question now to friend MGR who on 8 October [1972] spoke ill of the Kazhagam.' He added 'Yes. Ten years later, the betrayal that had appeared in Sampath's figure has now shown up in MGR's form. That's it.'[174]

However, in the aftermath of Sampath's departure, MGR said: 'I am not prepared to stay in the party or quit it based on whether people want me in or out. What matters is the policy my heart supports. My actions will be the result of that.'[175]

SADANANDAVATI'S DEATH

MGR's role was critical in the 1962 elections. He campaigned vigorously for the party, addressing close to forty meetings a day, even as his wife lay critically ill in a hospital. Whenever someone raced towards the stage, MGR dreaded that they would bring him bad news—that Sadanandavati had passed away.

Kalaignar had gone to Theni to take MGR to his Thanjavur constituency, explaining the uphill battle they faced against the Congress candidate.[176] In Anna's constituency, Kanchipuram, MGR had rightly sensed that the partymen's confidence was misplaced (Anna would eventually lose). On 24 February, the day of the polls, he toured polling stations and returned home at 5 p.m. Sadanandavati asked whether he needed to travel again, to which he replied laughingly that he would be with her until she wanted him to leave. She was using an oxygen tank to breathe. She asked if Anna would win; MGR asked her to keep quiet and not trouble herself. She slept peacefully, holding MGR's left arm with her right hand. MGR, tired, fell asleep in that position. The next morning, at about 4 a.m., as he tried to release her hand, it fell limp. Shouting 'Annae', MGR ran upstairs to Chakrapani.

MGR recorded how devastated he was. Many of the Kazhagam's leaders came to pay their condolences; he felt someone caressing his head even as he was crying. It was Anna; MGR was about to burst out on seeing him, but muffled his sobs with a towel. MGR recorded Anna's words of consolation: 'His [Anna's] mentioning, "What we don't wish for, happens" was somehow on my mind. Wiping my eyes, I asked Anna, "Isn't today the counting of votes?" Anna looked at me, astonished, and nodded his head. "You are here—what happens if something goes wrong there?" I said. He said, calmly, "There is nothing more to go wrong!"'[177]

RMV said that Anna's defeat greatly affected MGR, even more than his wife's death.[178]

The funeral rites had to be performed. Thousands called out 'annae' as he shouted 'ammukutti' and lit the pyre. Sadanandavati had departed, but MGR had long arrived.[179] Ganesan was there till the rites finished and he made sure that MGR ate.[180]

The twelfth day after Sadanandavati's death, MGR was back for the shoot of *Thaai Sollai Thattathey*, unable to stay at home, which was filled with her memories.[181] He would eventually move to Ramavaram Gardens for good.

MGR AS MLC

The 1962 election results were bittersweet for the party. Anna had been defeated, but fifty DMK members had been elected this time. MGR was nominated as a Member to the Legislative Council (MLC), only the second actor after KRR to be so nominated by the DMK. MGR later said that he did not wish for it.

After taking his oath as MLC, he called on his 'affectionate friend' Diraviam, who told him straight away that he could 'trust leader Kamarajar', who is not vengeful. 'But there is another one. You have to be cautious of him. He is like a snake, be careful,' the official had warned him, possibly of M. Bhaktavatsalam, the next in line to Kamaraj.[182]

On 1 May 1962, MGR made his maiden speech at the council, in which he bemoaned the lack of state sponsorship for the stage. He suggested minimum wages for the 1,00,000-odd cinema workers.[183] In a rare show of unity, the fans associations of MGR, Sivaji Ganesan and Gemini Ganesan felicitated MGR on his election to the council. He wished for the unity to last and invited members of the Sivaji Ganesan Fans Association to participate in the function to felicitate Sivaji Ganesan on his return from America.[184]

As the president of the Nadigar Sangam, he graciously hosted a farewell reception for Sivaji Ganesan and, on his return from the US, a public rally and reception. A special issue of Nadigan Kural, the mouthpiece of the Nadigar Sangam, was also brought out to fete Ganesan.[185] Ganesan was the first Indian artist to visit the United States at the invitation of the US government, an honour that had been accorded earlier only to Pandit Jawaharlal Nehru.[186] Here are a few excerpts of MGR's speech:

> I wish to point out that [Ganesan], who is at the pinnacle of fame as an artist, exhibited, even several years earlier, that he possessed basic skills—the elements of growth . . .
>
> Playing a good character, it is easy to find a place in people's hearts . . . But to take up a character who is hated by people and to succeed in finding a place in their hearts is not easy. In the film Thirumpipaar, his was a completely villainous character . . .
>
> When the question 'Who is Sivaji Ganesan?' comes up, lauded as the best actor in the Indian subcontinent, the answer we get is, 'His land is Tamil Nadu, his mother tongue is Tamil, his culture, Tamil!' Is any other qualification than this needed for everyone to praise him unanimously? . . .

This is a proud moment not accorded to a Tamil actor till
now . . .

I wish brother Ganesan's fame rises higher and higher, and I
pray my mother blesses him with a long life.[187]

■

Pasam released that year was a barometer for the MGR phenomenon.
His fans had begun to see him as immortal already. In the movie, MGR
is depicted as a thief who is hard on the edges, but with a golden heart,
who gives up thievery in the end. He also, however, dies at the end
of the movie. This ending would prove to be a mistake. Director T.R
Ramanna said later:

When we showed MGR dying in the last scene, I noticed a deadly
silence in the hall. That's all. The movie was dead! Not only that,
I began receiving hundreds of condemnatory letters from fans.
Pasam's ending not only made me understand MGR's dominance,
but also that one could not say things that are in contradiction
with people's sentiments.[188]

MGR RESIGNS AS MLC

The following year saw many hits, but *Kanchi Thalaivan*, scripted by
Kalaignar and released in late 1963, did not fare that well. Although
the movie's title was understood to refer to Anna, in less than two
years, MGR would create a serious controversy by calling Kamaraj his
'leader'.[189]

But MGR's controversial actions had already begun according to
Kalaignar when SSR ran for the presidency of the Nadigar Sangam.
Kalaignar wrote that MGR had conspired against SSR, but Anna felt that
since he had won, there was no need to make MGR's action an issue.[190]
In retrospect, Anna was only being diplomatic; MGR had grown too big.

The 1964 Pongal release *Vettaikkaran* proved to be a hit. In the
spring civic elections, Kamaraj would warn the voters that 'Vettaikkaran
will come, be watchful!', alluding to MGR and his campaign on behalf

of the DMK.[191] But within weeks of *Vettaikkaran*'s release, MGR would precipitate a crisis by unilaterally announcing his resignation from the council.

T.R. Ramanna recalled the day after the resignation. They were filming a song and it became a 'huge headache' for the filming crew as the DMK's senior leaders kept calling on MGR, urging him to withdraw his resignation, even as MGR told them 'Annan [M.G. Chakrapani] had instructed him against accepting any positions'. Chakrapani, Ramanna says, did not like partymen frequently seeking funds from MGR, and that the resignation was intended as a 'shock treatment'.[192] Anna for one was certainly 'shocked'. He considered MGR as someone who had a 'deep interest in the party and [had a lot of] affection for him'. But the matinee idol ignored the appeals of Nedunchezhian, NVN and others. Anna was interned for the anti-Hindi agitation. This news caused him much anguish and anxiety.

'Anna lamented the fact that he was not responsible for MGR's resignation, but that the consequent pain was wholly his. RMV, however, noted that MGR was irked by Anna's desire to nominate his classmate C.V. Rajagopal, not a career politician, to the council.[193] Clearly, MGR had wished to assert himself. He had shown that he could give up his seat and simultaneously deal a serious blow to the party, for the seat was lost to the Congress.[194] While SSR issued a statement condemning MGR, neither Anna nor the general council or the administrative board had the heart (read, courage) to pull him up.[195] On the other hand, Anna wrote: 'The affection between the Kazhagam and MGR was not a cultivated one, [it] was not a forced one; it was organic.' He added: 'Him leaving the Kazhagam or the Kazhagam without him is even an unthinkable idea. Therefore, even if he had left the council, I am confident that he will not quit the Kazhagam or my heart.'[196] The irony was that until 1968, MGR was not even a member of the party's executive council.[197]

En Kadamai (My Duty, 1964), released soon after, failed to draw crowds. In 1968, MGR said this had no connection with his resignation.[198] In any case, four months later, he appeared to have made amends when he sang Vaali's lines in his *Deivathaai* that his breath is in three letters, referring to the DMK:

In three letters is my breath
Even after it dies out, they will live
There will be a place called heart
And there will be a place in it for me*

KAMARAJ 'LEADER', 'MY GUIDE IS ANNA'

Yet, just when the dust had settled over the resignation, in July 1964, MGR would again court controversy, this time a bigger one, when he described Kamaraj as his 'leader', even as he referred to Anna as his 'guide'. T.R. Ramanna revealed that MGR played his recorded speech the following day at the film sets and sought the opinion of those there.[199] The speech caused much consternation within the party and party seniors condemned MGR.[200] Even as Madurai Muthu charged that MGR was seeking new pastures, an anonymous statement that heavily criticized MGR came out. Anna himself remained indifferent to all the commotion; that was Anna. Clearly, MGR appeared upset with Anna, and the speech demonstrated it. But MGR appeared unrepentant.

On 17 August, thirty-two days after his controversial speech, in a meeting at Krishnampet, Madras, to felicitate his charity to hut dwellers, MGR hit out at the anonymous 'VIP' and others who questioned his loyalty to the Kazhagam:

Who is the Kazhaga[m] 'VIP' who had issued a statement against me for my having taken part at the function to fete Kamarajar? Those who do not have the courage to come out with their names . . . Can they be a Kazhagam VIP? . . . All these show that the fifth columnists are growing within the Kazhagam! Our first job is to get rid of these fifth columnists! If Kazhagam were to score victories, it should first get rid of these fifth columnists.

---

* *Moondrezhuthil en moochirukkum*
  Athu mudindha pinaalum pechirukkum
  Ullam endroru oor irukkum
  Andha oorukkul enakkor paer irukkum

This event doesn't appear to be one organized to fete me. It appears more as though I have committed a crime that I should have not and that I should be brought before this forum for the people to believe that 'he is good' . . . How could we reach a shameful situation where Ramachandran, who has toiled for ten years, has to be introduced?

Erode Chinnasamy spoke here. He is a recent entrant to the Kazhagam. He too had joined the Kazhagam because of my efforts. And that Chinnasamy spoke as if he was introducing me. Why have we reached a stage where he should speak as though he were recommending me to you? I, a DMK worker, who had taken Anna as my guide had called Kamarajar as my leader. Immediately some commented that MGR would go away to the Congress, and the others engaged in wrongful propaganda as to MGR's role henceforth in the Kazhagam. Should I, who have throughout opposed Kamarajar, be considered a supporter of Kamarajar for praising him for his good attributes on his birthday? If that is the case, when Anna was interned, I worked very hard against Kamarajar for the Kazhagam's success! Who worked against the wishes of Anna who was in jail? I? Please think carefully . . .

When I spoke once in Madurai of Anna, I referred to Anna as someone 'who shows complete affection for me! Who is supportive of me!' The moment I sat down, Karunanidhi instantly asked me, 'Does it mean that we show you lesser affection?' I said: 'Your affection is that of a human. On some other occasion, you might get upset [with me]! But Anna is not like that. He showers his divine affection on me, forgiving me even if I were to do wrong. That is the truth.'

Suddenly there was a statement that the general council will take action against MGR. When asked who, [they say] VIP.

Similarly, there was this information that they would show me black flags! Who is this VIP who doesn't have the courage to reveal his name? We have ten to fourteen months for the elections. In that statement, the VIP has alleged that I cause trouble once a year. Who's that VIP?

I keep searching but I can't find [him]. I asked Navalar [Nedunchezhian] and also Mathi [Mathiazhagan]. They also don't know who this VIP is . . . One person had called me a coward, that

I had praised Kamarajar only to seek opportunities and luxury. He is also in our Kazhagam and I don't want to mention his name. If I were to, it would be of disgrace to us. Everyone says that I am at the pinnacle of filmdom. What more opportunity or luxury would I then seek? I, who spent all the money that I made for public cause, why should I save money any more? I, who do not have enough time to do the different things that I have to do here, what could I do going to a different place? People can speak as they wish, but there will be no honesty in it. I can only say this much now.[201]

Despite the strident talk, with time, MGR wished to make amends. At his behest, the head of his fans association, Musiriputhan, at a fans meet told Vaali to address the 'issue', saying that though the 'pouring had stopped, the drizzle continued'. Vaali then justified the use of the word 'guide' to suggest that MGR had elevated Anna to a 'messiah'. MGR hugged him on stage to show his pleasure, and his affection and fondness for Vaali grew after this.[202] In 1967, in his testimony against M.R. Radha after he was shot at, MGR said that he had not called Kamaraj his leader. This could be confirmed as the speech had been taped, he said.[203]

MGR IN CEYLON

In three months, Anna and the other leaders would be seeing MGR off to Ceylon for a visit from 22–28 October on the Davasa newspaper group's invitation. MGR travelled to his birth town, Kandy, to Jaffna, Batticaloa, Matale and Nuwara Eliya. He would pay a courtesy call on Prime Minister Dudley Senanayake. MGR and his entourage arrived a day early, on 21 October, and travelled in an open car to Galle Face Hotel, some 10 kilometres away on the seaside. Fans breached the police cordon to 'touch' their favourite star.

Crowds gathered wherever he went. Thousands waited outside Radio Ceylon to catch a glimpse of the actor, and some even stormed into the radio station. Earlier, speaking to the press, MGR referred to Anna telling him at the airport that there was no relationship between the DMK in Tamil Nadu and the DMK in Ceylon.

On 22 October, at the Colombo sports ground, lakhs gathered to felicitate MGR, despite the rains. Culture Minister Gamini Jayasuriya conferred the title 'Nrithya Chakravarthi' on MGR.[204]

On 25 October, Chelliah Rajadurai, Federal Party MP, greeted MGR in Batticaloa. In the north, where several Federal Party MPs received him, MGR travelled in an open car to the Jaffna sports stadium with a retinue of 200 cars in tow. A crowd of 1,50,000 had braved the heavy rains. Supreme Court judge Henry W. Thambiah, who welcomed him, said, 'I have not seen such a crowd in these parts in my life. MGR has proven that even in Ceylon he remains a crowd-puller.'[205] True to his nature and style, MGR had requested the collections from his events be donated to charity.

On 27 October, the Ceylon DMK hosted MGR for breakfast. That day, MGR addressed a meeting of plantation workers, visited Vijaya Studios and called on the leader of the Tamils, S.J. Chelvanayakam, at his residence. Speaking at the tea organized by the Ceylon Film Chamber, MGR said that he had come as an artist and not as a politician. In the evening, the local administration minister hosted him for dinner.

On 29 October, after addressing a meeting at Colombo's Sughathadasa Stadium, MGR reached Madras at 5.40 p.m. Anna welcomed him with a garland; Kalaignar and others were there to receive him. *Murasoli* reported the crowd shouted, 'Arignar Anna long live, MGR long live.'[206]

MGR considers *Enga Veetu Pillai* as his eighth break and says it proved that he was 'versatile'.[207] Cast in dual roles, where one is cowardly yet likeable, MGR was taking a risk but his fans extended the 'boundaries of appreciation', accepting the weakling, and him being beaten on screen.[208] The movie created a record, bringing in huge revenues to the government and a windfall to exhibitors.[209] The following song would become immortal and perhaps heralded MGR's ambition:

> If I were to command
> And if it is carried out
> The poor won't grieve here
> Throughout their lives
> There is no suffering

And they will not fall into the ocean of tears . . .

My future will arrive, my duty will arrive
I will finish this cabal's doings*

ENTER JAYALALITHAA

The year 1965 would bring MGR and Jayalalithaa together, his most-paired heroine and political successor. In the aftermath of MGR's death, in April 1999, she would tell her interviewer Simi Garewal, 'One-third of my life was dominated by my mother, the other part—a major one—was dominated by MGR. Two-thirds of my life is thus over. One-third remains, and this part of my life remains for myself . . .'[210]

Once 'terrified of meeting strangers' and hating the limelight, Jayalalithaa, in her own words, was 'propelled by fate into two high-profile careers'—films and politics—neither of which she really desired or liked, but then, as she said, once she put her heart into it, she gave her fullest. She described her introduction to MGR in the autobiographical series that she wrote for twenty-four weeks, beginning in late 1978, that was later aborted. On the first day, on the sets of *Aayirathil Oruvan* she greeted MGR who said 'welcome' to her. It was to be a no-holds-barred welcome. He became her 'mother, father, friend, philosopher and guide' and 'sort of took over [her] life'.[211]

MGR was of a 'very strong character', like her mother, and he 'dominated [her life] completely' after her mother. She said she was 'never in awe' of him but 'respected him a great deal'. She 'admired his intellect' and 'felt a lot of sympathy for him because he had a hard life', like herself.[212]

---

* *Naan aanai itaal*
   Athu nadanthu vitaal
   Ingu ezhaigal vethanai padamaatar
   Uyir ulla varai
   Oru thunbam illai
   Avar kaneer kadalile vizha maataar

   Ethirkaalam varum en kadamai varum
   Intha kootathin aatathai ozhipaen

MGR came to fill her mother, Sandhya's, shoes after her death. Jayalalithaa wrote about a time when she had been unwell for two–three days, at the end of which she fainted at home on the sofa. The only man at home, her uncle, was out of town and her two aunts did not know how to respond. Jayalalithaa's manager telephoned MGR for help. MGR called for a doctor and came over to Jayalalithaa's place. The doctor wanted Jayalalithaa to be hospitalized and MGR asked the aunts to get ready. As the aunts did not come down, MGR decided to see for himself what was keeping them. What he saw was the sad spectacle of the aunts fighting over the house keys. An angry MGR took the keys from them and asked them to come downstairs.

It took some hours for Jayalalithaa to regain consciousness at the hospital. MGR was patiently waiting around all this time at her bedside and when she woke up, she did so in MGR's presence. MGR handed over the house keys to her. She learnt of the circumstances only later. 'I will always remember this act with gratitude. Who would have taken such trouble? He wanted to protect me, and he guarded them and handed them over to me. If not, I don't know what all would have been lost! I cannot even imagine it,' wrote a grateful Jayalalithaa.

Karnan's (1964) director B.R. Panthulu offered Jayalalithaa a role in *Chinnada Gombe* (Gold Doll, 1964). Seeing the 'rushes' director C.V. Sridhar signed her up for his *Vennira Aadai* (White Dress, 1965), which became her debut Tamil film. Panthulu also signed up Jayalalithaa for *Aayirathial Oruvan*, as heroine opposite MGR.

MGR was shooting for *Panam Padaithavan* in the same studio that *Vennira Aadai* was being made. He entered the sets of *Vennira Aadai* one day and Jayalalithaa wrote that she was not aware that she had to greet the hero. Director Sridhar beckoned Jayalalithaa over and told her: 'MGR has come. You are to act in his film . . . He is a big hero. Go greet him and talk to him.' As Jayalalithaa folded her hands to say 'vanakkam', MGR motioned her to sit down. Jayalalithaa wrote that she did not remember what she was asked or what her response was.

She recalled seeing MGR as a young girl with her mother at the sets of *Baghdad Thirudan* (The Thief of Baghdad, 1960). The second occasion was when she performed at Loyola College, Madras. MGR, the guest, gave away his watch to the student mimic who had performed before Jayalalithaa, but had nothing for Jayalalithaa the danseuse. He sent someone to fetch a silver cup and presented it to her. *Aayirathil Oruvan* was only the third occasion. She would say later that the movie 'laid the base for [her] political life'.[213]

MGR saw the rushes of *Chinnada Gombe*. Behind him and the director sat Jayalalithaa and her mother, Sandhya. After seeing the rushes, MGR turned to Panthulu and said 'Okay' and left immediately. He had come in between a shoot and was still made up.[214]

In the first scene in *Aayirathil Oruvan*, instead of thanking MGR for having freed her, Jayalalithaa's character scorns him thus: 'You have bought me, making me a slave worth 2 lakhs.' As Jayalalithaa did the shot without any inhibition, MGR told her: 'You remind me of Bhanumathi madam. After a long time, I see her courage, spirit, enthusiasm and zest.' Jayalalithaa said 'Many thanks' in response.[215]

Jayalalithaa would usually go in before the others, be seated next to the director and read a book, and sometimes, she would even cross her legs. No one had taught her to stand up and greet MGR or the others on their arrival. Two or three days went by like this. But later, some busybody drew MGR's attention to this fact, persuading him that the behaviour was indifferent, if not disrespectful.* MGR appears to have spoken to Panthulu, who spoke to Sandhya, who in turn spoke to her daughter. Jayalalithaa grew upset, and said she would rather go back to college and quit acting. The following day, Jayalalithaa refused to come out of her room. Nambiar and MGR had already arrived at the set. As Sandhya enlisted Panthulu for help, he came home to plead: 'I am older and ask you to do this for me.' Jayalalithaa then said, 'I will do it for you.'

After this, greeting MGR became a preoccupation for her. Sometimes MGR went directly to the shot. Jayalalithaa would go over,

---

* MGR was very sensitive and took such things seriously. He did not like the fact that director K. Somu did not rise when he entered the hall in an event in the mid-1960s. Vijayan, S., *M.G.R. Kathai*, Chennai: Arulmozhi Pathippagam, 1992, part 1, p. 42.

He did not like a director crossing his legs and, in another case, an actor. He asked that the actor be dropped while the director was to be instructed through the producer on manners. Ravindar, K., *Pon Mana Chemmal*, Chennai: Vijaya Publications, 2009, p. 105

He reportedly disliked K.A. Mathiazhagan smoking in his presence (told to the author by late Nanjil K. Manoharan, July 1996); S.A. Asokan had said 'the old hag is delaying the movie', for which he punished him by further delaying the completion of his film *Netru, Indru, Naalai*. Vijayan, *M.G.R. Kathai*, part 1, 159.

hang around to catch his eye so that she could quickly wish him and return to her seat.[216]

On their first shoot for the song *Naanamo* (Are you shy?), she was to lie down on MGR, who was seated on a bed. It was their first night as per the movie. She said that until then no man had ever embraced her. The bed and the embrace made her shake involuntarily. MGR, who sensed that it was because of his embrace, asked her, 'Why? Why this much weakness? Why so much nervousness?'

She also possessed a strong fighting spirit. When the Tamil Nadu Cricket Association (TNCA) refused her membership, saying no woman had been independently given membership—only wives, daughters or siblings of males had been admitted—Jayalalithaa said that her father died when she was a year old and she could not bring him back to life for the sake of the membership nor could she marry just to become a member. 'Just because I don't have a dad or a husband, how could you refuse me the membership?' Of course she became the first woman member of the TNCA.

MGR appears to have been greatly fascinated by this brilliant convent-educated girl, who was indifferent to his superstar status, and the relationship proved most intense on and off screen.

She described their bond thus:

> Our relationship is very peculiar. Although he is so much older than me, every spare moment on the sets we would spend talking to each other, discussing every subject under the sun. We used to talk about science, philosophy, literature. Both of us are deeply interested in classical music, astrology and astronomy. We have so much in common.[217]

Among other things, they shared the same determination, charisma, crowd-pulling capability, and an interest in film and politics. But they were also very different, as time showed. While on the sets of *Raman Thediya Seethai* (Sita that Ram Sought, 1972), MGR, reading Jayalalithaa's palm, told her that she would enter politics. 'Me? In politics? No way,' said Jayalalithaa. 'Write it down, Ammu [Jayalalithaa]. My words will surely come true,' he replied.[218] Little did MGR know then that he would be the one to make those words come true.

In *Arasa Kattalai* (King's Command, 1967), Jayalalithaa had aptly acknowledged in advance MGR's future mentor status thus through Vaali's song:

> He is the one who made me sing
> He is the hero of my song...
>
> He is a man without blemish
> He is a god without a temple*

ANTI-HINDI AGITATION

Not everyone considered MGR blemishless though. MGR had turned down the Padma Shri Award then to protest the police action against the students participating in the 1965 Anti-Hindi Agitation.[219] Also, on 1 August 1960, in the Anti-Hindi Imposition Meeting, at Kodambakkam, Madras, Anna while reiterating the rationale for exemptions to students and certain professionals had said that MGR was unhappy that artists like him could not take part in the party's agitation:

> Students should not participate in agitations. Lawyers are needed to defend the DMK men when cases are booked. Doctors have a responsibility to save lives. If our artists were to participate and end up interned, then for another fifteen years, the film world will elude us. That is why they are being exempt. MGR, too, was upset with me for having exempted artists.[220]

However, all this failed to satisfy Kalaignar who after they fell apart would torment MGR asking repeatedly, 'What was this MGR doing during the 1965 Anti-Hindi Agitation? . . . Like Nero, who was playing his fiddle while Rome burnt, when Tamil Nadu was burning was not this MGR singing a "duet" in Goa?'[221] In 1978, MGR would point out that Anna himself

---

*   *Ennai paada vaiththavan oruvan*
    En paatuku avan thaan thalaivan...

    Oru kutramilladha manidhan
    Avan kovil illaadha iraivan

had termed the agitation as one led by students and not the DMK; and furthermore that Kalaignar himself had given in writing to the authorities that he had no connection to the agitation so that he could be released.[222]

MGR had also maintained that he wore a black flag at the shoots to mark the agitation. Nonetheless, Kalaignar would argue that MGR failed to fly a black flag on his house in Madras that day.[223]

THE CHANDRABABU–MGR FEUD

Similarly, in the film world, Kannadasan would charge: 'Destroyed by MGR, Chandrababu died vomiting blood.'[224]

In 1966, MGR consented happily to *Maadi Veetu Ezhai* to be directed by Chandrababu.[225] Already wary of each other, it remains unclear as to why they entered into such an unworkable partnership. Eventually, things came to a head, as charges flew thick and fast and tempers rose.

After two days of shooting and receiving an advance of 25,000 rupees, MGR began to dodge Chandrababu. The director began to visit Chakrapani a couple of times each day, seeking MGR's dates, only to have Chakrapani tell him, 'Do come tomorrow.' Not one to be fobbed off easily, Chandrababu confronted Chakrapani. Now, Chakrapani wondered how Chandrababu had stated in an interview that the two best actors were Sivaji Ganesan and himself, rather than MGR.[226] Heated words were exchanged. Chandrababu asked for the advance to be returned, only to hear that it had been settled. Tempers rose and Chandrababu lifted his iron chair to aim it at Chakrapani, only to be stopped by his friends. *Maadi Veetu Ezhai* thus died. Arurdhas blames Chandrababu for his haste and MGR for his irresponsible nature.[227]

With time, MGR and Chandrababu appeared to have made up; rather, they needed each other. They co-starred in *Parakkum Pavai* (Flying Girl, 1966),[228] *Kannan En Kadhalan* (Kannan My Lover, 1968) and *Adimaipenn* for which MGR gave Chandrababu a substantial sum.[229]

The year of Chandrababu's travails with MGR, 1966, saw his *Anbe Vaa*, a musical, become a runaway success.[230] *Anbe Vaa* took 30 lakh rupees to make and grossed 60 lakh rupees in earnings.[231] MGR was paid 3,25,000 rupees as remuneration.[232] In 1968, in his testimony in the shooting case, MGR said 1.5 lakh rupees was his highest fee and he had taken it for *Anbe Vaa*. Generally, his fee was not less than 55,000 rupees.

He said he had taken 23,500 rupees for *Aayirathil Oruvan*.[233] In 1963, Sivaji Ganesan's *Paar Magale Paar* (Look Daughter Look), was sold for a record 21 lakh rupees.[234]

THE 1967 ELECTIONS: THE DMK IN POWER

Success awaited MGR in the political arena as well. A line in *Arasa Kattalai* (King's Command, 1967), aimed at the general elections that year, went like this: 'The time that we have called him Anna, Anna will be left behind and the time to address him *mannaa mannaa* (king) will come', to indicate that Anna would capture power and become chief minister. MGR had been talking about such an eventuality for some years by then.[235] In early 1965, he said that he wished to tell the Opposition parties that the Kazhagam was not dependent on his money.[236] He was scathing in his criticism of the Congress. Here is an excerpt from a speech:

> We will be happy if you [the Congress] give your word that this year you will give one-and-a-half measures of rice, and subsequently, three measures of rice. We are taking over the rights (we will replace you) to relieve the poverty of the people.[237]

In another speech, he said they were all ready to follow Anna 'to the gallows' saying:

> What do they show in the Congress-propaganda films? They show in cinemas that in their rule they built so many schools, they built so many factories . . . In our Kazhagam-propaganda films, we show that they never built the required number of schools. They never built [the] required number of workshops. Which ones will the people see? Who will they support?
>
> I will tell them one thing.
>
> There will be lies in what you say; there will be truth in what we say . . .
>
> We only express what people need. We would show the [1965] self-immolation against Hindi . . . I would portray myself as going for self-immolation. Let us see you do that . . . We would portray a mother's tears on seeing her son shot in the agitation, portraying your shooting for [the] people to see.

You tell the reasons for the shooting; we will explain the reasons for being shot. Let us see which reason the people accept . . .

Let us see who succeeds in the year 1967.[238]

MGR'S ROLE

The DMK had stitched together a rainbow alliance, from the left to the right, to take on the Congress.[239] The DMK's treasurer, Kalaignar, declared open the four-day Virugambakkam election conference on 29 December 1966, handing over a sum of 11 lakh rupees to Anna as campaign funds—a record in the annals of the DMK history. Kalaignar had exceeded the target by 1 lakh rupees and Anna's appreciation would culminate in him euphemistically referring to Kalaignar as 'Eleven Lakhs' while announcing his candidacy for Saidapet.[240]

There was also another first. This time, the party had fielded MGR as a candidate. Noting that MGR was 'bashful' and 'reluctant' in one-to-one interactions with him, Anna said the screen hero was a completely different man when he addressed meetings. The cadres were like 'bees drunk with nectar' when they listened to MGR speak. At Virugambakkam, crowds would go wild at the sight of the matinee idol. Urging the audience to vote for the DMK, MGR said, 'We should all endeavour our best to definitely bring down the Congress government' and announced he would gift the equivalent of his fee for one movie to the party. Speaking after him, Anna said, 'Thambi Ramachandran said that he would gift his fee for a movie for the election funds. I don't want that. I seek from him the time that he gives for a movie. He should tour the state for a month. I know that if he shows his face, the Kazhagam would get 30,000 votes.'[241] Anna's words had echoed Christopher Marlowe's on Helen of Troy: 'Was this the face that launch'd a thousand ships / And burnt the topless towers of Ilium?' MGR's face would bring down the mighty Congress. None knew, however, that the matinee idol's potential would be tapped in a completely unexpected way.[242]

M.R. RADHA SHOOTS MGR

MGR had returned after an initial round of campaigning to Madras and his new film *Thaaikku Thalaimagan* was to be released on the eve of Pongal, 13 January, a Friday. The evening before the release, M.R. Radha shot MGR near his temple, before shooting himself. A wounded MGR turned out to be more potent than the swashbuckling screen hero.

Earlier, on 8 January, EVR had rebuked Anna, Rajaji and MGR for trying to bring down Kamaraj. M.R. Radha had mentioned MGR in his speech on that platform. RMV considered Radha's action had a political background.[243]

In the wake of *Petraal Thaan Pillayaa*'s success, producer Vasu and M.R. Radha had gone to see MGR at his Ramavaram Gardens to discuss a movie proposal. By 4.30 p.m. that fateful evening, the two were waiting in the reception.

As MGR entered the room, Radha got up from the sofa and, caressing his stomach, came to MGR's table. MGR inquired if he was all right. Radha said that he had eaten greens and rasam at Vasu's place, and he had flatulence as a result. As MGR wondered why they had wanted to meet him, Vasu explained their proposition: A Coimbatore-based producer wished to make a film with MGR, and would advance 2.5 lakh rupees to begin with and, later, another 2.5 lakh rupees. Vasu desired ten dates a month for six months from MGR. The actor offered him ten dates every alternate month, and promised to give more in the end if required. At this point, Radha came up to him and shot him. MGR felt something going through his ear. When he touched his left ear, he felt blood. And Radha was next to him holding a revolver.[244] Radha now stepped back and shot himself in the right temple, and then in the neck.

In court, Radha tried turning the tables on MGR, claiming that he had said, 'Brother, you are writing articles saying that I am conspiring to kill Mr Kamaraj. Thereafter, you are threatening to shoot me. What prevents me from talking on the same lines?' Radha said that he suddenly felt a sharp pain and when he looked up, MGR was holding a gun. He snatched it and shot MGR in return. In his testimony, Vasu refuted Radha's claim as a 'lie'.[245]

'I have been saved because of . . . loving hearts,' MGR said later. In an interview to film magazine *Bommai* in August 1967, MGR said that he was 'sacrificing [his] life for the sake of politics.'

The 'loving hearts' brought the city to a standstill and a prohibitory order was issued. The entire state was gripped by the issue. The

Congress office was set on fire, and the police had to provide protection to Kamaraj and EVR.

In his Pongal message, EVR tried to put things in perspective. He decried the hullabaloo following the incident between 'two lowly mountebanks'. He asked if a prohibitory order had to be clamped down, and if even he and Kamaraj had to be provided protection 'who could be safe then?'[246] *Murasoli*, of course, went with the flow:

> Tamilagam was tortured at the news! Many could not believe it!
>
> 'Did it happen to him? What happened?' countless cried!
>
> Countless wondered if this was not simply a tale! This was the talk in every place! People crowded around the Kazhagam's organ and the leaders' houses for news.
>
> Anna and other leaders were petrified; they had tears in their eyes! Within minutes of the news, people in the villages and towns were racked by anxiety . . .
>
> He had not harmed anyone. Did they intend to hurt such a man? Many, many lamented thus!
>
> Thus, Thamizhagam was rocked by the news of Puratchi Nadigar MGR being shot.
>
> Thankfully, our Puratchi Nadigar escaped death. If it had been otherwise . . . Even the thought of it makes our heart stop momentarily.
>
> Puratchi Nadigar
>
> Philanthropist
>
> People's darling
>
> Such are the people's epithets, in whose hearts MGR has established himself.
>
> His good heart has returned him to us safely. The efforts of the sinners have failed.
>
> Long live, MGR!
>
> Long live, Puratchi Nadigar![247]

The duty assistant surgeon, Abraham Sukumar, recollected later that MGR 'looked more handsome than he did on the screen' without make-up on, and was an embodiment of 'total nonchalance'. 'In real life, he proved to be as much the hero he was on the silver screen,' wrote Dr Sukumar. Radha was no different. He asked the doctors 'Are any of you Brahmins?' and was unconcerned about his wounds.

Dr Sukumar records that three men were present in the casualty theatre, watching over MGR. One of them, actor Asokan, was visibly upset. The other two, more calm and collected, were Kalaignar and Anna. Kalaignar, the doctor recorded, 'was youthful and handsome and, in spite of his being relatively small made, had presence'. Dr Sukumar aptly noted that he would have considered anyone who had suggested then that in front of him were three future chief ministers as mad.

MGR's wound was about half an inch in diameter and three inches deep. After the surgery, he was told not to speak for ten days.[248] While the bullets were removed from Radha's body, the bullet in MGR's was not disturbed as it was considered a risky move. For two days after the surgery, MGR was fed intravenously.

On 17 January evening, Kalaignar, and later Anna, had gone to see MGR. *Murasoli* said MGR held on to Anna's hands; MGR was asleep when Kalaignar visited him.[249]

Four years later, MGR said that all felt that he had died on 12 January and was reborn the next day. Several had donated blood for the surgery and ever since then MGR began his addresses with the famous line 'blood of my blood siblings'.[250]

In March 1971, in an election campaign meeting, MGR would talk of the incident thus:

What cruelty had I committed for one to shoot me? Let me explain. In a letter he wrote that we were attempting to prevent the continuation of Kamarajar's rule in this land. Therefore, he said, they had to be finished. People with such thoughts still exist in the syndicate [Congress led by Kamaraj].

MGR stayed in the hospital for two months. But the tragic event led to a spontaneous and unprecedented outpouring of love and many an act of kindness. Film producer Thevar's action shows both his humanity and what MGR could summon from his loyalists. Thevar had said that he would sign up MGR for his next venture on Pongal. He kept his word, showing up at the hospital where MGR was fighting for his life and pressing him to accept an advance for the film. MGR became extremely emotional every time he recounted this incident, reflecting Thevar's faith in him.[251]

Every day, Thevar brought offerings from the famous Agasthya temple in Madras. Sometimes he brought cash bundles wrapped in old newspapers. The largesse Thevar extended was not calculated. In all, he gave a staggering 10 lakh rupees to MGR. When his younger brother, Thirumugam, doubted if MGR would return the money, Thevar replied that if he lost the money, he would consider it as having lost one strand of hair. It was after *Thaai Sollai Thattathey* that they had begun to see money, he said, and assured his brother: 'He will surely get well. He will act in our films. Don't worry. All will be well.' MGR returned to do six more movies with Thevar.[252]

MGR'S CAMPAIGN

On 1 February 1971, MGR issued a statement from his hospital bed in which he said that voting for the DMK meant voting for 'true service and cultured politics' and for 'oneself'. He said that two decades of the Congress rule had only produced 'tears' and that they should entrust the administration to newcomers and expect 'novelty'. He promised to meet the public after his recovery and to continue to serve them. The consequent wave of sympathy for MGR would become an important factor in the DMK's victory.[253] MGR would file his papers from his hospital bed.[254] This would not be the first time he did so.

The statement was followed up with posters bearing MGR's image with his neck bandaged and palms folded together, seeking votes from his hospital bed. MGR, who wished only for his 'handsome face' to be displayed on posters, had reluctantly agreed to this idea.[255] Anna had made it clear that neither he nor the other leaders would campaign for P. Srinivasan, the DMK candidate pitted against Kamaraj. Srinivasan had turned to MGR for help and, after giving it some thought, the poster idea had sprung in to RMV's mind.[256] The day prior to the election, paid advertisements from the DMK saw MGR make the following appeal:

Respected motherfolk! Elders! Voters!

Prior to the elections, I was dying to see you all, but I am in bed because of a cruel act.

Death that came looking for me has fled. What chased it away was again your love, affection!

I was to come to your homes, but couldn't. Now I am asking for your hearts.

Tomorrow is election day. Please consider for one last time, for a moment, for whom to vote.

A rare opportunity to experience good governance after twenty years of suffering-filled Congress rule presents itself.

DMK's candidates, with good programmes and the help of the allies, are begging for your support.

If you support them:

Prices will come down!

Rice scarcity will go!

Poverty will leave!

Suffering will depart!

In total, certainly a new life will be assured!

I, who have been raised by you, I, who live because of you, kneel before your feet to seek just this one thing![257]

Anna campaigned in MGR's constituency. He said that he had not come to seek the people's votes but their hearts. He termed MGR's face as one that would make the audience 'dance with pleasure' and one that was 'made of gold'. He said with MGR in hospital, he was standing before them as a weak man, adding that MGR had wiped away his tears saying: 'Anna! Don't worry! The bullet has only gone this far. There is no danger.' 'Oh, it is our good fortune! The good man is safe. His philanthropy has saved him,' said Anna.[258] That year Vaali had in *Arasa Kattalai* penned the following lines about MGR:

His house has no doors

His entrance has no guards

He gave tens of millions
That king, long live*

MGR would return from St Thomas Mount in Madras with the most votes in the entire state. Although Kamaraj had vowed he would win hands down, it was MGR who did in the end.[259]

ANNA SEEKS MGR'S APPROVAL

A thoughtful Anna dispatched Era. Sezhian, Navalar Nedunchezhian's younger brother, with a list of his cabinet nominees, to MGR. The matinee idol was 'shocked' by the gesture but moved by Anna's acknowledgement of his significant role in the party's victory. One name on the list, however, made MGR 'angry' and he 'shouted', 'A minister's position for a man who until recently has been inimical to the Kazhagam and Anna? . . . How is this fair?' It was the nomination of C.P. Adithan, a barrister and press baron, that had troubled MGR. Adithan had disbanded his Naam Thamizhar (We Tamils) movement and had successfully run on the DMK ticket. His most popular Tamil daily, *Dinathanthi*, had played an important role in the run-up to the polls and Anna wished to acknowledge this contribution. But he was also aware that MGR could object to such a move. The daily had been hostile towards MGR, and the convalescing actor had reacted predictably. Furthermore, MGR recommended that the industries portfolio that was earmarked for C.P. Adithan be handed over instead to Navalar Nedunchezhian. 'I understand it is a ministry where one can get a lot of bribes. Therefore . . . let Navalar also handle this. Adithan was now listed for the Speaker's position in the revised list and Anna explained his reasons for the same. It is interesting that MGR referred to the industries portfolio in the way that he did. The rot had already set in and it would only get worse.[260] MGR himself was appointed vice chairman of the State Small Savings Advisory Board.

---

* *Avan veetukku kadhavugal illai*
  Antha vaasalil kaavalgal illai
  Avan koduththadhu eththanai kodi
  Antha komagan thirumugam vaazhi vaazhi

RETURNING WITH IMPAIRED SPEECH

Kavalkaran first showcased MGR's impaired speech, which was to become permanent. It was not clear if the audience would accept him. They did and the movie broke many previous records.[261] Women showed up in large numbers and special shows for women were screened at Globe Theatre. The movie became the first to run for 100 days there.[262] MGR considered *Kavalkaran* his ninth break.[263]

On 1 January 1968, Dr Sir A. Ramaswami Mudaliar unveiled Anna's statue on Mount Road on the occasion of the second World Tamil Conference. MGR had gifted the statue. Anna wondered at the conference: 'Isn't MGR, who is a combination of beauty and sentiment, a poem . . .'[264]

Kudi Irundha Koil and *Oli Vilakku* that followed *Kavalkaran* did very well. The former was his tenth break.[265] The eleventh turning point, *Oli Vilakku*, was in many ways a first.[266] In *Oli Vilakku*, he sang Vaali's song that praised Anna's government schemes of a measure of rice for one rupee and slum clearance thus:

> We are [a] new couple . . .
>
> When a measure of rice is available
> We don't have to go begging
>
> When the huts are becoming houses
> We don't have to live on the pavement
> When the government is with the poor
> We don't transgress any rules*

---

* *Naangha pudhusaa kattikkitta jodi thaanunga...*
Padi arisi kudaikkira kaalatthilae
Naanga padiyaeri picha kaetka povadhillae
Kudisaiyellaam veedaaghum naeratthilae
Naanga theruvoram kuriyaera thaevaiyillae
Sarkkaaru yaezhai pakkam irukkaiyilae
Naangha satta thittam meeri ingu nadappadhillae

In *Pudhiya Bhoomi*, MGR took the name Kathiravan (sun) to promote the candidature of the DMK candidate Tenkasi Kathiravan, aka Shamsudeen, who contested the by-election of Tenkasi during that time.

He sang Poovai Senguttuvan's song:

> I am your son
> This is well known
> My path is
> The path shown by Perarignar [Anna]*

MGR's career and political place seemed secure. But to a question around this time, 'If your mother had been alive today . . .', MGR said she would have pitied him and explained why:

> I don't have the peace of mind I had when I was earning little. Those who loved me then, without receiving any help from me, do not genuinely love me today, even though they received all manner of help from me. I say this with conviction: I have very few genuine friends. I know it for a fact. Do you think my mother could feel happy in these circumstances? She would naturally feel sorry for me.[267]

On 15 August 1967, Kalaignar began the one rupee for a measure of rice scheme in MGR's St Thomas Mount constituency. *Murasoli* said that for half an hour, Kalaignar was garlanded 'without a break'. MGR did not address the audience as he was still recuperating. In his brief speech, Kalaignar said that MGR would speak on Anna's birthday on 15 September.[268]

ANNA'S TERMINAL ILLNESS

MGR called Anna's passing away nature's 'huge conspiracy' against him.[269] Anna was 'puzzled' to see MGR on his flight to Bombay on his

---

*   *Naan Ungal Veetu Pillai*
    Idhu Oorarindha unmai
    Naan sellugindra paadhai
    Perarignar kaatum paadhai

way to the US for treatment. At the airport's waiting room, Anna asked MGR to check the oxygen cylinder. It was soon time to board the flight. Anna got up and sat in his bed. He asked Sezhian for the English books they had bought and chose Irving Stone's *Adversary in the House* and tore off its cover to give to MGR saying, 'Let it be with you.' Kalaignar and Nedunchezhian came in soon thereafter. Anna took the cover from MGR and gave it to Nedunchezhian, who looked at it and returned it to Anna, who then gave it to Kalaignar, who wondered if it was a design or a model for an advertisement. Anna said: 'Let it be with MGR' and returned the cover to him. MGR said he had wondered about Anna's action but did not get an answer.[270]

On 3 February 1969, Anna passed away. MGR lifted Anna's biological mother and put her next to her son's body. It was only then she knew that her son was no more.[271]

Anna's death would be an insurmountable loss for his thambis in particular and the Tamils in general. But it would also allow the former to come out of his shadow. Who would fill his big boots? MGR held the answer.

From Kingmaker to King

'After Anna, who?' was the question on everyone's mind after Anna's passing. Arignar Anna was a colossus. In 1956, he had famously said, 'Thambi vaa, thalaimai thaanga vaa (Younger brother come, come to lead us)', inviting Nedunchezhian to take over the reins of the party as general secretary from him. Nedunchezhian was next only to Anna in the Cabinet and, in Kannadasan's words, a 'complete human being (niraikudam)'.[1] MGR himself had characterized him as 'good and honest'.[2] But was Nedunchezhian the right one to fill Anna's big boots? He was known for his genteelness but his stint as general secretary was colourless; he lacked Kalaignar's charisma, skills, energy and the rapport with the cadres.

Kalaignar says he was under pressure from the party, ministers, legislators and parliamentarians to take on the job himself. Nedunchezhian, however, charged that Kalaignar had developed the 'great desire' to become chief minister, and had planned the takeover even as Anna was fighting for his life. According to him, MGR, C.P. Adithan, Anbil Dharmalingam, Mannai Narayanasamy, P.U. Shanmugam, K.A. Mathiazhagan and Sathyavani Muthu had begun to rally support for Kalaignar. C.P. Adithan, thus, spent 'much money' to woo legislators, and 'MGR invited many of the Kazhagam's MLAs to his Ramavaram Gardens for a meal and seriously engaged in canvassing for getting their support for Karunanidhi'.[3]

MGR's driver, Kaliyappan, later recalled, 'I still remember the day when MGR asked us to send in "Aasiriyar" (Kalaignar) immediately

---

*   Panruti S. Ramachandran, N. Ganapathi and Rama Subbiah were the few in favour of Nedunchezhian. When Arangannal explained the situation, Nedunchezhian 'shed tears'. Arangannal, *Ninaivugal*, part 2, pp. 37–9.

when he reached Sathya theatre [sic]. It was a time of political turmoil
and power struggle. After his arrival, I went to the hotel to get walnut
cake, a favourite of Aasiriyar. The next day, the newspapers informed us
about Aasiriyar becoming the chief minister.'[4] RMV writes that partymen
came to seek MGR's guidance and, 'Within half an hour, MGR was able
to convince them that Karunanidhi would be the right choice.'[5]

Sixteen years after the DMK's Lalgudi conference, MGR had risen
to become the kingmaker. On 1 April, MGR explained his role then
thus:

> When I consulted a majority as to who should be chief minister,
> all opined in favour of Kalaignar. Following this, I too insisted that
> he should take up the post. Even after all this, he did not consent.
> He sent Maran. The chief minister's position is not needed for
> Kalaignar [said Maran]. [And] Maran told us not to trouble him.
> We said . . . [it] was for the party and for the people.[6]

Three years later, in 1972, at the party's conference on 8–9 April 1972 at
Chengalpattu, MGR revealed:

> I have not mentioned till now in any public meeting what
> our Kalaignar said on taking over the chief ministership after
> Perarignar Anna's demise. I believe I can say that here. Kalaignar
> said, 'I don't wish to become the chief minister. I don't want it.'
> Not only that, he sent thambi [here a term of endearment] Maran
> to convey that he did not wish to have the position. Kalaignar's
> wife also said the same. However, it was we who rejected this.
> Therefore, Kalaignar neither wished [for] this position nor sought
> it. He became chief minister deferring to people's wishes. We
> together gave him the task of shouldering this burden. If he were
> to script dialogues for movies, he could earn in the thousands.
> Spurning that, he has assumed this responsibility for the sake of
> the masses.[7]

In May 1969, in his *Adimaipenn*, MGR's twelfth turning point in his
movie career, Jayalalithaa sang Vaali's song that was apposite to his
kingmaker's status:

> You had conquered time
> You had become an epic
> You are the victorious one . . .
> In working tirelessly, you are the sun
> In every household, you are the moon!*

MGR, true to his name, was the moon up until this point, reflecting the
DMK sun's light. But he would soon eclipse the sun. At the shooting of
Adimaipenn, someone gave him the white fur cap, to shield him from
the desert sun. It would become his signature look from this time on.
'In election campaigns, I had to go in the sun and rain. I used the cap.
Now, it has become a habit,' MGR said later. In response to a question
that the cap was to hide his bald pate, MGR asked: 'Let us assume that
I am bald. Would I then not be MGR? First I wore a *jubba* (kurta). Then
I wore a collared full-sleeved shirt. They criticized that. One day, the
shirt's sleeve was torn. I then folded up the sleeve. They said I have
folded it up like a rowdy. How can I respond to all this?'[8]

KALAIGNAR IS DMK'S FIRST PRESIDENT

On hearing of Kalaignar's selection, Prime Minister Indira Gandhi had
remarked, 'Oh, is it Karunanidhi? Will he cooperate with the Central
government? I have heard that he is a confrontationist!' Indira Gandhi's
fears would become a self-fulfilling prophecy, but for different reasons.
On 10 February, Kalaignar's first ministry was sworn in. MGR had
again objected to C.P. Adithan (minister for cooperation) being given a
ministership, but had been pacified.[9] Months later, when Indira Gandhi
unveiled Anna's portrait at Rajaji Hall, Madras, Kalaignar referred to her
concerns and famously declared, '*Uravuku kai kodupom, urimaiku kural
kodupom* (Extend a hand for cooperation, lend a voice for rights).' His

---

* *Kaalathai vendravan nee*
  Kaaviyamaanavan nee . . .
  Vetrithirumagan nee, nee

  Oayaamal uzhaipadhil suryian nee
  Ovvoru veetilum chandiran nee

intention, he said, was not to seek confrontation.[10] Kalaignar would be
as good as his word. He would support Indira Gandhi's nationalization
of banks in July, her candidate, V.V. Giri, as president in August and
the abolition of privy purses a year later. But things would begin to go
wrong afterwards.

On 17 March 1969, during the two-day visit to Delhi, the first
time as chief minister, Kalaignar said, 'In granting states more powers
[India's] unity will not be harmed' and he wished to resolve this issue
in a 'friendly way'. Way ahead of his times, Kalaignar would pay a
heavy price for his vision. Meanwhile, writing in his paper *Swarajya*,
elder statesman Rajaji exhorted Kalaignar to provide a clean, fair and
competent administration, a tall order indeed.[11]

But first, the intra-party battle with Nedunchezhian needed to be
settled. Having lost out in the chief ministerial race, he would queer the
pitch by declaring his candidacy for the general secretary's post. MGR
again rushed to Kalaignar's rescue:

> Ninety-nine per cent of the DMK desire Kalaignar as general
> secretary. Therefore they are pressing him to contest. [Thus] even
> the [question of his] withdrawal from the contest is not in his hands.
> When Navalar [Nedunchezhian]—who does not enjoy a majority—
> insists that his view should be accepted, it is tantamount to coercion.
> The Congress party became decadent because the party leadership
> was with one [person] while the administration rested with another.
> It is because I don't want such an eventuality for the DMK that I
> suggest that both positions should be vested in one person.[12]

It was a specious argument. Nedunchezhian had served as general
secretary under Anna before and the party had not become 'decadent'.
In deference to Kalaignar's wishes, a compromise formula was reached
to accommodate Nedunchezhian. In a throwback to the presidium
chairman era, the DMK would now have a president above the general
secretary. Nedunchezhian asserted later that Kalaignar wished to
be president.[13] Nonetheless, he had no compunctions then with the
proposed compromise. On 26 July, 320 of the 326 newly constituted
general council members chose Kalaignar as the party's first president,
Nedunchezhian as general secretary and MGR as treasurer. On MGR's
elevation, EVR remarked in private that 'Kalaignar had stepped on

something that he should have not'.[14] Even within the party, not all were happy with MGR's ascent. This team fielded A. Selvarasan, later a legislator, to compete against MGR, who won a significant number of votes.[15] A reconciled Nedunchezhian would soon join the Cabinet as minister of education and health.[16]

With no cadre or a popular base, Nedunchezhian had proved a walkover for the Kalaignar–MGR duo. But it was only a matter of time before competitive politics, ego, ambition and mutual distrust would turn these two friends into foes, and allies into opponents. For then, however, MGR, a Malayali, represented the party's Dravidian unity. Thus, on 26 July, in an event in Madras to hand over relief funds for the floods in Andhra Pradesh, Kalaignar remarked that the presence of his Andhra Pradesh counterpart Brahmananda Reddy, Karnataka's industries minister, Rajasekhara Murthy, and 'MGR belonging to Kerala' on the same dais made him feel that Dravida Nadu was present.[17]

LAUNCHING A POLITICAL CAREER

It is not clear if Anna's death had anything to do with MGR's political ambitions or if his kingmaker's role had made him more aware of his strength in the party. MGR told Nagi Reddy that he wished to make a film to help him find out about how people would respond to his entry into politics. The resultant *Nam Nadu*, a remake of a Telugu film, shows MGR, a municipal clerk, running successfully for elections in order to serve the people. MGR's name in the movie is Durai (after Annadurai). Comments on MGR, such as 'If there is a man like this one, the country will be all right' and another comparing MGR to the almighty, made *Nam Nadu* a special movie, even for the MGR genre of image-making films that showed him as a handsome do-gooder who is also generous, virtuous, valiant, successful, strong, chivalrous, a teetotaller, etc. Essaying such an image for two decades, the actor had become indistinguishable from the actual person.

Nagi Reddy and MGR watched the movie together at Mekala Theatre. In the movie, Jayalalithaa greets MGR after his electoral win in the song:

Welcome, oh teacher! We have come to welcome you
We, the poor, trust and look to you

Anna's younger brother, truth's comrade,
You are the poor's leader.'

Nagi Reddy said:

The audience rose as one man, cheering, clapping and whistling.
There were cries of 'We want to see the scene again! Repeat the
scene!' We advised the manager to oblige the audience. The reel
was rewound and the sequence was shown again. I turned to
MGR. His eyes were filled with tears of joy. He hugged me. 'Oh,
Reddiar! I have received the people's acceptance.'[18]

MGR himself sang '*Ninaithathai nadithiye mudippavan naan* (I accomplish
what I seek).'

MGR remembered 1970 as marking his thirteenth turning point,
with *Maatukkaara Velan*, a social entertainer. Jayalalithaa played the
heroine in it. MGR's Intelligence point man, K. Mohandas, first called on
him on the sets of *Velan*. On the cowherd being dressed in a suit, MGR
said: 'That is cinema, the world of make-believe. Mind you, the same is
true of politics.'[19] Mohandas said that he felt that MGR was turning into
a myth and would go places. The 1970s were to prove this true.

In *En Annan* (My Elder Brother, 1970), MGR sang '*Nenjam undu
nermai undu odu raja! Neram varum kathirundhu paaru raja* (You have a
heart, you have honesty, keep going! A time will come, wait)!' Was
MGR biding his time? In *Thedi Vandha Maapillai* (The Voluntary
Groom, 1970), his message was less subtle: '*Vetri meedhu vetri vandhu
ennai serum / Adhai vaangithantha perumai ellaam unnai serum* (Success
will succeed success in my case / all the credit for it belongs to you).'
Should Kalaignar have sung this?

---

* *Vangayya vaathiyarayya varaverka vanthomayya*
  Ezhaikal ungalai nambi ethir paarthu nindromayya...

  Annanin thambi unmaiyin thozhan
  Ezhaikkuth thalaivan neengalayya

KALAIGNAR'S TAMIL NATIONALIST AGENDA TAKES SHAPE

Kalaignar did not hide his ambition about translating into practice the DMK's ideals—both substantive and symbolic. He lost no time in establishing the Justice Rajamannar Committee on state autonomy—on 2 September 1969.[20] The A.N. Sattanathan Commission, the state's first Backward Classes Commission, was set up on 13 November 1969.

In the 22 February 1970 DMK conference in Trichy he gave the 'Five Great Declarations', one of which was 'Autonomy in State and Federalism at the Centre'. MGR had declared open the conference.[21] On 31 March 1970, the land ceiling was brought down from 30 to 15 acres.

The Kalaignar administration was equally daring when, in 1971, in keeping with EVR's views, it amended the Tamil Nadu Hindu Religious and Charitable Endowments Act 1959, to allow all, irrespective of caste, and those who qualified themselves, to become priests, and, for this purpose, set up two training schools. As the move faced a legal challenge, on 15 April 1974, the Tamil Nadu Legislative Assembly passed a resolution seeking a constitutional amendment to overcome the obstacles.[22] However, the progressive move became hostage to legal review and, on 15 December 2015, the Supreme Court might have dealt it a fatal blow when it said that the selection of priests, as prescribed by the agamas (treatises) does not violate the right to equality.[23]

Also in 1971, acting on the recommendations of the A.N. Sattanathan Commission, Kalaignar hiked the reservation for the backward classes from 25 to 31 per cent and for the scheduled castes and tribes from 16 to 18 per cent taking the total reservations up to 49 per cent. The government would discard the recommendations on what has come to be known as the 'creamy layer' or castes that had made progress and were therefore to be excluded from affirmative action; and to introduce an economic criteria (an annual income of 9000 rupees a year) to determine backwardness.[24]

The Slum Clearance Board, rehabilitation of the beggars and leprosy patients, assistance for the disabled, widows and free eye camps for the poor, abolition of hand rickshaws and the distribution of cycle rickshaws were some of the progressive schemes launched by the Kalaignar administration around this time. In 1973, buses were nationalized.[25]

Tamilness was not to be forgotten either: 'Tamil *thaai vazhthu*' was introduced as the official invocation song amidst stern opposition from Tamil savants, such as Ki. Va. Jaganathan, who termed the language a 'minor deity' and the move inappropriate.

Similarly, Dalmiapuram was officially renamed Kallakudi in 1970. Offering felicitations, MGR said: 'When Kalaignar left for the agitation, Anna said, "Go and come back." It was because he desired that Kalaignar should succeed him that he said that.'[26]

But MGR appears to have also reflected on his own political destiny around this time. In 1970, when thousands showed up for the procession at Vettaikaranpudur, next to Coimbatore, on seeing MGR in a contemplative mood, S.M. Subbiah Naidu wondered what was bothering him. MGR said:

> Nothing, annae! I am not sure where I am being led! If I knew my destination, then I could understand somewhat the reason and the consequences . . . Look how they praise me! Why is there such a mammoth crowd? What did I do? Which war did I fight or which country did I safeguard? . . .
>
> When I see all this . . . I am afraid. I am being taken somewhere. I don't know where. Will the end be dangerous or will it be peaceful? I have no clue! So many expect something big from me. How am I going to fulfil their needs?

Subbiah Naidu said that whatever is destined will happen.[27] Neither could have foreseen how destiny would unfold in this case.

COOPERATION AND COLD WAR

From around July 1970, MGR began to answer questions in the weekly *Dinamani Kadhir*, where he said that 'so far, [I] never failed to achieve something I have desired'. He described Kalaignar as 'a second edition of Anna' and 'Anna's heir'.[28] However, not all was well between them and a 'cold war' was brewing.[29] The Opposition and the press spoke of divisions within the DMK. MGR's 21 July

1970 speech, feting Kalaignar on his return after a three-week tour in western Europe hints at this:

> Kalaignar follows Anna's policy. From overseas, Kalaignar had written to ministers [and] friends in the Kazhagam. He had also handwritten his letter to me. That missive itself is a response to the foes critical of us. Whatever his circumstances, he has not forgotten the love and affection of his Tamil Nadu friends. We have a leader who possesses such unique traits; we wish for him to serve long. I also wish to speak about the prevailing situation in Tamilagam. Wherever I look, I see jealousy. Wherever I turn, I see opposition. As Kalaignar works to safeguard people—they (the Opposition) use the press to depict him as an enemy of the public. Kalaignar, who serves as the Kazhagam's leader, the chief minister and a party worker, has been entrusted with a great responsibility. We will overcome the conspiracies against the Kazhagam driven by competition, jealousy and selfishness. Those upstarts in political life are declaring that they will finish the Kazhagam.[30]

On 9 September, amidst allegations of corruption against some in the ministry, Kalaignar obtained the resignations of K.A. Mathiazhagan, M. Muthusamy and poet K. Vezhavendhan.[31] MGR seemed supportive of Kalaignar on this. In its aftermath, MGR summoned Vaali to ask him to change the line 'Mathiyai thanathu manam pol nadathum Thuglaqae! Vaa! ('Oh, Thuglaq, who treats his mind as he wishes, come)!' in the movie *Thuglaq* (1971). MGR felt that the line referred to Mathiazhagan, as the word 'mathi' meant both mind and moon.[32]

The first policy difference between Kalaignar and MGR may have been over prohibition. Anna had rejected the advice from officials on lifting prohibition saying 'revenue from liquor is like buying the butter from the hands of a very sick leper'.[33] However, a more pragmatic Kalaignar appeared to be veering towards the idea of lifting prohibition. On 13 September, MGR issued a statement in which he said that drunkards destroyed themselves and their families, and, among other things, he advocated an exclusive referendum nationwide for women on prohibition. MGR let the cat out of the bag when he said that the ideas were acceptable to Kalaignar, who would have issued a rejoinder otherwise.[34]

RELATIONSHIP WITH JAYALALITHAA

MGR's relationship with Jayalalithaa would also come under strain from now on. *Rickshawkaran* became his fourteenth break and the biggest box office hit ever.[35] In 1971, when Jayalalithaa was twenty-three years old, her mother died. MGR stepped in to fill that void.[36]

RMV, however, thought that the relationship was hurting MGR the leader and decided to separate them. He introduced seventeen-year-old Manjula in *Rickshawkaran*, and kept Jayalalithaa away from this and several other MGR films. But RMV did not have to try too hard. It appears that Jayalalithaa was also smarting at MGR's acute possessiveness of her. She told her interviewer, 'And after Mother, Mr MGR dominated my life completely.' When asked if he was 'very possessive' and stopped her from acting in certain movies, she hesitated for a split second before saying, 'Maybe, perhaps.' Her response, that 'after a point I stopped acting with other actors. But I did the most number of films with Mr MGR' said enough.[37] She wanted to do films with him and others, not solely with him as he appears to have wished. In 1968, she acted opposite Sivaji Ganesan in *Galatta Kalyanam* (Fun-filled Wedding). On Ganesan's request, Vaali had penned '*Nalla idam, nee vandha idam* (Good place, the place you have come)' meaning that she had moved from the MGR camp.[38] By cutting her off as MGR's exclusive heroine once and for all, RMV had helped greatly weaken their ties. But the relationship appears too convoluted for any straightforward analysis. She also said in the same interview when asked if she fell in love with him, 'I think everyone who met him fell in love with him. He was a charismatic figure.'[39] Therefore, it was no surprise that although she was not in the film, she would show up in Japan at the shooting of *Ulagam Sutrum Vaaliban* (Globetrotting Youth, 1973). RMV had pointed out that the talk of the town was that 'MGR was globetrotting with Jayalalithaa'. Yet, he could only bump her off in the movie and some others, and not until the autumn of 1973, when she would pair with him one last time in *Pattikaatu Ponnaiya* (Villager Ponnaiya, 1973). On a personal level,

Jayalalithaa herself would break free of MGR's suffocating embrace only to resume the association a decade later, after a rollercoaster, and later a reclusive, personal life.[40]

Rickshawkaran won the Bharat Award for Best Actor (later renamed National Award or Rajat Kamal Award for Best Actor) for MGR. Critics promptly said that the award was inspired by the DMK and *Blitz* alleged that he had paid 40,000 rupees for the award, a story that *Dinathanthi* carried with gusto. Threatened with legal action, *Blitz* would express regret for printing the story.[41]

In the movie, a fellow rickshawman falls ill and his family goes without food. Padmini sells meals to the rickshawmen. MGR buys all her food and sends it to the sick man's family. A labourer expresses disappointment that MGR had not eaten and the fellow labourer responds, 'Oh, his heart gets filled when the stomachs of others get filled.' MGR himself remarks: 'Can't trust the praise of individuals; but the praise of [full] stomachs can be trusted.'[42]

The trust deficit dogged the Bharat Award. *Blitz's* story was irrational but many believed that MGR did not deserve it. MGR shot back:

> Those who have not engaged in analysis whether the selections were just all these years when the Central government had awarded the Bharat awards are parsing it today after it has been awarded to me. What sin did I commit? . . .
>
> I want to ask those who think it is not just that I have been awarded this award one thing. For nearly thirty-six years I have been working with the film world. I don't wish to exalt myself by saying how many have gained because of me . . .
>
> At no time, have I run seeking position, title and fame. I have the belief that they should come looking for you.[43]

THE 1971 ASSEMBLY AND PARLIAMENTARY POLLS

They would come in a matter of years. But for now, the cold war between him and Kalaignar was no longer a secret. In April, the Tamil weekly *Kumudam* published a cartoon where a Sivaji Ganesan fan insinuated to an MGR fan that he was indirectly criticizing Kalaignar. MGR wondered about the weekly's ethics to 'deliberately' and 'stubbornly' pursue such a 'bad policy'.[44] But the *Kumudam* story was a smoking gun.

Meanwhile, Kalaignar had recommended the dissolution of the Assembly a year in advance to synchronize its elections with the 1971 parliamentary polls.[*45]

Once foes, the formidable Kamaraj–Rajaji duo had come together to form a 'grand alliance' against the DMK. EVR described it as a cart pulled by a horse of an inferior breed and a buffalo, and felt that Indira Gandhi favoured Kalaignar, and that Kalaignar could act as a 'check' on the Centre. Kalaignar did act as a 'check', but Indira Gandhi did not like it.[46]

At a mammoth meeting held at the Marina in Madras on 25 February, the Swatantra Party leader applied vermilion to Kamaraj's head, wishing him success. The picture was widely circulated in the press. The alliance's success appeared a strong possibility.[47]

MGR'S CAMPAIGN

Kalaignar undertook a thirty-day campaign. Comedian Thengai Srinivasan travelled with MGR on one of the pre-campaign trips for two days. He recorded:

> The bag [at my feet] contained bundles of 100-rupee and 10-rupee notes. I looked at him wondering at the huge [amount of] cash. He smilingly said, 'In two days, we have to go to three districts, address more than fifty meetings. I brought this for party expenses. In the general election, the DMK needs to get a majority of the seats. Furthermore, I had promised to assist many schools financially with their needs. Therefore, I brought this money to help [to] the extent I can.'

---

* Talks on an electoral understanding between the DMK and the Congress (I) would only be salvaged at the last minute. Consequently, Congress (I) would contest nine parliamentary seats in the state and the lone Pondicherry seat, but no Assembly seat.

When Srinivasan said, 'Money is like Goddess Lakshmi. How can you keep it under one's feet?' MGR responded: 'The Lakshmi in our car will take precedence in many households from tomorrow. If we keep it next to us, then we won't have the heart to part with it. That is why I kept it under my feet.'[48]

Huge crowds waited for hours on end to see and hear MGR. He urged people to 'hock' at those who gave money for their vote and throw the money away:

> The vote is to decide the nation's destiny. To sell it away for two, three, five rupees is disgraceful. The money that they give would help defray expenses for two or three. But I ask you to think of the difficulties that one would have to face for five years. Don't sell your honour. Only then will democracy survive.

This speech was made in 1971. Today, thanks to the two Dravidian parties, Tamil Nadu is the leader in vote buying and MGR must have turned over many times in his grave in his grave.[49]

However, MGR's campaign almost did not happen. As RMV insisted on his undertaking a campaign tour, MGR initially said he was busy, but then opened up to say that he had not received an invite from Kalaignar. RMV astutely pointed out that talk that the elections could be won without MGR must be avoided. Kalaignar disarmingly told RMV that MGR did not need an invite. In the end, the communication gap was bridged thanks to RMV and MGR's tour programme was announced and he set off.[50]

The results were stunning: The DMK won 184 of the 234 seats, the highest ever in its history. The Congress (O) won fifteen, Swatantra Party six and independents eight seats. Rajaji described it as the victory of vulgar licences, permits and money power.[51] Nedunchezhian recorded that MGR's cine fame, goodwill and propaganda were all behind the DMK's record victory.[52]

'MEDICAL MINISTER'

Kalaignar wrote that MGR had not expected such a 'massive' win. In fact, MGR was not the only one. Allegations of corruption had dented the DMK administration's image. The Kalaignar–MGR campaign and the sympathy wave from Anna's death had saved the party for the moment. At the time of the results, MGR was shooting in Kashmir for *Idhaya Veenai* (Heart's Veena, 1972). Kalaignar had declared open the shooting. By the time the film was released in 1972, however, they would become estranged. As MGR sang, '*Oru vaalumillai naalu kaalumillai, sila mirugam irukkudthu oorukullae* (There is no tail or four legs, but there are some animals in the town)!', his fans conflated the animals with the DMK leadership. Following the results, MGR reached Delhi on 14 March and hurriedly telephoned Kalaignar, suggesting that he consult him on ministry-making and subtly hinting that he wished to be 'Medical minister (sic)'. MGR refuted this as a mere 'story'.

> Karunanidhi is a good story writer and a powerful dialogue writer . . . Had he asked me not to act if I wanted to become a minister, could I have not asked him how he could continue to write stories and dialogues for films as chief minister? And if I really wanted a ministership, I could easily have requested the late Annadurai for one . . . In fact, many wanted me in the Cabinet, but I declined.[53]

If the request was irrational for a kingmaker, Kalaignar clearly saw an opportunity to show MGR his place and deny him the 'double role' off-screen. During their telephone conversation, Kalaignar said that he was willing to discuss anything that MGR wished to talk about once he reached Madras. However, in a show of independence, Kalaignar finalized and announced his Cabinet before MGR got there. Unable to get a seat on a regular flight, MGR had taken a chartered flight. Kalaignar said that he wished to accommodate MGR in his ministry but Nedunchezhian and the industries and law minister, S. Madhavan, wanted to have nothing to do with him. MGR's wish to continue his acting career made it more problematic for them. Madhavan came armed with the legal opinion that such duality was against convention. MGR now desired that Kalaignar 'insist' that Indira Gandhi amend the rules. (It would later transpire that there were no clear rules.) Kalaignar rightly said that a minister-actor would have looked 'odd' regardless. 'I have no objection to make you a minister. Can you kindly discontinue acting?' Kalaignar asked. MGR withdrew his request and, from then on, harboured a deep-seated resentment against him, according to Kalaignar. Nedunchezhian said MGR was 'disappointed' with Kalaignar.[54]

RMV, who saw this as the beginning of the parting of ways between the two, blamed Jayalalithaa for the fiasco:

> The problem with Jayalalithaa's association was that she made him [MGR] think that people would accept him, whatever [the] mistakes he made. Till then, his private life was a guarded one. This was the beginning of his downfall. After the results of the 1971 elections, people brought two big garlands, one for Karunanidhi and another for MGR. This man was missing. He had gone to Nepal with Jayalalithaa, [who was] dressed as a Muslim woman! It was due to her prodding that he asked, on his return, for a minister's post in Karunanidhi's Cabinet. A person who could form a government degraded himself by asking for a post. The wily Karunanidhi said, 'You leave acting in cinema and then come.' From then on the conflict began that ended in 1972 with MGR starting a new party.[55]

However, in the victory celebrations, MGR said that although Kalaignar was the Kazhagam's leader, as chief minister, he belonged to all. He described the poll as a 'class struggle' and a 'social revolution', and concluded that 'through state autonomy, Tamilagam is sure to rise [in its objective of a] classless society'.[56]

On 15 March 1971, the DMK's third, and Kalaignar's second, ministry took office.

Kalaignar would greatly regret making Mathiazhagan, the Speaker, and Panruti Ramachandran a minister for they would be the first ones to rebel.[57]

LIFTING OF PROHIBITION

Discussions about prohibition would again be in the air. Writing in his autobiographical series in *Ananda Vikatan* around this time, MGR said that Kalaignar's conviction about and traction to prohibition was superior to that of any party or person countrywide. He launched a frontal attack on the ruling Congress for not compensating the state for the loss it faced from prohibition and for not enforcing prohibition nationwide. Giving statistics of offenders from 1961 to 1970, MGR debunked the charge that the DMK regime's laxity had created drunks. MGR then pointed to the chief minister's budget speech, where he said that he would 'suspend' prohibition until the Centre would implement it nationally.[58]

The party's general council held in Coimbatore, later in the summer, would decide to 'suspend' prohibition for financial reasons.[59] At the general council, MGR had pointed out that lifting prohibition was 'temporary' and that the party should conduct a campaign on the ills of drinking.[60] Such a committee was subsequently formed with MGR as its head and former Madras mayor Sa. Ganesan as secretary. The chief minister was to launch the committee on 15 August, Independence Day.[61] MGR refuted the suggestion that his appointment was to soften his opposition to the move, and said he would make way for someone else if the committee's purpose was not to be served. The committee would not, however, even take off.[62]

When the DMK government lifted prohibition on 30 August 1971, MGR termed it a 'sad day' for the party and all those who advocated against alcohol.[63]

On 15 September, MGR had gone to Anna's mausoleum with his studio staff to undertake an oath to give up drinking. MGR reproached those magazines which had written that the show was poorly attended and that he had been let down by the DMK leadership. He ridiculed *Alai Osai* for the detailed head count of 150. He said he had no need to prove his popularity.[64]

MGR said he laughed at those who made it appear that he had failed as the advocacy committee chairman. He said some were even falsely claiming that he was working against the Kazhagam. He then released four letters where the writers asked that they be included in his advocacy.

However, despite his spirited defence of prohibition and Kalaignar's leadership, it was clear that the issue was a source of difference between the two. Busybodies and the press appeared to widen this cleavage. Cho. Ramaswamy's *Thuglaq* fortnightly carried a piece by a party official and *Alai Osai* editor, Vellore Narayanan, who lamented that the party leadership had not proceeded against MGR for his views against the party's decision on prohibition, after he had supported it at the

Coimbatore meet. Narayanan finally appeared to advise Kalaignar to safeguard his position. MGR responded to Narayanan almost point by point. He observed that Kalaignar was not in a 'pitiable' situation where he needed to safeguard his position.[65]

KALAIGNAR ESSAYS THE 'BEGINNING OF BETRAYAL'

But Vellore Narayanan was proved right. In a chapter in his autobiography titled the 'Beginning of Betrayal', Kalaignar gives his version of the events that led to the DMK's split in 1972. In a nutshell, he says that the Congress (I) schemed to divide the DMK and MGR, who had personal problems, went along to serve their end. But why would the Congress (I), which owed its electoral presence in Parliament to Tamil Nadu, do such a thing to the DMK? Kalaignar does not mince any words here: 'The one who sprang such a poisonous seed in Mrs Indira Gandhi's mind was Central minister Mohan Kumaramangalam. Having become a member of Parliament, thanks to the Kazhagam's support, he began to repay his debt thus.' Although a feudal by birth, Kumaramangalam turned an avowed communist. He was arrested for sedition and released in 1941. He joined Indira Gandhi following the Congress defeat in Tamil Nadu in 1967 and served as the minister for steel and mines before an air crash ended his promising public career in 1973.

Murasoli Maran described Kumaramangalam before and after he had the DMK's support. He had come to see the DMK leadership. '[Kumaramangalam] kept standing. There were enough seats. It was after Kalaignar and Navalar [Nedunchezhian] insisted that he sat down.' Maran said the demure Kumaramangalam later resolved to bring down the DMK government. He explained that when Kumaramangalam looked from his perch or 'summit', 'even the elephant appear[ed] like a cat!' Maran added: 'He is the scion of a zamindar! Within rises the wish to play with the constitutional instruments. "My position had been reduced to seeking the assistance of these ordinary [nonentities] guys. Let me first finish them!" he thinks,' wrote Maran.[66]

Kumaramangalam could have only viewed the rise of the DMK, the party that had appropriated the leftist agenda but, in his view, that was lumpen, with alarm. The belief that the once secessionist party had grown too strong for comfort and had to be taken down seemed perfectly understandable. A young and combative Kalaignar appeared to play into Kumaramangalam's hands. Imbued with his Tamil nationalist agenda, an idealistic Kalaignar and his militant followers were turning into a serious challenge for the Congress (I)'s centralized vision of subservient state administrations.

In his autobiography, Kalaignar mentions the labour dispute at the Simpson's plants in Madras, in early 1972, as when things began to go wrong.[67] In a conciliatory move, Kalaignar had asked the duly elected DMK union leader to step down, paving the way for elections and a compromise. However, historian and author A.R. Venkatachalapathy noted: 'Drunk with power after winning a brutal majority in the 1971 Assembly elections, the DMK regime suppressed people's movements and trade-union activities, exemplified by the handling of the workers strike in the Simpson's factory.'[68]

Central ministers Kumaramangalam and C. Subramaniam somehow felt that the DMK administration could do nothing right. The two ministers constantly, and severely, criticized the DMK administration, such that the 17 January 1972 party meet in Thanjavur authorized the DMK president and general secretary to take a decision on continuing ties with the increasingly antagonistic Congress (I) and Communist Party of India. Another resolution referred to Kumaramangalam's 'indifferent' and 'cavalier' attitude. MGR did not attend this meet; he was at a shoot. But there could have been more to his absence. Later, when Vellore Narayanan would make it an issue, MGR responded in his roundabout manner, asking Narayanan to convene the general council where he would place his response.[69] It could be that MGR did not wish to be identified with the raucous resolutions.

Kalaignar wrote that 'now almost inimical' to the DMK, the Congress (I) failed in its efforts to 'infiltrate' press tycoon and minister C.P. Adithan. What happened afterwards? Kalaignar explained:

> It was after this that Delhi's gaze fell on [my] friend MGR. They needed someone who was a strength for the DMK, but, at the same time, was weak and unable to face difficulties. MGR fitted the bill.
>
> Delhi circles began to interact with MGR, employing both compassion and fear-inducing tactics. 'Hushed stories' began to appear in some magazines as news. But MGR was vacillating.

He did not have the courage to betray the Kazhagam suddenly—at the same time, he had to act as the puppet of the Delhi men! To protect this secret, he presented himself as an ardent DMK warrior and full of affection for me in public meetings and the Kazhagam's conferences.[70]

In 1992 D.G.P. Mohandas wrote: 'In addition to persuasion, a veiled warning was communicated to MGR about his problems relating to income tax, and violations of the Foreign Exchange Rules, etc. MGR relented.'[71] On 23 March 1992, the Tamil magazine *Junior Vikatan*'s series 'Police Manithargal' or 'Police Folk' revealed the role played by the intelligence services in bringing MGR out of the DMK fold. The intelligence official who advised MGR to meet Indira Gandhi told the magazine:

We enacted a major drama to draw MGR out of the DMK . . . 1971 . . . then DMK had fifteen MPs (sic). It was a time when Karunanidhi was politically a superman . . . He was fiercely advocating state autonomy. He also claimed that his was the best-run state. These [comments] also reached the ears of the then prime minister, Indira Gandhi . . . Tamil Nadu remained an island in the DMK's hands. The support of the DMK MPs was needed for Indira Gandhi's government. At the same time, she also wished for Karunanidhi to be under her control.

She wondered what could be done towards this. She decided that if the DMK were [to] split, then it would seek the support of the Congress. She ordered senior intelligence officials to work towards this. An important Congress functionary was sent to assist them. That Congress functionary sat with intelligence officials and gave them a plan . . .

When we locked at the DMK's top leaders, MGR was the one at the forefront.

That is why we decided to wean him away from the DMK.

MGR was acting in a huge number of movies then . . . His income was also high.

Bearing this in mind, authorities such as the income tax, the income surveillance and enforcement directorate officials targeted him and gave him a very difficult time. At that time, he had returned from abroad after a film shooting [*Ulagam Sutrum Vaaliban*]. They questioned him on his accounts in relation to this as well. He did not, however, know that there was a huge agenda behind these moves questioning him. I was sent to speak to MGR at this time. He was very low when I saw him. I drew him into conversation and suggested that to resolve the problems, he should go to Delhi, meet with madam [Indira Gandhi] . . . and all [his] issues would be resolved.

MGR listened patiently to all this.

Then I, on my own, identified an important Congress functionary suggesting that he [MGR] meet 'amma' [Indira Gandhi] through him.

Accordingly, MGR met Indira Gandhi with the Congress functionary, and in the company of his lawyer and auditor.

MGR returned happy after the meeting.

This is how we slowly created an intraparty feud within the DMK and, in the end, in 1972, saw to it that MGR left the DMK.[72]

Nonetheless, till the end MGR would maintain his action was motivated by public good. Below is an excerpt of his speech made in the latter half of 1982:

If I spend the money earned and I cannot pay income tax.
I will not fall at anyone's feet; I will sell my property and settle it.
But not ask to favour me as Kalaignar did . . . [seeking withdrawal of Sarkaria spawned cases from Prime Minister Desai] . . .

But if I speak my conscience [as I did when I sought accounts] it is selfishness
Why should I have any selfishness?
Did not people give me huge support when I did films?
Did not producers give me money in lakhs?
I helped so many people – they say
They say that I have given more than I have
Where did this money come from?
It is black money
Why should I deny it?
Partly accounted and the rest unaccounted

That is what I spent for the party and people
Did party leaders not take this money from me? Did they not
know then that this was black money, illicit?
But what did I do for myself?[73]

And till the end Kalaignar insisted that it was personal gain. In his
autobiography, the DMK leader drew out a sequence of MGR's public
utterances that were adulatory to begin with but would turn defiant by
the end. In June 1971, MGR had named a place in his St Thomas Mount
assembly constituency as 'Karunanidhipuram'. On this occasion, he
said:

Tamil Nadu's chief minister, Kalaignar, and I go back twenty long
years . . .
    That relationship has resulted today in him being the
Kazhagam's president and I, its treasurer.
    It would be a gross mistake if anyone assumes that Kalaignar's
fame and name is because of his chief ministership. Even before
all these positions came looking for him, he was a personification
of fame and name . . .
    One cannot find anyone with such good attributes as Chief
Minister Kalaignar in any other party. For one of his acumen and
culture, this position will not do. A day will soon come where even
higher positions [will] come seeking him. To name this area after
this tall man's name—the one who is a mixture of compassion
and generosity—is a great pride.[74]

Kalaignar then listed MGR's speech at Kanchipuram at the DMK
conference at Chengalpattu on 8–9 April 1972. In his speech, MGR
described news reports of his disaffection with the DMK as 'lies' and
'requested' the audience not to trust them.

The DMK is a people's party. It is not an individual's party. Anna
built the Kazhagam; Kalaignar is preserving it. Some are trying to
divide the Kazhagam. I tell them: No one has ever been born to
divide the Kazhagam. No one will be born [to do so] in the future
as well.[75]

INCOME TAX ISSUES

But things were bound to go downhill quickly. In response to the campaign that he was an income-tax defaulter and the space that newspapers gave this news, MGR sarcastically wrote that it was his duty to thank those 'friends' who had introduced him to the people 'from a different angle'. He said that he had been receiving letters daily from his fans and released the contents of a letter that said that assuming there were approximately 16,000 fan clubs, and if each were to raise 500 rupees, 50 lakh rupees could be collected, and even if half this amount was collected, MGR's dues would be settled. Another letter came from Era. Sheriff, from Tindivanam, who offered to sell his house worth 40,000 rupees, towards MGR's dues, adding that his mother would give her life for him. MGR had to quickly send a telegram to stop Sheriff from doing so. MGR said later that he did not consider himself an orphan any more. He considered Sheriff's mother a human god. 'Let anyone cheat me, speak mockingly, criticize, hurt me. I will, henceforth, laugh at this with renewed vigour. Laugh and keep laughing.'[76] As chief minister, MGR would visit Sheriff's ailing mother twice.[77]

In June 1972, a district party official, S.S.M. Subramaniam wrote a letter on MGR's 'secret contacts' with Delhi, for possible publication in an Opposition magazine, which 'somehow' made it into the DMK leadership's hands. On MGR's insistence, Subramaniam was relieved of his primary membership for five years. Kalaignar interpreted 'secret contacts' as those in relation to MGR's foreign exchange and income-tax problems. In a different context, Kannadasan alleged that MGR took six times more than he accounted for as his fee.[78]

In November 1972, MGR asked his interviewer to reflect why actors took 'black money' or unaccounted money. He said there 'was no other go'. He pointed out that the income-tax ceiling was as high as 97 per cent for a slab of 1 lakh and a fee of 1 lakh entailed 97,000 rupees in taxes. It was believed that MGR was charging a few lakh rupees per film around this time. He asked, 'How could one live honestly?' He also pointed out that donations were taxed similarly and he was 'very angry' when, on an occasion, his gift of 1 lakh rupees was taxed.[79]

Kalaignar writes that 'it was with the passage of time that it became clear to all that [Subramaniam's] accusation was right and not unjust.'

Wondering in retrospect 'Did this person [MGR] act like this?', Kalaignar recorded excerpts of MGR's speeches and writings prior to

September 1972 to illustrate the change and the cause.[80] In his write-up in *Bommai*, MGR described Kalaignar as Anna himself. Here are excerpts on Kalaignar seeing him off on his overseas trip to shoot for *Ulagam Sutrum Vaaliban*:

> I was looking for Anna at the same airport where Anna had come and garlanded me earlier. Don't I know that Anna is no more? I know [this] very well! But my heart wished for 'Anna's send off!' Craving that, I looked around!
>
> There he was for the eyes that searched all around [for him]! Now he was close by! The police officials helped bring him near! Yes! Anna came in Kalaignar Karunanidhi's form!
>
> Kalaignar came! He was not in years older like Anna or me; yet, he who possessed the merits akin to Anna's, placed the garland around my neck . . .
>
> Suddenly, some police officials, who were outside, entered the flight. In Kalaignar Karunanidhi's form, Anna again came to me. He fondly embraced me.
>
> Tears welled up in our eyes . . .
>
> I had this huge consolation that finally my Anna had, in Kalaignar's form, come to where I was, to bless me . . .[81]

Similarly, on his return Kalaignar was there to greet him at the airport. MGR's flight reached Madras at 3 p.m. When the crowd finished garlanding MGR, it was 3 a.m. —a marathon twelve hours later.[82]

Yet, MGR had to give in to 'Delhi's threats' and, as Kalaignar put it 'was put in a situation where he had to describe me as Anna's foe [later]!'[83]

In July 1972, MGR led a delegation of artists on a tour to Singapore at the government's invitation to perform benefit shows for the country's development. They collected 100,000 dollars (after expenses). MGR travelled with Jayalalithaa and others. Traffic was stopped for MGR, only for the second time after Queen Elizabeth.[84]

BHARAT AWARD

MGR was at the shooting of *Idhaya Veenai* in Kashmir when news of the Bharat Award for *Rickshawkaran* reached him. He told Radio Kashmir that he had not expected it and could not believe it.[85] Others too could not believe that MGR would be awarded the prestigious prize.

On 28 July, MGR spoke at his felicitation ceremony for having won the Bharat Award for Best Actor that year for his movie *Rickshawkaran*. Here is an excerpt from his speech:

> Today if I address [M. Karunanidhi] as Doctor Kalaignar, one should note the huge change—the magnificent growth. At the Kallakudi agitation, Kalaignar risked his life. The one who risked his own life that person is today the Kazhagam's president. Even if we are to die—we are to do so with ideals and principles. We have a huge responsibility. We will strive to develop the Kazhagam.[86]

Kalaignar, for his part, said that MGR, his 'sibling in spirit', was 'fully deserving of the award'.[87]

At the felicitation by the Nadigar Sangam, MGR wished Sivaji Ganesan the Bharat Award and even better. Referring to whether he would serve under Ganesan, the Nadigar Sangam president, MGR said that Kalaignar was younger than him but he 'is DMK's president. I serve under him'.[88]

The most spirited speech was made at the DMK's Madurai district conference on 5 and 6 August. Earlier, MGR, Kalaignar wrote, had expressed his desire for a heroine of his to be invited and seated in the front row. Kalaignar, astounded, told him that the Dravidian movement would not digest such things and he should think through this patiently.* Kalaignar concluded that MGR grew bitter at this and Kumaramangalam exploited MGR's bitterness to divide the DMK. A day before the Madurai district conference, MGR met Kalaignar at his place in Madras. But neither spoke of what had transpired.

At the conference, MGR said that the DMK administration was clean. 'Congress men say that this is a corrupt administration; is it a corrupt government?' he asked the audience rhetorically. The audience's

---

* He had further said that Madurai Muthu (the secretary and the organizer) would not agree. MGR would not give up; he contacted Muthu. Muthu made it clear that he would stop the two (MGR and his heroine) at the very entrance. MGR abandoned the idea after S.S. Rajendran, Nedunchezhian and Anbazhagan registered their opposition.

response of 'No! No!' rent the sky. MGR then declared: 'The people's verdict is the verdict of god—this is not a corrupt administration!' On Kalaignar, he said:

> Kalaignar no longer walks as tall as before. He has begun to give in and give in for the sake of others . . . He has humbled himself and has become the epitome of modesty. He checks himself to see that he does not speak mockingly of anyone and has assumed humbleness. Anna taught all this to us.[89]

But the most provocative were the following lines:

> Friends said here that some people were trying to topple this government. They have provoked me to say what I have not said so far—have not spoken [of] till now.
>
>   If they wish for the elections to be held not when due but to create a situation for mid-term elections—if Mohan Kumaramangalam or C. Subramaniam instigates it, oh mothers, elders, Kazhagam's cadres, are you going to permit it?
>
>   If such a situation were to be created, Tamil Nadu would meet the army itself [at] the next moment.

After this, MGR declared loudly, 'Regional autonomy . . .' and the audience responded, 'We will get it . . .' and then he said aloud, 'Tamil Nadu's [DMK] administration . . .' and the audience chimed 'We will protect it! Protect it!' And then MGR said, 'Under Kalaignar's leadership . . .' and the people shouted, 'We will follow . . .' After this impressive performance, MGR left the stage. The crowd slowly began to disperse. Kalaignar, who did not address the gathering that day, said later that he could not make his plenary speech because of his throat and that MGR had stayed with him for an hour after delivering his speech.[90]

Kalaignar interpreted MGR's spirited speech then thus:

> Isn't it the case that those who choose to betray, profess themselves as absolutely loyal? Didn't Judas, who betrayed Jesus Christ, act so even at the last minute?[91]

The artist that the party had helped nurture had grown too big for his shoes. Newspapers wrote about the incident. MGR himself wrote nonchalantly later, 'Do not consider that this issue about me is passé. Even now, some get upset like the poet [Kannadasan]. What can I do about that?'[92]

CRITIC CHANDRABABU FINALLY SPEAKS OUT

Around this time, Chandrababu began to write a series in the movie tabloid *Filmalaya* about his bitter experience with MGR in his abortive attempt at making *Maadi Veetu Ezhai*. Titled '*Oru Maadi Veetu Ezhain Kanneerkadhai*' (The Tearful Story of a Poor of a Rich Household), Chandrababu said he had finally decided to pour his heart out as his situation was becoming intolerable. Declaring that he was not 'makkal thilagam' or 'people's darling', alluding to MGR, he swore on Mother Mary that he was merely telling his story. Chandrababu painted a dastardly picture of MGR in this series, in many ways completely contrasting to his public image as a good, kind and thoughtful man. MGR came out as a mean, low, sadistic individual, who put himself before anything else.[93]

Chandrababu admitted that he was an imperfect man, but his imperfections did not affect others, whereas MGR's shortcomings would push the naive, such as himself, out on the streets. In reply, MGR simply said that it was a 'story' and that he could not be responding to those who deliberately accused him all the time, and he hoped that Christ would give Chandrababu guidance.[94]

FIRST PUBLIC CRITICISM OF THE DMK: 8 OCTOBER MEETINGS

Heeding his 'conscience', as he would claim later, on 8 October, in a public meeting at Tirukazhukundram and later at Royapettah, Madras, that evening, MGR attacked the DMK head-on. He asked that Kalaignar and other top leaders submit accounts for the election expenses, along with the party and their personal accounts.[95] Nedunchezhian records that MGR had received some complaints of discrimination in the disbursal of campaign funds among candidates in the 1971 elections and Kalaignar took the stand that MGR should not be asking him for accounts—which saddened the thespian.[96]

MGR's speech at Royapettah is noteworthy:

The feelings that welled up inside me when I spoke at Tirukazhukundram . . . what provoked me to speak [there] . . . I see the same situation here.

I have come after unveiling Anna's statue there and making an address. I have met Anna and come here. I am speaking with Anna's permission . . .

I said, 'MGR meant DMK and DMK meant MGR.' Immediately, one person asked, 'Are we all not DMK then?' . . . You too have the right [to speak like I did] . . . Because you don't have the courage, don't make me a weakling! . . .

All these are needless issues. When Mathi [K.A. Mathiazhagan] spoke, he said that I should, in addition to my film career, give more of my time than now for the cause of public life.

Some cannot stomach even this minimal involvement! If I were to be more involved, what might happen to all? Such pathetic people! . . .

Gradually realizing that Anna's principles alone would bring a renaissance in the country, I came into the Kazhagam. When I knew Anna, I had holy ash smeared on my forehead and was sitting on the dais for two days during the proceedings of the Self-respect Conference, where Ayya [EVR] presided.

I have not been afraid of anyone in giving up my principles. I don't have such a need.

During electioneering, I sought votes for the DMK, promising the implementation of certain policies.

Am I not entitled to seek the implementation of what I promised?

I said, give your vote to the Kazhagam; we will do such and such, there will be no corruption; it will be clean. Don't I have the right to wish, say that such things should be part of the Kazhagam?

They are afraid to say that MGR would leave the DMK. Someone is troubled by my question. My question is causing confusion within someone.

We say that ministers, assembly, Parliament members should show their accounts. We are submitting accounts.

But why should the DMK general council not ask [for] the details of the assets of the kin of those people?

If Ramachandran [MGR] has a bungalow, did it come after coming to power or before that? Should I not ask this? If my wife or my relatives have bungalows, properties, how did that happen? How did the district, sub-district, branch Kazhagam functionaries acquire these [assets]?

Ramachandran is acting; he earns; if you earn, account for it!

The Opposition does not have to ask this [such questions]. Let us ask ourselves. I am going to bring this as [a] resolution in the general council. The people are with me. If I don't get support for my resolution in the general council, I will take it to the entire state, turning my question into a resolution. I will meet the people.

District secretaries, branch and sub-district secretaries, those in office—if they have bought properties for their family, they should submit accounts. They should explain how these were acquired.

The general council could pass a resolution, form a committee and to it each one can show that his hand is clean and [thus show this] to the people.

Those who cannot prove that they had not erred: We would bring them before the public to throw them out [of the party]. All those who had harmed Anna's ideals should be brought before the public and [be] thrown out [of the party]. I will see you after the 15.[97]

Kalaignar, who was in Madurai then, listened to the speech on a police wireless set as it unfolded.[98]

As chief minister, MGR explained his actions later:

As the treasurer of the DMK in 1972, it was my duty to know the party accounts. Certain sums of money were being received by the party, and were being spent without proper accounting to the general council. We were not aware of how it came and where it went. This was the first issue. The second was that people like Kamaraj and others were claiming that a lot of the DMK people had gained wealth and they wanted to know how. This was also the general impression [among the public of the party]. If these allegations were made against the party, they should have been

examined by a committee . . . This was my request, and I made
this request to clear doubts in the minds of the people about the
DMK. I sent a message to the party [the previous day] saying
that on 10 October [1972], I would come to the office [at 4 p.m.]
and the accounts of the party should be shown to me. But by
the morning of 10 October, I received a notice saying that I had
been suspended from the party for alleged anti-party utterances.
So there is a big difference between leaving the party and being
thrown out. I was sacked.[99]

I think that it is wrong to believe that our assets will be ours till
the end! Jupiter Somu was the first one to make me hero. This studio
was once his. We would be afraid to even stand in his presence. Now,
I am a partner of this studio. If he, who is so much more experienced
and talented, has been rendered thus, how long can I be the owner
of this studio? I understand this. But some think that they have the
protection of the law and hoard assets and money. What cannot be
protected by us, how long can it be protected by law?

Besides, who gave us these riches? The people? It is because
they have given them to me, I give in return. I consider the
happiness flowing from fruitful help rendered to others greater
than any happiness from money saved beyond one's need.[100]

S. Aranganaygam, later MGR's education minister, said that the
next day when he took the morning papers to Kalaignar, who was in
Coimbatore, Kalaignar had wondered why Anbazhagan had said what
he did: He had used the Tamil adage 'like the thread from the stem of
the banana tree tying the floral garland also smells of flowers' to say they
too were honoured because of their association with MGR.[101] Kalaignar
was clearly prepared for the revolt. 'There was no sudden exigency for
someone who held a very important position within the Kazhagam not
to air his views in the party executive or general council, and to do
so against party discipline in a public meeting,' Kalaignar wrote later,
questioning MGR's public stance and timing.[102]

But the DMK administration's idealistic sheen had disappeared.
Many of its leaders, from bottom up, were feathering their own nests
and MGR, like everyone else, knew of this. It seems plausible that his
compulsions made him discover this when he did so. His choice of

venue, a public forum, clearly showed that he had chosen to embarrass Kalaignar and, more importantly, jump ship. He had cornered Kalaignar, his friend, associate and leader. He had publicly avenged Kalaignar for having asked him to quit films to join the Cabinet.

However, the two had been moving away from each other, even otherwise, for MGR, the kingmaker, acted like a regent. He wanted to be consulted on everything, while Kalaignar tried to free himself from MGR's hold and assert himself.

MGR kept a watch on Kalaignar about which he could do nothing. But he would repay MGR in kind when he freed M.R. Radha on 29 April 1971, a month earlier than scheduled, much against the actor's wishes. Kalaignar had acknowledged that this was a reason for MGR's anger with him.[103]

Further, Kalaignar's attempts to promote his eldest son, M.K. Muthu, greatly peeved MGR. Ironically, Kalaignar had earlier asked him to advise Muthu against a career in films. 'Is [Karunanidhi] now attempting to bring his son [in] as my competition?' a highly troubled MGR vented to those close to him. Muthu called MGR 'periyappa', or elder father, and was a serious MGR fan. Greatly affected by MGR, he moved his arms and body uncannily like his hero. He also chose a hairpiece that resembled MGR's hairdo in films. He played a dual role in his first film, Kalaignar's home production *Pillayo Pillai*. MGR spoke thus at the inaugural: 'I believe Muthu wishes to see my movies and emulate [me]. Each one possesses individuality, acting talent. One should follow that. Muthu should chart out his own acting path and I wish that he grows into a good actor.'[104] When M.K. Muthu later changed his tune and said his 'guru' was Sivaji Ganesan, MGR sarcastically noted: 'Generally, in Tamil Nadu, we say [like] daughter like mother. He is [like] son like father.'[105]

In the movie, Vaali's song eulogized Muthu as the fountain spring of Muthamizh (literature, music and drama, the three artistic expressions of Tamil language) and the descendant of the Cheras, Cholas and the Pandyas—the three Tamil dynasties. MGR took Vaali to task for this.[106] Further, thanks to the DMK's Madurai strongman Muthu, M.K. Muthu rode the streets of Madurai, much like MGR had done in the aftermath of his *Nadodi Mannan*.[107] Worse still, MGR's fan clubs were slowly becoming Muthu's fan clubs, thanks to official patronage. MGR's public anguish would lead the chief minister to openly call for the dissolution of Muthu's fan clubs.[108] Of MGR's fifty-four allegations leading up to the

Sarkaria Commission, one said that Kalaignar had misused his official position to promote his son. But MGR need not have feared. M.K. Muthu was no MGR.

MGR'S EXPULSION (14 OCTOBER 1972)

The leadership was aghast by MGR's speech. He had clearly thrown down the gauntlet. Kalaignar hurriedly summoned the executive council on 10 October 1972. He sent telegram invites to the twenty-six members.[*] Nanjil Manoharan, Era. Sezhian, Murasoli Maran and Rama Arangannal just wished for an explanation, but no disciplinary action against MGR.[109] Five of the signatories, T.K. Srinivasan, Madurai Muthu, K. Rajaram, P.U. Shanmugam and S. Sathyavani Muthu, would later cross over to MGR's breakaway outfit.[110]

Of the twenty-six members of the council, a majority argued for MGR's expulsion. Kalaignar said that he adopted a moderate position. He wished to inform the press that the president and general secretary would confer with MGR, only to learn that, on Nedunchezhian's advice, N.V. Natarajan had already handed over the following statement to the press:

> Of late, as party treasurer, MGR's repeated actions violate the Kazhagam's discipline and discredit the party. He is suspended from his primary membership and other positions, including his treasurer's responsibility, of the party. Appropriate action will soon be instituted against him.

Nedunchezhian coolly explained his actions: 'Yes, I asked him to give it [to the press]. I expected that you would suddenly turn "soft" and,

---

* T.K. Srinivasan, Madurai Muthu, E.R. Krishnan, K. Rajaram, P.U. Shanmugam, K.T.S. Mani, Neelanarayanan, S.A. Rajamanickam, M. Selvaraj, H.L. Murugesan, Thoppur Thiruvengadam, S.S. Thennarasu, Azhagianambi, M.S. Venkatachalam, Era. Rajan, Sadiq Pasha, S. Sathyavani Muthu, K. Anbazhagan, Anbil Dharmalingam, Mannai Narayanasamy, N.V. Natarajan, Farooq Marickar, A.V.P. Asaithambi, T.P. Azhagamuthu, Kanchi Kalyanasundaram and C.V.M. Annamalai.

therefore, asked that it be handed out immediately!' A majority of the executive members cheered at this. 'Those who transgress party discipline, whomsoever [it is], cannot be forgiven!' a visibly red-faced Nedunchezhian thundered.

'After a majority of the executive members and the general secretary had reached a decision, is it not my duty to acquiesce to it!' Kalaignar wrote. In defence of his action, Nedunchezhian recorded later that he had, in the resolution, only 'noted' that MGR be suspended from all his positions and an explanation be sought from him. He gave this 'note' to Kalaignar who signed it, indicating his agreement. When asked by N.V. Natarajan if this could be given to the pressmen, Nedunchezhian said yes. Kalaignar, according to him, misrepresented this singular 'yes' to depict him as the one behind MGR's expulsion. He said that following the 1971 elections, relations between MGR and Kalaignar were strained, and Kalaignar wanted MGR out, and MGR knew the truth.

In any case then, as the general secretary, Nedunchezhian sent a show cause notice to MGR as to why he should not be expelled from the party. MGR had ten days to respond. The party had greatly underestimated MGR and would pay for it dearly.[111]

FANS' REACTION

On 10 October, MGR was shooting for Netru Indru Naalai; he remained calm and collected when he heard the news. He invited the reporters to have lunch with him. They said they had already eaten. He insisted that they take a little payasam (sweet pudding) at least. Helping himself to some payasam, MGR said, 'Today is the happiest day of my life.' He went on, 'Those twenty-six members who threw me out do not constitute the Kazhagam.' He wrote down a release and handed it over to his media manager, RMV. The release said, 'Conspiracy shall befall justice, but justice shall ultimately prevail . . . I will certainly win. [I] Will tell the world the truth.'[112] Comedian Thengai Srinivasan described that evening in detail. He had never seen such a large crowd in his life, and MGR accepted the crowd's 'command' to float his own party.[113] Although Srinivasan said MGR had acquiesced to his fans, it appears that MGR could not make up his mind at that point in time. Later that evening, a beaming MGR told actor Jaishankar, who visited him to commiserate, that he 'felt the peace and happiness of a man cured of his stomach ache'.[114] MGR continued shooting the film from 10 p.m. until 1 a.m.

MGR's fans stopped buses and trucks and, in some places, even set them on fire. The damage to state buses alone amounted to 60 lakh rupees.[115] Shops had to pull down their shutters, movie shows were cancelled, DMK flag posts were pulled down, and the rioting and protests continued for some three weeks, despite strident police action, which was termed by one scholar as 'repression'.[116]

On 11 October, Kalaignar said that the Kazhagam had 15 lakh members and 18,000 branches, and asked if it was important to save the party or his friend of twenty-seven years. 'He has been suspended from the party for saying in public that there is corruption in the Kazhagam.'[117] That day EVR justified Kalaignar's stand.

As planned earlier, the executive council met on 12 October. Kalaignar agreed to Nanjil K. Manoharan's suggestion that MGR be given a chance to express regret; Kalaignar decided that he be given a day to do so. The executive council then supported the idea of giving MGR another opportunity.[118]

At 11 a.m. the following day, EVR told the chief minister, who had called on him to confer a state award, to avoid a split. Two hours earlier, MGR had met EVR at the latter's request.[119] The actor reiterated that some MLAs were corrupt, the party was getting a bad name and he, as the treasurer, was not aware of the party's financial dealings.[120] EVR was firm that MGR had erred in going public and told him that he should express regret. MGR remained non-committal.

Acting on EVR's advice, Kalaignar sent Manoharan and Maran to MGR. RMV also spoke to him. Listening to their exhortation, MGR almost relented. But just then, the telephone rang and, following the call, MGR fought back saying he would not express regret and that he had not committed any wrong. (RMV said it was not a note of regret but a draft agreement.) As the intermediaries reported the failure of their mission, the 13 October executive unanimously recommended the expulsion of MGR from the general council. That day, EVR told press persons that he had advised MGR in a 'firm' manner just that morning. The following day, the DMK's 14 October 1972 general council saw 277 of the 310 members who attended voting unanimously on the executive's recommendation to expel MGR.[121] It was also decided to hold meetings in 200 places to explain this action.[122]

That day, the chief minister gave the number of those arrested till then as 1625, for the protests and violence that had begun on 11 October following news of MGR's suspension.[123] Kalaignar explained the hasty action against MGR to pressmen: 'To avoid the discussion turning into a heated one, swift action on MGR was taken.' But now the discussion had moved to the streets and tea shops.

The next day, on 15 October, at a public meeting at the Marina, called to explain the general council's decisions, Nedunchezhian said:

> MGR, who until now had not suspected our accounts, does so now. In 1969, Kalaignar decreed that legislators, their spouses and children should table their accounts in the legislature. There is no such law in any other state... Yet, we have been placing [our] accounts [in the legislature]. But MGR submitted [his] accounts only [in] the first year. For the last two years, he has not submitted accounts; this, despite notices sent to him thirteen times.

In his plenary speech Kalaignar said:

> My good friend, then and now, and I would always call him as my good friend, revolutionary actor MGR has through his unexpected criticism caused anguish to lakhs of Kazhagam's cadres, pain to the 18,000 branch secretaries, hurt to the 135 circle secretaries, anxiety to the 14 district secretaries, and to the executive and the general council...
>
> If we were to present the accounts of the 18,000 branch secretaries, can you imagine how hard it would be? Is it humanly possible to scrutinize them all? Is it practical?
>
> MGR, of course, is well aware of this. Yet, he asked why? His motive was that he should exit or be expelled. He wished for one of the two.
>
> The evidence to this is that when the twenty-six executive members petitioned for action against him, our eyes grew moist and our voices trembled as we reached this decision. We were saddened by the decision. But MGR was happy when he learnt of it ... He had payasam at the news ...

MGR says that others entertained doubts and, therefore, he does too. This is like the Ramayana.

A washerman suspects [his wife] and therefore Ram sends Sita to the forest! Ram can do it! Should Ramachandran wish to send the Kazhagam to the forest [exile]?

Can MGR have such an intention? Being part and parcel of the Kazhagam, claiming that he was following Anna's path and interacting with us as a sibling [though not a natural one], couldn't he have spoken to us in private?

He spoke for a month [in public]! He criticized Adithan. Spoke ill of [Adithan's] *Dinathanthi* and *Malai Murasu* newspapers. He said whatever he wished. He made personal allegations . . . We stomached this for a month. We were forced into an intolerable situation.[124]

Kalaignar also said in his speech that Anna had given his heart to MGR along with his 'heart's fruit', but a beetle had gotten into the fruit, and, if retained, would also bore into the heart. Therefore, the fruit had to be thrown out. 'Please forgive me, Anna!' he said.

THE NEW FLAG

MGR's fans would never forgive Kalaignar. The more enthusiastic ones had designed a flag with a lotus on it and, in some places, also hoisted the new party's flag. Reports of the flagpoles being brought down and the flags torn made it to the press. Later, revealing the officially designed flag MGR confidently noted, 'No one will tear our flag any more.' The reason was clear—Anna's image was at the centre. On MGR's instructions, art director Angamuthu, later member of the Legislative Council, had brought twenty different photographs of Anna. MGR chose one of them, which was later carried on the flag as a line drawing by Angamuthu.[125]

Kalaignar, however, claimed that Kumaramangalam's people helped design the name and even the flag for the new party, and were behind MGR in the founding of the ADMK.[126] MGR explained the rationale of Anna's prominence later:

When I was thrown out in October 1972 from the Anna-founded Kazhagam, Anna's enemies would not have expected that in our

organization's name, flag, policies, work programmes, Anna
would be ubiquitous. I was subjected to harsh criticism because
of that. But, one can see clearly where later developments placed
these critiques and where it has left me.

What is the cause behind this wonder? Notwithstanding
what those who love me say, that it is my strength, smartness and
politics, I wish to tell them all openly that it is the victory of the
force of the god that guides me—the immortal Perarignar Anna.[127]

MGR was devoted to Anna, and constantly invoked his name in his
speeches and writings. He was not shy of giving pride of place to Anna.
When the ADMK youth wing was to be named after him, he pressed for
it to be named Anna Youth Wing and only conceded after it was made
clear to him that his name would draw the youth.[128]

ANNA DRAVIDA MUNNETRA KAZHAGAM (ADMK) LAUNCHED

MGR, Aranganayagam said, could not avoid the ultimate decision.[129]
He remembered the frenzy that gripped Tamil Nadu. Fans had created
blockades, allowing only vehicles willing to sport the slogan 'MGR
vazhga!', or 'Long live, MGR', written in chalk, to go through. 'Even
ministers' vehicles were not spared.'

On 16 October 1972, Ismail, a youth from Udumalaipettai, set
himself ablaze at the public square shouting, 'MGR vazhga!' The self-
immolation spurred supporters from across the state to send telegrams
to MGR to found his own party.[130] We are to understand from what
RMV said that MGR was indeed a 'reluctant politician' and, but for
political developments and the machinations in the DMK, he would
not have floated his own party.[131] It was one thing to be a superstar, a
demigod and the third in a party, but it was something else to found,
politick and lead a party. MGR was very aware of what it entailed.

The 10 October payasam episode in the aftermath of the suspension
might have been bravado, for the 14 October expulsion had hit MGR
hard, and he 'confined' himself to his Sathya Studios. From there, a 'dazed'
MGR sought advice. 'Nathigam' Balu and V.N. Swami were two reporters
who had been requested, via telephone, to come over. When they met
him, on 15 October, they found that MGR feared that his political career

had been ruined. Nonetheless, he seized on Swami's idea to invite his fans' representatives across the state to confer, and instructed RMV to convene such a meeting. The refrain of the 2000 or so representatives who descended on Sathya Studios was that MGR found his own outfit. Buoyed, MGR indicated that he would heed their advice.[132]

However, Arangannal is of the view that E.V.K. Sampath, M. Kalyanasundaram and a Mylapore journalist (possibly *Ananda Vikatan's* S.V.S. Manian, popularly called '*Idhayam Pesugiradhu*' Manian) had played a role in his decision.[133] MGR himself would say in August 1977:

> If Perarignar Anna had been alive, the 10 October 1972 incident would not have happened in my life. A movement known as ADMK would have not been founded. The compulsion for me to become chief minister would not have arisen.[134]

On 18 October, MGR formally announced the launch of his new party, Anna Dravida Munnetra Kazhagam. Earlier, Anakaputhur Ramalingam from his fans association had told him, 'Leader, that is Karunanidhi's DMK. We are Anna's DMK.'[135] However, zealous supporters had turned DMK local units into ADMK units a day earlier. Consequently 17 October is marked as the party's foundation day.[136]

On 19 October, MGR told newsmen that his ADMK was the real DMK and noted that his party had been founded with 20,000 units—the fans associations had simply become party organs.*

Kalaignar commented:

> What he wished, what he had planned has happened . . . MGR wished to settle accounts with the DMK, not seek the accounts. Those who are joining MGR's party are not DMK people; they will move on to other parties.[137]

---

* The new party's workers would face severe hardships at the hands of a DMK administration bent on using force to nip the growing threat in the bud. The ADMK cadre would be the subject of organized violence and brutality at the hands of DMK men and even the police, not to mention the cases foisted on them and the prosecution they faced. These memories were fresh and deep, and could not be healed so easily. MGR would allude to this as a reason for changing his mind on the merger of the two parties later.

More than three decades later, in July 2015, to the question 'Did Indira
Gandhi use MGR to weaken the DMK?' Kalaignar said:

> The poisonous seed that some had planted in Indira's mind kept
> growing. The truth, therefore, is that she used whatever weapons
> fell into her hands to isolate, marginalize and debilitate the DMK.
> MGR became one of those instruments for Delhi. Till today, there
> is no clear answer as to whether MGR separated [from the party]
> on his own or he was encouraged and enthused to cause the split?[138]

On 20 October, MGR, the general secretary, named K.A. Krishnaswamy
(KAK) as the organizing secretary and his *Thennagam* as the party
mouthpiece.* On 29 October, in a public meeting, KAK said: '"Revolutionary
Actor" is a title given by the traitors. No need for it any more. Let us give a
new title—"Revolutionary Leader".'[139] The travesty of the idea of using the
word 'revolution' as an adjective was now complete.

In his first meeting as the 'Revolutionary Leader', MGR said:

> Chief Minister Kalaignar and a few aligned to him are ridiculing
> the ADMK, that it is a graft Kazhagam and [a] party of a few. This
> is neither a graft Kazhagam nor a party run by four people. The
> 5 lakh [people] who have assembled here and the huge support that
> has been exhibited [for it] throughout the state will make it clear
> that the Kazhagam has the goodwill of the Tamils and it espouses
> the aspirations of the 4 crore Tamils. The DMK's authoritarian
> leadership has patted itself [on its back] that it has thrown out the
> one who raised questions: [insisting that there be] no wrongs, no
> room for people to suspect, [and all] accounts be shown.
>
> Without me asking for it, the people's movement has
> organized itself against the DMK's dictatorship. Later, heeding
> my wishes, they are supporting the ADMK in a major way. My

---

* Under the by-laws the general secretary was to be elected directly by the
  grass-roots members and not by the general council. MGR was upset
  that the DMK general council, made up of a few hundreds, had been
  able to throw him out (Interview with P.H. Pandian, 27 August 2016,
  Madras). He held the post till the autumn of 1978, when he handed it
  over to Nedunchezhian on his first overseas tour as chief minister.

sympathies, thanks and tears with all those workers who have sacrificed their lives, engaged in this good work and, therefore, have been subjected to the cruelty of the rowdies and the administration's authoritarianism.

We will remove corruption and make it [the administration] clean without giving any room for people's suspicions. I had asked that [they] let us show the accounts to the people. I insisted [that] the DMK administration and the Kazhagam execute the people's wishes. Just because they support this and seek justice, people, students, children and women are all being subjected to unrestricted cruelty—beatings and firing. I ask Chief Minister Kalaignar and his partymen not to take their revenge against people; instead, to take revenge against this M.G. Ramachandran.

Is the chief minister ready to come forward and meet with the people and accept their judgement? He and I can resign, and can contest elections. Is he ready for the judgement of the electorate in Tamil Nadu?

Not just in one constituency. Let's ask for the people's vote in the whole of Tamil Nadu. Let the chief minister use his position, authority, money power and the rest and tour the state, and campaign that there is no need for an inquiry against corruption, and seek votes in support of it. I will not go anywhere to campaign. [Let us see] if people show [their] support and make me, who is asking for an inquiry commission, victorious. Let us see what the people's judgement is. Is Kalaignar ready to contest in the elections heeding the people's judgement? Let him analyse . . . I am ready; I need his response.

We have to immediately stop this authoritarianism [and] lawlessness that prevails in Tamil Nadu, where there is no more freedom of opinion and where students and women are being beaten up. We have to make room for an inquiry against corruption. Even if Kalaignar does not do so, Prime Minister Indira Gandhi should intervene and render justice to the people of Tamil Nadu, uphold law and order, establish peace and secure the nation's integrity.[140]

MGR welcomed support from all quarters for his demand. But support also came from the most unexpected quarters and with conditions.

On 21 October, the Communist Party of India (Marxist) (CPM) organ *Theekadhir* prophesied that seeking the cooperation of reactionary forces, such as the two Congress parties and the Swatantra Party, would result in MGR's 'political hara-kiri'.[141] MGR shot back: 'No party has any right whatsoever to dictate to any other party as to whom one should or should not befriend.'[142] But the Communist Party of India's (CPI) support came without any conditions.

On 22 October, Dindigul MP Rajangam, who had crossed over to the ADMK, died. MGR announced that the ADMK would contest the seat. On 5 November, speaking in Coimbatore, EVR alleged that Malayalis were dominant in Tamil Nadu's factories and wondered how Tamils would be protected if the DMK government were to fall because of MGR's 'betrayal' and the Centre's 'conspiracy'.[143]

On 25 October, the CPI resolution said, 'If Karunanidhi's government has lost the people's support, then it should resign.' At this juncture, CPI leader M. Kalyanasundaram cut short his visit to the Soviet Union to be beside MGR. In the beginning, as MGR feared for his life, Kalyanasundaram and the thespian would routinely exchange cars or travel in decoy cars.[144] Also, E.V.K. Sampath, by then with the Congress (O), went on a voluntary mission, for old times' sake, to Kalaignar to convey that MGR was very aware of the anger he had provoked in the average DMK worker because of his mission to destroy the very party that had built him, and was very concerned about the unpredictability of their actions against him. After a moment's pause, Kalaignar told Sampath: 'Please tell MGR that from this moment his safety is my concern.' MGR embraced Sampath when he broke the news to him. The three former DMK men and once friends had risen above their differences graciously.[145]

On 26 October, MGR said that he had told the DMK administration that its clampdown on the Simpson's factories, on farmers and power workers, and on the teachers' agitations had resulted in people's dissatisfaction and that it should look into the fairness of the demands, but the government did not accept his advice.[146] This was the first time that MGR revealed that he had offered such advice.

Unlike the CPI which had turned itself into a satellite of MGR, the CPM continued to be a thorn in MGR's flesh. On 28 October, CPM leader P. Ramamurti said that it appeared that the new party had no policy and asked that MGR announce its programme.

MGR responded:

I would like to tell leader P. Ramamurti that our party's programme is simply that of Perarignar Anna. Our party will strive to establish the egalitarian society that Perarignar Anna wished [to establish]. Our party will work constructively for the welfare of the working class, farmers and the middle class. Our party will fight against social evils. Our party will oppose violence, corruption, impropriety and caste–religious differences.[147]

CHARGES AGAINST THE DMK ADMINISTRATION

The CPI took MGR only at face value. On 31 October, MGR said that acting on M. Kalyanasundaram's advice he would present charges against the DMK administration to the governor. Fifty-four allegations of corruption were made against the DMK government, the DMK's district office-bearers and officials for 'abetting the crime of corruption by ministers'. Kalyanasundaram would later reveal that a team headed by M. Bhaktavatsalam, former chief minister, had put together the litany of charges.[148] Kalaignar wrote that Kumaramangalam helped compile the documentation to use as a basis for the 'unsubstantiated charges' and MGR was used as a 'vehicle', because of which he repeatedly disclaimed direct knowledge of the charges.[149]

The following day Kalaignar said:

Even if our government were toppled, the government to follow would be that of Kamarajar's. Kamarajar's government is that of a Tamil. We would wish for the rule by a Tamil and not that of enemies of Tamils ever in Tamil Nadu.[150]

Within twenty days of his expulsion, MGR had made Kalaignar accept Kamaraj as being Tamil enough to take over from the DMK. Until then, the party had consistently opposed Kamaraj on the grounds of not being sufficiently Tamil.

It was a sad day for the Dravidian movement. A man who was Malayali by birth but was, for all practical purposes, a Tamilian, was suddenly seen as non-Tamil and, worse still, anti-Tamil. MGR appeared cool about the insinuation, at least in the open. 'My wish is for Tamil rule in Tamil Nadu. Whom has Karunanidhi referred to as [the] enemies of Tamils? Only he can explain,' MGR said. He also smartly pointed out that the 'graft Congress' that Kalaignar had earlier referred to was actually the DMK. Had it not wished for Kamaraj's rule?[151]

Only six MLAs, including S.M. Durairaj and K. Kalimuthu, would leave the DMK to join MGR in the immediate aftermath of the split. By 1 November, in all, nine legislators and two parliamentarians, KAK and S.D. Somasundaram (SDS), had crossed over to the new outfit. But there was no exodus. Six months later, in April 1973, the ADMK had the support in total of only eleven MLAs. On 31 January 1976, when the DMK administration was dismissed, the ADMK's strength still was just sixteen as opposed to the DMK's 167 MLAs.[152]

K. Kalimuthu compared his dilemma to that of children who loved both quarrelling parents and were confused. He says he had a fever for a week because of the differences between Kalaignar and MGR, and it was finally on 29 October that he came to his 'mother' MGR, despite his 'devotion' and 'attachment' to Kalaignar.[153] But others were not 'confused'. They evaluated MGR as a passing cloud. They were clearly wrong.

On 4 November, MGR and M. Kalyanasundaram handed over the charges to Governor K.K. Shah, who clarified that he was constitutionally obliged to consult the chief minister before forwarding them to the President. On this, the two retracted their petition. MGR then boarded a flight to Delhi to meet the President. M. Kalyanasundaram, who was on the same flight, said it was a 'coincidence'. MGR handed his list of charges, running to thirty-two pages, to President V.V. Giri on 6 November in Delhi. (Kalyanasundaram presented his forty-page petition separately.) MGR opined in Delhi that if an inquiry commission were to be set up, then 'it would only be fair that the DMK ministry quits immediately. Any cultured government would do that.'[154]

The following day, a reporter wondered if it was proper to make KAK the organizing secretary of the party when his older brother, Speaker K.A. Mathiazhagan, had to quit the Cabinet as he was unable to account for the purchase of a house under both their names. MGR stoically maintained that the DMK leaders who had joined the ADMK were clean. He said the party was aware of their assets and liabilities at the time of entry and that a year later, he would review their finances.[155]

Kalaignar rightly termed MGR's demand to quit 'meaningless', pointing out that only two months earlier, in Madurai, MGR had said that if the Centre were to topple the DMK government, it would be improper. 'What is the need [to resign] now?' he asked.[156]

On 10 November, Speaker Mathiazhagan was seen witnessing the ADMK, CPI joint procession against the DMK government in Madras. The CPM organ termed the procession as 'mammoth', and said it took half an hour to cross a place. The marchers raised slogans such as 'Ministry which has lost people's support—resign!' Later, meeting newsmen, MGR clarified his demand: 'I did not say that the Tamil Nadu Legislative Assembly should be dissolved or that this DMK ministry should not be in office. But Karunanidhi must be removed from office.' By singling out Kalaignar, MGR intended to set the cat among the pigeons, for the organization and the elected officials were still with Kalaignar, who managed to keep his flock together till the very end.[157]

But MGR also received support from very respectable quarters.* Rajaji said that Kalaignar Karunanidhi and his men had surpassed Duryodhana and his brothers in defiling Tamil Nadu, and, continuing his hyperbole, said: 'At this juncture, just as Sri Krishna came forward to lend a helping hand to the Pandavas, MGR has come forward to assist those who fight the demonical rule of Karunanidhi.'[158] MGR promptly met Rajaji on 11 November, and he told MGR that he should have done this ten years earlier.[159] EVR wrote later that Rajaji's 'blabber' was akin to the words of 'a mad man who was also given some toddy'.[160] Rajaji's *Swarajya* advocated the imposition of President's Rule in the state.[161] EVR was not the only one who did not like Rajaji's stance. Kamaraj, too, was not happy with it and wanted Rajaji to stop. Only days earlier, on 8 November, at Thiruvathipuram, in Vellore district, Kamaraj had famously said that the two Kazhagams were barks soaked in the same pond.[162] It did not matter, for the same day MGR confidently claimed that 999 out of 1000 in Tamil Nadu were behind him.[163] And Rajaji's

---

* But it was not all support. The separation from the DMK would bring difficulties for his film career. Many feared antagonizing the DMK administration, and even an ardent producer like Thevar stopped making films with MGR and dissociated himself from him. Cinema hall owners were reluctant to screen his films. MGR understood their compulsions and did not hold it against them. Thus when Thevar called on him to congratulate him on his becoming chief minister, MGR was all grace. Interview with Arundhas, 26 May 2016, Madras.

query to Hande 'Were we able to unseat Karunanidhi?' when he brought Kamaraj's démarche to him showed that MGR's claim was not a tall one.[164]

TWO SPEAKERS: THE TAMIL NADU ASSEMBLY DISGRACED

Against this backdrop, the Assembly convened on 13 November. The question hour was to follow the message of condolences and the Speaker's announcement. Soon, MGR rose to say, 'Today's government has lost the confidence of its own party, as well as the confidence of the people. In this situation, is it within the rules and code of conduct that this ministry continues?' Essentially, MGR had tabled a no-confidence motion.

Kalaignar said that he silently watched the painful scenario of the 'calf attacking its keeper'. After a little while, MGR once again wondered if the ministry should continue. Speaker Mathiazhagan then commented that 'an extraordinary issue' has been raised. 'Thus, MGR is asking you if you are willing to face the people today. Does the chief minister wish to respond to that?' he helpfully explained. Amazingly, the Speaker had also recommended that Kalaignar face the people. He then suddenly adjourned the House until 5 December, thus setting the stage for one of the most shameful incidents in the House's history that would take place in the next few days.

MGR now called for a statewide shutdown on 15 November, which was partially successful. On 26 November, MGR's supporters visited the houses of the 166 DMK MLAs to petition that they resign or work to convene the Assembly in order to bring down the current ministry. If the MLA was not at home, the petition was stuck on the door.[165] On 28 November, MGR told the Statesman that the DMK had tried to finish him politically and professionally, necessitating the formation of the ADMK.[166] On 30 November, EVR called for a ban on the ADMK.[167]

On 2 December, the Assembly had to take up two no-confidence motions: One signed by 185 members against the Speaker, and the other by MGR against the government. Kalaignar said the Speaker would have taken up MGR's motion first, called for a voice vote, announced it had been carried out and then adjourned the House. He said that the Speaker's decision could not be challenged legally. Thus, according to him, the House and the administration's terms would have been brought to an end three years before they were due.

On that fateful day, the House began at 11 a.m. Following the question hour, Nedunchezhian pointed out that the Speaker should stand down when the motion on him was debated and proposed that the Deputy Speaker, P. Srinivasan, chair the House. Speaker Mathiazhagan took up the motion against the government and invited MGR to speak. MGR then went on to speak for two hours. The fact that his mic had been switched off did not deter him.

Kalaignar said since the Speaker did not leave his chair, another chair was temporarily placed in the middle of the House, with a mic. A DMK legislator took the bell on the Speaker's table and placed it before the Deputy Speaker. Thus, the Tamil Nadu Legislative Assembly saw the ugly spectacle of two Speakers conducting business at the same time. The MGR group's speeches went unrecorded.

The Deputy Speaker declared that the motion against the Speaker had been carried.[168] Kalaignar justified this as a pre-emptive move to stave off the constitutional coup the Speaker had planned. At 2 p.m., Mathiazhagan said that the House was adjourned and he left. Along with him, the ADMK, Congress (O), Congress (R), CPI and Swatantra members left. As he walked out, MGR famously said that democracy had died and that the legislature is dead, and he vowed to return only as a victor.[169]

P. Srinivasan then conducted the House for another hour and then adjourned it. On 4 December, Kalaignar moved a confidence vote, only the second time in the annals of the Tamil Nadu Legislative Assembly since 1952.[170] On 11 December, the ministry won the confidence vote. Kalaignar used that occasion to provide answers to MGR's charges to the President.[171] The irony is that in two years, on 18 December 1974, unable to get along with MGR, Mathiazhagan would return to the DMK and be accepted. S. Ramachandran said that Mathiazhagan had joined MGR not because of any 'loyalty or principle, but to seek revenge against Kalaignar. Mathi and others thought they could sway MGR. When they saw he was his own man they left.'[172]

For Kamaraj, the split was 'a stunt or drama'. He rightly saw that MGR contained in him the portents of an alternative to the DMK eclipsing his Congress (O). He lambasted MGR for keeping company with the corrupt DMK all this while, and his sudden discovery and crusade against its rot. In his packed meetings, Kamaraj was scathing in his criticism of MGR, questioning his credibility when it came to blaming others.[173]

On 14 December, Kalaignar came up with a response to the charges, the response running to 246 pages, and tabled it on the floor of the Assembly. Denying the allegations in toto, he described the charges as 'extremely frivolous, vexatious and false'. He noted that the 'state Cabinet is not accountable to the Union government' and that the Cabinet cannot be subject to a commission of inquiry. The ADMK and CPI would later present a 200-page rejoinder to Kalaignar's response.[174]

KEEPING UP THE HEAT

In just two months, MGR had shaken up the DMK and had clearly made heads turn. On 6 January 1973, Indira Gandhi visited Madurai for an official event. MGR and the CPI leaders decided to give their reply to Kalaignar's response to her. MGR chose to travel by train. The train was mobbed by his fans throughout, and it reached its destination five hours later, delaying all other Madurai-bound trains. 'Throughout the way, the welcome was so unprecedented it felt like I would swoon,' MGR said. He could not meet Mrs Gandhi that day. He would not have minded that at all. The spontaneous reaction of his fans and supporters was heady.[175]

That evening, addressing a meeting at Madurai, where only six months earlier he had vowed to follow Kalaignar's leadership, MGR lashed out at the DMK regime for forty-five minutes, seeking an inquest into the Kalaignar government's corruption and abuse of authority. Below is a piece from this speech:

I didn't leave the Kazhagam on my own. I was thrown out. What is the idea of showing me black flags instead of showing them to ministers who have not kept their promises?

'Vox populi, vox god,' said Anna. Similarly, people are suspecting you as corrupt. Hold an inquiry and prove that is not the case. I said only then would people's doubts go. Is it wrong?

The DMK folks say it is wrong. I was expelled because I said this. If I had given a promise and failed to keep it, if I had taken bribes I could be shown black flags. Did I take bribes or did the ministers?

I can also be interrogated. I am ready. Are you ready? Am I going to become the chief minister after the inquiry commission is set up and it begins its inquiry? Am I saying this for that? I am saying this so that the country does not become decadent . . .

Like those of the Opposition who underwent much torture under the administrations of Kamaraj and Bhaktavatsalam, today in the administration under Kalaignar, those who came to power after Anna's demise are being subjected to torture. Especially now the ADMK workers are being targeted and beaten up.

Many false cases are being foisted. Many have succumbed and died. Some police people are functioning without any conscience. They [the workers] asked for my permission to respond, saying that we are ninety ADMK workers in a 100 [people]. I said please be patient. I am telling them that the ministers will redeem them[selves]. The administration will be orderly.

Ministers only draw a salary [of] 500 rupees. But they have bungalows, land and assets. If they had this before 1967, people would not raise questions. These have happened after 1967. Not just ministers, but also the district [secretaries]. Therefore, I asked them to account for these; instead, they asked me to show my accounts.

Isn't it because [of the fact] that I showed my accounts that the income-tax authorities have sent me notices assessing my taxes? If I hadn't shown the accounts, would they be sending me notices? Alas, those who don't understand even this happen to be ministers. Some say that fearing income tax [problems], I founded the ADMK. I used to pay 2 lakh [rupees] as tax before. Now I have to pay 2.5 lakh [rupees]. Is paying 2 lakh [rupees] a problem? Is paying 2.5 lakh [rupees] a problem?

Some say that I am not marketable any more in the film world and therefore, I founded a party. Producers have issued a notice because I haven't been shooting for three months, saying they have been suffering losses. If this is the situation, have I founded this party because I don't have film opportunities? . . .

Set up an inquiry commission. If there is an inquiry commission and it investigates [the matter], are they going to sentence Karunanidhi to death by hanging? Why is Karunanidhi afraid? The Indian government should set up an inquiry commission soon. If they don't, then the situation will be created where the Tamils will suspect the Government of India and the Indira Gandhi government.

We have sent Indira Gandhi some photocopies with proof, with Karunanidhi's signature, that relate to the corruption charges. Only the Central intelligence police can understand this.

It's only after the inquiry commission conducts an inquiry will we know how many crores belonging to Tamil Nadu is in the homes of ministers.

I am willing to accept any punishment if it is proved that my charges are false. But why do you get scared at the mention of an inquiry commission? If you don't have skeletons in your cupboard, why should you worry? They accuse me, too, just because I accuse them!

I am not someone who is afraid of all these fear-inducing tactics.

You cannot destroy the ADMK like this. There are 21 lakh members in the ADMK.[176]

Again, this time around, he singled out Kalaignar, saying the ministers would redeem themselves. If the others were to rule as per Anna's ideals, the ADMK would support them from the outside, and if they were to contest in elections and come to power, the ADMK would support them. 'We don't want power,' he clarified. He admitted that Kalaignar had done the most for Tamil Nadu as compared to the other chief ministers—but then he was also the 'most corrupt' in comparison.[177] It was a clever ploy to isolate Kalaignar, but it was not working.

Instead, Kalaignar's administration slapped nine defamation cases against MGR. After completing the court formalities for the first case, MGR asked P.H. Pandian if his presence would be required for each of the cases. If the administration tried to pin him down to the courts, it did not work. Pandian obtained a stay after arguing that 'reputation could not be lost in instalments' and the eight other cases were thus redundant.[178]

But MGR's popular support greatly irked Kamaraj and his men more than the others, for MGR had come from behind unexpectedly, unlike in his movies where he fought a straight fight. Sivaji Ganesan was of the view that MGR should have gone to see Kamaraj.[179] On 17 January, his birthday, MGR responded sharply:

Rajaji and Anna had said that corruption and irregularities were there in Kamarajar's rule, the same Kamarajar's administration that we opposed, the same Kamarajar administration under which, when I was campaigning, I was shot. They formed a government owing to this . . . Kamarajar was the one who instigated the caste problem. He shot down only Thevars in Mudukulathur . . . Many of those who come to ADMK now are from the Indicate [Congress {O}]. It is because of this anger that Kamarajar and others oppose the ADMK.[180]

Only seven years earlier he had called him 'leader'. It was the heyday of Kamaraj then. If Kamaraj's stock had fallen, MGR's had since catapulted to new heights. In 1973, MGR was at the pinnacle of his fame. He had made a chief minister and was in the process of unmaking him. Why would he visit Kamaraj? MGR's emergence had snuffed out the dreams of the Congress (O) as an alternative to the DMK. And the dreams of a nationalist force to alternate with the Dravidian movement in the state. Kamaraj's diatribe and his angst that they did all the work and others were harvesting the crop only showed that time had passed by the aged leader. How could MGR align with someone who equated his party to championing cleanliness in public life to the DMK?

Probity had become an important issue, thanks to MGR. On 12 February Kalaignar introduced the bill 'Public Men's Conduct Enquiry Act'. The bill provided for up to seven years jail time if the person charged was found guilty. Any spurious complainant would be awarded three years in jail. The bill brought all, from the chief minister to members of the corporation council, former and present, under its purview. MGR understood that his party couldn't support the bill. All his arguments and charges would then fall flat. He knew Kalaignar was trying to checkmate him. He, therefore, described it as a 'black bill' and a smokescreen for corruption, even as the Jan Sangh's L.K. Advani,

The Hindu and the *Swarajya* lauded it. The bill was passed as law on 5 April. The ADMK voted against it.[181] On coming to power, the ADMK retracted it saying no one had come forward to use it.[182]

RETURNING THE BHARAT AWARD

On 21 March, MGR wrote to the minister of state for information and broadcasting, I.K. Gujral, returning the Bharat Award following Nedunchezhian's embarrassing claim in *Kumudam* that it was originally intended for Sivaji Ganesan and that Kalaignar had vigorously intervened to favour MGR. Nedunchezhian had hit below the belt.

MGR now turned the tables against the DMK. A reader had written to the weekly wondering how a chief minister could interfere thus and how a minister could speak so proudly of it. 'Isn't it strange?' the reader asked.

MGR said he had the credentials but could only accept an award whose selection was fair. He said that he was being heavily criticized because of his crusade for a clean administration and could not even imagine that the honour was given to him through improper means. Denying any knowledge of these events, he said he wanted to step away from the controversy in which the chief minister had played a major role.[183]

THE WOOING GAME

But the chief minister's strength remained unassailable as rank and file continued to stand by him. MGR left no stone unturned to exploit any dissatisfaction in the DMK. K. Manoharan, then DMK MP, wrote vividly about how MGR wooed him. It was 1972. One day, the phone rang in Delhi. MGR was on the other line and tried to persuade him, saying, 'I am asking you with affection—as an elder brother. You must be with me.' They agreed to meet on his return from Delhi, but Manoharan kept his visit quiet, in order to avoid MGR. The actor-politician had called him four–five times in between. Once he was back in Madras, MGR called that evening to see if they could meet. Although Manoharan did not oblige, the call caused much confusion as he was going through a rough time in the DMK then.

When they finally met, MGR, taking both his hands into his, insisted, 'Please join today itself.' MGR's embrace melted Manoharan's 'forceful rejections'. Instantly, pen and paper were placed before him, and he wrote and signed that he was joining the ADMK. MGR took the letter, felt it fondly and, keeping it in his pocket, told Manoharan, 'I will treasure this.'

When he came home, Manoharan's family wondered about his sudden decision. It was 'flash news' on the radio. Manoharan was delighted with the alacrity with which MGR had taken him into his fold. MGR's armoury was full of his charms.

MGR would call him at 6 a.m. Manoharan would still be asleep. Sometimes from his speech, MGR would figure out that Manoharan was not well. Manoharan's dismissals would be waved away with the line, 'Coming to your place is my right.' At 8 a.m. sharp, MGR would be at his residence. 'MGR genuinely had affection for me,' wrote Manoharan.[184]

The wooing game with relation to Swatantra Party leader and physician Dr Hande was different. Hande reminisced:

Kalaignar is a human being. He allowed me to criticize his administration as much as I wished [to]. He would then respond to my criticisms. In the event, I became a hero and caught MGR's attention.

One day, MGR called to say that he 'had the masses but not the intellectuals'. 'Rajaji is no more. Why don't you be with me?' he insisted. In June 1973, Hande joined MGR.[185]

MGR, too, appears to have been wooed by the Congress (I). Gundu Rao, then a Congress (I) legislator in Karnataka and later chief minister, would meet MGR to entice him to join the Congress (I). MGR apparently said that he was ready if Indira Gandhi would institute an inquiry against Kalaignar.[186] However, it never happened. As much as he was overawed by the Centre, MGR could not have been a vassal.

Despite these personal efforts undertaken behind the scenes and the obvious mass churning in MGR's favour, Kalaignar, elder leaders and his legislators believed that it was a passing phase and that the glamour of films would soon lose its sheen. Even seasoned politicians make misjudgements. Kamaraj did in the case of the DMK, and Kalaignar did in the case of MGR. Kalaignar underestimated MGR's popularity; he saw him as a mere dewdrop that would quickly be dried up by the DMK sun. He could not have been more wrong.

DINDIGUL BY-ELECTION—20 MAY 1973

The fledgling ADMK would create history with the 20 May 1973 Dindigul by-election, and would make India pause and look at MGR. The actor-politician knew the stakes involved in the maiden election and dealt his cards shrewdly. He said: 'It is not possible to negotiate with Kamaraj. He says things like that is a ghost, this is a spirit. Therefore, there is no basis for talks with him.' The CPM is laying down conditions before we can talk. It insists we declare that we will have no ties with the Congress (I). How can we talk to such people who have pre-conditions before talks? We are the true DMK. That is why we are contesting.'[187] However, on 24 October, as the CPM's N. Sankaraiah filed his nomination, MGR asked to see CPM leader P. Ramamurti and met him the following day. Later, he said that 'those who act against basic livelihood policies, be it the state government or the Centre . . . the ADMK would fight them to achieve its ideals'. The statement was still gnomic and MGResque. But three days later, the CPM said it would support MGR. Seeing the CPM's active support for the ADMK, Kalaignar would say 'my first job is to destroy the Marxist party'.[188]

Ulagam Sutrum Vaaliban would do its bit for the ADMK's success. In the story, MGR would take villain Nambiar's blows slowly and draw him out of a monk's house to tell him, 'I have seen your power. Don't you have to see my strength? Give me a chance.' At this, the entire cinema hall would go berserk. Fans simply transposed the situation to Dindigul.[189] The movie became the biggest box office hit of the '70s and ran for thirty-one

---

* Kamaraj would have never allied with MGR. In January 1973, MGR said he did not understand Kamaraj's opposition to him. By mid-April however, MGR was losing his patience with the Congress leader. When told that Kamaraj was calling him a 'mountebank', an upset MGR said that Kamaraj had called NSK a 'buffoon' on the latter's speeches on the Soviet Union's greatness, following his visit there. Yet, MGR said, a few years later, Kamaraj would repeat what NSK had said after his own visit to the Soviet Union. Kirubakaran, S, (ed.), *M.G.R. Paetigal*, Chennai: Vikatan Pirasuram, 2009, pp. 125–6; 133–4.

weeks. There wasn't a single poster advertising its release; this was for two reasons—one, to keep its release a secret from the DMK administration and the second, because the levies on it were trebled by the Madras Corporation. The film was released on 11 May and, nine days later, Dindigul went to polls. Madurai Muthu had said he would wear a sari if the movie was released as scheduled. MGR fans promptly sent him saris.[190]

Poet Pulamaipithan's song '*Namathu vetriyai naalai sarithiram sollum / Ippadai thorkin eppadai vellum* ('History will speak of our victories / If this army fails, which can win)?' in the movie was recorded and heralded the ADMK's victory and its arrival on the Tamil political landscape. Tamil savants believe that a poet's words usually come true.[191]

MGR had begun his campaign on 2 May. He spoke of the ADMK as a 'six-month-old baby' and that the voters should take the baby on their laps and honour it. Pointing to the support from the communists, he asked: 'Are these *sundakkai* parties? District parties? State parties?' He said the national parties supported the ADMK not because of him but because of its policies.[192] The next day, as he left for Madras, a local ADMK official was hacked to death in Vathalagundu. Speaking at the town later, P. Ramamurti condemned the DMK's 'rowdyism'.[193] MGR returned from his film shoot to pick up the campaign from 10 to 18 May. He travelled to the remotest corners of the constituency. Sivaji Ganesan would do the same. Kalaignar campaigned from 12 to 18 May. Six ministers, including Navalar Nedunchezhian, K. Rajaram, S. Madhavan and Anbil Dharmalingam, had camped in the constituency. Kamaraj campaigned from 5 to 10 May. The previous month, he had addressed several meetings in the constituency.

. ADMK's K. Mayathevar, fighting on the epochal twin leaves symbol,* secured 2,60,930 of a total 5,05,253 votes or nearly 52 per cent of the votes polled.[194] (His win was larger than that of his DMK

---

* Mayathevar recalled that he had chosen the twin leaves of the sixteen election symbols. When MGR wondered about the reason behind his decision he said prophetically in retrospect that it would be an easy symbol to take to the voters. http://tamil.thehindu.com/tamilnadu/ கட்சியையும்-ஆட்சியையும்-தன்வசம்-வைத்திராக்கும்-சசிகலா-தரப்பாக்கடே-இரட்டை-இலை-சின்னம்-இரட்டை-இலையை-அடையாளம்-காட்டிய-திண்டுக்கல்-மாயத்தேவர்-கருத்து/article9595048.ece?homepage=true&ref=relatedNews.

predecessor in 1971, when the DMK had contested along with the Congress (I), aided by an 'Indira wave'.) Kamaraj's candidate, V.C. Sithan, won 1,19,032 votes and took the second place. The DMK finished third, polling 93,496 votes. Women had overwhelmingly voted for MGR. The echoes of Dindigul were felt when, on 1 September 1974, Kalaignar reintroduced prohibition in two stages.[195]

Kalaignar attributed the ADMK's success to 'film glamour' that was merely localized, not a reflection of the entire state. On 22 May *Viduthalai* said that the Dindigul result was 'unexpected and the reason for it [was] difficult to comprehend'.[196] On 25 May, MGR issued a lengthy statement that demolished the claim that he was not a Tamil, and that it was cine glamour that had dazzled the voters and won him the election.[197]

Kalaignar recorded Dindigul as a 'great defeat in the DMK's history' and a speed breaker for all the future victories.[198] The mood in the DMK camp was sullen. *Theekadhir* published this trivia: 'Yesterday (21 May 1973) when the votes were being counted, DMK MP Murasoli Maran came out. A newsman had reportedly asked him about the trends. He had reportedly responded irritably, "In the next elections Jayalalithaa will win."'[199] Little could Maran have known then that his words would come true in less than two decades in 1991.

In the 10 June felicitation meeting at the Marina, in Madras, MGR said, 'People concluded that the Congress (I)'s slogan "remove poverty" was an empty one. All of us wish the unity that had happened for Dindigul should last.' However, in his heart of hearts, MGR wanted to be with the Congress (I). In the aftermath of rumours of the ADMK wooing Congress (I), on 30 June, CPM leaders A. Balasubramaniam and N. Sankaraiah met MGR. Avoiding any commitment, MGR simply said that he was ready for a discussion on his return from his overseas trip.

MGR left on 2 July for the USSR to attend the Eighth International Film Festival in Moscow.[200] En route, in Delhi, the CPI hosted a reception for him. MGR's political acumen was strongly evident when he told the press: 'If Congress (I) would accept that [the] ADMK is the next ruling party in Tamilagam, there is a possibility for an alliance. In Tamilagam, the Congress (I) could grow to be the second party.'[201]

Kamaraj, who had already sensed MGR's intentions, had said only days earlier:

> For the last six years we had galvanized all the [DMK] opposition sentiments and had prepared the people. We were the ones who worked, seeded, watered and did the weeding. Someone else is rushing [in] to harvest. That is thieving. He is stealing what we had saved. At least should not the people have sense?[202]

These were pretty harsh words, but they were true. If the Congress (O) party had thought that the split in the DMK would benefit them, MGR had destroyed their dreams of a comeback. The MGR menace had to be nipped in the bud. Hence, Kamaraj did the unthinkable. In early August, he met Indira Gandhi, setting off speculation of reconciliation. It would not happen, however, until Kamaraj breathed his last. On 3 October 1976, Jayaprakash Narayan (JP) wrote in his *Prison Diary* that Kamaraj was wary of a tie-up between the ADMK and the Congress (I), and, realizing that going it alone would be disastrous, he would have, in the end, 'thrown in his lot with Mrs Gandhi'.[203]

On 12 August, the ADMK launched a statewide anti-price rise agitation against both the state and the Centre. But, with MGR, inconsistency remained consistent. On 24 August, the ADMK, Congress (I) and the CPI decided to call for a shutdown on 6 September against price rise. However, with the Congress (I) deserting him at the last minute and MGR claiming that he would no longer invite the Congress (I), the CPM joined the shutdown call.[204]

On 17 September, despite the sharp criticism EVR had levelled against him, MGR, tactically, went over to wish him for his ninety-fifth birthday, gifted him 5000 rupees and ingeniously asked for his permission to put up a statue of him in Madras. Four years later, on 17 September 1977, as chief minister, MGR would unveil the statue.[205]

ANNAISM

On 30 September, the ADMK issued a twenty-nine-page programme, which largely went unnoticed. The document said it did not wish to 'become a prey to the confusion resulting from varied interpretations of the same "ism"'. Therefore, the 'ism' propounded was Annaism. However, the party's programmes were identical to that of its parent's, the DMK. It said that the party was founded to 'establish a casteless, socialist and rationalist society through democratic means'. It sought more power for the states, official language status for regional languages, continued the use of English as a link language and promised total prohibition. However, the word 'state autonomy' was conspicuous in its absence. Annaism included, inter alia, a cap on urban income, nationalization of banks, heavy industries, takeover of production and distribution of essential goods, and demonetizing of 100-rupee notes to get rid of black money. The contract system, the document said, was the capitalist system's exploitation of the 'working class' and the benefits of factory workers would be extended to contractual labour to overcome this. The party promised graduating students and the unemployed among them an 'assurance for a living'. Farmers were offered subsidies and assured that mortgaged land would not be confiscated on loan defaults and promised crop insurance. Handloom weavers and the backward classes found mention too. Women, the repository of 'Indian culture', were advised 'not to identify Western culture with progress'. Importantly, the party also sought a constitutional amendment to recall elected representatives who had failed to perform. An ADMK chief minister would have to seek an annual vote of confidence from the party general council.[206] It was MGR's turn to taunt the CPM now. 'Why have they not commented?' he asked in meetings and to pressmen. The DMK had already offered its view, with a minister saying that the CPI had finally found the time to draft the comments. Expectedly, the CPI welcomed the document. However, on 20 November, *Theekadhir* ran a lead story and, from 25 November, A. Balasubramaniam wrote a six-part article under the heading 'Annaism: A Critical Review'.[207]

MGR would famously explain 'Annaism' as follows the next year at the ADMK conference in Madurai, in August 1974:

> Annaism is one of the 'isms' like capitalism, imperialism, socialism, revisionism, Gandhism and Buddhism. In communism, there is room for ideals and philosophy. But there is no room for love and

humanitarianism. Annaism has both love and humanitarianism. I
am ready to debate on this with anyone.[208]

He would also claim that even the last worker of the party could explain
Annaism to anyone.

Earlier, the ADMK and its allies won the 24 February 1974
Coimbatore parliamentary and Coimbatore (West) assembly seat. In
Pondicherry, the ADMK won twelve seats with 60,812 votes or 39.28
per cent, the DMK won two seats and 47,823 votes or 24.29 per cent,
Congress (I) seven seats with 32,840 or 33.29 per cent of the votes and
Congress (O) five seats with 41,348 or 34.27 per cent votes.[209]

On 6 March, S. Ramasamy became the ADMK's first chief minister
of Pondicherry. The ADMK fell short of a majority and MGR, following
his meeting with Indira Gandhi, said that he 'obtained the blessings of
a motherly heart'.[210]

MGR had gone as a state guest to Mauritius to attend their Republic
Day celebrations on 15 March, the ides of March. On 26 March, the
Congress (I) voted for ending the first ADMK experiment within twenty
days. The 'motherly heart' had pulled the rug from under MGR's feet.

But MGR would be careful not to blame her[211] and say 'as far as
Pondicherry is concerned, I cannot yet believe that Prime Minister
Indira [Gandhi] had been two-faced.'[212]

On 3 May, MGR held a fast in Madurai with the CPM's A.
Balasubramaniam, drawing large crowds to protest price rise,
unemployment and other issues.

KALAIGNAR VERSUS THE CENTRE

Meanwhile, the differences between Kalaignar and Delhi were
growing. The DMK leader said that his participation at the Depressed
and Backward Classes Conference in Allahabad with the Opposition, in
October 1973, and his contact with JP were discomfiting to the Centre.
Further, on 29 January 1974, Kalaignar bitterly complained about
the fact he was not consulted on the India–Sri Lanka Agreement on
stateless persons. 'I cannot welcome this. This is not proper,' he told
the Legislative Council, calling for the pact to be denounced. He also
reiterated that Katchatheevu was part of Tamil Nadu.[213]

On 22 March, Kalaignar expressed his opposition to the Centre's idea to revive the southern food zone, saying it would be 'calamitous' and lead to 'famine', adding that he was ready for 'confrontation'.

In early April, the government announced pensions for the martyrs of the anti-Hindi agitation and passed orders for temple prayers (archanas) to be exclusively in Tamil. Tamil had been optional from 1971 and earlier only Sanskrit was used.

On 9 April, Kalaignar said he would follow a 'sons of the soil' policy, and that 'There cannot be two Keralas in India', and suggested 'those from other states [in Tamil Nadu] live [with that consciousness in mind]'. On 9 April, he unilaterally announced a partial takeover of production and trade in yarn for handloom centres in Tamil Nadu. The next day, the chief minister faulted the Centre for driving the state into famine-like conditions by freeing the movement of coarse grains.[214]

On 28 June that year, India ceded Katchatheevu to Sri Lanka. The island had been the subject of rival claims by both countries. Kalaignar conveyed the 'strong feelings' of 'his people' to the foreign secretary. MGR, however, said Kalaignar should quit. MGR was willing to conduct an agitation for the island and the party passed a resolution saying that it would 'gird its loins for Katchatheevu'.[215] On 21 August 1974, Kalaignar moved a resolution in the Assembly that requested the Centre 'to retain the sovereignty of India over Katchatheevu and thus give due consideration to the sentiments of the people of Tamil Nadu.[216]

RESOLUTION ON STATE AUTONOMY

However, the last straw was perhaps the 16 April historic Assembly resolution on state autonomy. Describing the states' status as 'internal colonies', the chief minister said that his party aimed to end this situation, terming the day it was achieved as 'golden' for him. The resolution, based on the recommendation of the 1971 Rajamannar Committee, called to 'effect immediate changes in the constitution of India . . . to establish a truly federal set-up with full state autonomy'.[217] On 20 April, the ADMK's deputy leader in the House, G.R. Edmund, termed the Rajamannar Committee's report as 'not worthy of study by the legislators; it has nothing that could be of use to even a high school student. It should be thrown into the dustbin.' The ADMK's H.V. Hande claimed that the DMK had forfeited its right to seek state autonomy and, if it was given, the evils in the state would be multiplied. When it was put to vote, the ADMK said that the five-day discussion was insufficient for seeking clarifications and, therefore, staged a walk out.[218]

In June, Aladi Aruna crossed over to the ADMK, taking the party's strength to fourteen against the Congress (O)'s thirteen, thus giving it the status of the principal Opposition. MGR's *Netru Indru Naalai* and *Urimaikural* would fare well at the box office.

MGR made up with Vaali, from whom he was estranged then, and drew up the content for the title song of *Netru Indru Naalai* and, in a first, listed the poet as Vaali and music director as M.S. Viswanathan on screen before he launched into the song.[219]

Little brother
I studied in Kanchi yesterday [earlier]—shall I
Give you the message today
Always the good will win tomorrow
This is the message given by scholar Anna

People's welfare, people's welfare, they declare
But they only think of their own children . . .

Don't think that the cheats are those who succeed
Don't forget that falsehood does not save one for long
One day all this will change
And that change will be brought by elections*

---

* *Thambi*
Naan padithen Kanchiyile netru — adhai
Naan unnakku sollatuma indru
Endrum nallavarkku kaalam varum naalai
Idhu Arignar Anna ezhudhi vaitha olai...

Makkal nalam makkal nalam endre solluvaar
Tham makkal nalam ondrethan manadhil kolluvaar...

The song would serve to electrify the cadre.

It was a time when rice had become scarce; smuggling and hoarding made rice unaffordable and the state government was unable to ensure the availability of the vital food grain. There was 75 per cent load shedding. MGR conducted agitations against the price rise and power shortages. He asked for, and obtained, the Congress (I)'s support.

PROMOTING THE ADMK: ADDRESSING US UNIVERSITIES

The University of Chicago's Department of South Asian languages and civilizations invited MGR to address their seminar on 31 October 1974, on 'The Anna DMK Party's Plans and Programmes'. US-based chemical engineer and Tamil writer, M.S. Udayamurthi recalls the origins of MGR's US visit. Against the backdrop of the elections in Dindigul, Coimbatore and Pondicherry, Professor Henry Hart at the University of Wisconsin, Madison, had wondered, 'Alas it looks like that MGR would win the next [general] elections?' Hart then proposed that an invitation for a US visit be extended to MGR, reasoning that the trip would help MGR in his administration later. Soon, the Universities of Wisconsin, Chicago, California at Berkeley and Pennsylvania sent out formal invites to him.

At Madison, MGR said the ADMK and the administration would never interfere with the due course of law, and then he compared his campaign to the Watergate Scandal.

> I did the same. I said I wish to bring a resolution in the general council. People are suspicious of us; the government has become corrupt. Our partymen and their relations are corrupt, and [they]

Aeipavarke kaalam endru enni vidadhe
Poi ethanai naal kai kodukkum marandhu vidadhe
Oru naal indha nilaimaikellam maarudhal undu
Andha maarudhalai seivadharkku therudhal undu

have become rich That is how people consider us. I said, 'Let us form an impartial judicial panel within the party. Enquire [into how the wealth was accumulated]. Punish the guilty. Let us prove that our party leaders are clean.' I said, 'Let us remove those rotten [people] who take bribes from the poor taxpayers and become rich from the party. Throw them out.' They threw me out [instead].

Udayamurthi said that MGR came across as a man of depth, strong in his moorings.

MGR met with professors of economics, economists, experts and entrepreneurs in Madison and Milwaukee, and took part in events in Chicago, Los Angeles and Washington. On MGR's belief that growth should begin from the villages, Professor U. Shankar of Milwaukee University would comment, 'It is only such people's leaders who can afford to fear not "how the votes would go", who could fearlessly do extraordinary things.'

In a symbolic gesture, MGR stayed at the Watergate Hotel. Many asked him during the tour: 'Have you not accepted Mathiazhagan into your party? How did his [mis]deeds become clean after he joined your party?' MGR was unfazed. 'When he joined our party, we did not give him any position. We did not give him any responsibility. He came as a member and left as a member.' When asked how he would provide a clean government, MGR said:

Before making any appointment, an impartial commission, headed by a judge, will be constituted to review the candidacy. Candidates will be appointed after it is proven that there is nothing against them. If suspected of having committed misdeeds, their case would go to court. Persons proved guilty would have to go to jail. Similarly, there are plans to recall ministers or elected representatives who do not perform their duty well.

We cannot permit the squandering of the tax-payers and public money any more. This has to be stopped immediately. The country should get a good government.

These statements remained mere talk and were never followed up. Udayamurthi said that the Tamils already treated MGR as the chief minister of Tamil Nadu.

On the west coast, MGR addressed UC Berkeley's South Asia department, met the media in San Francisco, visited the studios of Paramount, MGM and Twentieth Century Fox. He also made stops in Disneyland, Washington DC, Philadelphia and Pittsburgh. At the University of Pennsylvania he decried JP's methods as wrong and an attempt to run a parallel government. 'His is an illogical struggle.'

India's ambassador to the US, T.N. Kaul, hosted a major reception in MGR's honour. University presidents and Jack Joseph Valenti, president of the Motion Picture Association of America, and Foreign Secretary Kewal Singh were all present.

At Columbia University, MGR said: 'If my party were to take office, talent will be given first place. Separate training will be imparted and finances allocated for the advancement of the backward.'

Speaking about his plans for the party, he said:

My party may not have talent. I will not hesitate to go after the talented and the educated. I will form a brain trust with the educated and the experts. They will, after duly considering all aspects for the nation's welfare, give me suggestions, ideas and plans. A politician should use his goodwill, and the intellect and ability of the intelligentsia. For instance, what right do I have to suggest changes in education?

Udayamurthi was charmed by MGR's frankness.

At the Astoria Waldorf in New York, MGR met Gregory Peck. Slated for ten minutes, the meeting lasted for forty-five minutes. Peck said that he had read the New York Times's write-up on him. On 28 September 1974, on the eve of his US visit, the New York Times had run a half-page story on MGR. The thespian told its correspondent Bernard Weinraub in Madras, 'I believe in heroes who are pure and people do not want it any other way.' He said that he did not drink even coffee or smoke. 'I give my wealth to charity. I have an image of a good man.' On the DMK administration, MGR said, 'What they do best is lie, give false accounts and take money. They have corrupted a party that was once incorruptible.'[220]

Udayamurthi also recorded that people felt that MGR spoke in general terms about everything. Some wondered if he could keep his promises of a clean administration; how very clairvoyant of them. Some mocked Annaism.

Udayamurthi said that these were minor shortcomings of the man, and concluded that MGR was both a good person and a competent one.[221]

Back home, the communists, however, did not think so. The CPM issued a statement in December 1974:

> It is a pity that the ADMK leadership has been working on the sole objective of somehow allying with the Congress (I). Our efforts to make the ADMK take an ideological stand in opposition to the Congress (I) have so far not borne fruit.[222]

The CPI was blunter:

> The ADMK leadership is hesitant, that its workers will gain serious political awareness if they have a close relationship with the communist party and engage in agitations against price rise and to eradicate hoarding. Therefore, they don't come forward to participate in such agitations and, even if they do, they do so only symbolically.[223]

Indifferent to the criticism, MGR continued his propaganda. In *Pallandu Vazhga*, where the convicts turn over a new leaf after seeing a statue of Anna, MGR sang Pulamaipithan's song:

> Our god who lives in our hearts — Anna was born
> He lit the everlasting flame of ideals
> Let us follow that light, tread the path
> Tomorrow history could be made for us.*

---

* *Idhaya deivam namadhu Anna thondrinaar*
  Avar endrum vaazhum kolgai deepam aetrinaar
  Andha vazhi kaanalaam, sonna vazhi pogalam
  Naalai varalaaru namakkaga uruvaagalaam

In *Naalai Namadhae*, MGR says, 'En *vazhi, tani vazhi* (My path is special)', which would become a huge hit in 1999 when Rajinikanth mouthed the same in his blockbuster *Padayappa*.

In *Idhayakani* MGR, who plays an estate owner, is welcomed by his workers in a song penned by Pulamaipithan:

> You should be well so that the country could progress
> So that the lives of the poor of this country will improve*

In *Uzhaikkum Karangal* he sang:

> You should rule tomorrow
> Toiling hands
> Let the entire country see
> The blossoming of revolution†

In *Indru Pol Endrum Vazhga* he sang:

> This is the hand that protects the country
> This is the hand that protects the house
> This is the hand of the country's hope
> This is the future country's life‡

KALAIGNAR INVITES JP

Unlike MGR who was concentrated in his film career, Kalaignar was upping the ante against Indira Gandhi. In April, in a public meeting with the communists, Kalaignar called on 'all parties to come forward to prevent

---

* *Neenga nalla irukonum naadu munnera*
  Indha naatililulla ezhaigalin vazhvu munnera
† *Naalai ulagai aala vendum*
  Uzhaikum karangale
  Indha nadu muzhuthum
  Malara vaendum puratchi malargale
‡ *Idhu naatai kaakum kai*
  Idhu veetai kaakum kai
  Indha kai naatin namikkai
  Idhu edhirkala thayagathin vazhkai

Indira [Gandhi's] attempts to silence all political parties and establish dictatorship'. MGR had joined hands with the Congress (I) and had formed the rather paradoxically named Democratic Protection Front. The discord between the Centre and Kalaignar increased further when Kalaignar invited JP, spearheading the Opposition against Indira Gandhi, to declare open the Rajaji memorial. On 3 May, on the eve of JP's visit, MGR published an open letter in *Thennagam* asking JP to advise Kalaignar to either consent to an inquiry or conduct a referendum. The Congress (I) and CPI staged black flag protests against JP. Kalaignar, for his part, said that if JP were to point out shortcomings, the DMK administration would correct itself.

On 6 May, at a public meeting at the Marina, JP described the language of MGR's charges as low and bitter, and added that it was easy to accuse but difficult to prove. In his *Prison Diary*, JP recorded that Kamaraj was not happy with his speeches but he said that he could not 'condemn the DMK'. He added that Kalaignar was willing to discuss the charges with the Opposition, was ready for an impartial probe on them, enacted the Public Men's Conduct Enquiry Act and was open for a discussion on the Act. He said Kalaignar should be 'taken at his word'.[24]

DMK, KAMARAJ OPPOSE THE EMERGENCY—MGR CAPITULATES

On 12 June, the Allahabad High Court struck down Indira Gandhi's election from Rae Bareli citing campaign irregularities. As demands for her resignation grew, Kalaignar commented that he would have appreciated it if she had quit voluntarily. MGR, however, issued a statement asking: 'Should this fate befall the mother in the cradle of [Indian] democracy?' The Supreme Court conditionally stayed the judgement. Indira Gandhi now announced a twenty-point welfare–development programme. Kalaignar said his administration had not only implemented the schemes listed, but had, in fact, ensured people got more benefits and took out full-page advertisements in dailies of its schemes.*

---

* On 28 October 1975 Congress (I)'s A.R. Marimuthu would move a motion against the DMK government expressing disapproval 'for its failure to effectively implement the twenty-point programme'. The motion would be defeated. http://www.assembly.tn.gov.in/archive/reviews/Review_5_1971_1976.pdf

On 25 June, Indira Gandhi declared the internal Emergency. She justified it as defence against a conspiracy by reactionary forces to destabilize the country. On 28 June, Kamaraj registered his opposition in public meetings held that evening, which, however, went unreported because of the censorship regime. Earlier, on 27 June, the DMK's executive passed a resolution expressing 'anguish' and it termed the Emergency as the inauguration of dictatorship. Kalaignar had drafted the text himself in the early hours of that morning.[225] The next day, two presidential ordinances denied judicial recourse against arrests and exempted the government from providing reasons.

On 2–3 July, the Tamil Nadu Congress (O) passed a resolution against the Emergency.[226] On 2 July, K. Rajaram, minister of labour and housing, told the United States consul general in Madras that the DMK ministry could be dismissed and 'at the moment, we think we will go peacefully'.[227] At that meeting, Rajaram asked the consul general a 'leading question'. 'Would the United States give assistance to us, if Tamil Nadu decided to become independent?' The consul general said he 'would reply equally directly, and the answer was no; this was an internal affair of India and we supported the territorial integrity of India and other countries'. He then wondered if this was being considered seriously. Rajaram replied in the negative and pointed out that the party had given up the secession agenda long ago. He, however, noted that many of the younger DMK folks felt if Indira Gandhi triumphed, the communist sway would grow, and Tamil Nadu should then leave the Indian Union. The consul general reported that Rajaram did not return to the topic and he was 'inclined to take what he said at face value'.[228]

On 4 July, Kalaignar and Nedunchezhian met Kamaraj. Kalaignar recorded Kamaraj's words to them: 'The country is lost! The country is lost!' Kalaignar added that Kamaraj had advised them against quitting, as Tamil Nadu (with Gujarat) served as a haven for democracy.[229]

The same day, Murasoli Maran told the United States consul general that Indira Gandhi was wooing Kamaraj as it would be easier to move against the ministry with him by her side.[230] On 6 July, at the Marina, following a hard-hitting speech, Kalaignar asked the mammoth audience to take a vow to defend democracy and requested the prime minister to release the Opposition leaders and restore press freedom.[231] In 2015, on the fortieth anniversary of the Emergency, M.K. Stalin said that Kalaignar had, prior to the meeting, turned back the two emissaries from Indira Gandhi who sought that even if Kalaignar did not support the Emergency, he should not oppose it, and if he did not do so, the ministry would be dismissed.[232]

The US consul general's 7 July dispatch on the 4 July meeting with Maran assessed that Kalaignar was with the hardliners within the party who were against the Emergency 'particularly as his rival M.G. Ramachandran, supported by the CPI, has fallen in line completely behind the prime minister's actions'.[233] MGR had convened the ADMK executive and passed a resolution welcoming the Emergency and the economic measures, and, on 16 July, met Indira Gandhi to give her a copy of the resolution. Manoharan, SDS and Hande had accompanied MGR. The actor-politician refused to divulge what transpired at the meeting. *The Hindu's* N. Ram would later characterize MGR's 'role during the Emergency [as] shameful'.[234]

The US consul general dispatch on 21 July said that the DMK government was using the powers under the Emergency to arrest ADMK men on the excuse that they were antisocial elements. The same dispatch said that the DMK was 'reportedly' holding some 250 meetings daily in villages and towns to explain its stand on the Emergency.[235]

The ADMK proved no less vengeful. On 17 July, the ADMK mouthpiece *Thennagam* published the editorial, 'Did the Marxist handbill come to the attention of the state government?' suggesting that anti-Emergency literature was being allowed by the DMK government—one of the issues that would be cited in the reasons for its dismissal later.

Soon talks of discharging the Kalaignar government began doing the rounds. Kalaignar said: 'Perunthalaivar (Great Leader) Kamarajar stood in the way of Indira Gandhi's decision to dismiss the DMK government. He was sending messages that dismissal would not be democratic. Therefore, Indira Gandhi feared to dismiss the DMK government.'[236] JP wrote that 'for Kamaraj, the ADMK was even worse than the DMK' and he did not wish to 'weaken the DMK as otherwise the ADMK would be correspondingly strengthened'.[237]

In September 1975, MGR participated in a Maharashtra State Anti-Fascist Conference with CPI leader S.A. Dange, Chief Minister S.B. Chavan and Central minister Chandrajit Yadav. He stated: 'The regional parties in India only lead to disrupt the unity among people. It is wise that these parties join the national mainstream.' In September 1976, the ADMK would subsequently be rechristened as the All-India ADMK.

KAMARAJ PASSES AWAY

On 2 October, Kamaraj breathed his last. When A. Balasubramaniam met him on 30 September, two days before his death, he said he was still opposed to the Emergency.[238] Kalaignar wrote that some months prior to Kamaraj taking ill, the two met in a physician's place in Madras for three hours. Kamaraj had said then that, among other things, he would begin to advocate for more rights for states. But this was not to be.

On 5 October, speaking at a condolence meeting for Kamaraj in Delhi, Indira Gandhi said that Kamaraj had not criticized the actions under Emergency as he knew the challenges facing the country. She invited all Congress partymen to unite under one umbrella. As some held back, Kalaignar was suspected of blocking unity. Home Minister Brahmananda Reddy wrote, on 29 November, to Kalaignar with regard to this.

In his presidential speech at the Coimbatore state DMK conference from 25 to 28 December, Kalaignar referred to the imminent dismissal of his government and said that none could be more 'ecstatic' than he and his DMK if this were to happen.

Meanwhile CPI's P. Ramamurti was turning the heat on MGR. In December 1975,he challenged MGR publicly. He said:

> When MGR visited America, he told reporters who asked him what Annaism was: 'Socialism, communism and capitalism—a merger of all the three.'
>
> By putting together the three and confusing them, what they, in fact, brought [in] is fascism. Is this Annaism? You could have told the people of Tamil Nadu at the very beginning that it means 'Congress'. MGR is trying to push the ADMK workers into the Congress by confusing them bit by bit and speaking contrarily.[239]

DMK GOVERNMENT CHARGED AS SUBVERSIVE

In an interview published on 27 December, before the All India Congress Committee (AICC) meet from 29 December 1975 to 2 January 1976,

Indira Gandhi said that the Tamil Nadu and Gujarat governments 'are opposed to our party' and 'want to weaken the government at the Centre'. In her addresses to the AICC session on 30–31 December, she emotionally hit out at the DMK government (along with the Gujarat government and RSS) as an internal factor undermining India's unity. The meet would also resolve that parliamentary elections should be deferred by a year.[240]

On 2 January 1976, Sivaji Ganesan met Indira Gandhi in Delhi and, three days later, threw in his lot with her Congress. On 7 January, at a merger meeting, many Congress leaders underscored the union as necessary to fight separatist forces (the DMK).[241]

However, on 30 January, Governor K.K. Shah complimented the DMK administration for following Gandhi's ideals. The following day, at a private school event, Kalaignar said that 'most probably this would be the last event in which I participate as chief minister'.[242] He was right.

DMK GOVERNMENT DISMISSED

On 31 January 1976, President Fakhruddin Ali Ahmed signed an ordinance dismissing the DMK ministry. The state legislature was dissolved seven weeks later on 21 March 1976, when its term ended.[*][243] MGR said that it was a courageous act and that the ADMK welcomed it and it would support Indira Gandhi's attempts at protecting democracy. Kalaignar's statement to maintain peace in a spirit of duty, dignity and discipline was also reported.

A.V.P. Asaithambi, who had fiercely advocated for an independent Tamil state at the Coimbatore DMK party conference, was taken into custody, as were others from Madurai, under the Maintenance of Internal Security Act (MISA). The Army was posted at Fort St George to prevent any files from being removed. Soon enough, the police came looking for Kalaignar's son M.K. Stalin, who was in Madurantakam acting in a propaganda play. The next day, Kalaignar called the

---

* At the time of dissolution, the ruling DMK had 167 members in the House ADMK sixteen, and the two Congress parties had twenty members. http://www.assembly.tn.gov.in/archive/reviews/Review_5_1971_1976.pdf

inspector-general of police to come and fetch him. He did the same the following day, on Murasoli Maran's arrival from Delhi, asking for him to be taken into custody.[244]

Governor Shah's report charged the DMK administration with maladministration, corruption and misuse of power for partisan political ends, echoing what Congress president Dev Kant Barooah had said earlier: 'The DMK had institutionalised corruption in Tamil Nadu.' India Today opined that for years 'rampant corruption by members of the government and leading cadre of the party' had affected the government's credibility. The most glaring of the Governor's charges appeared in his references to the DMK's shrill demands and its leadership's militant speeches. 'Some of the DMK leaders have already given a threat of revolution in Tamil Nadu if the life of the state assembly is not extended,' Shah said. Furthermore, DMK leaders, including the chief minister, had indirectly threatened secession if state autonomy was not acceded to. Shah added that 'sinister comparisons have been made in their public utterances with the events in Bangladesh and the fate of Mujibar Rahman'. In conclusion, Governor Shah recommended a judicial inquiry.

India Today's cover story said, 'When some of his [Karunanidhi's] more foolish supporters began to describe him as another Mujibur Rahman, it was time to call his bluff.'[245]

On 2 February, Home Minister Reddy tabled Governor Shah's report in the Lok Sabha, and the minister of state for home affairs, Om Mehta, did the same in the Rajya Sabha. The next day, 3 February, Om Mehta announced a commission of inquiry, headed by Justice Ranjit Singh Sarkaria of the Supreme Court. It was to report to the President by 1 February 1977. The minister said that twenty-seven of the fifty-four allegations by M.G. Ramachandran and member of Parliament M. Kalyanasundaram, in December 1975, necessitated the move.[246] Senior police officials V.R. Lakshminarayanan and Mohandas would be transferred to Madras and later joint secretary, home, C.V. Narasimhan, would move to Madras to take over Anti-Corruption and Surveillance. From Delhi, M.K. Narayanan would monitor the progress of the Sarkaria inquiry.

On 3 February, the motion to extend the term of the Parliament by a year was placed. That day, which was also Anna's death anniversary,

Murasoli published a list under the heading 'Those unable to come to place wreaths at the Anna mausoleum'. In his unparalleled style Kalaignar had euphemistically listed those in custody under MISA. He wrote that 25,000 DMK cadre members were arrested soon after the dismissal of the government. A US consulate dispatch on 6 February said that thus far 7400 had been arrested in Tamil Nadu, according to police sources, and the arrests were continuing.[247]

It was perhaps the most difficult period in Kalaignar's public and personal life. If his son, nephew, close associates and cadre were interned, the Governor's report had completely disgraced his administration. Even within his own party, some saw the man who could not be distinguished from the party as a liability. On 11 February, S. Ramachandran claimed a 'sizeable section' of the general council wished for Kalaignar and the other ministers to step aside till proven innocent 'to prevent the DMK from disintegrating'. He said: 'No individual, however great, can ever be more important than the DMK, which had been built with the blood and tears of partymen.' Although S. Ramachandran indicated he would stay with the DMK, he would soon join MGR and become a leading light in the AIADMK. The situation in the AIADMK was not all that great either. The 13 February US report rightly noted the apprehension in the AIADMK that it might be treated no differently if the reunited Congress took the view that it could do without MGR's support.[248] MGR was fully aware that Indira Gandhi was 'ruthless' and he wished to avoid trouble.[249]

KAMARAJ'S 'LAST WISH'

Indira Gandhi made her first visit to Madras following the DMK ministry's dismissal on 14–15 February 1976. On 14 February, declaring the Kamaraj memorial open, she recounted her 'knowledge' of Kamaraj's 'last wish' as the merger of the two Congress parties. The US consul general's 18 February report on her visit should be quoted for posterity for both its poignance and poetry:

> Perhaps not all listeners were as sceptical as my West German colleague, who described the prime minister's speech as 'a fairy tale told quickly and with a bad conscience to a disbelieving

audience', but a number of people have commented privately
that 'dead men cannot answer back'.[250]

In his diary, JP mentions that Kamaraj had told him that 'he did not
trust Mrs Gandhi in the least and vice versa'.[251] The following day, she
spoke for seventy-five minutes at the Marina, where she continued
her fantastic claims that the DMK was planning serious violence in the
state. She also referred to corruption and maladministration.[252]

Another 18 February US dispatch said that Tamil Nadu's chief
secretary P. Sabanayagam refuted the allegations of violence, and
observed that Tamil Nadu was no different in corruption to the other
states. Sabanayagam felt that the public was sceptical of the charges,
was conscious of the DMK's welfare schemes, and that it was not for
Indira Gandhi but for the public to pass judgement. He, however,
expressed surprise that a party that had been built through much hard
work and little funds, and possessing a solid base, was giving way so
easily.* Sabanayagam appeared to proffer an explanation when he said
that DMK leaders had become 'too interested in money', from the top
down.

Sabanayagam thought that the allegations of separatist threats
stemmed from the Dravidar Kazhagam Conference in Thanjavur,
held between 22 and 24 January 1976. He said, 'We advised the chief
minister not to attend the conference', implying that by their presence,
the DMK ministers had played into the prime minister's hands. This 18
February US report opined: 'Despite all the indications to the contrary,
Mrs. Gandhi is now apparently able, without gulping, to make the
accusation of planned violence the major justification of her move
against the DMK government.'[253]

Indira Gandhi had viciously painted the DMK as violent and
separatist. On 18 February, Kalaignar dispatched K. Rajaram with a letter
to the home minister and his deputy that reiterated the DMK's credentials
of non-violence and extending cooperation to maintain law and order.
Earlier, Kalaignar had written a similar missive immediately following

---

* In contrast to Sabanayagam, the adviser to governor, P.K. Dave,
however, rightly felt that the DMK was not 'disintegrating'. https://
www.wikileaks.org/plusd/cables/1976NEWDE02455_b.html.

the dismissal of the government. The 19 February US consul general's dispatch noted that the DMK feared being banned for aligning with the CPM on its agitations and Kalaignar reportedly met Om Mehta, who was visiting with the prime minister. The DMK party leadership met on 17 February and had discussed ways to pre-empt any ban. Rajaram's visit to Delhi was a result of this.[254] On 2 March, Kalaignar said Om Mehta had replied that the release of the arrested would be considered 'with due regard to the developing situation in the state'.[255] According to a 3 March US consul general dispatch, Rajaram had indicated the pressure that Kalaignar was under to step down. Kalaignar had pointed out that two-thirds of the 600 members of the executive and the general council were in detention (1908 DMK men in detention under MISA, said the report) and there was nobody to send his resignation to.[256]

Fearing a shutdown, Kalaignar, a master at language play, now ran articles in Murasoli, which were seemingly innocuous but contained messages that the cadre understood. Kalaignar's daily letter to partymen had to be discontinued.[257]

Despite the overtures, the sword of Damocles continued to hang over the party's head. On 5 March, Nedunchezhian reaffirmed that the DMK had given up its secessionist plank for good since 1963.[258] On a visit to Madras in April, Home Minister Brahmananda Reddy made it clear that the DMK was being closely watched, and in response to a pointed question, Reddy said that 'only those parties which preached secession would be banned. . . The DMK has been declaring that it was not for separation . . . Its leaders have also been reiterating this point now more than in the past.' Meanwhile, more releases were effected, but only after members tendered written apologies for their activities and/or they quit the DMK. Those who would not bend stayed in custody.[259]

FIRST INDOOR MEETING OF THE DMK

But there were better tidings for the DMK around the corner. In its first indoor meeting in Madras, on 24 April 1976, the first since President's Rule, Kalaignar thanked Indira Gandhi for giving him an opportunity to judge who his friends were. He noted, 'Some branches of the sixty-year-old DMK might have been cut off, but as long as the trunk and the main root are there the party will live and grow strong. We want to build the

DMK by constructive methods and not by agitation.' He announced a membership drive and an 'Enquiry Commission Expenses Fund'. The US consul general report of 30 April said Kalaignar was trying to pull the party out of the morass it had sunk into.[260]

Then, Indira Gandhi toured the drought-hit areas in Tamil Nadu, where she repeated her now familiar charges against Kalaignar. On 15 September, Anna's birthday, Kalaignar responded to her, hinting that if he were gone, several Karunanidhis would take his place.[261]

LOYALTY TEST: THE TATTOO EPISODE

In 1976, MGR was concentrating on his film career. *Needhikku Thalai Vanangu* (Bow Your Head to Justice), *Uzhaikkum Karangal* and *Ooruku Uzhaipavan* all did relatively well. As MGR's loyalty to his own film career remained undiminished, those who were banking on him for their political careers to succeed grew restive. It was around this time that MGR called for his partymen to tattoo the party flag on their arm. His view was that it would help fellow partymen to identify each other, besides creating a sense of unity and facilitating coordination. He, however, told RMV the real reason: 'It will show if the partyman is [really] loyal.'[262] While many enthusiastically followed their leader's words, some protested. Kovai Chezhian, G. Viswanathan and P. Srinivasan said the idea was against the 'rational path'.[263]

After the protests, MGR did a volte-face. He said:

I have never compelled those who have quit, [those] who have been expelled to tattoo themselves. Since the rival parties doubt our cadre and our leaders' steadfastness towards our policies, I suggested this as a remedy. I took this decision after consultations with the senior leaders of the party. When I knew about a resolution, I asked that tattooing not be made mandatory. Such a resolution was never brought [in]. This is the truth. It cannot be construed that those who did not tattoo themselves did not like Anna's ideals or were not qualified to stay in the party. Hande, Srinivasan, Kovai Chezhian and Viswanathan have not spoken about this to me. They made this [the tattoo] the reason for their departure.[264]

Seeing Hande's protest letter, MGR immediately came over to his place. In their forty-five-minute discussion, Hande told him that many were heeding his advice 'but were cursing MGR'. (Nanjil Manoharan was one of them.) Hande said that he would be loyal to MGR, but could not be a 'slave'; at this point MGR's eyes grew moist and he held Hande's hand and said that was enough, and left. But the tattoo episode led to a hiatus between them.

He, however, would term Kovai Chezhian, G. Viswanathan and P. Srinivasan as 'separatists' and enemies of the twenty-point programme and expel them from the party.[265] They had written to MGR questioning the way he ran the party—his personalized style of leadership, the absence of audits for party funds, party elections and disciplinary measures that were not under any rules.[266]

An irked MGR said at a wedding that there were some 'plotters' around him and his tattoo suggestion was to single them out. 'Some think that they could threaten me, like Karunanidhi was. It will not happen with me.'[267] Later, at the stormy Coimbatore general council meeting in September 1976, MGR spoke thus:

> When I was thrown out I founded a new party. Didn't I? . . . Whom did I ask then?
>
> I named the party ADMK, whom did I ask? When I carried Anna's image on the party flag, whom did I ask? Now I ask that you be tattooed . . . I change the name to All-India . . . Why should I ask anyone about these? How much does it take to run the party? How much do I spend? Those who have questioned me, have they ever asked about these? Those who questioned me here are not bad, but they have listened to those who are![268]

Again in November, he said the tattoo episode had become a tool in the hands of those who wished to make it an excuse to paint him in a poor light.[269]

THE DMK'S DIFFICULTIES

MGR was facing a revolt and the DMK's difficulties were also on the rise. *Murasoli*, like other Opposition dailies, faced strict and often irrational censorship. Some 2000 from the DMK, DK and other parties were interned under MISA. Those who travelled with Kalaignar, like T.R. Baalu, later a Central minister, Bodi Surulivel, an MLA, S.M. Hussein, later an MLA, and L. Ganesan, later an MP, were taken into custody just for accompanying him. Reports of MISA detainees being beaten by warders and other convicts in the presence of senior officials began to surface. M.K. Stalin said that he lost consciousness because of the beatings. Yet, the convicts put to the task by warders continued beating him up. It was then that Chittibabu interceded, in vain, and later interposed himself between Stalin and them to take their blows. He would succumb to his injuries later in hospital, following a surgery. M.K. Stalin said he is alive because of Chittibabu who gave up his life instead.[270]

Kalaignar said that around this time, S. Ramachandran and SSR became prey to the Centre's scheme. He alleged that S. Ramachandran was a turncoat, identifying those who had to be taken into custody. Some senior leaders felt that if Kalaignar were to quit, the party would be saved from the Centre's scheme to destroy it.

At this point, Pulavar Govindan wrote to Kalaignar, urging him to leave. Kalaignar said they could have given him a little poison instead and said a good politician was akin to a captain who would not desert his sinking ship. He also wrote the same in *Murasoli*—that he would rather consume poison than quit the party.[*][271]

Actually, Kalaignar had become the party. In 1976, men and women travelled to Madras in buses and vans to meet their leader, get a photograph with him and give their contribution to the Enquiry Commission Expenses Fund. The governor's regime failed to break their resolve. When it created difficulties for them, the DMK men and women turned into pilgrims, tonsuring their heads and wearing pilgrims' clothes—only their shrine was Kalaignar's abode. When

---

* S. Ramachandran, for his part, said that in 1975, as the DMK ministry faced dismissal, MGR had issued a statement that he was ready to rejoin the DMK, but Kalaignar should quit power. It was then that Pulavar Govindan had written the letter. 'He was ready to die but not to quit his position. He was the first one who thwarted the reunification,' S. Ramachandran noted later. https://www.youtube.com/watch?v=EMMSGgR4Hgk.

party elders were so stricken with fear of associating themselves with Kalaignar, droves of families came every day to hold his hand, shed tears and assure him that they were with him. The DMK began paying the families of those interned a monthly sum of 200 rupees.

The excerpt from the US consul general's cable on Kalaignar at this juncture is worthy of being reproduced here:

> Despite the Damoclean sword hanging over his head, Karunanidhi has continued his travels throughout Tamil Nadu to be acclaimed by thousands, who have mobbed him at every stop and have donated small amounts to his legal defense fund. His tour programs are published in advance only in the DMK Tamil daily, *Murasoli*, or are spread by word of mouth. Karunanidhi uses functions such as marriages or funerals of party workers to meet the DMK faithful in various places and never misses such opportunities. For a man supposed to be disgraced and humiliated, a man who has faced every instrument that a determined government has been able to throw against him and his party short of incarceration, he tours the cities and rural areas undaunted by the forces arrayed against him. It may not be an exaggeration to say that Karunanidhi is probably the most complete and charismatic populist politician in India today. Consider a man who can say this to his people and move them to tears, as he did on August 20 in Coimbatore: 'Whether it is going to be criminal proceedings against me, or life imprisonment, or gallows, or any altar where I may be tortured or killed, I have this great confidence that I have a place in the altar of your hearts. Hence, I continue to speak to you and write to you.' And the people listen.[272]

But not all DMK men shared this view. The 3–4 July executive meet saw Mathiazhagan and others asking for him to quit.[273] On 6 July, Mathiazhagan, SSR, S. Ramachandran and DVN were suspended. Meanwhile, a 13 July US consul general report concluded that Kalaignar's detention looked imminent.[274]

Kalaignar said the witch-hunt against him was so bad that one day, as he was leaving his place, income-tax officials stopped him to ask if the house was purchased after he became chief minister. He told them that it was bought in 1956 and asked them, sarcastically, if MGR was not aware of even this. *Murasoli* was raided.

The saga of humiliation continued. One day income-tax officials raided his second residence. As he stepped into his house, the officials, who knew him well asked, 'Who are you, sir? What is your name?'

Chief Minister MGR

On 16 February 1977, the day after the DMK–Janata Party tie-up, the interim report of the Justice Sarkaria Commission was leaked to the press. (It was subsequently tabled in the Rajya Sabha on 2 March.) In his interim report, Justice Sarkaria characterized the evidence against Kalaignar and his former ministers as 'cogent, convincing and reliable', implicating Kalaignar and his ministerial colleagues Anbil Dharmalingam and S. Madhavan, who would both later join the AIADMK.[1] MGR and the CPI could not have been happier with this development. Kalaignar rued that 'with the legal cases [Indira Gandhi wished to] finish the DMK without a trace'.[2] The motive notwithstanding, the inquiry proved equal to the task and the weak-kneed would flee the DMK.

PARLIAMENTARY POLLS

Following Indira Gandhi's lifting of the Emergency and the call on 23 January 1977 for fresh elections, polling was scheduled for March 1977. Arangannal provided insight into how MGR chose the candidates in a different context (1980 parliamentary polls). The actor-politician said, 'Let us make a "list"' and then proceeded to suggest names.[3] KAK, however, noted:

> MGR would not reveal his preference. He would have a discussion, individually and collectively, and offer an explanation, even if one person differed. It is only after this that he would reach a decision. Whether it was an election,

announcement of candidates or party decisions, he would
consult and try to convince each one. He did not egoistically
stick to his decision, if it meant harm to the general good. He
was keen to see that no one should leave [the party].[4]

Despite his pharaoh-like status, MGR was open to suggestions and
discussions—at least up to a point. He surely had a soft corner for
the educated and the lawyers in particular, and did identify talent and
organizational abilities in the candidates he chose, taking on board
recommendations from the field and the leaders.[5] At times, he would
beamingly introduce his young ministers with their educational degrees
to visitors.[6] The election results would show that, in the end, it did not
matter how the AIADMK candidates were chosen. People voted for
MGR.

RMV revealed that he and Manoharan were keen on an electoral
alliance with the Congress (I), and that the talks were conducted by
an intelligence official on behalf of the prime minister. The formula
put forth by RMV and Manoharan was that the Congress (I) would
fight two-thirds of the parliamentary seats and the AIADMK a third,
and when it came to the Assembly, the AIADMK would contest
two-thirds while the Congress (I) would contest a third. When the
Congress (I) hesitated on giving away two-thirds of the Assembly
seats, MGR broke off the talks. In the end, however, RMV and
Manoharan's insistence would lead to an electoral understanding—
for the parliamentary polls.[7]

During the campaign, the DMK front advocated democracy,
but also ran advertisements that showed MGR as being anti-labour,
describing him as 'The actor noble who takes 1 lakh [rupees] that is
accounted for and many lakhs that are not.'[8]

MGR, expectedly, focused on the Sarkaria Commission's interim
findings and claimed that his ally Indira Gandhi faced danger: 'There is
danger for a mother's dignity. Let us protect the mother's dignity. Let
us save her leadership.'[9] When the results came in, the AIADMK had
won seventeen of the twenty seats contested, the Congress (I) fourteen
out of fifteen, the CPI won all the three seats contested, the DMK two

out of nineteen, Janata Party three out of eighteen, and the CPM didn't win either of the two seats it fought.[*]

The AIADMK took the lone Pondicherry seat. Its candidate polled 1,15,302 votes or 53.32 per cent against the Janata Party's candidate's 96,101 votes or 44.44 per cent.[10]

MGR's strong showing had come as a surprise, a 31 March US consul general's cable said, adding, 'The Centre's campaign to discredit Karunanidhi was more successful than anyone here had believed, and the DMK might be finished as an effective force in the state for some time.'[11] The party would prove the prophecy wrong with adversity bringing out the best in its leader and the cadre.

Who had voted for the AIADMK? Poet Kannadasan harshly stated:

> Even today, the irrational poor and fools among the educated are the only ones who trust him . . . In the elections that had been concluded, the uneducated and those who could think did not vote for him. He has firmly rooted himself in places where there has been no education or awareness.[12]

[*]

MAJOR PARTIES AND PERFORMANCE
MARCH 1977 PARLIAMENTARY ELECTIONS

Party	Contested	Won	Votes	Percentage
AIADMK	20	17	53,65,076	30.04
Congress (I)	15	14	39,77,306	22.27
CPI	3	3	8,22,233	4.60
CPM	2	0	2,79,081	1.56
DMK	19	2	33,23,320	18.61
Janata Party	18	3	31,56,116	17.67

http://eci.nic.in/eci_main/StatisticalReports/LS_1977/Vol_I_LS_77.pdf, 108.

Nedunchezhian attributed MGR's successes to 'film glamour'. Alluding to the women—MGR's support base—as politically naive,* he said, 'How can we change those who remain at home? We have learnt this now. Times are changing. Film glamour, too, will change.'[13] Ironically, it would be Nedunchezhian who would change and the womenfolk would continue to stand steadfastly with MGR.

But the Janata Party's national ascent and the eclipse of his ally, the Congress (I) in the north, had left MGR in an awkward position, and he rushed to Delhi to pledge his unconditional support for Prime Minister Morarji Desai.[14] The DMK, which had always accused MGR of being a Delhi 'stooge', lost no time in dissecting MGR's move. Nedunchezhian said:

> What did M.G. Ramachandran, who has pledged unconditional support for Morarji Desai today, say earlier? He asked if anyone knew Morarji! He said he had taken a bribe! He said if he were to come to power, he would impose Hindi! Do you know the reason for his surrender now? In 1972, Chittibabu, MP, had asked in the Lok Sabha if MGR had been sent a notice under the Foreign Exchange Regulations Act (FERA); and what was MGR's response to it? Central minister Ram Nivas Mirdha said that MGR had been served a notice, his reply was being studied and that appropriate

---

* Jayakanthan's short story in 1972, *Cinemavukku Pona Sithalu* (Madurai: Meenatchi Puthaga Nilayam, 2012), was on MGR's hold on the rural and unlettered womenfolk: Chellamuthu, a rickshawman and a diehard MGR fan, makes a living renting a rickshaw. Wishing to educate his village wife, Kamsalai, on lovemaking, Chellamuthu takes her to a movie—not just any movie, but MGR's movie. It proves to be Chellamuthu's undoing. Kamsalai takes a great liking to films and MGR, but not to Chellamuthu. On the rare occasions she cooperates as a wife, she is in a cinematic trance. It suddenly becomes clear to Chellamuthu that Kamsalai's embrace, kiss and acquiescence are not meant for him. How can his hero be responsible for his wife's fantasy? 'What would you do *vathiyarae* . . .' he remonstrates before the calendar from which his hero is smiling at him. He says it is not just Kamsalai but a whole lot of women like her are so 'drunk' with his vathiyar, who cannot, therefore, be held accountable. Chellamuthu stops her from watching films. Kamsalai loses herself in her quest to see MGR's films, lands up in a brothel and, finally, after seeing MGR knifed by the villain in a movie shooting and hospitalized, she turns mad.

legal action would be taken. The question was posed in August 1972. MGR left the party and began to support Indira Gandhi in October 1972 . . . There is now talk that there will be action. An alarmed MGR has run to Delhi and declared [the] unconditional support of his party MPs for Morarji.[15]

MGR's approach was to befriend prime ministers and those in power at the Centre. He desired no confrontation with an omnipotent Centre. Morarji would take a personal liking to MGR, who respected him, not in the least because the prime minister refused to heed to Kalaignar's pleas to wind up the Sarkaria Commission. While this was helpful in the short term, it would create complications later, as Indira Gandhi would bounce back into power. MGR himself openly justified his support for Desai, and later Charan Singh, to ensure they took a liberal view of projects and funding for the state.[16]

NEDUNCHEZHIAN DESERTS THE DMK

The DMK's electoral defeat, the portents of a harsh political road ahead and, importantly, MGR's arrival as a permanent fixture on the political firmament would see a flock of senior leaders desert the DMK. On 15 April, Nedunchezhian left the DMK, never to return. Launching the Makkal DMK (MDMK) on 8 May, he put forth a litany of charges against Kalaignar for the DMK's defeat and its sufferings.[17]

In less than five months, on 18 September, the MDMK merged with the AIADMK, bringing with it a rich haul of senior leaders to MGR's party. On 19 September, endorsing the merger, the AIADMK general council said that those accused of corruption should face a probe and, the next day, MGR announced the appointment of retired judge E.S. Venkatesan to conduct such probes. However, no such inquiry ever took place. That day, MGR announced that Nedunchezhian would be the presidium chairman of the AIADMK. Kovai Chezhian, too, had rejoined the party.[18]

MGR had offered the MDMK leaders lateral entry, guarding their seniority. Manoharan, the number two in the party till then, made the charge that the MDMK newcomers 'poisoned' the party and warned that they could betray MGR as easily as they did Kalaignar (strangely, it was Manoharan who left MGR). MGR told him: 'Nanjil [Manoharan],

I am doing this to isolate Kalaignar', at which Manoharan's heart 'fluttered'.[19] But Manoharan's acute sense of intellectual superiority and his indiscreet comments on MGR's competence appear to have done him in. As a distance developed between the two, Nedunchezhian eased into that gap. He proved adept at playing second fiddle to MGR, and was 'settled' with the recognition MGR accorded him in the party and, later, in the government.

ASSEMBLY ELECTION

The ruling Janata Party's hubris saw Desai say, on 6 May, in Bombay, that the Janata Party–DMK alliance was 'off'. Additionally, Home Minister Charan Singh indicated follow-up action on Sarkaria's findings.[20] With the DMK isolated, MGR increasingly behaved like a chief minister in waiting. The Congress (I) that had beseeched him for ninety seats[21] was offered forty and told to 'take it or leave it'. The CPI, which had asked for sixty-five seats, suffered the same fate. Clearly, the Congress (I) and the CPI desired a coalition government with the AIADMK.[22] MGR understandably had no need and therefore desire to accommodate them. Consequently, on 14 May, Kalyanasundaram said the way MGR treated his party was not proper, although MGR would later blame Kalyanasundaram and his CPI for the alliance talks failing with the Congress (I).[23]

MGR now wooed the CPM, which had also been treated shabbily by the Janata Party. Reciprocating MGR's overture, the party issued a lengthy statement in which it pointed out that the AIADMK was contesting against the Congress (I) and, besides, the practice of rallying the 'lakhs and lakhs of the AIADMK's poor and the simple folk behind the Congress [I]' has changed.[24] The CPM's political expediency had made it see virtue where there was none. *Dinathanthi*'s C.P. Adithan, who had made up with MGR by then, would be allocated the Sathankulam constituency.[25]

MGR's campaign drew mammoth crowds and people waited for twelve to eighteen hours as he got delayed at his previous meetings.[26] MGR played the AIADMK's propaganda song *'Vaasal engum irattai ilai kolam idungal* (Adorn your homes with the two leaves symbol)' after his speeches. Pulavar Pulamaipithan, its author, considers this an important element in the AIADMK's victory. Equally, two songs from *Indru Pol Endrum Vaazhga* written by poet Muthulingam were specially recorded in a company in Calcutta for the campaign.[27] They were:

This hand is the protector of the land
This hand is the protector of the home
This hand is the country's hope
This is the future homeland's life

And the second song:

I yield to affection
I yield to Tamil culture[*]

Released on 5 May, five weeks before the 10 June elections, the movie's songs greatly helped the campaign. In his campaign, Kalaignar said that 'Tamilagam should be ruled by a Tamil'.[28]

The AIADMK emerged as the clear winner, taking 130 seats. Clearly, a four-cornered contest had favoured the AIADMK, and MGR won by the biggest margin of 29,378 votes in Aruppukottai.[29] But equally, the DMK's performance of forty-eight seats belied all earlier analyses. Kalaignar's tireless work and leadership had achieved it.[†] The DMK leader pointed out that if the DMK and Janata Party had fought together, the potential to win 137 seats existed, and if they had allied

---

* *Idhu naatai kaakum kai*
  Indha kai naatin nambikkai
  Idhu edhirkaala thayagathin vazhkai

  Anbukku naan adimai
  Tamizh panbukku naan adimai

† MAJOR PARTIES AND PERFORMANCE
  JUNE 1977 ASSEMBLY ELECTIONS

Party	Contested	Won	Votes	Percentage
AIADMK	200	130	51,94,876	30.36
Cong (I)	198	27	29,94,535	17.50
CPI	32	5	4,96,955	2.90
CPM	20	12	4,77,835	2.79
DMK	230	48	42,58,771	24.89
Forward Bloc	6	1	50,831	0.30
Janata Party	233	10	28,51,884	16.67

http://eci.nic.in/eci_main/StatisticalReports/SE_1977/
StatisticalReportTamil%20Nadu77.pdf.

with the CPM, they could have won 150 seats.[30] But elections are better understood in hindsight, by which time it is too late.

MGR credited the good showing of the two DMKs to the trust of the people in the two parties, in relation to his party's language policy, but attributed the AIADMK's poor performance in Madras to the 'incidents' that prevented the middle class from voting—an allusion to the allegations that the DMK had created disturbances and violence to discourage the middle class from stepping out of their homes.[31] The truth remained that MGR's forte was the rural heartland. Madras, till the end, would remain a DMK stronghold.

MGR DESIRES MERGER WITH DMK

Three days prior to his swearing-in, MGR asked his journalist friend Solai if he had considered his earlier request and helpfully reminded him: 'I told you in Madurai . . . Go meet Kalaignar'. Solai remembered their conversation about Congress (I)'s machinations against the Kazhagams. When Solai advised that the issue could wait, MGR responded: 'We are not speaking after defeat. We are speaking from a position of strength after a victory.' Now Solai explained that he was personally not suited for the job and, instead, suggested Dravidar Kazhagam's general secretary, K. Veeramani. 'Will he be discreet?' asked MGR. 'Yes,' Solai assured him.

In his more than an hour-long meeting with MGR, Veeramani saw that he was keen on the unity of the two Kazhagams. MGR said that he had not wished to split the DMK, had achieved what he wanted and there was no need to prove anything to anyone any further. He noted that he had managed to draw the youth into the Dravidian movement's fold although some had left for the Congress (I). He asked Veeramani to tell Kalaignar that he desired unity; there was much hostility and antagonism between the cadre, because of the past, and the leaderships should prepare them, the process should not be rushed and must be organic.[32]

An incredulous Kalaignar said that Veeramani was the third messenger and warned that he might be the third one to be let down.[33] Veeramani assured Kalaignar that MGR appeared sincere. Kalaignar told Veeramani that he would drop a hint at the Assembly session to be convened two days later.[34] An accord was reached wherein the DMK leaders and the DMK would not be criticized and, in turn, the DMK men would not be harsh in their criticism of the AIADMK and MGR. It was also decided that MGR and Kalaignar would take part together in EVR's birthday celebrations. These, however, came to naught, not in the least because of vested interests and intelligence agencies, according to Solai.[35] Yet, the MGR–Veeramani meetings continued to happen on and off. These efforts would reach a culmination in the autumn of 1979, but because of an entirely unanticipated player. We will discuss this later.

MGR'S FIRST MINISTRY

MGR had once wished to be a minister and, yet, now, he seemed to be in no hurry to assume office as chief minister. Ostensibly, there were outstanding film shoots.[36] Kalaignar wrote that MGR had, however, acted on the advice of his astrologers.[37] Vidwan Lakshmanan marked the auspicious moment for the swearing-in in 1977 (and 1980), and MGR undertook a trip to Kollur Moogambika temple prior to his swearing-in on 30 June.[38] MGR had certain beliefs. He believed in car numbers, the shape and direction of the land plot, names of movie characters, and the propitious time for beginning the first shot of a movie. He believed number seven was favourable to him.[39] None of this, however, seemed to be of help as his government would be dismissed halfway through its term.

How did MGR pick his Cabinet? The actor-politician had an eye for talent and hard work. Earlier, during the campaign tour, MGR had told C. Aranganayagam, from the Kongu region, 'Kovai Chezhian would have been a minister if he had been with us.' He then began asking Aranganayagam about his qualifications and teaching experience. It later dawned on him that MGR might have actually interviewed him for a ministerial position. Aranganayagam found himself being selected as minister of education.[40] MGR chose S. Thirunavukkarasu (now Su. Thirunavukkarasar, TNCC [I] president) as Deputy Speaker, after he heard him at the AIADMK legislators' meeting emphasizing MGR's vision of a clean administration.[41] He tried to match talent, competence, interest and requirement with the portfolios.[42] But appointments were also made on the recommendation of senior leaders and out of other representational considerations, such as caste, district, gender and religion. RMV says Manoharan assisted MGR in preparing the Cabinet list.[43]

On 30 June, Governor Prabhudas Patwari administered the oaths of office to MGR and thirteen of his Cabinet colleagues in English, and they followed up in Tamil. As chief minister, MGR's first act was to garland his mentor Anna's statue on Anna Salai. Later that day, MGR said that the Centre–state relations 'would be very cordial. You need not have any doubts about it'.[44] MGR's cordiality and his zeal to replace the DMK as the Centre's ally sometimes reached comical proportions, like his stand in the 1979 Thanjavur and the 1981 Tirupattur by-elections, and in his support for the Charan Singh ministry. This cordiality and non-confrontation, however, also helped Tamil Nadu when it came to planning outlays, but not quite when it came to industrial or infrastructural development or support for MGR's welfare schemes or for prohibition. That evening, he thanked the voters in a rally at T. Nagar, Madras, with his allies present. Propaganda secretary S.D. Somasundaram presided over the rally.

MGR's first ministry consisted of:

1. M.G. Ramachandran: Chief Minister
2. (Nanjil) K. Manoharan: Finance
3. (Panruti) S. Ramachandran: Public Works
4. K. Narayanaswamy Mudaliar: Law
5. G.R. Edmund: Food and Cooperation
6. R.M. Veerappan: Information and Publicity
7. C. Aranganayagam: Education
8. K. Kalimuthu: Local Administration
9. S. Raghavanandam: Labour
10. P. Soundarapandian: Adi Dravida Welfare
11. C. Ponnaiyan: Transport
12. P.T. Saraswathi: Social Welfare
13. P. Kolandaivelu: Agriculture
14. K. Raja Mohammed: Handlooms and Textiles[45]

MGR had noticeably retained the ministry of health, which he had sought once upon a time, the portfolios of industries, where he thought there was room for corruption, and of revenue as well, perhaps for the same reasons. On 7 May 1978, in the course of a Cabinet expansion, he would hand over the health and revenue portfolios. Two years later, 26 January 1980, he would give away the industries portfolio as well.[46] Ironically, RMV, who would be suspected of harbouring chief ministerial ambitions from 1984 onwards, was not a member of either of the Houses and was reluctant to become a minister when he got the call.[47] The expanded Cabinet had S.D. Somasundaram (SDS) as revenue, commercial taxes and excise minister, K.A. Krishnaswamy as minister for cooperation, R. Soundararajan as minister for health and Subbulakshmi Jagadeesan as minister for handlooms, taking its strength to eighteen, the largest ever in the state's history.[48] He also appointed K. Rajaram as the government's special representative to Delhi.[49]

In a public ceremony that followed, MGR renewed his election vows of a clean and honest government. As he read out a pledge, his ministers repeated it after him, and, at the end of each sentence and the mention of Anna, the crowd broke out into a lusty cheer.

MGR said:

What we underwent at Rajaji Hall some time ago was an official swearing-in ceremony. But we consider it a great honour to swear by our great leader Anna's name in your presence. The proceedings of this ceremony are at your behest. 'Vox populi, vox god,' our Anna used to say often. In keeping with the spirit of what he had said, we take great pride in bowing to the wishes of the people in being sworn-in as ministers of the new government. On behalf of my colleagues in the Cabinet and the [All-India] Anna DMK, I wish to convey this message to the Tamil people in our state, in other Indian states and overseas countries: The Legislative Assembly . . . is here only to fulfil the wishes of the people and to transform those wishes into accepted laws of the land . . . [W]e assure all of you that we will run an administration free from all forms of corruption and [a] government that will not interfere in the working of the courts of law . . . [We will] govern by the principle that one who labours is supreme and I vow in the name of our Anna that we will fulfil the above promises at any cost and against all opposition, giving up, if necessary, even our body and soul.[50]

From there, MGR went with his entire Cabinet to his elder brother, M.G. Chakrapani, to get his blessings.[51]

The Hindu's 1 July Spotlight said: 'At sixty, a man of enormous physical grit and mental vigour. MGR is bubbling with enthusiasm for transforming the lot of the poorer sections of society.'[52] MGR's energies appeared equally focused on the DMK and its leader, Kalaignar.

IN OFFICE

A personalized style of politics and administration marked MGR's regime. He was clearly his own man and, until his party's defeat in the January 1980 parliamentary polls, behaved like a pharaoh. Mohandas said that MGR's 'native wisdom and ability to quickly grasp the essentials' impressed bureaucrats. He also quickly got over the shortcoming of his unfamiliarity with English. However, reflecting MGR's inexperience, the performance of his government in its first years was somewhat amateurish.

MGR considered his administration as a continuation of Anna's and began on a highly idealistic note.[53] His accent was on the rural poor. In his first interview as chief minister in August, to *Bommai*, he noted his pain at what he found out during his election campaign: That 'a majority of villages have the need for drinking water and many women [need] clothes to cover [themselves] above their waist.'[54] His welfare schemes catered to these weaker sections.

MGR wished to give a clean government, improve service delivery and enforce prohibition vigorously. He was against political interference in administration. He saw to it that private secretaries and personal aides to ministers were chosen carefully.[55] As for dealing with corruption, MGR's cinematic approach was brought out by an incident narrated by Mohandas. MGR beckoned him over to his side while in discussions with some ministers, only to suddenly rise and leave with Mohandas. In the car, MGR explained that his leaving in Mohandas's company would discourage one of the ministers suspected to be engaged in an act of corruption. Mohandas records that all three ministers anxiously called him later to inquire what transpired between the chief minister and him.[56]

Compared to his second and third terms, MGR's first term was relatively clean. Admissions to medical colleges—a yardstick by which corruption had come to be measured in the state then—was fair.

In trying to avoid political interference, he seemed to have, in turn, handed over the government to the bureaucracy. In trying to avoid wrongdoing, the chief minister sat on files of cases where foul play was suspected. The government moved very slowly. Soon, this idealism would give way to the harsh realities of exercising power, spreading the spoils and running a political party. Elected officials and partymen sought power, authority, patronage dispensation and prosperity. MGR yielded sooner than later, according to Mohandas, but his former Cabinet colleagues are unanimous in saying that his first term was without any blemishes. One pointed out that even during the second term, most legislators had no cars of their own and R. Soundararajan, once a minister, was seen standing in queue in a government hospital for medical help and died a poor man.[57] MGR shied away from being seen with 'those kind of industrialists', fearing talk of taking money from them during the first term. In the second term, however, MGR would invite the same industrialists and become their friend.[58] In the third term, he would happily declare open a liquor baron's medical college. Yet, MGR's messianic zeal in the first years in enforcing prohibition saw him enact unrealistic legislation to curb drinking, although he had, on 17 June, prior to his swearing-in, admitted that 'laws alone cannot curb violations'.[59] The offshoot was illicit liquor and bootlegging, which the state could not control, a police force that grew corrupt on this account, and a huge number of arrests and cases against breadwinners jeopardizing the livelihoods of tens of thousands of poor households.

Despite the fact his stature was akin to a sultan, none of the ministers or functionaries had to prostrate or genuflect before him. He surrounded himself with some of the best available talent, instead of political midgets or minions. However, sycophancy was rampant. Mohandas pointed out that two ministers, who had a view completely opposite to MGR's on some issue, went to the other extreme and bowed down to MGR's opinion. Mohandas said, 'In fact, all the MLAs and ministers were always conscious of the fact that they owed their position to MGR's grace. They were only too eager to please him, agree with him, laugh with him, play with him and even worship him.'[60]

MGR was, however, conscious of both his new station and how he had reached there. He stopped travelling by his larger cars and used only a green Ambassador car as a mark of simplicity. People recognized and greeted his TMW 4777 Ambassador, although they could not see MGR inside, because of its tinted glass. MGR could see them and often cupped his hands to reciprocate their greeting. He explained to his fellow traveller Valampuri John, who wondered on the usefulness of his gesture: 'Whether they can see me or not, I feel the need to greet them. I was a movie star. They have taken me to the [St George's] fort as chief minister.'[61] S. Ramachandran said that MGR would say, 'Coolie, farm labour paid their wages for tickets for my movies and made me what I am. I have to repay my debt.'[62] Similarly, he would often be moved by the trust that people had in him, and would wonder aloud how he would live up to this.[63]

MGR's humane and thoughtful nature was exemplary and was often exhibited in his dealings with his staff and other people. Govindan, one of the chief minister's drivers, died in a fatal car accident. MGR walked in to the funeral, went up to the cremation grounds, rendered financial assistance to his family and saw to it that the insurance for the deceased came through. It was then that the family realized why, against their wishes, MGR was insistent on the autopsy. MGR also ordered that Govindan's widow be granted a job on humanitarian grounds with the State Housing Board.[64]

Similarly, sometime around the end of 1978, MGR saw a woman among the morning crowd, got out of his car and went up to her, inquired about her husband, invited her to eat and asked that a car take her home. She was former Congress minister Kakkan's wife. Kakkan could not pay the 170 rupees rent and faced eviction from his government flat. Asking for a day's time, his wife had approached MGR who settled all the rental dues from his personal funds. The next day, a government order allocated free housing to Kakkan and granted him a monthly stipend of 500 rupees. MGR made sure that the housing, allowance and medical facilities were continued even after Kakkan's demise. Poet Kannadasan said, 'Any partyman would have to praise MGR who helps true martyrs like Kakkan.'[65]

The humane MGR was equally conscious of his godlike image and the fact that he was the AIADMK. He behaved as though he was Caliph

Harun al-Rashid of the *Thousand and One Nights* fame. Instead of doing nightly rounds like the Caliph, MGR, expectedly, used his sleuths to ascertain information about events and the dealings of individuals in the Opposition, his own ministers and, later, his own mentee, Jayalalithaa, if Salem Kannan, an MP, is to be believed. People around him were on tenterhooks, fearing when they might lose their god's grace. For a man of his popularity and stature, this was unnecessary. Despite his iconic status, and perhaps because of that, he remained a loner and totally capricious.[66]

But circumstances favoured him in a way that few could have anticipated, and MGR's image as a clean man, and a man who meant well, remained intact. Nothing stuck. Like the mythical Karna, born with his earrings and armour, MGR was granted the boon of a Teflon-like exterior when it came to his image. In fact, on 30 October 1981, Kalaignar would declare:

> MGR has this huge courage in him! However much Karunanidhi and the others speak about the rectified spirit scandal, shipping scandal, blending unit, bottling unit, arrack distillery, bottling factory scandals, corruption in the selection of district wholesale arrack dealership, shout at the top of their lungs, MGR is dreaming that he cannot be shaken.[67]

On a typical day, MGR woke up early in the morning and went for a brisk walk. On his return, he would go to the gym in the basement for about an hour.[68] Then, after a bath, he would pray in his prayer room before a portrait of his mother. After breakfast, at 7.30 a.m., he spent an hour seeing visitors, after which officials would brief him. Party functionaries with appointments then got to see him. If an unscheduled visitor arrived, MGR sent him away. But simple and poor folk, in their hundreds, travelled from far-off places just to catch a glimpse of him. They wanted nothing from him. But MGR saw to it that some sixty to seventy of them were offered breakfast or lunch. This daily ritual was carried out from his personal funds.

At 9 a.m., the chief minister travelled to his Arcot Road residence in T. Nagar, where he spent an hour discussing his day's programme with his aides, after which he proceeded to Fort St George, where people and files awaited him. People brought petitions and sought his intervention. If MGR pocketed the petition, it meant that he was not in its favour. If he gave it to an aide or an official, then it meant he viewed the request positively. At 2.30 p.m., MGR would return to his Arcot Road residence, where he would rest, read or listen to classical music or watch sports on television.[69] In the evening, MGR usually had a public engagement.

FIRST ASSEMBLY SESSION

On 7 July, the first Assembly session after MGR assumed office was held. In his address, Governor Patwari said that the MGR government stood for more powers to the states, while emphasizing harmonious relations with the Centre.[70] On 15 July, Kalaignar, as the leader of the Opposition, exhorted the treasury benches to seek state autonomy, introduce a resolution seeking legal status on Nehru's language assurance, implement the election promises made and set up an inquiry into the 'cruelties' of President's Rule. With a strident Tamil nationalist Opposition breathing down his neck, MGR's work was cut out for him. He rose to the challenge and said that the two parties would act as a 'double-barrelled gun', a metaphor used by Anna of the DMK and the parent DK when it came to opposing the imposition of Hindi.[71] Chief Minister MGR asserted:

> The Tamil Nadu government is committed to the two-language formula—Tamil for administration in the state and English as the link language. My party will be second to none in championing the cause of Tamil. The Tamil Nadu government will earnestly consider compensating those who suffered during the anti-Hindi agitations.
>
> Tamil Nadu is implementing the national policy on language, but this is not being done in other states . . . The language policy cannot be implemented by laws and threats, it needs a human approach. No government can impose any language on the people.

Efficiency in administration should be the main criteria for the language policy. The administration of the state has not suffered so far because of the absence of Hindi.

The language chosen should depend not on the majority of people who speak it but on the majority of administrators using it. English is known to all administrators and, in my opinion, it is the majority language. Hindi is not used in administration.

Linking language with employment opportunities is like propagating a British idea.[72]

MGR had to frequently refurbish his credentials when it came to opposing the imposition of Hindi, and he did so quite successfully. In the last term, he would get away with even disqualifying DMK MLAs protesting against Hindi.

RELATIONS BETWEEN THE CHIEF MINISTER AND LEADER OF THE OPPOSITION

MGR's relationship with Kalaignar and the Opposition was marked by capriciousness. Although in today's Dravidian politics, the actions of MGR then would pass off as respectable and even thoughtful, they were also equally tit for tat when it came to Kalaignar.

On the one hand, competitive politics and the five years of bad blood and bitter acrimony saw them constantly engaged in a game of one-upmanship. The two appeared obsessed with each other. If MGR tried to harass Kalaignar using the Sarkaria Commission findings and launching litigation, which often smacked of victimization, Kalaignar left no stone unturned to paint MGR as personally corrupt and his administration as anti-poor, anti-labour and ineffective. Thus, when allegations were made about admissions to medical colleges, an emotional MGR told the Assembly on 16 August, 'If it is proven that either I or ministers or ruling partymen had approached the selection committee to influence the committee, we will resign.'[73]

On the other hand, there were moments that showed that despite all that had happened between them, both Kalaignar and MGR professed much respect and civility for each other. The common struggle of more than a quarter century and their shared experience bound them. Those close to both may not have fully understood or liked this between them. What could hardly be imagined today was possible then. Even when they exchanged barbs and criticized each other in the Assembly, it was cultured and nuanced. On one occasion, Kalaignar said: 'Power is not new to us. You are tasting what we have eaten and left behind.' MGR's repartee was quick and pregnant with meaning: 'Yes. We have been voted to power to see how much you have eaten.'[74] Similarly, both the treasury benches and the Opposition were able to welcome the president or the prime minister at the airport, a practice that had been given the go-by long ago, thanks to the anomie in cultural values. And by all accounts, MGR gave a free rein to the presiding officers of the House and admonished any heavy criticism of Kalaignar or the use of the singular, identified in Tamil with impoliteness. In the Assembly, when an AIADMK member went about mentioning Kalaignar by just his name, 'Karunanidhi, Karunanidhi', MGR stopped him and advised him to say Kalaignar. 'He had been my leader,' MGR pointed out.[75] MGR wanted such remarks expunged and advised the treasury benches to behave with maturity and responsibility, regardless of the Opposition's actions.[76]

Both leaders would exchange greetings, smile and sometimes talk in a friendly manner to each other. In late August, in a public meeting in Neyveli, Nellikuppam Krishnamurthy, a DMK legislator, said the rapport between the two leaders had caused doubts in the minds of the cadre, who requested an explanation. In his clarification, Kalaignar cited traditions, the Periyar–Rajaji, Kamaraj–Anna relationships and the camaraderie between some in the DMK and the treasury benches. He said that their meetings were to discuss Assembly proceedings and not as 'suspected to look into the almanac for a date for the merger of the DMK and the ADMK'. It was, of course, a Freudian slip and a merger would almost happen in two years' time.[77]

On 15 August, in his first Independence Day speech at the celebrations in Fort St George, which Kalaignar attended as he had been invited, MGR said after hoisting the national flag:

I am obliged to mention this here . . . Up to a few years [ago] . . .
the governor would hoist this flag. I wish to commend Kalaignar
Karunanidhi for fighting to change that practice and for obtaining
this right for all the chief ministers.[78]

However, competitive politics meant that this bonhomie could not be maintained. Kalaignar and the DMK were determined to oppose MGR at every turn. MGR and his cohorts were determined to continue tarnishing the image of Kalaignar and his DMK. Thus, MGR's other side was seen when his government showed more than keen interest in taking the Sarkaria Commission's findings further. On 5 November, when asked whether he could not 'forgive and forget' (one of Anna's major sayings), he made it clear that cases were not being pursued in order 'to avenge' the difficulties inflicted on them in the past five years, and that one can 'never forgive' the crime of stealing public money.[79]

On occasions, MGR appeared to get personal. Unveiling EVR's statue on 18 September, MGR said, 'Karunanidhi's statue is on Anna Salai. The court will decide if it should be there or not. We will act according to the court's judgement. Until the matter can be lawfully dealt with, I ask that you stay patient. Do not do anything in anger.' An AIADMK man had legally challenged the installation of the statue.[80]

Kalaignar appeared to be an anathema. By the end of 1977, the government said that no public space or building should be named after the living. Soon thereafter, the name board of the Slum Clearance Board building at Nandanam, called Karunanidhi Maaligai, was removed. But it also led to some absurd situations when Anna's widow, Rani Anna's, name too had to be removed from a building named after her. Kalaignar wrote to the chief minister to make the order direct—asking just for the removal of his name but leaving the names of the rest of the living intact. In contravention of its own order, the MGR administration would later name government buildings, institutions and public places after the living, such as partyman R. Mohanarangam and Mother Teresa.[81]

Also, MGR denied permission 'at any cost' for a statue of EVR in Kanchipuram.* He insisted this was because of his high regard for the

---

* Despite his early familiarity with EVR's writings, MGR wondered thus while unveiling EVR's statue on 18 September 1977: 'How could Periyar, who had said that there should be no temples, have said that people from all castes could become priests?' Kalaignar pointed out that Periyar himself had said this on the occasion of the Vaikom (1924–25) struggle to throw open public streets to all, and such equal right of access extended to temples too. Kalaignar M. Karunanidhi, *Nenjuku Needhi*, vol. 3, Chennai: Thirumagal Nilayam, 2008, pp. 169–75.

senior Kanchi Shankaracharya. The DMK took the matter to court and, on 24 February 1980, unveiled the statue.[82]

MGR'S CHALLENGES

It was no surprise then that the most difficult challenge for the chief minister, in addition to the difficulties of administration, was his political nemesis, Kalaignar, who excelled as the leader of the Opposition and proved a formidable opponent, both in power and outside. He was sharp, able, engaged and tireless, and was on top of his brief. His politics kept the chief minister and his administration on edge.

Additionally, as chief minister, MGR faced the usual difficulties of administration. He often, and perhaps not unjustifiably, saw a DMK hand behind these. 'For two years instead of an agitation a day, they conducted three or four agitations in different places . . . Police could not catch thieves, provide security . . . prevent smuggling. Why? Because there was agitation, picketing everywhere. Strikes in transportation, electricity department, teaching . . .' MGR noted of this period later.[83] He dealt with agitations, strikes and demonstrations harshly, frequently saying that 'people will respond to them',[84] pitting his popular support against organized protests, whether it was non-gazetted officers (NGOs), teachers, farmers, transport staff or lawyers. He tried to crush their agitations with force, but, in the end, had to give in more than he would have wished to because of the strong Opposition, led by the DMK. Clearly, there was only so much his aura could achieve. This was not the movies, where he could always come out on top in the end.

The chief minister desired and felt the need to deny the DMK, in particular, political space, which led to situations where the administration refused to relent until the situation appeared to get out of control. The strike by the state-owned Pallavan Transport Corporation workers in late August–early September, after their demands were turned down, is an example. To break the strike, MGR ordered that a policeman be placed in each bus to provide security, and he asked his partymen to travel in the buses for the same reason.[85] Kalaignar also accused the MGR administration of requesting private bus operators to ply buses. An all-party meeting decided to hold protest meetings on 4 September and a shutdown on 6 September. Thankfully, three days before, on 3 September, an accord was reached, bringing the eight-day strike to an end.

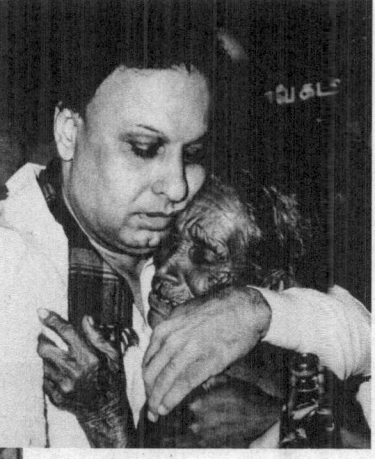

'Makkal Thilagam' MGR

K.R. Ramasamy to his left;
E.V.K. Sampath to his right

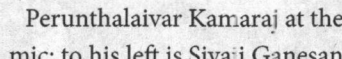

Perunthalaivar Kamaraj at the
mic; to his left is Sivaji Ganesan

At a South Indian
Artistes Association fast,
with comedian and critic
Chandrababu

(L to R) M.R. Radha, music director K.V. Mahadevan and MGR

MGR, film villain M.N. Nambiar (third from the right, wearing make-up), M.G. Chakrapani (far righ

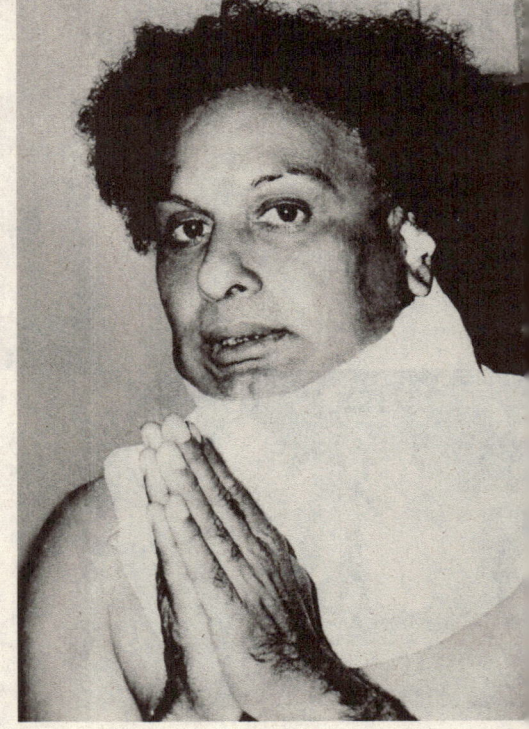

Appealing to voters from his hospital bed in 1967

A still from *Nam Nadu* (1969)

On the sets of *Thedi Vandha Maapillai* (1970): Singer TMS is to MGR's right, music director MSV and producer B.R. Panthulu are on his left. Standing (L to R): Lyricist Vaali and scriptwriter R.K. Shanmugam

At a function celebrating *Savaale Samaali* (1971). (L to R) Sivaji Ganesan, Kalaignar, MGR and Jayalalithaa

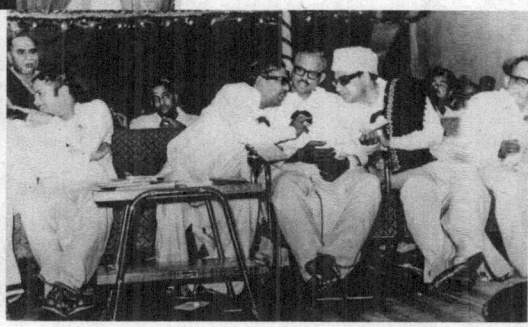

DMK conference in Madurai, in 1972. (L to R) Murasoli Maran, Kalaignar, Navalar Nedunchezhian, MGR, P.U. Shanmugam

With E.V.R. Periyar;
K. Veeramani is in the centre

Garlanding Rajaji in 1972

(L to R) CPI's
M. Kalyanasundaram
(wearing glasses),
K.A. Krishnaswamy
and MGR

The AIADMK leader
entering Anna's mausoleum

MGR's 'public' swearing-in ceremony

MGR—the people's CM

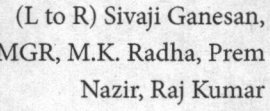

(L to R) Sivaji Ganesan, MGR, M.K. Radha, Prem Nazir, Raj Kumar

Garlanding his mentor Anna's statue on his return from the US; to the right are Navalar Nedunchezhian and Nanjil Manoharan

(L to R) MGR, music director S.M. Subbiah Naidu, Sivaji Ganesan and poet Kannadasan

With Kamal Haasan

With LTTE's Prabhakaran

MGR's 1980 ministry—Portraits (L to R): Rajaji, Kamaraj, EVR in the backdrop with Anna holding MGR's hands, Ambedkar and Muhammad Ismail Sahib

Sitting (L to R): C. Ponnaiyan, C. Aranganayagam, S.D. Somasundaram, S. Ramachandran, MGR, Governor Patwari, V.R. Nedunchezhian, K.A. Krishnaswamy, R.M. Veerappan, K. Kalimuthu

Standing (L to R): M. Vijayasarathy, Gomathi Srinivasan, S.N. Rajendran, Raja Mohammed, P. Kulandaivelu, S. Raghavanandam, H.V. Hande, S. Thirunavukkarasu, S. Muthusamy

(L to R) V.N. Chidambaram, K. Rajaram, PM Indira Gandhi, MGR and R M. Veerappan at the Madurai temple

Rajinikanth garlanding MGR

1982 ASIAD: MGR
seated between Jayalalithaa
and Janaki Ramachandran

Receiving PM Rajiv
Gandhi; Governor S.L.
Khurana is in the centre

The end of an er

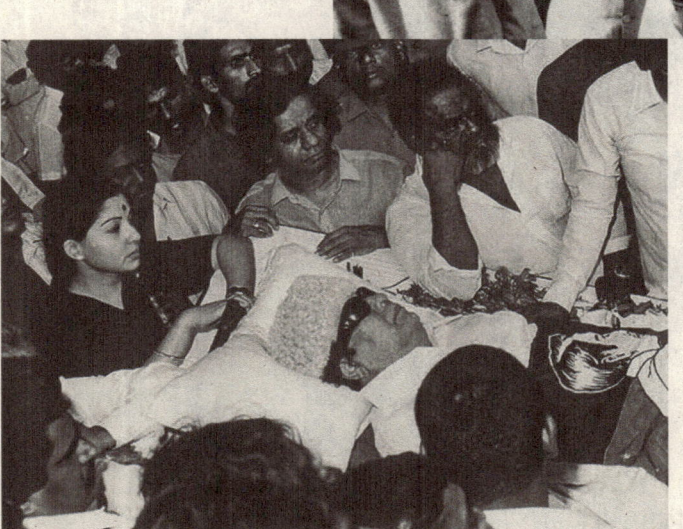

UNDOING THE DMK'S ANTI-CORRUPTION ACT

The obsession to continue to paint the DMK as a corrupt party and undo some of its legislations, however constructive they were, for political ends was rather evident in the first term. The MGR administration therefore decided to repeal the Public Men Conduct Enquiry Act, the precursor to today's Lokayukta idea, that Kalaignar had enacted in 1973. Then, the AIADMK fearing that the Act would weaken its charges against the DMK had termed it a 'black act' and a whitewash. Now, it tried to upend it to justify its earlier stand. The MGR government contended that the Act, which had come into force on 8 May 1974, 'was found to contain some basic defects' and 'also served no useful purpose'. The public was unwilling to depose against the accused and, during the tenure of the Act, the commissioner had not concluded any case. The DMK's contention that the baby was being thrown out with the bathwater and that the defects could have been rectified or a new, improved legislation could have been brought in went unheeded.[86]

ETHNIC ISSUE

The ethnic issue would become a bone of contention between the two parties from the early days of the MGR administration and the competition for championing the Sri Lankan Tamil cause would become a major preoccupation for both leaders. Violence in the third week of August 1977 in Sri Lanka saw the DMK call for a rally on 24 August and a closure in Madras, termed as 'redundant' by Manoharan, the Leader of the House. Kalaignar rightly said that the government did not wish the House to discuss the issue. On the morning of 24 August, tens of thousands of DMK men marched to the Sri Lankan Deputy High Commission in Madras. The Leader of the House moved an official resolution to coincide with the rally. Kalaignar indicated that the plans for the resolution were not disclosed even until the previous evening, probably to keep the DMK out of the loop. Clearly, the MGR administration was torn between not annoying the Centre on a foreign policy issue while not giving the DMK any room.[37]

THE FIRST TEST: INDIRA GANDHI VISIT

Indira Gandhi's two-day tour of Tamil Nadu on 29 and 30 October posed the first serious test for the MGR administration. The DMK's executive convened quickly on 27 October and decided to greet Indira Gandhi with black flags. Mohandas said that the Janata Party had put the DMK up to it.

Kalaignar said that lakhs of the cadre caressed the 'bloody scars caused by [the] Indira government's cruelty with one hand and held black flags in their other hand'! He recorded for posterity:

> 29.10.1977! This is the day when Indira Gandhi, and perhaps the whole of the Indian subcontinent, fully understood the DMK! The DMK workers showed to the world that they are the successors to the Self-respect Movement. On the 27th, the executive passed a resolution! Only a statement [followed]! Only an explanatory meeting in Chennai! On the 29th, the entire Tamilagam rose [as one]!

Although the black-flag demonstration was to begin in Madurai, zealous DMK men waved black flags and shouted 'Go back, Indira' even as she came out of the Madras airport on 29 October. Kalaignar recorded that the DMK men were beaten up and, to downplay the numbers, only twenty-five were arrested.

In Madurai, Indira Gandhi's car could not get past the black-flag cordon. As stones, eggs and sticks were thrown at her car, the police used sixteen rounds of tear gas and lathi charged the crowd, even as Indira Gandhi sat in her car. 'They [DMK] tried to attack her. I protected her. Not a single blow fell on her,' Congress (I) leader, P. Nedumaran would remark later. Sivaji Ganesan claimed that a 'plot was hatched to assassinate' her in Madurai. (Mohandas said that but for the police intervention, it would have been another Sriperumpudur [where Rajiv Gandhi was assassinated].)[88] On 30 October, Chief Minister MGR commented that Indira Gandhi 'would have died if she had been attacked'.[89]

Indira Gandhi cancelled her visit to the Meenakshi temple. She refused to comment on the incidents.[90] By now, prohibitory orders had been issued to prevent further demonstrations. Despite the ban, the DMK men greeted Indira Gandhi with black flags on her motor journey to Trichy. She, therefore, changed her route from Thoppampatti and travelled to Dindigul to board a train to Trichy. In Trichy, she managed to address the meeting scheduled for her, albeit briefly. Police had to burst tear gas shells to disperse the protesters.[91] She left by train for Madras.

In Madras, prohibitory orders had been issued for two days. Kalaignar and Anbazhagan were to lead the protests in Guindy, where a police bullet claimed its first victim. Kalaignar and the others were arrested at Saidapet before they could reach the picketing site; this fuelled further violence at Saidapet, where there was a second victim and the crowds halted Indira Gandhi's train in its tracks.

By the time Indira Gandhi's train pulled into Egmore station in Madras, the city was a war zone. A barrage of stones greeted Indira Gandhi as she got down from the train and Sivaji Ganesan said he had to point his revolver at the crowd, threatening to shoot if they drew near. He then drove her to the guest house.[92]

Indira Gandhi took a different route to Kanchipuram to avoid the protests and stopped at the town's outskirts to seek the blessings of the Kanchi Sankaracharya. In her public meeting in Madras later that day, Indira Gandhi said she was not shaken by the black-flag demonstration and would not be cowed by any instigation of violence. She left for Delhi early the following morning.[93] India Today said Indira Gandhi's '48-hour tour ended in a grand fiasco, leaving behind two dead, 200 wounded and over 1000 in jail'.[94] Kalaignar and others were later charged with, among other things, conspiracy to murder Indira Gandhi. But the wheels of justice turn slowly and, in 1995, the Supreme Court upheld the High Court's earlier dismissal of these cases. The wheels of politics, however, move at lightning speed. In a little over two years, Kalaignar and Indira Gandhi would be travelling in the same car, as political allies, during the 1980 parliamentary elections—evoking much criticism from observers that Kalaignar's political expediency had made him quickly forget the sufferings of the DMK and its men under Indira Gandhi's Emergency.

A peeved and spurned MGR would declare then, 'If the Congress (I) can have an alliance with a man like Karunanidhi, there is no reason why it cannot have one with someone like me who had ordered police firing to protect Amma from Karunanidhi's goons when she visited Madras four years ago.'[95]

THE SECOND TEST: A CYCLONE

If the first test was man-made, the second was of nature's making. On 12 November 1977, a cyclone, believed to be the biggest in twenty-five years, wreaked havoc in Tamil Nadu. The official death toll was in the hundreds (400 on 18 November), but CARE placed the actual death toll at over 2000. MGR convened an all-party meeting and sought support. The US consul general's cable of the time described relief efforts as 'quick, effective and efficient'.[96]

MGR issued a statement thanking all the parties but complained that the DMK was not helping and was, instead, agitating for the unconditional release of its leader. Kalaignar recorded that the DMK was treated with indifference by the government, as no senior official was available to accept its donation of 25,000 rupees, which was then handed over to the governor's secretariat. DMK lawmakers donated a month's salary, and the party suspended its agitation and asked for relief donations. As money orders poured in to Kalaignar in his prison cell, officials refused to accept them and advised that contributions be sent to the governor instead.

On 8 December, the DMK men's remand ended. The prosecution said it would not object to the detainees being let out on bail. Earlier, the DMK had announced picketing statewide from 9 December if they were not released. The defence counsel argued that the case was 'wholly politically motivated' and refused to move for bail. In the event, they were released. Kalaignar said that his 'friend MGR had given them forty days of good rest'.[97]

RETURN TO THE OLD WAYS!

At the December 1977 executive and legislature party meetings, MLAs observed that they had no say in the administration, complaining that officials baulk at even the genuine grievances they put before them. When MGR consulted him, Mohandas advised him to stay the course, but MGR 'looked unconvinced', and that evening, he advised his party officials and MLAs that they would soon have an 'effective role to play'. Mohandas wrote: 'I immediately knew that the die was cast. I told MGR that, for the first time since he took over as CM, I found him inclined to stray from the straight and narrow path. He did not like it.'[98]

However, in the essay he wrote on the completion of six months of his term, the chief minister had stated that he had taken to heart

Rajaji's advice to Anna—to keep partymen away from the corridors of the secretariat. Those immediately before him had discarded the advice and had paid for it. He took what had happened as a 'warning', and said that he had taken 'extreme care' to keep partymen (and corruption) away from the administration and had succeeded to 'some extent' in this.[99] Was this really so?

FIRST NO-CONFIDENCE MOTION

On 4 January 1978, the DMK moved a no-confidence motion that was debated for three days, starting from 4 January, with forty-two members taking part. Kalaignar charged that the administration was acting contrary to Anna's policies. He cited the AIADMK's support for the Emergency and its opposition to the DMK's resolution on state autonomy, and, perhaps taking a dig at MGR's purported desire for the merger, said that 'as some believe, there is no possibility for the two parties to unite as far as policy is concerned'. He said that over the past five months, some 25–30,000 people have been arrested by the administration. He charged that only 422 shops of the 16,000 fair price shops promised had been opened, that the promise of jobs for 1 lakh rural youth, for graduates, and for labourers to run factories that were closed down was yet to be fulfilled. He said that there was corruption in the awarding of contracts for undertaking relief works. Referring to the black-flag demonstration against Indira Gandhi, which he termed a 'duty', Kalaignar charged that the 'AIADMK implemented mini-MISA on Indira Gandhi's advice to finish [off] the DMK'.[100] MGR himself blamed the bureaucracy for some of the lapses.[101] The motion was defeated, with the communists and the Congress (I) opposing it, while the Janata Party abstained from voting.

The AIADMK general council meeting in 1978 saw partymen and MLAs again voicing their disappointment with officialdom. MGR buckled under their pressure and expanded his council of ministers in March with the appointment of eight parliamentary secretaries in an effort to curb the disgruntlement; thus reviving the system of parliamentary secretaries after a lapse of twenty-five years. A ninth parliamentary secretary was inducted in October.[102] Mohandas wrote of this time: 'MGR suddenly looked old and disappointed.'[103]

CORRUPTION IN THE SECRETARIAT

On 4 February, the chief minister revealed that on a file involving a land case, the concerned minister had written 'stay should not be granted' under the typed noting. However, below this, the words 'stay may be granted' were found handwritten. When MGR called the minister, he confirmed that he had not added anything to the typed noting. The chief minister said this showed how deep-rooted corruption was at the secretariat. He also said that when he met the prime minister and the home minister, they had pointed out that corruption was rampant in Tamil Nadu; the prime minister had, in fact, wondered if corruption was legally sanctioned in the state. MGR said the home minister, too, felt that corruption had become a 'right' in the state.[104] This instance gives an insight into MGR's reputed delay in disposing of files. In late 1981, justifying his taking time to clear files, MGR said:

> I don't take decisions unless I have all the details of a particular case with me. I can take a right decision only when I know everything about something, isn't it? You can't blame me in such cases, can you? During Karunanidhi's time, I am afraid the files were in a mess.
>
> This is causing us problems now. Just one example: A certain project cost 70 lakh rupees in 1970. Karunanidhi approved it in 1972. By the time work began on it, it was 1974. We will need over 330 lakh rupees to finish this project [now], thanks to my worthy predecessor's file-pushing efficiency. May I ask: What the hell was he doing sitting on the project for four blessed years?
>
> Files are often found missing. One wise official took eight months to fish out one file! Another just didn't know where his files were. The Sarkaria Commission had indicted one of Karunanidhi's officials for changing currency notes worth over 30 lakh rupees into notes of smaller denominations when there were rumours about [the] impending demonetization. This being so, can you really blame me for my so-called suspicious nature?[105]

ABUSE OF MINISTERIAL AUTHORITY

On 1 March, participating in the budget debate, Kalaignar listed incidents of interference in the administration by ministers and ruling partymen. He also pointed out how an official car allotted to the state's social welfare minister, P.T. Saraswathi, had been used by her mother and was seen at the Guindy Race Course. Chief Minister MGR seized the moral high ground here, intervening to say that his government should steer clear of any scandal. He added that the minister could participate in the House's proceedings only if she provided an explanation to clear herself of the charge. She duly expressed regret, saying that the incident had happened without her knowledge and the security man had escorted her mother, who was very old.[106] Today, the incident seems rather innocuous. But even such instances of open admissions of wrongdoings or errors in judgement are unthinkable, for we have reached a stage in our political culture where the ruling party can do no wrong and in the eyes of the Opposition, nothing right.

The MGR government dealt with agitations with an iron fist. NGOs carried out an agitation in February–March 1978, listing a number of demands. Kalaignar pointed out the chief minister's speech at a public event where he had said he would take to the streets and deal with the agitation with the help of the people. The Opposition staged a walkout.

The protesting NGO staff was attacked and an accident involving their leader was 'staged' as a warning. Finally, despite its tough talk, on 15 March, the government invited the NGOs for talks and succeeded in bringing them around. The raising of the age of superannuation to fifty-eight from fifty-five and the other concessions granted pleased the non-gazetted officers.[107]

Earlier, on 4 March, the government appointed the Krishnasamy Naidu Commission to probe the alleged improprieties committed during Kalaignar's second term that lasted from January 1972 to 31 May 1975. Kalaignar said it was in reaction to his 1 March speech, in which he had listed the improprieties of the treasury benches.[108]

THE DMK'S CONCILIATORY MOVES TOWARDS INDIRA GANDHI

On 2 April, in Madurai, Kalaignar remarked in a public meeting, for which tickets were sold and 50,000 rupees was collected for the party, that 'though he would unhesitatingly say that the Emergency promulgated by Indira Gandhi laid the foundation for dictatorship, atrocity . . . However, with the passage of time, Indira Gandhi herself appears to be slowly realizing this'. It was the first time Kalaignar had made a conciliatory comment about Indira Gandhi after the Emergency.

The following day, the industries minister, George Fernandes, said that Kalaignar knew well that Indira Gandhi was a fascist and that he would not do anything to support her. Kalaignar retorted on 11 April with a missive marked 'For Fernandes's Attention', which reminded him about the DMK government having provided refuge for many Janata Party ministers during the Emergency. Kalaignar also recorded his displeasure at the continuing Sarkaria probe, adding that he wanted those who preached to do some introspection themselves. He said that MGR had once called JP, Morarji Desai, Ashok Mehta and George Fernandes fascists. 'But now, George Fernandes says, "For me MGR is a friend; similarly Karunanidhi is also a friend."' This showed, Kalaignar declared, how political changes happen and how they were inevitable. Earlier, in February, Indira Gandhi had lamely explained in Trichy that her decision to dismiss the DMK government was owing to the advice she got from officers of the home ministry that the party's term was coming to an end.[109] If this was the case, then where was the need for dismissal?

Meanwhile, in the April biennial elections to the Rajya Sabha, the AIADMK gave its surplus votes to the Janata Party's Era. Chezhian and supported the Central government on the Banking Service Commission (Repeal) Bill in Parliament. MGR explained his support to the Congress (I) during the Emergency as support for its twenty-point programme. Now, he supported the Janata Party as its leaders continued the implementation of the programme. He explained his contradiction thus:

As far as I am concerned, my policies are single-minded and not concerned with what one [person] says. If our policy is one supported by Congress (I) or the Janata [Party] we appreciate it. For example, many points of Mrs Gandhi's twenty-point programme were good for the country, so we supported them. Many of the points are being reiterated by Janata [Party] leaders as well. Even family planning is being stressed by the present government. I have a letter from the prime minister saying that the family planning programme should be carried forward speedily.

So there is no question of special respect for Indira Gandhi then and none now. [It is] the same with Morarji Desai. It is only on the language issue that I have opposed Morarji Desai. Indira Gandhi assured us that she would preserve the assurances given by Pandit Nehru to non-Hindi speaking people—that Hindi will not be imposed upon them. Morarji Desai gave no such assurance. But after the resolution passed by the conference of south Indian chief ministers, the prime minister has given the assurance we demanded.[110]

MGR was playing a clever game, but Thanjavur would end his policy of riding two horses.

RELUCTANT POLITICIAN: RESUMING ACTING

Mohandas wrote that MGR was 'ill at ease' with his chief ministerial responsibilities and wished to resume acting.[111] On 12 February 1973, MGR announced in Madurai that he would go back to acting in two months as he could not repay his tax arrears from his salary.[112] MGR's flip-flops on this show his frustration and discomfort with officialdom, and the burden of politics, administration and governance. As early as December 1975, he had indicated that if he were to be voted to power he would defer to people's wishes and the law with regard to simultaneously continuing his film career.[113] S. Ramachandran denied that MGR was a reluctant politician, explaining that these announcements were the results of his 'frustration' at not being able to do much for the poor and the opposition that he encountered.[114]

MGR's explanations for his wish were inconsistent nonetheless. On the one hand, he said he needed the money to pay his tax dues. On the other hand, he credited the idea to DMK MLA Suppu, who had said that the money could be used for schemes, and that he had accepted it. Film-maker Muktha Srinivasan wrote that MGR was lost in 'deep thought' after he had suggested in a felicitation event, soon after the actor came into power, that he had settled for a 'job of simply pushing paper'. In his acceptance speech, MGR agreed with Srinivasan and announced that he would be an actor for fifteen days a month and chief minister for the remaining fifteen days. When Prime Minister Desai heard about this proposal, he called MGR up to advise him against this policy, saying it would not be dignified.[115] However, that year, MGR told *Rani*, a weekly, that he would not quit acting. He said he would manage both responsibilities.[116] In August, as MGR said he had paid back 13 lakh rupees of his income-tax dues, Kalaignar wondered about the source of the funds. To this MGR replied, 'If I had wrongly earned this money and paid back my dues, would the income-tax officials leave me alone?' He also asked how Kalaignar had arrears amounting to 80 lakh rupees and pressed him to reveal the details. He then refuted the widespread notion that he was not going back to acting to pay back his dues but to propagate his ideals.[117]

On 31 January 1979, he repeated the announcement that from April he would resume acting in his own film *Imayithin Uchiyil* (At Himalayas Summit), scheduled for a Deepavali release. He said if the law would not permit it, he would turn over his responsibility to 'friends' and take to acting.[118] In true MGR style, three days later, at Anna's death anniversary event, the chief minister reversed his words and said that 'until I am alive, I would not shun responsibility on any account'.[119] Yet in the same breath he cited the example of Dr B.C. Roy who continued his practice as a physician when he was chief minister of West Bengal.[120] MGR later wrote to Desai seeking permission, saying he had income-tax arrears and it was not possible to pay this back with his salary. Sivaji Ganesan welcomed MGR's move, but Kalyanasundaram opposed it.[121] On 5 June 1979, MGR said in Thanjavur that he had mortgaged his studios to raise 40 lakh rupees to pay the last tranche of his tax dues and, with this, had settled them.[122]

On 14 April, *Dinathanthi* ran the story that MGR would star in the movie *Unnai Vidamatten* (I Won't Leave You) on its first page. Sometime earlier, the telephone rang at Vaali's place. MGR asked him to check the newspapers. That day's *Indian Express* had featured a story that said the prime minister had no objection to MGR's film career, provided it did not interfere with his official duties. Vaali quickly prepared the screenplay and K. Shankar was to direct the film.[123] On the appointed day, Manoharan symbolically declared open the shooting at

Prasad Studios. Around this time, the police had opened fire on agitating farmers and MGR said that he, not wishing to make things difficult, had requested the governor, who was willing to attend the film event, to stay away. MGR said he would continue to act in movies that would serve the country well.[124] After this, *India Today* reported that one Monday, some top professionals went to the chief minister's office to invite MGR to preside over an event of much significance to Tamil Nadu's industrial growth. Initially, they learnt that the chief minister was too busy to see them, but when they insisted, they were told that he was at the campus of the Indian Institute of Technology, Madras. He was not there. Eventually, the chief minister was traced to a studio where *Unnai Vidamatten* was being shot. MGR was there from the morning till the evening, despite his announcement that he would keep his film work for after office hours. 'This incident just about sums up the kind of government activities that go on under the benign leadership of MGR,' the magazine commented.[125] On 6 December 1978, during his visit to Singapore, the chief minister made it clear that he had never made the transition to politics fully, 'I have not left the film world. Therefore, the question of when I will return does not arise. Without taking a salary from the government, I will continue to engage myself in acting.'[126] On his return on 9 December, the chief minister termed his nearly six-week-long trip as 'useful'. Among others, he indicated that Singapore had combated sea erosion successfully and this could prove useful as he was thinking of pushing back the sea in Royapuram and Tiruchendur.[127]

VIVASAYIGAL SANGAM AGITATION

The actor-chief minister could hardly get away from the pressing problems of the public. From the spring of 1978, the Vivasayigal Sangam (farmers' association) would become a thorn in his flesh.

In early 1978, the sangam agreed to pay land tax, but wanted the distraint proceedings to be dropped. When this was declined, the sangam representatives walked out of the government's high-power committee in March. However, Mohandas said that the sangam's leader, Narayanasamy Naidu, had bigger ambitions. In the first week of April, the sangam asked farmers not to pay their electricity bills, cooperative credit, land tax, etc., and put forth a nine-point charter of demands.

The nine-point agitation began and a statewide protest to condemn 'police repression' led to a sub-inspector's death in Tirunelveli. On 8 April, Narayanasamy Naidu was arrested in Dindigul for inciting violence. The agitation intensified and the police fired at the protesting farmers, including at Vedasendur, Nochiodaipatti, Udumalpet and Vagaikulam, killing five farmers.

On 11 April, in a statement, Kalaignar pointed out that if the government had monitored the situation carefully and had engaged with the sangam's representatives, such incidents could have been avoided. As more police firings followed, Kalaignar said that the government was 'obstinate' and standing on 'prestige'. The Army had been called in to deal with the situation and, by 20 April, *Dinamani* reported that 6000 people had been arrested.[128] On 24 and 25 April, MGR held talks with the representatives of the sangam. On 25 April, Narayanasamy Naidu developed chest pain at the venue of the talks and was admitted to a hospital. Earlier, on 19 April, the DMK called for a commission, made up of a high court judge and the public, to look into farmers' grievances and to release those detained immediately, and announced a week-long agitation of its own from 23 April. Mohandas wrote that on 30 April, the police used tear gas and batons on the sangam protestors at Valliyur village, in Chengalpattu district. However, Janata Party leaders alleged that the police ransacked the houses of the farmers and the media condemned the police 'brutality'. The chief minister and the minister for social welfare visited the place.[129]

On 22 May 1979, the chief minister announced twenty-five relief measures worth 40 crore rupees for 16 lakh farmers, including the writing-off of short-term loans.[130] Kalaignar called this move an 'eye wash'.[131] On 10 June, an exasperated chief minister declared that if some found that 40 crore rupees of relief was not enough, even 400 crore rupees would not satisfy them.[132]

ONE YEAR IN OFFICE

Meanwhile, Mohandas wrote that the rot was beginning to set in. MGR, however, thought differently. At the end of his eleventh month in office, he stated that the ministry had earned a good name because, in this short period, it had managed to remove corruption, at least at a small level. There was no corruption among the ministers, and likewise, among the MLAs, MLCs and MPs.[133]

The view from the outside was generally favourable to MGR. *Times of India* complimented the chief minister for his 'conciliatory approach' in the way he dealt with the non-gazetted officers' agitation. *National Herald* also praised MGR for weeding out corruption. However, it commented that economic growth in the state was unsatisfactory. *Statesman* felt that the government was mainly preoccupied with law and order. *Mail* also sang the refrain that MGR had contained corruption in high places.[134] *Sunday* and *India Today* said MGR was no match for Kalaignar, who exposed MGR's political naivety.[135]

India Today's scathing story was titled 'Administration: Cleanly inefficient'. It said that his charisma and popularity remained intact, but the government was stuck as MGR was guided by the principle that the best way to avoid corruption was not to act at all. It mocked the government's own advertisements of one year's achievements and rightly so. The upgrade of 'one post of superintendent of police designated as assistant inspector-general of police, sanctioned for the city for effective enforcement of "work in and around Madras"' had topped it. The administration, it said, did not know the difference between achievements and routine administrative actions. It concluded damningly that MGR's was a clownish administration and 'only a jester is lacking to make this medieval "Court of MGR" complete'.[136]

For a government run by a movie star with no administrative experience, MGR had actually done reasonably well. Although he lacked vision and treated routine administrative problems as if they were movie fights, he had performed much better than expected. He had been true to his prohibition policy, although the stringent punishments proved self-defeating. As for political corruption, *Times of India* said, 'Even the worst critics of the AIADMK government concede that MGR has rooted [it] out . . . No breath of scandal or complaint attends the selection of students to the professional colleges as in the past.'[137] S. Ramachandran noted that until 1980, MGR ran a tight ship and was very strict, and was 'penniless'. He conceded that some ministers might have been corrupt, but MGR himself was clean up to this point.

This was not the DMK's view. On 2 July, Kalaignar termed MGR's administration as corrupt. He alleged the government had collected 500 to 5000 rupees from cinema owners as 'extortion tax' and major irregularities had occurred in the grant of operating permits for bus routes, and he would prove this if there was an inquiry commission.[138]

ACTION ON SARKARIA'S FINAL REPORT

The Justice Sarkaria Committee findings were made public on 13 May. Sarkaria said Kalaignar's ministry was found guilty of misuse of official machinery to promote the DMK's ends. Among other things, Sarkaria held Kalaignar and Sadiq Pasha responsible for the wastage of 6 crore rupees in the Veeranam scheme.[139] But the commission had also implicated some others, like P.U. Shanmugam and C.P. Adithan, who had crossed over to the AIADMK or were allies of the party. Furthermore, it had not taken up the allegations involving Navalar Nedunchezhian, Sathyavani Muthu and Madurai Muthu, also with the AIADMK. Earlier, on 13 February Kalaignar had asked if 'MGR would arrange for an inquiry against them'?[140] In response, MGR said that if it was proven that they had taken money, action against them would be initiated as per the court's ruling.[141]

At the outset, Sarkaria had rejected fourteen of the twenty-eight charges as untenable. Of the fourteen taken up, Kalaignar was held responsible on two counts. Protesting the fact that cross-examination was not allowed with respect to all the witnesses, the DMK did not take part in the proceedings and the inquiry was concluded in its absence. Kalaignar said that in two-and-a-half years, the Veeranam scheme could have been concluded, as the feasibility study during President's Rule had favoured it, but it was left unexecuted with the aim of discrediting the DMK. He said MGR's main charge, that he had taken lakhs of rupees as bribes from the contractor, had not been proven. He said if all their requests for cross-examination had been allowed, even the allegations that apparently had been proven would have been demolished.[142] Dr M. Santhosham, vice president of the Janata Party in the state, said the findings were based on testimony of witnesses 'compelled by threats to speak against their conscience'.[143]

MGR was in Delhi, but rejected the chatter that he had gone there to discuss the Sarkaria findings. He said he had gone to discuss the loss of 146 crore rupees because of prohibition. On Sarkaria, he said that the 'law will take its course', famously reminding the DMK:

> I am, in fact, the person who submitted the memorandum. A lot of people had spoken to me with charges against Karunanidhi. They said they would provide evidence in the courts. In the future, when we begin proceedings against Karunanidhi in the courts, he can give us his version. He has the right.[144]

A year later, on 6 June 1979, during the Thanjavur by-election campaign, Kalyanasundaram, whose party was now allied to the DMK, said that, unlike him, MGR did not appear before the Sarkaria Commission. Earlier, MGR had asked if Kalyanasundaram had withdrawn the charges he had submitted against Kalaignar and Anbil Dharmalingam. He had also pointed out that MGR had not acted against those persons found guilty in the Sarkaria findings because some of them now held important positions within the AIADMK.[145]

On 29 May, when asked about Nedunchezhian, MGR said: 'Whoever it is, there will be impartial action; the court will decide whether they are guilty or not.' He denied allegations that he was being vindictive and stated that no party wished to ally with Kalaignar, who needed support. 'He has to instil confidence in his workers and [the] party. He cannot cheat them any more. I am not someone who knows politics well. But as far as I know, I have not seen any leader who speaks in such an imbalanced fashion as Karunanidhi.' He said that as a chief minister for seven years, Kalaignar, who was aware of the legalities involved, had calculated the punishment for the charges in relation to the incidents in Madurai during Indira Gandhi's visit. He sarcastically added that Kalaignar was talking as though they had decided to imprison him.[146]

PROHIBITION POLICY

Sarkaria was not the only issue that MGR found hoisted with his own petard. His prohibition policy, which was implemented with a messianic zeal, had only led to a robust bootlegging industry and illicit brewing.

Intensive raids on illegal liquor vends did not succeed in stopping the brewing. Besides, the campaign to win hearts and minds through village committees was going nowhere.[147]

MGR faced an uphill task because of the sobering ground reality. In the summer of 1978, Anbazhagan told the Assembly that some 2 lakh people were engaged in illicit brewing, another million in bootlegging and that every fourth person in the state drinks. The estimated 10 million consumers made the illicit liquor trade worth 800 crore rupees, and about 126 crore rupees was lost yearly in excise duty, even as the ruling partymen were believed to be profiting to the tune of 50 crore rupees.

On 18 September 1977, addressing a conference on prohibition, the chief minister said that the ban on alcohol was only on paper in the state and that his 'concern was that the poor should come out of this drinking habit'. He said bootleggers were running a 'parallel government', and a law like MISA, from the days of the Emergency, was required to deal with them. He said he had asked that the neighbouring states introduce a five-mile dry corridor and the prime minister was supportive of this idea. The states would, however, reject it. 'Without worrying about elections and votes, we will accomplish what has been entrusted to us well.'[148] MGR would eat his words later. On 1 January 1978, the chief minister announced in the Assembly that his administration was drafting a law, which would provide for severe punishment for prohibition offences, even death by hanging.[149]

In October 1978, an ordinance provided for stricter enforcement of prohibition, with a year's imprisonment for some offences, as well as expulsion from places of residence. And punishments were doubled in the case of government servants.

But MGR's prohibition policy was in shreds even as he valiantly filled the jails with the offenders. At one count, India Today said there were 30,000 registered cases but not one of them was a distiller. Critics said that the police were, however, having a field day.[150] Despite these problems, a stubborn MGR said on 27 May 1979 that he was willing to conduct a referendum, only for women, to decide on the question of total prohibition, which he advocated. He said he would never 'abandon' prohibition.[151] MGR's zeal would become muted after the 1980 poll reverses, and he would turn his own policy on its head from 1981 to 1986.

The caste violence in Villupuram, in July, between Adi Dravidas and caste Hindus led to twenty deaths—but it did not affect the fortunes of the AIADMK. Kalaignar said that the hands and legs of twelve Adi Dravidas were bound, and they were strangled and knifed. He added that 1000 people had become homeless as their huts were razed to the ground. On 2 August, Kalaignar visited the place. A parliamentary delegation's visit announced by the prime minister was called off as the chief minister said he had ordered a judicial inquiry and the visit would come in the way of it. As the Villupuram tragedy unfolded, MGR and his ministers were busy campaigning for the Madurai Corporation elections. It was only after five days that a minister visited the place and arranged for relief measures.[152] Despite this tardiness, the AIADMK won fifty of the sixty-four seats in the Madurai Corporation, the DMK won five and Congress (I), nine. *Statesman* commented that MGR had 'emerged as a political strategist to be reckoned with'.[153]

In 1978, the MGR government announced its year-long celebrations for EVR's birth centenary. A district, a university and a government building were named after EVR, and a highway was renamed after him EVR's revised Tamil script was adopted, and caste names were dropped in street names and other government accommodations. Importantly children born of inter-caste marriages were to be treated on par with scheduled classes for social benefits. On the occasion, those arrested or convicted for drunkenness under the Tamil Nadu Prohibition Act were set free. *India Today* commented it was done with the approaching elections in mind.[154]

RUMBLES WITHIN THE PARTY

On 31 October 1978, MGR toured Europe, the US, Japan, Hong Kong, Thailand, Malaysia and Singapore for six weeks. He said he would study the functioning of justice, the police and small industries in the US and other countries. He had heard about the independence of the judiciary in the US. He also wanted to study how after elections the Opposition there worked together with the government. He also sought to follow up his earlier idea of producing power from seawater and desalination plants. MGR's portfolios were distributed to six ministers. Nedunchezhian temporarily took over as general secretary, only to be confirmed in January 1979.[155] MGR said that Manoharan, who was the deputy general secretary, should decide whether he should continue to hold this post as well as his ministerial portfolio or hand over the party position to someone else. Clearly, not all was well between him and Manoharan.[156] On MGR's return, Nedunchezhian would be appointed full-time.

During his five-day stay in Japan, MGR signed a joint venture between Tuticorin Alkali Chemicals and a Japanese chemical firm.[157]

OPPOSITION TO IMPOSITION OF HINDI

The AIADMK would be obliged to follow the DMK's protest against imposition of Hindi. At the EVR centennial function, MGR rejected Kalaignar's earlier charge that he had not taken part in the DMK's 1965 anti-Hindi agitation as he was shooting in Goa. He pointed out that Anna had exempted actors from the agitation. He added Kalaignar was using Hindi to divert people's attention. MGR said English should be made a national language and then he administered an oath to the audience that Tamil Nadu would not accept Hindi as the sole official language.[158]

On 23 and 24 December, the DMK held an anti-Hindi conference in Trichy. Pushed to react, the AIADMK announced a similar conference in Coimbatore on 25 January 1979. It was, however, later redesignated as Language Martyrs Day. The DMK and DK had announced a black-flag demonstration against Hindi for 26 January 1979. The chief minister, meanwhile, called for an all-party conference, which Kalaignar attended. The conference unanimously decided that a resolution against the imposition of Hindi would be passed in the next legislative session.[159]

THANJAVUR BY-ELECTION

MGR supported Indira Gandhi's by-election in Chikmagalur in November 1978, politically and financially.[160] (By late December that year, the Janata Party had disqualified her as an MP.) It was a bold move on MGR's part as Indira Gandhi appeared to be in a political wilderness. He justified his actions by praising the Emergency for the discipline and order it brought to the country, the dismissal of the DMK ministry and for Indira Gandhi's democratic credentials. 'She had the right to stay in office for another year. Yet, didn't she announce the general elections? The election was democratic. Isn't the fact that Indira Gandhi lost proof of this?' he asked.[161] But this rare exhibition of political independence was to change in Thanjavur a year later, and Thanjavur would prove to be MGR's Waterloo. By-elections for the Thanjavur and Nagapattinam parliamentary seats were to be held on 17 June 1979. A week earlier, on 12 May, the AIADMK general council had indicated support for the Congress (I) candidate in Thanjavur.[162] On 19 May, Indira Gandhi, MGR and Tamil Nadu Congress (I) strongman G. Karuppiah Moopanar met in Delhi. The following day, newspaper reports said she would contest from Thanjavur.[163] S. Ramachandran said that after he had gone to bed, MGR met Morarji Desai around midnight, with Rajaram. Desai told him to choose between him and Indira Gandhi, but had no problems with his support for Congress (I).[164] Boxed into a corner, just when the formal announcement was awaited, a day before Indira Gandhi's visit to Madras, MGR declared that if she contested, it could give rise to a 'serious law and order problem' and he wanted to avert 'another Madurai'. Countering him, Kalaignar pointed out later that Indira Gandhi had visited the state several times post-Madurai safely. He termed MGR's reasons 'scare tactics'.[165]

On 22 May, MGR denied that there was 'any connection or relationship' between the decision and his meeting with Desai. He also argued that Desai could have easily stopped him from supporting the Congress (I) itself, and described the Congress (I) hand symbol as 'this hand is the hand that feeds, that embraces, that blesses and [is the] mother's hand'.[166]

Much earlier, on 6 May, Kalaignar had predicted in Thanjavur that if 'Prime Minister Desai were to summon the AIADMK leadership tomorrow and threaten them, they will ditch Indira Gandhi. Therefore, let Indira Gandhi not trust the AIADMK and be disappointed.'

MGR canvassed in both constituencies from 1 to 15 June, but the party lost in Nagapattinam. Earlier, on 24 May, Congress (I) leader R.V. Swaminathan had said the question of inviting MGR to campaign did not arise at all.[167] The next day, MGR, who had gone to Thanjavur uninvited, said, 'We will give our life to see that the Congress [I] candidate Singaravadivelu wins.'[168] The Congress won Thanjavur hands down, but Indira Gandhi took it as a personal insult and never forgave MGR for not backing her candidature. MGR's efforts to wean her away from the DMK and woo her would border on the tragicomic, and would not bear fruit till mid-1982.

Two years later, in October 1981, MGR maintained Indira Gandhi's life would have been in danger had she stood from Thanjavur and Kalaignar would have stood against her candidacy:

> There's been some misunderstanding between the Congress (I) and us. I decided against sponsoring Mrs Gandhi's candidature for the Thanjavur parliamentary election at the last minute because I had definite information that if she had fought from there, her life would have been in danger.
>
> Karunanidhi was to have been her opponent. The violence that had occurred during the Chikmagalur by-election would have paled into insignificance compared to the violence that would have erupted in Thanjavur had Amma contested from there. I acted in good faith.
>
> My opponents spread lies to say that I backed out in the last minute because Morarji Desai threatened me. That's rubbish. If that had been the case, why would I have backed a Congress (I) candidate at Thanjavur and ensured his victory? If I had incurred the wrath of some people in Amma's party because of my reluctance to back her candidature at that time, then I have no regrets. Only time will tell whether what I did was right or wrong.[169]

On 22 May 1979, Anbazhagan had indeed mentioned in a campaign meeting in Thanjavur that Kalaignar was planning to contest against Indira Gandhi.[170] In politics, there is no right and wrong, and, perhaps, there is no honour. With time, Indira Gandhi in 1980 would ally with the DMK she had completely discredited during the Emergency. However, as the alliance soured she would slowly move away from her 'dependable' ally, the DMK, yielding to MGR's craven wish to displace it.

On 10 June, speaking in Nagapattinam, Kalaignar charged that ministers had taken 60 lakh rupees from private bus operators and 30 lakh rupees from moneylenders and pawnbrokers as bribes.[171] In October 1981, he would say that private bus operators were permitted to have five, as opposed to three, buses and a bribe of 1 crore rupees was taken.[172]

Thanks to MGR's 'authoritarian style', both the CPI and CPM would move closer to the DMK. On 19 February, the DMK moved a no-confidence motion against the government, its second one, while the CPM, Janata Party and the Indian Union Muslim League (IUML) brought forward motions disapproving the government's policies on labour, law and order, and the minorities respectively.

Although defeated by 128 to sixty-four, the Opposition had faulted the government for failing to open fair-price shops as promised, its inability to address the grievances of farmers, labourers, NGOs, teachers and students, to tackle corruption, its interference in administration and the worsening law and order situation in the state. 'The treasury benches appeared to be on the defensive,' wrote Mohandas.[173]

RESERVATIONS ON ECONOMIC CRITERIA

On 2 July, the MGR administration committed a misstep. It came up with an official order limiting reservations to backward classes with an annual income limit of 9000 rupees. The timing of this could not have been more inappropriate. The state was celebrating the centenary of the architect of the social justice movement, EVR. The decision would have made EVR turn in his grave. MGR had brushed aside the advice to call for an all-party meet and announced this decision unilaterally in the Assembly. But as early as 1973, MGR had made his preference for the economic criteria known. He had said it should include Brahmins as well.[174]

Ironically, the prescription for exclusion had originally emanated from the DMK-appointed 1969 Sattanathan Commission. Sattanathan had wished to exclude the 'progressive section' in the backward castes that had crossed the 'borderline'—meaning those who were socially mobile. The exclusion of those who owned 10 acres of land and those with taxable income of 9000 rupees was recommended. The DMK understandably had not acted on the idea.

MGR defended his actions in the name of social justice and fairness. He said the rickshaw man's children should be preferred over the children of the affluent. Aranganayagam, his minister for education, spoke of excluding the 'neo-Brahminical cult' or the creamy layer.[175] Although Mohandas cited this as an instance of MGR's impulsive decision-making, it was not. It was something that MGR had always believed in and had espoused, even as early as 1973, soon after the founding of the party.[176] Anna had somewhat set a precedent when he announced free education up to the pre-university level for children of needy parents whose annual income was not above Rs. 1500, irrespective of caste.[177] The law minister, Ponnaiyan, said that MGR wished to eradicate caste from the hearts and minds of the younger generations. The AIADMK executive had discussed the issue a few times.[178] MGR's attempts to remove any caste traces in street names were in this direction. He also felt that the introduction of economic criteria would strike at the very root of the caste consciousness reinforced by reservations on that basis. But the constitution had only foreseen social backwardness and MGR was ahead of his time, and Manoharan and even Mohandas had warned him to expect stiff opposition.[179]

The DMK and the DK, expectedly rose up in arms. On 14 July, the DMK general council said that a certain percentage could be reserved under the general category for those deserving of affirmative action for economic reasons, regardless of their social status. By a majority decision, the Madras High Court however, upheld the government order. Yet, this victory would prove pyrrhic. The DMK–DK protests would have to be controlled by force, and MGR himself would do an about-turn and hike reservations.

AIADMK JOINS CHARAN SINGH'S MINISTRY

If MGR had underestimated the opposition to his economic criteria, he had grossly miscalculated the political developments in Delhi as well. The Janata Party proved to be a smorgasbord of the original parties that had come together to become the party, and quite a few of its egotistical stalwarts entertained prime ministerial ambitions. On 11 July, a no-confidence motion on the Desai ministry was taken up for discussion. Indira Gandhi said she would support the motion. On Cho. Ramaswamy's request, MGR had agreed to go to Delhi to assess the situation himself before making up his mind. MGR convened a meeting of his eighteen MPs to ascertain their views on whether to support Desai or his rival

Charan Singh. Rajaram took Cho. Ramaswamy, an advocate of Desai, aside and said: 'What is this? You are so naive! MPs and their views? If anyone gives his views, will he ever become an MP in this lifetime? Those who say, "The leader's view is my view. Why do I need a personal view?" alone can be an MP or become an MP. When that is the case, what will these people say?' Expectedly, all the MPs said that they would leave the decision to their leader.[180]

Meanwhile, Charan Singh's point man, Raj Narain, was meeting MGR every day to plead his boss's case. MGR asked Raj Narain about the contradictions in their stand with regard to seeking Indira Gandhi's support, whom Charan Singh had vowed to put behind bars, their stand on Hindi, et al. In the end, the AIADMK said it would oppose the motion against Desai. Cho. Ramaswamy wrote the reasons behind this were MGR's respect for Desai, Raj Narain's incredulous claims, Rajaram and Chezhian's reasoning and Karnataka Congress (I) leader Devaraj Urs's advice. But Desai stepped down on 15 July, avoiding a vote. With the other contender, Jagjivan Ram, stepping aside and the Congress (I's) unconditional support, Charan Singh looked like the next premier. However, Desai again contended with Charan Singh and, on 24 July, the AIADMK decided again in Desai's favour. The AIADMK's support was so coveted that Rajaram likened his party to 'a bride of sweet eighteen awaiting the groom'. Except, this bride had chosen the wrong groom again.

On 28 July, Charan Singh became prime minister. He had to prove his majority within forty days. MGR felt a little down that his support had failed to save the Desai ministry. As Charan Singh courted him and offered ministerial positions for his partymen, MGR said that the AIADMK's position to support stability in the Centre remained valid and, on 1 August, announced that the AIADMK would be part of the Charan Singh ministry. On 19 August, Sathyavani Muthu and Bala Pazhanoor became ministers for social welfare and petroleum respectively, and the first-ever ministers from a regional party in the Centre. Why MGR chose to be part of the Charan Singh experiment will remain one of the many unexplained mysteries. Bala Pazhanoor said that the AIADMK knew in advance that the Congress (I) would topple the ministry.[181] Cho. Ramaswamy's comment that the President had created the impression that Charan Singh's ministry would remain, provided a plausible reason for MGR's move. Nonetheless, despite the President's machinations the question of stability that MGR had spoken of remained precarious and patently absent. On 20 August, Charan Singh submitted his resignation as Congress (I) expectedly withdrew support from his government. He had been prime minister for twenty-four days. The AIADMK ministers continued as part of the caretaker government. MGR's desire to hitch his star to any prime minister would land him in a politically ungainly situation. His political nightmare was just beginning.

Jagjivan Ram now threw his hat into the ring and sought MGR's support, which he declined, making it clear that his earlier support was for Desai and not for the Janata Party. But when Desai pitched on behalf of Jagjivan Ram, MGR was pushed into a corner. After a great deal of hesitation, he asked that a delegation of senior Janata leaders meet him and seek his support in writing. He wished for someone who would understand Tamil in the delegation. Atal Bihari Vajpayee, Ravindra Varma and Subramanian Swamy, who understood Tamil, called on MGR. Vajpayee said that once MGR announced his support, the Akalis would follow suit and Jagjivan Ram could stake his claim. MGR agreed on the condition that the two ministers continue with their portfolios in the new ministry. Cho. Ramaswamy pleaded for an immediate announcement, while MGR said he would have to consult his MPs. That afternoon, as Cho. Ramaswamy had feared, President Sanjiva Reddy dissolved the Parliament, rendering MGR's potential support needless.[182]

Following the dissolution of the Parliament on 22 August, Congress (I)'s C. Subramaniam met MGR on 25 August. Later on 28 August, MGR clarified at Poompuhar that there was no need for doubts about the AIADMK–Congress (I) alliance, and, with beguiling insouciance, pointed out that they had favoured the Congress (I) in Thanjavur, even while supporting the Desai government. MGR said the DMK, facing charges of attempting to murder Indira Gandhi, felt its desire to ally with the Congress (I) was not inappropriate. 'Similarly,' said MGR, 'I wish to tell you something. Even though there are cases against Karunanidhi and other DMK friends, it does not mean that there should not be an AIADMK–DMK alliance. I am saying this for argument's sake. Electoral alliances will depend on how people's feelings change with time. If party workers have a view, what can leaders do?'[183] 'It did not need any extra intelligence to see that the entire exercise was aimed at sabotaging the DMK–Congress (I) alliance,' said *India Today*.[184]

If that was the intent, it was not working. Kalaignar now admitted that the possibilities of a DMK–Congress (I) tie-up to defeat the 'anti-people force, AIADMK' existed. That evening, speaking in Karaikal, MGR challenged Kalaignar publicly:

> Mr Karunanidhi, do not speak whatever [you want to] in order to encourage your cadre. I challenge you—if you were to align with Indira Gandhi, can you get the number of seats, we, the AIADMK, won in alliance with the Congress (I) in the 1977 elections? We won thirty-five seats. Are you willing to change your name if you cannot? If you are a true Tamil, if you are a true Dravidian cadre, capture all the seats. I will then garland you on a pedestal. I am not saying this out of conceit. Karunanidhi cannot [win as many seats]. In 1971, the DMK had twenty-five MPs. Could one of them become minister in Delhi?

Surely, MGR had either considered the AIADMK's place in the Centre as an achievement in itself or now made it appear so. On 6 September, MGR was in Delhi to meet Indira Gandhi. That morning, he called on Charan Singh and the Janata Party's Jagjivan Ram. Charan Singh told MGR that it would only be fair that he withdrew his ministers if he planned to ally with the Congress (I). In the end, MGR did not meet with Indira Gandhi. Congress (I) general secretary, C.M. Stephen, later said that the prime minister had made MGR 'tremble'.[185]

POLICE PROTEST FOR A UNION

Around this time, in October 1979, Nainar Das, a police sub-inspector, and another official John Britto began a stir demanding the setting up of a police union. Permission was denied for this even as phantom unions were granted recognition. MGR charged that Kalaignar was behind the protestors and that the AIADMK's 20 lakh members would sort them out. On 24 October, Nainar Das was arrested in Tirunelveli and 1000 protesting police personnel were taken into custody. The number would later rise to 3000. The Army was brought in and Mohandas wrote that the stir was suppressed badly. The scars, he said, were such that MGR would later concede to subsidize essential commodities for policemen up to the rank of inspector, grant risk allowance up to the rank of a superintendent and establish a police housing corporation. When MGR conferred with senior officials, Mohandas said he spoke for the agitators and raised his voice a little, and that it had a 'sobering effect on MGR and other officials'. When he apologized to MGR later, the chief minister graciously told him not to worry, and appreciated his knowledge of the problems and his concern for the policemen.[186]

THWARTED BULGARIA SHIP SCANDAL

The MGR administration came under a cloud when, on 3 November, in a debate on a censure motion, Kalaignar exposed what he described as the 'scandal of the century'. He accused the MGR administration of trying to make a neat 4 crore rupees, that was thwarted by a conscientious official, in a shipping deal. The government-owned Poompuhar Shipping Corporation had negotiated to buy three ships from Bulgaria at 8.4 crore rupees each. Kalaignar alleged that MGR's middleman agreed to buy the ships at 10.4 crore rupees each, 2 crore rupees more than their original price, with the intent of pocketing the additional sum, with the lion's share going to MGR. Tabling more than twenty telex messages and letters, Kalaignar said that the official had frustrated the plan by settling for the original price. It was a class act. After this, K.S. Ramakrishnan, an IAS officer, was relieved of his post, Jid Singh Bhango, another IAS officer, died suddenly, and H.N. Singh, the third member, awaited transfer. MGR lamely said that he would step down if it were proven that he or his partymen had made money, cited the charge as proof of weakness of the governmental machinery and agreed to face an inquiry. He also wrote to the chief justice of the Supreme Court to spare a sitting judge, a request that was rejected.[187] But in light of the exposé the government deferred the deal and, on 22 December 1980, the MGR administration filed defamation cases against Kalaignar and Murasoli Maran.[188] MGR would end up buying the ships in the summer of 1985 from Japan.[189]

The Madras High Court dealt the next blow to MGR's claim of a clean administration when it struck down ten admissions to medical colleges as 'arbitrary'. MGR, who had been personally involved in their selections, had justified their choice outside the prescribed norms. The High Court recorded its 'very strong disapproval in correcting a record after it was produced before the court. We have no doubt that whosoever was responsible for this correction should have done so with a clear intention of misdirecting the court by creating false evidence.' The Opposition called for the ministry's resignation.[190]

10 PLUS TWO, AND SELF-FINANCING COLLEGES

MGR's first term would be known for two major policy shifts in education. Acting on the Lakshmanaswami Mudaliar Committee's suggestions, MGR would scrap the Pre-University Course (PUC) and opt for Higher Secondary or 10 Plus Two–school education. His administration would also veer around to the idea of bringing in private partnerships for professional education, which would take shape in a major way in his second term. Aranganyagam credits the state's attraction for investors as a place of skilled human capital to these two major policy shifts.

The shifts were not easy. At the time, some 170-odd colleges, equipped with lab facilities, catered to PUC students. Schools needed to be equipped with science labs, which cost 1 lakh rupees each. As officials cited financial constraints against Plus Two being attached to schools the chief minister called Aranganayagam to ask him: 'You have recommended the Plus Two against the advice of the officials. Which of the two will serve the interests of the rural children?' Aranganayagam said that his recommendation would do so, as the children would not have to travel very far and MGR gave him the go-ahead. The money was gathered for the labs and higher secondary education began in 1978.[191]

The change would usher in a huge social revolution as education became accessible to the rural students. Rural pass rates jumped to 90 per cent, compared to the 40 per cent in PUC. Some 80,000 students sat for the PUC examination but 9 lakh wrote the Plus Two exams. But this revolution came at a price—the quality of teaching, infrastructure and environment had to be compromised. Colleges had to be found for the 9 lakh students who passed out. Tamil Nadu had only six engineering colleges, and education was in the state domain. But it was bereft of resources, even as there was a dire need to expand the educational infrastructure. MGR himself had wished to open more engineering and polytechnic colleges after his visit to Japan.[192] These reasons and the self-financing experience in neighbouring Karnataka and Maharashtra spurred the MGR administration to throw open education to private educationists, in most cases today a euphemism for pure entrepreneurs, but it was a mixed blessing in hindsight.

The requirements for this self-financing venture appear to have been carefully formulated: a 25 lakh rupee deposit, 25 acres of land and 50 per cent seats to the state. Aranganayagam said that in Delhi it came to be described as the 'MGR formula'. The management quota was 50 per cent of the seats. Yet, there were no takers. They had canvassed with industrialists such as Pollachi N. Mahalingam, Ramco Cements Ramasubramaniya Raja, and the likes. Aranganayagam said he was keen for the shift to result in the educational advancement of the four major communities—the Gounders, Nadars, Mukkulathors and Vanniyars. S. Jagathrakshakan and G. Viswanathan came forward to set up colleges in northern Tamil Nadu, a Vanniyar belt. Jagathrakshakan had to take loans, but the state did its bit to help such venturers. Thus, MGR provided 150 acres of land at a fixed price to Viswanathan for his Vellore Institute of Technology. Licences were awarded to Jeppiaar and A.C. Shanmugam. By 1983, sixteen polytechnics had come into being.

Engineering colleges would be started the following year. MGR had run into a Tamil Nadu parent seeking admissions in an engineering college in Bangalore. His son had failed to achieve the 90 per cent required in the state. MGR came back, had a discussion and then decided to emulate Karnataka. He sanctioned eight engineering colleges prior to his illness in 1984. At that point, the state had only ten government and government-aided colleges. Licences were then awarded for colleges of other disciplines such as nursing, dentistry, arts and medicine.

The rest is history. Three decades later, the results are remarkable, but mixed. Every village perhaps boasts of an engineer working overseas and the educational infrastructure in Tamil Nadu is one of the best in the country, with some 540 engineering colleges, more than 300 polytechnics, more than 400 arts and science colleges, twenty-five nursing schools and seventeen medical colleges.[193] Some of them are nationally well known. Tamil Nadu boasts of 2.5 lakh engineering seats, the highest in the country. However, of these engineering colleges, only 154 fulfil the three basic criteria of faculty, infrastructure and placement. The result is that almost half the seats go unfilled. Importantly, the quality of the engineers leaves much to be desired. Many 'educationists' see these institutions as money-making ventures, and few plough back the money that would make the institutions competitive and substantial.

The same could be said of medical and dental colleges or, for that matter, all self-financing colleges in the state. Despite all these shortcomings, MGR's vision indeed turned Tamil Nadu into one of the most attractive destinations for students around India for engineering education, and the spin-off effects in the social, industrial and economic spheres cannot be underestimated.[194]

MERGER TALKS COME INTO THE OPEN

In the autumn of 1979, Orissa leader and Central minister Biju Patnaik who desired a strong Opposition front, stepped in independently to reunite the Kazhagams. He was not aware of the on and off talks with Veeramani as a go-between. Solai now advised MGR that it was time for him to meet Kalaignar. Veeramani impressed the same on Kalaignar.[195] Patnaik felt that if both the Dravidian parties joined, then all forty seats could be won.[196]

One September evening, Patnaik telephoned Kalaignar to ask if he could come to Madras to see him. On 9 September, Kalaignar told reporters at Vellore, pointing out MGR's Poompuhar and Karaikal speeches, 'Let us wait and see.' Patnaik reached Madras on 12 September and met with Kalaignar, who posited six conditions for the merger: 1. The merged party would function as the DMK; 2. The party flag could be the AIADMK flag; 3. MGR should continue as chief minister; 4. DMK legislators do not require to be accommodated as ministers; 5. The issue of who is the president, general secretary, treasurer, etc. of the merged party could be decided at an appropriate time following the merger; and 6. Importantly, MGR should rescind the government order on reservations based on an economic order.[197] Buoyed by what he had heard, Patnaik was optimistic that MGR would agree to the conditions. He told the media that the Kazhagams' merger would keep 'political adventurers' out of Tamil Nadu.

MGR himself was for the merger, or so it appeared. Confrontational politics was taking Tamil Nadu nowhere and it must have been simply tiring for him. On the morning of 12 September, he talked to Mohandas about the benefits of the merger. The next morning, at 11 a.m., MGR entered the State Guest House fondly addressing Kalaignar in Patnaik's company as 'Aandavarae!' Anbazhagan was with Kalaignar, and MGR had taken Nedunchezhian and Panruti S. Ramachandran with him. Then, for forty minutes, the two leaders met privately, in which a pleasantly surprised MGR wondered if the conditions relayed by Patnaik were true. Kalaignar explained the reasoning behind the six conditions and MGR accepted all of them. He went a step further and assured Kalaignar that the executives and the general councils of the two parties could meet separately on a fixed day to pass the merger resolution.

The two leaders came out and informed Patnaik and the media of the conclusions of their talks. Kalaignar also recorded that the media reported that MGR had met with Karuppiah Moopanar that day. MGR was in talks with Karuppiah Moopanar at his Ramavaram residence, even as preparations were afoot for his talks with Kalaignar. That very evening, MGR also hosted a dinner for Desai's energy minister, P. Ramachandran. If MGR was keeping all his options open, Kalaignar was no different as we would see.

The next day, 14 September, the day prior to Anna's birthday, MGR addressed a public meeting in Vellore, in which he said that the AIADMK flag would be kept aloft for another millennia and that as long as he was alive there would be no merger. Further, his ministers spoke coarsely about the DMK and Kalaignar while MGR watched. MGR had killed the idea of the merger.

However, on 1 April 2009, in a public event, Kalaignar blamed the other Ramachandran for the failed merger: 'I know who had played spoilsport . . . I don't want to name him . . . But without his name, history would be incomplete . . . He was Panruti Ramachandran, who had travelled along with MGR to Vellore after our meeting on [the] merger took place at the State Guest House.[198]

S. Ramachandran said that when they were returning after the merger talks, they received the news that the MGR fans association head Musiriputhan had been attacked. He said that he told MGR that they could get together at the top, but the cadre at the lower level had undergone much hardship in the hands of the DMK men and the government—like violence, conflict and cases filed against them. When S. Ramachandran wondered how they could work together under the same DMK men, MGR decided against the reunification.[199] On 18 December 1981, a year later, the chief minister blamed Kalaignar for the failure of the talks and said that the DMK leadership had rejected his suggestion that a congenial atmosphere must be created for unity between the workers of the two parties.[200] Mohandas recorded that on the evening of 13 September itself, MGR had changed his mind, citing inspiration from his late mother.[201] RMV, however, said that MGR was sincere about the merger and insinuated that the blame lay elsewhere.[202]

In the meantime, C.M. Stephen, an Indira Gandhi confidant, had been in touch with Murasoli Maran asking that the party forget the past and ally with the Congress (I). Kalaignar termed this as a 'huge turning point in politics'. These talks had advanced to a stage where Kalaignar kept his scheduled 15 September visit to Delhi. Kalaignar and Indira Gandhi met that night after a period of four years and reached an electoral understanding. It was a daring move and MGR could only blame himself for this turn of events. His cryptic comment was: 'Let the wicked go with the wicked; we shall align with the righteous.'[203] MGR knew that he was doomed as his party had allied with the 'righteous' Janata Party.[204]

On 30 September, Indira Gandhi participated in the DMK's Periyar centenary celebrations. On that occasion, she cited her experience in Thanjavur to label MGR unreliable. Later, in a public meeting, Indira Gandhi reiterated that officials had told her that the DMK's term was coming to an end; she expressed regret for her wrongs and described the alliance as a new chapter.[205] Earlier, in a press meet, she said that the Sarkaria Commission was a result of CPI–AIADMK pressure and probably because of her own experience with the Shah Commission, added that the commission's inquiries would be entertaining if made and shown as a film. She also justified Nedumaran's suspension for he was against the alliance. So much for him protecting her in Madurai.[206] Kalaignar said, 'We believe that only Indira Gandhi can give us a stable government.'

'The days of Ramachandran's political hegemony are numbered' was the epitaph that *India Today* wrote for MGR.[207]

1980 PARLIAMENTARY POLLS AND PONDICHERRY ASSEMBLY POLLS

MGR's decision to ally with the Janata Party saw its first fallout. Charan Singh cancelled his visit to Madras, scheduled for 1 and 2 October, and, on 28 September, MGR met the prime minister in Delhi. Soon, the latter wrote asking that the two AIADMK ministers leave the Centre. MGR obliged this request. His ambition to project his party in Delhi had ended in mortifying circumstances. The time was not yet ripe for his vision to succeed. It would be another two decades before the Dravidian parties and other regional parties would become integral to government formation at the Centre.

Pushed into a corner, MGR, in a first, criticized Indira Gandhi, speaking harshly of the Emergency excesses and dictatorship, and said that if she were to come to power, elections would not be held for fifteen years.[208] In Pondicherry, he said that Indira Gandhi, who had ruled for eleven years, should step aside and advise the government.* Indira Gandhi responded in kind. She reminded MGR of the 1967, 1971 and 1977 elections, and described the AIADMK as one who went after those in the Centre for their livelihood.[209] Meanwhile, responding to Kalaignar's charges on the Bulgarian ship deal, MGR dramatically said,

---

* MGR's equivocal stand on Pondicherry's status in early 1979 would hurt the party for a long time. In January 1979, on a visit to Madras, Desai had indicated that Pondicherry would eventually have to merge with its neighbouring states. On 22 January, Pondicherry observed a shutdown against the prime minister's views. MGR spoke equivocally, noting that it was a decision for the Centre and that 'even if it was against the people's wishes some decisions have to be taken. However, I respect people's wishes.' The prime minister's views had led to such major disturbances that a curfew was enforced for two days. On 27 January, the prime minister clarified that no decision had been taken on the issue and all concerned would be consulted. http://indiatoday. intoday.in/story/pondicherry-heads-for-a-protracted-period-of-internal-strife/1/427993.html. Kalaignar, Karunanidhi, M., *Nenjuku Needhi*, Thiurmagal Nilayam, Chennai, 2008, vol. 3, pp. 325–26.

in Villupuram, that if the charges were proven he would leave the country.[210]

But H.V. Hande, who was with MGR when the results came in later, said that MGR was taken aback by the scale of the defeat. Hande said that 'MGR's reaction showed that he did not expect Indira Gandhi to bounce back.'[211] This possibly explains his harsh words against her. The Indira wave had swept away all but two of the twenty-four AIADMK candidates—from Gobichettipalayam and Sivakasi. The DMK–Congress (I)–Muslim League combine had won thirty-eight seats, including Pondicherry. Out of the 234 Assembly segments, the Congress (I) led in 119 and the DMK in eighty-three.[212]

In the Pondicherry Assembly elections, the DMK won fourteen seats, Congress (I) ten, the CPI one, Janata Party three and independents won two. The AIADMK failed to win a single seat.[213]

The DMK won all the sixteen parliamentary seats and was rewarded with G. Lakshmanan becoming the Deputy Speaker of the Lok Sabha. Kalaignar had said that the DMK would not seek ministerial berths, but would seek people's welfare schemes.[214] The Congress (I) won twenty-one of the twenty-three seats it had contested. MGR explained the DMK–Congress (I) victory as sympathy for Indira Gandhi. Kalaignar said while people wished for Indira Gandhi to return, it was also a statement that the thirty-month-old MGR administration's 'cruelties and scandals' had to end. Kalaignar also indicated that the idea of a merger was finished.[215]

*

MAJOR PARTIES AND PERFORMANCE – JANUARY 1980 PARLIAMENTARY ELECTION

Party	Contested	Won	Votes	Percentage
AIADMK	24	2	46,74,064	25.38%
Congress (I)	22	20	58,21,411	31.62%
CPI	3	0	6,60,940	3.59%
CPM	3	0	5,91,869	3.21%
DMK	16	16	42,36,537	23.01%
Janata Party	9	0	14,65,782	7.96%
Muslim League	1	1	2,32,567	0.08%

MGR put on a brave face saying that contesting 200 seats in the 1977 Assembly elections, the party had polled 52 lakh votes, while now it had polled 48 lakh votes, but had contested only twenty-two parliamentary seats. The AIADMK felt that strict prohibition, the price rise, and dissatisfaction of public servants and farmers were the reasons for the defeat. MGR himself did a volte-face, saying that from Indira Gandhi's interview to a foreign magazine, he was confident that she would 'never ever' postpone elections and that he would go to Delhi to congratulate her.[216]

Kalaignar claimed that MGR had lost the people's confidence, which MGR rejected, and said, 'What else can you expect from someone like Karunanidhi? He would say anything.'[217]

When asked if MGR should resign, Kalaignar responded: 'I am not insisting on it. At a public meeting at the Teynampet Congress grounds, MGR said that if Central Madras (constituency) were lost, it would be a matter of his personal dignity. Would the phrase personal dignity apply to one constituency or not to others?'[218]

MGR retorted that his words were intended for party workers, to enthuse them in that constituency.[219] But there would be no need for him to resign. His government would be dismissed on 17 February 1980, along with those of eight other states. That evening, an unfazed MGR watched M.K. Thyagaraja Bhagavathar's Sivakavi (1943) on television, and later expressed 'happiness' as his reaction to the dismissal.[220] Hande who was with MGR that day said that MGR was genuinely happy as he had been turned into a lame duck chief minister following the AIADMK's rout in the parliamentary polls. The situation was so bad that Central minister R. Venkataraman (RV) would directly give instructions to the police commissioner of Madras who would then ignore MGR's orders. 'The dismissal had ended the indignities at the hands of the Central administration for MGR,' noted Hande. MGR told Hande that he was at 'peace now'. In a statement, MGR, quoting poet Bharati, said, 'Treachery often engulfs righteousness; But lo! In the end, again right triumphs.' MGR asked that none should get angry, assuring them that it would be their administration again.[221] That evening, he took Hande and journalist Manian to the Drive-In Woodlands restaurant and ordered masala dosas for the three. 'Masala dosas are good here,' he said happily.[222]

Even prior to the dismissal, on 31 January, MGR had declared: 'Acting is an inseparable part of my life' and that he would resume his film career in April.[223] Clearly, the man was fed up with the burden of office. However, later, in 1984, when MGR would accuse him of being behind the dismissal, Kalaignar would allege that MGR had sent word that he was willing to give away 150 seats in the next elections, if his government was left intact.[224]

CLIMBING DOWN

On 19 January 1980, the now pumped-up DMK announced its plans for a three-phase agitation to force the government to rescind the economic criteria for reservations. Earlier, in a Cabinet meeting, MGR had sought the candid views of senior ministers such as SDS, KAK and Ponnaiyan on the issue. In an all-party meeting, where MGR had assembled all the secretaries of the government—which the DMK did not attend—MGR prompted the DK's Veeramani to speak on the issue and listened avidly to his explanation that the economic criteria was elastic and could change with the vagaries of income and, in the case of government servants, even with transfers (for instance a transfer from Chengalpattu to Madras, where she or he would be paid more, would render the civil servant ineligible for backward class concessions). KAK had half jocularly told Veeramani after the meeting that MGR had not dozed off, as he did sometimes, and was very contemplative during Veeramani's presentation.[225] Some three weeks later, on 24 January, the chief minister climbed down on his stand on reservations and the prohibition policy. He not only rescinded the economic criteria, but also upped the reservation quota for the backward classes from 31 per cent to 50 per cent. But, deep inside, MGR was not completely convinced. Three years later in December 1983, he would again indicate his government was considering reservations to all poor citizens. Kalaignar argued then that 'The Constitution recognizes only social and educational backwardness' and Veeramani suggested 'ameliorative measures for the economically weaker sections in general'. The chief minister maintained 'all backwardness ultimately boils down to economic backwardness'. He suggested that those who don't qualify as income-tax assessees could be considered poor. Veeramani pointed out that only 3 per cent paid income tax.[226] But for now, Veeramani thanked the chief minister, but the DMK in the Opposition felt it could not be seen as thanking him and announced 'victory celebrations'.[227]

Similarly, MGR diluted his prohibition policy—he brought down the age for drinking permits from forty-five to thirty, did away with the need for a medical certificate, rescinded the ban on government officials obtaining permits, reduced the fee to twenty-five rupees from 100, released prohibition offenders and said that the police would not act against those drinking in their homes or in hotels.[228] 'The government has revised its policy to save the innocent from unnecessary police harassment, remove corruption and stem the rot in the administration of prohibition,' he proclaimed. At the time of the relaxation, there were about 8000 permits and 3000 applications for Indian-made foreign liquor, which was expected to mushroom to 3,00,000; in the case of arrack permits some 6,00,000 applications were expected. Kalaignar said: 'MGR has now virtually opened liquor shops and made the Prohibition Act a dead letter.' The revenues estimated were 150 crore rupees. Some 80,000 people were to benefit from the withdrawal of cases and the commutation of sentences. Additionally, MGR had announced an unemployment dole, the release and reinduction of police personnel and withdrawal of cases against farmers.[229] Behind the scenes, a chastened MGR would successfully woo the disaffected like the farmers' sangam and the police. But, unsurprisingly, in true MGR fashion, he would simultaneously try to woo the Congress (I). Thus, on 5 February, MGR travelled to Delhi to meet Indira Gandhi. He could not meet her and returned to Madras. Kalaignar said that in not granting an audience to MGR, Indira Gandhi had made her anger with MGR clear. That week, Karuppiah Moopanar spoke of reports of the AIADMK's efforts for an understanding. On 15 February, a DMK–Congress (I) rally charged the AIADMK administration of corruption and the abuse of authority. The DMK was repaying its nemesis in kind.[230]

THE ILL-FOUNDED DMK–CONGRESS (I) ALLIANCE

Indira Gandhi had spurned MGR, but her handling of the alliance with the DMK for the Assembly polls was not much to write home about either. On 1 March, Indira Gandhi told the DMK delegation, led by Kalaignar, that RV would lead the talks on seats for the Assembly elections and informed that M.P. Subramaniam (MPS) would replace L. Ilayaperumal as the president of the state unit. M.P. Subramaniam's coolness towards Kalaignar was well known. As Kalaignar demurred on the appointment, Indira Gandhi promised to reconsider the proposal.

When they met RV later, he was visibly upset. As he walked in, RV said: 'Why, Kalaignar! You have spoiled all our plans!' RV was disappointed that MPS's appointment had been checkmated, albeit temporarily. (RV and others managed to achieve the change two weeks later.) An agreement was reached that the two parties would contest 109 seats each and the rest would be given to allies; it was also decided that the DMK would lead the government. RV now shook Kalaignar's hands. Even as their hands were locked, RV said: 'Kalaignar! We will together finish Moopanar.' Deeply embarrassed, Kalaignar says he quickly withdrew his hands, adding that if the party were to face the elections with such enmity, it would only lead to defeat.

MPS's appointment would prove to be a setback for the alliance. An E.V.K. Sampath sympathizer, MPS would, till the eleventh hour, deny any knowledge of the accord on the DMK leading the government. The Congress (I) dissension, and its anxiety to win a larger number of seats than its ally, the DMK, in order to deny its leadership in government would all lead to the alliance's defeat. On 20 April, Indira Gandhi finally confirmed the 1 March agreement.[231] But the damage had been done.

The AIADMK camp was not without its difficulties either. Janata Party leader P. Ramachandran lamented that MGR had offered it only twenty-six seats instead of their requested forty-six, and left. The AIADMK forged a sixteen-party alliance with the CPI, Kumari Anandan's Gandhi Kamaraj National Congress and P. Nedumaran's Kamaraj Congress, both unknown commodities, and other smaller parties. It was a brave decision on the part of MGR. However, he also appears to have sensed the public sympathy towards him.

If there was any doubt on this account, the 2 March rally of the AIADMK and its fifteen allies, which saw some 2 million protesting against his government's dissolution, should have made this clear to everyone. Noting the size India Today said the procession that preceded it 'had not been witnessed since Independence'. The march along Anna Salai saw attacks on Sivaji Ganesan's Shanthi Theatre and other shops.

and police action that followed left 1000 injured and turned the rally's participants into 'martyrs'.[232]

However, the rally failed to stop some ministers from leaving the party. Fearing lean times, Soundarapandian quit the party on 23 February. He had earlier resigned his ministership and the treasurer's post he held.[233] G.R. Edmund and P.T. Saraswathi left too, as did Bala Pazhanoor. Their refrain was that MGR 'continuously insulted, ignored and humiliated' them, and kept them under surveillance.[234] On 2 March, Manoharan quit too.[235]

Manoharan had been feeling slighted for some time and when his name was not initially included in the high-power committee on elections, he thought enough was enough and, on 3 March, joined the DMK.[236] Here are some excerpts of Manoharan's long statement:

> For the last two-and-a-half years, why even before that, I was humiliated, discarded and hurt. For the party brethren spread in the state, this is [something] new. In the recent party executive, criticism of the ministers was dominant. Some ministers were scolded by the leadership [read MGR]; others were crowned. When I met MGR separately, he shockingly said, 'I am not going to trust anyone henceforth.' I was filled with astonishment. MGR's past decisions, statements and criticism are not the result of consultations. I have not made the party suffer any blemish. I expected recognition, praise and confidence from MGR! I am also a human! When I realized that I would not get these, I was greatly troubled. I concluded that MGR needn't feel any compulsion . . . And I, a heavy heart. He himself might wholeheartedly welcome my decision. My respect for him is lifelong. I will continue, till my end, to preserve the flame that is [the] Dravidian movement.[237]

But Hande said that 'Manoharan thought that MGR was politically finished'.[238] S. Ramachandran added that 'Manoharan felt left out. Manoharan and some others thought that he [MGR] was after all an actor. Should he not listen to us? They overrated themselves.' Su. Thirunavukkarasar said that Manoharan's sometimes not-so-discreet comments about MGR, where he blew his own trumpet, did at times get back to MGR and soured the relationship.[239]

On 17 March, MGR, pointing to Manoharan's assessment that the AIADMK ministry was clean, posed ironically, 'Is this why he quit AIADMK?' MGR also said that he would come to meetings on time henceforth and had been late in the past because of various reasons. He also met Narayanasamy Naidu that day and they spoke for thirty minutes in private.[240] Subbulakshmi Jagadeesan joined the DMK on 5 March, the same day the vice chairman of the state planning commission, Kovai Chezhian, left MGR one more time, this time to join the DMK.[241] Kovai Chezhian would charge that the state had failed to capitalize on the programmes and assistance from the Centre and the World Bank, losing the 100 crore offered by the World Bank and 28 crore by the Centre for Madras's development. He said the government had not followed the 350 crore-rupee plan for the maintenance of the Vaigai and Cauvery rivers. He also alleged that the state had not responded to even one of the sixty-eight letters from the Centre on various projects to the chief minister.

A CHASTENED MGR REACHES OUT

Against this bleak backdrop Nedunchezhian said, 'The party will not disintegrate and MGR is bent on avenging the dismissal of his government.' He claimed that 'MGR is a totally different man today'.[242] While Nedunchezhian meant that MGR was inclusive and accommodative, the leader would also change otherwise for the worse—giving up his zeal for a clean government. It was a very difficult time for MGR. In fact, the dismissal showed who his friends were and that helped him. Cho. Ramaswamy said that MGR was 'hugely confident' that he would win. Hande added that MGR was sure about his victory.[243] But he did not want to take any chances.

On MGR's behalf, Solai got in touch with the CPM's A. Balasubramaniam who asked if MGR could be trusted. The question was not entirely out of place. MGR's political track record was not one of consistency and the non-Congress (I) opposition was only his second choice. On Solai's urging, two days later, AB, as A. Balasubramaniam was known, met MGR for an hour. AB spoke of the electoral strategy and the issues that needed to be placed before the electorate. MGR liked it and an alliance was born.

That very day, Solai met CPI state secretary, P. Manickam, and the following evening, Kalyanasundaram came to meet MGR. After this, Solai travelled to Vaiyampalayam, a sleepy village nineteen kilometres north-east of Coimbatore, the birthplace of Narayanasamy Naidu. As they were being served lunch, Naidu's daughter innocently asked Solai: 'Why, annan, would MGR come to our [humble] houses?' Narayanasamy Naidu's face brightened as Solai suggested that MGR would come to see her father. But the daughter's doubts persisted. 'Anna! If MGR comes, will he eat in our place?' 'Of course.' It was Narayanasamy Naidu's turn now: 'Solai? Will MGR really visit? Will he eat in our place?'

Solai next stopped at Dindigul to see the police association's John Britto and soon, MGR addressed his first public meeting at Salem, organized by district secretary Kannan. A mammoth crowd had assembled to hear their leader and the next day, MGR drove to Vaiyampalayam. Narayanasamy Naidu had invited his sangam's functionaries and lunch was served.

Narayanasamy Naidu's version of the wooing game differs from Solai's. Naidu was unwell and was recuperating. Kalaignar came over to inquire about his health. MGR sent word through T.R. Janarthanam, an MLC, that he wished to call on him too. Narayanasamy Naidu's rejection saw U.R. Krishnan, an MP, visit him with the same message. The third time, Aranganayagam showed up. The fourth was the visit by Ponnaiyan and Kolandaivelu. Narayanasamy Naidu relented and asked that MGR visit the following day, adding that it would not change the position of his sangam. The next day, Aranganayagam showed up to tell him that MGR would come at 10 p.m. Narayanasamy Naidu said that 2000 farmers had assembled in his place. He told Aranganayagam that they could not wait and the meeting could happen another time. Aranganayagam then brought MGR by 2.30 p.m. MGR blamed the officials for the raids on Narayanasamy Naidu's place and expressed regret, and sought his support, promising the manifesto the sangam wished for. MGR later visited Narayanasamy Naidu in Bangalore and showed him the AIADMK's election manifesto. Then Kalaignar visited him in Bangalore.

But MGR's visits and the manifesto had neutralized the sangam's stand which would aid the actor-politician. Narayanasamy Naidu would later say:

> Our sangam decided that when the AIADMK was not in power, we needn't talk against it. We don't have to get involved in a political controversy. [Besides] wherever he went, MGR promised that he would write off all the loans. Farmers believed it to an extent and were cheated. This is the reason why we kept an equal distance from both parties during the elections.[244]

He would repent later and say that Kalaignar would keep his word, while MGR's habit was to deny that he had even made the promise.[245]

Similarly, thanks to Solai, MGR met the police union functionaries in Trichy. Solai wrote that MGR was considered inaccessible, 'on the summit of the Himalayas', and these overtures helped overcome this negative image. MGR promised the recognition of the Tamil Nadu Police Subordinates Association as the sole representative of all ranks up to inspector in his manifesto.

MGR also promised 1 kilo of rice free for those who bought 5 kilos in the public distribution system, jobs for one member in every family, a fifty-rupee monthly allowance for unemployed graduates, a 100-rupee grant to the starving (regularity not specified), fifty rupees a month in the last trimester to the pregnant, and safe drinking water to all villages and towns. This was the content of the handouts promised.[246]

After careful consideration, MGR chose Madurai West as his constituency. Madurai was to be the nerve centre of the AIADMK's operations. The AIADMK and the CPM had won in many of the local wards, in the earlier elections, to local bodies. A small constituency that was easy to cover, it was considered a safe bet. In fact, MGR ended up addressing only two meetings there. The DMK was expected to field Pazhakadai Pandi, a local DMK heavyweight. What if Pandi were to be wooed into joining the AIADMK? Following a meeting with MGR, Pandi would do just that.

MGR did not wish to lose this election. Every seat was carefully analysed and a computer analysis projected 180 seats for the AIADMK front. Since Madras was considered a DMK fortress, it was allotted the least amount of time in MGR's programme.

Similarly, care was taken to pin down the important Opposition candidates to their constituency. Thus, MGR asked Valampuri John to contest in Purasawalkam against Anbazhagan. When John wondered what would happen if he lost, MGR said he would take care of him. He explained his choice thus: 'If you contest, Anbazhagan will not campaign across [the] state. That is enough for me.' John wrote that MGR was right. Anbazhagan issued a statement discontinuing his tour of the state. MGR spent both time and money in Purasawalkam. However, John did not win. But Anbazhagan could win only by 1400 votes.[247] In another instance, MGR pitted Dr H.V. Hande against Kalaignar. Kalaignar won by 699 votes, the lowest margin ever in his political career.[248]

Although MGR worried that he had no money for the elections, money did not determine the outcome of that election. Careful analysis, reaching out to allies and foes, planning and organization, and voter mobilization on the day of voting brought victory to AIADMK. 'What wrong did I commit? Why did you punish me?' he asked crowds. 'I worked only for you,' he cried. There were rains throughout Tamil Nadu that year and many places were flooded. AIADMK partymen said that the skies were crying for MGR. He won.[249]

The election taught MGR many lessons. The most important of them was that those who were expected to lend a helping hand, held back. They miscalculated that the AIADMK would not be victorious. They also did not wish to antagonize the Kalaignar–Indira Gandhi combination. MGR had begun his campaign with a measly 60,000 rupees and a loan of 1 lakh rupees from the owner of the lodge where he usually stayed in Coimbatore. He had pledged his Sathya Studios to movie mogul Nagi Reddy.[250] Cho. Ramaswamy wrote that MGR's only worry this time around was that he did 'not have enough funds' and this became his refrain.[251] Cho. Ramaswamy added that perhaps because of this, MGR's second term was an 'epitome of corruption' when the first term was an 'example of a clean government'.[252]

The AIADMK won 129 seats, the DMK thirty-seven seats and the Congress (I) thirty-one. MGR had almost single-handedly defeated the DMK–Congress (I) alliance.* *Ananda Vikatan* said in its lead story that the victory was a 'certificate from the people for MGR's clean, honest and non-corrupt rule'. It said people had rejected the Opposition's charges of corruption in MGR's rule.[253]

Kalaignar said that the lack of coordination between the two parties led to the defeat. Indira Gandhi obliquely suggested that projecting Kalaignar as chief minister had affected their chances. Kalaignar put on a brave face and said:

> But I do not interpret Mrs Gandhi's suggestion to mean that the alliance was rejected by the people on this count. Mrs Gandhi does not mean it that way. I, for one, do not think so. The fact is when she announced that I would be the chief minister, aspirants in the Congress (I) resented this forthright commitment. This resentment affected their relationship as electoral allies of the

---

*

MAJOR PARTIES AND PERFORMANCE
MAY 1980 ASSEMBLY ELECTION

Party	Contested	Won	Votes	Percentage
AIADMK	177	129	73,03,010	38.75%
Congress (I)	114	31	39,41,900	20.92%
CPI	15	9	5,01,032	2.66%
CPM	16	11	5,96,406	3.16%
DMK	112	37	41,64,389	22.10%
FBL	2	1	65,536	0.35%
GKNC	10	6	3,22,440	1.71%
Janata Party	95	2	5,22,641	2.77%
Kamaraj Cong +ind	11	6	4,88,296	2.6%

http://eci.nic.in/eci_main/StatisticalReports/SE_1980/ StatisticalReportTamil%20Nadu%201980.pdf.

DMK. This is what worried me, as it would hurt the alliance at the polls.[254]

On 3 June 1980, in a meeting to say thanks, the DMK chief spoke emotionally:

> If the child pees on the mother's forehead when she has lifted the child above her head in a display of affection, she does not drop the child. She will bring down her child slowly, give it a bath, change its clothes, and again tell the child lovingly 'my eyes' 'my jewel'. I take these election results in the same way. I wish to add one more thing. Oh, Tamils, if you throw me into the sea, I will float as a catamaran for you to use me to sail; if you throw me into the fire, I will become firewood so that you can cook and eat. If you strike me against a rock, I will not be reduced to smithereens. I will become like the coconut hurled on the ground, breaking into smaller pieces, turning into an eatable for you. Oh, Tamils, you can do whatever to me; I will always serve you.[255]

Prince of Populism

On 9 June 1980, Kalaivanar Arangam overflowed with humanity. MGR was sworn in as chief minister that day there. The stage backdrop sported portraits of leaders. A large painting of EVR watching over MGR and Anna adorned the centre of the backdrop. In the picture, MGR's head was slightly lowered towards his mentor, his palms brought together in respect, while Anna held his protégé's hands in a 'best wishes' gesture. Governor Prabhudas Patwari administered the oaths to MGR and his Cabinet. As chief minister again, MGR went up to his elder brother, M.G. Chakrapani, and former chief minister M. Bhaktavatsalam, seated in the audience, to seek their blessings. But the 'real swearing-in', as he said, was to follow. Like on the first occasion in 1977, MGR drove with his ministerial colleagues to Anna Salai 'to take oath'. It was 1.30 p.m. and the June sun was unbearable. But the 'sea of humanity' did not mind. MGR pledged to fulfil his election promises and uplift the poor.[1]

Once again, Vidwan Lakshmanan had marked the auspicious time for the official event. It proved unhelpful a second time around as well. The second term would prove more difficult than the first and would be punctuated by farmers' agitations, a shaky prohibition law, the lifting of prohibition, scandals and liquor barons and, worse still, MGR himself taking seriously ill.[2] However, it would also be the term where MGR would introduce the hugely popular Nutritious Meal Scheme, continue his vision of a welfare state and begin self-financing colleges—a mixed blessing.

His Cabinet had eighteen members of which seven were new. The eighteen were:

1. M.G. Ramachandran: Chief Minister
2. V.R. Nedunchezhian: Finance

3.   S. Ramachandran: Electricity
4.   K.A. Krishnaswamy: Rural Industries, Milk, Dairy Development
     and Registration
5.   S.D. Somasundaram: Revenue, Commercial Taxes, Excise
     and Census
6.   R.M. Veerappan: Information and Religious Endowments
7.   C. Aranganayagam: Education
8.   K. Kalimuthu: Agriculture
9.   C. Ponnaiyan: Cooperation and Law
10. P. Kulandaivelu: Local Administration
11. S. Raghavanandam: Labour
12. H.V. Hande: Health
13. K. Raja Mohammed: Irrigation
14. S. Muthusamy: Transport
15. S. Thirunavukkarasu: Industries
16. S.N. Rajendran: Handlooms and Khadi
17. M. Vijayasarathi: Adi Dravida Welfare
18. Gomathi Srinivasan: Social Welfare[3]

MGR had, at the outset, given away the ministries of health, industries and revenue this time. S.R. Radha, M.R. Govendhan and P. Vijayalakshmi would be inducted as ministers for fisheries, backward classes and khadi respectively from 1 July 1983. On 9 September 1983, K. Raja Mohammed, minister for irrigation, resigned and R. Soundararajan, Y.S.M. Yusuf, R. Arunachalam and K. Kalaimani were appointed as ministers for nutritious meals, irrigation, rural industries and fisheries respectively, taking the Cabinet's strength to twenty-four. On 8 July 1984, S.D. Somasundaram was given food and the ministries he was divested of were given to Nedunchezhian. On 3 September 1984, however, Somasundaram would be dropped from the Cabinet altogether. And his supporters T. Veerasamy and K.K.S.S.R. Ramachandran would be inducted as ministers of food and cooperation respectively. The Cabinet strength had gone up to twenty-five, the highest ever in Tamil Nadu's history.[4] Meanwhile, P.U. Shanmugam would take over as general secretary from Nedunchezhian in June 1980.[5]

His record win notwithstanding, MGR appeared uncomfortable in the political company of his smaller allies and was impatient to displace the DMK, the Congress (I)'s ally, even as the party tenaciously held on, sometimes under humiliating circumstances. Both Kalaignar and MGR rushed to Delhi to pay their last respects to Sanjay Gandhi, who was killed in an air crash on 23 June. MGR's allies, however, read more than commiseration into his gesture. Nedunchezhian's averment, 'Our relationships will be at three levels—Centre–state, AIADMK–Congress (I) and MGR–Indira Gandhi' only made their fears more credible. Kalyanasundaram pointed out that Indira Gandhi had taken twelve days to see MGR. However, MGR did not seem to mind.[6]

NUTRITIOUS MEAL SCHEME

In between all this political manoeuvring, MGR went ahead with his emphasis on the rural economy, cottage industries, strengthening last-mile connectivity[7] and, importantly, his social welfare measures. On 1 July, MGR joined the children of Pappakurichi village, in Trichy district, for lunch, to inaugurate the now celebrated Midday Nutritious Meal Scheme. The meal programme initially covered 56.9 lakh rural schoolchildren, providing them a meal of about 400 calories a day. Extended to the urban areas from September 1982, covering, in all, over 52,000 centres, including 31,000 schools, it took the number of beneficiaries up to 65.7 lakh children. The scheme provided employment to 1,80,119 persons, of which 1,58,387 were destitute women. The cost of the programme was 133 crore rupees per annum. Attendance at primary schools would go up to 96.2 per cent among the six to eleven age group and to 66.03 per cent in the eleven to fourteen age group. The nation had rarely seen a scheme of this magnitude. From 15 January 1983, the scheme would also cover 1,50,000 old age pensioners, orphans and destitute widows.[8] In 1987 Nedunchezhian would put the number of total beneficiaries from 1983 at 92 lakhs.[9]

Among the other measures MGR announced later were providing a job per family, on 2 September,[10] and free toothpowder for children, on 14 November 1982.[11] In 1987, plans for free footwear were afoot. The age of freebies had arrived.

MGR said on the launch of the lunch scheme:

This scheme is an outcome of my experience of extreme starvation at an age when I knew only to cry when I was hungry. But for the munificence of a woman next door, who offered a bowl of rice gruel to my mother and us, when we were starving for three days, and saved us from the cruel hand of death, we would have left this world long ago. Such merciful women, having great faith in me, elected me as chief minister of Tamil Nadu.

   To wipe the tears of these women I have taken up this project.[12]

MGR little realized that he had etched a permanent place for himself in history books with the launch of this scheme. 'It is epoch-making. Governments may come and go, but this scheme for 20,000 villages will go on,' Somasundaram, the revenue minister, had said prophetically.

   The scheme itself was not new. In 1920, two years after Kurichi Rangaswami Aiyangar had begun a lunch programme for students of the Hindu Theological School, the Justice Party's Sundarrao Naidu introduced free breakfast to pupils in a corporation preparatory school in Thousand Lights, Madras. Extended to four other schools by 1925, the paucity of funds saw an end to the avant-garde meal scheme and a consequent drop in school enrolment. On 17 July 1956, Chief Minister K. Kamaraj introduced the midday meal programme in Ettayapuram, Tirunelveli district. The scheme was gradually expanded and, by 1962–63, 27, 256 of the state's 28,005 aided or government-run schools were covered.[13]

   However, at the time of the launch of the new scheme, on 1 July 1980, the existing one covered only a third of the students for 200 days in a year. MGR had scaled it up twenty-five times. The new scheme covered all poor children for 365 days a year and the state bore the expenditure of 45 paise per head. MGR also set up and chaired a high-power committee to monitor the scheme's progress. Chief Secretary K. Diraviam served as member-secretary, with support from two dozen senior officials and a politician, and saw to the success of the scheme. Jayalalithaa, who was the politician in Diraviam's team, travelled across the state to spread the good word on the scheme. District collectors and party officials met her. On her return, she reported her findings on the administration and party affairs to the chief minister, who acted on them.[14] She would later attribute her elevation in 1983 as propaganda secretary to this work.[15]

   Ironically, when the scheme was discussed in the Cabinet, Nedunchezhian and others had opposed it, fearing corruption and wastage. MGR vetoed them, saying that any scheme would see a certain degree of corruption and that the baby cannot be thrown out with the bathwater. In MGR's scheme, education was secondary and feeding was primary.[16] When MGR suggested, 'Let us provide a hot meal with vegetable dishes to the pupils, akin to the lunch served in a middle-income family to the children by their mother', Aranganayagam was struck by his large heart and vision. A committee that included social worker Rajammal Devadas was formed; Devadas took a leaf out of the UN's World Food Programme book and adapted it to local needs. Greens and spinach were included and an ayah who had studied up to Class Ten was to take care of the preschool children.[17]

The scheme was ingenious and would do more than any of his other welfare measures to perpetuate his do-gooder image, leading DMK leader Murasoli Maran to perceptively comment:

> MGR is grossly exploiting the state's machinery and finances to project his own image by distributing alms. When he has failed on each front, he has started this to divert the people's attention from their hardships.

But Kalaignar had gone further, charging that MGR was turning children into beggars. Taking offence, he argued that Kalaignar should have instead offered advice on how to better implement the scheme.[18] Ironically, when the DMK came to power, they were compelled to continue the scheme, adding eggs twice a week and, in the 2016 elections, promising milk. So popular was the programme. Much later, on 28 November 2001, the Supreme Court, acting on a public interest litigation, would rule that government and government-assisted primary schools should provide cooked midday meals.

But the state had a deficit of 300 crore rupees and a determined MGR had to find nifty ways of funding the project, which were not all kosher.[19] A Chief Minister's Nutritious Noon Meal Programme Fund was created and donations to it were exempted from income tax. Contributions to it became a prerequisite for obtaining government clearances and for routine administrative orders.[20] Another 10 crore rupees was raised by way of a day's salary of government staff, one month's salary from ruling party MLAs and MPs, and the earnings from one show at cinemas. But money was also raised in many controversial ways, when, within a year, MGR would relax prohibition, although S. Ramachandran said that it was done towards filling the party's coffers.[21]

■

As MGR began his second term, his critic Cho. Ramaswamy certified that 'MGR is interested in earning a name by running a corruption free and clean administration. There is no need for him to hanker after anything including money.'[22] However, he would soon eat his words.[23]

The DMK's Manoharan said about MGR after his first term: 'During his first term of office, MGR was okay. But after he got re-elected in 1980, transport permits, admissions into medical and engineering colleges, everything, was turned into a money spinner.'[24]

Mohandas's testimony confirmed Manoharan's charge:

> I frankly told MGR that the tentacles of corruption were eating into the vitals of the administration during his second innings. I also informed MGR that people who mattered had begun voicing their opinion that the AIADMK government appeared to be more corrupt than the earlier DMK regime. MGR was annoyed but kept quiet. I felt that the 'sliding down' had started, and there was no way of stopping it, unless MGR had the political and personal will to avert the disaster.[25]

H.V. Hande tempered the criticism and placed it in context. He, however, began with the caveat that he could not speak the 'entire truth about anyone'. He said:

> MGR quietly allowed MLAs to make some money; he had the feeling that MLAs did require money. Corruption benefited the party functionaries marginally, and was there. It made things easier to move. MGR did not want anything for himself. To run a party, without collecting any money from industrialists, is impossible. I did not take money for medical seats. MGR would give from 2000 to 20,000 rupees as gifts to brides and grooms individually, depending on their status.[26]

Aranganayagam, who served in all three of MGR's Cabinets, also shared Hande's views.[27]

However, G. Viswanathan, who was elected an MLA that term, said that MGR gave AIADMK legislators a slush fund of 50 lakh rupees for local needs, like building schools, water facilities and roads.[28] Where did this money come from?

Hande also discounted the charge that MGR centralized authority or that civil servants ruled the roost. 'No health minister in the state has had as much power as I did under MGR. He was good at delegation. Each minister was independent, had responsibilities and functions, and civil servants did not have control.'[29]

'ENCOUNTERING' NAXALITES

But the police were definitely in control—perhaps too much in control—and the chief of Police Intelligence, Mohandas, continued to wield considerable influence over the chief minister.[30] Naxal violence had claimed eleven lives till then. MGR had given the police a 'free hand' although he was 'disturbed' by the sharp criticism he faced from civil rights groups. Mohandas congratulated himself and his deputy for finishing 'the job in twenty days and there has been no Naxalite activity in the area ever since.' On 27 August, the chief minister said, 'Whether the police act or not, [they are charged of] human sacrifice. This is a dangerous game played by politicians who are not serious.'[31] Later, in September 1981, citing the Hindu belief that one can kill an attacking cow in self-defence, he wondered how one could accept firing at the police and the possession of foreign firearms.[32] Mohandas complimented the chief minister for his 'foresight' in nipping the menace in the bud.[33] However, the police kept a tight lid on the reporting.[34]

HANDLING AGITATIONS: PART-TIME VILLAGE OFFICERS

On 13 November, by the stroke of a pen, a midnight ordinance sent 23,010 part-time 'village officers' packing. Many were believed to have empathized with the Vivasayigal Sangam. MGR explained his action, saying that they had become 'dictators' and 'had let loose repression on hapless people'. He had dispensed instant justice. MGR outlined plans to fill the positions full-time through the public service commission, which happened only two years later, in 1982.

He had not, however, thought of the immediate administrative vaccuum. The Supreme Court ordered the state government 'to avoid a deadlock and, at the same time, to protect the interests of the erstwhile village officers' and that no permanent appointments be made in the interim. The apex court criticized the 'high-handed' manner in which some village officers were forced out 'at odd hours'.[35] However, as the government undertook to absorb erstwhile staff who had minimum general education (a pass in the SSLC), the Supreme Court upheld the abolition.

MGR appeared to have dealt with the Vivasayigal Sangam in good faith initially and strove to keep his promises. His government wrote off short-term loans for small farmers, raised the exemption limit for land revenue from 5 to 10 acres for dry lands and waived agricultural income tax for non-cash crops. These benefits came up to some 60 crore rupees. However, sangam leader Narayanasamy Naidu termed these benefits as 'peanuts', demanding that all the loans, amounting to 302 crore rupees, be written-off.[36] Caught between a strict Centre that did not favour concessions and a defiant sangam, MGR divided the farmers into small and big, and dubbed Narayanasamy Naidu's programme 'a conspiracy of rich monopoly agriculturists to create conditions of anarchy by using poor farmers as pawns'.[37]

His administration now became tougher with the big farmers when it publicized the names and the dues owed by ten sangam members. Furthermore, a paid advertisement titled 'Do You Know?' warned defaulters to clear their dues in a week's time or face power disruption.[38] On 31 December, the sangam's call for a shutdown led to violence and police firing in four places in which four people died. MGR invoked the National Security Act against the farmers. In protest, the DMK held a rally on 1 January 1981.[39] MGR's allies too denounced such use of force. Nonetheless, MGR had started a war of attrition on the sangam as two major leaders left to form a new outfit—the fourth split since the sangam's founding.[40]

Slightly more than a year later, in the battle of wits between the sangam and MGR, Narayanasamy Naidu appeared defeated and accused the chief minister of three 'Os' against him: operation disconnection, operation collection and operation division. Under 'operation disconnection', an ordinance provided for deterrent punishment, including imprisonment for default of power dues, and helped realize 80 per cent of the electricity dues. Another ordinance threatened no-tax campaigners with a fine of 5000 rupees or five years' imprisonment, or both. Additionally, the Tamil Nadu Cooperative Land Development Bank Act and the Tamil Nadu Cooperative Societies Rules were passed to recover loans through distress procedures. The chief minister appeared to have beaten Narayanasamy Naidu at every turn and, worse still, had divided his sangam.[41] In 1983, Narayanasamy Naidu cited the failure of farmers' agitations in Karnataka and Maharashtra, and said, 'I abandoned these methods only after trying them to the limit. Is it our fate to always agitate after electing someone to power?'[42] In 1987, Nedunchezhian said in an op-ed piece in *Dinamani* that, in all, farm loans totalling 375 crore rupees had been waived. MGR would also allow agriculture produce in buses. Ironically, on the subsidies to farmers, a Madras Institute of Development study by S. Guhan, former finance secretary, who quit the IAS in 1979 during MGR's first ministry, said that his subsidies added up to 200 crore rupees annually and mostly benefited the rich farmers of the sangam.[43]

As a welfare measure for farmhands, the government distributed free saris and veshtis. Sometime before Pongal in 1981, civil servant Gopalkrishna Gandhi, grandson of both Gandhi and Rajaji, brought up the issue of some 80 crore rupees worth of stagnant handloom goods. The drought had affected agriculture, and farmhands did not have money to buy these goods. Without the stock moving, handloom workers could not produce or sell new goods. It was a vicious cycle. Gopalkrishna Gandhi suggested that the lower priced 'Janata' cloth, to the tune of 14 crore rupees, be given away free to farmhands, upon which Assembly Speaker Rajaram obtained Central clearance to use the famine relief funds for this purpose. MGR enthusiastically authorized this and it became the nucleus of the 1991 free sari, veshti scheme.[44]

TAMIL CONFERENCE

It was not all battle, there was also razzmatazz—the Fifth World Tamil Conference was held in Madurai from 4 to 10 January 1981.

The DMK boycotted the conference. Kalaignar wrote that they were not invited properly and, furthermore, MGR's ministers doubted his Tamil literary expertise. What a contrast it was to the Second World Tamil Conference that their mentor Anna had conducted. Anna's was a show of Tamil unity. Treating it as a family event, he invited Opposition leaders like Rajaji and Kamaraj personally, giving them due prominence and ensuring their attendance.

But times had obviously changed. In slightly more than a decade, egos and competitive Dravidian politics had left no room for Tamil unity or grace. The event was a vehicle for political mileage, and it was clear that MGR did not wish to share it with his rival Kalaignar. In the event, Tamil unity was sacrificed. The MGR government spent 10 crore rupees on the show. As much as he desired to keep Kalaignar away, MGR desired Indira Gandhi's attendance to add gravitas to the event and to show that she was warming up to him. Unsurprisingly, the DMK lobbied against him and she kept MGR guessing till the last minute. In the end, it was the senior Kanchi seer's interference that would secure her participation.[45] Kalaignar would commend her for denouncing the use of the National Security Act during the visit, after which he said the Vivasayigal Sangam's farmers were released. He would publicly charge that the conference money was swindled and hand over a letter on the government's 'misdeeds' to Indira Gandhi.[46]

The conference also showcased a performance by Jayalalithaa. Ironically, RMV, the man who had come between her and MGR once, was asked to facilitate the dance. Apparently, the ten-year hiatus between Jayalalithaa and her mentor was broken in the US, when MGR was on his official visit in late 1978 and she was there on a private visit.[47] Jayalalithaa would soon join the AIADMK. And the rest is history.[48]

CONVERSIONS AND CASTE TROUBLES

Hot on the heels of the Madurai World Tamil Conference was the Meenakshipuram incident. On 19 February 1981, Meenakshipuram, a tiny hamlet in Tirunelveli district, made headlines when some 150 Adi Dravidas chose to embrace Islam. In the aftermath of Meenakshipuram, figures revealed that over 2000 people had left the Hindu fold in an eight-month period as opposed to less than 1500 between 1944 and 1980. The following month, among others, BJP leader Atal Bihari Vajpayee visited the hamlet to ascertain the context. Indira Gandhi sent her minister of state for home, Yogendra Makwana, there. 'Her impression was that the Muslim leaders had the vision of a pan-Islamic empire connecting south India with Pakistan and the Middle East', wrote Mohandas.[49] MGR and his colleagues said that the conversions were achieved with money from outside the state. Uttharakosamangai, a village in Ramanathapuram, followed a month later. Rechristened Mohammadiapuram, 150 Adi Dravida families would take to Islam there.[50]

Mid-April saw caste clashes leaving five dead in Ramnad district. The chief minister cancelled his visit to Kuala Lumpur, where he was to attend the World Telugu Conference, and, instead proceeded to Ramnad, where he convened an all-party peace committee and restored calm.[51]

'YELLOW JOURNALISM': THE SCURRILITY LAW AND GOONDAS ACT

In a first, the MGR administration introduced the anti-scurrility amendment to the Indian Penal Code in early 1982, making scurrility a cognizable and non-bailable offence, leaving this to the judgement of a police inspector. As early as 1 August 1978, MGR had expressed his anger with 'yellow journalism', which he said was the result of some having lost power, in an oblique reference to the DMK. He justified the 1982 amendment thus: 'The Press Council takes its own time in dealing with cases, and delay is inevitable. What will happen to our prestige meanwhile?'[52] In the wake of stiff opposition, MGR set up a review committee, made up of seven ministers, officials and nine press persons, later that year. The committee met once in October 1982. But on 27 May 1983, when MGR dug in his heels, saying that the amendment is 'only a shield from the weapon of the press to protect people from slander' and will not be repealed, even those press persons close to him quit the committee. Following this, MGR said on 23 June that the amendment would be repealed, only to qualify the following day that he would only modify it. In true MGR speak, he explained:

Journalists themselves might become victims of scurrilous writing sometime or the other, and the Press Act was intended to protect them as much as the public. The provisions of the Indian Penal Code are not enough to deal with scurrilous writing. The editor of an Opposition-sponsored Tamil daily has the audacity to say that he will go on with his scurrilous writing, no matter how many times he is arrested. If journalists behave this way, I will perhaps be constrained to invoke the Goondas Act even.

Then, on 25 June, MGR told the press that the 1982 amendment would be withdrawn.[53] But it was finally on 6 March 1984 that law minister Ponnaiyan tabled the bill withdrawing the amendment.[54]

Similarly, the MGR administration would pass the Goondas Act, enabling preventive detention for up to a year on law and order and other issues. According to *India Today*, some fifty people were held on an average each month after the passage of the Act. On one occasion, the Madras High Court had intervened to release nearly 200 detainees.[55]

THE RECTIFIED SPIRIT SCANDAL

The biggest challenge to the administration's 'prestige' lay in its own handling of the diversion of rectified spirit. The 'great spirit scandal' as it came to be known would rock the state from January 1981, with the Opposition and media alleging that the MGR administration had been illegally diverting rectified spirit to Kerala after accepting bribes. On 4 July 1980, the joint commissioner for prohibition and excise had prohibited taking rectified spirit outside the state. This order was withdrawn on 28 August. In the meanwhile, a Kerala contractor named Ahmed Khan had allegedly influenced MGR to lift the ban in breach of the order. MGR himself admitted that he had only allowed 10 lakh litres but 15 lakh litres had been taken. A letter from Ahmed Khan to the Kerala government mentioning his Herculean efforts and expenses to get the permit from Tamil Nadu had let the cat out of the bag.[56] The DMK and Congress (I) parliamentarians promptly demanded a Central probe. On 10 February 1981, MGR appointed Justice Kailasam, a friend, to probe the issue, saying that Kalaignar's direct charges against him in the House had led him to respond thus.[57] The DMK termed it an 'eye wash' and carried out protests, Kailasam resigned and was replaced by Justice Sadasivam on 29 May.[58] The DMK now pointed out that the terms of reference had been extended to cover the events from 1969 to 76, when Kalaignar was in power, which the party said gave an insight into how the commission would function.[59]

Meanwhile, heeding the DMK, on 18 June 1981, the Centre appointed the Justice Ray Commission to probe the matter.[60] MGR had earlier said that he would resign if such a commission came into being. After a meeting with Indira Gandhi in Delhi on 25 June, Kalaignar, uncomfortably for MGR, reminded him of this.[61] MGR had gone a step further, visualizing dismissal, and said at a party meeting in Madurai: 'The Centre dismissed the AIADMK ministry last year without any valid reasons. It can do the same now also. We must be prepared for any eventuality' and indicated his cooperation with Ray. He instructed partymen not to criticize the Centre's decision, threatening disciplinary action. Following the turn of events, Kalaignar said that he would not ask for him to resign, but would simply remind MGR of his demand for Kalaignar to quit when he presented allegations against the DMK ministry.[62]

But MGR tried to stave off Ray and had tasked Hande to meet Indira Gandhi. On 16 June, when Hande met her, she told him unequivocally: 'Your chief minister should decide whether he wants me as his friend or foe.' She had expectedly pointed to a minister's vitriolic attack against her and the Congress (I). Hande delivered MGR's message: 'Madam, our leader has asked me to tell you that if this is an issue, he will drop the minister from the Cabinet.' The minister was Kalimuthu, who did MGR's bidding. Indira Gandhi was not pleased and, later that day, Home Minister Zail Singh told him: 'Dismissal, no. Commission, yes.'[53] Two days later, on 18 June, the Ray Commission came into being. The commission was to look into the eleven charges from the 6 February 1981 representations from the Tamil Nadu MPs and the nine charges stemming from representations from Kerala MLAs. In particular, as mentioned earlier, the commission was to probe if the chief minister had taken bribes for the permits.[64]

It was a trough in MGR's political graph. In the summer of 1981, the Centre would withdraw the CBI cases spawned by the Sarkaria investigation, against his political nemesis Kalaignar, saying that

important witnesses had retracted their testimony.[65] Mohandas said
that the development had shocked MGR.[66] His political career had
been built around the Sarkaria Commission, but, in the end, both the
way the commission came into being and its findings being discarded,
proved purely political. But MGR put on a brave face. He described
it as a 'huge blow' to the justice system. On 14 June, the AIADMK's
administrative committee, attended by seventy-five of the seventy-nine
members, condemned the withdrawal of the cases.[67]

CAPITAL CHANGE

Nature was also playing truant as eleven of the sixteen districts in Tamil
Nadu faced serious drought that year.[68] In response to the consequent
water shortage in Madras, on 15 March, MGR suggested building a new
capital in a central location between Trichy and Thanjavur, at a cost
of 400–500 crore rupees, like Chandigarh. To questions if the capital
should not be along the coast, MGR asked if Delhi and Washington DC
were along the coast.[69] He said the propertied who worried that their
assets would lose value were the ones questioning his idea. He pointed
out that his suggestion of a Supreme Court bench in the south was also
initially ridiculed.[70] Kalaignar, however, suggested that MGR was not
serious and it was a diversionary tactic. 'He is only keen on his capital,'
he concluded.[71] Kalaignar felt a new capital would require 1000 crore
rupees and when the state could not spend 50 crore rupees on drought
relief, he wondered 'is this effort necessary?'[72]

GOING BACK ON PROHIBITION

More loss of face was in store for MGR. On 1 May 1981, MGR went
back on his 1 December 1979 oath on his mother to retain prohibition
till his 'last breath'.[73]

MGR explained:

The law that was meant to wipe tears ended up swelling the eyes
of mothers and wives with more tears. I found that it resulted
in increased bootlegging, scores of deaths and thousands of jail
sentences. This meant that breadwinners in thousands of families

ended up in jail for breaking the law, thus reducing such families
to destitution. That's why I decided to change it.[74]

MGR said that 170 to 200 crore rupees was going to private enterprises
earlier, which the government was getting now, and the money was
being diverted for good causes like the nutritious meal scheme.[75]

But money also appeared to be coming into the party coffers
via dubious means. The Supreme Court directed fresh invites for
the wholesale distribution licences for Indian-made Foreign Liquor
(IMFL) for 130 places and the licences for the blending units. The
licences would fetch a cumulative annual profit of over 50 crore
rupees. In a seven-page affidavit in March 1981, R.N. Manickam,
a former inspector-general of police, averred that his brother
S. Sundarmurthy, son-in-law Shanmugam and their businessman friend
M. Ravindran were promised a licence for the wholesale distribution
of arrack and IMFL in return for a bribe of 10.75 lakh rupees, paid in
over four instalments to MGR's brother, Chakrapani, and his sons,
Sukumaran and Balan. They asked that their money be returned
when the licence did not materialize and, on 20 August, they received
a cheque from Sukumaran for 3 lakh rupees, which bounced. After
this, Manickam reached out to Chakrapani and MGR, and got two
promissory notes for 10.75 lakh rupees on 30 October, signed by
Chakrapani and Sukumaran. In March 1981, several Tamil newspapers
carried MGR's announcement that he had severed all ties with his
brother and his family. In hindsight, it appeared a pre-emptive move
against Manickam's charge.[76] The son of a neighbour and MGR's
advocate general, V.P. Raman, remembered that MGR had advised
him and his brother, even as children, to keep off his nephews.[77] From
the beginning MGR was firm that Chakrapani had to stay clear of the
AIADMK. He asked Solai: 'What will the world say? Won't it say that
the brothers are having it all for themselves?'[78]

After Manickam's sensational charge, the DMK and Congress (I)
MLAs and MPs demanded an inquiry. In response, on 30 October 1981,
a gazette notification on the Ramamurthi (later Ramaprasada Rao)
Commission said with disarming candour that the commission would
look into 'allegations [that] have been made both in the press and on
the floor of the House that Thiru M.G. Ramachandran, chief minister

of Tamil Nadu' or other ministers or public servants had 'collected huge amounts as illegal gratification' in connection with liquor licensing.

In two years, diversion of rectified spirit and the licensing of liquor would create a record three inquiry commissions—the MGR-appointed Sadasivam and Ramaprasada Rao Commissions and the Centre's Ray Commission. While the Sadasivam and Ray Commissions would get bogged down in legalities, in 1984, the MGR-appointed Ramaprasada Rao Commission would absolve the chief minister and his colleagues of any wrongdoing.

But the Ramaprasada Rao Commission's clean chit came in less than kosher ways. The commission had invited and received six affidavits by 3 February 1982, but extended the deadline to 25 March and received twenty affidavits in all. Except R.N. Manickam's affidavit, the rest supported MGR. The commission again extended the deadline for affidavits to 23 April and once more to 23 May 1982 and, in the interim, received over 225 pro-MGR affidavits. The hearings began finally in August. Of the 253 deponents, Manickam was the only deponent against the government.[79] MGR's lawyer said that the DMK counsel's demand for MGR to testify and subject himself to cross-examination was 'political'. In the event, the commission chose to go with the written depositions.[80]

On 15 March 1984, the commission cleared MGR and his Cabinet colleagues of any wrongdoing, and, on the same day, the Leader of the House, Nedunchezhian, read out selections from the report in the House. Terming it 'a blatantly one-sided and partisan report', Kalaignar declared that the DMK would burn the report. The following day, when a DMK legislator did just that and was duly expelled, and when a point of order by the DMK was disallowed, all parties, including the Congress (I), staged a walkout.[81] The Cabinet had read and approved the 476-page Ramaprasada Rao Commission report in just one hour. It had taken six months for the C.J.R. Paul Commission's 288-page report to be read and approved. (But then again Paul's report had not been favourable to the government.)[82] That day, in Erode, MGR described the Rao Commission report as a victory for 'justice and truth', and said that Kalaignar should have the 'frame of mind' to accept it.[83]

However, the Supreme Court would eventually strike down the state's award of IMFL wholesale dealerships. But the MGR administration's imagination came to the fore when the state turned this setback to an opportunity and, on 25 May 1983, floated two corporations—the now notorious Tamil Nadu State Marketing Corporation (TASMAC), for the wholesale marketing of liquor, and Tamil Nadu Spirit Corporation (TASCO), for the manufacture and to 'provide cheap and good quality liquor for those amongst the poor classes who consume and for protecting the health of the liquor consuming public'. By 1987, private companies took over manufacturing and TASCO was closed down.[84]

LIQUOR BARONS

TASMAC, however, would turn out to be a cash cow, with a turnover of 900 crore rupees in the next seven years. A three-member TASMAC board ran the operations, playing a key role in supporting and nourishing the new class of entrepreneurs that the MGR government had created—liquor barons.

Ignoring a Central ban on permits for new capacity, the MGR government would choose to allow the setting up of new breweries and distilleries: Ramasamy Udayar's Mohan Breweries and Distilleries was the first to set up a distillery. The 10 December 1981 application was cleared on 11 January 1982—in a record time of a month.

Then came Mohan Meakins, a firm from the north, which had tied up with Ramasamy Udayar and his family members, and only five months earlier was found unsuitable on its own. The sluice gates had been opened. The joint sector Southern Agrifurane, owned by the state and A.C. Muthiah, became the next to set up a distillery. Shiva Distilleries, Empee Distilleries and Balaji Distilleries joined the fray later.

Liquor barons had come into being and had come to stay. Kalaignar would point out that these barons would make 36 crore rupees a year. 'Do they go to those nine families or do they go [after being collected by these front families] to that one family?' he asked, insinuating that MGR pocketed all the money.[85] By 1989, the manufacturing five had supplied liquor and beer worth over 800 crore rupees to the state. An inquiry during the 1989 DMK administration would reveal the following:

- The five distilleries and breweries were allowed to manufacture IMFL and beer without Cabinet or the Central government clearance;

- Arrack and IMFL retail outlets were given away without tenders;
- Excise and sales tax concessions were given to manufacturers without prior Cabinet approval;
- Tax arrears were not recovered;
- Many arrack and IMFL shops were proxies, and they belonged to wholesalers;
- Despite the low excise duty, liquor prices were the highest in country, as prices were fixed by the sellers;
- More than 100 files on exemption of excise duties and recovery of arrears (of over 50 crore rupees) would go missing.

TASMAC paid the excise on liquor and Tamil Nadu became the first state in which manufacturers did not pay excise. According to one estimate, every month, some 5 crore rupees was lost in this way, with manufacturers paying thirty rupees less sales tax per twelve bottles, and on sales tax alone, the state was losing another 5 crore rupees monthly.

Again, in a first, the MGR administration exempted manufacturers from the excise duty of eight rupees per litre of rectified spirit and the vend fee of one rupee (a tax on the vendor for every bottle of liquor sold). Manufacturers made as much as fifty-six rupees per case.

The ultimate concession though was when the government allowed suppliers to fix the price of liquor sold. Consequently, manufacturers pocketed a neat 60 crore rupees yearly as profit.

The way retail sales dealerships were dispensed with was no better. Partymen had a field day when the government stipulated a measly fee of 20,000 rupees annually per outlet. Soon there were 2000 outlets. If these were auctioned, the state would have made an additional 25 crore rupees annually.

Despite all this, retailers owed the government 20 crore rupees as tax arrears. Most of them were found to be proxy outlets, with phantom addresses in Rajasthan and Madhya Pradesh. Additionally, more than 100 files on the exemption from licence fees went missing and, in 1989, former excise commissioner T.V. Venkataraman said he had personally delivered fifty-two files to MGR in 1986, and that none were ever returned.

In February 1989, when the DMK came to power, Chief Minister Kalaignar would declare in the Assembly that:

Rs 100 crore was being siphoned off year after year. There was a conspiracy to deprive the state of its legitimate revenue . . .

What was obviously bribe money will now be used to bridge the deficit in the state's finances.

He also revealed that the unholy alliance between the liquor barons and the MGR administration had caused the state a revenue loss of over 1000 crore rupees in seven years. Kalaignar would also tell the House, 'We have liquidated the liquor empire in the state within twenty days of coming to power.' This pronouncement would be revealed as to be tall talk when the DMK, later, created its own liquor barons and could not wholeheartedly commit to shut them down when it became an issue in the 2016 general elections to the Assembly.[86]

S. Ramachandran said that, sobered by the want of funds in the 1980 Assembly elections, MGR decided to open the taps 'promoting people like Ramasamy Udayar, A.C. Muthiah, and M.P. Purushottam and others'. P.H. Pandian, however, describes MGR as 'blemishless' and justified the development thus: 'Liquor business and the press— only the rich can run them. So money flowed in on its own.' It was not hard to surmise that the money flowed into the party coffers. However, S. Ramachandran and H.V. Hande said that MGR had designated a select few to collect party funds.[87]

MGR, S. Ramachandran added in the same breath, was very upset with these scandals for his 'image was his political asset'.[88] MGR need not have worried as these scandals barely seemed to affect his image. Despite him having given up acting, his films continued to perpetuate his image. By late 1981, it was estimated 100 out of his 136 films were still being shown across the state and their box office collections were better than the collections of the newer films. South Indian Film Chamber of Commerce (SIFCC) chief Ramanujam said that MGR's films kept rural cinema alive and an estimated half a million people watched them daily.[89]

But MGR took criticism personally. It would see him go back on his word to the Nadigar Sangam. In 1977, at MGR's request, Sivaji Ganesan had taken over the leadership on the condition that he would appoint new functionaries and that until the loan for the new building was settled, the sangam should not have elections. MGR declared open the building that had cost 22 lakh rupees. However, as the loan stared the sangam in the face, a sensitive MGR would stand up Sivaji Ganesan later.

Actor V.K. Ramasamy provided the context for MGR's change. It was at a time when the Congress (I), to which Sivaji Ganesan belonged, was seriously criticizing MGR's lifting of prohibition. Congress (I) speakers alliteratively asked: 'Appanaku saraayam. Pillaiku sathunavaa (Liquor for the father and nutritious meal for the child)?' As Sivaji Ganesan voiced these criticisms, MGR took it personally. 'Can thambi Sivaji speak like this? What does it mean if he himself criticizes me like this?' he demanded. V.K. Ramasamy tried to rationalize things with MGR and both kept repeating their positions. It was clear that MGR had taken Sivaji's criticisms to heart and would not relent. In the event, the Sivaji Ganesan administration resigned.[90]

WOOING THE CONGRESS (I): THE TIRUPATTUR BY-ELECTION

Despite its criticism of him, MGR still yearned for a Congress (I) alliance and sought to repair his ties with it. Prior to the Tirupattur Assembly by-election, the chief minister justified his craving thus:

> We have had some differences of opinion. That's why they went to the DMK. But it is we who have a more solid and meaningful relationship with the Congress (I). Our relationship is old and more durable.[91]

This urge saw him making every effort to woo the Congress (I)—from enlisting the services of Mohan Meakins to patiently courting ash-smeared sadhus considered close to Indira Gandhi. Nothing worked. 'Indira Gandhi refused to see MGR. It was Governor Khurana who finally took them to the prime minister,' said S. Ramachandran. He had accompanied the chief minister and the governor and recalled, 'She did not look in MGR's direction. When we were about to leave, she asked MGR, "How are you?" adding, "I can depend on junior Ramachandran but not [on] M.G. Ramachandran."'[92]

S. Ramachandran said that they then sent word through the Intelligence Bureau's M.K. Narayanan, that they would support the Congress (I) candidate in the Tirupattur by-election and that the Congress (I) should say that they welcomed support from anyone. In the first week of October, MGR punning on Tirupattur (*Thiruppam* means turning point in Tamil), said the elections there could be a turning point. Kalaignar responded sarcastically: 'He is capable of making changes easily. In the Thanjavur elections he took a decision at 10 p.m. At 10.30 p.m. he changed [it]. Therefore, I don't know what change he would bring this time.'[93]

MGR, however, was leaving no stone unturned to woo Congress (I). His party had offered support for the Centre's National Security Act and the Essential Services Maintenance Act. Besides, the DMK's agitational course on the ethnic issue was not entirely to the Congress (I)'s liking and, in September, during the thick of the agitation, Indira Gandhi had cryptically replied, 'Ask the local leaders,' when asked about the Congress (I)'s alliance with the DMK.

On 31 October, MGR flew to Delhi to meet Indira Gandhi, following which, on 4 November, she said in a statement that she welcomed support from all parties in relation to Tirupattur. When Kalaignar, in disgust, stayed away from the election campaign, he may not have realized that he was doing MGR a huge favour. Kalaignar recorded ironically that the Congress (I) had begun the 'chapter of gratitude' to the DMK.[94] Despite this humiliation, the party held on to its stand that it would not end the alliance on its own.

On 16 November, in Madurai, an AIADMK sixteen-member committee postulated the MGR doctrine to justify its support to the Congress (I) candidate: 'Except vacancies arising through the verdict of a court, in other cases, the party which won the seat in the previous election should be supported and the vacancy filled by that party.'[95] This was tantamount to making a mockery of democracy. Adding fuel to the fire, MGR stated that the AIADMK's support would depend 'on the need, situation and their [Congress (I)] request'.[96] True to his style, MGR was hunting with the hounds and running with the hares. He had summoned his allies to Madurai, but refused to heed their advice to field a candidate or support one of them. While the DMK stayed away, MGR not only campaigned vigorously for four days but also opened over a hundred AIADMK campaign offices. It was a sad day in Dravidian politics.[97]

But MGR had driven a wedge between the Congress (I) and the DMK. He would follow this up with his offer for government jobs to Congress (I) nominees. On 10 December 1981, the Tamil Nadu Congress Committee (I) executive said it would fight the elections to local bodies on its own. Subsequent to this, MGR met with some six Central ministers and TNCC (I) leaders a number of times, provoking a DMK leader to say: 'We are with Mrs Gandhi at the Central level but her supporters in the state are eating out of MGR's hands.'[98] But it would be a long time before a formal rapprochement occurred between MGR and Indira Gandhi.

ETHNIC ISSUE: 1981

The Sri Lankan Tamil issue had last attracted the state's attention in 1977. In the summer of 1981, the gutting of the Jaffna Public Library and the week-long violence in the country shocked Tamil Nadu. Again, the two Dravidian leaders would turn the issue into one of gamesmanship between them. Soon thereafter, MGR and Kalaignar met Indira Gandhi separately in Delhi and, on 21 August, the Tamil Nadu Assembly passed a unanimous resolution urging the prime minister to protect the Tamils. The MGR administration also called for a shutdown for 12 September. Clearly, the shutdown call had taken the wind out of the DMK's sails. (On a brief visit to Madras a day earlier, Indira Gandhi said she found the idea of government sponsorship of the shutdown 'odd'. The shutdown, however, proved total.)

The death of Dhanapathi, a Tamil Nadu tourist in Sri Lanka, would become the next point of competition between the Kazhagams. The DMK had given a solatium of 3000 rupees to his family and picketed outside the Sri Lankan Deputy High Commission. DMK picketers were arrested, but were not released, as had happened with the Congress men who had observed a fast defying a ban. The DMK now announced a daily picketing programme to culminate with Kalaignar's participation on 15 September. MGR called it a 'publicity stunt' and said that 'by courting arrest on Anna's birthday, Karunanidhi wants public attention to get focused on him rather than the government's birthday celebration programmes'. That day, MGR was laying the foundation stone for his other pet project, the

Tamil University in Thanjavur. On 15 September, Kalaignar was taken into custody and some 7000 DMK men in all were now behind bars. Kalaignar's arrest saw five people immolating themselves and six others suffering serious burns. MGR termed it a 'barbaric sacrifice',[99] but ordered the release of Kalaignar and the others on 29 September.

On his release, Kalaignar remarked, 'The self-immolations symbolize the awakening of the Tamil people. MGR had me arrested out of vengeance . . . And my party was singled out for this harsh treatment . . . MGR is bent on conducting the politics of hate.' As the AIADMK alleged there were personal reasons behind the deaths, Manoharan queried: 'Can MGR explain why people should try to commit self-immolation between September 15 and 28, and not before or after that?' Self-immolations continue to remain a low point of Dravidian politics and the Kazhagams have to be squarely blamed for idolizing these acts. When will Tamils learn to live to fight another day rather than consume themselves? On Dhanapathi, MGR said that the family had refused the DMK's relief and instead accepted the AIADMK's 25,000 rupees. Clearly, the ruling party had won this round.[100]

INDICTMENT BY THE PAUL COMMISSION

Kalaignar would, however, prove his resourcefulness with the Paul Commission report putting the MGR government in the dock. On 26 November 1980, C. Subramaniam Pillai, a temple verification officer, was found hanging in the inspection bungalow of the Tiruchendur Murugan temple. The temple trustees, mostly AIADMK men, accused Subramaniam Pillai, a man of a clean record, of pocketing 2850 rupees. An outraged town observed a shutdown on 2 December and, on 19 December, the C.J.R. Paul Commission was appointed to probe the death. Justice Paul had concluded 'homicidal violence' as the cause of Subramaniam Pillai's death and had recommended that the board of trustees be dismissed prior to any inquiry.[101] As MGR baulk, an editorial in Kumudam magazine aptly summed up the situation: 'Tamil Nadu is in MGR's hands; MGR is in a minister's [RMV was minister for Hindu Religious Endowment] hands; the minister is in the hands of the chairman of the temple trust.'[102]

On 24 November 1981, Kalaignar released the commission's adverse report to embarrass the government. Stung to the quick, the administration pressed a criminal case against Kalaignar and three associates for theft, accepting stolen property and violating the Official Secrets Act.[103]

On 13 February 1982, Kalaignar asked to bring the guilty to book, to which RMV said the government would proceed only after the Crime Branch investigated the case again, at which the DMK staged a walkout. Soon after this, MGR informed the Assembly that the trustees had sent in their resignations just then.

The DMK announced a '*Needhi Kaetu Nediya Payanam* (Long March Seeking Justice)' from Madurai to Tiruchendur from 15 February. En route, an official met Kalaignar in his train, at Villupuram, to give him the chief minister's letter appealing him to desist from his plans. Kalaignar, after consideration, nevertheless said that the chief minister was reluctant to punish the guilty and that his march would help him. The next day 30,000 workers assembled, considering it a huge honour and privilege to accompany their leader on the march. *Ananda Vikatan* said that one could not but be touched seeing 'these pure-hearted cadre'.

On the second day, Kalaignar's feet would develop boils and a music band stepped in to cheer their leader on. There was heavy, but discreet, police deployment. An ambulance had also been sent by a thoughtful MGR administration. The 200-kilometre march took eight days and culminated in Tiruchendur, and Kalaignar estimated that he had met some 15 lakh people on the way. On 24 February, the DMK also offered a solatium of 50,000 rupees to Subramaniam Pillai's family. The march galvanized the DMK cadre and 'generated public sympathy'.[104] A year later in the Tiruchendur by-elections in February 1983, MGR said the commission's findings were 'recommendations' and not 'judgement', and that Kalaignar was engaged in a 'smear campaign' for votes.[105]

JAYALALITHAA JOINS THE AIADMK

On 4 June 1982, Jayalalithaa enrolled as a party member. S. Ramachandran recalled that 'nobody' wanted her in the party. But MGR did and that was enough. In 1984, in what might be the most authentic version of the sequence of events that led her to entry into the AIADMK, she told *Ananda Vikatan* how she took to public life:

> I told Mr MGR that I wished to engage in politics. 'Do not be hasty . . . You have to read a lot,' he said. I have been interested in politics and have been observing developments. I showed more interest. In 1982, I again told Mr MGR of my wish. He gave me a book containing [the] AIADMK's principles, asking me to read it carefully. Two months after this, I joined the AIADMK.
>
> As someone who had read politics, there is no doubt that MGR had caught my attention. But, that is not the only reason . . . Gandhiji spoke of a village raj. Thirty-six years after Independence, no administration has helped the rural folk as [much as] MGR's administration has. In north India, there are villages where people cannot live because there is no water. Here, MGR had introduced a self-sufficiency water scheme . . . Now free nutritious meal scheme . . . The Centre is not helping a bit with these. They say MGR's administrative ability is inadequate. Which chief minister claiming administrative competence has been able to bring such schemes? Who stopped them? When even Congress [I] chief ministers did not care about Gandhiji's rural raj, these feats of MGR attracted me![106]

In 1999 she said she entered politics for his sake.

> I entered politics because of the influence of my political mentor, Mr MGR. I really came into politics just to be of help to him. Because he said he could not trust the people around him, and, at that time, his health was beginning to fail, and he wanted someone whom he could trust 100 per cent, someone who he thought could be totally dependable and reliable. I really came into politics just to be of assistance and help to him.[107]

But then both Jayalalithaa and MGR had come full circle. MGR needed her charisma, competence and crowd-pulling skills. He had pointed to her reading habits, her English, her potential to draw crowds and wondered to S. Ramachandran, 'Why can't we utilize her?'[108] He had once sought to 'own' her and she had freed herself. And now she was back after a tumultuous personal life and a film career that was behind her. And this time, ironically, she would ask for all the attention and often not get it, mostly because of her own doing. She had declared in 1984 that she would be his 'most loyal' follower.[109] But 'MGR felt that she often crossed the line,' said S. Ramachandran. But her loyalty to MGR itself would become suspect.

Time has shown that Jayalalithaa's entry into the party would prove a mixed blessing. While Jayalalithaa consolidated MGR's electoral legacy, she must have also made him turn in his grave daily— for pushing his memory completely into the background, turning into a megalomaniac, naming everything after herself, and perhaps also for being the only chief minister who had to quit office twice on charges of corruption. For a woman who was his heir and who claimed to carry his agenda forward, she would visit MGR's home in Ramavaram Gardens only after two decades, in 2010, when actor Vijayakanth posed a threat, laying claim to MGR's mantle.[110] The fact that MGR did not identify her as his successor till the end speaks volumes of his ambivalence towards her.

Su. Thirunavukkarasar acknowledged that MGR would suggest Jayalalithaa conduct public meetings, instead of him, as his health was not good. But P.C. Ganesan, one of her biographers, says that even MGR's files were sent to her 'for comments'.[111] Solai was given the task to train her in public speaking and to write her speeches. Valampuri John appears to have also assisted with her speeches. Solai recalled her reading the first speech he had prepared and repeating it on her request thrice. Solai was astonished when she was able to repeat the speech verbatim.[112]

Her debut speech was not political. MGR had asked her to give a talk on the 'Greatness of Women' at the Cuddalore party conference that year. But she turned it into a political speech, when she rhetorically posed the question: 'I am asking you; you tell me, aren't you all on the side of Puratchi Thalaivar MGR?' The crowd roared a 'yes' then.[113]

MGR seemed both possessive and eager to flaunt the star as a trophy. Equally, Jayalalithaa proved too impatient and eager to come out of MGR's shadow. Her independence, bordering on disobedience and disrespect to MGR, led to their relationship blowing hot and cold by turn, and her detractors taking advantage of her shortcomings to widen the chasm between the mentor and the mentee. But she always managed to climb back into his good books and take advantage of MGR's fascination for her. Her detractors like Valampuri John alleged that MGR was 'suspicious' and monitored Jayalalithaa's every move. It is not clear if MGR was suspicious, protective, possessive or a control freak. Salem Kannan too would have us believe that MGR watched her.[114] S. Ramachandran said that MGR monitored the size of her meetings, the reception and the content of her speeches.[115]

It is true that Jayalalithaa had to take instructions and approval for her activities. But she took her job seriously. She was given the green light then to attend the party office and go on a tour once in ten days. Her debut political meeting on 17 October 1982 happened at Mangollai, in Mylapore, Madras. She criticized the Centre for not involving itself in the Cauvery issue because of the elections in Karnataka. She also said that if Karnataka were to claim ownership of the Cauvery water then a situation would arise where Tamil Nadu might claim ownership for the oil discovered on its shores.[116] That day, MGR met Indira Gandhi in a one-to-one meeting in Delhi for twenty minutes, among others, seeking her intercession for the release of 2600 crore cubic feet of Cauvery water, and the prime minister had said that 'she wanted to help'.[117] *Ananda Vikatan* reported that there was a heavy police presence around the meeting venue and policemen locked arms to form a human chain, preventing entry even to residents of the street where the meeting was held. Jayalalithaa wore a black blouse and a dark red silk sari, and spoke last of all, with notes. Sometimes, when she tried to raise her voice to pose a challenge to the Opposition, it sounded muffled because of its femininity. She enlisted the measures to tackle the difficult water situation in the state, and her speech was full of statistics and data. Some police officials were seen taking notes. Others recorded her speech. At the end of the meeting, it began to pour outside. 'Anni (elder brother's wife) Jayalalithaa and the rain have come, see!' a woman flower vendor outside said, holding up the garland that Jayalalithaa had given her.[118]

On 23 November, the media would carry a picture of the chief minister flanked by his wife to the left and Jayalalithaa to his right, watching the ASIAD in Delhi, highlighting the chief minister's wish to exhibit her as an equal to his wife.*[119]

In 2008, Jayalalithaa said that MGR had asked her to promise that she would never leave the cadre, whatever the hardships they faced, hinting that he wanted her to lead the AIADMK.[120] On 16 October 2012, on the forty-first anniversary of the founding of the AIADMK, she issued a statement in which she said:

> MGR's appeal was that I dedicate my life to protect his followers. He obtained a vow to this effect from me . . .
>
> To protect you, the Kazhagam's siblings, I have dedicated my life to the Kazhagam and you. To be in Tamil Nadu's political life as a woman is not an easy task. This is a river of fire. It is a script of ingrates, full of deceit and intrigue. Yet, I understood at the very beginning that I should not abandon my duty fearing these.[121]

But one 'sibling in spirit' would become dear, from 1982, and Jayalalithaa would protect her until the end. Civil servant Chandralekha introduced Sasikala Natarajan, a video rental and filming facility owner, soon to become the 'sister that I have never had' to Jayalalithaa, in 1982, during the centenary celebrations of poet Subramania Bharati. Sasikala's husband, M. Natarajan, a public relations officer, who was not yet estranged from his wife, worked with Chandralekha. 'Jayalalithaa's programmes were covered by Sasikala's team . . . Through that some good association developed,' M. Natarajan would say, in an understatement later.[122]

PERIYAKULAM BY-ELECTION

Indira Gandhi sent Shankar Dayal Sharma (later President of India) to Madras to see if MGR would do a Tirupattur again. Under the Tirupattur MGR doctrine, the seat should have gone to the DMK, whose incumbent had died. This was, of course, out of the question. MGR drove a hard bargain with Sharma: He might concede the seat,

---

* S. Ramachandran recalled his conversations with MGR about the public impression that Jayalalithaa was 'MGR's other wife'. Interview with S. Ramachandran, 27 August 2016, Madras.

but the Congress (I) should sever its ties with the DMK. The Congress (I)
was not ready to do so yet and, in the event, said a by-election would
not make any difference to it, a party with a two-thirds majority.
MGR turned this line of thinking to his advantage in the campaign. 'If
AIADMK wins, its representatives will . . . urge the Centre to help the
state in keeping up the tempo of development.'

The AIADMK worked hard. It extended the midday meals to the
urban centres and women were to be recruited, and an ordinance
cancelled the private debts of the poor. The Congress (I), for its part,
expedited Central projects and more than a dozen Central ministers
launched projects, including the important Tuticorin–Madurai broad
gauge line.[123] The AIADMK's S.T.K. Jakkaiyan won, polling 2,52,377
votes against the DMK, which finished second with 1,83,177 votes.
Nonetheless, the DMK had polled more votes on its own than when
it fought in alliance with the Janata Party in 1977 (1.23 lakh) and
almost close to the 1.9 lakh votes it won in 1980 in the company of
the Congress (I). The Congress (I) candidate lost his deposit.[124] Indira
Gandhi wasted no time in sacking M.P. Subramaniam on the very day
the results were out. M.P. Subramaniam conceded that he had made a
mistake in going it alone.[125]

MGR suddenly announced that Kalaignar's physical safety was
important amidst alleged attempts on his life and his government had
a duty to provide protection. Furthermore, on 30 October 1982, MGR
and Kalaignar showed up at the wedding of Tamilisai Soundararajan,
the BJP Tamil Nadu chief today, at 6 a.m., holding hands and smiling.
The invitees cheered the sight. In his speech, the chief minister advised
the couple to emulate his relationship with Kalaignar, saying they knew
'when to fight and when to put their arms around the other's shoulder
and unite'.[126] Mohandas commented that all this was 'real politik'. Soon
enough, during a tour of Andhra Pradesh, Indira Gandhi spoke against
regional parties and said that her alliance with the Dravidian parties
came under difficult circumstances. When Mohandas told the chief
minister that there was no need to provoke Indira Gandhi, he made a
thumbs-up sign, saying his shot had hit the bull's eye.[127]

Earlier, on 15 October 1982, MGR organized a statewide shutdown to draw the the Central government's attention to Karnataka's reluctance to release Cauvery water to the delta.[128]

Meanwhile, Kalaignar Karunanidhi participated in the Opposition conclave in Srinagar.[129]

JAYALALITHAA NAMED PROPAGANDA SECRETARY

On 28 January 1983 Jayalalithaa was named propaganda secretary. She saw her appointment as the result of her hard work as a member of the high-power midday meal committee.[130] However, the party's first propaganda secretary, S.D. Somasundaram, and others were not too happy at this development.[131] In the March 1983 Tiruchendur by-elections, her maiden campaign, she drew large crowds like MGR. The AIADMK retained the Tiruchendur seat by a small margin of over 1710 votes.[132] Jayalalithaa's official portal has this to say about her maiden campaign:

> In February 1983, she was chosen by Dr MGR to conduct her maiden election campaign . . . Her election campaign was a trailblazer, securing an astounding victory for the party candidate against all odds.[133]

Only a decade later, MGR had got for Jayalalithaa what he could not obtain for her in the DMK. With her mentor's backing, Jayalalithaa would rise in the pecking order so rapidly and so high (she would claim after his death that she was the fifth highest-ranking official in the party), that ministers were instructed to rise for her and civil servants were asked to receive her.[134] Senior ministers avoided the ignominy by not attending events with her. She proved ambitious, but also willing to rough it out in what was traditionally a male preserve. When her mentor fell ill in 1984, those who could not do much about her mentor's fascination with Jayalalithaa, would strike back hard. But, for now, as the DMK ridiculed the AIADMK for having to learn about policies from Jayalalithaa, on MGR's instructions, RMV, who would turn into her principal antagonist, explained her role:

Jayalalithaa does not make policies. She is to spread them. What credentials are required to spread the party's ideals? One should have the ability to draw large crowds. All would agree that Jayalalithaa has that credential and competence. That is why MGR has appointed her as propaganda secretary.[135]

Later, RMV would openly spearhead the opposition to Jayalalithaa, and of the ministers, only Era. Nedunchezhian, S. Ramachandran, C. Aranganayagam, S. Thirunavukkarasu and K.K.S.S.R. Ramachandran would be with her.[136]

REVVING UP INDUSTRIAL GROWTH

On 25 January 1983, the chief minister complained that when industrialists from the state approached the Centre for licences, they were told that if they were to set up their industries in Uttar Pradesh, all facilities would be extended immediately; otherwise licences would not be issued.[137] On 7 February, at the inauguration of a 3.6 crore-rupee plant for automobile accessories at Sriperumbudur, the chief minister expressed the hope that the defence minister, R. Venkataraman, would show interest in the state's industrial development and its welfare. MGR also said that his government was keen on turning the state into a leader in industry, but licensing from the Centre, which took time, and other issues had to be surmounted first. In response, Venkataraman pointed out that the state had no mineral resources or water, but had skilled labour and this should be kept in mind while planning for industrial growth.[138]

On 29 January, the industries minister, Thirunavukkarasu, pointed out that the Centre had earmarked eighty-seven districts as zero-industries districts, but not one in Tamil Nadu; three or four sub-districts (taluks) made up a district in the north and this should be changed so that Tamil Nadu could also become eligible. Agriculture minister Kalimuthu charged that the Centre's policy was basically 'deliberately ignoring Tamil Nadu'—it would blame the state for the lack of industrial growth, on the one hand and, on the other, came up with policies that were not enabling such growth. 'Small industries here and big industries there,' said Kalimuthu and wondered if this was the way to national unity. He said the Centre's expectations on Tamil Nadu were akin to asking for an omelette without breaking the egg. In response, Congress (I) MLA Thirumayam Sundarrajan said, 'You have no right to say that the Centre has ignored you as you have failed to attract the many factories that wished to set up shop in Tamil Nadu.' He said Ashok Leyland's expansion and the Integral Coach Factory's expansions had gone to other states only because of the state government's 'ineffectiveness'.[139]

On 21 February, the chief minister, responding to a Congress (I) leader's charge of unemployment and the lack of jobs, said that 31 lakh people found jobs after the AIADMK came to power and wondered how this would have been possible without industrial growth, as charged. He said that small industries had grown in number from 18,000 to 40,000, and more than twenty-seven new major businesses have been set up.[140] Su. Thirunavukkarasar referred to the enterprises that were set up during the AIADMK's administration: the SIPCOT Guindy Industrial Estate, Gummidipoondi, Tuticorin, Pudukottai, Manamudurai, Cuddalore, the Hosur SIPCOT expansion, five to six sugar mills, six to seven textile mills, cement factories, the Tamil Nadu Cement Corporation, Tamil Nadu Minerals Ltd and Tamil Nadu Pugalur Newsprint.[141] In May 1982, in response to R. Venkataraman's observation that after 1967 there had been no major industries set up in the state, MGR would point to the establishment of the Southern Petrochemical Industries Corporation (SPIC), the Tuticorin thermal station, Salem Steel, and the caustic soda factories, and would argue that the usage of high-tension power before and after 1967 and the sales-tax receipts would reveal the situation.[142]

However, MGR's truncated two-and-a-half-year first term, his lack of rapport with Indira Gandhi till mid-1983 in the second term and his illness from late 1984, not to mention his emphasis on rural growth, had indeed seen Tamil Nadu register lacklustre industrial growth during his ten years as CM.

FOODGRAIN SHORTAGES: MGR'S FAST

Despite MGR's focus on rural growth, there was a severe shortage of foodgrains at this time. On 9 February 1983, MGR parked himself at the Marina beach and undertook a seven-hour fast, from 10 a.m. to 5 p.m., against the Centre's inadequate foodgrain allocations to the state. The previous day, he blamed the Central agriculture minister, Rao Birendra Singh, for the desperate situation and, describing the Centre as being indifferent, he said that his patience had worn thin and he had finally decided to subject himself to this 'suffering'.[143] To the Congress (I) charge that it was a 'stunt', MGR responded they were not aware of how dire the situation was.[144] Thousands of fans, admirers and curious onlookers filed past the chief minister. When Rao Birendra Singh, who had termed MGR's demand as 'unfair', called to urge him to give up the fast and invited him to Delhi for talks, the chief minister said the fast could not be given up 'since it has already begun'. The state's public distribution system required some 90,000 tonnes of rice every month. Another 17,000 tonnes of rice were needed for the nutritious meal scheme. The state had just two months of stocks.

Two consecutive years of vicious drought and the drop in the state's rice production from 58 lakh tonnes a year to only about 38 lakh tonnes in 1982 had led to the situation. Pleas for more grains went unheeded. The minister of state for home, P. Venkatasubbaiah, asked: 'How can the state look to the Centre during difficult times when it had not supplied any rice to the Centre on its part?'

Tamil Nadu maintained it had supplied rice whenever it had a surplus and, on several occasions, the Food Corporation of India had been tardy in lifting the stocks. MGR also pointed out that Kerala, which did not contribute to the national pool, was allocated rice.[145] When the agriculture ministry said that the state had been injudicious in its management of the food stocks, MGR retorted: 'If there was any injudicious food management, it should be put on the state government, taking seriously one of the main points of the Prime Minister's twenty-point programme, which stresses the need for an effective public distribution system to ensure supply of essential food items to the people at fair prices.' The fast had come against this backdrop and against the reported refusal of the Reserve Bank to allow imports from Thailand.[146]

On 15 February, the chief minister met the agriculture and food ministers, Prime Minister Indira Gandhi and others, and expressed 'happiness' at the end of the talks. He refused to answer any other questions.[147] The relationship with Indira Gandhi was still frigid.

SOUTHERN CHIEF MINISTERS' CONCLAVE

On 20 March 1983, Karnataka Chief Minister Ramakrishna Hegde convened the Southern Chief Ministers' Conference. Andhra Pradesh Chief Minister N.T. Rama Rao (NTR), MGR and the DMK chief minister, D. Ramachandran, of Pondicherry participated. The Congress (I) chief minister of Kerala, K. Karunakaran, stayed away. The four chief ministers were closeted in deliberations for ten hours, after which they announced the formation of the Southern Chief Ministers Council. The council emphasized the need for a commission on Centre–state relations in the economic sphere.

Ramakrishna Hegde said the meeting was 'a step in the right direction' and aimed at sorting out issues 'between states at their own level'. If only this had come true, the four southern states could have resolved their problems smoothly, without recourse to legal means as in the issues of water sharing of the Cauvery and the Mullaiperiyar dam. MGR, the brain behind the council, termed it 'a good augury'. He added, 'The council was constituted as a pioneering step, to show the way to the rest of the country. Today we are four, tomorrow we may be twenty-two.' N.T. Rama Rao said: 'We support a strong Centre, but we want the limbs to be strong too so that the country is in good physical form.'[148]

Four days later, on 24 March, Indira Gandhi announced the Sarkaria Commission on Centre–state relations. Both Kalaignar and MGR welcomed it. MGR hoped that the commission would recommend suitable constitutional changes.[149] The conclave achieved little else. And the commission itself would prove to be a damp squib, belying MGR's hopes. On 29 March, Kalaignar suggested that the Assembly pass a resolution on state autonomy.[150] On 29 May, MGR participated in the Opposition conclave in Vijayawada, but did not criticize Indira Gandhi there.[151] This would be the last time that MGR would have anything to do with the Opposition. On their return from Vijayawada, S. Ramachandran asked him if he wished to be prime minister, to which MGR replied in the negative. 'In that case, it is not important as to who becomes the prime minister at the Centre. If your strategy is to ally with anyone except Kalaignar Karunanidhi, why should we have any truck with these people?' S. Ramachandran asked his leader. MGR would then cut his tenuous ties with the Opposition.[152] This would see him sending a telegram to assure N.T. Rama Rao that 'justice would prevail', but not openly condemn the 16 August 1984 coup against the NTR ministry.

KRISHNA WATERS: APRIL 1983

Prior to Vijayawada, on 19 April, NTR and MGR signed an agreement in Hyderabad, with Prime Minister Indira Gandhi witnessing it, to bring Krishna waters over 550 km into Madras for the city's drinking water needs. Following this, on 27 April, MGR and NTR laid the foundation stone for the project in Cuddapah district.[153] On 25 May, MGR would hand over 30 crore rupees to NTR in an event in Madras. Indira Gandhi along with the Central irrigation minister and the chief ministers of Karnataka and Maharashtra would participate in the event.[154]

Ironically, the agreement was delayed, among other reasons because of NTR's objections to the efforts of the Congress (I)'s K. Vijayabhaskara Reddy, charging that it was at the expense of the state's own needs. But MGR's personal equation with NTR and the responsibility of office would see him moderate his stand. After his victory in January 1983, NTR had come to get MGR's blessings. And MGR, the ultimate host, had thrown a grand dinner party for NTR and his entourage. NTR gave up his earlier opposition and the two chief ministers agreed to pursue the Telugu Ganga scheme. MGR had earlier suggested that NTR name his party Telugu Desam Party instead of Telugu Rajyam, saying, 'It will be appropriate.' NTR saw MGR as a 'guru'.[155] Hande's recollection of NTR's visit is different. He said that MGR had invited NTR over for breakfast and welcomed him warmly. Even at the outset, NTR had asked MGR: 'Annagaaru (elder brother), please tell me what I should do?' MGR then spoke of the Krishna waters and the 1000 million cubic feet needed. The prepared files were also handed over. NTR did not hesitate one moment. He said: 'You want water to quench your thirst. As a neighbouring state, when annagaaru asks, will we refuse?' NTR okayed the scheme then and there.[156]

This was an achievement for the MGR government, but Kalaignar found nothing to celebrate in it. In his critique of the Krishna scheme, he pointed out that the interest on the money given by Tamil Nadu to Andhra Pradesh alone came to 24 crore rupees a year and, MGR's arrangement for water for eight months (excluding the monsoon) thus cost 24 crore rupees annually. He said the 'clever younger brother had conned the older brother' and that the waters should have come at no cost.[157] On 13 May, the chief minister would charge Kalaignar for having noted in a file that Tamil Nadu need not participate in the committee formed in 1969 on Krishna waters, saying that if he had supported it then, by now Krishna waters would have reached Madras. He also said he was looking for an opportune moment to strike a deal on the sharing of the waters from the west-flowing rivers with Kerala.[158] Alas, that moment would never come.

MGR did not wish to continue his predecessor's Veeranam scheme—that would bring in water through a 218-kilometre-long pipeline. More than 22 crore rupees had already been spent on that project. Another 180 to 190 crore rupees would have to be spent to complete the project. But MGR had said that he did not wish to make Tamil Nadu a 'debtor', spending such a big sum borrowed from the World Bank to bring only 250 mn cubic feet of water.[159] The author of the scheme, Kalaignar, responded that Veeranam could have been an interim solution and when the Krishna waters arrived, they could serve the villages through which they passed. Yet, the scheme was politically untouchable. MGR's own idea, to bring water from Kattalai near Trichy through a 425-kilometre channel, at the cost of 450 crore rupees, had to be dropped as farmers protested against diverting Cauvery water.

History is difficult to predict and even more difficult to decipher. Kalaignar would play a critical role in ensuring the completion of the Krishna project later. It would, however, not be before the year 2000, or seventeen years later, that the first drops of water would reach Madras. In 2002, godman Sai Baba extended a 200 crore-rupee gift to the Tamil Nadu government headed by Kalaignar Karunanidhi, to extensively rebuild the Kandaleru–Poondi Canal and the many reservoirs. When the project was completed in 2004, the Poondi reservoir received Krishna water for the first time.[160]

PONDICHERRY DMK–CONGRESS GOVERNMENT FALLS

Two months later, there would be more good news for MGR with Pondicherry turning out to be the proverbial last straw in the DMK–

Congress (I) relationship. Tirupattur, where the Congress (I) kept off the DMK, and Tiruchendur and Periyakulam, where it fielded its own candidates, were hurtful enough to the DMK. But the DMK had stomached these insults. When it chose to hit back by sending its Pondicherry chief minister to the Southern Chief Ministers' Conference, the farce could not be maintained any longer. As the Congress (I) withdrew its support, the DMK ministry fell, bringing down with it the uneasy alliance. Kalaignar said if the DMK's participation in the conclave was the reason, then the party was proud of its stance as it had always stood for state autonomy. Three days later, G. Lakshmanan resigned as Deputy Speaker of the Lok Sabha, signifying that the tenuous relationship had reached the point of no return.[161] Earlier, in a public meeting in Trichy, Chief Minister MGR had welcomed the 'new climate of understanding' between his party and the Congress (I). Clearly, MGR's persistence, patience, not to mention his flexibility to go to any length and the DMK's peeve with the Congress (I), had helped him finally achieve his goal of displacing the DMK as the Congress (I)'s ally.

MGR'S ASSISTANCE TO THE LTTE

The July ethnic riots in Sri Lanka would bring the MGR and Indira Gandhi administrations closer. The riots sparked outrage and sadness in Tamil Nadu. At a 27 July DMK rally, Kalaignar would demand that the Indian Army be sent to Sri Lanka.[162] The following day, an all-party delegation would meet to discuss the issue. Both MGR and Kalaignar would participate—a rare occasion—and agree that a delegation led by the chief minister would meet the prime minister with regard to this.[163] On 1 August, the Tamil Nadu memorandum to the prime minister would suggest, among other steps, a UN peacekeeping force be sent to Sri Lanka.[164]

Indira Gandhi felt the need to reassure Tamil Nadu, to mitigate any sense of alienation. Therefore, derogating from India's established view, she declared that the ethnic issue concerned India. Till then, India had only exerted jurisdiction over the Indian-plantation Tamils. Jayewardene's biographers correctly attribute this departure as 'a concession to Tamil Nadu sentiment'.[165] Even so, Indira Gandhi did not accommodate Tamil Nadu all the way. She refused to ask for a

United Nations presence in Sri Lanka, owing to the traditional Indian wariness over foreign presence in South Asia, India's traditional sphere of influence. Similarly, Indira Gandhi's son and successor, Rajiv Gandhi, halted the Sri Lankan advance against Jaffna in the spring of 1987, ordering the airdrop of food for the Tamils in order to stave off any unilateral action by Tamil Nadu. But, neither Rajiv Gandhi nor his mother could grant the demand by the Dravida Munnetra Kazhagam for a Bangladesh or Cyprus-style intervention or to establish Eelam (a separate Tamil state). They were afraid that India's own territorial integrity and unity, sacred in any foreign policy calculation, might be compromised. This is where MGR's role was seen as fundamental to balance and moderate the DMK's demands and the popular sentiments. MGR played a very smart game. Some of his ministers, like S.D. Somasundaram and K. Kalimuthu, almost echoed the DMK line, even as MGR himself appeared an epitome of moderation. His arguments against the DMK's demands and tactics were brilliant, albeit specious sometimes. In the open track, Indira Gandhi's emissary, G. Parthasarathi attempted to forge a political solution even as the prime minister and her defence minister, R. Venkataraman, clandestinely sponsored a 'train and equip' programme for the militants (after consultations with MGR) to keep the pressure on Jayewardene.[166]

Thus, the political alliance between one of the two principal Dravidian parties of the state and the ruling party at the Centre provided both possibilities and limitations for peddling the state's influence. Besides, the coercive strength and the blandishments of the Indian state should not be ignored while assessing MGR's cooperative attitude. S. Ramachandran, MGR's point man on the ethnic issue, put it bluntly that any hard-line position would have led to the removal of the state government.[167]

The DMK called for a protest before Central government offices on 4 August and a rail-stop agitation the following day. Not to be outdone, the AIADMK government sponsored a shutdown on 2 August, which was total. MGR outlined the loss the state faced due to the shutdowns, how even daily-wage earners had lost much, but noted that compared to the sufferings of the Sri Lankan Tamil brethren this was 'very ordinary'.[168] Trains were cancelled on 5 August. On 10 August, Kalaignar and K. Anbazhagan resigned from their Assembly seats to urge the Centre to 'act'.[169] MGR said: 'Even when they suffered unbearable cruelties, Sri Lanka's Tamil MPs did not come forward to resign [from] their seats.' It was a clever argument wondering how Kalaignar could be more papal than the Pope.[170] He would later announce that his party would not put up candidates against Kalaignar and Anbazhagan if they chose to contest again.[171] But he also suggested that Kalaignar was frustrated and the pretext of 'sacrifice' was to avoid the ignominy of losing his leader of the Opposition status. The ethnic issue would become a game of one-upmanship.

Uncomfortably for Indira Gandhi, Tamil Nadu's memorandum reminded her of the Bangladesh precedent. And the DMK tenaciously kept up the demand. Thousands of its partymen filled the jails, some, overcome with emotion, immolated themselves and the party collected 10 million signatures urging UN intervention in Sri Lanka.[172]

In turn, beginning 16 August, MGR and his Cabinet would sport black shirts for a month and, on 26 August, MGR sent a telegram asking the prime minister to raise the issue in the UN.[173] Two days later, on 28 August, Kalaignar threw down the gauntlet when he said at a public rally on the Marina: 'If the Indian Army were to go to Sri Lanka and create a Tamil Eelam, the Congress (I) can rule Tamil Nadu. For ten years the DMK will not make an effort to come to power.'[174]

On 27 October, the chief minister responded. He said that when Sri Lanka's Tamil leaders and the militants had not sought the Indian Army's presence, 'how would it be appropriate for some here to demand so?'[175] It was an ingenious argument, but MGR knew that the Sri Lankan Tamils could never make such a demand and expect to go back to their country—nothing could be more treasonous for them.

The chief minister also declared that ministers S.D. Somasundaram and Kalimuthu 'will not speak bypassing me . . . They may speak passionately. If there is no unity we will dissolve this ministry and exit.'[176] It was a cinematic class act, but the truth of the matter was that SDS and Kalimuthu were bettering Kalaignar's demands on Sri Lanka. While Kalimuthu wanted the Indian Army dispatched, SDS wanted the LTTE and Eelam recognized. On 7 November, the chief minister himself said that 'at no point would the AIADMK government betray the Tigers or any individual fighting for a separate Eelam'.[177] Five months later, on 9 April 1984, MGR would tell the House that if Tamil Nadu had to act on its own to save the Tamils, it would do so.[178]

MGR–PRABHAKARAN

Mohandas says 'an instant rapport was established between MGR and [LTTE supremo] Prabhakaran'. He had arranged the meeting.[179] The 1982 shoot-out between Prabhakaran and his adversary, People's Liberation Organization of Tamil Eelam's (PLOTE) leader, Uma Maheswaran, in Madras, embarrassingly brought to light the militants' presence in the state. Sri Lanka promptly sought Prabhakaran's extradition. In response, an all-party meeting told the Centre to reject the request. Meanwhile, the militants were beginning to be romanticized as freedom fighters in the Tamil media and political discourse, and the extradition issue quietly petered out.

The LTTE's Anton Balasingham wrote that they first met MGR in April 1984. Following MGR's public invite to them, Kalaignar had also openly invited them. Thus, he would have met them before the chief minister. Prabhakaran wisely avoided the Kalaignar meeting. That evening, DIG A.X. Alexander met Balasingham to say that MGR was upset with those who had met Kalaignar, but wanted to see them later that evening. The police official added that if they chose to antagonize MGR, it would be difficult for them to operate in the state.

When the Balasingham delegation met MGR, he said he was 'anxious' to see Prabhakaran. Pleased to hear Balasingham's response interpreting Kalaignar's invite to the militants as competing with him, MGR appreciatively said: 'You have understood Tamil Nadu's politics well.' He then asked about the disunity between the various groups, the rivalry between Uma Maheswaran and Prabhakaran, the LTTE's ideology and if they were part of the Centre's training programme. Balasingham portrayed the LTTE's ideals as noble and the organization as a disciplined freedom fighting force. In answer to the chief minister's question, Balasingham said that the LTTE was not the favourite of the Indian intelligence agencies because of its fierce independence.

After this, MGR pleasantly surprised them when he asked about the assistance they expected from him. As Balasingham indicated it was financial, MGR asked, 'How much do you expect?' to which Balasingham said, 'A huge amount.' MGR asked him to specify the amount. When Balasingham hesitated, his colleague Shankar suggested a minimum of 2 crore rupees to impart training for 1000 cadre and for arms. 'Okay. Only 2 crore [rupees]? I will give it tomorrow itself,' said MGR. Hearing this, their jaws dropped. While Balasingham said that Prabhakaran was not there in that meeting, the LTTE leader said he was there. In his eulogy, he noted that MGR understood the ethnic issue well, wished to give them full support, including providing them with arms, had special respect for them and that they 'could have not grown this far if not for his help'.[180]

The next evening, when Balasingham and his colleague arrived at 10 a.m., MGR took them by lift to the basement, which opened out to a large room with boxes neatly stacked up to a height of ten feet. It was a strongroom. MGR showed his two fingers and gave instructions in Malayalam to his aides. They loaded ten boxes in the lift, and it was then transferred to the Tigers' vehicle. The following week, Prabhakaran went to see MGR and the chief minister took a liking to him.[181] This personal relationship would help the LTTE immensely and MGR, for his part, would appear key to a solution to the ethnic problem. However, the personal relationship ebbed and flowed with the vicissitudes of political developments. Prabhakaran's intransigence would see MGR fail repeatedly. In the months prior to the accord, MGR himself was frail, and senility might have also set in by then, if Mohandas is to be believed. MGR was disappointed that Prabhakaran and the LTTE were 'not listening to me and come for their favours', while the LTTE felt that MGR was trying to please Delhi, without showing full appreciation and understanding of their situation.[182]

On one occasion, MGR helped clear a ship bearing arms for the Tigers from the Madras port.[183] But on the second occasion, the financial assistance he extended would prove controversial. This time, MGR made available the chief minister's relief funds of 4 crore rupees collected for the Tamil refugees. The Indian Express, however, broke the news the next day and on President Jayewardene's objections, Rajiv Gandhi called up MGR to express his displeasure. MGR, Balasingham writes, was upset with both Jayewardene and Rajiv Gandhi, whom he termed as 'not courageous'. He now promised the '4 crore [rupees] from my personal money'.[184] While this incident is romanticized by Balasingham, one cannot help wonder how the chief minister could have had this kind of money of his own.

JUDGES COMPLAIN OF SURVEILLANCE

On 27 April, in an unprecedented manner, judges of the Madras High Court passed a resolution condemning the state surveillance that was on them since February. (Earlier, in 1983, *India Today* had reported that seventy orders had been issued to gather information about over 200 people. This included Kalaignar and some DMK district party functionaries.)[185]

Earlier, on 2 February, MGR had said, 'The courts in Tamil Nadu are giving a stepmotherly treatment to the state government. They give *ex parte* stays on government measures. They don't give due consideration to the point of view of the government. However, we take care of the security of the judges.' Days later, MGR repeated his allegation in the Assembly: 'It is the law which speaks in the courts and not conscience.'

Jayalalithaa amplified this issue further: 'The chief minister's complaint is completely justified. Some of the latest judicial pronouncements amount to interference in state matters . . . The judiciary should not spring rude surprises on the government.' Law minister Ponnaiyan said: 'We want the judiciary to listen to us before giving *ex parte* orders.' In an April judgement, the High Court blamed the government for the 1.5 lakh-odd cases pending till the end of 1982. The government, the respondent in a majority of the cases, frequently delayed its reply or did not attend hearings.[186]

JAYALALITHAA: EMERGING FROM MGR'S SHADOW

Within a year as propaganda secretary, much to the delight of the cadre and the discomfiture of many senior leaders, Jayalalithaa had managed to create a niche for herself and had begun to seriously assert herself. However, the opposition to her remained underground and would not surface until later that year. She, too, would sing the praises of these leaders who were opposed to her, calling them 'elder leaders', whom, she said, 'have been affectionately patting me for my work as propaganda secretary. Workers have developed enthusiasm . . . As for the party, what Mr MGR says is policy. I only speak his thoughts on stage. I reflect his thinking . . . These are the guidelines.'[187] Jayalalithaa said that she was filling in for the chief minister when it came to his party work; and when the general secretary was away, she acted as the interface between the workers and the leadership. She also said that she pulled up errant partymen, such as speakers who fail to turn up at meetings, and that 'party workers are satisfied, proud and confident that such questions are being asked on their behalf.' But the fact that she had pulled up the very senior Madurai Muthu did not go down well with the higher-ranking members.[188]

Asked whether she had the strength to bear failure in politics, she said:

- Only time can tell. I will submit myself to MGR's leadership in all situations.
- I will always be the most loyal worker. I will not run away from defeat.

And when asked about the absence of a democratic second-rung leadership, she answered:

Why don't we have leaders? They asked after Nehru who? Didn't leaders emerge? They asked after Anna who? Didn't MGR emerge? People say he is the one who follows Anna. Even Karunanidhi becoming chief minister in the interregnum was because of MGR!

When asked whether she was an extra-constitutional authority like Dhirendra Brahmachari, Jayalalithaa responded:

How can you compare me with him? Dhirendra Brahmachari was no one. Now he is a *crorepathi*. I worked . . . I sweated my brow in cinema, hurt my hands and legs, and shed blood and earned my bread. I have not come into politics with the motive of profit. I have come with the true ideal of service. I am not the one to piggyback a ride on MGR. I did not come seeking profit. I already have much name and fame . . .[189]

She expressed her reservations about some of the DMK speakers' uncultured remarks:

In the beginning, Kalaignar responded to my speeches at Tiruchendur. He referred to me as 'star with a tail [shooting star]'. But those around him must have said, 'Why do you have to respond to her [in the singular, used in Tamil to address an inferior or subordinate]?' Therefore, he may have stopped referring to me. He has no courage to respond to my speeches and questions. He makes others, his henchmen—to be precise, his underlings—to respond to me. This is cowardice. He cannot answer a single question of mine. I never talk at a personal level. DMK speakers speak so lowly in 'filthy language' about me. Let us forget other things . . . Is it right to speak so lowly about a woman? Is this cultured?[190]

Sadly, some of her own 'elder leaders', like RMV would stoop low, even lower than the DMK, once her mentor took ill. But in the post-MGR phase, Jayalalithaa's comments on the 'elder leaders' and the DMK leadership would prove that she was no better either.[191]

But for now, MGR was well, and, in February, had nominated Valampuri John and Jayalalithaa to the Rajya Sabha. RMV and Raghavanadam were uncomfortable with MGR's decision.[192] She took the same seat that Anna was given: seat number 185. In her maiden speech, she said she deemed it a 'great honour to stand here and speak on the floor of the very same Rajya Sabha, where, twenty-two years ago, in 1962, our great departed leader Anna rose to make his forceful maiden speech, which electrified the entire nation . . .'

She added that her mission was:

My leader, the chief minister of Tamil Nadu, Dr MGR, the founder–leader of the All-India Anna Dravida Munnetra Kazhagam, to which I have the honour to belong, has sent me here . . . to echo the voice of the people of Tamil Nadu . . .[193]

The echo was more about herself, and not so much the people of Tamil Nadu. MGR could have hardly imagined that Jayalalithaa's head would become so swollen after her sojourn in Delhi or that she would use it as an effective perch to advance her political ambitions at a later time. He kept a close watch on her, according to John. She would, one day, seek Prime Minister Rajiv Gandhi's intercession to fill in as chief minister or help MGR as his deputy, given MGR's debilitating illness. One of her first displays of independence was when, after a meeting with Indira Gandhi on an alliance between the two parties, she did not report on the successful outcome of the talks to the 'anxious' MGR immediately. MGR had called Solai to learn of the details. Solai said that MGR felt that she was taking him for granted.[194] Jayalalithaa listed Indira Gandhi as one of her two benefactors in politics.[195] But she was being disrespectful and indifferent to the first one—MGR. RMV goes further to allege that she bad-mouthed MGR to Indira Gandhi, and later to Rajiv Gandhi, and that MGR had received her resignation letter as MP.[196] No surprise then that, according to Salem Kannan, Jayalalithaa's 'sister in spirit', Sasikala, was also used to track her activities and that copies of her letters to Kannan on her political moves ended up with MGR.[197] It was a difficult relationship and she would allude to it later.

MGR SPEAKS UP FOR THE STATES

On 14 December, MGR asked the Opposition to drop its plan of a rail-stop agitation to protest price rise, saying he would 'manage it with people's support'.[198] On 8 January 1984, MGR's valedictory speech at the four-day seminar on Centre–state relations at the Tamil Nadu Academy of Political Sciences could have passed off for Kalaignar's views on Centre–state relations. This is what he said:

> When others express the ideas of the nation's leaders, they are being accused of seeking separation. State autonomy is neither a new policy nor a new demand that we raise. We are seeking the implementation of the same that was announced by the nation's leaders at the time of Independence and during the Constituent Assembly sessions . . . We, the states, take the leftovers now. Please remember that the people who have elected the state governments are the same people who have elected the Central government. A single party government throughout the country is not good for the country. If such was the case, then there would be no one to speak like [I am doing] here now.

MGR complained that there was no assistance for the nutritious meal scheme because it was outside the plan outlays, even as the state was told not to include it as part of the annual plan. 'We will bring the nutritious meal scheme in the five-year plan. Let them say that we cannot include it.' He pointed out that the Centre demanded that the state raise power tariffs, even as the Congress in the state agitated against a raise. 'This is akin to pinching the baby and then rocking the cradle [to stop it from crying],' he said.[199]

HIGH COURT ORDERS INCREASE OF MEDICAL SEATS

Meanwhile, on 30 April 1984, the Madras High Court directed that as many as eighty-six of the 200 candidates who had filed a writ application challenging their non-admission to the MBBS course, should be admitted to it. The candidates had not been assessed properly in the interviews for admission.

Kalaignar said:

The government's corrupt practices have resulted in the denial of seats to 100 meritorious students, and the judgement is a proof of the various malpractices for which MGR and Dr Hande should own responsibility and quit their posts immediately.

But the judges themselves explained: 'We are unable to accept the sweeping contention that the interviews were conducted in a haphazard manner and that the marks awarded bore no relation to the performance.'[200]

FOUR ASSEMBLY BY-ELECTIONS

If the judges' ruling was favourable to MGR, the results of the 20 May by-elections were not at all favourable to him. The DMK took the Mayiladuthurai seat from AIADMK and retained Annanagar—Kalaignar's earlier constituency by an additional 9000 votes over its last count. Annanagar was a 'slap in the face' as MGR had described the fight as 'between me and Karunanidhi'. But he would later say that he had said the same from 1973.[201] Congress (I) took Thanjavur from the DMK. The AIADMK held on to Uppiliapuram. In its wake party general secretary P.U. Shanmugam would admit, 'We have been wounded in the by-elections', and MGR himself publicly proclaimed efforts would be made to cleanse the party of 'racketeers, liquor barons and capitalists'.[202] The poor choice of candidates, conceit and the crass display of money power had mauled the AIADMK. The party had been in power for seven years by then. Corruption was embedded in every aspect of the administration now. Mohandas said that for the 'first time, MGR felt that his mass base was getting eroded' and this became a reason for his declining health. He now wished to personally assess the various developmental works. The DMK was jubilant considering it prematurely as an augury to the next general elections.[203]

On the heels of the electoral setback came more bad news when Congress (I) general secretary Rajiv Gandhi, on a visit to the state, said that 'we will not enter into alliances with any regional parties'. MGR said the AIADMK was an 'all-India party, having representatives in the Lok Sabha and even in the Karnataka Assembly'.[204] On 22 May, in response to Rajiv Gandhi terming the nutritious meal scheme a short-term measure, MGR pointed out that Rajiv Gandhi should have said that Tamil Nadu's poor and hapless children were having at least one meal. He pointed out that Congress (I) chief ministers had praised the scheme and, internationally, others were believed to have come forward to emulate the scheme. He wondered, 'Why should Rajiv Gandhi be angry against such people?'[205]

On 1 July, Jayalalithaa would claim in Trichy that even if the AIADMK were to contest alone, it would be voted in to power. She would also say that she had received 'several letters with death threats'.[206]

S.D. SOMASUNDARAM CHARGES CORRUPTION

Despite MGR's all-India claims, the party was shaking from within. The first signs that all was not well surfaced that summer, when SDS began making veiled attacks on MGR. He was one of the first two MPs to cast their lot with MGR, was known to have built the party organizationally in Thanjavur, and enjoyed a relatively clean image and a small following of his own. Not taking kindly to Jayalalithaa's ascent, he was now trying to wreck the party from within by getting deep under MGR's skin. Su.

Thirunavukkarasar said SDS felt peeved that he was being bypassed in his district. But MGR did not wish to lose SDS. He had gently told SDS in a Cabinet meeting to avoid going to Trichy, and if he had to, not to talk to press persons. The chief minister was indirectly urging SDS not to criticize him.[207] As SDS continued to do so, MGR had to be seen as taking action and, on 8 July, he relieved SDS of the commercial taxes portfolio. But SDS had not said anything new or what the chief minister had not already expressed.

An effective minister, SDS saw liquor revenues jump to 230 crore rupees from 150 crore rupees, and commercial taxes rise from 250 to 750 crore rupees. His Benami Land Bill, believed to have been aimed at proxy landowners with the Congress (I), got passed unanimously, but failed to get the President's assent. SDS's stridency against the Congress (I) and the Centre was even otherwise well known. Kalaignar said SDS's wings had been clipped because 'MGR has been going out of his way to cultivate the Congress (I) by humiliating Somasundaram. If Somasundaram has self-respect he should leave the AIADMK.'[208] SDS would not leave on his own and would cause as much damage as possible, to force MGR's hand and throw him out.

The chief minister himself had remarked at a wedding earlier that the AIADMK had turned into a party of liquor barons and moneybags. He said, 'I know who is using the party for self-aggrandizement. I am going to remove them.' Coincidentally, on 8 July, he would say he had already done so.[209] On 20 July, SDS said in a statement that he was not voicing his views against MGR and that he accepted MGR's leadership.[210] 'The chief minister was exerting pressure directly' on behalf of the blending units, SDS claimed later. On 27 August, SDS said that MGR should take action against the liquor barons and moneybags, and people should know this.[211] He added that MGR had asked at a Cabinet meeting, six months earlier, 'Can we now face the people with a clear conscience? Okay, even if you accept money, should you not do it with a certain discreetness?'[212]

The cinema hero avoided direct engagement with SDS and employed proxies. Thus, AIADMK men demonstrated and carried signature campaigns against SDS. On 2 August, partymen waved black flags at SDS at the Trichy railway station and later kept him away from a public meeting in a village in the district. SDS later accused the chief minister of orchestrating these events,²¹³ against which MGR had to issue a statement. On 12 August, MGR said SDS was not shown black flags anywhere and said that the 'SDS issue was not an issue at all and there was no question of disciplinary action against anyone'.²¹⁴ But clearly there was much turmoil within the party. On 16 August, the entire Cabinet sent in its resignation, professing loyalty to the chief minister.

On 17 August, MGR set up a five-member ministerial committee under him to inquire into complaints against legislators and ministers, and a secret cell made up of himself, the chief secretary and the home secretary, to investigate allegations against senior officials and politicians. 'The sub-committee which I am heading will inquire into the allegations against Somasundaram's handling of the excise and revenue portfolios, and take whatever follow-up action is to be taken.'²¹⁵ On 28 August, Jayalalithaa questioned SDS's authority to issue policy statements. SDS had voiced his opposition to the party allying with the Congress (I).²¹⁶ That day, SDS faced an angry crowd of partymen at the Erode railway station. Two days later, on 30 August, SDS said that people suspected the integrity of those at the very top in the administration²¹⁷ and, on 1 September, on Jayalalithaa, he said:

> The one who came to the party in 1983 is levelling charges against those who came to the party in 1972. [She] Is taking disciplinary action [against them]. Perhaps Jayalalithaa has enacted such new rules for the party! Veerappan (RMV) has called me a traitor. When MGR founded his new party, Veerappan declined to sign the membership form. At one juncture, MGR himself was saddened by this.²¹⁸

On 20 August, MGR wrote, in his circumlocutory style, to SDS engaging him directly:

> In the flowing crystal clear water of the Cauvery River, can we separate the water that flowed first and the water that flowed later? We can remove the impurities from the water, but can we reject the water itself as being unclean?

No one had mounted a challenge before to MGR's authority as SDS had and no one had accused him of corruption so openly. The Kovai Chezhians and Manoharans complained of his leadership style and effectiveness, but had not questioned his clean image. MGR felt that SDS had betrayed him and had exceeded Kalaignar in his criticisms.[219] Hande and Aranganayagam did not know why SDS protested, or why he was protesting so hard. SDS would return to MGR, on his insistence, before MGR's death and later serve as a minister under Jayalalithaa from 1991–96. Hande rightly described SDS as 'an ass'.[220]

But the same day MGR wrote his missive to SDS, Jayalalithaa wrote to MGR saying that she was stepping down as propaganda secretary:

> Only after holding discussions with senior party leaders like finance minister Nedunchezhian, electricity minister S. Ramachandran, respected S.D. Somasundaram and party general secretary P.U. Shanmugam did you appoint me as propaganda secretary of the party. But now the impression is gaining ground that you thrust me on the party, and that esteemed party leaders like Somasundaram are thinking of leaving the party because they resent my position.

In January 1985, Jayalalithaa said that she had acted under MGR's instructions, and he dictated the resignation letter to her over the phone, promising to reinstate her soon and terming the resignation as 'political'.[221]

On 21 August, MGR said that Jayalalithaa would have to continue until the position was filled. The position was not filled and she would return to it a year later.[222]

On 1 September, the expected reaction against SDS came. That day the AIADMK executive passed a resolution, moved by Jeppiyar, an MLC, that accused SDS of anti-party activities, misuse of the office to amass wealth in proxy names, committing grave corruption and, afraid of being exposed, of bringing charges against the administration. He was dismissed from both the party and the Cabinet 'for anti-party activities' and on 'corruption charges'.[223]

On that day, MGR also asked whether it is 'deserved, just and moral' for SDS to accuse him of corruption, when he had borrowed

40 lakh rupees from a moneylender for interest to pay off his income-tax arrears. An emotional MGR said that he wished to ask with 'pain', 'how [SDS], who makes this abominable accusation, will live well?'[224]

SDS reacted:

> People have come to know of MGR's true face now. They have begun to understand that the film MGR and the real MGR do not possess the same attributes. People believe that he is taking bribes, committing wrongs. He cannot escape saying he does not take bribes. I have the appropriate proof . . .[225]

On 3 September, SDS was dismissed from the ministry. That day, T. Veerasamy replaced SDS as food minister and K.K.S.S.R. Ramachandran as cooperation minister, both followers of his, taking the Cabinet's strength to twenty-five.[226] Even a year earlier, in 1983, to mute his influence, SDS supporters like S.R. Radha and others had been inducted into the Cabinet. More than a dozen MLAs and party workers were already chairmen of various state-owned corporations. SDS rightly wondered about the price MGR had had to pay to keep hold of the party:

> At what price MGR has been able to retain his control of the legislature party? Every fourth MLA is either a minister or chairman of a corporation. What is MGR's personal gain is Tamil Nadu's loss. He may be able to sustain himself temporarily, but ultimately people will show him the door.[227]

On 5 September, SDS founded his Namadhu Kazhagam (Our Kazhagam). That day, three MLA supporters of SDS were expelled from the party.[228]

On 15 September, the chief minister said that he was 'an open book' and that he does not have the need to 'collect wealth because I have no children'. He repeated that he was indebted to the tune of 40 lakh rupees, which the party would settle following his death.[229]

Two weeks later, on 19 September, SDS dealt a master blow when he alleged that MGR wanted him to collect the 50-rupee bribe per case from liquor wholesalers, and, since he had refused, MGR relieved him of the excise portfolio. The former minister also questioned MGR's claim of having taken a personal loan to settle his income-tax dues: 'Who has given him 40 lakh rupees? What are the terms of repayment? Has he repaid anything? Let there be an inquiry on the loans raised by him.'[230]

SDS was not the only one who got under his skin. MGR seemed equally upset with Jayalalithaa's show of independence and what he regarded as immaturity. According to the party organ *Anna*, MGR had almost disowned his protégé:

> It is my fault that I placed Jayalalithaa in a position that was beyond her qualifications and age. We did not found this movement depending on her. In the 1977 and 1980 elections, madam was not with us. To issue statements without my permission and in my name, especially on the dismissal of N.T. Rama Rao's government in Andhra Pradesh, is to be condemned. None of these views were a result of discussions with me or the party. I cannot tolerate her using my name in many places without my knowledge any more. Jayalalithaa is working on moving to another party. I am also not concerned with those who believe that they could get their work done [through her by] going behind her.[231]

On 21 August, *Dinamani* reported that Jayalalithaa had withdrawn a telegram to Chittoor district AIADMK bodies six hours later condemning the 'unconstitutional act' of the NTR government's dismissal.[232]

Jayalalithaa would disclaim any such happening in the general council, adding that '99 per cent' had given signed letters, and speaker after speaker had urged their leader not to accept her resignation.

> MGR collected these letters. He was very happy that I had captured the hearts of the partymen. Then, on October 2, Gandhiji's birthday, MGR had assured ministers K.A. Krishnaswamy and K.K.S.S.R. Ramachandran that I would be reappointed propaganda secretary within a few days. But then, sadly, he had to get hospitalized before that. So the claim that MGR had criticized me at the general council is all false.[233]

It is clear that MGR did lament his decision about Jayalalithaa. What is not clear is how the chief minister was able to articulate all of this with his speech impairment. However, in the see-saw battle of intrigues and counter-intrigues, MGR the ultimate arbiter, favoured one over the other, to keep the balance within the party, and, at times, showed his displeasure at both factions. This was one such occasion.

MGR FALLS ILL

Politically, MGR would never be shown the door. In a bizarre manner nature would intervene to save him politically, but ruin him physically. SDS had 'mentally tortured MGR', said Hande. 'He was half responsible for MGR falling ill,' he added.[234] But SDS alone was not to blame. MGR a diabetic, was childishly defiant when it came to eating sweets or high-calorie foods. The first signs of his health difficulties became apparent in Thanjavur on 16 September, at the Big Temple, at the celebrations of Raja Raja Chola's thousandth coronation anniversary. Feeling unsteady, he simply sat down on the stage, although he collected himself in a few minutes and resumed business. On his return to Madras, he ignored pleas to check into a hospital. He was also taken aback by the dismissal of the NTR government and was apprehensive that such a fate awaited him.[235]

On 5 October, past midnight, MGR was admitted to Apollo Hospital after suffering a cardiac asthma attack, with breathing difficulties. But even in this state, an acutely image-conscious MGR said, 'Don't tell anyone I am here, don't let anyone know that I have been brought to hospital.' Even a delay of a few minutes would have been fatal for him. The doctors worked hard to rid their VIP patient of his breathlessness. A grateful MGR asked Apollo chairman, Dr Prathap C. Reddy, 'Do you do this for all your patients?'[236] He had also suffered renal failure and had to undergo peritoneal dialysis.[237]

---

* Rajaram (Speaker 1930–84) recorded that MGR was apprehensive that if he cleared a hospital that would serve the rich, it would bring disrepute to him. Rajaram pointed out that the government hospitals were not equipped with the latest medical instruments and Dr Reddy had left his lucrative career back in the US to found a hospital that would fill this gap in Madras. The hospital was cleared and opened in 1983. Dr Reddy showed his gratitude by treating MGR free. Rajaram, K., *Oru Saamaniyianin Ninaivugal*, Nakkheeran Publications, 2014, pp. 371–72.

MGR instructed that other than Janaki, no one else should be allowed to see him, and, reluctantly, he agreed to a daily medical bulletin. The official bulletin admitted to little more than 'slight asthmatic trouble', causing breathlessness and leading to 'mild renal impairment'. The next two weeks saw MGR's health see-sawing, giving his doctors anxious moments and much grief to the Tamils. Hande's 13 October statement cryptically said that MGR was getting better.[238] However, that evening, past midnight, MGR suffered a stroke which paralysed his right side and placed him in a semi-comatose stage.[239] Dr Reddy indicated that the situation was critical. RMV was for transparency, even as Nedunchezhian counselled that MGR's condition should not be publicized. In the end, Hande revealed to the media that MGR was not that conscious.[240] MGR, through his negligence and his acuity in keeping his health a private affair, had brought this upon himself. On 15 October, Kalaignar visited the hospital and inquired from Janaki, Assembly Speaker Rajaram and other ministers after MGR's health.

Three experts were flown in from the United States and Japan. As MGR fought for his life, only the second time after 1967, the outpouring of affection was overpowering. Unable to bear their idol's suffering, at least twenty of his fans immolated themselves. More rational ones prayed and supplicated for divine intervention.[*]

Kalaignar, a declared rationalist, penned a tender missive in his *Murasoli*, captioned 'I Too Am Praying'.

My sweet friend!

The fact that my eyes turned to streams [of tears] when I learnt about your illness is a sign that the forty-year-old friendship had melted the twelve-year enmity today like ice! Our differences did

---

[*] Earlier, on 19 January 1984, laying the foundation stone for a polytechnic college at a religious institution, the chief minister had said that Kalaignar had denigrated believers, characterizing those who went to temples as 'fraudsters'. Describing himself as a 'believer', MGR said that he was considered guilty if he kept his temple visit a secret and when he announced this, they asked why he was visiting. *Dinamani*, 20 January 1984.

not dissolve in that stream! But the bitterness has disappeared without a trace!

I was about to sink into the crowd when I reached Egmore station, Madras, following my release after six months in Trichy jail for the Kallakudi agitation! It was your arms that extended towards me, as the 'protective hands'! You grabbed and embraced me, lifting my body on your shoulders, to navigate the sea-like crowd! Then, your expensive watch was gone in that crowd! Oh my gosh, when I think of those events, and that too now, what can my heart and lips pronounce but to seek your recovery?

My sweet friend! May the prayers for you be answered! Oh, affectionate comrade of my earlier days! Please come back, donning your old smile! It is enough if you get well and come to see us! 'Prayer' does not mean 'worship' alone; 'request' is also its meaning! In that sense, let me too pray. Our differences notwithstanding, get up quickly to come to give [me] the joy of pleasant talk! Let your illness leave you like the mist that melts with the sun!

Ever your friend,
M.K.

On 16 October, Indira Gandhi paid a short visit—destined to be her last visit to the star and Tamil Nadu. She said that MGR recognized her and smiled at her words of comfort.[241] Sivaji Ganesan had told her private secretary, R.K. Dhawan, earlier that day that 'Madam . . . must come immediately'. 'And she came that day itself,' an emotional Sivaji Ganesan would recall later.[242] On her instructions, a customized plane was chartered to fly MGR overseas for treatment if necessary. Indira Gandhi had proved to be gracious towards the man who dropped her like a hot potato in Thanjavur. Two weeks later, on 31 October, Indira Gandhi was assassinated. MGR would not know of her death or Rajiv Gandhi's succession until many months later.

Four doctors from the US attended to the chief minister on the 17 and 18 October.[243] On 20 and 22 October, two Japanese doctors attended to the chief minister, to look into the swelling of his brain.[244]

On 5 November, MGR was flown by a special plane to Brooklyn State Hospital, New York. Twenty-one people—including ten doctors, two nursing superintendents, two security officers, wife Janaki and Health Minister Hande—accompanied him. Home Minister Narasimha Rao, the chairman of the Policy Planning Committee, G. Parthasarathi, and G.K. Moopanar, the AICC (I) general secretary, flew down to Madras to see MGR off. Thirunavukkarasu had, at Jayalalithaa's request, arranged to see the three of them. Both Rao and G. Parthasarathi assured Jayalalithaa that she was a mass leader and she would not be sidelined, and that they would look after her interests, something that Rajiv Gandhi repeated to them when they met him later.[245] On 19 November, MGR received a kidney from his niece Leelavathi, while continuing to be treated for paralysis and speech impairment.

Janaki had, through Cho. Ramaswamy, consulted three astrologers while MGR was at Apollo. They had uniformly predicted MGR's overseas treatment, his recovery and his continuing importance in politics.[246] S. Ramachandran suspected that Janaki began to harbour political ambitions from the moment MGR fell ill and that, along with RMV, tried to hijack the party from then on. MGR sensed their machinations and would apparently close his eyes, pretending to be asleep sometimes, according to his aide Manickam.[247] Academician, and later industrialist, Palani G. Periasamy, who organized MGR's treatment in the US and was with him throughout, said that MGR did not wish for others, including Janaki, to know of his discussions with him and would raise the TV volume when the two spoke.[248]

CONSTITUTIONAL QUESTIONS AND INFIGHTING

When MGR slipped into coma, it would lead to serious constitutional issues and Jayalalithaa's marginalization. The framers of the Constitution had not anticipated a scenario of a chief minister being unwell for a while and Governor Khurana admitted that 'the Constitution is silent on all these issues'. Officials and politicians from Delhi, therefore, flew down to discuss 'these issues' with their counterparts. Interestingly, Mohandas wrote in a matter-of-fact tone that when his views were sought, he had said that Nedunchezhian 'could assume responsibility for the day-to-day administration'. In relation to party affairs, he had suggested a 'top-level committee', made up of the secretaries of the party headquarters and heads of the different wings, which would have included Jayalalithaa. A majority of the AIADMK leadership was against her as she was not senior enough and they pointed out that MGR himself had removed her as propaganda secretary and had expressed his disapproval of her at the September general council. RMV, her most vocal opponent, said that Jayalalithaa was ambitious and thought of herself as the successor to MGR in both the government and the party, and that senior leaders had their misgivings about her activities since she became propaganda secretary. That MGR removed her from the post had made them 'very happy'.[249]

On the morning of 19 October, ministers Nedunchezhian, S. Ramachandran, KAK and RMV met the governor, and, later that day, a release from the governor's office said that Nedunchezhian would look after the chief minister's files. That day, when the ministers came together in a meeting, *India Today* reported that Chief Secretary Chockalingam was asked to leave in the middle of it. Nedunchezhian's efforts to become the acting chief minister, however, were shot down.[250] On Advocate-general R. Krishnamurthy's advice, an interim solution that ministers could informally get together, transact business but would take no major policy decision, had been reached. But as MGR remained indisposed, the charade had to end sooner rather than later. On 20 and 21 October, Nedunchezhian, the chief secretary and the private secretary to the chief minister, wrote to the governor stating that MGR had orally instructed him to look after his portfolios. The advocate-general said this was 'advice'. This would not be the first time that MGR's oral advice would be cited. Thus, the governor assigned MGR's portfolios to Nedunchezhian, who would also convene and preside over Cabinet meetings. A constitutional precedent had been set. Kalaignar wondered when the governor met the chief minister, and if he was unable to talk, how could he orally give advice?[251] On 25 October 1984, Nedunchezhian was allocated the subjects the chief minister dealt with.[252]

On 15 November, the DMK executive questioned the news of MGR's good health from the US, calling it a 'fraud' committed on the people and said a delegation of MPs would meet the President seeking an explanation for the 'extraordinary' situation in Tamil Nadu caused by the chief minister's illness.[253]

Elections for the Parliament and Tamil Nadu Assembly were announced for 24 December.[254] Nedunchezhian said this, too, was on MGR's instructions. But this was not true.[255]

On 23 November, MGR, who could neither speak nor sign, filed his nomination for the Andipatti constituency in the presence of the Indian consul general in New York, Arun Patwardhan. He had put his left thumb impression on the papers, as he could not sign them. It was reported that MGR also took the oath, as was required by law. Kalaignar said that the Centre facilitated these controversial moves and termed the consul general's act as 'shameful to India's honour'.[256] But, being politically correct, he also added that the DMK would not field a candidate against the ailing chief minister. However, political correctness could only go so far and the DMK asked for a judicial inquiry into the chief minister's condition and promised the same in its election manifesto. On 6 December, RMV called the DMK's promise 'inhumane'. He also released three photographs, the first since MGR's surgery, showing him reading a newspaper and greeting some people.[257]

RMV, a consummate operator, had become the most important person in the vacuum caused by MGR's illness and his absence. Nedunchezhian commanded little following and his fate too, despite his seniority, hung in RMV's hands. For now, they seemed to need each other. Nedunchezhian's seniority and status as number two in the ministry helped him serve as a frontman. Moreover, Nedunchezhian, never known for his organizational abilities or following, hoped to use RMV to finally reach the pinnacle of power, if and when the occasion arose. Those who had smarted at Jayalalithaa's rise now tried to show her her place. She, of course, had her own supporters and was very ambitious. Commercial taxes minister S. Thirunavukkarasu, the minister for cooperation and public works, K.K.S.S.R. Ramachandran, and Salem Kannan, the MP, were behind her. Thirunavukkarasu took her to the hospital, but she was not allowed to see MGR.

As the RMV faction kept her away, she used a different tack, reportedly approaching Rajiv Gandhi to see that she became chief minister, as MGR could not discharge his duties. Kannan, John,

Thirunavakkarasu and RMV all alleged that Jayalalithaa entertained such ambition.[258] These efforts came to naught.

And when the elections were announced, her plea for Delhi's intercession was pre-empted by RMV, who had filled the AIADMK party list with his loyalists and he announced it before the scheduled date. The barbs, invectives and vulgar comments that were thrown at Jayalalithaa by Kalimuthu, otherwise one of the finest Tamil orators, were shameful. RMV described her as a 'fourth-rate lady' in a public meeting and would assume for himself the 'moral duty to destroy her evil force'.[259] But the Dravidian movement would show that it was capable of even more shameful behaviour and Jayalalithaa herself would prove no better in the coming years.[260]

MGR'S VIDEO CAMPAIGN

Following his surgery, MGR's recovery was quick. His mind was agile and politically aware. Thus, when Sivaji Ganesan wished to call on him, MGR hesitated, wondering how it would be interpreted back home. Periasamy said it took some convincing for MGR to see him.[261] Actor Bhagyaraj would be the other visitor who would manage to see him.[262] From his hospital bed, he carefully followed the happenings back home. His routine was to read the newspapers thoroughly and surf the TV. His private secretary, M. Paramasivam, would read out a daily bulletin, to be followed by a police official's briefing. If the versions of an incident differed, MGR would instruct Periasamy to call Nedunchezhian, RMV, Muthusamy, Ponnaiyan or Chief Secretary Chockalingam, and listen to the conversation on another receiver. Periasamy would interpret MGR's gestures and pass on the messages to the other end. One day, Rajaram had called. Knowing MGR was listening, he declared that they were going to win the elections hands down. MGR was pleased to hear this. But later, Rajaram would tell Periasamy that he did not wish to 'hurt [MGR's] feelings'; the truth was that the situation was bad as the Opposition maintained that MGR was dead and was preserved in an icebox, and the public was buying this argument. According to RMV, it was Jayalalithaa who had planted the seed of the disinformation.[263] Periasamy then came up with the plan of making a video of MGR's activities. With a friend's help, they shot this video of MGR.[264] On

9 December, the video was shown to press persons.[265] As was the case in 1967, an MGR in the hospital, and again fighting for his life, would prove more of a vote-getter than the healthy MGR. The slick video showed MGR holding and reading newspapers, eating and smiling. Indira Gandhi's funeral footage was attached to it and Valampuri John provided the commentary. Titled *Vetrithirumagan* (The Victorious), the video evoked a huge emotional response wherever it was screened.[266]

But the video would not be sufficient to win the elections. A person of mass appeal had to be drafted for the campaign. S. Ramachandran had impressed on all concerned that Jayalalithaa was the only one who could counter Kalaignar's mass appeal. S. Thirunavukkarasu issued a public statement echoing similar sentiments, only to be promptly told off over the phone by Janaki from the US. When he asked, 'Amma do you want [to] come back as the chief minister's wife or the ex-chief minister's wife?' she hung up on him.[267]

However, when they eventually gave in, possibly also because of pressure from Delhi, Jayalalithaa sought RMV's good wishes prior to the campaign. In her campaign, Jayalalithaa would assure that her leader was well and would return to give them good governance.[268] (Actor Bhagyaraj would do the same.)[269] She drew large crowds, but conspicuously skipped the Madurai East constituency, where K. Kalimuthu was contesting. Former industries minister C. Ponnaiyan skipped an election meeting that she addressed for him.[270] This is what her official portal says of that time and her role: 'In the absence of Dr MGR, she took his place and spearheaded the alliance of the AIADMK and the Congress (I), securing a massive victory for the alliance.'[271]

She had replaced MGR. Kalaignar, for his part, had a formidable task before him in trying to overcome the sympathy wave for the ailing chief minister. He rose to the occasion. 'I will be the sandals to your feet,' he implored, asking the crowds to 'care for [their] feet'. He asked them to entrust the chief minister's chair to him in trusteeship, only to hand it over to MGR on his return.[272] Kalaignar said any wrongs that might have happened when he ruled 'may have happened without his knowledge'.[273] In the end, voters heeded the rhyming call, '*Saavuku oru votu; Novuku oru votu*' meaning a vote for the death of Indira Gandhi and a vote for the illness of MGR. The AIADMK–Congress (I) alliance won thirty-seven of the thirty-nine parliamentary seats, and 193 of the

234 Assembly seats.' Congress (I) won the lone Pondicherry seat. P. Shanmugam polled 1,59,376 and 58.86 per cent of the votes. The DMK candidate, who finished second, polled 97,672 and 36.07 per cent.[274]

The AIADMK won 132 of the 234 assembly seats (elections were countermanded in two constituencies). Except for the former minister for Adi Dravida Welfare, M. Vijayasarathy, the entire Cabinet came into power again. MGR won by a big margin of 32,000 votes over his nearest Forward Bloc rival P.N. Vallarasu in the Andipatti constituency of Madurai district. In Madras, the DMK's M.K. Stalin lost by a narrow 2292 votes to the former minister for dairy development, K.A. Krishnaswamy. The AIADMK faction's superficial unity would end on

---

*

MAJOR PARTIES AND PERFORMANCE
DECEMBER 1984 PARLIAMENTARY ELECTION

Party	Contested	Won	Votes	Percentage
AIADMK	12	12	39,68,967	18.36
Congress (I)	26	25	87,55,871	40.51
CPI	3	0	7,38,106	3.41
CPM	3	0	6,14,893	2.84
DMK	27	2	55,97,507	25.90

http://eci.nic.in/eci_main/StatisticalReports/LS_1984/Vol_I_LS_84.pdf.

ASSEMBLY ELECTION

Party	Contested	Won	Votes	Percentage
AIADMK	155	132	80,30,809	37.03
Congress (I)	73	61	35,29,708	16.28
CPI	17	2	5,67,527	2.62
CPM	16	5	59,762	2.76
DMK	167	24	63,62,770	29.34
Janata Party	16	3	4,93,374	2.28

http://eci.nic.in/eci_main/StatisticalReports/SE_1984/StatisticalReportTamilNadu84.pdf.

31 December when Jayalalithaa would be unceremoniously turned out of the VIP suite in Tamil Nadu House in Delhi.

The governor, meanwhile, told the media that he had written to MGR on 3 January to consider an interim solution until he was ready to return as chief minister. On 4 January, Nedunchezhian and Chief Secretary Chockalingam travelled to New York, and they brought back MGR's reply that he would return by January-end and the caretaker arrangements should be continued till then.[275] But the governor had received legal advice against giving any such time. Nedunchezhian, RMV, S. Ramachandran and KAK travelled to Delhi to seek Prime Minister Rajiv Gandhi's support through President R. Venkataraman.[276] On 13 January, Jayalalithaa and Salem Kannan met Nedunchezhian on his return from the US in Delhi.[277] On 14 January, Nedunchezhian handed over a sealed letter, advising the governor to relieve Thirunavukkarasu of the portfolios of excise, handlooms and textiles, and instead, he would be given the nutritious noon meals scheme portfolio from the next day.[278] Nedunchezhian was to take over his portfolios. Thirunavukkarasu now said he would go to New York to personally satisfy himself 'that the decision was his [MGR's] own'. Nedunchezhian responded, 'It is not proper to suspect MGR's thinking.'[279] Thirunavukkarasu himself admitted later that Janaki and RMV had obtained MGR's consent to divest him of the portfolios, telling him that 'he was causing trouble'.[280]

In December, Thirunavukkarasu started *Ponmanam*, a daily, on Jayalalithaa's advice, to reflect her views correctly as *Anna* had been 'captured' by the Janaki–RMV faction. In a bizarre turn of events, M.G. Chakrapani would launch it and MGR himself would treat it as an official organ after his return.[281]

However, two days prior to Thirunavukkarasu's journey to New York, a telex message from MGR arrived with this advice: 'Heard that you plan to visit New York to see me. You may please wait till my arrival in Madras by the end of the month.' Meanwhile, the media reported that 100 party workers of the Jayalalithaa faction had been removed. Additionally, Mohandas was transferred and K. Radhakrishnan was posted as Director of Vigilance in his place. Mohandas attributed his transfer to 'certain bureaucratic circles', and said that Nedunchezhian was not 'acting on his own' and the changes in the portfolios and the party had MGR's approval, 'willing or otherwise'.[282]

RMV announced that the swearing-in would be decided after MGR's return. The governor admitted, 'It is a very difficult situation and the choice before me seems limited. The leader of the majority party is unable to assume office immediately and nobody else seems to command a sufficient following.' Jayalalithaa and Thirunavukkarasu had met Rajiv Gandhi prior to these developments.[283]

A few days after taking over as prime minister, Rajiv Gandhi offered the Deputy Speaker's position to the AIADMK. MGR was vehemently opposed to it. He wanted Rajiv Gandhi to know that the AIADMK's support was not based on any expectation. When the prime minister said he would not fill the post then, MGR asked Periasamy to go through the AIADMK MPs' curriculum vitae. They were looking for someone who could speak English. M. Thambidurai, assistant professor of economics, caught their eye. When Periasamy said that he should speak English fluently, MGR said that Thambidurai knew a little bit of Hindi as well. He ticked Thambidurai's name on the list.[284]

JAYALALITHAA REMOVED AS DEPUTY LEADER IN PARLIAMENT

On 20 January, the AIADMK parliamentary board elected R. Mohanarangam as party leader and Aladi Aruna as deputy leader, replacing Jayalalithaa in the Rajya Sabha. Valampuri John was elected as party whip. That day, Thirunavukkarasu met G. Parthasarathi to bat for his leader.[285] Earlier, RMV refused to comment on Thirunavukkarasu's visit.[286] On 22 January, Jayalalithaa said that she was not aware of the election and had not been notified. Furthermore, she contested that the elections had been held under MGR's advice, claiming that Janaki and a 'cabal of conspirators' were holding MGR 'prisoner', and sought an impartial inquiry. When asked pointedly, 'Is your enemy DMK leader Karunanidhi or Veerappan?' she said, 'Karunanidhi belongs to the Opposition. He is not a personal enemy. But Veerappan sees me as an enemy' and added that RMV had not enjoyed a cordial relationship with MGR 'in the recent years'. She said that she met the prime minister to extend greetings for the New Year and that she had discussed nothing with any other party leaders. Not everyone, especially Kalimuthu, was persuaded.[287]

Kalimuthu responded as follows:

> Jayalalithaa has relations with Opposition parties . . . She needs to
> be expelled from the party, but because of his magnanimity, MGR
> has only removed her from the post of [AIADMK] Rajya Sabha
> deputy leader. Jayalalithaa gathered supporters to take over the
> party even as early as when MGR was at Apollo Hospital.

Solai recollected: 'Jaya was so ambitious that she wanted to become
the chief minister when MGR was hospitalized.' On 17 January 2015,
Kalaignar would tweet the alleged letter she wrote to Rajiv Gandhi,
asking that he intercede to make her chief minister as MGR was
incapacitated.[288] RMV said that 'from the very beginning, Jayalalithaa
had wished to be part of the Cabinet and become chief minister'.[289]

And on 24 January, Kalimuthu chastised Jayalalithaa in extremely
foul and revolting language, and said: 'Please do not give Jayalalithaa
the opportunity to meet Rajiv Gandhi on a one-to-one [basis]—she is
a cruel woman, ready to do anything to oppose our recovering golden
leader.'[290]

As he went after her, she lamented Kalimuthu's 'vulgar speeches'
and said Tamils should hang their heads in shame because of him. That
very day, Kalimuthu, in a statement, told the cadre, 'Don't betray leader
MGR and the party [by] trusting Jayalalithaa.' The CPM's Nallasivan,
in a statement, pointed out that Jayalalithaa had said that the 'Central
government cannot keep quiet seeing the drama played out in Tamil
Nadu to cheat the people' and added that she had the backing of the
Centre.[291]

Jayalalithaa, in turn, charged that the 'gang of four'—Nedunchezhian,
P.U. Shanmugam, RMV and Janaki, whom she described as 'the lady in
New York who is the de facto chief minister'—was taking advantage
of MGR's medical condition to remove her. Nedunchezhian, who met
MGR in the US, said that 'he is in full possession of his faculties and is
also able to utter monosyllables'.

Shanmugam said MGR had instructed him through a letter, which
a 'friend' had brought. Jayalalithaa said: 'I am convinced that this letter
is bogus. They are producing letters and telexes like rabbits from a
magician's hat. I wish to meet MGR face-to-face, and ask him what

crime I have committed.' Jayalalithaa said that the gang of four would 'expel' her from the party and that she 'can't even demand to see MGR even after he returns'. She said they were acting under the belief that MGR was 'not going to regain his mental faculties'. She said that she was fighting to save MGR's good name and for MGR.[292]

She was actually fighting for herself. Her interview in *Savvy* magazine made clear her real thougths about MGR in the aftermath of her being relieved of her post:

> MGR has been a great influence in my life, I don't deny that. But now I am my own person. I have evolved. Hereafter, I am responsible only for myself. Never again will anybody influence me to such an extent that all my thoughts and actions and statements are influenced and made in a particular way, just because someone else wants it that way.[293]

In 1999, she said, without any sense of irony, that he had not identified her as his successor or helped her succession:

> Now if you look at all the other women leaders who have made it to the top in Asia, they were all the daughters, wives or widows of former prime ministers or presidents. Because if you're a wife, automatically so much respect is given to you. People talk about you, refer to you, with respect. But such wasn't the case with me. Though Dr MGR introduced me to politics, he certainly didn't smoothen the way for me, he didn't make anything easy for me. I had to fight and struggle my way up every inch of the way . . .[294]

Why would MGR, who had introduced her, not identify her? She deflected this question, as seen above. Especially, as she would point out that she had lived the first third of her life for her mother and the second third for MGR:

> You see, for most of my life, I'd say for one-third of my life, I was entirely dominated by my mother. I'd do everything that she wanted. I could never do anything I really wanted. Then, for the other part of my life, I was entirely dominated by Mr MGR. First, I

had to enter films for my mother's sake, then I had to enter politics for Mr MGR's sake. Now I'm passing through the last phase of my life. Two-thirds of my life is over, one-third remains.[295]

She also noted, 'As long as he was there, he was the leader. I only had to follow his instructions.'[296] But did she really, especially after he took ill? And would she in the future?

An MGR Not In Charge

On 4 February 1985, it was much like in his movies at the Mohite Stadium in Madras. Returning after a three-month absence in the US, MGR stepped out of his sky-blue Ambassador, ecstatically waving with his once-paralysed right hand to the delirious crowds. Visibly buoyed by their adulation, MGR brushed aside Nedunchezhian's repeated entreaties to take his seat. Spotting Speaker Rajaram and Council Chairman M.P. Sivagnanam, MGR beckoned them to the stage. *Frontline* said, 'Except that he was a shade slower, emotionally brittle and tired, there was no visible impairment in his movements.'[1]

Jayalalithaa had come with a large and impressive garland—but to the Anna international airport at Meenambakkam. RMV had kept even MGR's landing site a secret from her. After waiting for over three-and-a-half hours at the VIP lounge, she returned, disappointed.[2]

MGR did not address the gathering. His speech impairment would, regretfully, prove permanent. Yet, MGR had defied all odds and predictions, and was there in flesh and blood, as energetic and strong as ever, making the specially designed vehicle for him redundant (RMV said that the transport minister, S. Muthusamy, had arranged the vehicle).[3] Only three days earlier, on 1 February, the governor had asked RMV how he could appoint someone who could not speak or function fully as chief minister. Under the circumstances, he said, RMV was the most apt person to take over the reins. Asking the governor to never repeat such a thing, RMV assured him that his leader would return fit enough to take over as chief minister again.[4] MGR's physicians and surgeons would attribute 70 per cent of this miraculous recovery to the star patient's willpower and limit their own contribution to just 30 per cent.[5] In July 1985, MGR would ask for contributions to reimburse his medical expenses, branding it as 'one more opportunity for the

Tamil people to demonstrate their affection for me'. Only MGR could say such things. The response was staggering and, on 30 July 1985, the party paid back the 96,90,375 rupees.[6]

Despite his miraculous recovery, MGR was living on borrowed time. Heavily dependent on medication, the chief minister probably yearned for his past physical and mental prowess. He grew reclusive and, in the evening of his life, seemed to wallow in self-pity and would break down often on account of his debilitating condition. Like him, his administration faltered, sputtered and gasped for breath. Intra-party squabbles and the ethnic issue consumed the chief minister's time. The rebellion against his authority was stark and directly proportional to his lack of physical and mental strength. The threats of resignation, the Cabinet shake-ups and the dismissal of almost half the Cabinet gave away the shaky nature of his grip over the party apparatus. Although he smarted at Jayalalithaa's ambition and oscillated between her and her detractors, in the end, he was overcome by his fondness for his protégé. Yet, he would not identify her as his successor. To be fair to Jayalalithaa, perhaps these things are possible only in the matter of succession as a religious head.

As chief minister, MGR seemed alert and played a constructive role in moderating and channelling Tamil sentiments in relation to the ethnic issue. Nonetheless, for all his personal rapport with the Liberation Tigers of Tamil Eelam leader, Prabhakaran, MGR was unable to make the all muscle and no mind organization, and its leader, heed him or the ground realities. He showed his displeasure twice by ordering a police swoop at dawn and later seizing their communications equipment. Similarly, when it came to criticism and the Opposition, the chief minister's tolerance levels appeared to have reached a new low, bordering on meanness, such as when he stood by as the *Ananda Vikatan* editor, S. Balasubramaniam, was jailed by an Assembly resolution over a cartoon or when he went along with the disqualification of the ten DMK MLAs for their protest against Hindi imposition, not to mention abolishing the Legislative Council to deny Kalaignar a platform.

After MGR regained consciousness, both Mohandas and RMV had dispatched news of developments, frequently at odds with each other, and similarly, the information from the US to the two also differed. According to Valampuri John, this was deliberate, with MGR trying to ascertain the loyalty of his key people.[7]

On his return, MGR lost no time in piecing together the events that transpired during his absence. He beckoned S. Ramachandran into his car on his way to his Ramavaram residence from the stadium. 'Janaki had told MGR that his transplanted kidney had been purchased from a donor in Singapore for 3 lakh rupees. MGR wept when he learnt the truth—that his brother's daughter Leelavathi was the donor—and he promptly fetched her from Kerala to thank her,' said S. Ramachandran, who also told MGR about Jayalalithaa's effective electoral campaign that had saved the day for the AIADMK as well as the RMV–Janaki shenanigans.[8] Later that day, when S. Thirunavukkarasu, who was earlier stopped from travelling to the US, called on him at Ramavaram, MGR gestured Janaki and Nedunchezhian out of the room. He then wondered why Thirunavukkarasu had stood by Jayalalithaa when everyone was against her. Thirunavukkarasu said, 'They all decided to chase her away in your absence. You brought her [to the party] and I thought you should decide.'[9]

According to John, MGR's inquiries had led him to believe that RMV had harassed and victimized Jayalalithaa. But he also learnt that his mentee aspired to be the chief minister now. S. Ramachandran explained that 'she was at the height of [her] insecurity and needed protection and security, and saw the chief minister's position as offering it, given MGR's incapacitating condition'. He was her protective amulet. She had seen the RMV–Janaki machinations against her. She asked MGR, 'Why can't you make me chief minister?' This upset MGR. 'He told me we could use her for the party, but should not allow her to rule,' said S. Ramachandran.[10]

MGR was angry with a number of his ministers and party functionaries, said John. But it appears that he also easily forgave them. At the 1985 launch of the songs of the movie *Poovukul Bhoogambam* (An Earthquake in a Flower, 1988), days after his return, John asked movingly as to how MGR could suspect his loyalty to him. An obviously touched MGR asked actress 'Silk' Smitha, seated next to him, to make room for John near him once he finished his speech. Later, when the event concluded, MGR hugged John, opening the door for Jayalalithaa's most vocal and obstreperous critic Kalimuthu to speak to MGR, who was all grace to him.

On his way back, in the car, MGR first asked Solai about what had transpired in his absence. Not wishing to agitate the convalescing leader, Solai suggested that nothing against MGR had taken place. Not fully convinced, MGR now turned to S. Ramachandran, who spoke favourably of Jayalalithaa. Aranganayagam's response that they had to be protective of Jayalalithaa greatly pleased him.[11]

THIRD-TIME CHIEF MINISTER

On 4 February, after calling on him at his Ramavaram residence, Governor Khurana, who had all along doubted MGR's speech, physical and mental abilities said: 'He is all right; both mentally and physically, he is all right.'[12] On 6 February, Khurana told MGR who came to see him that he did not have to repeat the entire oath and it would suffice for him to say just said four words. That day, MGR met his party MPs and MLAs at his residence. S. Ramachandran said that MGR noticed the MLAs rise as RMV entered, got upset and, pointing to the then Mylapore MLA, he said: 'Who gave tickets to such guys to become MLAs? We should dissolve the House and have fresh elections.' Obviously, it was a rebuke to RMV.[13]

On 10 February, MGR was sworn in as chief minister for the third time. In being sworn in alone and in charge of all the ministries without a council of ministers, MGR had set a precedent, although P.H. Pandian said that there had been other instances of this.[14] MGR read out the first few words of the oath and then affixed his signature thrice.[15] The event, closed to the media, was attended by the Speaker, Legislative Council chairman, the chief justice and the AIADMK's Lok Sabha Deputy Speaker. MGR had asked for Mohandas on the occasion.

When Mohandas met him at his residence later, MGR asked that he return to his post. The following day, the chief minister drove to Fort St George to sign a single file reinstating Mohandas as director-general of Police, Crime and Intelligence.[16]

CHIEF MINISTER MGR RESUMES CHARGE

Except for his speech impairment, MGR appeared to be normal and observed a busy routine, at least for the first year. He travelled to his Fort St George office regularly and perused files at home in the evenings. With his hand having steadied over the course of the following weeks, the chief minister appeared to relish the ability to write again and made copious notes on files on even simple matters. But the same could not be said about his speech and, till the end, he would rely on gestures and a smattering of words. Yet, he was able to chair and hold Cabinet meetings, arriving on the dot, bowing and taking his seat, attentively listening to discussions gesturing and sometimes whispering to his neighbour to convey his message to the Cabinet. The impediment also helped put an end to MGR's vacillation in matters and, when briefed, MGR took decisions on the spot.[17]

He also kept open house in the mornings. Touching his heart and waving out to the visitors, he would assure them that he would look into their concerns. When he did not follow what they were saying, he would close his fist and shake it to ask for clarification. He was so mentally agile that on one occasion he spotted a visitor who had come many years previously, and flashed a smile at him and assured him by waving his hand that he would sort out his problem.

MGR dissolved the parliamentary board, began a membership drive, altered party rules and pressed a committee to look into the case of the eighty partymen dismissed during his absence. *India Today* concluded: 'If anything, precisely because he can't speak much, MGR has become quicker and sharper at his job.' But *India Today* had spoken too soon.[18]

Four days later, the twenty-five-member Cabinet was appointed in stages: sixteen ministers on 14 February, seven on 3 March and one on 18 March. These were the Cabinet ministers and their portfolios.

1. M.G. Ramachandran: Chief Minister
2. V.R. Nedunchezhian: Finance
3. S. Ramachandran: Electricity
4. K.A. Krishnaswamy: Labour
5. R.M. Veerappan: Information and Religious Endowments
6. C. Aranganayagam: Education
7. K. Kalimuthu: Agriculture
8. C. Ponnaiyan: Law
9. H.V. Hande: Health
10. S. Muthusamy: Transport
11. S. Thirunavukkarasu: Food

12. R. Soundararajan: Housing and Local Administration
13. M.R. Govendhan: Backward Classes
14. Gomathi Srinivasan: Social Welfare and Nutritious Meals
15. Vijayalakshmi Palanisamy: Khadi and Handlooms
16. Y.S.M. Yusuf: Public Works
17. K.K.S.S.R. Ramachandran: Cooperation and Rural Industries
18. K. Rajaram: Industries
19. V.V. Swaminathan: Handlooms and Textiles
20. T. Veerasamy: Commercial Taxes
21. N. Nallusamy: Housing
22. Anoor P.G. Jagadeesan: Rural Industries
23. T. Ramasamy: Rehabilitation and Employment
24. A. Arunachalam: Adi Dravida Welfare
25. P.U. Shanmugam: Local Administration[19]

The third term would see several Cabinet reshuffles, and, in the end, almost half of the Cabinet would be dropped. In March 1985, S. Raghavanandam, who did not make it to the Cabinet this time, would become general secretary.[20] In the autumn of 1986 when the party was in the thick of infighting MGR would take over as general secretary from him.

JAYALALITHAA WISHES TO BE DEPUTY CHIEF MINISTER

Mohandas said that Jayalalithaa expected to be rewarded with a ministerial berth, but MGR chose to ignore her. He suspected that MGR was putting her 'loyalty and affection' to the test. She actually wished to be the deputy chief minister and took umbrage at MGR for testing her thus. She told S. Thirunavukkarasu: 'I was responsible for his coming back. [By] countering Kalaignar. He is seeing everyone. Does he not remember me? Can't you tell him about my work?'[21] She would say later that when MGR was alive, she 'could not dream of getting carried away because he gave her a knock on the head to bring her down to earth'. More such knocks were in store. But that MGR's heart was still with Jayalalithaa became clear when he finally agreed to her calling on him. Earlier, RMV, her bête noire, had disputed her claim of closeness to MGR, pointing out how MGR had not asked for her at Apollo Hospital and wondering, 'Why not now, that he's alert?' RMV had spoken too soon.

Salem Kannan, said he handed over Jayalalithaa's 'endearing' letter to MGR at the secretariat and how 'after reading it, he broke down'. He added, 'Madam [Jayalalithaa] met him at the secretariat and sorted out the differences.'[22] S. Ramachandran, who was present at that 19 February meeting, exactly two weeks after MGR's return, said that Solai would come on her behalf with letters to MGR, which he then took to the chief minister with his recommendation that he see her. These letters were very personal, stoking nostalgia and professing loyalty yearning and undying love.'[23] MGR grudgingly yielded. 'She came and fought to be named the deputy chief minister,' said S. Ramachandran. The chief minister gestured to him to indicate, 'Didn't I say so?' When Thirunavukkarasu showed up soon after she left, he asked S. Ramachandran to tell him what had transpired in the meeting.[24] That evening, there was a statement from MGR, saying that no significance should be attached to a routine courtesy call. Ironically, the statement achieved just the opposite.[25]

In ten days' time, Jayalalithaa's ambition to be deputy chief minister would get the better of her. On 28 February, MGR greeted Prime Minister Rajiv Gandhi at the Madras airport at 3 a.m. Rajiv Gandhi repeatedly asked him why the ailing chief minister had troubled himself, when the governor was there to receive him. MGR simply said that it was only appropriate and later also travelled to the Raj Bhavan for an unscheduled meeting with the prime minister. He told Rajaram on their way back in the car that he was aware that Jayalalithaa would be meeting the prime minister there. Jayalalithaa had asked the prime minister to intervene with MGR to name her as his deputy.[26]

As MGR stonewalled her, she wrote to Rajiv Gandhi alleging that he was 'jealous' of her popularity and was doing everything to 'eliminate me from the political scene and public life'. She added, 'No one can oppose him as they are "zeroes" without him.'[27] Four years later, just ten days prior to the 21 January 1989 general elections, on 10 January 1989, *Makkal Kural* and *Malai Murasu* carried the letter on their front pages, but she alleged that Kalaignar had fabricated the letter.[28]

---

* RMV said that an MGR aide brought these letters, found next to MGR's pillow, and gave them to him after his death and that he destroyed them. Interview with RMV, 15 September 2016, Madras.

But MGR could have done with a deputy. After his illness, he operated through his secretary and personal staff. The key man was MGR's secretary, M. Paramasivam, IAS. Vying with him as the closest confidant was the deputy secretary in the chief minister's office, T. Pitchandi. Undersecretary T.S. Sivakolundu was the third member of MGR's immediate team. After his illness, MGR was also dependent on Janaki.[29]

But this personalized and individualistic style of leadership meant veering away from collective decision-making and established constitutional practices. Expectedly, in June, the governor wrote to him objecting to unilateral policy decisions without reference to the Cabinet. Governor Khurana refused to elaborate on what else he wrote in the letter.[30]

On 25 July 1985, the chief minister left for Japan for a medical check-up and to purchase three ships for coal. From there, he went, on 8 August, to the US for medical treatment.[31] His portfolios were distributed to Nedunchezhian, S. Ramachandran and RMV, who was given home.[32] In the US, he invited the diaspora to invest in Tamil Nadu.[33] On 22 August, MGR would meet Rajiv Gandhi in Delhi. He would also consent to a meeting with Jayalalithaa while in Delhi and return to Madras on 24 August.[34]

PROPAGANDA SECRETARY FOR THE SECOND TIME

Thanks to the Delhi meeting, after a year in the cold, Jayalalithaa made a triumphant return on 5 September 1985 as propaganda secretary.[35] Magnanimous in her success, Jayalalithaa would call on RMV to seek his good wishes before her visit to the party headquarters where S. Raghavanandam, the party's general secretary, awaited her with a garland and said later, 'It is our revolutionary leader MGR's order and I am only too willing to implement it.' Jayalalithaa herself could not contain her emotions: 'I am overjoyed. I owe everything to my leader, MGR,' she said. She clarified that MGR had asked her to resign earlier in order to assuage the fears of some in the party, promising that her position would be restored after some time. But it had taken a year and a meeting in Delhi for it to happen. Also, around this time, the chief minister assumed the information portfolio held by RMV, who was given planning, archaeology and passports instead.[36] RMV, who prided himself on having sensed that Jayalalithaa was an 'evil force' as early as 1970, said that his sixtieth birthday celebrations in Pudukottai, an event to fete him organized by a party MLA, and the fact that policemen saluted him when he was holding the home portfolio were all used by Jayalalithaa to 'sabotage' MGR's trust in him. He said boards and festoons that proclaimed RMV as the next chief minister were 'planted' by Jayalalithaa's people in the MLA-organized event, and it was filmed and sent to MGR, who grew 'very upset'.[37]

On 11 September 1985, the chief minister would inaugurate a medical college set up by liquor baron and MGR's suspected sponsor, Ramasamy Udayar. The MGR administration also sanctioned the establishment of three private medical colleges.[38]

He could not sanction yet the two factions fighting under his very nose. Agriculture minister K. Kalimuthu alleged that the CBI was trying to connect him to a bank fraudster Robin Mayne, who had cheated banks out of 56 lakh rupees. On his complaint that the police were harassing Mayne to 'falsely implicate' him, the chief minister, accompanied by his law minister, Ponnaiyan, visited some police stations on 16 October, including Egmore where Maine was held, to ascertain the condition of lock-ups himself.[39] Mayne was in the CBI office, however, when the chief minister came calling Jayalalithaa termed Kalimuthu's charge that she was behind the CBI action—as she found him 'an obstruction to her ambitions'—as 'fertile imagination', adding that she 'cannot be made a scapegoat for a fraud committed by someone else'.[40]

All this must have been too much for the chief minister. On 28 October, after a Cabinet meeting lasting a couple of minutes, and when the officials had left, MGR shocked his ministerial colleagues when he declared: 'I am resigning. Please elect some other leader of your choice,' and then left. RMV knew that it was aimed at him and he gave an emotional speech about his association with MGR, his indebtedness to him and that if he suspected him, MGR should change his mind.[41] RMV recorded that his detractors had succeeded in planting the 'poisonous seed of doubt' in MGR's mind—that he was aspiring for the chief minister's chair.[42]

MGR's announcement saw the ministers huddling together to decide to send in their individual and collective resignations, affirm their loyalty only to him, and send Nedunchezhian and Rajaram as their emissaries to pacify him. The following day, Nedunchezhian said MGR had agreed to continue as chief minister.[43] In the Cabinet that day, it was decided that no one would issue statements to air their differences,[44] even as many ministers took this opportunity to complain about Jayalalithaa.[45] Famous for his literary analogies, Kalimuthu said in its aftermath: 'MGR, like Lord Shiva, has swallowed poison to save the party.' But that Kalimuthu himself was unconvinced of his own analogy was clear when soon thereafter he pointed out in an interview: 'To say that we partymen should unquestioningly accept whatever MGR does is not good for MGR himself. To say "yes" to everything that the leader does, temple cows can be appointed as ministers.' Furthermore, Kalimuthu said, he and eighty-five MLAs were opposed to any plan to make Jayalalithaa deputy chief minister. On 1 November, the chief minister lamely said that Kalimuthu's interview was probably before the 29 October Cabinet meeting even while clarifying that he was not planning to have a deputy.[46] Asked if the storm had subsided, he said: 'Even a gentle breeze was not there.'[47] But soon thereafter, Jayalalithaa's tour programme to the North Arcot and Erode districts would be cancelled, demonstrating just the opposite.[48] Mohandas had suggested naming a number two around this time, to which MGR said: 'There will be no party after me. After me [comes] the deluge.' MGR had greatly underestimated his image's shelf life and his protégé.[49]

The travesty of Dravidian politics is that Kalimuthu would join the Jayalalithaa faction after MGR's death, become the party's deputy general secretary and, later, an MP. In 1990, he would cross over to the DMK, only to return to the AIADMK soon thereafter. In 2001, he would become the Speaker of the Legislative Assembly in Jayalalithaa's government and, in April 2005, when the Supreme Court asked him to face trial in the Mayne case, Jayalalithaa, of all people, would come to his defence on the floor of the House, rejecting the demand for his resignation.[50]

The MGR pendulum was now swinging back in RMV's direction as Jayalalithaa was kept away in the 16 February 1986 Cheyyar by-election campaign. MGR himself campaigned for the RMV loyalist he had fielded. The AIADMK won the seat.[51] On 24 January 1986, RMV was given back his information portfolio.[52] More disconcertingly for

Jayalalithaa, in a signed statement on the front page of *Anna*, the party's official newspaper, the chief minister said: 'Associations like Jayalalithaa Peravai [Jayalalithaa Assembly], and Jayalalithaa Narpani Manram [Jayalalithaa Good Deeds Club], and similar associations, started in Ms Jayalalithaa's name should be immediately wound up. The starting of such associations is a breach of party discipline, and persons who continue to run them will face disciplinary action.' The eponymous Peravai had been formed courtesy of Salem Kannan, even as Jayalalithaa denied any hand in it and Kannan claimed she was fully aware of it. A greatly upset MGR stopped Jayalalithaa from acting as propaganda secretary for a second time and got a defiant Kannan expelled a week prior to the local body polls. 'When I met MGR, he was very cryptic in telling me not to support [her],' said Kannan.[53]

Mohandas wrote that MGR worried that he was not in control of the party any more and thought the February 1986 civic elections would help restore order.[54] This was not the most brilliant idea. In the end, the infighting would do the party in, as Jayalalithaa's rebel candidates fought the official nominees in at least a sixth of the places.[55] Jayalalithaa was not included in the selection panel and instead, on RMV's suggestion, MGR appointed Nedunchezhian, Raghavanandam and RMV as the selection committee.[56] Additionally, MGR gave away the subjects of molasses and deputy collectors to the law minister, Ponnaiyan, considered an RMV associate, around this time.[57] 'MGR's actions are now clear. You can draw the obvious conclusions from them and you will be right,' said a minister formerly close to Jayalalithaa. But he had jumped to a hasty conclusion as the March AIADMK general council and executive would demonstrate.[58]

Voters failed to be enthused by the promises of the reintroduction of prohibition in 1987 and a housing scheme for the weaker sections of society. As Kalaignar questioned the veracity of the prohibition assurance, the AIADMK issued a commercial in major dailies asking: 'If in January 1987 the liquor shops are closed, is Karunanidhi ready to quit politics?' On 21 February, speaking at Periyakulam, Kalaignar responded that he would not talk about politics for a year if they did so, and wondered if the government was willing to enact an ordinance the next day.[59] A campaign video, titled 'We Will Hoist the Flag of Victory', with MGR appealing to the voters directly, failed to do the trick in MGR's absence this time.

The DMK won sixty-four of the ninety-seven municipalities in these elections that were held after sixteen years. The DMK's allies— the communists, Indian Union Muslim League and the Forward Bloc—took another eight seats, bringing the DMK alliance's total to seventy-two municipalities. The AIADMK and Congress (I) won eleven each, and independents won the rest. Kalimuthu, however, said that the people had not considered it a contest between his leader and Kalaignar.

The RMV and Jayalalithaa camps blamed each other for the party's dismal performance. Certainly, the vote was also a statement against the lack of governance.[60] Mohandas said that although MGR had expected a poor performance owing to the infighting, the results came as a jolt to him.[61] According to RMV, MGR's trust in him began to shake again.[62] It appears that his trust in Jayalalithaa was not any stronger either and was at its lowest.

COUP AGAINST JAYALALITHAA FAILS

Su. Thirunavukkarasar said that MGR wished to expel Jayalalithaa from the party at this point. On his summons, Raghavanandam showed up with a dossier that listed her 'anti-party activities'. Thirunavukkarasu, who was also summoned, asked for a private meeting and, in the hour-long discussion, said that MGR was above the two factions, adding that if MGR had personal reasons for axing her, it was up to him. MGR said that he would think think the matter over. Raghavanandam lamented to Thirunavukkarasu that he had scuttled his hopes of salvation for the party.[63]

Thus, the two-day March executive and general council meeting, which was to have been a coup de grâce against Jayalalithaa, got botched.[64] But there was more to MGR's decision than Thirunavukkarasu's advice. Kannan said that thirty-three MLAs supporting Jayalalithaa had met around this time and planned to seek Rajiv Gandhi's intercession to stave off the impending danger for their leader. Kannan added:

This meeting was wrongly reported by the state intelligence as a move to float a rival party. A bitter and sad MGR could not stomach his protégé breaking away. The sacking of Jayalalithaa was struck off the general council's agenda and madam was invited to speak at a public rally that evening [in Royapuram].[65]

MGR's fondness for her ensured that he swung in Jayalalithaa's favour again. Three days prior to the party meeting, MGR unexpectedly postponed a Cabinet meeting for a three-hour-long meeting with Jayalalithaa. Subsequently, the party meeting, attended by 522 members and 142 special invitees, did not discuss Jayalalithaa at all. Instead, participants were given a form asking them to evaluate the performance of ministers and to list complaints. MGR had exclusive access to the filled forms. The tables had been turned quickly. Speakers criticized P.U. Shanmugam, K. Rajaram, C. Ponnaiyan and N. Nallusamy and, as a result, some of RMV's followers would turn on each other. The second day, Nedunchezhian announced that the chief minister would be dropping ten or eleven ministers from party work. And, if all this was not enough, Jayalalithaa gave the concluding remarks, where she took the moral high ground and appealed for unity. What a contrast to the April 1984 general council, where MGR himself had regretted his decision to give her responsibility. In two years, the wheel had turned a full circle. M. Natarajan claimed he had advised Jayalalithaa to address the council, to put her point of view across, even if she was not listed as a speaker. He and his wife, Sasikala, were becoming more and more integral to Jayalalithaa's political career.[66]

In the evening's public meeting at Royapuram, a first for MGR since October 1984, Jayalalithaa maintained the momentum of her advance when she said, 'Though I wasn't invited by the organizers [the Madras unit] to speak here, I have come at MGR's behest and am speaking at his wish.' In his seven-minute slurred speech, MGR warned his ministers to shape up or face the music. 'I will not hesitate to throw out the corrupt, however big the posts they occupy.' The following day, MGR would again cancel the Cabinet meeting for a closed-door discussion with Jayalalithaa.[67] Meanwhile, on 9 April, MGR, even as he was in Delhi, sent instructions relieving KAK of the labour portfolio and leaving him with animal husbandry, milk, and registration and stamp papers. Unpleasantly surprised, KAK resigned and said he would renounce politics. The next day, however, he changed his mind.[68]

MGR'S HEALTH AND ITS EFFECT ON ADMINISTRATION

'The fact that he has been unable to speak either in public or in the Assembly over the last sixteen months has raised serious questions about his ability to govern the state,' complained DMK legislator Rahman Khan. In the Assembly, the chief minister conveyed his messages through Nedunchezhian; sometimes, he could not make himself understood and had once given up after some minutes. But it was obvious that MGR and the administration were not well. Some fifty files were said to reach him daily, but the chief minister could not get to them. Some 8000-plus files were still pending for want of a decision. A minister had admitted to *India Today* that the 'administration is practically paralysed'.

An important file between the Tamil Nadu Electricity Board and the Neyveli Lignite Corporation had been pending for some months and the chief minister's clearance was obtained after intervention. A minister, who had waited for a month, got the nod by presenting a fait accompli—he announced a welfare scheme. Then the media stated that for eleven weeks, during the floods, MGR's phone had been disconnected.[69]

Mohandas said that MGR was conscious of the fact that, given his condition, he would not live long, and had become a 'little senile', and was losing interest in the government and the party.[70] On 20 May, a letter from the governor revealed the state of affairs:

My dear Chief Minister,

Of late, I find that I learn about policy decisions through the newspapers. If legislation is involved, I know only when the Governor's message is sought. Article 167 of the Constitution indicates the role of the Chief Minister regarding the furnishing of the information to the Governor.

Article 166(3) says that the Governor shall make rules for convenient transaction of the business of the state. Rule 35(2) gives the classes of cases that shall be submitted by the Chief Minister to the Governor before the issue of the orders. Clause 2 of this rule lists the cases pertaining to the questions of policy.

Where change of policy or practice is involved the Governor has to be kept informed. Even the minutes of the Council of Ministers relating to a meeting held on October 28, 1985, were received by me in March 1986. No meeting of the Council of Ministers seems to have been held after December 3, 1985, except a meeting held on March 11, 1986, to consider the budget.

None of the policy decisions taken recently seemed to have been discussed in the Council of Ministers as visualised in Clause 16 of the Second Schedule of the Business Rules. You may examine this so that major items of policy do come up before the Council of Ministers and minutes are sent to me immediately thereafter as visualised in Article 167(1) of the Constitution.

Frequent contacts and frank exchange of views between the Chief Minister and the Governor are the essence of the Constitutional requirements. I presume that you would have inferred that my role as head of the state has throughout been constructive and in the best interest of the state. Unfortunately in the recent past when a number of major decisions have been taken I find that I have been kept in the dark. I do hope that this position will be rectified.

Ten days later MGR replied:

Dear Governor,

I received your letter of May 20, 1986. I learn that you have not been informed about some of the decisions taken recently. I have been under the impression that everything has been going on according to the rules and procedures prescribed in the Business Rules. If there has been any omission, I feel, these could have been averted had I been properly advised by the chief secretary in such matters.

I assure you that they are absolutely unintentional. The chief secretary and the senior officials in the secretariat have, therefore, been instructed suitably to strictly adhere to the rules and procedures and the constitutional requirements that are already in vogue. I fully agree with you that frequent meetings between the Chief Minister and the Governor are very much imperative and useful in the interest of the state and I can assure you of my fullest cooperation in this regard.

In fact, I have always deemed it a pleasure to meet you often and discuss with you all important matters. I am proud to say that in all the meetings I had with you, I felt as if I had met a personal friend from home. I have always got valuable advice and guidance. I have got the highest regard for you and great admiration for a constructive role you are playing as head of the state.[71]

MGR's reply had not addressed the issue of Cabinet meetings and had simply made the chief secretary a scapegoat. RMV, however, explained the whole saga as part of Jayalalithaa's machinations in spreading the canard that MGR was 'dysfunctional' and unable to carry out his duties.[72]

THE DOWNWARD SLIDE HASTENS

Then came the All-world MGR Manrams conference in Madurai on 14 July 1986. MGR travelled with Janaki and Jayalalithaa, in the same flight, to Madurai. Jayalalithaa flagged off the procession and later spoke before MGR's plenary speech. Presenting a six-foot, gold-polished sceptre, she touched MGR's feet. MGR surprised his audience by making no announcement on Jayalalithaa, which had been expected, although she would later claim that it was this event where MGR identified her as the successor when he returned the sceptre to her.[73] But the event is best remembered for MGR's exhortation to his fans to carry a knife 'when the police cannot take action against the enemy, this would help for self-defence'.[74] Kalaignar said, 'MGR has lost the right to govern the state . . . He has given an open call to lawlessness. He should be sacked.' MGR was unfazed by the criticism. He had said that his cadre could not rely on the police 'because violence may come very suddenly from the squads being raised by the DMK'.[75]

But peeved by MGR's indifference, Jayalalithaa had unburdened herself to her 'sister in spirit', Sasikala, over the phone. Obviously, the speech had been recorded by MGR's intelligence people and placed before her leader, who refused to grant her audience for a week. As she sensed the cold, she did what she was best at—she poured her heart out in a six-page letter expressing her regret, seeking his forgiveness if she had hurt him by speaking ill of Janaki, promising never to repeat it, adding that the events of Madurai had 'greatly hurt' her, that she had no one and 'if he too hurt her, where would I go?' and asking for a meeting the next day and to not 'punish me further'. The letter had ended on an intimate, passionate and emotional note.[76] MGR would eventually yield.

He was also slowly yielding to his ailments. The media reported that MGR had had blood transfusions and, on occasion, suffered epileptic seizures. That he was not in control of his party became public when the government ran two paid advertisements in the chief minister's name in June. The first, issued on 13 June, directed civil servants not to oblige his wife or other close relatives vis-à-vis official matters. Apparently, a police constable owed his appointment to Janaki. The second advertisement said that there was no 'personal and confidential cell' in the chief minister's office, and cautioned officials to beware of letters on such a letterhead.[77]

Before his illness, the chief minister would speak personally to senior officials or use an intercom to communicate with them. But that had stopped now. 'Most of us are totally cut off from him now and we have no means of cross-checking anything or to confirm which decisions are his own,' a senior official had said then. A week after his Madurai speech, and soon after the publication of his letter to him, MGR met the governor to move chief secretary T.V. Anthony out and appoint him as vice chairman of the planning commission, a nondescript job.[78] But the Cabinet had not convened even in the aftermath of the governor's letter. Congress (I) leader Rangarajan Kumaramangalam said, 'If we allow this mess to continue, we will be doomed.'[79] Cho. Ramaswamy said, 'There is no doubt that MGR has lost control over his executive.' But he was not in control of his partymen either. Kalimuthu refused to apologize for having described P. Chidambaram as a 'tout of the Central government', and MGR himself expressed regret on his behalf.[80]

TIRUNELVELI AND ARUPPUKOTTAI BY-ELECTIONS

On 17 August 1986, M.G. Chakrapani passed away. MGR would break down and cry his heart out.[81] He would announce publicly in 1987 that he would not celebrate Pongal that year, requesting followers, friends and fans not to come to wish him that day.

On 31 August 1986, by-elections were held for the Tirunelveli and Aruppukottai Assembly constituencies. MGR made a snap decision, all on his own, and nominated RMV for the Tirunelveli seat and V.S. Panchavaranam, a panchayat president, for the Aruppukottai seat. *India Today* said that MGR attempted to give the news himself to local dailies on the phone, but could not because of his speech problem.[82] Keeping Jayalalithaa away from the campaign, MGR addressed some thirteen rallies himself, sometimes reading from a text. In one meeting, he said: 'I am one of you. You can say whatever you want of me, but the DMK politicians are heaping undeserved blame on me. They are alleging that I have amassed Rs 24 crore of illegal wealth. They should prove it.' His audience, in response, held up two fingers in a V, as support for the party's twin leaves. Yet, RMV's win was only by 13,324 votes, some 5000 and 10,000 less than on the previous occasions respectively. Kalaignar said: 'It is not a mandate against us, but a show of emotional sympathy for an ailing leader. The tide is on the wane and will disppear by the next election.'[83]

When MGR worried about the party and the warring factions after he passed away, Mohandas reminded him that he had said there would be no party after him, at which a 'ghost of a smile crossed his face', which was 'so pathetic'. Mohandas suspected that MGR, in the autumn of his life, wanted to return to the tinsel world where he was the undisputed king.[84]

ASSERTING HIS AUTHORITY

On 21 October, MGR dropped ten of his twenty-four ministers—RMV, C. Aranganayagam, K. Kalimuthu, H.V. Hande, T. Veerasamy, N. Nallusamy, M.R. Govendhan, Gomathi Srinivasan, Vijayalakshmi Palanisamy and Y.S.M. Yusuf. This was long coming since the March general council.[85] MGR, however, saved RMV's and Kalimuthu's dignity by saying, 'The services of senior party leaders like Veerappan and Kalimuthu are now required to give the party a new thrust and enthusiasm. That is why I have spared them ministerial work.' If anyone read it as MGR's message to the RMV camp, the portfolio changes that resulted sent confusing signals. V.V. Swaminathan, an RMV follower, was given the information, tourism, prohibition and electricity portfolios. Former electricity minister, S. Ramachandran, was given charge of food. KAK was reinducted as minister for labour, his former portfolio, only to be dropped again on 16 March 1987, along with Anoor Jagadeesan.[86] CPM's Nallasivan said that the act had not cleansed the party.[87] CPI's P. Manickam felt the chief minister's move 'shows that the factional squabbling in the ruling party is at its peak'. S. Ramachandran said there was no 'substantial' reason for MGR's action, while Su. Thirunavukkarasar maintained it was to 'keep the balance within the party'.

Expectedly Kalimuthu said that the reshuffle was Jayalalithaa's handiwork. But he clarified: 'I am not cribbing about my having lost the ministerial post. I will serve my leader MGR to the end and will do whatever he ordains.'[88] On 6 November, MGR took over as general secretary of the party from Raghavanandam making him a deputy general secretary. Hande was also made a deputy general secretary. Whether these moves restored any of his authority is a moot point; MGR had spoken and that was enough.

RMV would have to wait until 5 November 1987 to be reinducted into the Cabinet, as minister for local administration. Prior to that, RMV had complained to MGR that he was under surveillance.[89] This was MGR's last Cabinet change.[90] RMV said that in his last days, MGR was ready to 'atone' and reverse the decisions he had taken under the influence of others. He added that MGR was convinced that Jayalalithaa was 'evil', and it was only a matter of time before he would have thrown her out.[91]

DISQUALIFICATION OF TEN DMK MEMBERS

MGR now left for the US for a check-up. In his absence, the DMK would hold an anti-Hindi conference on 8 and 9 November in Coimbatore. Subsequently, on 17 November, in Madras, Anbazhagan symbolically burnt copies of the constitutional provisions on Hindi as the official language.

On 24 November, Speaker P.H. Pandian informed the House that he had decided to disqualify the DMK legislators for the act. Anna would have turned in his grave at Pandian's words and DMK legislator Madurantakam Arumugham pointed out the hideous irony of the Speaker's decision:

> How can you judge so, sitting under Anna's portrait? Is it fair? Didn't Anna himself attempt to burn the copy of the constitutional provision? If you indeed wish [to], you should remove Anna's portrait and then issue such a decision.

Taking a purely legalistic view, P.H. Pandian said he had already warned DMK leader Manoharan. When Congress (I)'s M. Palaniyandi and the Muslim League's Abdul Samad met MGR to work out a compromise, he simply told them to go by the Speaker's advice. When they met Kalaignar later that night, he told them that he would announce his decision the following day in the House. The next day, when MGR gestured to Kalaignar for his decision and sensed his reluctance to change his party's stance, he then signalled this to the Speaker. Pandian said that no one was elated at the decision to uphold the disqualification.[92]

Undeterred, the DMK continued its agitation and one of its MPs Vaiko took part in the protests on 9 December (but the Parliament would not disqualify him). Meanwhile, on 22 December, following an acrimonious four-hour-long debate, a government resolution to disqualify the ten DMK legislators who were in jail was adopted. The AIAMDK had issued a whip and all the 131 AIADMK members voted in favour. The DMK and its allies voted against the whip, while the Congress (I) walked out. The DMK's strength in the Assembly had been reduced from twenty-four to fourteen.

Ananda Vikatan said 'mud has been thrown at the face of democracy'. Terming the chief minister a 'dictator', Manoharan claimed that MGR's 'life's ambition is to destroy the image of the DMK and its leader M. Karunanidhi'. CPI leader P. Manickam charged that MGR was trying to 'eliminate every political opponent and build himself up'.[93] Kalaignar, the disqualified MLAs and close to 20,000 party workers were interned and charges were pressed under the Prevention to National Honour Act. Kalaignar was given a ten-week prison term. However, they were released sixteen days before their term ended, on MGR's orders.[94]

ABOLITION OF THE LEGISLATIVE COUNCIL

There was more disappointment in store for the DMK and Kalaignar. On 14 May, Nedunchezhian introduced a one-sentence resolution in the Assembly, in the chief minister's name, invoking the constitutional provision to abolish the Legislative Council. After being in existence for sixty-six years, one of the two oldest councils in the country ceased to function from 1 November.[95] Nedunchezhian said the chief minister had arrived at the decision after consulting ministers, such as himself, in the course of the past seven to eight months. He did not explain why it had nominated three members in April—the film actress 'Vennira Aadai' Nirmala, MGR's counsel N.C. Raghavachari and G. Swaminathan. On 23 April, Nirmala was to have taken oath. Then things began to unravel. Nirmala had been declared insolvent in 1981 and owed 10 lakh rupees to her creditors. As the Madras High Court admitted a writ petition challenging her nomination, Nirmala came up with the 10 lakh rupees and cleared herself the same day. After the governor asked MGR to explain her nomination, without adequate scrutiny, Nirmala resigned.

On 13 May, M.P. Sivagnanam, the council chairman, allowed adjournment motions by the DMK and others. Kalaignar said on that occasion: 'If this council will not be abolished and will continue . . . If I am not there to preserve this council's legacy and for the benefit of the other members, I am willing to resign my position [as the leader of the Opposition]. Let the chief minister [relax that] Karunanidhi has gone, there is nothing to worry, and come forward to make the decision to let the council without him continue.' Elected to the council on 6 March 1984, Kalaignar said the abolition move was to pre-empt him becoming the leader of the Opposition.[96] While the ruling party members voted the council out, the Congress (I) stayed away, facilitating the vote.[97]

Six weeks later, on 29 June, the MGR administration marked its tenth anniversary. Mohandas said, 'MGR was not personally very enthusiastic . . . He was slowly withdrawing into himself and spent his leisure hours watching videotapes of his old movies.'[98]

Cho. Ramaswamy said on that occasion:

Corruption has been institutionalized under MGR's rule. Apart from all the scandals which have been written about, the chief

minister has recently begun gifting wads of currency notes to the
bride and bridegroom of every wedding he is invited to preside
over. You should remember that MGR once said he had no
money to pay his income tax.[99]

Jayalalithaa, however, would blame it on Janaki and RMV: 'Until 1984,
the MGR government was free of corruption. It was only after his
return from America in 1985 that corruption grew under the coterie led
by Janaki and Veerappan.'[100]

PROHIBITION OF ARRACK—FAVOURING IMFL

On 1 January 1987, MGR shut down some 16,000-odd retail arrack and
toddy shops as promised during the February 1986 local bodies polls.
Excise and information minister V.V. Swaminathan admitted that
they had earlier relaxed prohibition 'temporarily'. The temporariness
had lasted five years and had left a huge backlog of cases relating to
infractions of the dry law. Thus, at the time of the announcement,
courts were dealing with a whopping 1.2 lakh excise cases and another
60,000 were under investigation. Civil rights activists worried that the
new ban would leave the police to have a field day—as in the pre-1981
period, when there were times the police planted liquor in someone's
vehicle to charge him later of an offence.

Swaminathan said that they 'have now decided to enforce
[prohibition] more forcefully. It is a commitment our leader, MGR,
gave to the people of Tamil Nadu'. However, Swaminathan was being
disingenuous. The MGR administration had not only left the IMFL
business intact, but it was keen to see it flourish.

Kalaignar charged:

Liquor trade means money. This government has made frequent
changes in the excise policy only to help a few people. We
want total prohibition, but under the new law, rich people and
expensive liquor have been left out. It is patently obvious that it
has been designed to help the IMFL trade.

The inordinate delay in the selection process further lent credence to
the suspicion that the move was in order to create a monopoly for

IMFL. Although 1900 applications had been received by 31 July 1985, allotments were not made before September the following year—fourteen months later. Besides, in the four months prior to the arrack ban, 953 new licences had been awarded, almost doubling the total IMFL outlets to 1931, making it clear that there was a strong emphasis to favour IMFL sales.

In addition to the exponential rise in the number of retail outlets sanctioned, the arrack ban had also made available 500 lakh litres of raw alcohol, the source of IMFL for its producers both local and major, based in other states.[101]

ANANDA VIKATAN BALASUBRAMANIAN'S ARREST

The intolerance of the AIADMK, increasingly under siege, was growing. On 28 March, P.H. Pandian informed the House that some members had drawn attention to the fact that *Ananda Vikatan* had published a cartoon on its cover page 'aimed and calculated to damage the reputation of the members of the House, in general and more so the ministers in particular'.[102] He ruled that the weekly should publish its apology on the front page, failing which the House would pass a summary sentence.

That week's *Ananda Vikatan* cover had carried a cartoon picturizing two persons, in which one was asking the other, 'Of the two persons on stage, who is the MLA and who is the minister?' and the other responded, 'The person who looks like a pickpocket is the MLA and the person who looks like a masked dacoit is the minister.' Editor S. Balasubramanian said he would not express regret, even as he sarcastically explained the reasons behind the cartoon to his readers. He also pointed out that even a murderer gets to offer an explanation with regard to his actions. On 4 April, the House adopted a resolution asking Balasubramanian to apologize or face three months' rigorous imprisonment. Within three hours, Balasubramanian was put in Madras Central Jail. Criticism was unanimous, and Kalaignar and the press said that they would boycott the Assembly on 6 April if he was not released forthwith.

On 6 April, the Speaker announced that he was freeing the editor as the chief minister, in all his 'magnanimity', had requested so. Cho. Ramaswamy said that there was no magnanimity involved as, in the first place, MGR was behind the arrest. Pandian said that 'it was their

perception . . . But MGR was truly magnanimous'. The irony was that
Balasubramanian had directed MGR in the movie *Sirithu Vazha Vendum*
and his father, S.S. Vasan, had produced MGR's hundredth film, *Oli
Vilakku*. S.S. Vasan had stood by Janaki during her messy divorce
from her former husband Bhatt. One of MGR's advisers was *Ananda
Vikatan* Manian. Yet, MGR appears to have been stung to the quick
and went along with P.H. Pandian's actions. With its fierce impartiality,
Ananda Vikatan remained a thorn in the MGR administration's flesh.
Earlier, in 1980, the weekly had invited Kalaignar for its golden jubilee
celebrations. On the invite, Kalaignar's name had figured twice and
MGR's only once. In the event, MGR stayed away. *Vikatan* had also
been fair (read, critical) in its observations on the MGR administration.
In a full bench judgement in 1994, the Madras High Court awarded
a token compensation of 1000 rupees to Balasubramanian for gross
violation of law and natural justice.[103]

VANNIYAR SANGAM AGITATION

On 5 August, MGR left for the US for his medical treatment and
returned on 31 October.[104] In his absence, the Vanniyar Sangam, led by a
physician, Dr S. Ramadoss, brought northern Tamil Nadu to a standstill
for a week, in a roadblock agitation starting from 17 September.
Twenty persons were killed in police firing and in clashes between the
Vanniyars and Adi Dravidas, and over 20,000 persons were arrested.
The Vanniyars' (considered the most numerous community in Tamil
Nadu) two earlier protests—on 6 May 1986, when roads were blocked,
and on 19 December, when buses and trains were stopped—failed to
push the government into action. Prior to these agitations, the Vanniyar
Sangam claimed that it had made numerous representations to the
chief minister, including sending twenty-five letters to which there had
been no response. Their demands included a 20 per cent reservation
in education and jobs in the state, and a 2 per cent reservation in the
Central services.

Although the MGR government had increased the size of the
affirmative action pie for the backward classes to 50 per cent, it had
also added another thirty-nine to the list of forty-two communities who
would benefit from this move. While S. Ramachandran (a Vanniyar

himself) railed against the agitation, Nedunchezhian laid down conditions to the Vanniyar Sangam.[105] A paid advertisement in MGR's name, as the AIADMK's general secretary, listed the government's welfare measures for the Vanniyars and the backward classes. Among other things, it pointed out that Vanniyars were appointed to the High Court as judges for the first time by the MGR government and that of the 234 MLAs, twenty-one from the AIADMK and sixteen from the Congress (I) were Vanniyars, and that the AIADMK and its allies had won in Vanniyar-majority areas in the last three general elections. However, it pointed out that the current system of reservations should not be changed to a caste-based one, as demanded by the Vanniyars, as that would 'create new confusions and problems'.[106]

On 25 November, MGR met the Vanniyar Sangam representatives led by Dr Ramadoss. The sangam gave a nine-page memorandum detailing their demands and a month for the MGR government to fulfil them.[107] MGR's death would see the Vanniyar Sangam wait to get its demands met by Kalaignar as chief minister later.

INVOKING THE NON-BRAHMIN CARD IN JUDICIAL APPOINTMENTS

Earlier, in October, while MGR was still being treated in the US, the AIADMK administration tried to burnish its non-Brahmin credentials. Law Minister Ponnaiyan called a press conference to accuse Chief Justice M.N. Chandurker of sponsoring only Brahmins to the bench, and that four names of scheduled caste and backward class candidates would be sent to the Centre on MGR's return. Eight months earlier, on 25 February, MGR had recommended the governor to forward the name of a senior judicial officer, P.K. Sethuraman, who also enjoyed the backing of the chief justice, to Delhi. Alongside, MGR had sponsored K. Kaliyaperumal, V.C. Palanichami, T.M. Kuppuswami and T. Kothandaramasamy of the scheduled caste and backward classes. If it was an attempt to circumvent the chief justice, it did not work. In his 6 March response, the governor insisted that the views of the chief justice on the candidates were required.[108] Ponnaiyan recalled that the House passed a resolution backing the candidates as Chandurker was perceived to be a pro-Brahmin RSS man.[109]

INDO-SRI LANKA ACCORD

The governor and the chief justice were not the only ones who refused to oblige MGR. His nominal protégé, the LTTE's Prabhakaran, also refused to heed his advice or pressure with respect to a peace deal. Mohandas said that policymakers in Delhi knew that MGR was under their control as he was beholden to both Indira Gandhi and her son for facilitating his overseas medical treatment and, secondly, because of the 'many skeletons in his cupboard'.[110] However, this is how the Centre saw MGR; in Natwar Singh's words:

> In the next few months after the summit, Minister of State P. Chidambaram and I made several trips to Sri Lanka. On the way, we made it a point to visit M.G. Ramachandran, a former film star who, apart from being head of the government, had a huge personal following in the state. It was widely alleged that he covertly supported and financed the LTTE and their cadre were being given military training in Tamil Nadu. He also considered Jaffna an extension of Tamil Nadu. Prime Minister Rajiv Gandhi realized that we had to keep MGR on board and he was right in doing so, because to by-pass so formidable a Chief Minister would only add to our problems.[111]

MGR had been a hugely moderating force and *The Economist* aptly wrote in MGR's aftermath that 'no new state government will be able to match the late chief minister's ability to hold the line [on the ethnic issue]'.[112]

Rajiv Gandhi was keen to reach a settlement while MGR was still alive.[113] However, the LTTE refused to accommodate MGR's wishes on substantive issues—beyond a point. On the evening of 16 November 1986, on the margins of the SAARC summit in Bangalore, MGR, who had been brought in to persuade Prabhakaran, asked S. Ramachandran why the Tamil east should be divided. S. Ramachandran explained the ethnic demographics behind the proposal. In response, the LTTE's Balasingham argued that the east had undergone 'Sinhala colonization'. After this, MGR asked S. Ramachandran: 'The Tamil areas are for Tamils. The Sinhala areas are for the Sinhalese. Isn't this the Indian government's stand?' S. Ramachandran nodded in the affirmative. The discussion then took a bizarre turn when MGR pointed out that the majority in the north were Tamils, and Indian Tamils were substantial in number in the southern plantations. S. Ramachandran agreed. MGR now suggested the Tamils were a majority in Colombo and S. Ramachandran, rather doubtfully, agreed to this. 'In the whole of Sri Lanka, the Tamils are spread out. Right?' 'Yes,' said the minister. 'Then in that case, as per the Indian government's stand, should not the entire island become that of the Tamils? Then why should the Tamil lands be divided? Should not the entire Sri Lanka be given to the Tigers?' asked MGR. S. Ramachandran was aghast at this curious logic. As he kept quiet, MGR persisted. 'Why? Isn't there fairness in my contention?' S. Ramachandran meekly said yes. MGR now turned to Prabhakaran and Balasingham to tell them that they could leave, saying that he would not force them to accept the accord. S. Ramachandran had to run to tell them that MGR was merely being rhetorical when he suggested that the entire island go to the Tigers and requested that they didn't divulge this to the media.[114]

As S. Ramachandran told this author, 'It was Balasingham's perception of events.' Prabhakaran's intransigence in Bangalore led to MGR responding with 'Operation Tiger' on 8 November—seizing their arms and placing them under house arrest briefly.[115] MGR, initially happy, was worried about the fallout of this with Prabhakaran.[116] And two weeks later, he ordered Mohandas to seize their sophisticated wireless equipment. It was Prabhakaran's turn to be upset with MGR now. As Prabhakaran undertook a 'fast unto death', MGR, who was in Salem, disclaimed prior knowledge of this action. P. Chidambaram indicated that the Centre was neither consulted nor informed, while Kalaignar condemned the seizure.[117] In a complete volte-face, MGR returned the arms seized earlier. Mohandas decided to go on leave at this point and Prabhakaran moved back to Jaffna.

On 27 April 1987, MGR announced that 4 crore rupees would be provided as 'humanitarian aid' to the Sri Lankan Tamils who were facing siege. MGR told the Assembly on the occasion: 'Tamil groups are spearheading the fight against the fascist action of the Jayewardene regime, and they should be congratulated and helped.' Earlier, President Jayewardene had called the LTTE 'the private army of Mr M.G. Ramachandran, the present chief minister of Madras'.[118]

Both Nedumaran and Veeramani of the Kalaignar-headed Tamil Eelam Supporters Organization (TESO), founded on 13 May 1985, commended this largesse to the LTTE[119] while Jayewardene objected.[120] But, as the fall of Jaffna appeared imminent, MGR, in a message to Rajiv Gandhi on 27 May, said, 'The people of Tamil Nadu are deeply agitated, shocked and profoundly concerned.'[121] Kalaignar warned Rajiv Gandhi that 'history will find you guilty of permitting the genocide' and asked for a Cyprus-like solution.[122] MGR would air-dash to Delhi.[123] On 4 June the Political Affairs Committee of the Union Cabinet met and the meeting lasted till 4 a.m. and met again that morning after Rajiv Gandhi's discussions with MGR, who was specially flown in from Madras. The chief minister, *India Today* reported, brought with him 'a brief-case full of telegrams from citizens of his state pleading with him to "save" the Jaffna Tamils'. That afternoon India would undertake 'Operation Poomalai (Floral Mountain)' and unilaterally airdrop twenty-five tonnes of food. While Sri Lankan leaders were furious Kalaignar urged Delhi for a 'Cyprus-like' solution.[124]

After this, MGR and Prabhakaran would meet one last time in Delhi, days before the July 1987 Indo-Sri Lanka Accord. President R. Venkataraman recorded that Rajiv Gandhi had told him of MGR's good offices and that Prabhakaran had told Rajiv Gandhi later that the chief minister had convinced him.[125] This was, of course, not the case, although Natwar Singh also believed that MGR had knocked some sense into Prabhakaran.[126] On 26 July, MGR was flown by the prime minister's special aircraft to Delhi to deal with the Tigers. S. Ramachandran said that MGR returned disappointed with Prabhakaran's intransigence, leaving him behind in Delhi to assist with the talks. It was then that the LTTE negotiated an assistance of 50 lakh rupees per month from the Centre and other favours to overcome 'practical problems' as Natwar Singh told the Parliament later. S. Ramachandran suggested that Prabhakaran, who had indicated agreement, resiled because of his internal differences with senior commander Mathaya.[127]

Mohandas said that MGR looked 'weak and forlorn', but was not happy that the LTTE was not party to the accord.[128] MGR wished to avoid the Congress (I)'s 2 August Marina rally to welcome the Indo-Sri Lanka Accord as he felt he 'had no role in it'. He half-heartedly returned from the airport on Rajiv Gandhi's call requesting his participation in the gathering.[129] There however, he made a fifteen-minute speech in which he asked that 'everyone support the accord'. He said the accord would facilitate Sri Lanka's Tamils 'to live without fear and in security' and the Indian Peace Keeping Force (IPKF) had been sent so that 'Jaffna's Tamils could live without fear'.[130] When Rajiv Gandhi said that 'without his [MGR's] sagacity, profound humanism, rock-like support and the deep understanding that he has shown, we could not have reached this agreement', MGR rose and held his hand to thank him. *Dinamani* reported that they stood in a 'state of ecstacy' for some moments.[131]

On 5 August, MGR left to the US for the last time. When the hostilities between the IPKF and LTTE began, an unhappy MGR described the developments as 'unfortunate'.[132] From his hospital in the US, MGR wrote to Rajiv Gandhi, who was attending the Commonwealth Conference in Vancouver, expressing his distress and concern over the turn of events.

Kalaignar began condemning the accord as 'an altar built to sacrifice the interests of Tamils in the island'.[133] As MGR's health failed, Prabhakaran wrote on 13 October to Kalaignar for support, dubbing S. Ramachandran as a 'traitor'.[134] The DMK responded with rallies and protests.[135] On 19 October, MGR travelled from Baltimore to meet Rajiv Gandhi in a reception in Washington DC, turning down the prime minister's offer to visit him instead. This was the time when the death of nineteen LTTE cadre at sea had become an issue. MGR had asked for the views of some Opposition leaders like Veeramani and Nedumaran. A list of nineteen points was drawn up, and he signed it and handed it over to Rajiv Gandhi, who studied them, and promised to act on them as soon as he reached Delhi.[136] Mohandas said that MGR had called him from the US with regard to Sri Lanka and he had to 'gently' remind the chief minister that he was no longer the intelligence chief.[137]

On 2 November, MGR sent Rajiv Gandhi a telegram, asking for a grace period of forty-eight hours for the LTTE to surrender arms, and to remind him that he wished to continue the discussions on the ideas they had exchanged during their meeting in Washington DC. Earlier, Rajiv Gandhi had sent a message advising the chief minister to rest well and not exert himself.[138] MGR reputedly framed the message and kept it at his bedside. In reply to MGR's telegram, the Centre reiterated its stance that it wanted the LTTE to announce its acceptance of the accord. Following the Centre's message, MGR met the LTTE's Kittu and some others on 4 November.[139] Nedunchezhian told the Assembly on 11 November that MGR alone could decide how much detail could be revealed of the talks with Kittu. That day, MGR issued a statement that his views on the ethnic issue were final and were corroborated by the party and the government. The previous day, the AIADMK's MP Aladi Aruna had said in the Rajya Sabha to leave the matter to MGR, who would settle it if the Centre could not, and that the militants should not be forced at gunpoint to accept the accord, but should be cajoled through talks.[140] Balasingham wrote that Kittu had met MGR on 23 November, and had received both financial assistance and the chief minister's advice that Prabhakaran should reach a truce and begin talks with India.[141] On 24 December, the day of MGR's death, the IPKF announced a ceasefire in his honour. Balasingham and his wife used the ceasefire to exit Jaffna quietly. Balasingham concluded that even in his death MGR had stood by the Tamils of Sri Lanka.[142] Prabhakaran declared, 'He was like a brother. He understood our issue. He wished to give us full support. He had a special respect for us. We could have not grown this far but for his help.'[143]

MGR'S DEATH

The President of India was to launch the Dr MGR Medical University on 25 December. The previous evening, MGR had busied himself with details of the public reception he was to have hosted for R. Venkataraman on his first visit as President to Madras. Ironically, the statute that MGR had introduced in his first term, that no names of living persons could be used for government premises and buildings, had to be amended so that the university could be named after a living person.[144] Alas, there was no need for it in the end.

At 5 p.m. on the evening of 23 December MGR had used the bathroom and then said he felt tired. He asked for BRS, his personal physician. The previous day, Rajiv Gandhi had unveiled a statue of his grandfather, Jawaharlal Nehru at Kathipara, Madras, thus fulfilling one of MGR's long-expressed wishes. The event would be MGR's last public appearance. When BRS arrived, MGR's heartbeat was irregular.

But then MGR had had no prior heart complications. Both MGR and Janaki turned down BRS's suggestion to go to the hospital, saying he had no pain and was not sweating. Jayalalithaa would later blame Janaki for this decision.[145] So a team of doctors, including cardiologist Dr K.M. Cherian, descended on MGR's residence to be of assistance At 8 p.m., when approached to go to the hospital again, MGR jovially declined. This time around, though, he was defying death at his own peril. BRS was worried that MGR might suffer a silent heart attack. As a diabetic, MGR's peripheral nerves were dead and thus, he would not feel the attack, he would only feel unease. MGR had some porridge at 8 p.m. and then some buttermilk at 10 p.m. He then said he was going to bed. Two duty doctors kept watch, while BRS and the others waited downstairs. Two hours later, feeling uneasy, the chief minister got up, passed 400 cc of urine and had a plate of rice gruel. A little after midnight, at around 12.50 a.m., the ECG became irregular and ten minutes later stopped completely. Resuscitation measures were attempted until 3 a.m. Although, the heartbeat resumed intermittently, MGR's body had gone cold and anoxia had set in. His death was confirmed as having occurred at 3 a.m. and, at 6 a.m., formalin was injected to preserve his body. MGR, who had been waging a losing battle with his kidney, had however, died of cardiac arrest. Nedunchezhian remarked poignantly: 'It is the end of an institution, the end of an era.'[146]

KALAIGNAR PAYS HIS RESPECTS

Kalaignar could not bear the news of his over four-decade-old friend's death. He was returning from a tour by train from Periyar district when he heard of MGR's passing away. Thoughts of their times spent at Singanallur, a Coimbatore suburb, tugged at his heart. It was still early and the news had not spread widely. When he reached Ramavaram Gardens from Egmore Station, the entrance doors were closed. Former minister S. Madhavan came to take him inside to the body. Kalaignar rightly recorded that if he had not proceeded immediately after hearing the news, he could have never paid his respects. The enmity between the parties was so deep.

Violence gripped the city as news of the death spread. Kalaignar's statue was broken and pulled down. He issued a statement asking for calm among the DMK cadre and suspended DMK programmes for a week, and ensured that the DMK flag flew at half mast.

Jayalalithaa had also rushed to MGR's house immediately, only to find the door shut in her face. She had to keep banging the door with her fists before she was let in, but from 'then onwards it was another series of Herculean efforts'.[147]

MGR'S WILL AND TESTAMENT

In his last days, MGR preferred to be on his own as he could not speak. He would get up suddenly from his bed and take Janaki or Manickam, the help, by the hand and walk around the garden sighing heavily. Then, one day, a poor worker's daughter brought her eight-year-old girl who could not speak. MGR then asked his speech therapists and doctors to treat the girl. Surprisingly, within eight weeks, the girl gained a fair ability to speak and MGR was immensely happy. The thought of aiding such children occurred then and led him to put down in his will that, except the house, the rest of the 7.5 acres of his Ramavaram residence should be used for a school for poor children who could not hear or speak, to be maintained from the income of Sathya Gardens and Sathya Studios. MGR registered his will on 18 January 1987.[148]

FUNERAL CORTÈGE

Prime Minister Rajiv Gandhi was informed of the death before 4 a.m. and he immediately set off for Madras (he was to meet with the visiting Afghan President, Dr Najibullah, around lunchtime in Delhi). A day of national mourning was observed and Doordarshan covered the funeral extensively. Kalaignar said his eyes brimmed over as he watched the final journey of his friend on television.

The Union Cabinet passed a resolution saying, 'For a long time, Mr Ramachandran provided inspiring leadership to his State. While representing hopes and aspirations of the people of Tamil Nadu, he always kept them in the mainstream of national life.' The resolution said that the chief minister symbolized 'the principle of unity in the midst of diversity, which is the keynote of our national life'.[149]

The Indian Air Force planes flew seven sorties to bring men and material for the funeral.[150]

After the body was displayed for twenty-nine hours for people to pay their respects, the three-hour funeral procession to the Marina began at 1:30 p.m. Clad in a white sari, Jayalalithaa had stood for thirteen hours on the first day and eight hours on the second by MGR's body as it lay in state in Rajaji Hall. She said she suffered 'mental and physical torture' on the second day at the hands of seven or eight women, who stamped on her feet, dug their nails into her skin, pinched her and attacked her everywhere except her face. Then, she was not allowed to be present when the last rites were performed. She said she 'didn't mind that'.

When she attempted to get on to the gun carriage bearing MGR's body at the start of the cortège, Janaki's nephew Deepan hit her on the forehead and again beat her when she tried to get back on to the carriage, and he pushed her away, forcing her to leave. She said she was 'injured and bruised all over'. In a 26 December statement, she denied the allegation that she had shouted hysterically at those who asked her to leave. She said both Deepan and her party MLA K.P. Ramalingam had flung the most obscene words at her and did so again when military men helped her climb on to the gun carriage. She, therefore, 'against my conscience', decided not to join the last journey. *Dinamani* said that at the sight of trouble, Nedunchezhian had rushed to advise her that it was against convention to be on the gun carriage, that RMV was seen saying something, moving his hands agitatedly, and Jayalalithaa was seen speaking 'caustically' to some in English.[151] She got into her car and left for her Poes Garden residence, where legislators, parliamentarians and others later called on her to affirm their loyalty.

At 4.30 p.m., with 'Abide With Me' playing behind, MGR's mortal remains were laid to rest in a six by four foot grave, by the side of his mentor Anna's mausoleum. R. Venkatraman's tribute that 'MGR was the most charismatic leader in the country' was never truer.[152] *The Economist* said matter-of-factly that MGR's death had driven 'several mourners to suicide'.[153]

THE AFTERMATH

Jayalalithaa addressed her supporters the next day from her balcony and was given the sobriquet 'the balcony maiden' by her detractors.

S. Ramachandran recalled that when he called on Janaki a day after MGR's death, she said, 'All of them say that I should become chief minister.' Hearing this, he said that he 'got the shock of my life'.[154] RMV recorded that Janaki sent the same message to him through her astrologer, at which he readily agreed to propose her name as chief minister.[155]

Despite these behind the scenes moves by Janaki, on 28 December, Nedunchezhian formally made a bid to succeed MGR. On 29 December, Nedunchezhian, S. Ramachandran, K. Rajaram, S. Thirunavukkarasu and C. Aranganayagam did not attend the consultations held by Janaki. Meanwhile, Nedunchezhian, rooting for himself, said that the status quo should continue till the end of the term.[156] He said later that even from the day of MGR's death, thirty 'senior party leaders decided to propose Veerappan's name as legislature party leader.'[157]

Meanwhile, on 30 December, in her second address to her supporters from her balcony, Jayalalithaa said:

> You have expressed the wish that I should become chief minister
> and take over the leadership of the party. As far as I am concerned,
> I do not have a desire for office. Neither do I need wealth and
> pleasure . . . I will complete the tasks he had left behind.[158]

The next day, Janaki threw her hat in the ring openly and asked for Nedunchezhian's support.

With his chief ministerial dream being snuffed out one more time, Nedunchezhian switched sides. He, S. Ramachandran, Aranganayagam, Thirunavukkarasu and K.K.S.S.R. Ramachandran rallied behind Jayalalithaa, selecting her as the general secretary. On 1 January 1988, Jayalalithaa said she 'assumed general secretaryship of the party'.[159] When asked about a successor, Jayalalithaa pointed out that Anna had not named one. She promised to carry Anna's and MGR's message to the people. 'When Anna died, MGR was only the treasurer of the DMK, number four in the party. Now, without MGR, as party propaganda secretary, I am number five,' she noted.[160]

On 6 January, with ninety-seven MLAs behind her, Janaki Ramachandran became chief minister. She was required to prove her majority on 28 January.

In the third week of January 1988, Jayalalithaa told an appreciative crowd in Madras, 'Janaki Ramachandran was meant to be a housewife, counting [her] beads and chanting Sri Rama Jayam [the name of

God] . . . Instead of doing this, she is now signing on government bills. This is a tragedy.'[161] But there was more tragedy waiting to happen as Janaki tried to win the confidence vote without the numbers, and by any means, on 28 January. She and Jayalalithaa had both travelled to Delhi—she seeking Congress (I)'s support in the vote of confidence and Jayalalithaa lobbying against it. As the DMK and the Congress (I)* stayed clear, and even as less than half the members were present in the House, P.H. Pandian declared Janaki had won the vote.[162] That day, she had unsuccessfully sought the DMK's support, making a mockery of her late husband's politics from 1972 till his death. The resultant violence in the Assembly had to be broken up by the police and was described by *Hindustan Times* as 'the worst of their kind in the history of parliamentary democracy in India'. Terming the episode 'sickening' and 'shameful', the daily wanted the government dissolved.[163] On 30 January, the ministry was dismissed. Janaki had been chief minister for twenty-four days, the shortest in the state's history.

CONCLUSION

MGR's success ought to be an inspiration for today's young and for the young to come. The early death of his father, abject poverty, lack of formal education, living in an adopted state, his belated opportunity as hero—MGR allowed nothing to stand between him and success.

He was only the second actor-turned-politician after Ronald Reagan who managed to take centre stage. Few could read the masses as he did. Not surprisingly, none before or after has been deified like MGR.

From the mid-1950s, when his hero status had become secure, a group of image-makers—scriptwriters and lyricists—spun stories of his fight for justice, invincibility and acts of kindness towards the poor, morphing the reel with the real. Such a concerted effort was made possible as MGR was socially conscious and politically committed as none other.

MGR was a modern-day Karna.

---

* Mani Shankar Aiyer alleged she tried to 'buy' Congress (I) MLAs instead of trusting Rajiv Gandhi. 'That dished her.' http://www.ndtv.com/opinion/rajiv-gandhi-jayalalithaa-and-i-1634795.

When he broke company with them, DMK leaders downplayed the record crowds he drew as 'film glamour' that would pass. They were still in disbelief when he was voted to power in 1977. It was only then that leaders began deserting the DMK ship.

Originally a Congress man, MGR changed Tamil Nadu's politics into a contest between two Dravidian forces, instead of the Dravidian movement versus a nationalist movement. MGR's positioning of himself as the rival to the DMK, from 1972, upended a nationalist alternative in Tamil Nadu for decades now. Kamaraj had feared exactly this.

MGR was greatly underestimated by his political rivals. But he defied political gravity by not depending on caste, religion or language for votes. His image, charisma and political appeal transcended such electoral considerations. He mostly chose good candidates who were able to relate with their constituents. His was a party where there was room for those with an interest to serve—regardless of their background. He proved to be an astute and consummate politician, except for his occasional gaffes. He had the confidence to surround himself with some of the best minds. His godlike status made him ride the political scene as a colossus. As Su. Thirunavukkarasar once famously said, 'MGR is the one and all his associates are [political] zeroes.' He overcame political adversity with clumsy overtures, but he came out on top in the end. The course of Dravidian political history would have been very different if his avowed intent to merge with his parent party had come true.

Competitive politics saw MGR stoop down, but only to conquer. But there is no doubt the man was indeed a great humanist. The longest serving chief minister till then, with three consecutive, albeit truncated, terms, he, nonetheless, left a very mixed record. He laid the foundations for Tamil Nadu turning into a welfare and freebie state.

His poverty and difficult childhood made him think of the rural poor especially in the short term. His genius captured the imagination of the masses. His schemes providing a nutritious noon meal, free tooth powder, uniforms and footwear, among others, made him true to his popular name 'Darling of the Masses'. His administration made education up to the Plus Two stage free. According to Nedunchezhian, nutritious midday meal scheme saw 92 lakh children and others in need eat one hot lunch every day, at a cost of 185 crore

rupees per annum. The scheme's spin-offs were varied—including a
rise in school attendance and a reduction in the number of dropouts,
and immediately led to the creation of employment for 2 lakh women.
Sixty-two lakh children received free uniforms at an annual expenditure
of 62 crore rupees and free textbooks at 14.5 crore rupees per annum.
In 1987, more than 3 lakh old-age destitutes, differently abled people,
widows, farm labourers and deserted wives were receiving financial
assistance earmarked for the elderly. From 1982 onwards, farmers with
less than 5 acres of land were given free power. No other state had
provided such a concession. Similarly, those who owned above 5 acres
of land, depending on the capacity of their motors, were charged a flat
annual tariff of 75 rupees per horsepower. Likewise, more than 8.5 lakh
huts were provided free power, costing the state 250 crore rupees per
annum. One crore and 18 lakh ration cardholders received 16 kilos of
rice per card for 1.75 rupees a kilo per month. Plans had been made to
provide free footwear to 1.5 crore children and poor women. Between
1979 and 1987, the MGR government waived the interest and penalty
interest on farmers' cooperative loans to the tune of 375 crore rupees.[164]
On Deepavali in 1987, a man who never celebrated the festival, gifted
veshtis and saris and 2 kilos of rice to every landless farm labour family,
which cost the state 20 crore rupees. The distribution of plastic pots
to the slum dwellers in water-starved Madras helped slake the thirst
of those waiting in long queues. Similarly, he provided financial
assistance to needy artists and artisans, and introduced insurance for
the unorganized sector. While the human development index showed
promise, all of this welfare, and arguably a culture of dependency, came
at a price, with more than three-fourths of the budget being devoted
to subsidies. Critics contended that many of the schemes came at the
expense of industrial and infrastructural development.

His reign witnessed relative industrial harmony and peace. The
vision to partner the private sector in education would transform the
state forever. However, while it had spawned some quality institutions
and skilled manpower, it had also fuelled corruption and mediocrity.

His administration had the best of relations with the Centre,
especially the prime minister. MGR had a good personal rapport
initially with Morarji Desai and later with Rajiv Gandhi. This cordiality
was mostly reciprocated by the Centre's liberalness while making

allocations for the annual plan outlays, and assistance for water supply and the public distribution system.[165] For instance, for the fiscal year 1986–87, MGR managed to get 20 per cent more than the previous year's allocation.[166]

MGR's reign was much like that of Caliph Harun al-Rashid. Caliph Rashid, in disguise, went out on walks in the nights to find out the truth, and dispense justice later. He was usually accompanied by Masrūr, the executioner, as well as friends like Jaffar the Barmakid and Abū Nuwas, the brilliant poet. MGR used his police and others to eavesdrop on his own ministers and even his protégé, not to mention the members of the Opposition or judges whom he considered were not in line. He personalized incidents, issues and people, and brooked little criticism. His fascination for the Intelligence was complete, and he trusted the last person who had his ear. But information for MGR was a one-way street. A highly private man, his administration was opaque. MGR's anti-scurrility law was fruitless as it failed to silence his Opposition, but he banned government officials from divulging any information to the press, because of which, sometimes, even routine statistics became hostage.

He ran an administration that was woven around him and centred on him. Between 1947 and 1977, only one IAS officer quit. MGR's administration had the dubious distinction of seeing twenty officers resign in his ten years.

MGR was the architect of the Sarkaria Commission probe against Kalaignar, his colleagues and administration. However, it did not take long for the MGR administration's puritanical zeal to crumple and it reverted to business as usual. His first term is considered clean by many. But by the end of the first term, he would be directly accused of kickbacks from an aborted ship deal. After the stormy waters he faced due to the allegations, his administration would run aground because of its private bus policy and then reek foul of its liquor policy.

But, before this, MGR's zeal for temperance saw him turn into a contrarian on the liquor policy and run an administration that bordered on the tragicomic, with his harsh laws that sent tens of thousands behind bars for drinking and led to the burgeoning of an illicit liquor mafia and a more corrupt police. He then did an about-turn. How a man wedded to prohibition could go to the other extreme, where he midwifed liquor barons, who in turn bankrolled his party and his private acts of largesse, defies comprehension. When MGR died, he left behind ten distilleries, hundreds of IMFL outlets, and an arrack blending and bottling unit in every district. For a man who had promised a clean administration, swearing on his mentor, and prohibition, swearing on his mother, and a probe by a judge before admitting leaders into his party, this must have been déjà vu of his time with the DMK. But, until the end, he insisted that he and his administration were clean. And, to his credit, none of the charges stuck to him.

He was open enough about his religious beliefs for which he had taken people to task in his years with the DMK. The timings of his first two swearing-in ceremonies were fixed by his astrologer, ghostwriter and friend Vidwan Lakshmanan. MGR himself was a regular devotee at the Mookambiga temple in Karnataka. His reign heralded the resurgence of exhibitionist Hinduism, which reached its zenith when, in October 1984, AIADMK partymen offered public prayers for MGR and performed popular Hindu practices from eating *mann soru* (eating food without a plate from the ground to propitiate the gods) to rolling on the floor in circumambulation. At least two ministers proudly tonsured their heads.

His good relations with NTR helped and the Krishna waters project became a reality. However, MGR made no sustained effort to convert his personal and political capital to try to forge lasting agreements on the water front. (His attempts at the southern chief ministers' conclave were to score a political point.) Perhaps it is a harsh indictment of the man, for the issue is an extremely complicated one and without all-round goodwill, courage, vision and magnanimity, it will not be resolved. A legal approach has resulted in awards that are trophies for Tamil Nadu, but little else.

Farmers were at constant war with his government till 1982. So were the others. Few in the organized sector seemed happy. Yet, MGR did wield influence over the people. His charisma and hold over them could have been used productively to bring Tamil Nadu on par with Maharashtra in industrial growth or Punjab in agriculture. While he seemed to have had the intent, the general degeneration in public life, realpolitik stemming from competitive politics, an entrenched bureaucracy, his own dilution of values, not to mention his illnesses, let him waste the opportunity of a lifetime, much like his protégé, Jayalalithaa.

With all his international exposure, the chief minister could have done more for industrial growth, investments and infrastructure. One study said that Tamil Nadu, which was third in industrial production when he took over, had fallen to the thirteenth place when he left. The state's growth rate was lower than the national average. Power and water were, and still are, chronic problems. The state income was less than the national average of 3.5 per cent.

MGR's administration could thus boast of no major developmental projects, industrialization, infrastructure or modernization of agriculture or tourism. His rural vision held back Tamil Nadu's industrial growth and infrastructural development.

Nedunchezhian, the number two in his ministry, however, in a résumé of the ten-year MGR administration in an 11 October 1987 op-ed in *Dinamani*, said that small industries had grown from 18,000 in 1977 to 32,000 in 1987 and large-scale industries from 8000 to 13,000. From 232 crore mW, Tamil Nadu produced 613 mW; Tamil Nadu grew at 4 per cent, while India grew at 3.9 per cent; in 1972–73, 59.7 per cent lived in poverty and by 1983–84 it had decreased to 39.6 per cent. The national industrial growth was 6.2 per cent in 1971–86, while Tamil Nadu's was 7.2 per cent. Tamil Nadu GDP in 1976–77 was 4.307 crore rupees, but in 1985–86, it grew to 12,625 crore rupees. The per capita income in 1976–77 was 944 rupees and in 1985–86, it was 2403 rupees.[167]

Yet, despite Nedunchezhian's claims, studies are clear that half the state remained below the poverty line after MGR's ten-year rule. Worse still, he did not take from the rich to pay the poor, but took from the poor themselves. Economist S. Guhan's analysis indicates that the MGR government hurt the very poor it intended to serve. In 1975–80, excise was only 1 per cent of the tax revenue. In 1980–85, it grew to 13.9 per cent, and four-fifths of it came from the country liquor consumed by the poor. Direct taxes, which came from assets and wealth, stood at 4.6 per cent of the total tax base during 1975–80. From 1980–85, it fell to 1.9 per cent. However, according to a working paper of the Madras Institute of Development Studies, 40 per cent stayed below the poverty line, and their situation failed to improve and unemployment grew.[168] Government land was given away for a song, wrote *Aside*.[169] MGR's government had a poor record when it came to the redistribution of wealth, said M.S.S. Pandian.[170]

On the ethnic issue, while cultivating and funding the Liberation Tigers of Tamil Eelam's V. Prabhakaran, he also helped balance the DMK's shrill demands. However, his influence over Prabhakaran was greatly overrated. He held the line on Sri Lanka with his carefully calibrated policy, catering both to popular sentiments and yet keeping these passions in control.

He was ambivalent about Jayalalithaa as his successor. If he had not brought her into the AIADMK, politics after him would have moved on to a non-charismatic, collective leadership phase, perhaps under someone like Nedunchezhian, as Tamil Nadu is witnessing now on the AIADMK side. Politics between the two Dravidian parties would have also remained relatively cultured, and not diabolically and irrationally adversarial. The merger was not meant to be.

In 1991, when Jayalalithaa became chief minister she turned into a Caesar and her aide Sasikala Natarajan, the high priestess. They behaved like the East India Company, slowly colonizing Tamil Nadu. The state's public life sank to new lows. MGR was a 'great influence' on Jayalalithaa. Yet, she had imbibed none of his selflessness or greatness.

As early as 2002, the Supreme Court asked that candidates, among others, furnish details of their and their family's assets. Sadly, even those who have had no need for such wealth, change when they reach the dizzying heights of power. The late Jayalalithaa was a classic example of this.

Much was expected of her—Jayalalithaa's cult-like personality, charisma, intelligence and the fact that, like her mentor, she did not have a family of her own. She could have transformed the state easily, making it one of the most prosperous in the country. Instead, thanks to her and her 'sister in spirit', it soon ranked first in corruption.

The 14 February 2017 Supreme Court decision on the Disproportionate Assets case has laid bare our own morals and values— Jayalalithaa was buried with all the state honours. Yes, she was the chief minister when she died. We did not pause to consider that the nation's flag was on the woman whose morality and honesty still hung in the balance. Partly our excruciatingly slow judicial system is to blame. But we should also hang our heads in shame for the words of eulogy and the paeans of praise that we heaped on her—partly in the tradition that no ill should be spoken of the departed, but also because our bar has become so low and most of our leaders have become adept pretenders. But when the AIADMK, founded by MGR, sought that the nation's highest honour be bestowed on Jayalalithaa, it begs the question—what were they thinking? Jayalalithaa symbolizes all that has gone wrong with our idea of a public career, and especially with the Dravidian movement. It is time to press the reset button to return the movement to its idealistic and egalitarian moorings.

Although his protégé disappointed him, providence did not. Whenever MGR's political stock appeared low, fate helped draw sympathy and support for him. Despite the scandals that dogged his years in power, his whittling down of the Dravidian ideals of secularism by his temple visits, his image as a clean man or a Dravidian leader could not be dented.

It would be appropriate to include excerpts of Prime Minister Rajiv Gandhi's condolences, which aptly captures the man whose life would remain an inspiration if not a message:

The nation mourns the passing away of one of her great sons. Mr M.G. Ramachandran was above all a patriot, imbued with a deep feeling for his country, a profound pride in her glorious heritage and love for all her people. To him, the unity of India was sacrosanct, and the preservation of her integrity a sacred duty . . .

His mind soared above all narrow divisions and petty loyalties. To him, the service of the people of Tamil Nadu was the service to the people of India. His life's work exemplified the ethical and moral values which have kept our nation united through all these centuries—Sathya, Ahimsa, Karuna and the concept of *Vasudaiva kudumbakam*.

M.G. Ramachandran's name was synonymous with the struggle for justice, rights for the poor and the deprived, most specially the oppressed women of India, the sufferings of her mothers and sisters. With his powerful tongue, he articulated their grievances.

From the charity of his heart, he showered upon them his generosity. When he became the chief minister, he channelled the energies and resources of the state in the direction of those most in need. The people adored him live as on the screen, for they saw mirrored in his concerns his compassion for their cause.

He will be mourned by not only the people of India, but also the people of Sri Lanka . . .

He is no more, but his work lives on.[171]

Anna said that 'it will take a thousand years for another Tamil to reach his place' about Perunthalaivar (Great Leader) Kamaraj. About his protégé, Anna would have said, 'It will take a thousand years for another to enjoy such adulation from Tamils.' Anna would know, for he was one such man himself.

Notes

Preface

1 https://www.britannica.com/biography/Harun-al-Rashid.

2 The film based on a tale from the *Arabian Nights* is known for MGR's fighting sequences, especially the one with a tiger. Comedian and co-star in the film Chandrababu, in a moment of pique with MGR, revealed years later as to how the actor-politician fought the drugged tiger and how the sequence continued to be filmed, showcasing MGR still locked in fight with the animal, although he had long exited the cage and was watching the shoot sitting next to Chandrababu. Mugil, *Kanneerum Punnagaiyum*, Chennai: Kizhakku Pathippagam, 2005, pp. 37–49.

3 MGR was originally from Kerala.

4 Court report produced verbatim in *The Hindu* (14 Feb 2017): http://www.thehindu.com/news/national/tamil-nadu/article17300801.ece/BINARY/DAcase.

5 http://www.thehindu.com/news/national/tamil-nadu/I-am-against-bans-be-it-on-bulls-or-my-films-says-Kamal-Haasan/article17087632.ece?homepage=true.

Chapter 1: The First 'Stage'

1 https://www.youtube.com/watch?v=X2c7LMEXd1U.

2 Pritish Nandy, 'Was It Foul Play?', *The Illustrated Weekly*, 1 May 1988.

3 Pandian, M.S.S., *The Image Trap*, New Delhi: Sage Publications, 1992, p. 17.

4 *Dinamani*, 31 July 1985.

5 Ibid.

6 Karunanidhi, Kalaignar M., *Nenjukku Needhi*, vol. 3, Chennai: Thirumagal Nilayam, 2008, pp. 521–22.

7 Lakshmanan, Vidwan V., *Makkal Thilagam*, Chennai: Vanathi Pathippagam, 2002, p. 22. *Dinathanthi*, 22 February 2014, p. 23.

8   Arurdhas, *Kodambaakathil Arubadhu Aandugal*, Chennai: Vikatan
     Pirasuram, 2006, pp. 21–22.

9   Raju, Pulavar, *MGR Oru Thamizharae*, Chennai: Megathudan
     Pathippagam, 2010, p. 172; p. 187.

10   Kirubakaran, S., (ed.), *Naan Aanaiyitaal . . .!*, Chennai: Vikatan
     Pirasuram, 2014, p. 256; Arurdhas, *Naan Mugam Paartha Cinema
     Kannadigal*, Chennai: Kalaignan Pathippagam, 2002, pp. 50–51.

11   http://www.youtube.com/watch?v=rRj7oJ8bI2k.

12   Vidwan, *Makkal Thilagam*, p. 21; *Gundoosi*, November 1949, cited in
     Arandhai Narayanan, *Dravidam Paadiya Thiraipadangal*, Chennai: New
     Century Book House, 1994, p. 13.

13   Vidwan, *Makkal Thilagam*, pp. 21–22.

14   Nivedita, Charu, *Theerakkaathali*, Chennai: Uyirmai Pathippagam,
     2008, pp. 124–25; Muthukumar, R., *Vadhyar*, Chennai: Kizhakku
     Pathippagam, 2010, pp. 13–14.

15   Raju, *MGR Oru Thamizharae*, p. 185.

16   Vidwan *Makkal Thilagam*, p. 22; Sri Kantha, Sachi, 'MGR Remembered,
     Part 1', 12 December 2012, http://sangam.org/mgr-remembered-part-1.

17   Raju, *MGR Oru Thamizharae*, p. 185.

18   MGR, *Naan Yaen Pirandhen?*, part 1, Chennai: Kannadhasan
     Pathippagam, 2015, p. 259.

19   According to another account, family disputes had led to division of
     property and Gopala Menon's family had become poor. *Gundoosi*, cited
     in Arandhai Narayanan, *Dravidam Paadiya Thiraipadangal*, Chennai:
     New Century Book House, 1994, p. 13.

20   Vidwan, *Makkal Thilagam*, p. 23.

21   Vidwan, *Makkal Thilagam*, p. 23; , S., *M.G.R. Kathai*, part 2, Chennai:
     Arulmozhi Pathippagam, 1992, p. 38.

22   Vidwan, *Makkal Thilagam*, p. 23.

23   Kirubakaran, S., (ed.), *Naan Aanaiyitaal . . .!*, p. 220.

24   Nivedita, *Theerakkaathali*, pp. 126–27.

25   MGR, *Naan Yaen Pirandhen?*, part 1, pp. 225–32.

26   http://www.vikatan.com/news/coverstory/56762-mgrs-interview-
     by-jayalalitha.art.

27   MGR, *Naan Yaen Pirandhen?*, part 1, p., 220.

28   http://www.thehindu.com/arts/cinema/article2899646.ece.

29   http://www.vikatan.com/news/coverstory/56762-mgrs-interview-
     by-jayalalitha.art.

30   MGR, *Naan Yaen Pirandhen?*, part 1, pp. 515–56; Copper Cochin, *Profile – MGR a hero on and off the screen*, Spotlight on Tamil Nadu, pp. 27–31.

31   MGR, *Naan Yaen Pirandhen?*, part 1, pp. 515–56.

32   Ibid., pp., 523–26.

33   http://www.vikatan.com/news/coverstory/56762-mgrs-interview-by-jayalalitha.art.

34   MGR, *Naan Yaen Pirandhen?*, part 1, pp., 403–04.

35   Doctor Udayamurthi, *Americargal Paarvayil Mudhalvar Anna Makkal Thilagam M.G.R.*, Chennai: Vidwan Pathippagam, 2003, pp. 62–104.

36   MGR, *Naan Yaen Pirandhen?*, part 1, p., 484.

37   Ibid., pp. 338–40.

38   http://www.thehindu.com/todays-paper/tp-features/tp-fridayreview/gone-but-not-forgotten/article805318.ece?css=print.

39   MGR, *Naan Yaen Pirandhen?*, part 1, pp. 401–08.

40   KRR made his film debut with *Gumasthavin Penn* (Clerk's Daughter, 1941), but obtained an early break with *Poompavai* (The Flower Girl, 1944). Anna's *Velaikaari* (Servant Maid, 1948) and *Oar Iravu* (One Night, 1951) would add to his fame. His success, philanthropy and devotion to Anna and the party were unparalleled. In acknowledgement of KRR's histrionic gifts, 'Navalar (The Eloquent)' Era. Nedunchezhian of the DMK would later confer the title 'Nadipisai Pulavar (Exponent of Acting and Singing)' on him.

41   Santhanakrishnan, T., 'Kollywood Mudhal Hollywood Varai: Thirai Ulaga Athisayayngalum Arputhangalum', *Dhinathanthi*, 26 March 2016; Ramasamy, V.K., *Enadhu Kalaippayanam*, Chennai: New Century Book House, 2002, pp. 212-14; http://www.thehindu.com/features/cinema/k-r-ramaswamy-the-man-who-started-the-trend/article6429708.ece; Also see: Hardgrave, Robert L., 'Politics and the Film in Tamil Nadu', *Asian Survey*, March 1973, vol. 13, p. 289.

42   MGR, *Naan Yaen Pirandhen?*, part 1, pp.409–22; T.K.S. Brothers' company was reputed for its discipline and caring of its staff. Kannusamy Pillai was associated with the Madurai Thathuva Meenalosani Vithuva Bala Sabha of Sankaradas Swamigal. His third son, T.K. Shanmugam, excelled in theatre and the brothers—T.K. Sankaran, T.K. Muthusamy and T.K. Bagavathy—together came to be known as T.K.S. Brothers. Kalaivanar N.S. Krishnan, actors K.R. Ramasamy, S.S. Rajendran, D.V. Narayanasamy and director A.P. Nagarajan are some who were

mentored by the brothers. http://www.britannica.com/EBchecked/
topic/556016/South-Asian-arts/65263/Modern-theatre#ref532760;
http://www.thehindu.com/todays-paper/tp-national/tp-
tamilnadu/avvai-shanmugams-centenary-passes-off-without-fanfare/
article3366107.ece.

43 Kirubakaran, S., (ed.), M.G.R. Paetigal, Chennai: Vikatan Pirasuram,
    2009, p. 11.

44 MGR, Naan Yaen Pirandhen?, part 1, p.118.

45 Ibid., pp.430–46.

46 Ibid., pp. 109–10.

47 Ibid., pp.542–47.

48 Ibid., p. 343.

49 Ibid., pp.107–20.

50 Kirubakaran, S., (ed.), M.G.R. Paetigal, p. 11.

51 MGR, Naan Yaen Pirandhen?, part 1, p.447.

52 Ibid., p. 450.

53 Ibid., pp. 449–55, 464–70.

54 MGR, Naan Yaen Pirandhen?, part 2, p. 1420–26.

55 Ibid., pp. 1 391–92.

56 Mugil, Radhayanam, Chennai: Kizhakku Pathippagam, 2007, pp. 18–19.

57 Mugil,   Radhayanam,   pp.   20–3;   http://cinema.maalaimalar.
    com/2012/06/16112442/mr-radha-life-story.html.

58 Arurdhas, Naan Mugam Paartha Cinema Kannadigal, pp. 15–16.

59 'Radhayanam', Kumudam, 1960, cited in Arandhai Narayanan , 1–6, 38,
    42; Mugil, Radhayanam, pp. 44–45.

60 MGR, Naan Yaen Pirandhen?, part 2, pp. 1392, 1407–11.

61 MGR, Naan Yaen Pirandhen?, part 1, pp. 149–50.

62 MGR, Naan Yaen Pirandhen?, part 2, pp. 1415, 1422–26.

63 Ibid., pp. 853–62.

64 http://www.thehindu.com/todays-paper/tp-national/tp-tamilnadu/
    a-silent-witness-to-the-journeys-of-stars/article5356770.ece.

65 Kumudam, 27 April 2016, 47.

66 Doctor, Vikram, '1962 India-China war: Why India needed that
    jolt', 7 October 2012, http://economictimes.indiatimes.com/news/
    politics-and-nation/1962-india-china-war-why-india-needed-that-jolt/
    articleshow/msid-16703076,curpg-2.cms?from=mdr.

67 http://tamil.thehindu.com/opinion/blogs/100-6/article8271377.ece.

68 Dinamani Kathir, 14 August 1970.

69 Vijayan, M.G.R. Kathai, part 2, p. 43.

70 Raju, MGR Oru Thamizharae, p. 208.

71 Indian Express, 28 April 1987.

72 Balasingham, Anton, Viduthalai, Surrey: Fairmax Publishing Ltd, 2003, pp. 24–25.

73 Ibid., pp. 2–17; https://www.youtube.com/watch?v=ASx21@L03y0.

74 Arurdhas, 'Cinemavin Marupakkam', Dinathanthi, 22 February 2014, p. 23.

75 Vijayan, M.G.R. Kathai, part 2, pp.142–49.

76 Ibid., p. 60.

77 Ranimaindhan, RMV Oru Thondar, Chennai: Rajarajan Pathippagam, 2005, pp. 346–48.

78 Malai Murasu, 6 July 1987, cited in Pandian, The Image Trap, p. 103.

79 MGR, Naan Yaen Pirandhen?, part 1, pp. 636–41.

80 Balasingham, Viduthalai, pp. 14–17.

81 http://tamil.thehindu.com/opinion/blogs/எம்ஜிஆர்-100-11-என்என்ஸ்கிருஷ்ணன்-எனாம்-ஆசான்/article8298343.ece?ref=sliderNews.

82 https://www.youtube.com/watch?v=b6ISEImE240.

83 Kannadasan, Kavignar, Arangamum Andarangamum, Chennai: Kannadhasan Pathippagam, 2010, p. 8.

84 http://tamil.thehindu.com/cinema/tamil-cinema/எம-100-13-கண-வர-ஆணழகன/article8308866.ece.

Chapter 2: Stepping Into Cinema and Marriage

1 Kirubakaran S. (ed.), Naan Aanaiyitaal . . .!, Chennai: Vikatan Pirasuram, 2014, pp. 78–79.

2 MGR, Naan Yaen Pirandhen?, part 1, Chennai: Kannadhasan Pathippagam, 2015, p. 289.

3 Ibid., p. 343.

4 Ibid., p. 323–24.

5 In one of his articles in 1966, MGR says she kept the note at the bottom of Vishnu's image. Kirubakaran, S., (ed.), Naan Aanaiyitaal . . .!, p. 82.

6 Ibid.

7 In the autobiography, Kandasamy Mudaliar asks Marudachalam Chettiar to give the advance to the brothers and wish them well.

MGR, *Naan Yaen Pirandhen?*, part 1, pp. 291–97; Ravindar, K., *Vizha Nayagan MGR*, Chennai: Vijaya Publications, 2009, p. 28.

8   Barnouw, Erik and Krishnaswamy, S., *Indian Film*, New York: Columbia University Press, 1963, p. 173.

9   MGR, *Naan Yaen Pirandhen?*, part 1, p. 305–07.

10 Ibid., pp. 150–58.

11 Ibid., pp. 326–28; 483–84.

12 Bhaskaran, S. Theodore, *Message Bearers*, Chennai: Kizhakku Pathippagam, 2009, pp. 17–37

13 Thirunavukarasu, K., *Needhikatchi Varalaaru*, Chennai: Nakkheeran Pathippagam, 2013, p. 64.

14 MGR, *Naan Yaen Pirandhen?*, part 1, pp. 318–22.

15 Ibid., pp. 301–03.

16 MGR, *Naan Yaen Pirandhen?*, part 2, pp. 791–800, 807–10, 842–46; Kirubakaran, S., (ed.), *M.G.R. Paetigal*, Chennai: Vikatan Pirasuram, 2009, p. 21.

17 MGR, *Naan Yaen Pirandhen?*, part 1, pp. 293–95, 308–17.

18 Ibid., pp. 328–33.

19 Dungan, Ellis, *A Guide to Adventure: An Autobiography*, Pittsburgh: Dorrance Publishing Co., 2001, p. 103.

20 Arurdhas, *Kottaiyum Kodambakkamum*, Chennai: Vikatan Pirasuram, 2006, pp. 42–43.

21 MGR, *Naan Yaen Pirandhen?*, part 1, pp. 345–48.

22 Ibid., pp.893–95.

23 Ibid., pp.901–02.

24 Ibid., pp. 101–02.

25 Mentioned to the author by former mayor Sa. Ganesan, March 2015, Madras.

26 MGR, *Naan Yaen Pirandhen?*, part 1, p. 104.

27 MGR, *Naan Yaen Pirandhen?*, part 2, pp. 1413–14; http://www.outlookindia.com/magazine/story/the-ghost-who-talked/281007; http://cineplot.com/master-vithal-d-1969/.

28 MGR, *Naan Yaen Pirandhen?*, part 1, pp.122–26.

29 Ravindar, K., *Pon Mana Chemmal MGR*, Chennai: Vijaya Publications, 2009, pp. 148–50; Ravindar, *Vizha Nayagan MGR*, Chennai: Vijaya Publications, 2009, pp. 28, 31; http://tamil.thehindu.com/opinion/blogs/-100-4-/article8256809.ece; Rajaram, K., *Oru Saamaniyianin Ninaivugal*, Chennai: Nakkheeran Pathippagam, 2014, pp. 346–48.

30   MGR, *Naan Yaen Pirandhen?*, part 2, pp. 903–22.

31   http://www.youtube.com/watch?v=rRj7oJ8bI2k.

32   http://www.vikatan.com/article.php?aid=19576&sid=531&mid=1# cmt241.

33   MGR, *Naan Yaen Pirandhen?*, part 1, pp.235–36.

34   Ibid., pp. 237–80.

35   Ibid., pp. 136–38.

36   Ibid., p.88.

37   MGR, *Naan Yaen Pirandhen?*, part 1, pp.162–81; http://mgrperannews. blogspot.com/p/new-attractions-from-mgr-peran-blog.html.

38   MGR, *Naan Yaen Pirandhen?*, part 1, p. 186.

39   After two years of marriage, Thangamani's parents took her back, as life at her in-laws' place was unbearable because of the poverty. Twenty days later she died. Vijayan, *M.G.R. Kathai*, part 1, Chennai: Arulmozhi Pathippagam, 1992, p. 12.

40   Arurdhas, 'Cinemavin Marupakkam', *Dinathanthi*, 22 February 2014.

41   MGR, *Naan Yaen Pirandhen?*, part 2, pp. 948–74.

42   Ibid., pp. 1427–43.

43   Ibid., pp. 48–89.

44   MGR, *Naan Yaen Pirandhen?*, part 2, p. 1082.

45   Ibid., p. 1095.

46   Kirubakaran, S., (ed.), *Naan Aanaiyitaal . . .!*, pp. 27–29.

47   Ibid., pp. 27–28.

48   Ibid., p. 168.

49   Bharathan, M.S., *Nadigar MGR Pithalaatangal*, Chennai: Jhansirani Pathippagam, 1977, p. 12.

50   Vaali, *Enakkul M.G.R.*, Chennai: Kumaran Pathippagam, 2013, p. 127; http://www.thehindu.com/todays-paper/tp-features/tp-cinemaplus/ saalivaahanan-1945/article2135380.ece.

Chapter 3: The Lure of the Dravidian Movement

1   Parimalam (ed.), *Perarignar Annavin Than Varalaaru*, Chennai: Bharati Pathippagam, 1997, p. 47.

2   Kannadasan, Kavignar, *Vanavasaam*, Chennai: Vanathi Pathippagam, 2000, pp. 66, 113.

3   Kamaraj's mentor S. Satyamurti pioneered the use of the stage for political propaganda. He performed on stage and roped in other

artists such as singer–artist K.B. Sundarambal, the first actor MLC, to Congress meetings to rouse nationalist fervour.

4   Barnouw, Erik and Krishnaswamy, S., *Indian Film*, New York: Columbia University Press, 1963, p. 175.

5   Kirubakaran, S., (ed.), *M.G.R. Paetigal*, Chennai: Vikatan Pirasuram, 2009, p. 133.

6   Mugil, *Radhayanam*, Chennai: Kizhakku Pathippagam, 2007, pp. 138–39.

7   Ganesan, Sivaji, *Autobiography of an Actor*, Chennai: Sivaji Prabhu Charities Trust, 2002, p. 70.

8   http://www.frontline.in/arts-and-culture/cinema/cinema-for-a-cause/article5189240.ece.

9   Kirubakaran S. (ed.), *Naan Aanaiyitaal . . .!*, Chennai: Vikatan Pirasuram, 2014, pp. 19–23.

10 MGR, *Naan Yaen Pirandhen?*, part 2, Chennai: Kannadhasan Pathippagam, 2015, pp. 1052–53.

11 MGR, *Naan Yaen Pirandhen?*, part 1, p. 633; In an article on Anna in 1983, MGR noted the year as 1944. http://www.vikatan.com/news/coverstory/58518-anna-is-nationalist-mgr.art;   Thirunavukarasu, K., *Thi Mu Ka Varalaaru*, vol. 1 Chennai: Nakkheeran Pathippagam, Chennai: 2015, pp. 103–04.

12 Natarajan,M., (ed.), *Perarignar Annavin Sorpozhivugal*, vol. 2, Chennai: Tamil Arasi Pathippagam, 2001, p. 680.

13 http://www.ibef.org/industry/information-technology-india.aspx.

14 Doctor Udayamurthi, *Americargal Paarvayil Mudhalvar Anna Makkal Thilagam M.G.R.*, Chennai: Vidwan Pathippagam, 2003, p. 39.

15 MGR, *Naan Yaen Pirandhen?*, part 1, p. 633.

16 Narayanan, Arandhai, *Dravidam Paadiya Thiraipadangal*, Chennai: New Century Book House, 1994, pp. 81–82.

17 Natarajan, M., (ed.), *Perarignar Annavin Peruraigal*, p. 295.

18 http://tamil.thehindu.com/opinion/columns/அதிமுக-வெற்றி-பெறும்-என்பது-கற்பனை-ஆர்எம்வீரப்பன்-நேர்காணல்/article8429087.ece?homepage=true.

19 Karunanidhi, Kalaignar M., *Nenjuku Needhi*, vol. 2, Chennai: Thirumagal Nilayam, 2009, p. 98.

20 Thirunavukarasu, *Thi Mu Ka Varalaaru*, vol. 1, p. 119; Interview with Arurdhas, 26 May 2016, Chennai.

21 Kirubakaran, S., (ed.), *Naan Aanaiyitaal . . .!*, pp. 19–23.

22   Rajendran, S.S., *Naan Vandha Pathai*, Chennai: Agani Veliyeedu, 2014. p. 65; Interview with Arurdhas, 26 May 2016, Chennai.

23   MGR, *Naan Yaen Pirandhen?*, part 2, pp. 1059–60.

24   Arurdhas, *Naan Mugam Paartha Cinema Kannadigal*, Chennai: Kalaignan Pathippagam, 2002, p. 39.

25   Ganesan, *Autobiography of an Actor*, p. 221.

26   Ibid., pp. 14–33.

27   Ibid., p. 44.

28   Kirubakaran, S. (ed.), *M.G.R. Paetigal*, p. 16.

29   Ganesan, *Autobiography of an Actor*, pp. 74–80; Deenadhayalan, P., *Sivaji Nadigar Mudhal Thilagam Varai*, Chennai: Kizhakku Pathippagam, 2006, pp. 27–28.

30   Kirubakaran, S. (ed.), *M.G.R. Paetigal*, p. 22.

31   MGR, *Naan Yaen Pirandhen?*, part1, pp. 77–88.

32   Arurdhas, *Naan Mugam Paartha Cinema Kannadigal*, p. 99.

33   MGR, *Naan Yaen Pirandhen?*, part 1, pp. 73–88

34   Kirubakaran, S. (ed.), *M.G.R. Paetigal*, p. 93.

35   MGR, *Naan Yaen Pirandhen?*, part 1, pp. pp. 88–90.

36   T.S. Balaiah claims that he was booked as the hero initially and MGR was to play the villain. MGR pleaded with him to let him have the hero's role, as Balaiah could excel in any role, unlike him who depended on fights. Balaiah says he gave in to MGR, disregarding his family and friends' advice. Bharathan, M.S., *Nadigar MGR Pithalaatangal*, Chennai: Jhansirani Pathippagam, 1977, pp. 12–3.

37   MGR, *Naan Yaen Pirandhen?*, part 1, pp. 82–98.

38   Vijayan, S., *M.G.R. Kathai*, part 1, Chennai: Arulmozhi Pathippagam, 1992, p. 7; MGR, *Naan Yaen Pirandhen?*, part 1, pp. 569–70.

39   Kalaignar, *Nenjuku Needhi*, vol. 1, pp. 94–95.

40   Ibid., pp. 33–34.

41   http://tamil.thehindu.com/opinion/columns//article8450136.ece?homepage=true&theme=true.

42   Kalaignar, *Nenjuku Needhi*, vol. 1 Chennai: Thirumagal Nilayam, 2000, pp. 69–72

43   Ibid., pp. 43–45, 72–73.

44   Ibid., pp. 53–63.

45   Ibid., pp. 64, 73–75; Karunanidhi, Kalaignar M., *Kalaignarin Pasumai Ninaivugal*, Chennai: Bharathi Pathippagam, 2010, pp. 22–3.

46   Kalaignar, *Nenjuku Needhi*, vol. 1, pp. 80–83.

47 Ibid., pp. 77–80, 85–92.

48 In June 1971, at the opening of 'Karunanidhipuram', a housing settlement, MGR noted that their friendship had begun in Coimbatore. Owing to the spread of plague, Kalaignar had sent his family away and had come to board with him. http://www.vikatan.com/anandavikatan/Exclusive/28943-vikatan-medai-stalin.html#cmt241.

49 Kalaignar, *Nenjuku Needhi*, vol. 1, p. 95.

50 Ibid., pp. 99–100.

51 Arangannal, *Ninaivugal*, Chennai: Andal Pathippagam, 2000, part 1, pp. 66–67, 78–79.

52 Kalaignar, *Nenjuku Needhi*, vol. 1, pp. 101–07; Arangannal, *Ninaivugal*, part 1, pp. 9–10.

53 The Dravidian movement celebrated its people. Sampath was called 'Sollin Selvar (Silver-tongued Orator or Wordsmith)' by party men and Arangannal was the first to use the title Kavignar or poet before Kannadasan's name in *Dravida Nadu*. Arangannal, Ninaivugal, part 1, pp. 168–9.

54 MGR, *Naan Yaen Pirandhen?*, vol. 2, pp. 1458–59.

55 Kalaignar, *Nenjuku Needhi*, vol. 1, pp. 130–34.

56 MGR, vol. 2, 1248.

57 https://www.youtube.com/watch?v=X2c7LMEXd1U.

58 MGR, *Naan Yaen Pirandhen?*, vol. 2, p. 1257; a coy MGR does not openly say that he recommended Kalaignar.

59 Kannadasan, Kavignar, *Vanavaasam*, Chennai: Vanathi Pathippagam, 2000, pp. 113–14.

60 http://www.thehindu.com/features/cinema/naam-1953/article4252688.ece; Vijayan, S, *M.G.R. Kathai*, part 1, pp. 48–53.

61 MGR, *Naan Yaen Pirandhen?*, part 2, pp. 1323–28.

62 Arurdhas, *Sivaji Vendra Cinema Rajyam*, Chennai: Vikatan Pirasuram, 2009, p. 81.

63 Kalaignar, *Nenjuku Needhi*, vol. 1, pp. 141–43.

64 Vijayan, *M.G.R. Kathai*, part 2, p. 33.

65 Ibid., pp. 142–49.

66 MGR, *Naan Yaen Pirandhen?*, part 2, p. 1248.

67 http://www.frontline.in/arts-and-culture/cinema/cinema-for-a-cause/article5189240.ece; Initially KRR and the Telugu screen evergreen hero A. Nageswararao were considered, says Arurdhas. Arurdhas, *Sivaji Vendra Cinema Rajyam*, p. 83.

68   http://www.frontline.in/arts-and-culture/cinema/cinema-for-a-cause/
      article5189240.ece; Deenadhayalan, *Sivaji Nadigar Mudhal Thilagam
      Varai*, 31; Rajendran, *Naan Vandha Pathai*, p. 99; Once, at the time of the
      making of *Parasakthi*, when Kalaignar, poet Karunanandam and Sivaji
      Ganesan came to see Anna in Kanchipuram. Anna met them, but did not
      talk to them. He simply kept reading his journals and writing. Clearly,
      something had upset him. However, Kalaignar was tormented by this
      indifference that he cried on Arangannal's shoulders. If Anna was upset,
      his habit was to not speak. Arangannal, *Ninaivugal*, part 1, pp. 162–63.

69   Ganesan, *Autobiography of an Actor*, p. 77.

70   Ganesan, *Autobiography of an Actor*, pp. 74–80; Krishnan Panju, *Ennai
      Iyakkia Kadhanayagaral*, Naagai Dharuman (ed.), Chennai: Vijaya
      Publications, 2010, pp. 68–73; http://www.thehindu.com/features/
      cinema/parasakthi-1952/article1761261.ece.

71   Deenadhayalan, *Sivaji Nadigar Mudhal Thilagam Varai*, p. 123.

72   Ibid., p. 124.

73   Arangannal, *Ninaivugal*, part 1, pp. 176–77.

74   Ganesan, *Autobiography of an Actor*, p. 221.

75   Narayanan, *Dravidam Paadiya Thiraipadangal*, pp. 163–4.

76   Ibid., pp. 171–72.

77   http://www.thehindu.com/features/cinema/a-brief-history-of-
      nadigar-sangam/article7877460.ece.

78   Kalaignar, *Nenjuku Needhi*, vol. 5, pp. 664–65.

79   http://cinema.malaimalar.com (Transcripts of MGR's testimony)
      31 May–15 June 2012. In his testimony, MGR said that he was a
      'sympathizer' (and not yet a member), even at the time of the 15 July
      1953 Kallakudi agitation.

80   Thirunavukarasu, *Thi Mu Ka Varalaaru*, vol. 1, p. 540; Arangannal,
      Ninaivugal, part 1, p. 175.

81   In September 1953, at the second Tirunelveli district conference,
      Anna indicated that the Kazhagam as a social movement conducted
      conferences that attacked superstition and backward thinking. He
      said that it was artists who had helped spread backward beliefs and
      their songs and acting and make-up and dialogues had brought the
      country to the current lowly state. 'Therefore, for them to take back
      the poison they had planted, I have them with me. I bring them along!'
      Karunanandam, Kavigar, *Anna Sila Ninaivugal*, Chennai:Poovazhagi
      Pathippagam, 2012, pp. 199–201.

82 MGR, *Naan Yaen Pirandhen?*, part 1, pp. 571–75; *Dinamani Kadhir*, 28 August 1970.

83 *Dinamani Kadhir*, 28 August 1970.

84 MGR, *Naan Yaen Pirandhen?*, part 1, pp. 576, 585–87; 591–92.

Chapter 4: 'God On Earth': The Zealous Convert

1   Kirubakaran, S., (ed.), *M.G.R. Paetigal*, Chennai: Vikatan Pirasuram, 2009, p. 14.

2   Ibid., p. 42.

3   https://web.archive.org/web/20141121080016/http://tamil.thehindu.com/cinema/cinema-others/எம்ஜிஆர்-இல்லாமல்-நடந்த-எம்ஜிஆர்-படப்பிடிப்பா/article5812252.ece.

4   Arurdhas, 'Cinemavin Marupakkam,' *Dinathanthi*, 2 March 2013, p. 23.

5   Vijayan, S., *M.G.R. Kathai*, part 2, Chennai: Arulmozhi Pathippagam, 1992, p. 93.

6   Kirubakaran, S., (ed.), *M.G.R. Paetigal*, pp. 41–42.

7   Vaali, *Naanum Indha Nootraandum*, Chennai: Kalaignan Pathippagam, 1995, pp. 252–53.

8   Vijayan, *M.G.R. Kathai*, part 2, pp. 113–14.

9   Arangannal, Rama, *Ninaivugal*, Chennai: Andal Pathippagam, 2000, part 1, p.177; Ranimaindhan, *RMV Oru Thondar*, Chennai: Rajarajan Pathippagam, 2005, pp. 80–83; Rajendran, S.S., *Naan Vandha Pathai*, Chennai: Agani Veliyeedu, 2014, pp. 229–30.

10 Ranimaindhan, *RMV Oru Thondar*, p. 424.

11 Vijayan, *M.G.R. Kathai*, part 2, p. 120.

12 Ibid., pp. 114–15.

13 Ibid., p. 125.

14 Ibid, p. 130.

15 Ranimaindhan, *RMV Oru Thondar*, pp. 85–86.

16 MGR, *Naan Yaen Pirandhen?*, Chennai: Kannadhasan Pathippagam, 2015, part 2, p. 1138.

17 Vijayan, *M.G.R. Kathai*, part 1, p. 109.

18 Ibid., 121.

19 Ibid., 122.

20 Vijayan, *M.G.R. Kathai*, part 2, pp. 117–18.

21 MGR, *Naan Yaen Pirandhen?*, part 2, p. 1172.

22 Sudangan, *Suttachu Suttachu*, Chennai: Kizhakku Pathippagam, 2005, p. 234, 252.

23 Arurdhas, *Kottaiyum Kodambakkamum*, Chennai: Vikatan Pirasuram, 2006, pp. 130–31.

24 Arurdhas, *Naan Mugam Paartha Cinema Kannadigal*, Chennai: Kalaignan Pathippagam, 2002, pp. 87–88.

25 MGR, *Naan Yaen Pirandhen?*, part 2, pp. 923–27, 932–35; http://www. hindu.com/mp/2010/04/05/stories/2010040550910400.htm

26 MGR, *Naan Yaen Pirandhen?*, part 1, pp. 923–24.

27 Deenadhayalan, P., *Sivaji Nadigar Mudhal Thilagam Varai*, Chennai: Kizhakku Pathippagam, 2006, p. 92.

28 MGR, *Naan Yaen Pirandhen?*, part 2, pp. 1248–54.

29 The song followed the path set by Jupiter's *Kanjan* (Miser, 1947) in which Coimbatore C.A. Ayyamuthu's song '*Indha ulaganil ulla maandharil ezhiluduyoan engal Thamizhan* (In the world's people, our Tamils are the handsome ones)' played everywhere, and later the "*Vaazhga Vaazhgave valamaai emadhu Dravida Nade*' song of Bharatidasan in *Parasakthi* to propagate the DMK's ideals of Tamil/Dravidian pride and, initially, a homeland.

30 MGR, *Naan Yaen Pirandhen?*, part 1, pp. 25–45.

31 Sudangan, *Suttachu Suttachu*, p. 218.

32 Kalaignar, M., Karunanidhi, *Nenjuku Needhi*, vol. 1, Chennai: Thirumagal Nilayam, 2000, pp. 196–207, 254–5.

33 Kalaignar,, *Nenjuku Needhi*, vol. 3, pp. 521–22.

34 MGR, *Naan Yaen Pirandhen?*, part 1, p. 651

35 Vaali, *Enakkul M.G.R.*, Chennai: Kumaran Pathippagam, 2013, p. 140–42.

36 Interview with RMV, 15 September 2016, Madras.

37 Vaali, *Enakkul M.G.R.*, p. 142.

38 http://tamil.thehindu.com/opinion/blogs/என்னராமலை-தே·ரழி-25-நடிகையின்-கதை/article9518884.ece?widget-art=four-rel.

39 http://www.vikatan.com/article.php?aid=10240&sid=281&mid=1.

40 Doctor Udayamurthi, *Americargal Paarvayil Mudhalvar Anna Makkal Thilagam M.G.R.*, Chennai: Vidwan Pathippagam, 2003, pp. 62, 104.

41 The *New York Times*, 28 September 1974.

42 *Dinamani*, Deepavali issue, 1997, cited in P. Deenadhayalan's *Sivaji Nadigar Mudhal Thilagam Varai*, p. 119.

43 Ganesan, Sivaji, *Autobiography of an Actor*, Chennai: Sivaji Prabhu Charities Trust, 2002, p. 90.

44 Vijayan, *M.G.R. Kathai*, part. 2, pp. 154–55.

45 http://indiatoday.intoday.in/story/politics-like-films-is-a-matter-of-communicating-with-the-people-mgr/1/434435.html.

46 goondukilihttp://www.dinamani.com/junction/kanavukkannigal/2016/01/23/ட.-ர-3.க/article3239597.ece.

47 Vaali, *Enakkul M.G.R.*, pp. 202–03.

48 Kavigar Karunanandam, *Anna Sila Ninaivugal*, Chennai: Poovazhagi Pathippagam, 2012, pp. 43–44.

49 Udayamurthi, *Americargal Paarvayil Mudhalvar Anna Makkal Thilagam M.G.R.*, pp. 62–104.

50 http://www.vikatan.com/article.php?aid=19576&sid=531&mid=1#cmt241.

51 Vaali, *Enakkul M.G.R.*, 202–04.

52 Vijayan, *M.G.R. Kathai*, part 2, p. 100.

53 Vaali, *Enakkul M.G.R.*, pp. 205–08.

54 Arurdhas, *Naan Mugam Paartha Cinema Kannadigal*, pp. 36–39.

55 Mohandas, K., *MGR: The Man and the Myth*, Bangalore: Panther Publishers, 1992, p. 16.

56 Ranimaindhan, *RMV Oru Thondar*, p. 160.

57 Arurdhas, *Kottaiyum Kodambakkamum*, pp. 180–81.

58 Kirubakaran, S., (ed.), *M.G.R. Paetigal*, p. 70.

59 Mugil, *Kanneerum Punnagiyum*, Chennai: Kizhakku Pathippagam, 2005, pp. 37–49.

60 http://tamil.thehindu.com/opinion/blogs/எம்ஜிஆர்-100-68-சினிமாவிலாம்-பின்பற்றிய-தர்மம்/article8629442.ece?ref=relatedNews.

61 Kavignar Kannadasan, *Arangamum Andarangamum*, Chennai: Kannadhasan Pathippagam, 2010, p. 10.

62 Vaali, *Naanum Indha Nootraandum*, p. 253

63 Ravindar, K., *Pon Mana Chemmal MGR*, Chennai: Vijaya Publications, 2009, p. 104.

64 http://tamil.thehindu.com/opinion/blogs/எம்ஜிஆர்-100-11-என்எஸ்கிருஷ்ணன்-எனாம்-ஆசான்/article8298343.ece?ref=sliderNews.

65 http://tamil.thehindu.com/cinema/tamil-cinema/எம-100-13-கண்வர-ஆணழகன/article8308866.ece; http://www.thehindu.com/features/cinema/article3363973.ece.

66 Ibid.

67 http://tndipr.gov.in/memorials/kaviarasarkannadasanmanimandapam.html.
68 Vaali, *Enakkul,* pp. 234–59.
69 Ibid., pp. 123–24.
70 Vaali, *Enakkul,* pp. 39–44.
71 Ibid., pp. 44–45.
72 Ibid., pp. 45–46.
73 Mugil, *Kanneerum Punnagiyum,* pp. 58–63.
74 Vijayan, *M.G.R. Kathai,* part 2, p. 93.
75 Ibid., pp. 82–90.
76 MGR, *Naan Yaen Pirandhen?*, part 2, pp. 1196–97.
77 http://www.thehindu.com/todays-paper/tp-features/tp-cinemaplus/article3023424.ece.
78 *The Hindu* (Tamil), 29 April 2016.
79 Kirubakaran, S., (ed.) *M.G.R. Paetigal,* p. 39.
80 Sudangan, *Suttachu Suttachu,* p. 115.
81 Ganesan, *Autobiography of an Actor,* p. 110.
82 Narayanaswamy, T.S., ed., *Sivaji Ganesan: Enadhu Suya Saridhai,* Chennai: Sivaji Prabhu Charities Trust, 2002, p. 134; Arurdhas, *Sivaji Vendra Cinema Rajyam,* Chennai: Vikatan Pirasuram, 2009, p. 47; Poet Kannadasan published a still from Ganesan's *Tenaliraman* (1956), for which he had penned the dialogues, showing Ganesan buried neck deep, waiting to be trampled by an elephant, with the caption 'Sivaji Ganesan's Future'.
83 Kirubakaran, S., (ed.), *M.G.R. Paetigal,* p. 14.
84 Ibid., pp. 51–2.
85 Kalaignar, *Nenjuku Needhi,* vol. 2, pp. 95–96.
86 Arangannal, *Ninaivugal,* part 1, p. 203.
87 Ganesan, *Autobiography of an Actor,* p. 221.
88 Ibid., p. 116.
89 Ibid., p. 175.
90 http://mgrroblogspot.com/2014/01/great-chief-minister.html.
91 http://tamil.thehindu.com/opinion/blogs/எம்ஜிஆர்-100-26-படம்-ஓடினால்-மன்னன்-ஓடாவிட்டால்-நாடோடி/article8384172.ece.
92 *DMK Silver Jubilee Souvenir,* pp. 55–6, 159.
93 Rajendran, *Naan Vandha Pathai,* pp. 127–28.
94 Kalaignar, *Nenjuku Needhi,* vol. 1, p. 351.
95 MGR, *Naan Yaen Pirandhen?*, part 2, pp. 1449–51.

96   MGR, *Naan Yaen Pirandhen?*, part 1, pp. 628–32.

97   Lakshmanan, Vidwan -V., *Makkal Thilagam*, Chennai: Vanathi Pathippagam, 2002, p. 14.

98   http://www.thehindu.com/todays-paper/tp-miscellaneous/dated-august-31-1957-ns-krishnan-dead/article1902218.ece.

99   Kirubakaran, S., (ed.), *M.G.R. Paetigal*, p. 13–16.

100 Rajendran, *Naan Vandha Pathai*, pp. 121–23; http://tamil.thehindu.com/opinion/blogs/எம்ஜிஆர்-100-7-பே·ராட்டமுவிமர்சனமும்/article8274942.ece?homepage=true.

101 MGR, *Naan Yaen Pirandhen?*, part 2, pp. 1112–16.

102 Ibid., pp. 1177–82.

103 Kirubakaran, S., (ed.), *Naan Aanaiyitaal . . .!*, Chennai: Vikatan Pirasuram, 2014, p. 101.

104 Vaali, *Enakkul M.G.R.*, pp. 213–14.

105 Kirubakaran, S., (ed.), *Naan Aanaiyitaal . . .!*, p. 130.

106 Ravindar, *Pon Mana Chemmal*, p. 33; Kirubakaran, S., (ed.), *Naan Aanaiyitaal . . .!*, p. 111.

107 Arurdhas, 'Cinemavin Marupakkam', *Dinathanthi*, 2 February 2013, p. 19.

108 But they did act together in *Raja Desingu* (1960) and *Kanchi Thalaivan* (1963), and MGR honoured her with the Kalaimamani award in 1983. He also appointed her as principal of the Tamil Nadu Music College. An overjoyed Bhanumathi rang MGR up and, later Janaki, to express her thanks. Arurdhas, 'Cinemavin Marupakkam', *Dinathanthi*, 26 January 2013, p. 21.

109 Kirubakaran, S., (ed.), *Naan Aanaiyitaal . . .!*, p. 133, 174.

110 Ranimaindhan, *RMV Oru Thondar*, pp. 110–11.

111 Jagathrakshakan, S., *MGR: A Phenomenon*, Chennai: Apollo Veliyeetagam, 1984, p. 64.

112 Kirubakaran, S., (ed.), *M.G.R. Paetigal*, p. 115.

113 Vidwan, *Makkal Thilagam*, p. 39.

114 The first one was at Thyagaraja College in north Madras, a bastion of the DMK. Finance Minister C. Subramaniam presided over the 28 September event, with an estimated 50,000 people in attendance. Thirunavukarasu, K., *Thi Mu Ka Varalaaru*, vol. 3 Chennai: Nakkheeran Pathippagam, Chennai: 2015, pp. 1760–62.

115 Vidwan, *Makkal Thilagam*, p. 41–47; Thirunavukarasu, *Thi Mu Ka Varalaaru*, vol. 3, pp. 1763–7.

116 Vidwan, *Makkal Thilagam*, p. 47–48.

117 Villalan, Thillai, 'Arnavin Idhayam', *Porvaal* Anna special issue, 1980, vol. 22; Ranimaindhan, *RMV Oru Thondar*, p. 117.

118 Ranimaindhan, *RMV Oru Thondar*, p. 122–23.

119 Kirubakaran, S., (ed.), *M.G.R. Paetigal*, p. 197.

120 Kirubakaran, S., (ed.), *Naan Aanaiyitaal . . .!*, p. 169–70.

121 Kirubakaran, S., (ed.), *M.G.R. Paetigal*, p. 32–33.

122 MGR, *Naan Yaen Pirandhen?*, part 1, pp. 657–58.

123 Kirubakaran, S., (ed.), *M.G.R. Paetigal*, p. 32–33.

124 MGR, *Naan Yaen Pirandhen?*, part 2, p. 1121.

125 Ibid., p. 1121.

126 Ibid., pp. 1143–44.

127 Ibid., p. 1121.

128 Bhaskaran, Theodore, *The Eye of the Serpent: An Introduction to Tamil Cinema*, Chennai: Tranquebar Press, 2008, p. 239.

129 Vidwan, *Makkal Thilagam*, p. 14.

130 MGR, *Naan Yaen Pirandhen?*, part 2, pp.1116–21, 1126–36.

131 MGR, *Naan Yaen Pirandhen?*, part 1, pp. 603–05.

132 Ibid., pp. 642–44.

133 Ranimaindhan, *RMV Oru Thondar*, p. 125.

134 Arurdhas, *Kottaiyum Kodambakkamum*, pp. 75–77.

135 Ranimaindhan, *RMV Oru Thondar*, p. 137–9.

136 Kirubakaran, S., (ed.), *M.G.R. Paetigal*, p. 26.

137 MGR, *Naan Yaen Pirandhen?*, part 2, pp. 1459–62.

138 Ibid.

139 Ibid

140 Ibid.

141 Arurdhas, *Naan Mugam Paartha Cinema Kannadigal*, pp. 167–68.

142 Interview with Arurdhas, 26 May 2016, Madras.

143 Ibid.

144 Ibid.

145 http://tamil.thehindu.com/opinion/blogs/எம்ஜிஆர்-100-89-நடிகர்-நலனில்-அக்கறை-கொண்டவர்/article8744629.ece?ref=relatedNews.

146 http://tamil.thehindu.com/opinion/blogs/எம்ஜிஆர்-100-97-பொய்க்காலில்-அல்ல-பாகழ்க்காலில்-நிற்கும்-உயரம்/article8791605.ece?ref=relatedNews.

147 Arangannal, *Ninaivugal*, part 1, p. 198; B.R. Panthulu who had made *Kattabomman* (1959), *Kappalotiya Thamizhan* (The Tamil who Launched

Shipping, 1961) and *Karnan* (1964) had left him to make *Ayirathil Oruvan* (One in a Thousand, 1965) and *Nadodi* (Nomad, 1966), while G.N. Velumani who had done *Bagapirivanai* (Property Partition, 1969) and *Paalum Pazhamum* (Milk and Fruit, 1961) went over to MGR to do *Panathoattam, Padagoti, Kalangarai Vilakkam* (Light House, 1965) and *Chandrodhyam* (Moon Rise, 1966). P.S. Veerappa who did *Aalayamani* (Temple Bell, 1962) and *Andavan Kattalai* (Lord's Orders, 1964) had gone over to MGR to do *Ananda Jothi* (Flame of Happiness, 1963). A.P. Nagarajan who did *Navarathiri* (Nine Nights, 1964), *Thiruvilayadal, Thiruvarutchelvar* (1967) *Thillana Mohanambal* (1968) had gone over over to MGR to do *Navarathinam* (Nine Jewels, 1977) during his lean times. Sridhar who did *Nenjirukkum Varai* (Until the Heart Lasts, 1966) and *Sivandha Mann* (Red Sand, 1969) turned to MGR to make *Urimaikural* (The Voice of Rights, 1974). Interview with scriptwriter Arurdhas, 25 May 2016, Madras.

148 Arurdhas, *Kottaiyum Kodambakkamum*, pp. 142–47.
149 Ibid, pp. 167–68.
150 Arangannal, *Ninaivugal*, part 1, p. 200.
151 MGR, *Naan Yaen Pirandhen?*, part 1, pp. 52–57.
152 Arurdhas, *Naan Mugam Paartha Cinema Kannadigal*, p. 98.
153 Ibid., pp. 96–99.
154 Kannadasan, *Arangamum Andarangamum*, p. 4.
155 Ibid., 5.
156 Ibid.
157 Ibid, p. 11.
158 Kavignar Kannadasan, *MGR'in Ullum Puramum*, Chennai: Muthiah Publisher, 1974, pp. 39–41.
159 Interview with Arurdhas, 26 May 2016, Madras.
160 Kavignar Kannadasan: *Santhithaen Sinthithaen*, Chennai: Kannadhasan Pathippagam, 2013, pp. 89–92.
161 MGR, *Naan Yaen Pirandhen?*, part 1, pp. 46–65.
162 MGR, *Naan Yaen Pirandhen?*, part 2, pp.1177–82.
163 Vijayan, *M.G.R. Kathai*, part 1, p. 64.
164 MGR, *Naan Yaen Pirandhen?*, part 2, pp. 1177–82.
165 *Thenral*, 25 February 1961.
166 Kirubakaran, S., (ed.), *M.G.R. Paetigal*, pp. 49–50
167 Ganesan, *Autobiography of an Actor*, p. 128.
168 Kalaignar, *Nenjuku Needhi*, vol. 2, p. 366.

169 MGR, *Naan Yaen Pirandhen?*, part 1, pp. 654–56.

170 Kalaignar, *Nenjuku Needhi*, vol. 2, pp. 23–24.

171 Arangannal, *Ninaivugal*, part 1, pp. 210–11.

172 Kannan, R., *Anna: The Life and Times of C.N. Annadurai*, Delhi: Penguin Viking, 2010, p. 248.

173 Kavignar, *MGR'in Ullum Puramum*, pp. 11–12.

174 Kalaignar, *Nenjuku Needhi*, vol. 2, pp. 369–76; see Kannan, *Anna*, pp. 234–54.

175 Kirubakaran, S., (ed.), *M.G.R. Paetigal*, p. 44–45.

176 Rajendran, *Naan Vandha Pathai*, pp. 244–45.

177 MGR, *Naan Yaen Pirandhen?*, part. 2, p. 1239.

178 Ranimaindhan, *RMV Oru Thondar*, p. 180.

179 MGR, *Naan Yaen Pirandhen?*, part. 2, pp. 1228–42.

180 Kirubakaran, S., (ed.), *Naan Aanaiyitaal . . .!*, p. 235.

181 Vijayan, *M.G.R. Kathai*, part 2, pp. 2–3.

182 MGR, *Naan Yaen Pirandhen?*, part 2, p. 1208.

183 Kirubakaran, S., (ed.), *Naan Aanaiyitaal . . .!*, p. 36–37.

184 Ibid., pp. 38–42.

185 Vidwan, *Makkal Thilagam*, pp. 13–6.

186 http://www.rediff.com/movies/dec/24siv.htm.

187 Kirubakaran, S., (ed.), *Naan Aanaiyitaal . . .!*, pp. 20, 43–45, 47–48.

188 Vijayan, *M.G.R. Kathai*, part 1, p. 95.

189 http://www.frontline.in/arts-and-culture/cinema/cinema-for-a-cause/article5189240.ece.

190 Kalaignar, *Nenjuku Needhi*, vol. 1, pp. 635–36.

191 Kannan, *Anna*, p. 277.

192 Vijayan, *M.G.R. Kathai*, part 2, p. 99.

193 Interview with RMV, 15 September 2016, Madras.

194 Sudangan, *Suttachu Suttachu*, pp. 213–14.

195 Ibid.

196 Kannan, *Anna*, pp. 279–81.

197 Sudangan, *Suttachu Suttachu*, pp. 222–23.

198 Ibid., p. 217.

199 Vijayan, *M.G.R. Kathai*, part 2, p. 99. For the speech, see *Maalai Malar*, Kamarajar Birthday Special Issue, 2010, p. 21.

200 Sudangan, *Suttachu Suttachu*, p. 105.

201 Kirubakaran, S., (ed.), *Naan Aanaiyitaal . . .!*, p. 63–66.

202 Vaali, *Enakkul M.G.R.*, pp. 172–79.

203 *Murasoli*, 1967, http://murasoli.in:8080/murasoli/home.jsp.

204 http://tamil.thehindu.com/opinion/blogs/எம்ஜிஆர்-100-93-சிறந்த-க⸱⸱ட⸱யாளி/article8768435.ece?ref=relatedNews.

205 Ibid.

206 *Murasoli*, 19, 23, 26, 27, 29, 30 October 1965, http://murasoli.in:8080/murasoli/home.jsp; Sachi, Sri Kantha, http://sangam.org/mgr-remembered-part-32/.

207 MGR, *Naan Yaen Pirandhen?*, part 2, pp. 1177–82.

208 Kirubakaran, S., (ed.), *Naan Aanaiyitaal . . .!*, p. 70.

209 MGR, *Naan Yaen Pirandhen?*, part 2, pp. 1177–82.

210 https://www.youtube.com/watch?v=DzqLo_1SPZg.

211 Ibid.

212 Ibid.

213 http://tamil.thehindu.com/opinion/blogs/எம்ஜிஆர்-100-2-எம்ஜிஆரின்-அக்கறை/article8247753.ece.

214 Jayalalithaa, 'Manam Thirandhu Solgiraen', *Kumudam*. (Do we have a date here?) NO. It is from late 1978 for 24 weeks. The photocopy I have has no dates regretfully.

215 Ibid.

216 Ibid.

217 Vaasanthi, *Amma: Jayalalithaa's Journey from Movie Star to Political Queen*, Delhi: Juggernaut, 2016, p.38.

218 http://tamil.thehindu.com/opinion/blogs/எம100-2-எம-அக/article8247753.ece.

219 Kirubakaran, S., (ed.), *M.G.R. Paetigal*, p. 102.

220 http://tamil.thehindu.com/opinion/blogs/எம்ஜிஆர்-100-7-இந்தி-எதிர்ப்பு-போராட்டமாம்-விமர்சனமாம்/article8274942.ece?homepage=true.

221 Manimozhi and N. Manimaran, *Hindi Adhika Ethirpu Poril Puratchithalaivar*, Chennai: Pudhiya Bhoomi Pathippagam, 1987, p.141; Kalaignar, *Nenjuku Needhi*, vol. 1, p. 635.

222 Kirubakaran, S., (ed.), *M.G.R. Paetigal*, p. 235.

223 *Kumudam*, 6 November 2013, pp. 54–6; Manimozhi and Manimaran, *Hindi Adhika Ethirpu Poril Puratchithalaivar*, pp. 142–43.

224 Kavignar, *Arangamum Andarangamum*, p. 8.

225 http://www.thehindu.com/books/the-tragic-story-of-a-comedian-jp-chandrababu/article4313909.ece.

226 Mugil, *Kanneerum Punnagiyum*, pp. 131–33.

227 Arurdhas, *Naan Mugam Paartha Cinema Kannadigal*, pp. 190–99.

228 Mugil, *Kanneerum Punnagiyum*, p. 131.

229 http://tamil.thehindu.com/opinion/blogs/எம100-2-எம-அக/article8247753.ecehttp://tamil.thehindu.com/opinion/blogs/எம்ஜிஆர்-100-31-சந்திரபாபா-நட்பா/article8408679.ece.

230 Jagathrakshakan, *MGR: A Phenomenon*, p. 117.

231 http://web.archive.org/web/20160629143536/http://cinema.dinamalar.com/cinema-news/26078/special-report/Anbe-Vaa-in-50th-Year.htm.

232 M. Saravanan: *AVM.60 Cinema*, Chennai: Rajarajan Pathippagam, 2006, pp.159–79; http://web.archive.org/web/20141006211657/http://articles.economictimes.indiatimes.com/2010-03-20/news/27598199_1_avm-productions-hindi-films-ms-guhan.

233 http://murasoli.in:8080/murasoli/home.jsp.

234 Arurdhas, *Naan Mugam Paartha Cinema Kannadigal*, p.166.

235 *Murasoli*, 13 January 1965 http://murasoli.in:8080/murasoli/home.jsp.

236 *Murasoli*, 1 April 1965 http://murasoli.in:8080/murasoli/home.jsp.

237 Kirubakaran, S., (ed.), *Naan Aanaiyitaal . . .!*, p. 51.

238 Ibid., pp. 96–7

239 It would take six hours for the conference procession to pass through. An estimated 15,000 bicycles, 500 buses, and many lakhs of people took part in the rally. It was a spectacular show. Kavignar Karunanandam, *Thanthai Periyar Vazhkai Varalaaru*, Chennai: Arulbharathi Pathippagam, 2012, pp. 423–29.

240 Kalaignar, *Nenjuku Needhi*, vol. 1, pp. 663–64.

241 Ranimaindhan, *RMV Oru Thondar*, p.198.

242 Kannan, Anna, pp. 300-01.

243 Ranimaindhan, *RMV Oru Thondar*, p. 198–99.

244 http://murasoli.in:8080/murasoli/home.jsp; *Murasoli*, 10 August 1967 http://murasoli.in:8080/murasoli/home.jsp .

245 *Murasoli*, 10 August 1967, http://murasoli.in:8080/murasoli/home.jsp.

246 Mugil, *Kanneerum Punnagiyum*, pp. 138–39.

247 *Murasoli*, 1967, http://murasoli.in:8080/murasoli/home.jsp.

248 *Murasoli*, 4 September 1967, http://murasoli.in:8080/murasoli/home.jsp.

249 *Murasoli*, 1967, http://murasoli.in:8080/murasoli/home.jsp.

250 Jagathrakshakan, *MGR: A Phenomenon*, p. 196.

251 MGR, *Naan Yaen Pirandhen?*, part 2, pp. 568–9.

252 Interview with Arurdhas, 26 May 2016, Madras.

253 Kannan, *Anna*, pp. 300–01.

254 Ranimaindhan, *RMV Oru Thondar*, p. 200.

255 *Dinamalar*, 30 April 2016, p. 7.

256 Ranimaindhan, *RMV Oru Thondar*, pp. 202–04.

257 *Dinathanthi*, 17 April 2016, p. 15.

258 http://murasoli.in:8080/murasoli/home.jsp.

259 *Dinathanthi*, 17 April 2016, p. 15.

260 Kannan, *Anna*, pp. 305–06.

261 Interview with RMV, 15 September 2016, Madras.

262 http://tamil.thehindu.com/opinion/blogs/எம்ஜிஆர்-100-18-ஆங்கிள்-பார்த்த-எம்ஜிஆர்/article8335068.ece?homephttp://tamil.thehindu.com/opinion/blogs/எம்ஜிஆர்-100-91-ரசிர்களளுக்கு-மதிப்பளித்து-மகிழ்ச்சிப்படுத்தியவர்/article8759640.ece

263 MGR, *Naan Yaen Pirandhen?*, part 2, pp. 1177–82.

264 http://tamil.thehindu.com/opinion/blogs/எம்ஜிஆர்-100-1-அண்ணா-குறிப்பிட்ட-கவிதை/article8244262.ece?homepage=true.

265 MGR, *Naan Yaen Pirandhen?*, part 2, pp. 1248–54.

266 Ibid.

267 Kirubakaran, S., (ed.), *M.G.R. Paetigal*, p. 80

268 *Murasoli*, 16 August 1967.

269 MGR, *Naan Yaen Pirandhen?*, part 2, p. 631.

270 Ibid., 631–37.

271 Arangannal, *Ninaivugal*, part 2, p. 33.

Chapter 5: From Kingmaker to King

1 Kavignar Kannadasan, *Vanavasaam*, Chennai: Vanathi Pathippagam, 2000, p. 190.

2 Kirubakaran, S., (ed.), *M.G.R. Paetigal*, Chennai: Vikatan Pirasuram, 2009, p. 75.

3 Nendunchezhian, Navalar Era., *Vazhvil Naan Kandathum Kaethaum*, Chennai: Navalar Nedunchezhian Kalvi Arakattalai, 2000, pp. 476–77.

4 http://www.thehindu.com/news/cities/chennai/a-silent-witness-to-the-journeys-of-stars/article5355453.ece?homepage=true.

5   Vaasanthi, *Cut-Outs. Caste and Cine Stars: The World of Tamil Politics,*
     Delhi: Penguin, 2006, p. 69.

6   Karunanidhi, Kalaignar M., *Nenjuku Needhi*, vol. 2, Chennai:
     Thirumagal Nilayam, 2009, pp. 27–28.

7   Ibid., pp. 344–45.

8   *Dinamani*, 28 April 2016.

9   While discussing the ministerial representative for Chengalpattu
     district he would, in the end, ask why the discussants had not suggested
     him. I am grateful for this information to the late DMK functionary
     Karikalan who was at the meeting.

10   Kalaignar, *Nenjuku Needhi*, vol. 2, pp. 28–29, 195–96.

11   Ibid., pp. 28–29, 31, 39.

12   Ibid., p. 145.

13   Navalar, *Vazhvil Naan Kandathum Kaethaum*, p. 483.

14   Karunanandam, Kavignar, *Thanthai Periyar Vazhkai Varalaaru*,
     Chennai: Arulbharathi Pathippagam, 2012, p. 667.

15   Arangannal, Rama, *Ninaivugal*, part 2, Chennai: Andal Pathippagam,
     2000, p. 42–43.

16   Kalaignar, *Nenjuku Needhi*, vol. 2, pp. 146–51.

17   Ibid., p. 177.

18   http://www.thehindu.com/todays-paper/tp-features/tp-metroplus/
     a-small-tribute-to-a-big-legend/article5994347.ece.

19   Mohandas, K., *MGR. The Man and the Myth*, Bangalore: Panther
     Publishers, 1992, p. 4.

20   Kalaignar, *Nenjuku Needhi*, vol. 2, p. 211.

21   Ibid., p. 226.

22   http://www.assembly.tn.gov.in/archive/reviews/
     Review_5_1971_1976.pdf.

23   http://www.thehindu.com/news/national/tamil-nadu/priest-
     appointments-to-tn-temples-only-as-per-agama-sastra-supreme-
     court/article7995839.ece.

24   https://www.countercurrents.org/radhakrishnan100212.pdf.

25   Kalaignar, *Nenjuku Needhi*, vol. 2, pp. 429–31.

26   Arunan, *M.G.R: Nadigar Mudhalvar Aanadhu Eppadi?*, Madurai:
     Vasantham Veliyeetagam, 2006, p. 109.

27   MGR, *Naan Yaen Pirandhen?*, part 1, Chennai: Kannadhasan
     Pathippagam, 2015, pp. 621–25.

28   *Dinamani Kathir*, 14 and 21 August 1970.

29 Interviews with Pulavar Pulamaipithan, 21 May 2012, and S. Ramachandran, 27 August 2016, Madras. Vaali, *Enakkul M.G.R.*, Chennai: Kumaran Pathippagam, 2013, p. 142,

30 Kalaignar, *Nenjuku Needhi*, vol. 2, pp. 261–62.

31 Ibid., pp. 268–69.

32 Vaali, *Enakkul M.G.R.*, pp. 263–66

33 http://www.vikatan.com/news/article.php?aid=49833.

34 MGR, *Naan Yaen Pirandhen?*, part 1, pp. 719–20.

35 MGR, *Naan Yaen Pirandhen?*, part 2, pp. 1177–82.

36 http://www.newindianexpress.com/states/tamil-nadu/2016/dec/06/i-dont-think-anyone-has-taken-more-criticism-than-i-have-jaya-told-simi-garewal-1546016.html.

37 https://www.youtube.com/watch?v=DzqLo_1SPZg.

38 http://tamil.thehindu.com/opinion/blogs/என்னரா மலை-தோழி-18-அன்றே-கொடுத்த-ஷீல்டு/article9501139.ece?ref=relatedNews.

39 http://www.newindianexpress.com/states/tamil-nadu/2016/dec/06/i-dont-think-anyone-has-taken-more-criticism-than-i-have-jaya-told-simi-garewal-1546016.html.

40 Ranimaindhan, *RMV Oru Thondar*, Chennai: Rajarajan Pathippagam, 2005, pp. 225, 234–5; interview with RMV, 15 September 2016, Madras.

41 MGR, *Naan Yaen Pirandhen?*, part 2, pp. 1350–52.

42 http://tamil.thehindu.com/opinion/blogs/எம்ஜிஆர்-100-20-அசைவ-உணவைப்-பிரியர்/article8345864.ece#comments.

43 Kirubakaran, S., (ed.), *Naan Aanaiyitaal . . .!*, Chennai: Vikatan Pirasuram, 2014, pp. 163, 166–69.

44 MGR, *Naan Yaen Pirandhen?*, part 1, pp. 672–73.

45 Kalaignar, *Nenjuku Needhi*, vol. 2, pp. 277–82.

46 Karunanandam, *Thanthai Periyar Vazhkai Varalaaru*, p. 602.

47 Arurdhas, *Kodambaakathil Arubadhu Aandugal*, Chennai: Manivasagar Pathippagam, 2011, pp. 159–60.

48 Vijayan, S., *M.G.R. Kathai*, part 2, Chennai: Arulmozhi Pathippagam, 1992, p. 56–57.

49 http://murasoli.in:8080/murasoli/home.jsp.

50 Ranimaindhan, *RMV Oru Thondar*, pp. 244–47; interview with RMV, 15 September 2016, Madras.

51 Karunanandam, *Thanthai Periyar Vazhkai Varalaaru*, p. 609.

52   Vaasanthi, *Cut-Outs, Caste and Cine Stars: The World of Tamil Politics*, Delhi: Penquin, 2006, p. 69) http://eci.nic.in/eci_main/StatisticalReports/SE_1971/StatReport_TN_71.pdf; http://en.wikipedia.org/wiki/Tamil_Nadu_Legislative_Assembly_election,_1971.
     Navalar, *Vazhvil Naan Kandathum Kaethaum* 493.

53   *India Today*, 1–15 August 1978, pp. 39–40.

54   Navalar, *Vazhvil Naan Kandathum Kaethaum*, p. 494.

55   Vaasanthi, *Cut-Outs, Caste and Cine Stars: The World of Tamil Politics*, 71.

56   Kirubakaran, S., (ed.), *Naan Aanaiyitaal . . .!*, pp. 160–62.

57   Kalaignar, *Nenjuku Needhi*, vol 2, pp. 283–91.

58   MGR, *Naan Yaen Pirandhen?*, part 1, pp. 721–54.

59   Ibid.,pp. 812–13.

60   Ibid., *Naan Yaen Pirandhen?*, part 2, p. 1166.

61   Ibid., pp. 812–13.

62   Ibid., pp. 880–87.

63   Ibid., p. 880. Prior to lifting prohibition, Kalaignar had asked the Centre to grant assistance to continue prohibition, only to receive the explanation that states where prohibition was already in place would not be given any subsidy. 'Is this the punishment for enforcing prohibition?' he demanded. When criticized for his actions, Kalaignar said that Tamil Nadu was like camphor surrounded by a ring of fire—referring to the wet neighbouring states.
     Earlier, on 20 July, Rajaji had visited Kalaignar at his residence and pleaded for the retention of the status quo. Neither leader spoke of the twenty-minute meeting. Subsequently, the Kalaignar government was charged with 'trampling' on Anna's 'avowed wishes'. Kalaignar hit back, pointing to Congress-ruled states without prohibition. 'Does it mean they have all given up the Gandhian ideology or [have] forgotten Gandhiji?' he asked. Kalaignar said the government would get a revenue of 26 crore rupees annually. The yearly revenue from taxes then was around 210 crore rupees. When he reintroduced prohibition in 1973, he asked for a central assistance of 29 crore rupees, which did not come through and prohibition was again lifted for financial reasons. http://www.vikatan.com/news/article.php?aid=49833.

64   MGR, *Naan Yaen Pirandhen?*, part 2, pp. 880–87.

65   MGR, pp. 1164–74.

66   Murasoli Maran, *Manila Suyatchi (State Autonomy)*, Chennai: Murasoli, 1974, pp. 496-7.

67 Kalaignar, *Nenjuku Needhi*, vol 2, p. 338.

68 http://www.thehindu.com/news/national/tamil-nadu/it-was-an-opportunity-for-dmk-to-cleanse-itself/article8177113.ece.

69 MGR, *Naan Yaen Pirandhen?*, part 2, p. 1167.

70 Kalaignar, *Nenjuku Needhi*, vol. 2, p. 342.

71 Mohandas, *MGR: The Man and the Myth*, p. 7.

72 http___archives_Archives_JV_1992_Mar_25-3-92_25031992aJV.jpg.

73 https://www.youtube.com/watch?v=SfPO9j3A9BM.

74 Kalaignar, *Nenjuku Needhi*, vol. 2, pp. 348–49.

75 Ibid., pp. 344–45.

76 MGR, *Naan Yaen Pirandhen?*, part 2, pp. 1223–27.

77 http://tamil.thehindu.com/opinion/blogs/எம்ஜிஆர்-100-90-படத்துக்கொண்டே-நடித்தவர்/article8755472.ece?ref=relatedNews.

78 Kannadasan, Kavignar, *MGR'in Ullum Puramum*, Chennai: Muthiah Publisher, 1974, p. 7.

79 Kirubakaran, S., (ed.), *M.G.R. Paetigal*, pp. 105–06

80 Kalaignar, *Nenjuku Needhi*, vol. 2, p. 345.

81 Ibid., pp. 346–48.

82 Vijayan, *M.G.R. Kathai*, part 2, pp. 80–81.

83 Kalaignar, *Nenjuku Needhi*, vol. 2, p. 348.

84 Kirubakaran, S., (ed.), *Naan Aanaiyitaal . . .!*, pp. 181–84;

85 http://tamil.thehindu.com/opinion/blogs/எம்ஜிஆர்-100-80-ஆஸ்திரலேய-இயக்குநரின்-பாராட்டு/article8700507.ece.

86 Kalaignar, *Nenjuku Needhi*, vol. 2, pp. 352–53.

87 Muthukumar, R., *Thamizhaga Arasiyal Varalaaru*, vol. 1, Chennai: Kizhakku Pathippagam, 2013, p. 289.

88 Kirubakaran, S., (ed.), *Naan Aanaiyitaal . . .!*, pp. 179–80.

89 http://www.vikatan.com/juniorvikatan/Politics/27344-kalukar-answer.html#cmt241.

90 *Murasoli*, http://murasoli.in:8080/murasoli/home.jsp; interview with H.V. Hande, 8 May 2016, Madras.

91 Kalaignar, *Nenjuku Needhi*, vol. 2, p. 357.

92 MGR, *Naan Yaen Pirandhen?*, part 2, pp. 1457–62.

93 Mugil, *Kanneerum Punnagiyum*, Chennai: Kizhakku Pathippagam, 2005, p. 139.

94 Kirubakaran, S., (ed.), *M.G.R. Paetigal*, p. 133, 136.

95 Ibid.

96   Navalar, *Vazhvil Naan Kandathum Kaethaum*, pp. 494–5.

97   Kalaignar, *Nenjuku Needhi*, vol. 2, pp. 354–62.

98   Interview with RMV, 15 September 2016, Madras.

99   *India Today*, 1–15 August 1978, pp. 39–40; https://www.youtube.com/watch?v=LJwLKXxmgec.

100 http://www.vikatan.com/news/miscellaneous/57771-the-reason-to-avoid-mgr-act-as-sivaji-character.art.

101 Interview with C. Aranganayagam, 9 May 2016, Madras.

102 Kalaignar, *Nenjuku Needhi*, vol. 2, p. 347.

103 Arurdhas, *Kottaiyum Kodambakkamum*, Chennai: Vikatan Pirasuram, 2006, pp. 119–23; *Kodambaakathil Arubadhu Aandugal*, p. 46; http://www.thehindu.com/news/cities/chennai/the-day-mr-radha-shot-mgr/article4229865.ece?homepage=true.

104 Arunan, *M.G.R: Nadigar Mudhalvar Aanadhu Eppadi?*, p. 128.

105 Kirubakaran, S., (ed.), *M.G.R. Paetigal*, p. 133.

106 Vaali, *Naanum Indha Nootraandum*, Chennai: Kalaignan Pathippagam, 1995, pp. 261–62.

107 Arurdhas, *Kottaiyum Kodambakkamum*, pp. 114–16.

108 Kalaignar, *Nenjuku Needhi*, vol. 2, p. 379.

109 Navalar, *Vazhvil Naan Kandathum Kaethaum*, p. 497.

110 Arangannal recorded that he had resisted the idea, saying that the party would split and that MGR could be spoken to. He said that Navalar Nedunchezhian was against the idea. So were Madurai Muthu, P.U. Shanmugam and N.V. Natarajan. He added that Murasoli Maran was supportive and was against the resolution. Era. Sezhian was also supportive and Kalaignar himself was willing to defer the issue. Arangannal, *Ninaivugal* part 2, p. 55.

111 Kalaignar, *Nenjuku Needhi*, vol. 2, pp. 363–68; Navalar, *Vazhvil Naan Kandathum Kaethaum*, p 501.

112 Ranimaindhan, *RMV Oru Thondar*, p. 258.

113 Vijayan, *M.G.R. Kathai*, part 2, pp. 58–59.

114 Ibid.

115 *Dinamani*, 5 December 1972, cited in Pandian, M.S.S., *The Image Trap*, New Delhi: Sage Publications, 1992, p. 18.

116 Pandian, *The Image Trap*, p. 18.

117 Karunanandam, Kavignar, *Thanthai Periyar Vazhkai Varalaaru*, p. 665.

118 Kalaignar, *Nenjuku Needhi*, vol. 2, p. 368.

119 Rajaram, K., *Oru Saamaniyanin Ninaivugal*, Chennai: Nakkheeran Pathippagam, 2014, p. 216.

120 Interview with K. Veeramani, 8 September 2016, Madras.

121 Kalaignar, *Nenjuku Needhi*, vol. 2, p. 370 71;.https://www.youtube.com/watch?v=LJwLKXxmgec; Ranimaindhan, *RMV Oru Thondar*, p. 259.

122 Karunanandam, *Periyar Vazhkai Varalaaru*, p. 665; Arangannal records that some had deliberately made MGR rethink his decision, saying that the Madras district secretary had destroyed his hoardings and that it was the same in Madurai as well. Arangannal, *Ninaivugal*, part 2, pp. 55–56

123 Kalaignar, *Nenjuku Needhi*, vol. 2, pp. 372–73.

124 Ibid., 384.

125 http://tamil.thehindu.com/opinion/blogs/எம்ஜிஆர்-100-22-மதியஉகத்தின்-மறுபெயர்/article8360253.ece.

126 Kalaignar, *Nenjuku Needhi*, vol. 2, p. 385.

127 http://www.vikatan.com/news/coverstory/58518-anna-is-nationalist-mgr.art.

128 Interview with Su. Thirunavukkarasar, 23 August 2016, Madras.

129 Interview on 9 May 2016 with C. Aranganayagam, Madras.

130 Jagathrakshakan, S., *MGR: A Phenomenon*, Chennai: Apollo Veliyeetagam, 1984, p. 2.

131 Interview with RMV, 15 September 2016, Madras.

132 Narrated by V.N. Swami, 18 February 2017, Madras.

133 Arangannal, *Ninaivugal*, part 2, p. 56, 80.

134 *Kumudam*, 8 June 2016, p. 118.

135 http://www.vikatan.com/anandavikatan/2017-apr-05/politics/130018-history-of-aiadmk-politics.html.

136 http://www.thehindu.com/opinion/op-ed/The-prince-of-populism/article17046215.ece; Jagathrakshakan, *MGR: A Phenomenon*, p. 85–86.

137 Arunan, *M.G.R: Nadigar Mudhalvar Aanadhu Eppadi?*, p. 141.

138 http://www.writersamas.blogspot.in/2015/07/blog-post.html#more.

139 Arunan, *M.G.R: Nadigar Mudhalvar Aanadhu Eppadi?*, p. 138.

140 Kirubakaran, S., (ed.), *Naan Aanaiyitaal . . .!*, pp. 185–87

141 Arunan, *M.G.R: Nadigar Mudhalvar Aanadhu Eppadi?*, p. 143.

142 Ibid., p. 154.

143 Karunanandam, *Thanthai Periyar Vazhkai Varalaaru*, p. 672.

144 Interview with C. Aranganayagam, 10 May 2016, Madras.

145 Narrated by Iniyan Sampath, 6 February 2017, Madras.

146 Arunan, *M.G.R: Nadigar Mudhalvar Aanadhu Eppadi?*, p. 145.

147 Ibid., p. 146.

148 Ibid., p. 148.

149 Muthukumar, *Thamizhaga Arasiyal Varalaaru*, vol. 1, p. 303.

150 Arunan, *M.G.R: Nadigar Mudhalvar Aanadhu Eppadi?*, p. 147.

151 Ibid.

152 http://www.assembly.tn.gov.in/archive/reviews/
     Review_5_1971_1976.pdf.

153 Kalimuthu, K., *Ennai Naan Paarkiraen*, Chennai: Anuragam, 1999, p. 278.

154 Kirubakaran, S., (ed.), *M.G.R. Paetigal*, p. 117.

155 Karunanandam, *Thanthai Periyar Vazhkai Varalaaru*, p. 672.

156 Karunanandam, *Thanthai Periyar Vazhkai Varalaaru*, p. 672.

157 Arunan, *M.G.R: Nadigar Mudhalvar Aanadhu Eppadi?*, p. 148–49.

158 Jagathrakshakan, *MGR: A Phenomenon*, pp. 87–88.

159 Kirubakaran, S., (ed.), *M.G.R. Paetigal*, p. 134.

160 Karunanandam, *Thanthai Periyar Vazhkai Varalaaru*, p. 676.

161 Ibid., p. 674.

162 Muthukumar, *Thamizhaga Arasiyal Varalaaru*, p. 308.

163 Kirubakaran, S., (ed.), *M.G.R. Paetigal*, p. 117.

164 Interview with H.V. Hande, 8 May 2016, Madras.

165 Arunan, *M.G.R: Nadigar Mudhalvar Aanadhu Eppadi?*, p. 152.

166 Karunanandam, *Thanthai Periyar Vazhkai Varalaaru*, p. 677.

167 Ibid., p. 677.

168 http://www.assembly.tn.gov.in/archive/reviews/
     Review_5_1971_1976.pdf.

169 *Dinamani*, 26 December 1987; Jagathrakshakan, *MGR: A Phenomenon*,
     p. 89.

170 http://www.assembly.tn.gov.in/archive/reviews/
     Review_5_1971_1976.pdf.

171 Kalaignar, *Nenjuku Needhi*, vol. 2, pp. 374–403; Arunan, *M.G.R: Nadigar
     Mudhalvar Aanadhu Eppadi?*, pp. 154–55.

172 Interview with S. Ramachandran, 27 August 2016, Madras.

173 Jagathrakshakan, *MGR: A Phenomenon*, pp. 87–88.

174 Sastry, Ramaswamy, K., 'A Chronicle of the DMK Split', *Economic &
     Political Weekly*, 30 March 1974.

175 Jagathrakshakan, *MGR: A Phenomenon*, pp. 89–90.

176 Kirubakaran, S., (ed.), *Naan Aanaiyitaal . . .!*, pp. 195–97.

177 Ibid., pp. 198–9.

178 Interview with P.H. Pandian, 27 August 2016, Madras.

179 Arunan, *M.G.R: Nadigar Mudhalvar Aanadhu Eppadi?*, pp. 157–58.

180 *Theekadhir*, 19 January 1973, cited in Arunan, *M.G.R: Nadigar Mudhalvar Aanadhu Eppadi?*, p. 159.

181 http://www.assembly.tn.gov.in/archive/reviews/Review_5_1971_1976.pdf.

182 Kalaignar, *Nenjuku Needhi*, vol. 2, pp. 445–52.

183 Kirubakaran, S., (ed.), *Naan Aanaiyitaal . . .!*, pp. 201–03.

184 Manoharan, Nanjil, *Medum Pallamum*, Chennai: Poompuhar Pirasuram, 1988, pp. 166–72.

185 Interview with H.V. Hande, 8 May 2016, Madras.

186 Ramasamy, Cho., *Adhirshtam Thanta Anubhavangal*, Chennai: Alliance Publishers, 2015, pp. 237–39.

187 http://lh3.googleusercontent.com/-VXPlrfj2vhU/VgOkgBM2VxI/AAAAAAAAIro/GAFT-0771-s/s1600-h/dindukal_election1_1973-04-04%25255B4%25255D.jpg.

188 Arunan, *M.G.R: Nadigar Mudhalvar Aanadhu Eppadi?*, p. 163.

189 http://tamil.thehindu.com/opinion/blogs/எம்ஜிஆர்-100-22-மதியஉஉகத்தின்-மறுபெயர்/article8360253.ece.

190 Jagathrakshakan, *MGR: A Phenomenon*, p. 92; http://tamil.thehindu.com/opinion/blogs/எம்ஜிஆர்-100-57-ஏவுஈகணகைகளையே-ஏணிப்படிகளாக்கியவர்/article8554726.ece?ref=relatedNews.

191 Interview with Pulavar Pulamaipithan, 4 January 2013, Madras.

192 http://lh3.googleusercontent.com/-4N-Bqx2Uz8g/VgOkqJqcz2I/AAAAAAAAIso/-1YApyOY9g8/s1600-h/dindukal_election5_1973-05-02%25255B4%25255D.jpg.

193 Arunan, *M.G.R: Nadigar Mudhalvar Aanadhu Eppadi?*, p. 163.

194 http://mgrroop.wordpress.com/2011/11/20/dindukal-election-victory.

195 http://indiatoday.intoday.in/story/call-for-relaxation-of-prohibition-in-tamil-nadu-likely-to-remain-a-cry-in-the-wilderness/1/435982.html

196 Karunanandam, *Thanthai Periyar Vazhkai Varalaaru*, p. 692; Arunan, *M.G.R: Nadigar Mudhalvar Aanadhu Eppadi?*, p. 166; https://wikileaks.org/plusd/cables/1973NEWDE06010_b.html.

197 Arunan, *M.G.R: Nadigar Mudhalvar Aanadhu Eppadi?*, p. 166.

198 Muthukumar, *Thamizaaga Arasiyal Varalaaru*, vol. 1, p. 314.

199 Arunan, *M.G.R: Nadigar Mudhalvar Aanadhu Eppadi?*, p. 167.

200 Jagathrakshakan, *MGR: A Phenomenon*, p. 93.

201 Arunan, *M.G.R: Nadigar Mudhalvar Aanadhu Eppadi?*, p. 163.

202 *Theekadhir*, 28 June 1973, quoted in Arunan, *M.G.R: Nadigar Mudhalvar Aanadhu Eppadi?*, p. 169.

203 Narayan, Jayaprakash. *Prison Diary*, Delhi: Gian Publishing House, 1988, p. 85.

204 *Thennagam*, 11 September 1973, cited in Arunan, *M.G.R: Nadigar Mudhalvar Aanadhu Eppadi?*, p. 171.

205 Karunanandam, *Thantnai Periyar Vazhkai Varalaaru*, p. 707, 759.

206 Sastry, 'A Chronicle of the DMK Split', *Economic & Political Weekly*, 30 March 1974; *Economic & Political Weekly*, 10 November 1973.

207 Arunan, *M.G.R: Nadigar Mudhalvar Aanadhu Eppadi?*, pp. 171–72.

208 Ibid., pp. 192–93.

209 http://eci.nic.in/eci_main/StatisticalReports/SE_1974/Statistical%20Report%201974%20Pondicherry.pdf.

210 *Theekadhir*, 4 April 1974, quoted in Arunan, *M.G.R: Nadigar Mudhalvar Aanadhu Eppadi?*, p. 177.

211 *Theekadhir*, 30 March 1974, quoted in Arunan, *M.G.R: Nadigar Mudhalvar Aanadhu Eppadi?*, p. 178.

212 *Theekadhir*, 8 April 1974, quoted in Arunan, *M.G.R: Nadigar Mudhalvar Aanadhu Eppadi?*, p. 178.

213 https://wikileaks.org/plusd/cables/1974NEWDE01638_b.html.

214 https://wikileaks.org/plusd/cables/1974NEWDE05411_b.html; Arunan, *M.G.R: Nadigar Mudhalvar Aanadhu Eppadi?*, p. 183.

215 https://wikileaks.org/plusd/cables/1974NEWDE08674_b.html; Arunan, *M.G.R: Nadigar Mudhalvar Aanadhu Eppadi?*, p. 191.

216 http://www.assembly.tn.gov.in/archive/reviews/Review_5_1971_1976.pdf.

217 Ibid.

218 Kalaignar, *Nenjuku Needhi*. vol. 2, 209; p. 211, 429–44; https://wikileaks.org/plusd/cables/1974NEWDE05411_b.html; http://www.assembly.tn.gov in/archive/reviews/Review_5_1971_1976.pdf.

219 Arunan, *M.G.R: Nadigar Mudhalvar Aanadhu Eppadi?*, pp. 218–19; Vaali, *Enakkul M.G.R.*, pp. 267–70.

220 *New York Times*, 28 September 1974.

428   Notes

221 Doctor Udayamurthi, *Americargal Paarvayil Mudhalvar Anna Makkal Thilagam M.G.R.*, Chennai: Vidwan Pathippagam, 2003, pp. 62–104.

222 *Theekadhir*, 25 December 1974, cited in Arunan, *M.G.R: Nadigar Mudhalvar Aanadhu Eppadi?*, p. 194.

223 *Theekadhir*, 28 January 1975 quoted in Arunan, *M.G.R: Nadigar Mudhalvar Aanadhu Eppadi?*, p. 195.

224 Jayaprakash Narayan, *Prison Diary*, pp. 83–84.

225 *Murasoli*, 26 June 2015, http://murasoli.in:8080/murasoli/home.jsp.

226 Arunan, *M.G.R: Nadigar Mudhalvar Aanadhu Eppadi?*, p. 208.

227 https://wikileaks.org/plusd/cables/1975NEWDE08932_b.html.

228 https://wikileaks.org/plusd/cables/1975NEWDE08889_b.html.

229 Kalaignar, *Nenjuku Needhi*, vol. 2, pp. 473–80.

230 https://wikileaks.org/plusd/cables/1975NEWDE09016_b.html.

231 Kalaignar, *Nenjuku Needhi*, vol. 2, pp. 479–80.

232 *Murasoli*, 26 June 2015, http://murasoli.in:8080/murasoli/home.jsp.

233 https://wikileaks.org/plusd/cables/1975NEWDE08833_b.html.

234 *India Today*, 1–15 August 1978, pp. 40–41.

235 https://wikileaks.org/plusd/cables/1975NEWDE09777_b.html.

236 Kalaignar, *Nenjuku Needhi*, vol. 3, p. 40.

237 Narayan, *Prison Diary*, pp. 84–85.

238 Arunan, *M.G.R: Nadigar Mudhalvar Aanadhu Eppadi?*, p. 208.

239 *Theekadhir* 14 December 1975 cited in Arunan, *M.G.R: Nadigar Mudhalvar Aanadhu Eppadi?*, p. 209.

240 https://www.wikileaks.org/plusd/cables/1975NEWDE17294_b.html; https://www.wikileaks.org/plusd/cables/1976NEWDE00308_b.html; https://www.wikileaks.org/plusd/cables/1976NEWDE00308_b.html.

241 https://wikileaks.org/plusd/cables/1976NEWDE12284_b.html/.

242 Kalaignar, *Nenjuku Needhi*, vol. 2, p. 522.

243 https://wikileaks.org/plusd/cables/1976NEWDE01514_b.html.

244 https://wikileaks.org/plusd/cables/1976NEWDE01515_b.html; Kalaignar, *Nenjuku Needhi*, vol. 2, p. 526; *Murasoli*, 26 June 2015, http://murasoli.in:8080/murasoli/home.jsp.

245 *India Today*, 29 February 1976, 9-10; *India Today*, 29 February 1976, pp. 8–9; https://wikileaks.org/plusd/cables/1976NEWDE01750_b.html.

246 The report said: 'Several senior South Indian GOI officials, while reserved in their comment, were evidently unhappy over the GOI action. South Indian newspaperman (para 6) recalled a whole series

of alleged slights and acts of favoritism for north in recent months,
including sharp decline in number of southern joint secretaries in GOI
ministries (which has indeed occurred), passing over of two southern
admirals for naval chief-of-staff (also true), and a steady decline in
acceptances into the IAS of southern candidates over the last 2-3 years
(of which we are uncertain). Sanjay Gandhi is alleged to be "anti-
south", and this is said to be causing serious concern to many south
indians.'https://wikileaks.org/plusd/cables/1976NEWDE01666_b.
html.

247 https://www.wikileaks.org/plusd/cables/1976NEWDE01666_b.
   html.
248 https://wikileaks.org/plusd/cables/1976NEWDE02264_b.html.
249 Interview with H.V. Hande, 8 May 2016, Madras.
250 https://wikileaks.org/plusd/cables/1976NEWDE02489_b.html.
251 Narayan, *Prison Diary*, p. 35.
252 https://wikileaks.org/plusd/cables/1976NEWDE02457_b.html;
   https://www.wikileaks.org/plusd/cables/1976NEWDE02455_b.
   html;
   https://wikileaks.org/plusd/cables/1976NEWDE03310_b.html.
253 https://wikileaks.org/plusd/cables/1976NEWDE02457_b.html;
   https://www.wikileaks.org/plusd/cables/1976NEWDE02455_b.
   html;
   https://wikileaks.org/plusd/cables/1976NEWDE03310_b.html.
254 https://wikileaks.org/plusd/cables/1976NEWDE02551_b.html.
255 https://wikileaks.org/plusd/cables/1976NEWDE02455_b.html.
256 Ibid.
257 https://wikileaks.org/plusd/cables/1976NEWDE03310_b.html.
258 https://wikileaks.org/plusd/cables/1976NEWDE03523_b.html.
259 https://wikileaks.org/plusd/cables/1976NEWDE05685_b.html.
260 https://wikileaks.org/plusd/cables/1976NEWDE06326_b.html.
261 https://wikileaks.org/plusd/cables/1976NEWDE13883_b.html.
262 Ranimaindhan, *RMV Oru Thondar*, p. 300.
263 http://tamil.thehindu.com/opinion/blogs/எம்ஜிஆர்-100-25-
   திரையாலகில்-மாபிசஇடா-மன்னர்/article8374291.ece.
264 Interview with H.V. Hande, 8 May 2017, Madras; http://tamil.
   thehindu.com/opinion/blogs/எம்ஜிஆர்-100-25-திரையாலகில்-
   மாபிசஇடா-மன்னர்/article8374291.ece; http://www.vikatan.com/
   news/tamilnadu/59726-tattoos-culture-is-not-new-to-aiadmk.art.

265 Arunan, *M.G.R: Nadigar Mudhalvar Aanadhu Eppadi?*, pp. 215–16; https://wikileaks.org/plusd/cables/1976NEWDE15757_b.html; http://tamil.thehindu.com/opinion/columns/ஞாயிறு-அரங்கம்-ஐயெலலிதாவாதல்/article8320357.ece?homepage=true.

266 Muthukumar, *Thamizhaga Arasiyal Varalaaru*, vol. 1, p. 398–400.

267 Ibid., p. 396.

268 Ibid., pp. 397–98; MGR would compare his compulsions to Anna's compulsions in 1962, saying he was leaving it for future historians to judge him. He added that it would not be an exaggeration to say that the ADMK acquiring a national form was on the lines of Anna taking a nationalist approach in 1962. http://www.vikatan.com/news/coverstory/58518-anna-is-nationalist-mgr.art

269 Kirubakaran, S., (ed.), *M.G.R. Paetigal*, p. 214.

270 *Murasoli*, 26 June 2015, http://murasoli.in:8080/murasoli/home.jsp.

271 Kalaignar, *Nenjuku Needhi*, vol. 2, pp. 540–51.

272 https://wikileaks.org/plusd/cables/1976NEWDE13883_b.html.

273 Sundaram, V., *Nadigamani D.V. Narayanasamy*, Chennai: Sekar Pathippagam, 2000, p. 46; Rajendran, S.S., *Naan Vandha Pathai*, Chennai: Agani Veliyeedu, 2014, pp. 334–37.

274 https://wikileaks.org/plusd/cables/1976NEWDE10284_b.html.

Chapter 6: Chief Minister MGR

1   http://indiatoday.intoday.in/story/sarkaria-commission-karunanidhi-partially-guilty/1/435472.html; Karunanidhi, Kalaignar M., *Nenjuku Needhi*, vol. 3, Chennai: Thirumagal Nilayam, 2008, p. 226.

2   Ibid., pp. 50–51.

3   Arangannal, Rama, *Ninaivugal*, part 1, Chennai: Andal Pathippagam, 2000, pp. 88–90.

4   *Dinamani*, 30 December 1987.

5   Interview with Su. Thirunavukkarasar and RMV, 24 August and 15 September 2016 respectively, Madras.

6   Interview with K. Veeramani, 8 September 2016, Madras.

7   Ranimaindhan, *RMV Oru Thondar*, Chennai: Rajarajan Pathippagam, 2005, pp. 300–02.

8   *Dinamani*, 18 March 1977. In his novel *Arangamum Andharangamum* (The Exterior and the Interior), poet Kannadasan painted his hero Chandrasuriyan (MGR) as being a narcissist and sadist rather than

a leader, and his aura being a result of the poet's and Kalaignar's mistakes. Bordering on the vulgar and abusive, Kannadasan wrote that after the 1961 Thiruvottiyur DMK guards meeting, he lamented to Anna about MGR the 'deity' overshadowing those who had built the party, and Anna allegedly responded that the public would think deeply before they could believe their accusations against MGR. Kannadasan, Kavignar, *Arangamum Andarangamum*, Chennai: Kannadhasan Pathippagam, 2010, p. 10–11.

9   *Theekadhir*, 20 February 1977, cited in Arunan, *M.G.R: Nadigar Mudhalvar Aanadhu Eppadi?*, Madurai: Vasantham Veliyeetagam, 2006, p. 220.

10   http://eci.nic.in/eci_main/StatisticalReports/LS_1977/Vol_I_LS_77.pdf, 108.

11   https://www.wikileaks.org/plusd/cables/1977NEWDE04586_c.html.

12   Kavignar, *Arangamum Andarangamum*, p. 3.

13   Kalaignar, *Nenjuku Needhi*, vol. 3, p. 87.

14   Interview with S. Ramachandran, 27 August 2016, Madras.

15   Kalaignar, *Nenjuku Needhi*, vol. 3, pp. 87–89.

16   *Dinamani*, 26 December 1987.

17   *Dinamani*, 9 May 1977.

18   *Dinamani*, 21 September 1977; Kalaignar, *Nenjuku Needhi*, vol 3, p. 178.

19   Manoharan, Nanjil, *Medum Pallamum*, Chennai: Poonjolai Pirasuram,1986, pp. 172–74.

20   http://indiatoday.intoday.in/story/tamil-nadu-assembly-elections-mgr-rides-again/1/435597.html; *Dinamani*, 7 May 1977.

21   Half of the 234 seats, says Jagathrakshakan. Jagathrakshakan, S., *MGR: A Phenomenon*, Chennai: Apollo Veliyeetagam, 1984, p. 12.

22   Interview with S. Ramachandran, 27 August 2016, Madras.

23   *Dinamani*, 6 June 1979.

24   *Theekadhir* 22 May 1977, cited in Arunan, *M.G.R: Nadigar Mudhalvar Aanadhu Eppadi?*, p. 227.

25   Rajaram, K., *Oru Saamaniyianin Ninaivugal*, Chennai: Nakkheeran Pathippagam, 2014, p. 317.

26   Jagathrakshakan, *MGR: A Phenomenon*, p. 8.

27   http://www.thehindu.com/news/national/tamil-nadu/hit-songs-that-won-polls-for-aiacmk/article5845441.ece?homepage=true.

28   Arunan, *M.G.R: Nadigar Mudhalvar Aanadhu Eppadi?*, p. 229.

29 http://www.assembly.tn.gov.in/archive/reviews/
    Review_6_1977_1980.pdf.
30 Kalaignar, *Nenjuku Needhi*, vol. 3, p. 25.
31 Kirubakaran, S., (ed.), *M.G.R. Paetigal*, Chennai: Vikatan Pirasuram,
    2009, pp. 227–29.
32 Interview with K. Veeramani, 8 September 2016, Madras.
33 Ibid.;
34 http://news.oneindia.in/2009/04/01/panruti-blocked-dmk-aiadmk-
    merger-m-karunanidhi.
    Interview with K. Veeramani, 8 September 2016, Madras.
35 Solai, *Sangapalagai*, Chennai: Nakkheeran Publications, 2012, pp. 186–91.
36 *Meenava Nanban's* (Fisherman's Friend, 1977) climax, a boat chase in
    the rain, was his last shoot, although the dubbing work for *Maduraiai
    Meeta Sundara Pandian* (Sundara Pandian Who Re-conquered Madurai,
    1977) also held up his swearing-in. Lakshmanan, Vidwan V., *Makkal
    Thilagam*, Chennai: Vanathi Pathippagam, 2002, pp. 206–08. MGR had
    accepted a salary of 45 lakh rupees, the highest ever in the south till
    then. http://tamil.thehindu.com/opinion/blogs/எம்ஜிஆர்-100-89-
    நடிகர்-நலனில்-அக்கறை-கொ·ாண்டவர்/article8744629.ece.
37 Kalaignar, *Nenjuku Needhi*, vol. 3, p. 130.
38 Vidwan, *Makkal Thilagam*, pp. 206–08.
39 http://tamil.thehindu.com/opinion/blogs/என்னராமதே-தே·ாழி-
    27-மனை-மாட்சி/article9525752.ece?widget-art=four-rel.
40 Interview with C. Aranganayagam, 8 May 2016, Madras.
41 Interview with Su. Thirunavukkarasar, 24 August 2016, Madras.
42 Interview with RMV, 15 September 2016, Madras.
43 Ibid.
44 https://www.wikileaks.org/plusd/cables/1977NEWDE09401_c.
    html.
45 http://www.assembly.tn.gov.in/archive/reviews/Review_6_1977_
    1980.pdf.
46 Ibid.
47 Ranimaindhan, *RMV Oru Thondar*, pp. 308–09.
48 http://www.assembly.tn.gov.in/archive/reviews/Review_6_1977_
    1980.pdf; *Dinamani*, 7 May 1977.
49 Kalaignar, *Nenjuku Needhi*, vol. 3, p. 276; http://indiatoday.intoday.in/
    story/in-just-nine-months-as-tamil-nadu-cm-mgr-finds-his-popularity-
    on-the-wane/1/434322.html.

50 http://www.vikatan.com/article.php?aid=11713&sid=320&mid=2S;
    Jagathrakshakan, *MGR: A Phenomenon*, pp. 10–11.

51 Solai, *Netru, Indru, Nealai*, Chennai: Nakkheeran Publications, 2012,
    p. 136.

52 Jagathrakshakan, *MGR: A Phenomenon*, p. 100.

53 Kirubakaran, S., (ed.), *M.G.R. Paetigal*, p. 244.

54 *Kumudam*, 1 June 2016, p. 139; https://www.google.iq/search?q=MG
    R's+swearing+in+on+1977&biw=909&bih=715&tbm=isch&tbo=u
    &source=univ&sa=X&ved=0ahUKEwi_29uP_-vRAhVHQBQKHTh
    KBfwQsAQIGw&dpr=1#imgrc=eAeZ3un9YlhrfM%3A.

55 Mohandas, K., *MGR: The Man and the Myth*, Bangalore: Panther
    Publishers, 1992, p. 22.

56 Ibid., p. 53.

57 Interview with P.H. Pandian, 25 August 2016, Madras.

58 Ramasamy, Cho., *Adhishtam Thantha Anubhavangal*, Chennai: Alliance
    Publishers, 2015, pp. 355–56.

59 *Dinamani*, 17 June 1977.

60 Mohandas, *MGR: The Man and the Myth*, pp. 52–53.

61 John, Valampuri, *Vanakkam*, Chennai: Nakkheeran Publications, 2010,
    p. 110.

62 Interview with S. Ramachandran, 27 August 2016, Madras.

63 Interviews with H.V. Hande, Su. Thirunavukarasar, P.H. Pandian, C.
    Ponnaiyan, Pulavar Pulamaipithan, RMV and KAK, Madras.

64 http://tamil.thehindu.com/opinion/blogs/எம்ஜிஆர்-100-27-
    மனிதரை-மனிதராக-மதிப்பவர்/article8388770.ece.

65 http://tamil.thehindu.com/opinion/blogs/எம்ஜிஆர்-100-
    9-தியாகி-கக்கணக்கு-செய்த-உதவி/article8284655.
    ece?homepage=true.

66 Mohandas, *MGR: The Man and the Myth*, pp. 19–20.

67 *Murasoli*, 31 October 1981.

68 https://srimgr.wordpress.com/category/chief-minister/.

69 Jagathrakshakan, *MGR: The Man and the Myth*, p. 17, 120–23.

70 http://www.assembly.tn.gov.in/archive/Resumes/06assly/06_01_1.
    pdf.

71 http://indiatoday.intoday.in/story/janata-partys-sweeping-success-
    marred-by-aiadmk-in-tamil-nadu/1/436021.ahtml; Kalaignar, vol. 3, 154.

72 http://indiatoday.intoday.in/story/no-government-can-impose-any-
    language-on-the-people-m.g.-ramachandran/1/436069.html.

73   *Dinamani,* 17 August 1977.

74   http://tamil.thehindu.com/opinion/blogs/100-3-/article8252363.
     ece?homepage=true.

75   http://www.vikatan.com/new/article.php?module=magazine&
     aid=89124.

76   Interview with Su. Thirunavukkarasar and P.H. Pandian, 24 and 26
     August 2016 respectively, Madras.

77   Kalaignar, *Nenjuku Needhi,* vol. 3, pp. 189–91; 161–62; I had provided
     the information to R. Kolappan for his story in *The Hindu* on this.

78   Kalaignar, *Nenjuku Needhi,* vol. 3, pp. 161–62.

79   *Dinamani,* 6 November 1977.

80   Kalaignar, *Nenjuku Needhi,* vol. 3, pp. 169–75.

81   Ibid.,pp. 226–27, 236–37.

82   Muthukumar, R., *Thamizhaga Arasiyal Varalaaru,* vol. 2, Chennai:
     Kizhakku Pathippagam, 2013, pp.47–49.

83   https://www.youtube.com/watch?v=6lTYd7mo3pQ&t=6s.

84   Manoharan, *Medum Pallamum,* p. 179.

85   *Murasoli,* http://murasoli.in:8080/murasoli/home.jsp.

86   Kalaignar, *Nenjuku Needhi,* vol. 3, pp. 188–89.

87   Ibid., pp. 179–83.

88   http://www.rediff.com/news/1999/oct/12gandhi.htm;   Ganesan,
     Sivaji, *Autobiography of an Actor,* Chennai: Sivaji Prabhu Charities Trust,
     2002, p. 197; Mohandas, *MGR: The Man and the Myth,* p. 26; *Dinamani,*
     30 October 1977.

89   *Dinamani,* 31 October 1977.

90   *Dinamani,* 30 October 1977.

91   Ibid.

92   Ganesan, *Autobiography of an Actor,* p. 197.

93   *Dinamani,* 31 October 1977.

94   http://indiatoday.intoday.in/story/indira-gandhis-two-day-tour-of-
     tamil-nadu-ends-in-a-grand-fiasco/1/435308.html.

95   Mohandas, *MGR: The Man and the Myth,* p. 28; Kalaignar, *Nenjuku Needhi,*
     vol. 3, pp. 284–87; http://indiatoday.intoday.in/story/karunanidhi-does-
     not-exist-without-congressi-support-m.g.-ramachandran/1/402339.html.

96   https://www.wikileaks.org/plusd/cables/1977NEWDE17175_c.html.

97   Kalaignar, *Nenjuku Needhi,* vol. 3, pp. 201–22; http://indiatoday.
     intoday.in/story/m.g.ramachandran-no-match-for-dmk-chief-m.k.-
     karunanidhi/1/434041.html.

98   Mohandas, *MGR: The Man and the Myth*, pp. 28–29.

99   Kirubakaran, S., (ed.), *Naan Aanaiyitaal . . .!*, Chennai: Vikatan Pirasuram, 2014, pp. 209–10.

100 *Dinamani*, 5 January 1978.

101 Mohandas, *MGR: The Man and the Myth*, p. 31.

102 K. Rajaram Naidu was parliamentary secretary in 1952–53 to the then minister for finance and food, C. Subramaniam, in the Rajaji cabinet.

103 http://www.assembly.tn.gov.in/archive/reviews/Review_6_1977_1980.pdf; Mohandas, *MGR: The Man and the Myth*, pp. 32–33.

104 *Dinamani*, 5 February 1978.

105 http://indiatoday.intoday.in/story/karunanidhi-does-not-exist-without-congressi-support-m.g.-ramachandran/1/402339.html.

106 http://indiatoday.intoday.in/story/karunanidhi-writes-film-scripts-tinged-with-bitter-political-attack-on-mgr/1/434896.html; Kalaignar, *Nenjuku Needhi*, vol. 3, pp. 250–51.

107 Mohandas, *MGR: The Man and the Myth*, pp. 40–44.

108 Kalaignar, *Nenjuku Needhi*, vol. 3, p. 253.

109 Ibid., pp. 270–72, 276–77.

110 http://indiatoday.intoday.in/story/politics-like-films-is-a-matter-of-communicating-with-the-people-mgr/1/434435.html.

111 Mohandas, *MGR: The Man and the Myth*, p. 32.

112 *Dinamani*, 13 February 1978; Muthukumar, *Thamizhaga, Arasiyal Varalaaru*, vol. 2, p. 30

113 Kirubakaran, S., (ed.), *M.G.R. Paetigal*, p. 155.

114 Interview with S. Ramachandran, 27 August 2016, Madras.

115 *Kumudam*, 31 August 2016, pp. 24–29.

116 Kirubakaran, S., (ed.), *M.G.R. Paetigal*, p. 231.

117 Ibid., p. 238.

118 *Dinamani*, 1 February 1979.

119 *Dinamani*, 4 February 1979.

120 Kirubakaran, S., (ed.), *M.G.R. Paetigal*, p. 231.

121 http://indiatoday.intoday.in/story/tamil-nadu-cm-mgr-to-launch-his-own-film-imayathin-uchiyil-with-himself-in-the-lead/1/409484.html.

122 *Dinamani*, 6 June 1979.

123 Vaali, *Naanum Indha Nootraandum*, Chennai: Kalaignan Pathippagam, 1995, pp. 351–55.

124 http://indiatoday.intoday.in/story/karunanidhi-writes-film-scripts-tinged-with-bitter-political-attack-on-mgr/1/434896.html, Kalaignar, *Nenjuku Needhi*, vol. 3, pp. 272–73.

125 Kalaignar, *Nenjuku Needhi*, p. vol. 3, 276; http://indiatoday.intoday.in/story/in-just-nine-months-as-tamil-nadu-cm-mgr-finds-his-popularity-on-the-wane/1/434322.html.

126 *Dinamani*, 8 December 1978.

127 *Dinamani*, 10 December 1978.

128 *Dinamani*, 21 April 1977.

129 Gurusamy, S., 'Peasant Politics in Tamilnadu Dina: A Socio-political Analysis of a Pressure Group', thesis, Gandhigram Rural Institute (deemed) University, http://shodhganga.inflibnet.ac.in/bitstream/10603/16237/8/08_chapter%202.pdf;

Kalaignar, *Nenjuku Needhi*, vol. 3, p. 2881; Mohandas, *MGR: The Man and the Myth*, pp. 40–44.

130 *Dinamani*, 23 May 1979.

131 *Dinamani*, 23 May 1979.

132 *Dinamani*, 11 June 1979.

133 *Dinamani*, 30 May 1978.

134 Mohandas, *MGR: The Man and the Myth*, pp. 33–34.

135 http://indiatoday.intoday.in/story/m.g.ramachandran-no-match-for-dmk-chief-m.k.-karunanidhi/1/434041.html; Kalaignar, *Nenjuku Needhi*, vol. 3, pp. 230–31.

136 http://indiatoday.intoday.in/story/clean-and-honest-administration-a-far-cry-in-mgr-government/1/434434.html.

137 Mohandas, *MGR: The Man and the Myth*, pp. 33–34.

138 *Dinamani*, 3 July 1978.

139 *Dinamani*, 13 May 1978.

140 *Dinamani*, 14 February 1978.

141 Kirubakaran, S., (ed.), *M.G.R. Paetigal*, p. 236.

142 *Dinamani*, 14 May 1978.

143 http://indiatoday.intoday.in/story/tamil-nadu-cm-m.g.-ramachandran-fails-to-corner-dmk-chief-karunanidhi/1/434783.html; http://indiatoday.intoday.in/story/sons-alleged-indiscretions-puts-tamil-nadu-minister-shanmugam-in-a-tight-spot/1/354102.html.

144 *Dinamani*, 15 May 1978.

145 *Dinamani*, 7 June 1979.

146 *Dinamani*, 30 May 1978.

147 http://indiatoday.intoday.in/story/call-for-relaxation-of-prohibition-in-tamil-nadu-likely-to-remain-a-cry-in-the-wilderness/1/435982. html.

148 *Dinamani*, 19 September 1977.

149 *Dinamani*, 8 January 1978.

150 http://indiatoday.intoday.in/story/in-dry-tamil-nadu-two-lakh-people-engaged-in-illicit-brewing-a-million-in-bootlegging/1/427183. html.

151 *Dinamani*, 28 May 1979.

152 http://indiatoday.intoday.in/story/breasts-of-a-harijan-girl-spark-off-orgy-of-violence-in-villupuram-tamil-nadu/1/434470.html; Kalaignar, *Nenjuku Needhi*, vol. 3, pp. 308–09.

153 Mohandas, *MGR: The Man and the Myth*, p. 35.

154 *Dinamani*, 20 September 1978; http://indiatoday.intoday.in/story/dmk-shuns-e.v.-ramaswami-naickers-ideals-the-go-by-one-after-another/1/427703.html.

155 http://www.thehindu.com/news/national/tamil-nadu/Sasikala-is-the-sixth-person-to-be-AIADMK-generalsecretary/article16968191 ece/ucbrowser?hbt=uc&utm_source=UCbrowser&utm_ medium=Referal&utm_campaign=UCBrowser.

156 *Dinamani*, 29 October 1978.

157 *Dinamani*, 3 December 1978.

158 *Dinamani*, 20 September 1978.

159 *Dinamani*, 24 January 1979; Kalaignar, *Nenjuku Needhi*, vol. 3 pp. 322–25.

160 Mohandas, *MGR: The Man and the Myth*, p. 45.

161 Muthukumar, *Thamizhaga, Arasiyal Varalaaru*, vol. 2, pp. 36–37.

162 Kalaignar, *Nenjuku Needhi*, vol. 3, p. 331.

163 http://indiatoday.intoday.in/story/indira-gandhi-looks-at-thanjavur-in-tamil-nadu-to-make-a-bid-to-return-to-parliament/1/427291.html.

164 Interview with S. Ramachandran, 27 August 2016, Madras.

165 *Dinamani*, 23 May 1979.

166 *Dinamani*, 23 May and 11 June 1979.

167 *Dinamani*, 25 May 1979.

168 *Dinamani*, 26 May 1979.

169 http://www.thehindu.com/news/national/tamil-nadu/when-mrs-gandhi-favoured-thanjavur/article5797407.ece; Mohandas, *MGR: The Man and the Myth*, p. 40–42; Kalaignar, *Nenjuku Needhi*, vol. 3, pp. 331–34;

http://indiatoday.intoday.in/story/karunanidhi-does-not-exist-without-congressi-support-m.g.-ramachandran/1/402339.html.

170 *Dinamani*, 23 May 1979.

171 *Dinamani*, 11 June 1979.

172 *Murasoli*, 31 October 1981.

173 Mohandas, *MGR: The Man and the Myth*, p. 37.

174 Kirubakaran, S., (ed.), *M.G.R. Paetigal*, p. 126.

175 Radhakrishnan, P., 'India's Affirmative Action Politics as Seen Through Tamil Nadu's Specious Quota Law', http://www.countercurrents. org/radhakrishnan100212.pdf.

176 Kirubakaran, S., (ed.), *M.G.R. Paetigal*, p. 126.

177 Kannan, R., *Anna: The Life and Times of C.N. Annadurai*, Delhi: Penguin Viking, 2010, p. 312.

178 Interview with C. Ponnaiyan, 25 August 2016, Madras.

179 Manoharan, *Medum Pallamum*, p. 172; Mohandas, *MGR: The Man and the Myth*, p. 24.

180 Ramasamy, *Adhirshtam Thantha Anubhavangal*, p. 317.

181 'I knew they (Congress (I)) were going to topple this ministry and would allow it to function only for three or four months at the most.' http://indiatoday.intoday.in/story/national-problems-can-be-solved-only-by-understanding-them-aravinda-bala-pajanor/1/427689.html; Ramasamy, *Adhirshtam Thantha Anubhavangal*, pp. 327–8, 331.

182 Ramasamy, *Adhirshtam Thantha Anubhavangal*, pp. 344–51.

183 Kalaignar, *Nenjuku Needhi*, vol. 3, p. 358.

184 http://indiatoday.intoday.in/story/coming-together-of-dmk-and-congressi-threatens-stability-of-aiadmk-administration/1/427731.html.

185 Kalaignar, *Nenjuku Needhi*, vol. 3, pp. 358–59; http://indiatoday. intoday.in/story/coming-together-of-dmk-and-congressi-threatens-stability-of-aiadmk-administration/1/427731.html.

186 Mohandas, *MGR: The Man and the Myth*, p. 38–39.

187 *Dinamani*, 14 January 1981.

188 http://indiatoday.intoday.in/story/after-10-years-of-ramachandran-rule-tamil-nadu-presents-a-very-sorry-picture/1/337294.html; *India Today*, 1–15 December 1979, pp. 32–5; http://www.assembly. tn.gov.in/archive/reviews/Review_6_1977_1980.pdf;   http:// indiatoday.intoday.in/story/dmk-leader-karunanidhi-charges-m.g.-ramachandran-government-with-shipping-deal-scam/1/427545.html; Kalaignar, *Nenjuku Needhi*, vol. 3, p. 377.

189 *Dinamani,* 25 July 1985.

190 http://indiatoday.intoday.in/story/dmk-leader-karunanidhi-charges-
     m.g.-ramachandran-government-with-shipping-deal-scam/1/427545.
     html.

191 Interview with C. Aranganayagam, 8 May 2016, Madras.

192 http://timesofindia.indiatimes.com/city/chennai/mgrs-
     100th-birth-anniversary-hero-of-the-poor-manager-of-talent/
     articleshow/56607132.cms.

193 http://eduhelp.in.

194 Interview with C. Aranganayagam, 8 May 2016, Madras; Abdullah
     Nurullah, 'MGR's edu reforms cemented TN's tech base', *Times of
     India,* Madras, 31 March 2016; Ganesan, S., 'Only 30% of engg colleges
     achieve 60% admission rate', *Times of India,* Madras, 25 May 2016.

195 Arangannal, *Ninaivugai,* part 2, p. 95.

196 Interview on 27 August 2016 with S. Ramachandran, Madras.

197 Kalaignar, *Nenjuku Needhi,* vol. 3, p. 360.

198 Solai, *Sangapalagai,* pp. 186–91; http://www.newindianexpress.com/
     states/tamil_nadu/article53096.ece?service=print.

199 https://www.youtube.com/watch?v=EMMSGgR4Hgk; Arangannal,
     Ninaivugal, part 2, p. 95.

200 *Dinamani,* 19 December 1981.

201 Kalaignar, *Nenjuku Needhi,* vol. 3, pp. 359–62; Mohandas, *MGR: The
     Man and the Myth,* p. 25; http://www.newindianexpress.com/states/
     tamil_nadu/article53096.ece?service=print;   http://indiatoday.
     intoday.in/story/coming-together-of-dmk-and-congressi-threatens-
     stability-of-aiadmk-administration/1/427731.html.

202 Interview with RMV, 15 September 2016, Madras.

203 http://indiatoday.intoday.in/story/coming-together-of-dmk-and-
     congressi-threatens-stability-of-aiadmk-administration/1/427731.html.

204 Solai, *MGR'in Theerkatharisanam,* Chennai: Nakkheeran Publications,
     2010, p. 24.

205 http://indiatoday.intoday.in/story/congressis-poll-prospects-in-
     southern-and-northern-states-acquire-a-definable-form/1/427637.html.

206 Muthukumar, *Thamizhaga, Arasiyal Varalaaru,* vol. 2, p. 51.

207 Kalaignar, *Nenjuku Needhi,* vol. 3, pp. 364–71; http://indiatoday.
     intoday.in/story/coming-together-of-dmk-and-congressi-threatens-
     stability-of-aiadmk-administration/1/427731.html; Mohandas, *MGR:
     The Man and the Myth,* p. 35, 38; http://indiatoday.intoday.in/story/

congressis-poll-prospects-in-southern-and-northern-states-acquire-a-definable-form/1/427637.html.

208 *Dinamani,* 1 January 1980.

209 Muthukumar, *Thamizhaga, Arasiyal Varalaaru,* vol. 2, p. 53.

210 *Dinamani,* 2 January 1980.

211 Interview with H.V. Hande, 31 August 2016, Madras.

212 http://indiatoday.intoday.in/story/pm-indira-gandhi-dismisses-governments-in-nine-states-looks-to-put-congress-in-power/1/409511.html.

213 http://indiatoday.intoday.in/story/pm-indira-gandhi-dismisses-governments-in-nine-states-looks-to-put-congress-in-power/1/409511.html.

214 *Dinamani,* 9 January 1980.

215 *Dinamani,* 9 January 1980.

216 *Dinamani,* 10 January 1980.

217 *Dinamani,* 10 January 1980.

218 Kalaignar, *Nenjuku Needhi,* vol. 3, p. 383.

219 *Dinamani,* 10 January 1980.

220 http://tamil.thehindu.com/opinion/blogs/-100-4-/article8256809.ece; *Dinamani,* 18 February 1980.

221 http://www.vikatan.com/new/article.php?module=magazine&aid=92334.

222 Interview with H.V. Hande, 8 May 2016, Madras.

223 http://indiatoday.intoday.in/story/tamil-nadu-cm-mgr-to-launch-his-own-film-imayathin-uchiyil-with-himself-in-the-lead/1/409484.html

224 *Dinamani,* 10 July 1984.

225 Interview with K. Veeramani, 8 September 2016, Madras.

226 http://indiatoday.intoday.in/story/tamil-nadu-cm-mgr-stirs-a-hornets-nest-with-his-concessions-for-all-proposal/1/371274.html.

227 Ibid.

228 Kalaignar, *Nenjuku Needhi*, vol. 3, pp. 38485.

229 http://indiatoday.intoday.in/story/tamil-nadu-chief-minister-m.g.-ramachandran-waters-down-his-prohibition-law/1/409471.html; http://indiatoday.intoday.in/story/tamil-nadu-governor-prabhudas-patwari-puts-congressi-in-a-fix/1/409631.html

230 Kalaignar, *Nenjuku Needhi*, vol. 3, pp. 388–89.

231 *Dinamani,* 21 April 1980.

232 Kalaignar, *Nenjuku Needhi*, vol. 3, pp. 395–96; http://indiatoday.
intoday.in/story/aiadmk-led-protest-rally-in-madras-comes-under-
wanton-police-attack/1/409565.html

233 *Dinamani*, 24 February 1980.

234 'Tamil Nadu: A fallen idol', *India Today*, 15 May 1980, http://
indiatoday.intoday.in/story/sizeable-chunk-of-m.g.-ramachandran-
cabinet-leaves-for-greener-pastures/1/409661.html; Mohandas, *MGR:
The Man and the Myth*, pp. 49–50.

235 *Dinamani*, 3 March 1980.

236 Manoharan, *Medum Fallamum*, p. 172.

237 Kalaignar, *Nenjuku Needhi*, vol. 3, pp. 393–94.

238 Interview with H.V. Hande, 8 May, 29 August 2016, Madras.

239 Interviews with Su. Thirunavukkarasar, 24 August 2016 and
S. Ramachandran, 27 August 2016, Madras.

240 *Dinamani*, 18 March 1980.

241 *Dinamani*, 6 March 1980.

242 'Tamil Nadu: A fallen idol,' *India Today*, 15 May 1980, http://
indiatoday.intoday.in/story/sizeable-chunk-of-m.g.-ramachandran-
cabinet-leaves-for-greener-pastures/1/409661.html.

243 Ramasamy, *Adhirshtam Thantha Anubhavangal*, p. 355; Interview with
H.V. Hande 31 August 2016, Madras.

244 Kalaignar, *Nenjuku Needhi*, vol. 3, pp. 424–25.

245 Ibid., p. 426.

246 *Dinamani*, 17 August 1984; http://indiatoday.intoday.in/story/aiadmk-
helped-by-overconfidence-of-dmk-and-congressi/1/409816.html.

247 John, *Vanakkam*, pp. 35–36.

248 http://www.thehindu.com/news/national/tamil-nadu/tiruvarur-
gifts-highestever-victory-margin-to-karunanidhi/article2021813.ece.

249 Solai, *MGR'in Theerkatharisanam*, pp. 177–84; http://www.vikatan.
com/new/article.php?module=magazine&aid=92334.

250 Interview with S. Ramachandran, 27 August 2016, Madras.

251 Ramasamy, *Adhirshtam Thantha Anubhavangal*, p. 355.

252 Ibid.

253 Muthukumar, *Thamizhaga Arasiyal Varalaaru*, vol. 2, pp. 67–68.

254 http://indiatoday.intoday.in/story/aiadmk-govt-in-tamil-nadu-
recommends-assembly-dissolution-and-simultaneous-polls/1/361175.
html.

255 Kalaignar, *Nenjuku Needhi*, vol. 3, p. 408.

Chapter 7: Prince of Populism

1   *The Hindu*, 9 June 1980, 1; http://lh4.ggpht.com/-ZAQ9OMvOCds/
    Uc-P_iTiNUI/AAAAAAAAEpo/8mui-AHmoto/s1600-h/
    secondterm4.jpg.

2   Lakshmanan, Vidwan V., *Makkal Thilagam*, Chennai: Vanathi
    Pathippagam, 2002, pp. 206–08.

3   http://www.assembly.tn.gov.in/archive/7th_1980/7threvi
    ew_80-84.pdf.

4   Ibid.

5   http://www.thehindu.com/news/national/tamil-nadu/Sasikala-is-
    the-sixth-person-to-be-AIADMK-general-secretary/article16968191.
    ece/ucbrowser?hbt=uc&utm_source=UCbrowser&utm_
    medium=Referal&utm_campaign=UCBrowser.

6   http://indiatoday.intoday.in/story/aiadmk-not-likely-to-spearhead-
    any-agitation-against-the-centre/1/409838.html.

7   http://timesofindia.indiatimes.com/city/chennai/mgrs-
    100th-birth-anniversary-hero-of-the-poor-manager-of-talent/
    articleshow/56607132.cms.

8   Kirubakaran, S., (ed.), *Naan Aanaiyitaal...!*, Chennai: Vikatan Pirasuram,
    2014, p. 222; Jagathrakshakan, S., *MGR: A Phenomenon*, Chennai: Apollo
    Veliyeetagam, 1984, p. 110; also see Swaminathan, Padmini, Jeyaranjan,
    J., Sreenivasan, R., Jayashree, K., 'Tamil Nadu's Midday Meal Scheme:
    Where Assumed Benefits Score over Hard Data', *Economic and Political
    Weekly*, 30 October 2004, pp. 4811–24 for the inconsistencies with data
    from the different departments; *Dinamani*, 25 November 1982.

9   Nedunchezhian, Era., 'Makkal Aadharavae Aatchiku Valimai',
    Dinamani, 11 October 1987.

10 *Dinamani*, 3 September 1980.

11 *Dinamani*, 14 November 1982.

12 Kirubakaran, S., (ed.), *Naan Aanaiyitaal...!*, p. 220.

13 *Viduthalai*, 21 July 1956; http://shodhganga.inflibnet.ac.in/
    bitstream/10603/30267/8/chapter2.pdf; http://pibmumbai.gov.in/
    English/PDF/E0000_H12.PDF; http://www.thehindu.com/news/
    cities/Madras/chen-columns/one-small-meal-for-children-one-giant-
    leap-for-literacy/article3570254.ece.

14 http://www.vikatan.com/news/tamilnadu/74365-emotional-
    memories-of-jayalalithaa.art.

15   http://news.vikatan.com/?nid=10825#cmt241.

16   Interview with S. Ramachandran, 27 August 2016, Madras.

17   Interview with C. Aranganayagam, 10 May 2016, Madras.

18   https://www.youtube.com/watch?v=6h-CYmotfKI.

19   *India Today*, 15 March 1984, pp. 28–31.

20   Ibid.

21   http://indiatoday.intoday.in/story/mgr-midday-nutritious-meal-
     scheme-a-shrewd-political-move/1/392281.html.

22   http://indiatoday.intoday.in/story/aiadmk-helped-by-
     overconfidence-of-dmk-and-congressi/1/409816.html.

23   Vaasanthi, *Cut-Outs, Caste and Cine Stars: The World of Tamil Politics*,
     Delhi: Penguin, 2006, p. 81.

24   http://indiatoday.intoday.in/story/after-10-years-of-ramachandran-
     rule-tamil-nadu-presents-a-very-sorry-picture/1/337294.html.

25   Mohandas, K., *MGR: The Man and the Myth*, Bangalore: Panther
     Publishers, 1992, pp. 60–61.

26   Interview on 8 and 9 May 2016 with H.V. Hande and C. Aranganayagam
     respectively, Madras.

27   http://indiatoday.intoday.in/story/after-10-years-of-ramachandran-
     rule-tamil-nadu-presents-a-very-sorry-picture/1/337294.html.

28   http://timesofindia.indiatimes.com/city/chennai/mgrs-
     100th-birth-anniversary-hero-of-the-poor-manager-of-talent/
     articleshow/56607132.cms.

29   Interview with H.V. Hande and C. Aranganayagam, 8 and 9 May 2016
     respectively, Madras.

30   Mohandas, *MGR: The Man and the Myth*, pp. 128–29.

31   *Murasoli*, 28 August 1980.

32   Kirubakaran, S., (ed.), *M.G.R. Paetigal*, Chennai: Vikatan Pirasuram,
     2009, pp. 256–57.

33   Mohandas, *MGR: The Man and the Myth*, pp. 56–57, 125.

34   http://indiatoday.intoday.in/story/seven-alleged-naxalites-killed-in-
     so-called-encounters-in-tamil-nadu/1/410107.html.

35   http://indiatoday.intoday.in/story/mgr-government-sacks-part-
     time-village-officers-in-tamil-nadu/1/401430.html.

36   Cooperative loans amounted to 200 crore rupees, land revenue and
     government loans 70 crore rupees and electricity dues 32 crore rupees.

37   Small farmers with less than five acres saw power tariff reduced from
     16 paise a unit to 12 paise. For the others it was 14 paise.

38 http://indiatoday.intoday.in/story/farmers-in-tamil-nadu-karnataka-andhra-pradesh-on-the-warpath/1/410242.html; http://indiatoday.intoday.in/story/from-west-to-north-india-farmers-agitation-continues-to-smoulder-for-three-weeks/1/410246.html.

39 Karunanidhi, Kalaignar M., *Nenjuku Needhi*, vol. 3, Chennai: Thirumagal Nilayam, 2008, pp. 423–24.

40 http://indiatoday.intoday.in/story/tamil-nadu-agriculturists-association-president-to-contest-panchayat-elections/1/391327.html.

41 In January 1982, Naidu pulled off an impressive rally in Coimbatore, but it came with a price, as usual. Eight farmers died in police firings. http://indiatoday.intoday.in/story/tamil-nadu-agriculturists-association-president-to-contest-panchayat-elections/1/391327.html.

42 Gurusamy, S., 'Peasant Politics in Tamilnadu: A Socio-political Analysis of a Pressure Group', 1991 thesis, shodhganga.inflibnet.ac.in/bitstream/10603/16237/.../08_chapter%202...shodhganga.inflibnet.ac.in/bitstream/10603/16237/.../09_chapter%203...

43 Pandian, M.S.S., *The Image Trap*, New Delhi: Sage Publications, 1992, p. 22.

44 Rajaram, K., *Oru Saamaniyianin Ninaivugal*, Nakkheeran Publications, 2014, pp. 371–72, pp. 264–65; Aranganayagam narrated an incident where he and the secretary, Gopalkrishna Gandhi, met Chief Minister MGR, who said, 'Why limit it to poor weavers? Make it common to all the poor.' This is how the scheme of free veshtis and sarees for Pongal began. Interview with C. Aranganayagam, 8 May 2016, Madras.

45 Vaali, *Naanum Indha Nootraandum*, Chennai: Kalaignan Pathippagam, 1995, p. 207.

46 Muthukumar, R., *Thamizhaga Arasiyal Varalaaru*, vol. 2, Chennai: Kizhakku Pathippagam, 2013, p. 80.

47 Vaasanthi, *Amma: Jayalalithaa's Journey from Movie Star to Political Queen*, Delhi: Juggernaut, 2016, p. 36.

48 Kalaignar, *Nejuku Needhi*, vol. 3, pp. 427–30; Mohandas, *MGR: The Man and the Myth*, p. 58.

49 Mohandas, *MGR: The Man and the Myth*, p. 61.

50 http://www.indiatvnews.com/news/india/flashback-how-800-dalit-hindus-were-converted-to-islam-33-years-45123.html; http://www.rediff.com/news/special/meenakshipuram-33-years-on-muslims-happy-hindus-not/20150112.htm; http://timesofindia.indiatimes.com/home/sunday-times/deep-focus/The-other-conversion-story/articleshow/45747192.cms; http://indiankanoon.org/doc/1108533/.

51 http://indiatoday.intoday.in/story/untouchability-is-far-from-eradicated-in-tamil-nadu/1/401780.html.

52 http://indiatoday.intoday.in/story/press-faces-fresh-assault-from-tamil-nadu-cm-m.g.-ramachandran/1/371721.html.

53 http://indiatoday.intoday.in/story/tamil-nadu-cm-m.g.-ramachandran-does-a-u-turn-on-anti-scurrility-act/1/371803.html; *Dinamani*, 26 June 1984.

54 *Dinamani*, 7 March 1984.

55 http://indiatoday.intoday.in/story/after-10-years-of-ramachandran-rule-tamil-nadu-presents-a-very-sorry-picture/1/337294.html.

56 Muthukumar, *Thamizhaga Arasiyal Varalaaru*, vol. 2, pp. 81–85. I am indebted to the author for enabling a better understanding of the issue.

57 *Dinamani*, 11 February 1981.

58 *Dinamani*, 31 May 1981.

59 *Dinamani*, 2 June 1981.

60 *Dinamani*, 19 June 1981.

61 *Dinamani*, 26 June 1981.

62 http://indiatoday.intoday.in/story/tamil-nadu-cm-m.g.-ramachandran-plays-safe-with-centre-on-spirit-deal-commission-issue/1/401975.html.

63 Interview with H.V. Hande, 31 August 2016, Madras.

64 Muthukumar, *Thamizhaga Arasiyal Varalaaru*, vol. 2, pp. 86–87.

65 *Dinamani*, 17 May 1981.

66 Mohandas, *MGR: The Man and the Myth*, p. 60.

67 *Dinamani*, 21 May 1981; *Dinamani*, 15 June 1981.

68 http://indiatoday.intoday.in/story/severe-drought-hits-11-of-16-districts-of-tamil-nadu/1/401713.html.

69 *Dinamani*, 16 March 1981.

70 Kirubakaran, S., (ed.), *.G.R. Paetigal*, pp. 256–57.

71 http://indiatoday.intoday.in/story/wave-of-violence-envelops-tamil-nadu-after-karunanidhis-arrest/1/402336.html.

72 *Dinamani*, 18 March 1981; http://indiatoday.intoday.in/story/severe-drought-hits-11-of-16-districts-of-tamil-nadu/1/401713.html.

73 *Anna*, 2 December 1979.

74 http://indiatoday.intoday.in/story/karunanidhi-does-not-exist-without-congressi-support-m.g.-ramachandran/1/402339.html.

75 *Dinamani*, 9 October 1981.

76 http://indiatoday.intoday.in/story/liquor-scandal-may-cost-tamil-
    nadu-cm-much-of-his-political-credibility/1/371802.html.

77 Interview with Mohan Raman, 2 November 2016, Madras.

78 Solai, *Netru, Indru, Naalai*, Chennai: Nakkheeran Publications, 2012,
    pp. 135–36.

79 http://indiatoday.intoday.in/story/former-hc-judge-to-head-one-
    man-commission-to-probe-tamil-nadus-liquor-problem/1/392189.
    html.

80 http://indiatoday.intoday.in/story/mgrs-illness-makes-it-difficult-for-
    opposition-to-criticise-him-or-question-his-honesty/1/361151.html.

81 *Dinamani,* 17 March 1984.

82 http://indiatoday.intoday.in/story/liquor-licences-corruption-case-
    mgr-and-other-cabinet-ministers-get-clean-chit/1/360646.html;
    Kalaignar, *Nenjuku Needhi,* vol. 3, pp. 468–69.

83 *Dinamani,* 17 March 1984.

84 http://thewire.in/29736/the-politics-of-prohibition-in-tamil-nadu/;
    http://www.thehindu.com/elections/tamilnadu2016/tamil-nadu-
    prohibition-politics/article8460791.ece;   http://www.vikatan.com/
    article.php?module=magazine&aid=108702; *Dinamani,* 28 May 1983.

85 http://www.vikatan.com/article.php?module=magazine&
    aid=108702; https://www.google.iq/#q=Kalaignar+Karunanidhi%2
    7s+interview+to+karthigai+selvan+in+may+2016+in+puthiya+tha
    laimurai.

86 I owe this section's details and the chronology of events to *India
    Today*'s articles on this issue and in particular to http://indiatoday.
    intoday.in/story/karunanidhi-govt-initiates-steps-to-take-over-liquor-
    industry-destroy-liquor-barons-clout/1/323292.html.

87 Interview with S. Ramachandran, 27 August 2016, Madras.

88 Ibid.

89 http://indiatoday.intoday.in/story/wave-of-violence-envelops-tamil-
    nadu-after-karunanidhis-arrest/1/402336.html.

90 Ramasamy, V.K., *Enadhu Kalaippayanam,* Chennai: New Century
    Book House, 2002, pp. 429–34; http://www.thehindu.com/features/
    cinema/a-brief-history-of-nadigar-sangam/article7877460.ece.

91 http://indiatoday.intoday.in/story/karunanidhi-does-not-exist-
    without-congressi-support-m.g.-ramachandran/1/402339.html.

92 Interview on 27 August and 31 August with S. Ramachandran and
    with H.V. Hande respectively, Madras.

93   Kalaignar, *Nenjuku Needhi*, vol. 3, p. 461.

94   Ibid., *Nenjuku Needhi* p. 463.

95   Ibid., *Nenjuku Needhi* pp. 463–64.

96   *Murasoli*, 9 November 1979. On 8 November, Kalaignar wondered, even if this was to be accepted for the sake of argument, what would happen in case the incumbent was an independent.

97   http://indiatoday.intoday.in/story/congressi-terminates-alliance-with-dmk-indirectly-welcomes-support-of-aiadmk/1/402394.html.

98   http://indiatoday.intoday.in/story/periaulum-seat-could-be-another-watershed-in-tamil-nadus-political-kaleidoscope/1/392106. html.

99   http://indiatoday.intoday.in/story/battle-of-wits-between-aiadmk-and-dmk-degenerates-into-street-fights-over-sri-lanka-tamils/1/402276.html.

100 Kalaignar, *Nenjuku Needhi*, vol. 3, p. 436–55; http://indiatoday.intoday. in/story/wave-of-violence-envelops-tamil-nadu-after-karunanidhis-arrest/1/402336.html.

101 http://indiatoday.intoday.in/story/after-tirupattur-by-election-triumph-congressi-decides-to-go-solo-in-tamil-nadu/1/391292.html

102 Muthukumar, *Thamizhaga Arasiyal Varalaaru*, vol. 2, p. 105.

103 http://indiatoday.intoday.in/story/dmk-president-karunanidhi-blatantly-refuses-to-appear-in-court/1/354071.html.

104 http://indiatoday.intoday.in/story/temples-in-tamil-nadu-face-serious-crisis-due-to-political-interference-by-state-govt/1/361359. html; http://indiatoday.intoday.in/story/murder-or-sucide-judicial-inquiry-ordered-into-c.-subramaniam-pillais-death/1/401651.html; Kalaignar, *Nenjuku Needhi*, vol. 3, 465–68; Mohandas, *MGR: The Man and the Myth*, pp. 62–64; http://indiatoday.intoday.in/story/dmk-president-karunanidhi-blatantly-refuses-to-appear-in-court/1/354071. html.; *Ananda Vikatan*, 18 August 2010.

105 *Dinamani*, 28 February 1983.

106 http://www.vikatan.com/news/article.php?module=news&aid=25095; http://news.vikatan.com/article.php?module=news&aid=25828.

107 http://www.rediff.com/news/1999/apr/01jaya.htm.

108 Interview with S. Ramachandran, 27 August 2016, Madras.

109 http://www.vikatan.com/news/article.php?module=news&aid=25828.

110 http://zeenews.india.com/home/im-the-political-heir-of-mgr-jayalalitha_418718.html.

111 Interview with Su. Thirunavukkarasar, 23 August 2013, Madras; http://
archive.tehelka.com/story_main10.asp?filename=Ne020505The_
Enigma.as

112 Vaasanthi, *Amma*, p. 37; http://www.hell-man.de/proxy/index.php?q
=aHR0cDovL3d3dy5vdXRRsb29raW5kaWEuY29tL21hZ2F6aW5lL3N
0b3J5L3RoZS1yb2FkLXRvLWFtbWFob29kLzI3MDg1OA%3D%3D.

113 http://www.newindianexpress.com/states/tamil_nadu/Vote-
AIADMK-in-War-to-Protect-Democracy/2014/03/24/article2127051.
ece;   http://indianexpress.com/article/explained/j-jayalalithaa-m-
karunanidhi-tamil-nadu-assembly-polls-2016-2807205/.

114 http://www.outlookindia.com/magazine/story/the-life-and-times-
of-jayalalitha/205450

115 Interview with S. Ramachandran, 27 August 2016, Madras.

116 *Dinamani,* 19 October 1982.

117 Ibid.

118 *Ananda Vikatan,* 18 August 2010; http://www.vikatan.com/article.ph
p?aid=14524&sid=394&mid=2&uid=34071&#.

119 *Dinamani,* 24 November 1982.

120 http://tamil.oneindia.com/news/2008/02/14/tn-mgr-got-assurance-
from-me-says-jayalalitha.html.

121 https://www.google.iq/#q=தொ்ண்டர்களை+காப்பாற்ற+எம்.
ஜி.ஆர்.+சத்தியம்+வாங்கினார்:+ஜெ.

122 http://www.ndtv.com/elections-news/i-broke-contact-with-
jayalalithaa-554634

123 http://indiatoday.intoday.in/story/periakulum-seat-could-be-another-
watershed-in-tamil-nadus-political-kaleidoscope/1/392106.html.

124 Mohandas, *MGR: The Man and the Myth*, pp. 68–70.

125 Kalaignar, *Nenjuku Needhi*, vol. 3, p. 491.

126 *Dinamani,* 31 October 1982.

127 Mohandas, *MGR: The Man and the Myth*, p. 71.

128 Ibid.

129 http://www.csmonitor.com/1983/1013/101342.html

130 http://www.vikatan.com/news/article.php?module=news&aid=25095;
http://news.vikatan.com/article.php?module=news&aid=25828;

131 Interview with Su. Thirunavukkarasar, 23 August 2016, Madras.

132 http://indiatoday.intoday.in/story/congressi-gets-another-drubbing-
in-the-south-wins-only-two-seats-in-assembly-by-polls/1/371495.
html; *Dinamani,* 30 January 1983.

133 http://www.tn.gov.in/government/keycontact/18358

134 Interview with R.M. Veerappan, 15 September 2016, Madras.

135 Muthukumar, *Thamizhaga Arasiyal Varalaaru*, vol. 2, p. 118.

136 Interview with Su. Thirunavukkarasar, 23 August 2016, Madras.

137 *Dinamani*, 26 January 1983.

138 *Dinamani*, 8 February 1983.

139 *Dinamani*, 30 January 1983.

140 *Dinamani*, 22 February 1984.

141 Interview with Su. Thirunavukkarasar, 24 August 2016, Madras.

142 Kirubakaran, S., (ed.), *M.G.R. Paetigal*, pp. 259.

143 *Dinamani*, 9 February 1983.

144 *Dinamani*, 10 February 1983.

145 Ibid.,

146 http://indiatoday.intoday.in/story/with-crop-failure-looming-large-
     tamil-nadu-govt-gets-embroiled-in-relief-row-with-centre/1/392337.
     html; http://indiatoday.intoday.in/story/tamil-nadu-faces-foodgrain-
     crisis-cm-mgr-undertakes-seven-hour-working-day-fast/1/372349.
     html 28 February 1983.

147 *Dinamani*, 16 February 1983.

148 http://indiatoday.intoday.in/story/conclave-of-four-southern-
     non-congressi-chief-ministers-surprisingly-low-key/1/371529.html;
     Dinamani, 21 March 1983.

149 *Dinamani*, 25 February 1983.

150 *Dinamani*, 30 March 1983.

151 *Dinamani*, 26 December 1987.

152 Interview with S. Ramachandran, 27 August 2016, Madras.

153 *Dinamani*, 28 April 1983.

154 *Dinamani*, 25 May 1983.

155 Kirubakaran, S., (ed.), *Naan Aanaiyitaal . . .!*, p. 231; http://tamil.
     thehindu.com/opinion/blogs/எம்-100-14-எம்-எ/article8312829.ece;
     However, in May 1982, when it was pointed out that NTR had said
     he was following him, MGR responded: 'That's wrong. I have been
     in politics for thirty-five years from 1937. It won't be correct to follow
     one. It depends on the state.' Kirubakaran, S., (ed.), *M.G.R. Paetigal*,
     p. 258.

156 Interview with H.V. Hande, 8 May 2016, Madras.

157 *Dinamani*, 29 April 1983.

158 *Dinamani*, 14 May 1983.

159 *Dinamani*, 25 October 1978.

160 http://www.thehindu.com/todays-paper/tp-national/tp-tamilnadu/
      article1785242.ece; http://www.thehindu.com/2004/12/01/
      stories/2004120113280300.htm; http://indiatoday.intoday.in/story/
      tamil-nadu-and-andhra-pradesh-sign-pact-to-bring-krishna-waters-
      over-550-km-into-madras/1/371584.html; May 15, 1983http://
      indiatoday.intoday.in/story/telugu-ganga-project-turns-out-to-be-
      a-financial-sink-hole/1/354174.html; http://tamil.thehindu.com/
      opinion/blogs/தம-100-14-தம-எ/article8312829.ece.

161 http://indiatoday.intoday.in/story/coalition-government-in-
      pondicherry-collapses-as-congressi-pulls-out/1/371763.html;
      Kalaignar, *Nenjuku Needhi*, vol. 3, pp. 505–07.

162 *Dinamani*, 28 July 1983.

163 *Dinamani*, 29 July 1983.

164 *Dinamani*, 1 August 1983.

165 de Silva, K.M., Wriggins, Howard, *J.R. Jayewardene of Sri Lanka: A
      Political Biography: From 1956 to His Retirement*, vol. 2, Honolulu:
      University of Hawaii Press, 1995, p. 570.

166 Nedumaran's deposition, Jain Commission, no. 5, chapter 16.

167 Interview with S. Ramachandran, February 1994, Madras.

168 *Dinamani*, 3 August 1983.

169 *Dinamani*, 11 August 1983.

170 *Dinamani*, 28 October 1983.

171 *Dinamani*, 15 August 1983.

172 'The Tamils are being duped,' interview by M. Karunanidhi, *Frontline*,
      7–20 March 1987, p. 105; 'Eelam State Only Solution: DMK,' *The
      Hindu*, 28 August 1983, p. 13.

173 *Dinamani*, 20 August 1983; *Dinamani*, 27 June 1983.

174 Kalaignar, *Nenjuku Needhi*, vol. 3, pp. 494–99;

175 *Dinamani*, 28 October 1983.

176 *Dinamani*, 28 October 1983.

177 *Dinamani*, 8 November 1983.

178 Muthukumar, *Thamizhaga Arasiyal Varalaaru*, vol. 2, p. 144.

179 Mohandas, *MGR: The Man and the Myth*, pp. 78–79.

180 https://www.youtube.com/watch?v=ASx21WL03y0.

181 Balasingham, Anton, *Viduthalai*, Surrey:Fairmax Publishing Ltd, 2003,
      pp. 2–17.

182 Interview with S. Ramachandran, 27 August 2016, Madras.

183 Balasingham, *Viduthalai*, p. 21.

184 Ibid., pp. 24–25.

185 http://indiatoday.intoday.in/story/furore-in-rajya-sabha-over-tamil-nadu-govt-order-authorising-police-to-open-dmk-leader-mail/1/372256.html.

186 http://indiatoday.intoday.in/story/madras-hc-judges-condemn-m.g.-ramachahdran-government-for-keeping-surveillance-on-them/1/371635.html.

187 http://www.vikatan.com/news/article.php?module=news&aid=25095; http://news.vikatan.com/article.php?module=news&aid=25828.

188 Interview with Su. Thirunavukkarasar, 23 August 2016, Madras.

189 http://www.vikatan.com/news/article.php?module=news&aid=25095; http://news.vikatan.com/article.php?module=news&aid=25828.

190 http://www.vikatan.com/news/article.php?module=news&aid=25095; http://news.vikatan.com/article.php?module=news&aid=25828.

191 http://www.outlookindia.com/magazine/story/the-life-and-times-of-jayalalitha/205450.

192 John, Valampuri, *Vanakkam*, Chennai: Nakkheeran Publications, 2010, p. 114.

193 http://www.newindianexpress.com/states/tamil-nadu/2016/dec/05/the-powerful-speeches-of-late-aiadmk-supremo-jayalalithaa-1545887.html.

194 Vaasanthi, *Amma*, pp. 42–43.

195 http://www.vikatan.com/news/tamilnadu/74365-emotional-memories-of-jayalalithaa.art.

196 Interview with RMV, 15 September 2016, Madras.

197 http://www.outlookindia.com/magazine/story/the-life-and-times-of-jayalalitha/205450.

198 *Dinamani*, 15 December 1983.

199 *Dinamani*, 9 January 1984. http://indiatoday.intoday.in/story/mgr-gives-new-twist-to-possible-aiadmk-congressi-electoral-alliance/1/360416.html.

200 http://indiatoday.intoday.in/story/madras-hc-judgement-to-ensure-medical-education-for-almost-a-hundred-more-students/1/360692.html.

201 *Dinamani*, 24 May 1984.

202 http://indiatoday.intoday.in/story/will-alliance-between-congressi-and-aiadmk-continues-for-ever/1/360795.html.

203 Kalaignar, *Nenjuku Needhi*, vol. 3, p. 510; http://indiatoday.intoday. in/story/by-elections-congress-loses-key-contests-in-well-entrenched-citadels/1/360723.html; Mohandas, *MGR: The Man and the Myth*, pp. 90–91.

204 http://indiatoday.intoday.in/story/will-alliance-between-congressi-and-aiadmk-continues-for-ever/1/360795.html.

205 *Dinathanthi*, 23 May 1983.

206 *Dinamani*, 2 July 1984.

207 Interview with Su. Thirunavukkarasar, 23 August 2016, Madras.

208 http://indiatoday.intoday.in/story/tamil-nadu-cm-m-g-ramachandran-goes-out-of-his-way-to-please-congressi/1/361394. html; http://indiatoday.intoday.in/story/by-elections-congress-loses-key-contests-in-well-entrenched-citadels/1/360723.html.

209 *Dinamani*, 9 July 1984.

210 *Dinamani*, 21 July 1984.

211 *Dinamani*, 28 August 1984.

212 http://indiatoday.intoday.in/story/there-is-no-democracy-within-aiadmk-s-d-somasundaram/1/360998.html.

213 *Dinamani*, 7 September 1984.

214 *Dinamani*, 13 August 1984.

215 *Dinamani*, 7 September 1984; http://indiatoday.intoday.in/story/ tamil-nadu-cm-m.g.-ramachandran-faces-major-crisis-following-sacking-of-s.d.-somasundaram/1/360984.html.

216 *Dinamani*, 29 August 1984.

217 *Dinamani*, 31 August 1984.

218 http://indiatoday.intoday.in/story/there-is-no-democracy-within-aiadmk-s-d-somasundaram/1/360998.html; *Dinamani*, 2 September 1984.

219 Mohandas, *MGR: The Man and the Myth*, pp. 93–94; Kalaignar, *Nenjuku Needhi*, vol. 3, p. 519.

220 Interview on 8 and 9 May 2016 with H.V. Hande and C. Aranganayagam respectively, Madras.

221 http://indiatoday.intoday.in/story/riven-by-internal-dissension-ruling-aiadmk-government-virtually-splits/1/360977.html; http:// indiatoday.intoday.in/story/they-are-tarnishing-the-name-of-the-aiadmk-and-mgr-jayalalitha/1/353860.html.

222 *Dinamani*, 22 August 1984.

223 *Dinamani*, 2 September 1984.

224 *Dinamani,* 3 September 1984.

225 Kalaignar, *Nenjuku Needhi,* vol. 3, pp. 517–19, *Dinamani,* 2 September 1984.

226 http://www.assembly.tn.gov.in/archive/7th_1980/7threvi ew_80-84.pdf; *Dinamani,* 4 September 1984.

227 http://indiatoday.intoday.in/story/tamil-nadu-cm-m.g.-ramachandran-faces-major-crisis-following-sacking-of-s.d.-somasundaram/1/360984.html.

228 *Dinamani,* 6 September 1984.

229 *Dinamani,* 16 September 1984.

230 http://indiatoday.intoday.in/story/tamil-nadu-cm-m.g.-ramachandran-faces-major-crisis-following-sacking-of-s.d.-somasundaram/1/360984.html, Mohandas, *MGR: The Man and the Myth,* pp. 93–94; Kalaignar, *Nenjuku Needhi,* vol. 3, pp. 517–19.

231 Ibid., p. 593.

232 Dinamani, 21 August 1984.

233 http://indiatoday.intoday.in/story/they-are-tarnishing-the-name-of-the-aiadmk-and-mgr-jayalalitha/1/353860.html.

234 Interview on 8 and 9 May 2016 with H.V. Hande and C. Aranganayagam respectively, Madras.

235 Mohandas, *MGR: The Man and the Myth,* pp. pp. 93–96.

236 http://indiatoday.intoday.in/story/mgrs-illness-leads-to-massive-emotional-upsurge-political-turmoil-in-tamil-nadu/1/361134.html.

237 *Dinamani,* 10 October 1984.

238 *Dinamani,* 14 October 1984.

239 *Dinamani,* 15 October 1984; http://indiatoday.intoday.in/story/mgrs-illness-leads-to-massive-emotional-upsurge-political-turmoil-in-tamil-nadu/1/361134.html.

240 Interview with H.V. Hande, 31 August 2016, Madras.

241 *Dinamani,* 17 October 1984.

242 http://indiatoday.intoday.in/story/mgrs-illness-leads-to-massive-emotional-upsurge-political-turmoil-in-tamil-nadu/1/361134.html.

243 *Dinamani,* 19 October 1984.

244 *Dinamani,* 23 October 1984.

245 Interview with Su. Thirunavukkarasar, 24 August 2016, Madras.

246 Ramasamy, Cho., *Adhirshtam Thantha Anubhavangal,* Chennai: Alliance Publishers, 2015, p. 401.

247 Interview with S. Ramachandran, 27 August 2016, Madras.

248 Periasamy, G., Palani, *Heartbeats: My Unforgettable Life Experiences*, Chennai: Vanathi Pathippagam, 2016, p. 157.

249 Mohandas, *MGR: The Man and the Myth*, pp. 100–01.

250 http://indiatoday.intoday.in/story/mgrs-illness-leads-to-massive-emotional-upsurge-political-turmoil-in-tamil-nadu/1/361134.html.

251 *Dinamani*, 28 October 1984.

252 http://www.assembly.tn.gov.in/archive/8th_1985/8threview_85-88.pdf.

253 *Dinamani*, 16 November 1984.

254 Ibid.

255 Interview with H.V. Hande, 31 August 2016, Madras.

256 *Dinamani*, 4 December 1984.

257 *Dinamani*, 7 December 1984.

258 http://www.outlookindia.com/magazine/story/the-life-and-times-of-jayalalitha/205450.

259 http://indiatoday.intoday.in/story/m.g.-ramachandran-is-back-and-back-to-stay/1/354271.html.

260 http://www.outlookindia.com/magazine/story/the-life-and-times-of-jayalalitha/205450.

261 Periasamy, *Heartbeats*, p. 158.

262 https://www.youtube.com/watch?v=hIj49FXT1aI.

263 Interview with RMV, 15 September 2016, Madras.

264 Periasamy, *Heartbeats*, pp. 170–6; however, Mohandas and RMV also claim that it was their idea. See, Mohandas, *MGR: The Man and the Myth*, pp. 105–06; Ranimaindhan, *RMV Oru Thondar*, Chennai: Rajarajan Pathippagam, 2005, pp. 370–72.

265 *Dinamani*, 10 December 1984.

266 Mohandas, *MGR: The Man and the Myth*, pp. 105–06; John, *Vanakkam*, p. 153.

267 Interview with Su. Thirunavukkarasar and S. Ramachandran, 24 and 31 August respectively, Madras.

268 http://www.vikatan.com/news/tamilnadu/74365-emotional-memories-of-jayalalithaa.art.

269 https://www.youtube.com/watch?v=hIj49FXT1aI.

270 Mohandas, *MGR: The Man and the Myth*, pp. 106–07.

271 http://www.tn.gov.in/government/keycontact/18358.

272 John, *Vanakkam*, p. 158; http://www.vikatan.com/juniorvikatan/Politics/29139-Kaluzhu-answer.html#cmt241

273 *Murasoli*, 8 December 1984.

274 http://eci.nic.in/eci_main/StatisticalReports/LS_1984/Vol_I_
     LS_84.pdf

275 *Dinamani*, 12 January 1985.

276 Ranimaindhan, *RMV Oru Thondar*, pp. 375–76.

277 *Dinamani*, 16 January 1985.

278 *Dinamani*, 16 January 1985; http://www.assembly.tn.gov.in/archive/
     8th_1985/8threview_85-88.pdf

279 *Dinamani*, 19 January 1985.

280 Interview with Su. Thirunavukkarasar, 23 August 2016, Madras.

281 Ibid.

282 Mohandas, *MGR: The Man and the Myth*, pp. 109–110; http://
     indiatoday.intoday.in/story/tamil-nadu-cast-decisive-vote-aiadmk-
     congressi-combine-sweeps-the-polls/1/353775.html.

283 http://indiatoday.intoday.in/story/while-mgr-recuperates-in-us-
     aiadmk-heads-for-a-split-jayalalitha-gets-a-rude-shock/1/353861.
     html; Interview with Su. Thirunavukkarasar, 24 August 2016, Madras;
     http://www.vikatan.com/new/article.php?module=magazine&
     aid=32557.

284 Periasamy, *Heartbeats*, pp. 177–79.

285 *Dinamani*, 21 January 1985.

286 *Dinamani*, 20 January 1985.

287 *Dinamani*, 23, 24 January 1985.

288 https://twitter.com/kalaignar89/status/556706498147930112?lan
     g=en;   http://blogs.timesofindia.indiatimes.com/Madrastalkies/
     jayalalithaa-her-hero-s-rival/.

289 Interview with RMV, 15 September 2016, Madras.

290 Kalaignar, *Nenjuku Needhi*, vol. 3, pp. 530–31.

291 *Dinamani*, 23, 24 January 1985.

292 http://indiatoday.intoday.in/story/they-are-tarnishing-the-name-of-
     the-aiadmk-and-mgr-jayalalitha/1/353860.html.

293 http://www.outlookindia.com/magazine/story/the-life-and-times-
     of-jayalalitha/205450.

294 http://www.newindianexpress.com/states/tamil-nadu/2016/
     dec/06/i-dont-think-anyone-has-taken-more-criticism-than-i-have-
     jaya-told-simi-garewal-1546016.html.

295 Ibid.

296 Ibid.

Chapter 8: An MGR not In-charge

1   *Frontline*,   5–22   February   1985,   http://mgrroop.blogspot.
    com/2009/01/hero-returns.html.
2   *Frontline*,   5–22   February   1985;   http://indiatoday.intoday.in/
    story/tamil-nadu-cm-m.g.-ramachandran-returns-home-health-
    speculations-laid-to-rest/1/353919.html.
3   Interview with RMV, 15 September 2016, Madras.
4   Ranimaindhan, *RMV Oru Thondar*, Chennai: Rajarajan Pathippagam,
    2005, pp. 378–79; Interview with RMV, 15 September 2016, Madras.
5   Mohandas, K., *MGR: The Man and the Myth*, Bangalore: Panther
    Publishers, 1992, pp. 102–03.
6   *Dinamani*, 31 July 1985.
7   John, Valampuri, *Vanakkam*, Chennai: Nakkheeran Publications, 2010,
    pp. 163–64.
8   Interview with S. Ramachandran, 27 August 2016, Madras.
9   Interview with Su. Thirunavukkarasar, 23 August 2016, Madras;
    http://indiatoday.intoday.in/story/m.g.-ramachandran-is-back-and-
    back-to-stay/1/354271.html.
10 Interview with S. Ramachandran, 27 August 2016, Madras.
11 John, *Vanakkam*, pp. 162–64.
12 Muthukumar, R., *Thamizhaga Arasiyal Varalaaru*, vol. 2, Chennai:
    Kizhakku Pathippagam, 2013, p. 172.
13 Interview with S. Ramachandran, 27 August 2016, Madras.
14 Interview with P.H. Pandian, 24 August 2016, Madras.
15 http://indiatoday.intoday.in/story/tamil-nadu-cm-m.g.-
    ramachandran-returns-home-health-speculations-laid-to-
    rest/1/353919.html.
16 http://indiatoday.intoday.in/story/tamil-nadu-cm-m.g.-
    ramachandran-returns-home-health-speculations-laid-to-
    rest/1/353919.html.
17 http://indiatoday.intoday.in/story/m.g.-ramachandran-is-back-and-
    back-to-stay/1/354271.html.
18 Ibid.
19 http://www.assembly.tn.gov.in/archive/8th_1985/8threvi
    ew_85-88.pdf.
20 http://www.the hindu.com/news/national/tamil-nadu/Sasikala-is-
    the-sixth-person-to-be-AIADMK-general-secretary/article16968191.

ece/ucbrowser?hbt=uc&utm_source=UCbrowser&utm_medium=Referal&utm_campaign=UCBrowser.

21   Interview with Su. Thirunavukkarasar, 23 August 2016, Madras.

22   http://www.outlookindia.com/magazine/story/the-life-and-times-of-jayalalitha/205450.

23   http://www.vikatan.com/news/coverstory/71371-jayalalithaa-pleads-mgr--from-mysuru-to-81-poes-garden-travel-story-of-jayalalithaa--episode-17.html.

24   Interview with Su. Thirunavukarasarar and S. Ramachandran on 24 and 27 August respectively in Madras.

25   http://indiatoday.intoday.in/story/is-tamil-nadu-cm-ramachandran-losing-grip-over-state-government-and-aiadmk/1/353996.html; http://www.outlookindia.com/magazine/story/the-life-and-times-of-jayalalitha/205450.

26   Rajaram, K., *Oru Saamaniyianin Ninaivugal*, Nakkheeran Publications, 2014, pp. 460–61.

27   https://twitter.com/kalaignar89/status/556706498147930112?lang=en.

28   http://www.the hindu.com/the hindu/2003/02/14/stories/2003021406540100.htm.

29   http://indiatoday.intoday.in/story/m.g.-ramachandran-is-back-and-back-to-stay/1/354271 html.

30   'M.G. Ramachandran, The Glitter is Gone', *India Today*, 31 July 1986, http://indiatoday.intoday.in/story/tamil-nadu-cm-m.g.-ramachandran-once-indestructible-image-takes-a-heavy-battering/1/348679.html.

31   *Dinamani*, 25 July 1985; *Dinamani*, 25 August 1985.

32   *Dinamani*, 27 July 1985.

33   *Dinamani*, 15 August 1985.

34   *Dinamani*, 25 August 1985.

35   *Dinamani*, 6 September 1985.

36   *Dinamani*, 6 September 1985.

37   Interview with RMV, 15 September 2016, Madras.

38   *Dinamani*, 11 September 1985; *Dinamani*, 12 September 1985.

39   *Dinamani*, 17 October 1985.

40   http://indiatoday.intoday.in/story/succession-battle-erupts-between-veerappan-and-jayalalitha-as-mgr-falls-ill/1/354722.html.

41   Ranimaindhan, pp. 388–89.

42   Ibid.

43 *Dinamani*, 29 October 1985; *Dinamani*, 30 October 1985; http://
    indiatoday.intoday.in/story/succession-battle-erupts-between-
    veerappan-and-jayalalitha-as-mgr-falls-ill/1/354722.html;   Kalaignar,
    vol. 3, 547–8.
44 *Dinamani*, 30 October 1985.
45 *Dinamani*, 3 November 1985.
46 http://indiatoday.intoday.in/story/aiadmk-mp-jayalalitha-
    makes-her-come-back-as-propaganda-secretary-to-thundering-
    applause/1/354783.html.
47 *Dinamani*, 2 November 1985.
48 *Dinamani*, 3 November 1985.
49 Mohandas, *MGR: The Man and the Myth*, p. 122.
50 http://www.the hindu.com/news/cities/Madras/a-case-that-rattled-
    mgr-and-fuelled-dissent/article8170252.ece.
51 Mohandas, *MGR: The Man and the Myth*, p. 122.
52 http://www.assembly.tn.gov.in/archive/8th_1985/8threvi
    ew_85-88.pdf.
53 http://www.outlookindia.com/magazine/story/the-life-and-times-
    of-jayalalitha/205450.
54 Mohandas, *MGR: The Man and the Myth*, p. 130.
55 http://indiatoday.intoday.in/story/aiadmk-suffers-unprecedented-
    defeat-in-municipal-polls-dmk-romps-home-a-clear-winner/1/348250.
    html.
56 Ranimaindhan, *RMV Oru Thondar*, pp. 386–87.
57 http://www.assembly.tn.gov.in/archive/8th_1985/8threvi
    ew_85–88.pdf.
58 http://indiatoday.intoday.in/story/r.m.-veerappan-steals-a-march-
    over-his-political-foe-jayalalitha/1/348162.html.
59 Karunanidhi, Kalaignar M., *Nenjuku Needhi*, vol. 3, Chennai:
    Thirumagal Nilayam, 2008, p. 549.
60 http://indiatoday.intoday.in/story/effect-of-mgrs-failing-health-
    began-to-show-on-the-administration/1/348354.html.
61 Mohandas, *MGR: The Man and the Myth*, p. 130.
62 Ranimaindhan, *RMV Oru Thondar*, p. 387.
63 Interview with Su. Thirunavukarasar, 24 August 2016, Madras.
64 http://www.outlookindia.com/magazine/story/the-life-and-times-
    of-jayalalitha/205450.
65 Ibid.

66   http://www.ndtv.com/elections-news/i-broke-contact-with-jayalalithaa-554634.

67   http://indiatoday.intoday.in/story/aiadmk-politics-resemble-theatre-of-the-absurd-as-leaders-feud-for-ascendancy-in-the-party/1/348389.html.

68   RMV explained that MGR was unhappy with KAK's elder brother Mathiazhagan, deceased in 1983, and sometimes this spilled over to KAK. Interview with RMV, 15 September 2016, Madras.

69   http://indiatoday.intoday.in/story/effect-of-mgrs-failing-health-began-to-show-on-the-administration/1/348354.html.

70   Mohandas, *MGR: The Man and the Myth*, pp. 122–23.

71   http://indiatoday.intoday.in/story/unfortunately-i-have-been-kept-in-the-dark-tamil-nadu-Governor/1/348653.html.

72   Interview with RMV, 15 September 2016, Madras.

73   http://www.vikatan.com/news/tamilnadu/74365-emotional-memories-of-jayalalithaa.art

74   *Murasoli*, 15 July 1987.

75   *India Today*, 15 August 1986, pp. 64–65.

76   http://www.vikatan.com/news/coverstory/71371-jayalalithaa-pleads-mgr--from-mysuru-to-81-poes-garden-travel-story-of-jayalalithaa--episode-17.art; Vaasanthi, *Amma: Jayalalithaa's Journey from Movie Star to Political Queen*, Delhi: Juggernaut, 2016, pp. 52–53.

77   http://indiatoday.intoday.in/story/tamil-nadu-cm-m.g.-ramachandran-once-indestructible-image-takes-a-heavy-battering/1/348679.html.

78   Ibid.

79   *India Today*, 15 August 1986, pp. 64–65.

80   http://indiatoday.intoday.in/story/tamil-nadu-cm-m.g.-ramachandran-once-indestructible-image-takes-a-heavy-battering/1/348679.html.

81   Interview with artist Mohan Raman, 2 November 2016, Madras.

82   http://indiatoday.intoday.in/story/tamil-nadu-by-elections-omens-not-propitious-for-ruling-aiadmk/1/348760.html.

83   http://indiatoday.intoday.in/story/mgrs-near-mystical-hold-on-tamil-nadu-politics-on-the-wane/1/348873.html.

84   Mohandas, *MGR: The Man and the Myth*, pp. 137–38.

85   http://www.assembly.tn.gov.in/archive/8th_1985/8threview_85-88.pdf.

86   Ibid.
87   *Murasoli,* 25 October 1987.
88   http://indiatoday.intoday.in/story/tamil-nadu-cm-m.g.-
     ramachandran-displays-his-authority-as-undisputed-boss-of-
     aiadmk/1/348984.html.
89   Ranimaindhan, *RMV Oru Thondar,* p. 414.
90   Interview with Dr. H.V. Hande and C. Aranganayagam, 8 and 9 May
     2016 respectively, Madras.
91   Ranimaindhan, *RMV Oru Thondar,* p. 422; interview with RMV, 15
     September 2016, Madras.
92   Interview with P.H. Pandian, 27 August 2016, Madras.
93   *India Today,* 15 January 1987, pp. 45–47.
94   *India Today,* 31 January 1987, pp. 31–32; Kalaignar, *Nenjuku Needhi,* vol.
     3, pp. 571–78.
95   http://www.assembly.tn.gov.in/archive/8th_1985/8threvi
     ew_85-88.pdf;   http://www.the   hindu,.com/todays-paper/tp-
     national/tp-tamilnadu/legislative-council-had-chequered-history/
     article746386.ece; *Dinamani,* 6 March 1984.
96   *Dinamani,* 6 March 1984.
97   http://indiatoday.intoday.in/story/objections-raised-to-nomination-
     of-actress-to-legislative-council-mgr-abolishes-council/1/348518.
     html; Kalaignar, *Nenjuku Needhi,* vol. 3, pp. 557–61.
98   Mohandas, *MGR: The Man and the Myth,* p. 131.
99   http://indiatoday.intoday.in/story/after-10-years-of-ramachandran-
     rule-tamil-nadu-presents-a-very-sorry-picture/1/337294.html.
100 http://indiatoday.intoday.in/story/dmk-is-my-enemy-number-one-
     in-tamil-nadu-jayalalitha/1/330176.html.
101 http://indiatoday.intoday.in/story/tamil-nadu-chief-minister-m.g.-
     ramachandran-reintroduced-prohibition/1/336631.html.
102 http://www.assembly.tn.gov.in/archive/8th_1985/08_04_02.pdf.
103 http://www.assembly.tn.gov.in/archive/8th_1985/8threview_85-88.
     pdf; http://www.the hindu.com/2003/11/16/stories/2003111602121000.
     htm; http://indiatoday.intoday.in/story/arrest-of-ananda-vikattin-editor-
     another-press-vs-ramachandran-government-battle/1/336963.html;
     Kalaignar, *Nenjuku Needhi,* vol. 3, pp. 579–80.
104 *Dinamani,* 1 November 1987.
105 http://irdp.info/journals/j2/volume2/IJMRSS_212.pdf;   http://
     indiatoday.intoday.in/story/agitation-by-backward-vanniyar-
     community-rocks-tamil-nadu/1/337588.html.

106 Interview with S. Ramachandran, 27 Madras.

107 *Dinamani*, 26 November 1987.

108 *Dinamani*, 26 November 1987.

109 Interview with C. Ponnaiyan, 25 August 2016, Madras.

110 Mohandas, *MGR: The Man and the Myth*, pp. 113–14.

111 Singh, Natwar, K., *One Life Is Not Enough*, Delhi: Rupa Publications, 2014, p. 254.

112 *The Economist*, 9 January 1988.

113 Interview with S. Ramachandran, February 1994, Madras.

114 Balasingham, Anton, *Viduthalai*, Surrey: Fairmax Publishing Ltd, 2003, p. 315.

115 *The Hindu*, 9 November 1986, p. 1.

116 Mohandas, *MGR: The Man and the Myth*, pp.147–48, 155.

117 'Karunanidhi condemns police action,' *The Hindu*, 23 November 1986, p. 12; for the version of the man who ordered the seizure see, Mohandas, *MGR: The Man and the Myth*, pp. 155–57.

118 *Time*, 11 May 1987.

119 *The Hindu*, 18 May 1987.

120 *The Hindu*, 2 May 1987; De Silva, K.M and Wriggins Howard, *J.R. Jayewardene of Sri Lanka: A Political Biography: From 1956 to His Retirement*, Honolulu: University of Hawaii Press, 1995, pp. 107–08.

121 *The Hindu*, 28 May 1987.

122 *The Hindu*, 4 June 1987; *The Hindu*, 7 June 1987.

123 Ibid.

124 http://indiatoday.intoday.in/story/indias-decision-to-airdrop-supplies-over-jaffna-opens-up-a-diplomatic-pandora-box/1/337218.html.

125 Singh, *One Life Is Not Enough*, p. 260.

126 Ibid.

127 Interview with S. Ramachandran, 27 August 2016, Madras; Singh, *One Life Is Not Enough*, pp. 263–64.

128 Mohandas, *MGR: The Man and the Myth*, p. 163.

129 *Dinamani*, 2 August 1987; Interview with S. Ramachandran, 27 August 2016, Madras.

130 *Dinamani*, 3 August 1987; Mohandas, *MGR: The Man and the Myth*, pp. 147–48, 162–63.

131 *Dinamani*, 3 August 1987; *Frontline*, 8–21 August 1987, p. 15.

132 Interim report of the Jain Commission, no. 5, chapter 27. 'Violation of Accord, says TULF', *The Hindu*, 8 October 1987, p. 9.

133 *The Hindu,* 12 October 1987; *Dinamani,* 14 October 1987.

134 http://indiatoday.intoday.in/story/m.g.-ramachandran-death-marks-the-passing-of-an-era-of-stability-in-tamil-nadu/1/328814.html.

135 *The Hindu,* 14 October 1987.

136 Interview with K. Veeramani, 8 September 2016, Madras; *Dinamani,* 21 October 1987; Periasamy, G. Palani, Dr, *Heartbeats: My unforgettable life experiences,* Chennai: Vanathi Pathippagam, 2016, pp. 191–93.

137 Mohandas, *MGR: The Man and the Myth,* pp. 163–64.

138 *Dinamani,* 3 November 1987.

139 *Dinamani,* 5 November 1987.

140 *Dinamani,* 12 November 1987.

141 *Dinamani,* 25 November 1987.

142 Balasingham, *Viduthalai,* p. 44.

143 https://www.youtube.com/watch?v=ASx21WL03y0

144 Vijayan, S., *M.G.R. Kathai,* part 1, Chennai: Arulmozhi Pathippagam, 1992, pp. 80–84; http://indiatoday.intoday.in/story/m.g.-ramachandran-death-marks-the-passing-of-an-era-of-stability-in-tamil-nadu/1/328814.html; *Dinamani,* 25 December 1987.

145 *Illutstrated Weekly,* 1 May 1988.

146 http://indiatoday.intoday.in/story/deepan-pushed-me-beat-me-and-threw-me-out-jayalalitha/1/328800.html.

147 Ibid.

148 http://www.vikatan.com/article.php?aid=10240&sid=281&mid=1.

149 *The Hindu,* 25 December 1987.

150 http://indiatoday.intoday.in/story/m.g.-ramachandran-death-marks-the-passing-of-an-era-of-stability-in-tamil-nadu/1/328814.html.

151 *Dinamani,* 27 December 1987; *Dinamani,* 26 December 1987.

152 http://indiatoday.intoday.in/story/m.g.-ramachandran-death-marks-the-passing-of-an-era-of-stability-in-tamil-nadu/1/328814.html.

153 *The Economist,* 9 January 1988.

154 Interview with S. Ramachandran, 27 August 2016, Madras.

155 Ranimaindhan, *RMV Oru Thondar,* p. 428–31.

156 *Dinamani,* 30 December 1987.

157 http://indiatoday.intoday.in/story/tamil-nadu-janaki-ramachandran-is-chief-minister-but-can-she-survive/1/328843.html.

158 *Dinamani,* 31 December 1987.

159 http://www.thehindu.com/news/national/tamil-nadu/Jayalalithaa-vs-Janaki-The-last-succession-battle/article17284902.ece.

160 http://indiatoday.intoday.in/story/deepan-pushed-me-beat-me-and-threw-me-out-jayalalitha/1/328800.html.
161 http://articles.philly.com/1988-01-28/news/26282958_1_janaki-ramachandran-madras-tamil-nadu.
162 http://indiatoday.intoday.in/story/tamil-nadu-janaki-governments-foundations-cave-in/1/328934.html.
163 http://www.nytimes.com/1988/01/31/world/gandhi-dissolves-state-rule-after-assembly-brawl.html.
164 Era. Nedunchezhian, 'Makkal Aadharavae Aatchiku Valimai', Dinamani, 11 October 1987.
165 http://www.frontline.in/politics/end-of-an-era/article6805204.ece.
166 Chand, Attar, M.G. Ramachandran: My Blood Brother, Delhi: Gian Publishing House, 1988, p. 49.
167 Era. Nedunchezhian, 'Makkal Aadharavae Aatchiku Valimai', Dinamani, 11 October 1987.
168 Guhan, S., 'State Finances in Tamil Nadu: 1960–85: A Review of Trends and Policy', Working Paper 77, MIDS, p. 345.
169 Aside, 16 June 1988.
170 Pandian, M.S.S., The Image Trap, New Delhi: Sage Publications, 1992, p. 24.
171 The Hindu, 25 December 1987.

Bibliography

Arangannal, Rama, *Ninaivugal*, Chennai: Andal Pathippagam, 2000.

Arunan, *M.G.R.: Nadigar Mudhalvar Aanadhu Eppadi?* Madurai: Vasantham Veliyeetagam, 2006.

Arurdhas, *Cinema Nizhalum Nijamum*, Chennai: Arundhati Nilayam, 2000.

———, *Naan Mugam Paartha Cinema Kannadigal*, Chennai: Kalaignan Pathippagam, 2002.

———, *Kottaiyum Kodambakkamuml*, Chennai: Vikatan Pirasuram, 2006.

———, *Sivaji Vendra Cinema Rajiyam*, 2nd edn. Chennai: Vikatan Pirasuram, 2009.

———, *MGR-Sivaji En Iru Kangal*, Chennai: Manivasagar Pathippagam, 2011.

———, *Kodambaakathil Arubadhu Aandugal*, Chennai: Manivasagar Pathippagam, 2011.

———, *Oru Kadhai Vasanakarthavin Kadhai*, 2nd edn. Chennai: Manivasagar Pathippagam, 2013.

———, *Cinemavin Marupakkam*, Chennai: Dinathanthi Pathippagam, 2016.

Balasingham, Anton, *Viduthalai*, Surrey: Fairmax Publishing Ltd, 2003.

Bharathan, M.S., *Nadigar MGR Pithalaatangal*, Chennai: Jhansirani Pathippagam, 1977.

Barnouw, Eric and S. Krishnaswamy, *Indian Film*, New York: Columbia University Press, 1963.

Baskaran, Theodore, S.

———, The Eye of the Serpent: An Introduction to Tamil Cinema, Chennai: Tranquebar Press, 2008.

Chand, Attar, *M.G. Ramachandran: My Blood Brother*, Delhi: Gian Publishing House, 1988.

Charu, Nivedita, *Theerakkaathali*, Chennai: Uyirmai Pathippagam, 2008.

Copper Cochin: Profile – MGR, a hero on and off the screen: Spotlight on Tamil Nadu – Special Publication released on the occasion of the 5th World Tamil Conference, Madurai, January 1981.

De Silva, K.M. and Wriggins, Howard, *J.R. Jayewardene of Sri Lanka: A Political Biography: From 1956 to His Retirement*, Honolulu: University of Hawaii Press, 1995.

Dixit, J.N., *Assignment Colombo*, Delhi: Konarak, 1998.

Deenadhayalan, P., *Sivaji-Nadigar Mudhal Thilagam Varai*, Chennai: Kizhakku Pathippagam, 2006.

Dungan, Ellis with Smik, Barbara, *A Guide to Adventure: An Autobiography*, Pittsburgh: Dorrance Publishing Co., 2001.

Ganesan, Sivaji, *Autobiography of an Actor*, Chennai: Sivaji Prabhu Charities Trust, 2002.

Guy, Randor, *Starlight, Starbright: The Early Tamil Cinema*, Chennai: Amra Publishers, 1997.

Guhan, S., 'State Finances in Tamil Nadu: 1960-85: A Review of Trends and Policy,' Working Paper 77, Madras Institute of Development Studies, Madras, 1988.

Gurusamy, S., 'Peasant Politics in Tamilnadu - A Socio-political Analysis of a Pressure Group,' thesis, 1991, shodhganga.inflibnet.ac.in/bitstream/10603/16237/.../08_chapter%202.p...shodhganga.inflibnet.ac.in/bitstream/10603/16237/.../09_chapter%203.p...

Hardgrave, Jr, Robert L., 'Politics and the Film in Tamilnadu: The Stars and the DMK,' *Asian Survey* (JSTOR) March 1973, vol. 13, no. 3, pp. 288–305.

Harriss, Barbara, 'Meals and Noon Meals in South India: Food and Nutrition Policy in the Rural Food Economy of Tamil Nadu State,' Development Studies Occasional Paper No. 31, School of Development Studies, University of East Anglia, October 1986.

Jagathrakshakan, S., *MGR: A Phenomenon*, Chennai: Apollo Veliyeetagam, 1984.

Jayakanthan, *Cinemavuku Pona Sithaalu*, 9th edn., Chennai: Meenakshi Puthaga Nilayam, 2012.

Jayalalithaa, *Manam Thirandhu Solgiraen*, Kumudam, 1978-79.

John, Valampuri, *Vanakkam*, 3rd edn., Chennai: Nakkheeran Publications, 2010.

Kalimuthu. K, *Ennai Naan Paarkiraen*, Chennai: Anuragam, 1999.

Kannadasan, Kavignar, *M.G.R. in presumably Ullum Puramum*, Chennai: Muthiah Publisher, 1974.

_____, *Manavaasam*, 13th edn., Chennai: Vanathi Pathippagam, 2000.

_____, *Vanavaasam*, 23rd edn., Chennai: Vanathi Pathippagam, 2000.

_____, *Naan Paartha Arasiyal*, 11th edn., Chennai: Kannadhasan Pathippagam, 2007.

_____, *Arangamum Andharangamum*, 13th edn., Chennai: Kannadhasan Pathippagam, 2010.

_____, *Sandhithaen Sindhithaen*, 2nd edn., Chennai: Kannadhasan Pathippagam, 2013.

Kannan, R., *Anna: The Life and Times of C.N. Annadurai*, Delhi: Penguin Viking, 2010.

Karunanandam, Kavignar, *Thanthai Periyar Vazhkai Varalaaru*, Chennai: Arulbharathi Pathippagam, 2012.

_____, *Anna Sila Ninaivugal*. 3rd edn., Chennai: Poovazhagi Pathippagam, 2012.

Karunanidhi, M. Kalaignar, *Nenjuku Needhi*, 7th edn., Vol. 1, Chennai: Thirumagal Nilayam. 2000.

_____, *Nenjuku Needhi*, 8th edn., vol. 2, Chennai: Thirumagal Nilayam, 2009.

_____, *Nenjuku Needhi*, 6th edn., vol. 3, Chennai: Thirumagal Nilayam, 2008.

_____, *Nenjuku Needhi*, vol. 4, Chennai: Thirumagal Nilayam, 2003.

_____, *Nenjuku Needhi*, vol. 5, Chennai: Thirumagal Nilayam, 2013.

_____, *Kalaignarin Pasumai Ninaivugal*, 4th edn., Chennai: Bharati Pathippagam, 2010.

Krishnan, Panju. *Ennai Iyakkia Kadhanayagaral*, ed., Naagai Dharuman, Chennai: Vijaya Publications, 2010.

Kirubakaran, S., ed., *M.G.R. Paettigal*, Chennai: Vikatan Pirasuram, 2009.

Lakshmanan, V. Vidwan, *Makkal Thilagam M.G.R.*, 4th edn., Chennai: Vanathi Pathippagam, 2002.

Manoharan, K. Nanjil, *Thamizhagath Thalaivar Kalaignar*, Chennai: Poompuhar Pirasuram, 1988.

_____, *Medum Pallamum* Chennai: Poonjolai Pirasuram, 1986.

Maran, Murasoli, *Manila Suyatchi (State Autonomy)*, Chennai: *Murasoli*, 1974.

Meiyappan, A.V. *Enadhu Vaazhkai Anubhavangal*, 4th edn., Chennai: Vanathi Pathippagam, 2000.

Mohandas, K. *MGR: The Man and the Myth*, Bangalore: Panther-Publishers, 1992.

Mugil, *Kanneerum Punnagaiyum*, Chennai: Kizhakku Pathippagam, 2005.

_____, *M.R. Radhayanam*, Chennai: Kizhakku Pathippagam, 2007.

Muthukumar, R., *Dravida Iyakka Varalaaru*, two vols. Chennai: Kizhakku Pathippagam, 2010.

_____, *Vadhyar*, Chennai: Kizhakku Pathippagam, 2009.

_____, *Thamizhaga Arasiyal Varalaaru*, Chennai: Kizhakku Pathippagam, 2012.

Manimozhi and Manimaran, N., *Hindi Adhika Ethirpu Poril Puratchithalaivar*, Chennai: Pudhiya Bhoomi Pathippagam, 1987.

Narayan, Jayaprakash, *Prison Diary*, Delhi: Gian Publishing House, 1988.

Narayanan, Arandhai, *Dravidam Paadiya Thiraipadangal*, Chennai: New Century Book House, 1994.

Narayanaswamy, T.S., ed., *Sivaji Ganesan: Enadhu Suya Saridhai*, Chennai: Sivaji Prabhu Charities Trust, 2002.

Nedunchezhian Era, Navalar, *Vazhvil Naan Kandathum Kaethaum*, Chennai: Navalar Nedunchezhian Kalvi Arakattalai, 2000.

Natarajan, M. *Perarignar Annavin Peruraigal*, four vols., 2nd edn., Chennai: Tamil Arasi Pathippagam, 2001.

Pandian, M.S.S., *The Image Trap: MG Ramachandran in film and politics*, New Delhi: Sage Publications, 1992.

Parimalam, Anna, ed., *Perarignar Annavin Than Varalaaru*, Chennai: Bharati Pathippagam, 1997.

Periasamy, G. Palani, Dr, *Heartbeats: My Unforgettable Life Experiences*, Chennai: Vanathi Pathippagam, 2016.

Phadnis, Aditi, *Political Profiles of Cabals and Kings*, Delhi: Business Standard Books, 2009.

Rajaram, K. *Oru Saamaniyanin Ninaivugal*, Chennai: Nakkheeran Pathippagam, 2014.

Rajendran, S.S. *Naan Vandha Paadhai*, Chennai: Agani Veliyeedu, 2014.

Raju, S. Pulavar, *MGR Thamizharey*, Chennai: Megathudan Pathippagam, 2010.

Ramachandran, M.G. *Ulagam Sutrum Vaaliban Undaana Kadhai*, Chennai: Vijaya Publications, 2009.

_____. *Naan Yaen Pirandhen?*, Chennai: Kannadhasan Pathippagam, 2015.

_____, ed., *Naan Aanaiyitaal*, 2nd edn., Chennai: Vikatan Pirasuram, 2014.

Ramasamy, V.K., *Enadhu Kalaippayanam*, Chennai: New Century Book House, 2002.

Ramaswamy, Cho., *Adhirshtam Thanta Anubhavangal*, 6th edn., Chennai: Alliance Publishers, 2015.

Ranimaindhan, *Mellisai Mannar M.S.V,* Chennai: Rajarajan Pathippagam, 2003.

_____, *R.M.V. Oru Thondar,* Chennai: Rajarajan Pathippagam, 2005.

Ravindar, K., *Pon Mana Chemmal MGR*, Chennai: Vijaya Publications, 2009.

_____, *Vizha Nayagan MGR*, Chennai: Vijaya Publications, 2009.

Sachi, Sri Kantha, https://www.researchgate.net/publication/292502450_Minimum_Guarantee_Ramachandran_A_Life_in_Cinema_and_Politics DOI: 10.13140/RG.2.1.1703.7847

Saravanan, M., *AVM 60 Cinema*, Chennai: Rajarajan Pathippagam, 2006.

Shrikanth, Veeravalli, *MGR-A Biography*, Delhi: Rupa Publications, 2013.

Singh, Natwar, *One Life Is Not Enough*, Delhi: Rupa Publications, 2014.

Sivagnanam, Ma. Po., *MGR Udan Enakirundha Thodarbu*, Chennai: Poongodi Pathippagam, 1995.

Solai, *Netru-Indru-Naalai*, Chennai: Nakkheeran Publications, 2012.

_____. *MGR in Theerkatharisanam*, Chennai: Nakkheeran Publications, 2010.

_____. *Sangapalagai*, Chennai: Nakkheeran Publications, 2012.

Subramanian, N., *Ethnicity and Populist Mobilization: Political Parties, Citizenship, and Democracy in South India*, Delhi: Oxford University Press, 1999.

Sudangan, *Suttachu Suttachu*, Chennai: Kizhakku Pathippagam, 2005.

Sundaram, Vellaiyaampattu, *Nadigamani D.V. Narayanasamy*, Chennai: Sekar Pathippagam, 2000.

Thirunavukarasu, K., *Thi Mu Ka Varalaaru*, vols. 1, 2, 3, Chennai: Nakkheran Pathippagam, Chennai: 2015.

_____, *Needhikatchi Varalaaru*, 3rd edn. Chennai: Nakkheran Pathippagam, 2013.

Udayamurthi, M.S., Doctor, *Americargal Paarvayil Mudhalvar Anna Makkal Thilagam M.G.R.*, Chennai: Vidwan Pathippagam, 2003.

Vaali, *Naanum Indha Nootraandum*, Chennai: Kalaignan Pathippagam, 1995.
_____. *Enakkul M.G.R.*, Chennai: Kumaran Pathippagam, 2013.
Vaasanthi, *Cut-Outs, Caste and Cine Stars: The World of Tamil Politics*, Delhi: Penguin, 2006.
_____. *Amma: Jayalalithaa's Journey from Movie Star to Political Queen*, Delhi: Juggernaut, 2016.
Vivekanandan, Iniyan Kalpanadasan Sampath, *E Ve Ke Sampathum Dravida Iyakkamum*, Chennai: Iniyan Sampath Pathippagam, 2013.
Vijayan, S., *M.G.R. Kathai*, 3rd edn., Chennai: Arulmozhi Pathippagam, 1992.

Widlund, I., *Paths to Power and Patterns of Influence: The Dravidian Parties in South Indian Politics* Uppsala: Acta Universitatis Upsaliensis, 2000.

Index

Aasiriyar. *See* Karunanidhi, Muthuvel (Kalaignar)

Aayirathil Oruvan (1965), 91n, 113, 128, 129–30, 134

Abhimanyu (1948), 1, 60, 55

Adi Dravida Welfare, 347

Adi Dravidas, 259, 376; embrace Islam, 296–97

Adimaipenn (1969), 89n, 91, 133, 146–47

Adithan, C.P., 141, 145, 147, 162, 179, 228, 256

Advani, L.K., 193–94

affirmative action. *See* reservation

Ahmed, Fakhruddin Ali, 213

Aiyangar, Kurichi Rangasami, 290

Aiyer, Mani Shankar, 387n

Alai Osai, 160

Alexander, A.X., 326

Alibabavum 40 Thirudargalum (1956), 69n, 77

All India Anna Dravida Munnetra Kazhagam (AIADMK), 2, 52, 89, 92, 113n, 215, 227, 231, 236, 243, 255, 267, 271–73, 279, 292–93, 296, 299, 300, 301, 355, 356, 382, 391, 393–94; Assembly elections (1977), 228–30; and Congress, alliance/ relations, 224, 267, 289, 307, 318, 346–47, 349, 364, 375, 377; Constitutional question and infighting, 342–45; alleged corruption, 256, 268–69, 278, 301–4, 333–34, 336, 338, 370; joined Charan Singh's Ministry, 264–67; supported Emergency, 247, 250; ethnic issue, 308–9; four assembly by-elections, 332–33; and general elections (1977), 223–25;—(1980), 281, 282–85; intra-party squabbles, 342–45, 354–64; invoking non-Brahmin card in judicial appointments, 377; and Janata Party, relations, 250; Jayalalithaa joins, 310–16; leadership against Jayalalithaa, 343, 345; and Karunanidhi, 240, 241; and LTTE, 324–25, 382; and Madurai Corporation elections, 259; municipal elections (1986), 362–64; opposition to imposition of Hindi, 260–61; parliamentary polls and Pondicherry assembly polls (1980), 274–76; Periyakulam by-election, 314–15; prohibition, 276; reservation issue, 264; action on Sarkaria Commission,